A SPLENDID EXCHANGE

William Bernstein is a financial theorist and historian whose books include *The Birth of Plenty*, published in 2004 to critical acclaim. He lives in the United States.

A SPLENDID EXCHANGE

How Trade Shaped
the World

WILLIAM BERNSTEIN

Atlantic Books
LONDON

First published in the United States of America in 2008 by
Grove Atlantic Ltd.

First published in hardback in Great Britain in 2008 by Atlantic
Books, an imprint of Grove Atlantic Ltd.

This paperback edition published in Great Britain in 2009
by Atlantic Books

1 3 5 7 9 10 8 6 4 2

A CIP catalogue record for this book is available from the British
Library.

ISBN: 978 1 84354 803 4

Maps by Matthew Ericson

Printed in Great Britain by Clays Ltd, St Ives plc

Atlantic Books
An imprint of Grove Atlantic Ltd
Ormond House
26–27 Boswell Street
London WC1N 3JZ

www.atlantic-books.co.uk

To Jane

CONTENTS

MAPS

INTRODUCTION

The circumstances could not have been more ordinary: a September morning in a hotel lobby in central Berlin. While the desk clerk and I politely exchanged greetings in each other's fractured English and German, I casually plucked an apple from the bowl on the counter and slipped it into my backpack. When hunger overtook me a few hours later, I decided on a quick snack in the Tiergarten. The sights and sounds of this great urban park nearly made me miss the tiny label that proclaimed my complimentary lunch a "Product of New Zealand."

Televisions from Taiwan, lettuce from Mexico, shirts from China, and tools from India are so ubiquitous that it is easy to forget how recent such miracles of commerce are. What better symbolizes the epic of global trade than my apple from the other side of the world, consumed at the exact moment that its ripe European cousins were being picked from their trees?

Millennia ago, only the most prized merchandise—silk, gold and silver, spices, jewels, porcelains, and medicines—traveled between continents. The mere fact that a commodity came from a distant land imbued it with mystery, romance, and status. If the time were the third century after Christ and the place were Rome, the luxury import par excellence would have been Chinese silk. History celebrates the greatest of Roman emperors for their vast conquests, civic architecture, engineering, and legal institutions, but Elagabalus, who ruled from AD 218 to 222, is remembered, to the extent that he is remembered at all, for his outrageous behavior and his fondness for young boys and silk. During his reign he managed to shock the jaded populace of the ancient world's capital with a parade of scandalous acts, ranging from harmless pranks to the capricious murder of children. Nothing, however, commanded Rome's attention (and fired its envy) as much as his wardrobe and the lengths he went to flaunt it, such as removing all his body hair and powdering his face with red and white makeup. Although his favorite fabric was occasionally mixed with linen—the so-called *sericum*—Elagabalus was the first Western leader to wear clothes made entirely of silk.[1]

From its birthplace in East Asia to its last port of call in ancient Rome, only the ruling classes could afford the excretion of the tiny invertebrate *Bombyx mori*—the silkworm. The modern reader, spoiled by inexpensive, smooth, comfortable synthetic fabrics, should imagine clothing made predominantly from three materials: cheap, but hot, heavy animal skins; scratchy wool; or wrinkled, white linen. (Cotton, though available from India and Egypt, was more difficult to produce, and thus likely more expensive, than even silk.) In a world with such a limited sartorial palette, the gentle, almost weightless caress of silk on bare skin would have seduced all who felt it. It is not difficult to imagine the first silk merchants, at each port and caravanserai along the way, pulling a colorful swatch of it from a pouch and turning to the lady of the house with a sly, "Madam, you must feel this to believe it."

The poet Juvenal, writing around AD 110, complained of luxury-loving women "who find the thinnest of thin robes too hot for them; whose delicate flesh is chafed by the finest of silk tissue."[2] The gods themselves could not resist: Isis was said to have draped herself in "fine silk yielding diverse colors, sometime yellow, sometime rose, sometime flamy, and sometime (which troubled my spirit sore) dark and obscure."[3]

Although the Romans knew Chinese silk, they knew not China. They believed that silk grew directly on the mulberry tree, not realizing that the leaves were merely the worm's home and its food.

How did goods get from China to Rome? Very slowly and very perilously, one laborious stage at a time.[4] Chinese traders from southern ports loaded their ships with silk for the long coastwise journey down Indochina and around the Malay Peninsula and Bay of Bengal to the ports of Sri Lanka. There, they would be met by Indian merchants who would then transport the fabric to the Tamil ports on the southwest coast of the subcontinent—Muziris, Nelcynda, and Comara. Here, large numbers of Greek and Arab intermediaries handled the onward leg to the island of Dioscordia (modern Socotra), a bubbling masala of Arab, Greek, Indian, Persian, and Ethiopian entrepreneurs. From Dioscordia, the cargo floated on Greek vessels through the entrance of the Red Sea at the Bab el Mandeb (Arabic for "Gate of Sorrows") to the sea's main port of Berenice in Egypt;

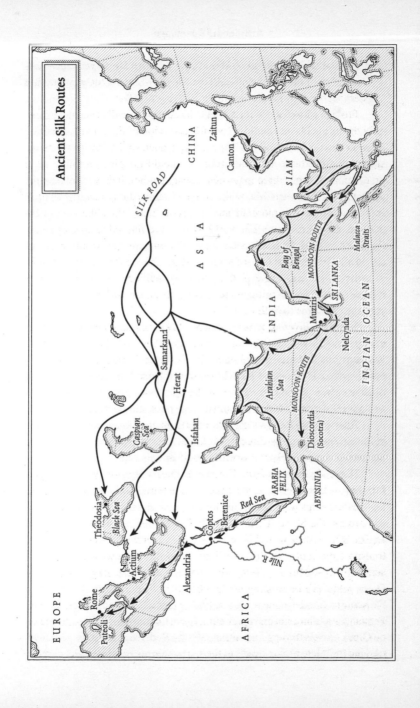

Ancient Silk Routes

then across the desert by camel to the Nile; and next by ship downstream to Alexandria, where Greek Roman and Italian Roman ships moved it across the Mediterranean to the huge Roman termini of Puteoli (modern Pozzuoli) and Ostia. As a general rule, the Chinese seldom ventured west of Sri Lanka, the Indians north of the Red Sea mouth, and the Italians south of Alexandria. It was left to the Greeks, who ranged freely from India to Italy, to carry the greatest share of the traffic.

With each long and dangerous stage of the journey, silk would change hands at dramatically higher prices. It was costly enough in China; in Rome, it was yet a hundred times costlier—worth its weight in gold, so expensive that even a few ounces might consume a year of an average man's wages.[5] Only the wealthiest, such as Emperor Elagabalus, could afford an entire toga made from it.

The other way to Rome, the famous Silk Road, first opened up by Han emissaries in the second century of the Christian era, bumped slowly overland through central Asia. This route was far more complex, and its precise track varied widely with shifting political and military conditions, from well south of the Khyber Pass to as far north as the southern border of Siberia. Just as the sea route was dominated by Greek, Ethiopian, and Indian traders, so would be the overland "ports," the great cities of Samarkand (in present-day Uzbekistan), Isfahan (in Iran), and Herat (in Afghanistan), richly served by Jewish, Armenian, and Syrian middlemen. Who, then, could blame the Romans for thinking that silk was manufactured in two different nations—a northern one, Seres, reached by the dry route; and a southern one, Sinae, reached by water?

The sea route was cheaper, safer, and faster than overland transport, and in the premodern world had the added advantage of bypassing unstable areas. Silk originally reached Europe via the land route, but the stability of the early Roman Empire increasingly made the Indian Ocean the preferred conduit between East and West for most commodities, silk included. Although Roman commerce with the East tapered off during the second century, the maritime route would remain open until Islam severed it in the seventh century.

The seasonal metronome of the monsoon winds drove the silk trade. The monsoons also dictated that at least eighteen months separated the embarkation of the fabric from south China and its arrival at Ostia or Puteoli. Mortal peril awaited the merchant at every point, especially in the hazardous stretches of the Arabian Sea and the Bay of Bengal. The loss of lives, bottoms, and cargoes was so routine that such tragedies were usually recorded, if at all, with the short notation: "Lost with all hands."

Today, the most ordinary cargoes span such distances with only a modest increase in price. That the efficient intercontinental transport of even bulk goods today seems so unremarkable is in itself remarkable.

Our high-value items fly around the globe at nearly the speed of sound, conveyed by crews manning air-conditioned cockpits and greeted at journey's end with taxis and four-star hotels. Even those tending bulk cargoes serve on vessels stocked with videos and bulging pantries that provide a degree of safety and comfort unimaginable to the premodern sailor. Today's aircraft and freighter crews are highly skilled professionals, but few would recognize them as "traders." Neither would most of us apply that term to the multinational corporate sellers and buyers of the world's cornucopia of commerce.

Not so long ago, the trader was simple to identify. He bought and sold goods in small amounts for his own account, and he accompanied them every step of the way. On board ship, he usually slept on his cargo. Although most of these traders left us with no written records, a vivid window into premodern long-distance commerce can be found in the Geniza papers, a collection of medieval records stumbled on in a storage room adjacent to Cairo's ancient main synagogue. Jewish law required that no document containing the name of God be destroyed, including routine family and business correspondence. Since this rule applied to most medieval written material, great quantities of records were stored in such repositories at local synagogues—the *geniza*. Cairo's Jewish population thrived in the relatively prosperous and tolerant atmosphere of the Muslim Fatimid Empire of the tenth to twelfth centuries, and that city's arid climate preserved the papers (typically written in the Arabic language but with Hebrew script) well enough that they survived into the present. This routine correspondence among relatives and business partners, strung from Gibraltar to Alexandria to India, provides a rare glimpse into the slow, perilous, grim, gritty world of the peddlers who bought and sold merchandise.

Preparation was onerous even before the journey began. Traders did not venture abroad without letters of introduction to expected business

contacts, or without letters of safe conduct from the local rulers along
their route. Otherwise, they were certain to be robbed, molested, or
murdered. Further, all travelers in the medieval Muslim world required
a *rafiq,* or companion, usually another trader. The trader and the *rafiq*
entrusted their personal security to each other. Few catastrophes en route
were worse than the death of one's *rafiq,* since the local authorities
would assume that the traveler was now in possession of the *rafiq*'s
money and belongings, a virtual guarantee of confiscation and torture.
To send a relative or guest on a journey without a *rafiq* was considered
a disgrace.[6]

In this world, travel was faster, cheaper, safer, and more comfortable
by ship than by land. "Faster," "cheaper," "safer," and "more comfortable,"
however, are all relative terms. Before the advent of the European caravel
and the carrack in the Iberian peninsula in the fifteenth century, vessels
that moved primarily under sail were reserved for bulky, low-value cargoes; passengers and precious freight moved on oared craft, which provided the most rapid and reliable method of maritime transport. A galley
150 feet in length might carry up to five hundred oarsmen, not counting
other crew, officers, and passengers. Cramming so much humanity into
a small space utterly lacking in sanitation turned such craft into floating
sewers. "I suffered terribly because of the diseases of my fellow travelers and their disgusting odors," reported an anonymous merchant on a
Nile River boat. "Things went so far that three of them died, and the last
of them remained on the boat for a day and a half until he became putrid."[7] The captain's reluctance to land and bury the corpse on the day of
death, a severe violation of Muslim custom, hints at the danger awaiting
passengers and crew on shore.

Basic hygiene aside, the captain and crew were often themselves
sources of danger. Shipboard robbery and murder were not uncommon,
and merchant ships provided corrupt government officials with easy targets. After paying an official the despised "head tax" before leaving port,
our Nile River merchant was still suspicious that the same official would
return to shake him down a second time:

> I left the boat and went ahead, overtaking it at al-Rumayla, where I
> boarded it again after its arrival. I learned indeed that my apprehen-
> sions had been justified. After I had left, the policeman had appeared
> again to arrest me.[8]

Such hardships and peril were not unique to Muslim boats. Egyptian merchants often had the option of traveling on Italian or Byzantine vessels; these offered no additional safety or comfort. Any boat might fall casualty to murder, piracy, or disease and then drift without aim for lack of control. These "ghost ships" bore horrifying witness to the human cost paid by crews and passengers, particularly on the remote Indian Ocean spice routes.

Yet however expensive, unpleasant, and perilous medieval sailing was, traders preferred it to the overland route. Even along main roads in the heart of the Egyptian Fatimid Empire, a letter of safe conduct did not protect against bedouin raids. Weeks on a heaving, rancid deck were still preferable to months on the lookout for brigands from the back of a donkey or camel.

The Geniza papers also describe the high expense of land transport. For most of recorded history, the primary manufactured trade commodity was cloth. The total transport costs from Cairo to Tunisia for a bale of "purple" (a camel's load of textiles, weighing roughly five hundred pounds) was eight gold dinars. This sum was equivalent to about four months' living expenses for a medieval Egyptian lower-middle-class family. Half of this cost covered the relatively short 120-mile ground segment from Cairo to Alexandria, and the other half the twelve hundred–mile sea route from Alexandria to Tunisia. Thus, mile for mile, ground transport was ten times more expensive than maritime transport.[9] Given the enormous costs, risks, and discomfort of the dry route, merchants chose it only when they could not go by sea: for example, when the Mediterranean was "closed" for the winter season.

Were the trader lucky enough to complete the journey with his cargo and person intact, ruin could still come at the hands of a fickle marketplace. Prices were wildly unpredictable, often brokered with caveats that "Prices follow no principle," and "The prices are in the hand of God."[10] Why would anyone risk life, limb, and property on journeys that might carry him from hearth and home for years on end, yielding only meager profits? Simple: the grim trading life was preferable to the even grimmer existence of the more than 90 percent of the population who engaged in subsistence-level farming. An annual profit of one hundred dinars—enough to support an upper-middle-class existence—made a trader a rich man.[11]

* * *

Adam Smith wrote that man has an intrinsic "propensity to truck, barter, and exchange one thing for another," and that this happy tendency was nothing more than human nature "of which no further account can be given."[12] Yet few other historical inquiries tell us as much about the world we live in today as does the search for the origins of world trade—if we ask the right questions. For instance, from the dawn of recorded history there was a vigorous long-distance commerce in grain and metals between Mesopotamia and southern Arabia. And going back even further, archaeologists have found strong evidence of the prehistoric conveyance over long distances of strategic materials such as obsidian and stone tools. While other animals, particularly primates, groom and share food with each other, systematic exchanges of goods and services, particularly over great distances, have not been observed in any species besides *Homo sapiens*. What drove early man to trade?

Evolutionary anthropologists date the origins of modern human behavior in eastern and southern Africa to around 100,000 years ago.[13] One of these behaviors, the innate tendency to "truck and barter," has yielded an ever-increasing volume and variety of goods. Although world trade grew in tandem with the technological innovations of land and sea transport, political stability was even more important. For example, soon after Octavian's forces defeated those of Anthony and Cleopatra at the battle of Actium in western Greece in 30 BC and greatly expanded the ambit of the Roman Empire, Rome was flooded with pepper, exotic animals, ivory, and precious jewels from the Orient. Chinese silk was the most famous and coveted of these new commodities, yet no native of the Italian peninsula had ever met a Chinese person, and, as we've already seen, even Roman cartographers were unaware of China's precise location. Then, just as rapidly as the trade between Rome and the East had swelled during the early empire, it abruptly decreased to a trickle as Rome began a long decline after the death of Marcus Aurelius in the late second century. The silk of Elagabalus was in fact one of the rare luxuries to arrive from India after that period.

The dramatic increase in long-distance trade following the battle of Actium and its waning two hundred years later had nothing to do with changes in maritime technology. Certainly, the Roman, Greek, Arab, and Indian traders who plied the Indian Ocean trade routes did not suddenly lose their maritime abilities after the reign of Marcus Aurelius.

Now consider the contribution of trade to our planet's agricultural bounty. Try to imagine Italian cuisine without the tomato, the highlands around Darjeeling without tea plants, an American table without wheat bread or beef, a café anywhere in the world beyond coffee's birthplace in Yemen, or German cooking without the potato. Such was the world's limited range of farm produce before the "Columbian exchange," the invasion of billions of acres of cropland by species from remote continents in the decades following 1492. How and why did this occur, and what does it tell us about the nature of trade?

During the seven centuries between the death of the Prophet Muhammad and the Renaissance, the Muslim states of Europe, Asia, and Africa outshone and towered over western Christendom. Muhammad's followers dominated the great conduit of long-range world commerce, the Indian Ocean, and in the process spread his powerful message from west Africa to the South China Sea. Then, with breathtaking speed, a newly resurgent West took control of global trade routes in the decades following the first roundings of the Cape of Good Hope by Bartholomew Diaz and Vasco da Gama. Can we understand these events under the larger banner of the history of trade?

The great national trading organizations, particularly the English and Dutch East India companies, spearheaded Europe's commercial dominance and made world trade the nearly exclusive province of large corporate entities and, in the twentieth century, of the multinational corporation. Today, these organizations—fountainheads of Western, and particularly American, cultural and economic dominance—are often objects of virulent resentment and animosity. What are the roots of the modern international corporate giant, and is today's trade-related cultural conflict, with its rampant anti-Americanism, a new phenomenon?

The world's increasing dependency on the continuous flow of trade has made us both prosperous and vulnerable. A major disruption of the Internet would wreak havoc in the international economy—an amazing circumstance, considering that its widespread use is merely a decade old. The developed world has become addicted to fossil fuels from the world's most unstable nations, the greatest share of which flows through a single narrow strait guarding the entrance to the Persian Gulf. Does the history of trade offer us any landmarks that can guide us through these dangerous waters?

Today's conventional wisdom has it that the communications and transportation revolutions of the late twentieth century have for the first time brought nations around the world into direct economic competition with each other. We shall see, however, that this is nothing new. In previous centuries, this leveling—the "flattening" of the world—produced both winners and losers, who, not unsurprisingly, tended, respectively, to favor or oppose this process. What does the history of previous trade revolutions tell us about today's titanic political struggle over globalization?[14]

How, then, did we get from the world of the ancient silk trade and the Geniza papers, in which the trader's job was so solitary, expensive, and heroic that only the most precious of cargoes paid their way, to the modern corporate world of wines from Chile, cars from Korea, and apples from New Zealand?

Stable countries are trading countries. Commerce between Rome and East Asia took off after Octavian's victory at Actium and ushered in nearly two centuries of relative peace throughout the Mediterranean and Red Sea trade routes. While the Romans controlled, at most, the western third of the route between Alexandria and India, their influence was felt as far east as the Ganges.

Although individual merchants rarely carried goods all the way from India to Rome, there were frequent face-to-face diplomatic contacts between various Indian states and Rome. Within a few years of Octavian's ascension as Augustus, Indian rulers honored him with elaborate embassies and wondrous gifts—snakes, elephants, precious gems, and gymnasts, all of which the emperor exhibited at home—and in India itself, temples were built to honor him. Most significantly, Roman citizens were granted free passage through much of the subcontinent; an archaeological site excavated near Pondicherry between 1945 and 1948 revealed evidence of a Roman trade colony that had functioned until about AD 200.[15]

Local goods in India were purchased with durable gold and silver coins, each dated by the image of the emperor. Caches of these coins are still being discovered in south India, offering us a glimpse of trade patterns two thousand years ago. They include gold and silver coins from the reigns of Augustus and Tiberius (27 BC to AD 37), suggesting a vigorous trade in a large volume of goods. After the death of Tiberius, the composition of the Indian coin caches changes. Significant numbers of only gold, but not silver, coins bearing the heads of Caligula, Claudius, and Nero (AD 37–68) are found. According to the historian E. H. Warmington, this absence of silver coins suggests a trade mainly in luxury goods during that period. Few Roman coins of any type are found after the death of Marcus Aurelius in AD 180.[16] When Roman and Han authority finally collapsed around AD 200, trade with the East came to an almost complete standstill.

The other great advance in commerce during this period came from Greek sailors who exploited the summer southwest monsoon of the western Indian Ocean. Initially, the Greeks used the monsoons, which drove them out into the open sea, merely to avoid pirates off the Persian coast. By about 110 BC, however, they were making the treacherous summer blue-water passage directly east across the Arabian Gulf from the Red Sea entrance at Bab el Mandeb to India's southern tip and beyond in just under six weeks, one thousand years before the Chinese invented the magnetic compass. Legend has it that a navigator by the name of Hippalus "discovered" the Arabian Gulf trade winds (hence the origin of the term), although they were undoubtedly also well known to Indian and Arab sailors. The willingness of the Greeks to drive themselves directly across vast open stretches of the Indian Ocean before the terrifying seasonal monsoons, rather than creep along thousands of miles of endless coasts, was a major factor in the expansion of long-range maritime trade.

After clearing Bab el Mandeb in late spring or late summer, the mariner headed east on the following wind. If his goal was the Indus basin (in present-day Pakistan), he might steer north, and if he was heading to the Malabar Coast in southwestern India, he might steer south. Midsummer, when storms were the fiercest, was generally avoided, and the Malabar route held the additional risk of passing south of the subcontinent, usually a fatal mistake. The return journey on the cool and relatively calm northeast monsoon was safer; missing the Bab el Mandeb by even a wide margin to the north or south could be more easily tolerated, since that took the sailor to shelter and supplies in either Arabia or east Africa.

The Greek traders of Ptolemaic Egypt had the additional advantage of metallurgical expertise, enabling them to bind their ships with iron nails. (The timbers of early Arab and Indian vessels were stitched together with coconut fiber, which fell apart in rough seas.) Nailed hulls proved critical during the southwest summer monsoon, whose ferocious storms would occasionally tear apart even the most solidly bound vessels. Until the nineteenth century brought the clipper ship and steam, the seasonal dance of the monsoons—southwest in summer, northeast in winter—would dictate the annual rhythm of trade in the Indian Ocean.

If man's innate desire to challenge nature at sea paid handsome dividends, his decision to do so on land, by rescuing the slow, large, and defenseless camel from the brink of oblivion, reaped similar rewards. Already extinct in North America, and quickly headed for extinction in Eurasia, the camel was first valued, about six thousand years ago, solely for its milk. Not until twenty-five hundred years later, around 1500 BC, would humans begin to exploit the camel's ability to carry hundreds of pounds of cargo across otherwise impenetrable territory. Without the domestication of the camel, the trans-Asian silk and trans-Arabian incense routes would have been impossible.

It is a little-known fact that the progenitors of the modern camel (along with the horse) originated in North America and migrated east across the Bering Strait land bridge to Asia. Although swift herds of camels or horses might manage the perilous journey from the heartland of North America to that of Eurasia in a matter of decades, it was a much tougher trek for fragile plant species from a temperate area. Such plants had little chance of surviving an accidental intercontinental journey via ocean currents or thousands of years of haphazard migration across the frigid land bridge from their North American habitat to a similar one in Eurasia. Thus, whereas animal species might migrate across the Bering Strait during the ice ages, crop species could not.

That all changed in 1493 with Christopher Columbus's second voyage, which would turn the agriculture and the economies of both the Old World and the New World upside down. Columbus's seventeen vessels were Iberian Noah's arks, carrying to the New World around 1,300 colonists and nearly the entire Western inventory of crops and domesticated animals. They spread like wildfire. Even exchanges of "minor" crops—squashes, pumpkins, papaya, guava, avocado, pineapple, and cocoa from the western hemisphere; and grapes, coffee, and a battery of fruit and nut trees from Europe—assumed major economic importance.

Of all the plant and animal passengers on the second expedition, none had more immediate impact than the pig. Far closer in appearance and temperament to the mean, lean, fast wild boar than to the modern farm hog and capable of transforming 20 percent of feed weight into protein (versus only 6 percent for cattle), these prolific herbivores fed voraciously on the New World's plentiful tropical grasses, fruits, and roots. Further, large predators had nearly disappeared from both North and South America following the arrival of the first native Americans, and no serious diseases threatened the animals. In such a paradise, the pigs soon became independent of the expedition's swineherds and multiplied swiftly, not only on Hispañola (the object of the 1493 expedition, the island containing modern-day Haiti and the Dominican Republic) but also on Cuba and Puerto Rico, and on many smaller Caribbean islands. The Spaniards soon found that tossing a breeding pair of the animals onto a promising uninhabited island guaranteed an abundance of pork there within a few years. In such an agreeable habitat, not only pigs but also horses and cattle thrived without human intervention. From their increasingly well-stocked bases in Hispañola and Cuba, the Spanish now had the wherewithal to attack the mainlands of the Americas. Their columns of Caribbean-bred horses and war dogs were followed by enormous herds of swine, a veritable "commissariat on the hoof."[17] Armed with guns and swords of steel, this fearsome mounted war machine would destroy far larger native formations with near impunity.

Within a few decades after the conquests of Cortés and Pizarro, the cattle population of Spanish America doubled as rapidly as every fifteen months. From Mexico to the pampas of Argentina, the vast open spaces of the New World swarmed black with livestock. One French observer in Mexico wrote in wonderment at the "great, level plains, stretching endlessly and everywhere covered with an infinite number of cattle."[18]

The tiny local populations could consume but a minuscule fraction of the burgeoning mountain of beef, almost all of which was left to rot after the skin and hooves, the only salable parts of the animal, had been secured. By 1800, a million hides per year were being exported from Argentina alone.

The advent of the refrigerated ship late in the nineteenth century changed all that and gave the Continent access to cheap steak. This damaged European butchers in the same way that the twentieth-century flood of cheap textiles and electronics from Asia hurt American manufacturers. If the *New York Times*'s columnist Thomas Friedman had been writing in 1800, he would have had little trouble explaining the flattening of world commerce to European tanners; neither would European cattlemen have had any problem with the concept in 1900.

With plenty often comes tragedy. For thousands of years, Europeans dwelled in close proximity to their highly specialized domesticated animals and became immune to many virulent pathogens, to which America's indigenous peoples were highly susceptible. The sword and the musket worked side by side with smallpox and measles, which in many cases arrived hundreds of miles in advance of the white man's physical presence. One Spaniard remarked that the Indians "died like fish in a bucket."[19] Worse, substantial damage was also done to the local ecosystems, as livestock eroded the landscape by overgrazing and monotonous stretches of European crops and weeds displaced diverse local species.

Native American seed stock, particularly potato and corn, changed the diet of Europe. Both crops produce far more calories per acre than wheat; the potato will grow in poor soils and in a wide variety of environments, from sea level to ten thousand feet. Corn is more fastidious, requiring rich soil and long stretches of hot weather, but it can grow in "in-between" climates too dry for rice but too wet for wheat. An impoverished swath of southern Europe stretching from Portugal to the Ukraine filled this bill precisely. By 1800 it had become one of the world's largest corn growing regions.

Corn and potatoes not only allowed Europe to escape from the deadly jaws of the Malthusian trap but directly stimulated trade. At the dawn of the Industrial Revolution, these crops provided Europeans with excess food to exchange for manufactured goods and freed agricultural laborers for more productive manufacturing. The increased crop yields, in turn, created a vast demand for fertilizer, which was initially met by stripping Latin American and Pacific islands of guano. Similarly, the introduction of yams, corn, tobacco, and peanuts into China allowed the newly ascendant Qing (or Ching) dynasty to expand its influence in the seventeenth and eighteenth centuries.[20]

"Globalization," it turns out, was not one event or even a sequence of events; it is a process that has been slowly evolving for a very, very long time. The world did not abruptly become "flat" with the invention of the Internet, and commerce did not suddenly, at the end of the twentieth century, become dominated by large corporations with worldwide reach. Beginning at the dawn of recorded history with high-value cargoes, then slowly expanding into less precious and more bulky and perishable goods, the markets of the Old World have gradually become more integrated. With the first European voyages to the New World, this process of global integration accelerated. Today's massive container ships, jet planes, the Internet, and an increasingly globalized supply and manufacturing network are just further evolutionary steps in a process that has been going on for the past five thousand years. If we wish to understand today's rapidly shifting patterns of global trade, it serves us very well indeed to examine what came before.

For the past decade or so, I've been involved in the world of finance and economics; during this period, I've written three books. The first was a treatise on theoretical and practical finance through which ran a strong historical theme. With each successive title, I've moved further into historical territory. My third book, *The Birth of Plenty,* dealt with the institutional origins of the global prosperity that occurred after 1820. Few readers found the book's basic premise—that the recent wealth of the modern world was underpinned by the development of property rights, rule of law, capital market mechanisms, and scientific rationalism—at all controversial. The failure of the communist experiment and the current wealth and poverty of individual nations testify to the power of these critical institutions.

This book enjoys no such ideological shelter. The pain and dislocations in the lives of individuals, industries, and nations caused by the globalization of the planet's economy are real, and the debate is rancorous. In the language of economics, human well-being is affected not only by the mean (the prosperity of the average citizen) but also by the variance (the increasing dispersion between rich and poor). In plainer English, the incentives and equal opportunity afforded by free trade simultaneously improve the overall welfare of mankind *and* increase socially corrosive disparities of wealth. Even if trade slightly improves the real income of those at the bottom, they will feel the pain of economic deprivation when they fix their gaze at the growing wealth of those above them.

And as long as we're throwing statistical terms around, the synonymous terms "mean" and "average" have of late begun to carry their own ideological freight. The political right embraces the mean, but rarely uses a different bit of jargon, the median—that is, the income or wealth at the fiftieth percentile, the "person in the middle." When Bill Gates walks into a roomful of people, their mean income skyrockets while their median income changes hardly at all—a concept usually ignored by pro-market conservatives.

But this is not a book about numbers; if you want detailed data on trade volume and commodity prices through the ages, they can be found in the book's reference sources. The history of world trade is best told through carefully selected stories and ideas. My fondest hope is that the narratives and concepts contained herein will inform participants and challenge assumptions on both sides of the great ideological divide over free trade.

This book is organized as follows: Chapters 1 and 2 deal with the origins of world trade, beginning with the first fragmentary evidence of long-range commerce during the Stone Age. The unmistakable footprints of trade in the earliest Mesopotamian records tell of the exportation of surplus grain and cloth from the rich land between the Tigris and Euphrates rivers, as well as the importation of strategic metals, particularly copper, utterly lacking in its alluvial soil. This earliest axis of trade ran three thousand miles from the hills of Anatolia, through Mesopotamia, out the Persian Gulf, across the shores of the Indian Ocean, and up the Indus River. The hubs of this trade were the successive great centers at Ur, Akkad, Babylon, and Nineveh (all located in modern Iraq). The volume and sophistication of trade through these cities slowly expanded over time, first in the Middle East, then spread westward through the Mediterranean and out into Europe's Atlantic coast, and eastward all the way to China. By the time Rome fell, goods moved through scores of hands, all the way between London and the Han Chinese capital at Chang-an. The end of the Roman Empire in the West provides a natural caesura between the world of vigorous ancient trade and the era that followed.

Chapters 3 through 6 trace the rise of trade in the Indian Ocean. This story properly begins in remote western Arabia in late antiquity and recounts the explosive spread of the religion of trade, Islam, whose influence ranged from Andalusia to the Philippines, and whose chosen conduit of divine revelation, the Prophet Muhammad, was himself a trader. Islam provided the glue that held together an advanced system of great commercial ports, where tangles of local and mercantile families and castes from far and wide mingled together with one purpose: profit. This system, we might add, was almost completely devoid of Europeans, who had been excluded from the Indian Ocean for nearly a millennium by Muslim conquests in Arabia, Asia, and Africa. Each one of the nations in this system faced the basic "trilemma" of trade—to trade, to raid, or to protect. Then, as now, how each government, from that of the humblest city-state to that of the grandest empire, approached these three choices dictated the shape of the trading environment and, indeed, the fates of nations.

Chapters 7 through 10 recount how this vast multicultural trade system was shattered when Vasco da Gama outflanked the Muslim "blockade," which had previously stopped European merchants at the western gates of the Indian Ocean. The Portuguese rounding of the Cape of Good Hope ushered in the current era of Western commercial dominance. Within a few decades after that momentous event, Portugal took the commanding heights of the Indian Ocean at Goa and sealed its eastern and western choke points at Malacca and Hormuz. (It would, however, fail to take the Red Sea entrance at Aden.) A century later, the Portuguese were shoved aside by the Dutch, who in their turn were eclipsed by the English East India Company.

Whereas the ambitions of kings and merchants and the religion of the Prophet drove premodern history, secular ideologies have largely propelled the modern era. Chapters 11 through 14 examine today's global trade in light of its underlying modern economic doctrines. As so famously put by Keynes:

> Practical men, who believe themselves to be quite exempt from any intellectual influences, are usually the slaves of some defunct economist. Madmen in authority, who hear voices in the air, are distilling their frenzy from some academic scribbler of a few years back.[21]

Trade's modern scribblers—David Ricardo, Richard Cobden, Eli Heckscher, Bertil Ohlin, Wolfgang Stolper, and Paul Samuelson—will help us to understand the massive upheavals seen in our ever more integrated global system.

Although the structure of this book is chronological, its many interwoven narratives will supersede the flow of mere dates and events. For example, two closely related stories, the south Arabian incense trade and the domestication of the camel, both span thousands of years. At the other extreme, the memoirs of medieval travelers who left us extensive and intact records of their journeys—Marco Polo, the Moroccan

legal scholar Ibn Battuta, and the Portuguese apothecary Tomé Pires—
will provide isolated but detailed snapshots of world trade spanning only
a few decades.

Ultimately, two deceptively simple notions anchor this book. First,
trade is an irreducible and intrinsic human impulse, as primal as the needs
for food, shelter, sexual intimacy, and companionship. Second, our urge
to trade has profoundly affected the trajectory of the human species. Simply by allowing nations to concentrate on producing those things that their
geographic, climatic, and intellectual endowments best enable them to
do, and to exchange those goods for what is best produced elsewhere, trade
has directly propelled our global prosperity. Ricardo's law of comparative advantage tells us it is far better for the Argentinians to grow beef,
the Japanese to make cars, and the Italians to turn out high-fashion shoes
than for each nation to attempt to become self-sufficient in all three areas.
Moreover, over the centuries camels and ships have conveyed in their
packs and holds history's fabulous stowaways, the intellectual capital of
mankind: "Arabic" (actually, Indian) numerals, algebra, and double-
entry bookkeeping. Without the need for long-range navigation, accurate
watches and clocks would surely not have become available until much
later; without the desire to transport large amounts of perishable foodstuffs long distances, it is unlikely that the unsung but essential household refrigerator would grace virtually every home in today's developed
world.

Modern life flows on an ever-rising river of trade; if we wish to
understand its currents and course, we must travel up its headwaters to
commercial centers with names like Dilmun and Cambay, where its origins can be sought, and its future imagined.

A Note to the Reader

Uncertainty shrouds more than a few of the topics covered here. Further,
I have found it difficult to completely ignore the myriad of fascinating
minutiae surrounding many of the tales. In order to maintain narrative
flow, I have consigned areas of controversy and engaging trivia to the
endnotes; interested readers are encouraged to consult these. They can
otherwise be safely ignored.

The events described herein took place in many places around the world. Rendering the names of them into Latin script was often problematic; in each case, I have employed the most commonly used spelling in the English-language academic literature as determined by the online database Journal Storage (JSTOR).

There is also the issue of money over the millennia. The basic unit of currency of the premodern world was remarkably constant: a small gold coin weighing approximately four grams—one-eighth of an ounce—and about the size of a present-day American dime, appearing in various times and places as the French livre, Florentine florin, Spanish or Venetian ducat, Portuguese cruzado, dinar of the Muslim world, Byzantine bezant, or late-Roman solidus. At the current price of gold, this corresponds to a modern value of roughly eighty American dollars. The three major exceptions to this rule were the Dutch guilder, which weighed about one-fifth as much, and the English one-pound sovereign and the early Roman aureus, each of which weighed twice as much. The Muslim dirham, Greek drachma, and Roman denarius were silver coins of roughly the same size and weight, each equivalent to the daily wage of a semiskilled worker, with a value ratio of about twelve to one between the gold and silver coins.

1

SUMER

The messages we receive from [the] remote past were neither intended for us, nor chosen by us, but are the casual relics of climate, geography, and human activity. They, too, remind us of the whimsical dimensions of our knowledge and the mysterious limits of our powers of discovery.—Daniel Boorstin[1]

Sometime around 3000 BC, a tribe of herders attacked a small community of Sumerian farmers at harvest time. From a safe distance, the attackers used slingshots, spears, and arrows that allowed them to achieve surprise. The farmers responded by closing in on the attackers with maces. The mace—a rounded stone attached to the end of a stout stick, designed to bash in the head of an opponent—was the first weapon specifically intended for use solely against fellow humans. (Animals had thick, angulated skulls that were rarely presented at an ideal angle to mace wielders.) Capable of crushing a man's fragile, round skull whether he was coming toward an attacker or running away, the mace proved especially effective.[2]

There was nothing unusual about an attack at harvest time; the herders' goats and sheep were highly sensitive to disease and the vagaries of climate, and thus the nomadic tribe's survival required frequent raids to take grain from its more reliably provisioned crop-growing neighbors. In this particular battle, the herders wore a strange, shiny piece of headgear that seemed to partially protect them. Hard, direct mace blows, once lethal, now merely stunned, and many blows simply glanced off the headgear's smooth surface. This protective advantage radically changed the tactical balance of power between the two sides, enabling the herders to devastate the defending farmers.

After the attack, the surviving farmers examined the headgear from the few fallen herders. These "helmets" contained a sheet, one-eighth inch thick, of a wondrous new orange material fitted over a leather head cover. The farmers had never seen copper before, since none was produced in the flat alluvial land between the Tigris and Euphrates. Their nomadic rivals had in fact obtained the metal from traders who lived near its source hundreds of miles to the west, in the Sinai Desert. It was not long before Sumerian farmers obtained their own supplies, enabling them to devise more lethal spiked copper-headed maces, to which the herders responded with thicker helmets. Thus was born the arms race, which to this day relies on exotic metals obtained through commerce.[3]

How did these farmers and herders obtain the copper for their helmets, and how was this trade conducted over the hundreds of miles between their farms and pastures and the copper mines? Paleoanthropologists believe that the best place to begin is about sixty to eighty thousand years ago, when the first genetically modern populations of humans in Africa began to develop more complex tools, pierce shells (presumably used in necklaces), and produce abstract images with pieces of red ochre. About fifty thousand years ago, small numbers of them probably migrated via Palestine into the Fertile Crescent and Europe. At some point prior to this trek, language developed, enabling more complex, uniquely "human" behavior: adroitly carved animal bone and antler tools, cave paintings, sculpture, and refined missile technologies, such as the atlatl, a specially crafted stick used to improve the range and accuracy of the spear. These increasingly sophisticated skills probably made possible yet another activity characteristic of modern humans: long-distance trade in the new weapons, tools, and knickknacks.[4]

Historians, on the other hand, traditionally start with Herodotus's description, written around 430 BC, of the "silent trade" between the Carthaginians and "a race of men who live in a part of Libya beyond the Pillars of Hercules" (the Strait of Gibraltar), most likely today's west Africans:

> On reaching this country, [the Carthaginians] unload their goods, arrange them tidily along the beach, and then, returning to their boats, raise a smoke. Seeing the smoke, the natives come down to the beach, place on the ground a certain quantity of gold in exchange for the goods, and go off again to a distance. The Carthaginians then come ashore and take a look at the gold; and if they think it represents a fair price for their wares, they collect it and go away; if, on the other hand, it seems too little, they go back aboard and wait, and the natives come and add to the gold until they are satisfied. There is perfect honesty on both sides; the Carthaginians never touch the gold

until it equals in value what they have offered for sale, and the natives never touch the goods until the gold has been taken away.[5]

Alas, Herodotus's description of the decorum displayed on each side has an aroma of myth.[6] Yet he probably got the basic scenario right. On some unrecorded occasion deep in prehistory, a man, or several men, initiated early long-distance trade by setting out on the water in boats.

Hunger most likely got man into those primitive craft. Twenty thousand years ago, northern Europe resembled modern Lapland: a cold, uncultivated panorama dotted with fewer and smaller trees than are there today. Europe's first *Homo sapiens,* probably fresh from wiping out their Neanderthal rivals, subsisted primarily on large game, particularly reindeer. Even under ideal circumstances, hunting these fleet animals with spear or bow and arrow is an uncertain enterprise. The reindeer, however, had a weakness that mankind would mercilessly exploit: it swam poorly. While afloat, it is uniquely vulnerable, moving slowly with its antlers held high as it struggles to keep its nose above water. At some point, a Stone Age genius, realized the enormous hunting advantage he would gain by being able to glide over the water's surface, and built the first boat. Once the easily overtaken and slaughtered prey had been hauled aboard, getting its carcass back to the tribal camp would have been far easier by boat than on land. It would not have taken long for mankind to apply this advantage to other goods.

Cave paintings and scattered maritime remains suggest that boats first appeared in northern Europe around fifteen thousand years ago. These early watercraft were made from animal skins sewed over rigid frames (most often antler horns) and were used for both hunting and transport, most commonly with a paddler in the rear and a weapon-bearing hunter or passenger in front. It is no accident that the reindeer-bone sewing needle appears simultaneously in the archaeological record, since it is necessary for the manufacture of sewn-skin vessels. These first boats predate the more "primitive" dugout canoe, for the cold, steppe-like vista of northern Europe could not grow trees wide enough to accommodate a fur-clad hunter.

Only the most durable remnants, mainly stone tools, survive to provide hints about the nature of the earliest long-range commerce. One of the earliest commodities traded by boat must have been obsidian, a black volcanic rock (actually, a glass) that is a favorite of landscapers and gardeners around the world. Prehistoric man valued it not for its aesthetic properties, but rather because it was easily chipped into razor-sharp, if fragile, cutting tools and weapons. The historical value of obsidian lies in two facts: first, it is produced in only a handful of volcanic sites, and second, with the use of sophisticated atomic fingerprinting techniques, individual samples can be traced back to their original volcanic sources.

Obsidian flakes dating to over twelve thousand years ago found in the Franchthi Cave in mainland Greece originated from the volcano on the island of Melos, one hundred miles offshore. These artifacts must have been carried in watercraft, yet there are no archaeological remains, literary fragments, or even oral traditions that inform us just how the obsidian got from Melos to the mainland. Were these flakes conveyed by merchants who traded them for local products, or were they simply retrieved by expeditions from the mainland communities who valued them?

Obsidian atomic fingerprints have been used to examine flows of the material through regions as disparate as the Fertile Crescent and the Yucatán. In the Middle East, the researcher Colin Renfrew matched up sites with sources dating from around 6000 BC. The amount of obsidian measured at each excavation site fell off dramatically with distance from its source, strongly suggesting that this was a result of trade. For example, all the stone blades found in the Mesopotamian sites came from one of two sites in Armenia. At a site 250 miles away from its volcanic source, about 50 percent of all of the chipped stone found was obsidian, whereas at a second site five hundred miles away from the source, only 2 percent of the chipped stone was obsidian.[7]

These Stone Age obsidian routes put into modern perspective the costs of prehistoric commerce. Transporting a load of obsidian between Armenia and Mesopotamia was the prehistoric equivalent of sending a family Christmas package from Boston to Washington, DC. But instead of paying a few dollars and handing the package over to a brown-clad clerk, this ancient shipment consumed two months (including the return trip) of a single trader's labor—very roughly, about $5,000 to $10,000 in current value.

With the advent of agriculture, this new maritime technology spread to settled farmers, who adopted the skin-and-frame design for river travel. A pattern of commerce commenced that would remain unchanged for thousands of years: traders from advanced farming communities would transport grain, farm animals, and basic manufactured items such as cloth and tools downriver to exchange for the wares, mainly animal skins, of the hunter-gatherers. Archaeologists usually find the remains of these prehistoric markets on small, unforested river islands. This is no coincidence; these locations not only took advantage of boat transport but also minimized the odds of a successful ambush.

Ax and adze (chisel) blades, dating to about 5000 BC, survive as the main evidence of this Stone Age waterborne commerce. Archaeologists have identified Balkan quarries as the source of the ax and blade material, fragments of which are found all the way from the mouth of the Danube at the Black Sea to the Baltic and North seas. These durable stone artifacts, found far from their identifiably unique sources, attest to a lively long-distance exchange in a rich multitude of goods.[8]

Water transport is by its nature cheaper and more efficient than land carriage. A draft horse can carry about two hundred pounds on its back. With the help of a wagon and a good road, it can pull four thousand pounds. With the same energy expenditure, the same animal can draw as many as sixty thousand pounds along a canal towpath, a load that could be managed by small ancient sailing ships.[9]

Herodotus also described similar sewn-skin vessels carrying wine "stored in casks made of the wood of the palm-tree." The ships were "round, like a shield," made of hide, and propelled by two Armenian merchants down the Euphrates to Babylon. Here, then, is the direct descendant of the earliest cargo ship used in maritime trade, a vessel relatively round in shape—and thus slow—so as to accommodate the most weight with the smallest crew and the minimal amount of building material. (By contrast, warships since ancient times have been narrow and fast, with smaller carrying capacities.)

The largest of these boats carried about fourteen tons and came equipped with several donkeys, so that at journey's end the wood frames could be scrapped and the precious skins packed up and carried back to Armenia on the beasts. Herodotus explains:

> It is quite impossible to paddle the boats upstream because of the strength of the current, and that is why they are constructed of hide instead of wood. Back in Armenia with their donkeys, the men build another lot of boats to the same design.[10]

After returning to Armenia, the farmers would refit the skins over new frames and load the boats with fresh cargo, and the several-month journey to bartering centers would begin anew. No doubt, the Stone Age hunter-gatherers and farmers of northern Europe also paddled their goods downstream and packed their craft upstream in similar fashion.

Such were the likely beginnings of trade. Yet out of the desire to attack (or defend) territory was born one of the earliest and most enduring motifs of its history—the exchange of grain from advanced farming communities living in alluvial areas for metals, generally found in less fertile locales.

Around six thousand years ago, man figured out how to purify the abundant copper ore found just below the layers of the pure metal of the first virgin mines. Not long after, the Ergani mines in mountainous Anatolia (modern-day Asian Turkey) began shipping copper to the early settlements at Uruk (in what is now southern Iraq, about a hundred miles west of Basra). The Euphrates River connected Ergani and Uruk, and although the vessels of the day could easily float several tons of copper downstream to Uruk in a few weeks, the transport of hundreds of tons of grain to Anatolia, against the current, would have been much more problematic.[11]

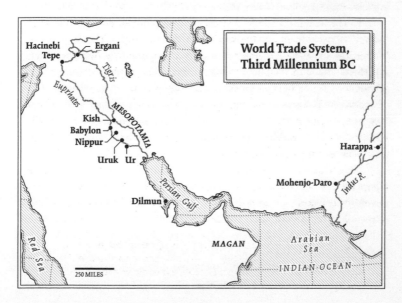

World Trade System, Third Millennium BC

Later Mesopotamian civilizations took advantage of more favorably placed Persian Gulf mineral sources. The appearance of written records just before 3000 BC offers fleeting glimpses of a massive copper-grain trade that flourished along this route. The land of milk and honey from the ancient Sumerian creation myths was a place known as Dilmun, celebrated for its wealth and probably located in modern-day Bahrain. Its prosperity, however, came not from its relatively fertile soil, but rather from its strategic position as a trading post for copper produced in the land of Magan, in what is today Oman, just outside the entrance to the Persian Gulf at the Strait of Hormuz.

Not far from modern-day Qalat al-Bahrain, the archaeological excavation of ancient Dilmun's likely location has yielded a treasure trove of Bronze Age objects. The site covers only about fifty acres but contained a population of about five thousand, probably far more than could have been supported by the city's agricultural hinterland. Cuneiform texts record that small shipments, usually consisting of a few tons of barley, began to travel down the Gulf toward Dilmun and Magan around 2800 BC. By the end of the millennium, these grain cargoes increased to as much as several hundred tons per shipload. At an astonishingly early point, history affords an ancient equivalent of Las Vegas—a large population living in relatively barren surroundings whose very survival depended on large amounts of food imported from hundreds of miles away.[12]

The excavation of Dilmun provides a tantalizing, and often highly personal, window on what the Sumerian trade in grain and copper in the Persian Gulf might have looked like. The town sat on an island and was supplied with a generous spring issuing what the ancients called "sweet," or fresh, water. By 2000 BC, the city walls enclosed an area almost the size of the biggest Mesopotamian city, Ur. In its center sat a municipal square, one end of which opened on the sea gate; at the other end stood a building filled with seals and scales, almost certainly a customs house. Piled high around the square would have been huge baskets of barley and dates from the banks of the Tigris; the more precious cargo—Mesopotamian cloth as well as ivory and ingots of copper bound for Ur—stood just outside the customs house, guarded by nervous sailors while their officers argued with, bribed, and cajoled the officials inside.

If the year was 1800 BC, these ingots would probably have been bound for the warehouses of Ea-nasir, the largest copper merchant in Ur, where archaeologists have discovered a large cache of clay tablets detailing this strategic trade.[13] One tablet records a shipment of twenty tons of the metal; another bears the complaint of a client, one Nanni:

> You said, "I will give good ingots to Gimil-Sin." That is what you said, but you have not done so; you offered bad ingots to my messenger saying "Take it or leave it." Who am I that you should treat me so? Are we not both gentlemen?[14]

The curiosity and drive of the first metal-craftsmen who produced the copper in Ea-nasir's warehouses must have been remarkable. The process in which sulfur, oxygen, chlorine, or carbonate, depending on the type of ore, are removed from it to yield the pure metal—smelting—first saw the light of day in approximately 3500 BC. The metallurgists of the Fertile Crescent soon began mixing their local copper with an exotic imported metal, tin. Not only was the new hammered copper-tin alloy as hard and durable as that of the previous copper-arsenic and copper-antimony alloys, but it melted at a much lower temperature than pure copper. Better yet, it did not bubble and was thus easily cast.

The magical new alloy was bronze, and it quickly became the standard for a vast array of weapons, cooking utensils, ceremonial objects, and agricultural implements. Not coincidentally, the early Sumerian Ur dynasties, which had pioneered organized agriculture, were also the first to discover the optimal ratio of copper to tin, ten to one, around 2800 BC.[15]

Only two things are certain about the Sumerians' supply of tin: unlike arsenic and antimony, which were locally available and cheap, tin was extremely expensive to procure, and it traveled to them across a great distance. The price of tin was about ten times that of copper, a ratio that held well into the early twentieth century. But where did tin come from? Brittany and Cornwall began producing tin well before 2000 BC, but no record of navigation beyond the Pillars of Hercules (the Strait of Gibraltar) exists until about 450 BC, when a Phoenician navigator, Himilco, ventured into the open Atlantic and brought back tin from these northern European mines.[16] Historians hypothesize that tin traveled from northern Europe to the Fertile Crescent via multiple land routes through France, particularly along the valley of the Garonne River, which runs northwest from its sources in the coastal ranges above the Mediterranean to modern-day Bordeaux on the Atlantic. By this period, central Asia was also yielding supplies of the precious metal. All three routes—by sea through Gibraltar, overland through France, and from central Asia—were probably used.

Here and there, archaeologists have found tantalizing hints. In 1983, the marine archaeologist Don Frey was showing some slides to Turkish sponge divers, who often provide academics with information about sunken wrecks. After the talk, one of them came up to Frey and told him about a pile of ingots on the ocean bottom at the base of a cliff off the western Turkish coastal city of Bodrum, at a site called Ulu Burun. An expedition there uncovered a wreck from about 1350 BC yielding an abundance of ancient cargo: unworked elephant and hippopotamus ivory, early glass, and a mass of copper ingots. Among these exotica they also found some fragments of tin ingots, the earliest known specimens of the metal. Archaeologists estimate that about a ton of tin went down with the vessel, in addition to ten tons of copper; this estimate corresponds to the ideal ratio of copper to tin in bronze: ten to one.[17] The nationality of the vessel, let alone the source of the tin, remain unknown.[18]

If the evidence for a long-distance tin trade in the early ancient world sounds highly speculative, that's because it is. Since the first Sumerian cuneiform tablets date from 3300 BC—just after the earliest evidence of copper smelting but before the appearance of bronze—we have only scant archaeological evidence of trade in goods before that date. But if there was long-range trade in tin around 3000 BC, there must also have existed a similar long-range barter for other valuable materials, such as linen, frankincense, myrrh, tigers, ostrich feathers, and a thousand other sights, sounds, and smells now lost to history.

While the modern West worries about its dependency on oil from the most politically unstable regions of the planet, the plight of ancient Mesopotamia was far worse. The flat, alluvial land between the rivers possessed only water and soil in excess, and so yielded an abundance of barley, emmer wheat, fish, and wool. This cradle of ancient civilization was, however, nearly completely devoid of the era's strategic materials: metals, large timbers, and even stone for building. The very survival of Mesopotamia's great nations— the Sumerians, Akkadians, Assyrians, and finally the Babylonians—hinged on the exchange of their surplus food for metals from Oman and the Sinai, granite and marble from Anatolia and Persia, and lumber from Lebanon.

As the ambits of these civilizations spread during the ensuing eras, so did long-distance trade. By the fourth millennium BC, the Fertile Crescent was not the only region of coalesced communities; organized agricultural, military, religious, and administrative activity had also begun to appear in the Indus Valley, in what is now Pakistan. Even before written records, there is evidence of trade between these two regions. Archaeologists have discovered lamps and cups in Mesopotamia dating from the late fourth millennium BC and made from conch shells found only in the Indian Ocean and the Gulf of Oman. Since transportation costs along this route must have been astronomical, it is not surprising that these shells were found only in palaces or in the graves of high-status individuals.

By 2500 BC, tastes had changed, as new status symbols—jars, tools, and jewelry made of copper—replaced conch cups and lamps. At this early stage, shipping costs were still prohibitive, and ordinary people used stone, not metal, tools. Even if they could afford the superior copper implements, these high-end products were probably reserved for the ruling elites and the military.

In another five hundred years, metal became more abundant, and copper tools finally came into widespread use in Mesopotamia. Because of its high value, copper was used for barter (along with cattle and grain) throughout the Bronze Age. Several centuries later, around 2000 BC, increasing copper supplies devalued the metal. This abundance mandated a shift toward the use of silver as a medium of exchange, or as we call it today, "money."

The rise of silver as internationally recognized currency itself lubricated commerce, because it facilitated the purchase and sale of other staples. Without it, trade required barter between pairs of commodities. For example, with ten different items, there are forty-five possible exchange pairs (and thus prices). The widespread use of silver money, by contrast, requires only ten different prices—one for each of the different goods. Moreover, the subjectivity of deciding whether a cow was worth fifty or fifty-five chickens made barter too unreliable for large-scale transactions.

Nanni and Ea-nasir, the two merchants we met a few pages ago, witnessed the rise of early financial markets. The businessmen who ran the trade in metals and grain, the so-called *alik-Dilmun* (literally, "go-getters of Dilmun"), had to purchase massive amounts of agricultural products and then outfit and man ships large enough to transport them to Dilmun.

This necessitated capital from outside investors, who in turn expected a handsome return. A contract executed on a clay tablet gives us a rare insight into one such financial transaction, a loan from a wealthy man identified as "U" to two trading partners, "L" and "N":

> Two mina of silver, [which is the value of] five gur of oil and thirty garments for an expedition to Dilmun to buy there copper for the partnership of L and N. . . . After safe termination of the voyage, U will not recognize commercial losses; the debtors have agreed to satisfy U with four mina of copper for each shekel of silver as a just price.[19]

In other words, U has lent the traders L and N 120 shekels (two mina) of silver, for which he expects to be paid back with 480 mina (roughly a quarter ton) of copper; if the voyage fails, the traders L and N will absorb the loss.

Whereas there clearly were extensive imports into Mesopotamia, including ivory, jewels, slaves, perfumes, and oils, we know far less about what, beyond grain, was exported. Since Mesopotamia was the world's richest agricultural area, it must have shipped out vast amounts of "invisible exports," such as fish and wool.[20] The historian Christopher Edens notes that our knowledge of early trade to the north and south of the Tigris and Euphrates is

> one-sided, and built on a narrow foundation of documents that are few in number and disparate in context. . . . The economic documents reflect Mesopotamian but not foreign enterprises. . . . Other sources indicate the arrival of foreign vessels but do not reveal their cargoes.[21]

Still, historical fragments suggest a system of roadways and sea-lanes along a three-thousand-mile arc extending from the mountains of Anatolia, southeast throughout Mesopotamia and the Persian Gulf, eastward through the near-shore waters of the Indian Ocean, and northeast up present-day Pakistan's Indus Valley.[22] Trade along this vast network—version 1.0 of the World Trade Organization, if you will—must have been indirect (as would be much later connections between imperial Rome and Han China), involving dozens, if not hundreds, of individual journey segments, intermediaries, and transactions. Although the Anatolians and the people of the Indus Valley knew each other's products, it is not known whether or not they met each other face-to-face; rather, they would have been separated by an unknown number of middlemen. Whenever possible, traders exploited the efficiency of water transport; where there was none, the first animal domesticated for transport, the pack donkey, was used.[23]

Government and temple officials in both Sumeria and Egypt carried out these earliest transactions, but by 2000 BC long-range Sumerian commerce had fallen largely into private hands (such as those of Ea-nasir), while in Egypt it remained under the direction of the state. What is unclear is whether this three-thousand-mile trading arc was home to the first "trade diasporas"—permanent colonies of foreign merchants who facilitated commerce between their native and adopted homes, middlemen trusted in the cities in which they were guests as well as in their homelands.

Tantalizing hints abound, especially a cache of seals, uncovered in Mesopotamia, of a sort commonly used in the Indus Valley; and animal-headed pins, native to Mesopotamia, found in the Indus Valley. The stone seal functioned as the ancient version of shrink-wrap; the merchant placed a lump of wet clay over the closure of a container, then rolled or pressed the seal across the lump, impressing it with his mark. Left to dry and harden, the seal informed the purchaser that the merchant had guaranteed the contents of the container, and that it had not been tampered with in transit. Smaller stone tokens were often used to add to the seal information about the type and quantity of goods.[24] Government officials employed their own designs, and both the trading and the governmental seals of different civilizations were quite distinct, so that "Indus Valley" seals found in Mesopotamia strongly suggest the presence of a colony of Indus Valley traders in the land between the rivers.

The strongest evidence for early trade diasporas is found at the western end of the arc. During the 1990s, the archaeologist Gil Stein excavated a site in Anatolia at Hacinebi Tepe, at the northernmost navigable point of the Euphrates. There, he found evidence for an advanced local culture dating back to 4100 BC, including extensive housing, mortuaries, and, most tellingly, distinctive flat stone seals. His team also uncovered a small area within this site containing artifacts characteristic of Uruk civilization dating to 3700 BC; these artifacts included typical Mesopotamian cylindrical seals and the bones of goats carrying the marks of a "Mesopotamian" pattern of butchering. Although it is possible that the colony represented an occupying force from the south, this seems unlikely for several reasons.

First, this colony was quite small; second, it was unwalled; third, upstream transport from Mesopotamia was tenuous; and fourth, the Anatolians were at least as militarily advanced as the Mesopotamians. It is difficult to avoid the conclusion that Stein uncovered the earliest known trade diaspora, perhaps simultaneous with the birth of the local copper industry.[25]

The advent of the written word around 3300 BC lifted history's curtain and revealed an already well-established pattern of long-distance trade, not only in luxury and strategic goods, but in bulk staples such as grain and timber as well.

By 3000 BC the Persian Gulf served as a major artery of commerce. As civilization spread slowly west into Egypt, Phoenicia, and Greece, another maritime route assumed increasing importance—out the Red Sea and into the Indian Ocean through the Red Sea's southern exit at Bab el Mandeb, past what is now Yemen. For over four thousand years, the Egypt–Red Sea nexus served as a pivot point of world trade, and with it, Egyptians profited mightily.

Pre-Ptolemaic Egypt, with abundant quarries and easy access to the copper mines of the nearby Sinai desert, did not depend on trade with other countries for vital strategic materials as much as did the Sumerians. The most important exception to the Egyptians' self-sufficiency was wood, which they could easily import via the efficient Mediterranean Sea route from Phoenicia, whose lumber was prized for its resistance to decay.

Egyptian ships plied the Red Sea route as far as the "country of Punt" (modern Yemen and Somalia), over 1,500 miles to the south.[26] There are hints of such voyages as early as 2500 BC, and a lucky archaeological find gives us the powerful story of one such expedition occurring around 1470 BC, ordered by Queen Hatshepsut.

After 1479 BC, Hatshepsut ruled as regent to the son of her deceased husband (and half-brother) by a commoner. She left a mortuary sanctuary at Deir el-Bahri (on the Nile, just across from Luxor), whose painted relief carvings and narrations depicted a commercial expedition to Punt.

The story is told in four panels, the first showing several galleys, each perhaps eighty feet long and equipped with sails and teams of rowers. The second panel depicts the unloading of what are presumably bales of Egyptian grain and textiles in Punt; the third, large plants or trees being

Figure 1-1. Expedition of Queen Hatshepsut. (Begin at the lower right and proceed clockwise. Second panel occupies only a small corner at lower left.)

loaded; and the fourth, the vessels returning home. Above this frieze is the following inscription:

> The loading of the ships very heavily with marvels of the country of Punt: all goodly fragrant woods of God's land, heaps of myrrh-resin, with fresh myrrh trees, with ebony, and pure ivory, with green gold of Emu, with cinnamon wood, khesyt wood, with ihmut-incense, sonter-incense, eye-cosmetic, with apes, monkeys, dogs, and with skins of the southern panther, with natives and their children. Never was brought the like of this for any king who had been since the beginning.[27]

Following the decline of the Egyptian dynasties after Hatshepsut's reign, the Phoenicians took over the Red Sea trade. Distant relations of the Canaanite sea-peoples, they settled in what is now Lebanon. With that land's abundant timber and strategic location between Mesopotamia and Egypt, no ancient race was as well positioned to excel at trafficking goods by sea. Their supremacy in commerce in the eastern Mediterranean lasted over a thousand years. It is likely that the Phoenicians were the first people to engage in *direct* long-distance trade. The first book of Kings records:

> And King Solomon made a navy of ships in Eziongeber, which is beside Eloth, on the shore of the Red Sea, in the land of Edom. And Hiram sent in the navy his servants, shipmen that had knowledge of the sea, with the servants of Solomon. And they came to Ophir, and fetched from thence gold, four hundred and twenty talents, and brought it to King Solomon.[28]

Translation: The long-distance trading of Solomon's kingdom, near the beginning of the first millennium BC, was carried out by the Phoenicians (Hiram being the king of Tyre, the dominant Phoenician city-state). "Eziongeber" was most likely a port city at Tall al-Khulayfah, near Elat ("Eloth"), on the Gulf of Aqaba (the northeastern tip of the Red Sea). "Ophir" was probably India, as suggested by the goods imported from it: precious metals, peacocks, ivory, and apes.[29] The 420 talents of gold mentioned weighed about thirteen tons and would be worth approximately $270 million in current value—real money, even by today's standards.

By 400 BC, most of the western European coastline, as well as the coasts of both eastern and western Africa, were familiar to the Phoenicians.[30]

This was, in the ancient world, an incredible trading range. Such was Phoenicia's dominance in long-distance commerce that around 600 BC the Egyptian pharaoh Necho commissioned Phoenician mariners to circumnavigate Africa. Herodotus writes:

> The Phoenicians sailed from the Arabian Gulf into the southern ocean, and every autumn put in at some convenient spot on the [African] coast, sowed a patch of ground, and waited for the next year's harvest. Then, having gotten their grain, they put to sea again, and after two full years rounded the Pillars of Hercules in the course of the third, and returned to Egypt. The men made a statement which I do not myself believe, though others may, to the effect that as they sailed on a westerly course round the southern end of [Africa], they had the sun to their right—to the northward of them.[31]

What prompts doubt in Herodotus—that the sun could be seen on the right, that is, in the north, while one was traveling west—persuades the modern reader. That the ancient historian was probably unaware of how the sun moves in the southern hemisphere makes the story of intrepid Phoenicians rounding Africa's southern cape, over two thousand years before Vasco da Gama, all the more convincing.[32]

In the coming centuries, power shifted eastward into Persia, which had set its sights on the Aegean area. Seeking an alternative to the arduous overland route north through the Hellespont (the modern Dardanelles), Darius the Great completed a canal at Suez (originally contemplated by the pharaoh Necho), linking the Nile, and thus the Mediterranean, with the Red Sea.[33] However, Persia's Aegean ambitions were thwarted in the early fifth century BC at the battles of Marathon, Salamis, and Platea, allowing the Greeks to burst onto the Mediterranean political, trading, and military scene.

Although the independent Greek and Phoenician city-states both traded and colonized widely in the Mediterranean Sea and the Black Sea (with the Phoenicians occasionally venturing well beyond the Mediterranean), their routine commerce spanned neither continents nor oceans. The Athenians' imperial ambition would eventually trigger the Peloponnesian War, devastating the Greek world and paving the way for Alexander the Great's spectacular conquest of all of Greece, Egypt, and west Asia in the late fourth century BC. It was this occupation that hellenized the Western world and greatly expanded the scope of ancient global commerce.

Alexander's most enduring legacy would be the founding of the cosmopolitan Alexandria, for centuries the base for the profitable commerce with Arabia, India, and China. The center did not hold long after his death in 323 BC, as his empire fragmented into warring successor states. One of them, Egypt, ruled by his general Ptolemy, inherited the sailing and trading traditions of the preceding dynasties, as well as Phoenician shipbuilding technology, which centered on hulls of cedar planks. This enabled the Egyptians to pioneer the Red Sea waterway into the Indian Ocean, and thence regular blue-water commerce to India itself. Their priority, however, was not trade, but the acquisition of elephants, the "tanks of the ancient world," from Ethiopia for use against the rival post-Alexandrian Seleucid Greek empire in Persia.[34] With this in mind, Ptolemy II attempted, with little success, to reopen Darius's old canal, which had silted up.

Because of Egypt's strategic position between the Mediterranean Sea and the Indian Ocean, via the Red Sea, the canal would have been an ideal route for shipping Ptolemy's elephants. The dream of a sea-level canal across the Suez beckoned to rulers as far back as Necho in 600 BC. Multiple difficulties plagued the project. The massive undertaking—a deepwater canal sixty to eighty miles long—would have strained even the wealthiest of states, ancient or modern. Herodotus records that Necho's attempt resulted in the deaths of more than 120,000 conscripts. Worse, the Nile was used as the canal's western terminus. When the river was at flood stage, it deposited sediment into the canal. Alternatively, when the Nile was low, its level would fall below that of the Red Sea, allowing seawater to flow into the river and poison the drinking and irrigation sources with salt. Additionally, there was the ever-present fear that enemies would use the canal to surround Egypt—the reason Necho never completed it.

But the temptation was strong, and successive canals were attempted by the ancient Persians, Ptolemies, and Romans, and the early Muslim empires.[35] All the canals, except the last, followed essentially the same route, from the easternmost arm (Pelusiac Branch) of the Nile delta via a dried riverbed, Wadi Tumilat, to the northern end of what is now the Great Bitter Lake, just north of the present-day Gulf of Suez. By the time of the caliphate, the Pelusiac Branch of the Nile had silted up, forcing Arab engineers to originate their canal on a more southerly arm of the delta. In biblical times, Great Bitter Lake was connected by a narrow channel at its southern end to the Gulf of Suez, and from there to the Red Sea. Later efforts to connect the Nile and Great Bitter Lake mainly involved dredging out and enlarging the silted remains of earlier canals.

The channel between Great Bitter Lake and the Gulf of Suez was shallow and tenuous; a brisk east wind combined with a low tide often rendered it high and dry. (Such a circumstance could easily have afforded Moses and his followers their probably mythical crossing. Shortly thereafter the water could have swallowed up the pursuing Egyptians. This channel between Great Bitter Lake and the Gulf of Suez finally closed off permanently around AD 1000, likely as the result of an earthquake.)

Although apparently the Persian and Abbasid canals each operated for more than a century, it is not clear whether, or for how long, any of the others functioned. And even an operational canal merely served to expose mariners to the many drawbacks of the Red Sea route, where stiff headwinds in its northern half impeded northbound travel. Further, ships sailing in either direction faced murderous shoals. If the winds and reefs weren't discouraging enough, pirates infested the entire route, especially its upper portion.

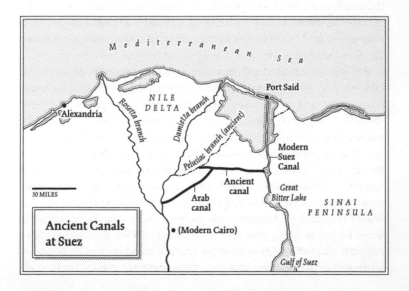

We can now return to the story of Ptolemy's elephants. His minions marched them from their home in the African heartland east to Ethiopia, where the elephants were put on boats and shipped to the Egyptian port of Berenice, about two-thirds of the way north up the Red Sea. They then marched across the desert toward the start of the navigable portion of the Nile at Coptos or Caenopolis, and from there continued by boat about three hundred miles north to Alexandria.

Alone among the world's great rivers, the Nile flows north, and it is also fanned by a year-round northerly wind. These two circumstances allow ships to float north downstream and to sail south upstream. The route via the Nile, desert, and Red Sea to and from the Indian Ocean would remain one of the "grand trunk roads" of commerce until the advent of steam power, which not only freed sailors from the vagaries of the wind but also drove the construction of the modern canal, which avoided the silt-ridden Nile delta altogether.

After 200 BC, Ptolemaic Greek merchants gradually extended their trading activities eastward toward India. A century later, an ambitious sea captain, Eudoxus of Cyzicus, traveled directly from Egypt to India via the long coastwise route out through Bab el Mandeb. He first hugged the southern and then the eastern Arabian shores to the Strait of Hormuz at the mouth of the Persian Gulf and finally navigated the coasts of what are now Iran and Pakistan to the southern Indian trading centers—a total distance of about five thousand miles. This feat led the way to the momentous "discovery" of the Indian Ocean monsoon.

The huge Indian Ocean functions as a heat reservoir, remaining at approximately the same even temperature when the Asian landmass heats up in summer and cools down in winter. Since heat produces low pressure and cold produces high pressure, the prevailing winds tend to blow from the area of high pressure (cold) to the area of low pressure (hot)—that is, more or less from the south in summer (the southwest monsoon) and more or less from the north in winter (the northeast monsoon).

It fell to the Egyptian Greek mariner Hippalus (who was quite possibly Eudoxus's navigator) to harness these seasonal winds, which enabled Greek traders to cross the Arabian Sea directly from Bab el Mandeb to India in a matter of weeks. The result was a flourishing of large, ethnically diverse hubs such as Socotra and the Malabar ports—polyglot communities where trade diasporas of many nations and races mingled,

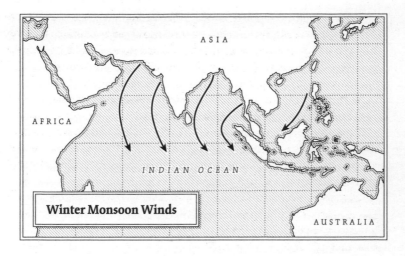

Winter Monsoon Winds

managed cargoes, made fortunes, and satisfied an unquenchable Western (i.e., Roman) demand for such Oriental luxury goods as silk, cotton, spices, gems, and exotic animals.

Octavian's accession to power prepared the ground for the two centuries of Pax Romana, the environment of stability in which ancient long-range trade blossomed. It would not be long before Indian ambassadors

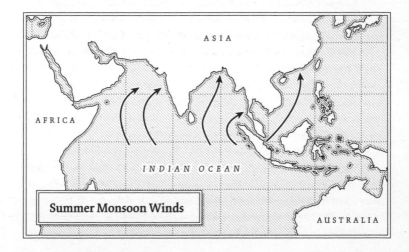

Summer Monsoon Winds

appeared in Rome bearing exotic gifts. These new luxuries—Chinese silk and Indian wildlife borne on the trade winds—electrified the empire's affluent. Monkeys, tigers, cockatoos, and rhinoceroses were not uncommon sights in the capital; Latin-speaking parrots became all the rage; and Romans prized the tusks of both Indian and African elephants, using the ivory to adorn furniture, weaponry, chariots, jewelry, and musical instruments. The Stoic philosopher and playwright Seneca is said to have owned five hundred tripod tables with ivory legs—no small irony, since he was a vocal critic of the empire's extravagances.

Not all imported goods were luxuries. Oceangoing ships needed ballast, and so-called "ballast goods" such as wine, lumber, and even jugs of water were traded in great volume. Filling the holds of many a Greek ship, pepper arrived in bulk to flavor the otherwise bland wheat- and barley-based Mediterranean cuisine of rich and poor Romans. It proved so popular that when the Goth Alaric held Rome for ransom in AD 408, he demanded three thousand pounds of the black spice.

The Western Ghats, a range of low mountains, rise up from southwestern India's Malabar Coast and capture the moisture of the summer monsoon. The resultant abundant rainfall produces a lush, tropical climate ideal for growing the fruit of *Piper nigrum* and *Piper longum*—black pepper and the more potent, and thus more expensive, long pepper, respectively.

Malabar peppers eventually would find their way into huge *horrea,* or warehouses, in Ostia, in Puteoli, and of course in Rome. Although the modern image of the imperial city is dominated by the ruins of the Coliseum and the Forum, the economic life of ancient Rome centered on side streets filled with apartments, shops, and *horrea.* Probably none was more important than the *horrea piperataria,* or spice warehouses, just off the Via Sacra, the capital's main street, which today runs through the site of the Forum. As was typical in the premodern world, the trade in a given commodity tended to cluster in one area. From the *horrea,* pepper was distributed to smaller retail shops in the "spice district" of the Via Sacra neighborhood, where it was sold in small packets to wealthy and middle-class families. (By contrast, the more precious wares of India—pearls, ivory, fine hardwood furniture, and Chinese silk—were sold inside the Forum itself.) The one surviving cookbook from the era, apparently written by a Roman named Apicius, called for pepper in 349 of its 468 recipes;

the Romans poured pepper not just into their main courses, but also into their sweets, wines, and medicines.[36]

What investment banking is to the ambitious and acquisitive today, the pepper trade was to the Romans—the most direct route to great riches. In the early empire, a greedy person was commonly referred to as being "the first to take the fresh-bought pepper from the camel's back."[37] The poet Persius wrote:

> *The greedy merchants led by lucre, run*
> *To the parched Indies, and the rising sun;*
> *From thence hot Pepper, and rich Drugs they bear,*
> *Bart'ring for Spices, their Italian ware.*[38]

Pliny wrote: "To think that its only pleasing quality is its pungency and that we go all the way to India to get this! Both pepper and ginger grow wild in their own countries, and nevertheless they are bought by weight like gold or silver."[39] Pliny's moral outrage, as well as that of Seneca and other critics of Roman decadence, mirrors what is commonly understood today: that the East-West trade contributed to the fall of the Roman Empire by draining it of its gold and silver to pay for fleeting luxuries. The most infamous of Roman emperors, Nero, certainly played his part in this ancient version of the current accounts deficit; according to Pliny, "Good authorities declare that Arabia does not produce so large a quantity of perfume in a year's output as was burned by the Emperor Nero in a day at the obsequies of his consort Poppaea."[40] The English historian E. H. Warmington gave an entire chapter of his epic volume on the Indian-Roman trade to this "adverse balance":[41]

> Not only did Italy consume more than she produced, not only was Rome a city and Latium a district poor in manufactures . . . but the Empire taken as one unit was often unable to offer to foreign regions in general and to oriental nations in particular sufficient products of its own to balance the articles imported from them in large quantities, and the result of this was the draining away from the Empire of precious metals in the form of coined money without any adequate return.[42]

Yet the conventional wisdom that Rome went broke buying pepper and silk may not be correct. Nature blessed the empire with an abundance of both base and precious metals, and the Romans also exported prodigious quantities of bulk goods. To India went red Mediterranean coral and the world's finest glass (also popular in China). Lead from Spain and copper from Cyprus filled the ballast holds of many a Greek ship. Tin from Cornwall traveled directly from England to Alexandria for onward shipment, and Italian vessels bound for Egypt and India groaned with large cargoes of fine wine. Just as climate and natural resources gave China and India dominance in proffering high-value agricultural goods such as silk and pepper, advanced civil engineering techniques gave Rome large advantages in mining. Further, China and India strongly preferred silver to gold. While silver flowed east, gold from India moved west in impressive quantities. We know, for example, that in the late seventeenth century, an ounce of gold in China bought only five or six ounces of silver, whereas in Spain it bought twelve ounces.[43] (Marco Polo reported that in Burma during the late thirteenth century, one weight of gold bought only five of silver.[44]) This disparity between East and West in the exchange rate for gold and silver had existed since at least Seneca's day; thus it would have been insane for a Roman merchant to pay for Chinese goods in any other coin but silver. In the words of the economic historians Dennis Flynn and Arturo Giráldez, "There was no imbalance of trade—East-West, North-South, Europe-Asia, or otherwise—for which monetary resources had to flow in compensation. *There was just trade.*"[45]

The end of the western Roman Empire slowed the expansion of world trade outward from its cradle in the Indian Ocean. But it didn't stop it. A powerful new monotheistic religion—Islam—would arise and propel this renewed expansion of trade through the Indian Ocean, across the broad plains of Asia, and to the very extremities of the vast Eurasian landmass. The trade along the Han-Roman axis spanned huge distances, but it was still poorly integrated: between origin and destination, cargoes bounced among merchants of many races, religions, cultures, and most important, legal traditions.

The coming of the Prophet would sweep away this fragmented and pluralistic pattern of trade in the ancient world. Within a few centuries of Muhammad's death, one culture, one religion, and one law would unify the commerce of the Old World's three continents nearly a millennium before the arrival of the first European ships in the East.

2

THE STRAITS OF TRADE

And so against these men, our greatest enemies, disorganized as they are and betrayed by their own fortune, let us go into battle with anger in our hearts; let us be convinced that in dealing with an adversary it is most just and lawful to claim the right to slake the fury of the soul in retaliation on the aggressor, and also that we shall have that greatest of all pleasures, which consists, according to the proverb, in taking vengeance on an enemy.—Gylippus, Spartan commander, on the eve of the defeat of the Athenian naval force at Syracuse harbor[1]

Whoever is lord of Malacca has his hand on the throat of Venice.—Tomé Pires[2]

Few stories from classical antiquity stir the modern soul as does that of the destruction of the Athenian expedition to Sicily during the Peloponnesian War. On the plains above and in the harbor below the eastern Sicilian port of Syracuse, the Spartan-led forces of that far-flung outpost of Greek civilization picked off soldier after Athenian soldier and ship after Athenian ship. Thucydides, a meticulous observer not given to overstatement, minced no words, "This was . . . the greatest action that we know of in Hellenic history—to the victors the most brilliant of successes, to the vanquished, the most calamitous of defeats."[3]

Just what does the Peloponnesian War have to do with the history of trade? A great deal indeed, because the reasons that drove Athens to seek empire sprang directly from the commerce in that most basic of commodities—grain—and in the peculiar geography of the Hellenic cradle of Western civilization. Further, just as the cultural and institutional foundations of Western civilization first saw the light of day in ancient Greece, so did the obsession of the modern West with the control of vital sea lanes and strategic maritime choke points derives from Greece's unique agricultural and geographic configuration, which left it dependent on imported grain. The forces that drove Britain and the United States to control the world's shipping lanes in the nineteenth and twentieth centuries, respectively, first saw light of day in Greece's need to feed itself with imported wheat and barley.[4]

The question of why proud Athens overreached the limits of its power and resources and suffered defeat on the remote shores of Sicily has vexed Western historians since Thucydides, a cashiered Athenian general, first wrote his famous chronicle. It is no accident that modern-day interest in this ancient conflict intensifies as history's greatest superpower becomes ever more mired on the battlefields of the Middle East. It is hard not to associate today's principal foreign policy advocates with the main Athenian actors: the arrogant, brilliant, and perfidious hawk Alcibiades, and the cautious and loyal dove Nicias, whom the Syracusans captured and executed.

But what drove Athens toward empire in the first place? Ancient Greece consisted of hundreds of more or less independent small city-states arrayed in a kaleidoscopic and ever-changing pattern of alliances, almost continuously at war with one another. "Greece" was a cultural and linguistic concept, not a nation. Only external threats of the first order, such as the Persian invasion at the beginning of the fifth century BC, could unify this fractious brotherhood into a coherent whole, and even then, only briefly.

A brief look at a map of the Aegean area sets the scene. Greece's coastline is convoluted, a tapestry of innumerable islands, peninsulas, inlets, bays, and channels. This complex topology, combined with the relatively mountainous landscape of Greece, dictated that almost all trade went by sea.

Along with geography, the other key player in Greek trade was the poor soil of almost all its city-states, most of which existed hard by famine's precipice. The first human civilizations that took root in the fertile land between the Tigris and Euphrates and along the lush banks of the Nile were blessed with some of the world's most productive farmland. Not so mountainous Greece, which lacked the rich alluvial valleys of the two older societies and possessed only a thin, limestone soil watered by an average of just sixteen inches of rain per year. Because of limited agricultural opportunities, its population clustered on the coasts and engaged in fishing, manufacturing, and trade.

While a traditional Greek farm might not grow grain adequate even for its own needs, it could produce sufficient wine and olive oil to ex-

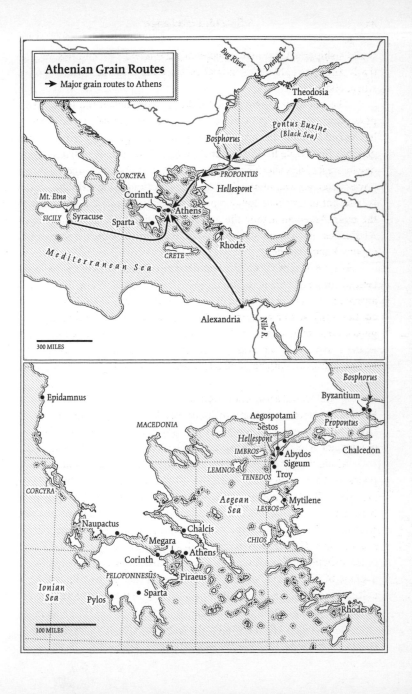

change for more abundant wheat and barley from abroad. Thus the Greek farmer depended on trade not only to feed his family, but also to allow him enough excess income to afford the time and resources needed for participation in the assembly and in the basic local military unit, the hoplite formation.[5]

At about the same moment that some of the Greek city-states first developed as democracies in the early first millennium BC, they also began to outrun their food supply. Even for Greece, the soil of Attica—the territory ruled from Athens—was especially poor. Thucydides thought that the infertility of the soil made Athens unappealing to invaders, thus affording it a sturdy political climate. This "stability of poor soils," he felt, attracted those of wealth, power, and knowledge from wealthier and more powerful, but fractious, city-states.[6]

Greece's barley production was probably adequate, at least early on, for subsistence needs, but over time the increasingly prosperous and discriminating Greek palate began to demand wheat. The cultivation of this crop, which requires well-timed watering for germination, proved especially difficult in an environment with scant and unreliable rainfall. As with the English medieval folk hero John Barleycorn, the ceremonial sacrificial bread of both Greece and Rome was cake of barley, which is much easier to grow in a dry climate and in poor soil. Until the advent of active grain trade in the sixth century BC, wheat bread was eaten only on Greek feast days.[7]

Where did the demanding Greek homemaker get wheat? Before the sixth century BC, mainly from Egypt, granary of the Mediterranean. Herodotus records that the pharaoh Amasis[8] gave the city of Naucratis on the Canopic arm of the Nile delta to the Hellenes as a trading city for merchants from many Greek cities.[9]

The Greeks also colonized Sicily in order to take advantage of the rich volcanic soil around Mount Etna on its eastern coast. Syracuse itself was founded south of its peak in the late eighth century BC by colonists from Athens's powerful rival just to its southwest, Corinth. But it would be in the vast, rich hinterlands of the Black Sea's northern shore that the Greeks found pay dirt, so to speak. At about the same time that Corinthian farmers were founding Syracuse, the Aegean city-states began sending large numbers of colonists to the extraordinarily fertile valleys of the Bug and Dnieper rivers, in what is now the southern Ukraine (hereafter, the "Pontus," after the Greek Pontus Euxine—the modern Black Sea).

As Greek citizens began to acquire grain from the colonies in the Pontus and Sicily, simple geography dictated that one group of states—Athens and its allies in the Aegean islands—sent ships northeast to the Pontus for additional grain supplies. It also dictated that a second group—Sparta, Corinth, and Megara (which lay midway between Athens and Corinth), and their allies—looked west to Sicily. Corinthian and Megaran ships could sail directly west out the Gulf of Corinth toward Sicily, or take the longer route south around the Peloponnese. Both routes ran through narrow waterways, and were thus highly vulnerable to rival city-states and pirates. For example, vessels from Corinth and Megara sailing to and from the Gulf of Corinth could easily be blocked at its western entrance, which is only about a mile wide. The southern route to Sicily was also exposed to enemy states and pirates as it passed through the island-studded strait between the southern Greek landmass—the Peloponnese, which contained Sparta—and the island of Crete.

The grain supplies of the Athenians and their Aegean allies were even more vulnerable. The route to their breadbasket in the Pontus threaded through not one, but two perilously constricted passageways between the Aegean Sea and the Black Sea: the Dardanelles (the Hellespont—"bridge of the Greeks") and just to the north, the even tighter Bosphorus. Further, maritime traffic to and from Piraeus, Athens's port city, had to pick its way through straits among the islands forming the outlet of the Saronic Gulf. By the middle of the seventh century BC, Attica's infertile valleys provided an ever smaller portion of the food supply of a burgeoning Athens. The city-state found itself increasingly dependent on foreign grain obtained in exchange for its sophisticated crafts goods and cash crops—pottery, textiles, olive oil, and wines.

Athens thus depended for its very survival on one of the most tenuous supply routes on the planet. Worse, tempestuous seas and cloud cover "closed" the sea most of the year, constricting the sailing season to between early May and late September—just four and a half months.[10] (Before the invention of the magnetic compass, overcast skies largely prevented open-water navigation, particularly at night.)

As Greece grew ever more populous, the competition for increasingly scarce grain supplies and its fractious geopolitical atmosphere conspired to split it into two rival groups: one led by Athens, one by Sparta.

These two alliances squared off again and again, and their rivalry culminated in the catastrophic Peloponnesian War.

As early as 700 BC, the "Great Game" of the Hellenes, the fight for
control of the Hellespont and Pontic grain, was well afoot. Around 660 BC,
Megara—Athens's archrival and neighbor, and an ally of Sparta—founded
Byzantium and Chalcedon, the guard dogs of the Bosphorus. Not long
after, the western Aegean city-state of Mytilene occupied Sigeum, at the
mouth of the Hellespont, just a few miles from the ruins of Homeric Troy.

Athens counterattacked by seizing Sigeum from Mytilene in about
600 BC. In 535 BC, the Athenian tyrant Peisistratus began an extensive
program of colonization around the Black Sea and fortification of the
straits (along with the other development projects of his thirty-three year
reign, which included a municipal water system and the first public library in Athens).

Peisistratus also secured the three islands just south of Sigeum that
commanded the southwestern approach to the Hellespont: Tenedos,
Imbros, and Lemnos. In 506 BC, Athens seized the fertile western coast
of the western Aegean island of Euboea from the city-state of Chalcis; this
acquisition had the dual effect of improving its grain supply and completing a "marine superhighway" through which ships could sail unmolested
between Piraeus and the Hellespont. On a number of occasions, the Persian invasions of the late sixth century and early fifth century BC temporarily interrupted the Black Sea trade. But Athens never took its eye off
the ball, finally ejecting the forces of the Persian emperor Xerxes from
Sestos, inside the Hellespont, two years after defeating the emperor's navy
at Salamis (an island just southwest of Athens) in 480 BC.

Athens had barely survived the Persian attack, the city having been
evacuated during the battle of Salamis. Chastened by this harrowing experience, the Athenians built the "long walls." Consisting of two parallel
ramparts a hundred or so yards apart, they ran four miles south of the city
to its port at Piraeus, allowing Athens to survive a land-based siege in-
definitely with supplies landed at the docks from overseas.

Ultimately, however, the "long walls" merely shifted Athens's
vulnerability from land to sea. In 476 BC, Sparta made a lunge for the
jugular of Athens at the Hellespont and Bosphorus when the Spartan
commander Pausanias seized both Sestos and Byzantium, respectively.
Athens ejected the Spartans from these cities almost immediately.

By 450 BC, in order to secure its trading routes, the greatly enlarged Athenian navy began patrolling the Black Sea in strength more or less continuously, an unheard-of action in a world of part-time soldier-citizens and temporary armies and navies. Pericles himself led a squadron of warships in a show of force on its waters.

During peaceful years, Athenian merchants shipped over a million bushels of grain through the Hellespont. In times of famine, shipments to Athens swelled to as much as three million bushels per year. Most of this Pontic grain was loaded at Theodosia, situated east of the juncture of the Bug and Dnieper rivers.

The coasts and hinterlands of the Black Sea also provided Greece with cattle, wool, fish, and timber. In turn, the less sophisticated local populations valued manufactured Greek wares far more than the civilized and jaded Egyptians. Because Greek traders obtained a better return on their investment in the Pontus than in Egypt, commerce gradually shifted north.

By this point, Athens realized that merely becoming a naval power would not suffice. The ease with which an enemy could blockade the narrow straits of the Aegean, Hellespont, and Bosphorus led it to acquire political control of the tightest points along those routes. Moreover, simply capturing a few cities and forts was not enough; other states in the region were just as dependent on the same sea-lanes and choke points, and all needed to contribute men and resources to police them. The only way to accomplish this was with a cohesive, centrally directed group of like-minded states, which gradually coalesced into the Athenian Empire.

How Athens accomplished this feat—the velvet glove covering the mailed fist—will be ominously familiar to the modern American reader. Athens aided its friends in the Aegean Sea and the Black Sea by helping them fend off pirates and attacks from the local "barbarians" who had the temerity to try to reclaim the land taken from them by Greek settlers. In turn, Athens collected tribute from these allied states and also forgave export duties on grain bound for Piraeus. Contrariwise, control of the Aegean sea-lanes enabled Athens to punish its enemies—Sparta, Corinth, and Megara. At the beginning of the Peloponnesian War, for example, Athens established a base at Naupactus at the narrow western entrance to the Corinthian Gulf in order to blockade shipping to and from Corinth and Megara.[11] Athens used this full range of political and military tools to retain wavering allies, such as Rhodes (located just off the southwest coast of what is modern

Turkey), and the western Aegean islands of Chios and Lesbos. It could even manipulate the price of grain and maintain a reserve for use in times of blockade or plague; any merchant, Athenian or foreign, caught trying to corner the market or reexport grain found himself on trial for his life.

Like World War I, the Peloponnesian War began in 431 BC over a relatively minor conflict, in this case a struggle between oligarchs and democrats in the tiny city-state of Epidamnus (present-day Durrës, on the Albanian coast). The democrats appealed for help to Corcyra (present-day Corfu), which had founded Epidamnus and was also a naval power allied with Athens. Corcyra refused to help the democratic forces, who then requested and received a fleet from Corinth.

The Corcyrans, angered by the Corinthians' interference in their former colony, proceeded to defeat the Corinthian fleet. The Athenians grew alarmed that the Corinthians might join forces with their Spartan allies to capture the large Corcyran fleet and tip the balance of power against them. This triggered a naval conflict between Athens and Corinth, which quickly mushroomed into the great "global conflict" of the Greek world.

Initially, things went well for the Athenian Empire, which won a victory at Pylos in the southwestern Peloponnese, where they captured a large number of Spartan soldiers. At this point the Spartans, chronically short of manpower with which to suppress their large population of helot slaves, would probably have made a generous peace with the Athenians in order to recover the captured soldiers. Instead, the Athenians let the war drag on.

In 415 BC, the brash young expansionist Alcibiades and the older, cautious veteran warrior Nicias debated the invasion of Sicily. Alcibiades cited the value of its grain to Athens; Nicias argued that its bounty was a reason *not* to invade: "The greatest advantage they have over us is . . . the fact that they grow their own corn and do not have to import any."[12]

The hawks won the debate, and the resulting devastation to the expeditionary force to Sicily left the home city vulnerable to attack. The great Spartan admiral Lysander, rather than attacking Athens directly, once again went for the empire's exposed throat at the Hellespont. Slowly, the wily commander gathered his forces and waited until the high summer of 405 BC, when the largest number of grain ships were preparing to head south with their precious cargoes before the sea closed. At precisely the right moment, he fell on the remains of the Athenian fleet at Aegospotami, inside the Hellespont near Sestos. The Spartans sank or captured almost all of the Athenian ships and slew thousands of troops. The Athenian sacred galley survived and raced home with the dreadful news; when word of the defeat arrived in Piraeus, "The lamentations spread . . . up the long walls of the city, one man passing on the tidings to another so that night no man in Athens slept."[13]

At that point, an invasion of Athens was no longer necessary, for the cruel sword of starvation could defeat Athens more efficiently and cheaply than the fearsome Spartan hoplites. In the humiliating peace settlement, Athens kept its independence, but just barely; it abandoned its remaining fleet, razed the fortifications of Piraeus, and tore down the "long walls" that until then had made it immune to siege. As a final indignity, it was forced to become an ally of Sparta.

Athens would rise again, and it would even reassert dominance over the Black Sea trade from the weakening naval forces of Sparta, but it would never regain its former heights of power and influence. Its next challenger was Thebes, which took control of the straits in 360 BC, though Athens reoccupied them just three years later. Soon after, Philip of Macedon, father of Alexander the Great, attacked the Hellespont at Perinthus (a small city on the Propontis, the inland sea between the Hellespont and the Bosphorus) and then at Byzantium itself. Once again the Athenians, rallied by the orator Demosthenes, held on. Athens had once again regained its lifeline, albeit just barely.

Alexander pledged freedom of the seas for Greek shipping, although this promise did not prevent him from occasionally seizing the odd freighter to demonstrate just who really held the straits. In the ensuing centuries, Athens, while remaining nominally independent, no longer commanded its lifelines or its fate. Just as it had invented many Western institutions and intellectual and artistic endeavors, so did it pioneer a less glorious tradition. In the centuries following the Peloponnesian war, Athens became the first in a long line of senescent Western empires to suffer the ignominious transformation from world power to open-air theme park, famous only for its arts, its architecture, its schools, and its past.

If Greece was the cradle of Western civilization, then surely its peculiar strategic geography informs the core of Western naval strategy, which emphasizes the security of maritime routes. Venice, then Holland, and then England became, respectively, the Athens of the thirteenth, seventeenth, and nineteenth centuries—nations which had outgrown their domestic food supplies and whose prosperity and survival hinged on control of sea-lanes and of strategic choke points as far-flung as the Kattegat (the strait between Jutland and Sweden), the English Channel, Suez, Aden, Gibraltar, Malacca, and, again and again, the Hellespont and Bosphorus.

Today, as the ever-increasing output of the vast oil fields of Saudi Arabia, Iraq, and Iran flows through the Persian Gulf, defense ministries in Washington, London, New Delhi, and Beijing need no reminders of the importance of maintaining free navigation through its narrow waters. The great medieval trading nations of Asia, on the other hand, lulled by the open geography of the Indian Ocean, never learned that lesson. The forces of Islam were indeed able for centuries to shut out the weakened and backward European states from the heart of the world's long-distance trade in the Indian Ocean. However, this was entirely due to their conquest of the landmass of the Middle East, which denied Europe access to the Indian Ocean's "back doors" at the Persian Gulf and at Bab el Mandeb. For example, the mighty Abbasid caliphate in Baghdad did little to protect its vital Persian Gulf choke point at Hormuz, allowing pirates to flourish there. (Nor did the early Arab empires consider the building and maintenance of roads to be within their brief.)

Whereas the Mongols and the Ming Chinese did make naval forays toward Japan, Indonesia, and the Indian Ocean, they did relatively little to secure the Strait of Malacca, which controlled trade to all points west. India's Muslim rulers all but ignored their sea-lanes until the Portuguese were upon them, at which point Malik Ayaz, the Muslim governor of the Gujarati city of Diu on India's west coast, frantically appealed to the Mamluk rulers of Egypt for help in ejecting the Portuguese. In 1508, the combined Mamluk-Indian fleet surprised a Portuguese flotilla in the harbor at Chaul (just south of modern Mumbai) and inflicted a stinging defeat on the Europeans. The next year, the Portuguese marshaled a larger fleet off Diu and reversed their setback, opening up the door for European domination of the vital spice trade, previously a Muslim monopoly.

Naval strategy and strength matter little when two monsoons can blow a cargo over an unobstructed Indian Ocean from Basra to Malacca. The easy, open geography of the Indian Ocean left the Muslim trading powers insufficiently prepared for the European onslaught.

The West's ascendancy in the Indian Ocean would not be a rout; as the Muslims had already demonstrated at Chaul, they would not be rolled over as easily as the Native Americans of the New World. A few years after their defeat at Diu, a rebuilt Egyptian fleet was able to hold off the Europeans at Aden, and the Prophet's forces retained control over the strategic Bab el Mandeb until the English finally took the port from the Ottomans in 1839. But despite the ferocity and technical sophistication of the Muslim navies, they would ultimately prove no match for the alumni of the rough schools of the Hellespont, the Kattegat, Gibraltar, and the Channel.

It is not hard to see the ghost of the Athenian obsession with the Hellespont reflected in the presence of the U.S. Navy at Bab el Mandeb and in the straits of Gibraltar, Hormuz, and Malacca, or the temporary defeat of the Portuguese at Chaul recalled by the attack on the USS *Cole* in Aden. But we have gotten well ahead of our story. Almost a millennium separated the Peloponnesian War from the fall of Rome, and there was yet another millennium between Rome's demise and the dawn of Western hegemony announced by the appearance of the Portuguese in the Indian Ocean.

For most of the period following the fall of Rome, the adherents of a powerful new monotheistic religion dominated medieval long-distance commerce as completely as the West dominates such commerce today; the legacy of that former dominance is still all too visible.

3

CAMELS, PERFUMES, AND PROPHETS

Almost invariably, artists and illustrators portray camels in profile. . . . Seen from the front, a camel's nose is a bulbous, rubbery snout with its upper lip sliding forward beneath it, pouching over its teeth, bulging above its shorter lower lip in such a way that as I squint, I no longer see an animal that looks anything like the way I expect a camel in profile to look full face. What I see is some other creature, something like a sea serpent or a dog-faced dinosaur.—Leila Hadley[1]

The technique of desert raiding should be studied by all travelers. An approaching party may be friend, but is always assumed to be foe. . . . Raiding parties are of two kinds, that whose tribe and yours have no blood-feud, and that where a blood-feud exists. Both want your camels and arms, the second your life as well.—Bertram Thomas[2]

If we are to believe recent geological and paleontological research, the dinosaurs met a sudden, dark, and frigid end when an enormous asteroid hit the Gulf of Mexico about sixty-five million years ago and triggered an ice age. Our warm-blooded mammalian ancestors, better adapted to the cold, enjoyed a resurgence. Around forty million years ago, one of these, the rabbit-size *Protylopus,* arose in North America. At the beginning of the Pleistocene epoch, about three million years ago, the Isthmus of Panama formed, allowing *Protylopus* to migrate to South America, where its descendants, the llama, alpaca, guanaco, and vicuña, thrive in the Andes. In North America, perhaps five hundred thousand years ago, *Protylopus* also gave rise to the modern camel.

The Pleistocene, which ended just ten thousand years ago, was marked by periods of intermittent but vast glaciation. During these frozen interludes the accumulation of ice in the earth's expanding polar caps caused the sea level to drop by as much as several hundred feet, more than enough to expose the bottom of the Bering Strait, at present less than two hundred feet deep in places. This land bridge, Beringia, allowed the movement of plant and animal species between the eastern and western hemispheres.

During these exchanges in the late Pleistocene, two momentous migrations would occur: human beings moved east from Siberia into the New World, and the camel and horse crossed over in the opposite direction to Asia and onward into Africa. Both these hooved species soon disappeared from North America—perhaps falling prey to large saber-toothed cats, perhaps because of change in their forage caused by climatic oscillation, or perhaps because of the depredations of prehistoric man. Although the horse would be spectacularly reintroduced to the Americas by the Spanish conquistadors, the camel never regained its original birthplace.

Neither did the camel initially thrive in its new home in the Old World. Unlike the fleet horse, the defenseless camel has a top speed of only about twenty miles per hour—an easy meal for the lion or for any other large, swift predator. In Asia's driest regions, particularly Arabia, the camel developed its signature evolutionary advantage: the ability to store and preserve water, enabling it to exist for long periods in the desert far from oases, where large carnivores gathered.

Camels do not store water in their humps, as is commonly supposed, but rather distribute it uniformly throughout their bodies. They are easily able to go days and, in exceptional circumstances, weeks, without water by drinking huge amounts—up to fifty gallons at a time. They conserve fluid through the remarkable ability of their kidneys to efficiently concentrate urine. The first Asian camels were two-humped (Bactrian), but in the hotter Arabian and African deserts, the species evolved toward its familiar single-hump (dromedary) configuration, which reduced its surface area, thus decreasing water evaporation. The dromedary also evolved another water-conserving mechanism, the ability (unusual for a mammal) to passively raise its body temperature up to six degrees Fahrenheit during the heat of the day, minimizing water loss from sweating. To this day, dromedaries predominate in Arabia and Africa, while the Bactrian dwells in Asia.[3]

Initially, both varieties fought a losing battle and were saved from extinction only by the fortuitous appearance of humans. The camel is one of the few animals that can be domesticated. To be bred by humans, a species must simultaneously possess several relatively unusual characteristics:

the provision of appealing and nutritious food, ease of herding, docility, lack of fear of people, resistance to human diseases, and, most critical of all, the ability to breed in captivity. Only a few animals qualify on all counts. Goats and sheep were the first livestock to be domesticated, around ten thousand years ago, followed by chickens, pigs, cattle, and finally, camels. (The donkey, horse, and dog were domesticated primarily for their transport, hunting, and military usefulness, but often wound up in the food chain as well.)[4]

We have little idea of how the most common crop and animal species were first domesticated, and the camel is no exception. On the basis of anthropological evidence, it seems likely that humans began drinking camel milk about five thousand years ago in the Horn of Africa, or perhaps just across the Red Sea in southern Arabia. To this day, Somalis refuse to ride camels, believing that the large, slow, ungainly beasts make their riders easy targets. Today, this region is home to the world's largest population of camels, which are still kept only for their milk. Gradually, mankind discovered other uses for the animal: meat and leather from the males, hair from both genders, and, last but not least, transport.

Until about 1500 BC, the donkey had been the pack animal of choice. Thereafter, nomadic tribes bred camels for transport in huge numbers. If the donkey was a family sedan, able to convey light loads over smooth hard surfaces, then the camel was a Land Rover, whose huge padded hooves allowed it to carry roughly twice as much and twice as fast over long stretches of trackless waste. This capability revolutionized trade over the sands of the Middle East and through the steppes of Asia.[5]

A single camel driver, conducting three to six animals, can transport one to two tons of cargo between twenty and sixty miles in one day. When Tiglath-pileser III of the Assyrians defeated the Arabian queen Samsi about 730 BC, his booty included twenty thousand cattle, five thousand bundles of spices, and thirty thousand camels.[6]

A trader cannot simply sling heavily laden bags across a camel's back. The animal's soft, nonsupportive hump and swaying motion require a frame-and-mattress saddle that distributes the weight of the cargo over its back. Between about 1300 BC and 100 BC, pre-Islamic Arabian nomads refined saddles to the point where they allowed the average pack camel to carry more than five hundred pounds, and in excess of one thousand pounds for the strongest animals. The ultimate configuration, the north Arabian saddle, has been in continuous use in the Middle East for the past two thousand years.

The Bactrian camels of central Asia are just as highly specialized and carefully bred as those of the Arabian desert, having been domesticated for transport at more or less the same time, around 2500–2000 BC. The slightly cooler and wetter climates of the Asian steppes, Iran, and India favor two-humped design. But whereas the desert Arabs valued the dromedary not only for its transport ability but also for its milk, meat, and hair, central Asians did not. In that part of the world, settled agriculture had already established itself and had spread widely. Central Asians found sheep's wool superior to camel hair, and cow's milk and meat more plentiful and better-tasting. Further, the ox and water buffalo gave the camel a run for its money over short distances, particularly in wet climates, where camels do not thrive.

Thus, as the ancient era wore on, both the size and the range of the more highly valued dromedary population increased and began to impinge on the domain of the Bactrians: first in Syria and Iraq, then in Iran, then in India, and finally in central Asia itself. When the two populations came into contact, the laws of hybridization worked their typical magic. The two types are similar enough to interbreed, and the first-generation offspring of a Bactrian and dromedary (the so-called F1 hybrid) is, as so often happens, a beast possessed of remarkable stamina and strength, perfectly suited to the long distances of the central Asian overland trade. All along the Silk Road, demand mushroomed for these crossbred "super camels," capable of carrying up to half a ton of cargo from China to the western fringes of Asia.

Such beasts of burden can be bred with a Bactrian stallion servicing a large population of female dromedaries, or the other way around. The pairing of a Bactrian stallion and a dromedary mare, however, is used almost exclusively, since one Bactrian stallion can service a large number of dromedary mares, the latter being far more common, even in central Asia. (A similar situation occurs with the powerful all-purpose western pack animal, the usually sterile mule, which is the offspring of a female horse and a male donkey, but for a different reason. The "reversed" F1 hybrid between a stallion and female donkey—the hinny—is rarely bred, because of the difficulties of delivering the large offspring through the birth canal of the smaller donkey mare.)

The inexorable logic of animal husbandry also demands that hardy first-generation crossbreeds *not* mate, as their second-generation offspring are most often small and degenerate; the Arabic and Turkish words for this second-generation crossbreed both translate as "runt." Consequently, the dromedary and the crossbreed predominate in almost all of Africa and Asia; only in the highest and coldest mountains of central Asia, where even the hardy crossbreed cannot thrive, are pure Bactrians bred in any number.[7]

The animal's continued widespread use from Morocco to India to western China attests to its extraordinary transport efficiency. In the modern era, the availability of well-paved roads allows for the even more efficient camel-and-wagon arrangement. The UN Food and Agricultural Organization estimates the present-day world camel population at just shy of twenty million (including 650,000 feral beasts in the Australian outback, whose services became redundant with the advent of the railroad).[8]

Although an exceptional animal and driver might cover as much as sixty miles per day, a more typical day's span is approximately thirty miles. Given the "safe" three-day water capacity of the camel, oases and caravanserais needed to be spaced about one hundred miles apart; this greatly restricted possible routings, particularly in central Asia. Further, since camels cannot negotiate steep, narrow grades, donkeys were required through the mountain passes of the Asian route.[9]

We've already encountered one commodity, silk, that could be shipped great distances in camel packs. But for thousands of years before silk traveled from China to Rome on camels, as well as in ships, another precious cargo found its way thousands of miles from the vast Arabian desert to the ancient world's great centers of civilization in the Fertile Crescent.

The trademark, and the curse, of the Arabian Peninsula is its hot, dry climate. Scarcely a permanent creek penetrates its desert vastness. There are only their ghosts, the parched, meandering wadis (equivalent to the arroyos of the American Southwest), often missed by even experienced travelers until these dormant streams rage as torrents during storms separated by decades.

One part of the peninsula, however, was known in classical antiquity as Arabia Felix—literally, "happy Arabia." The name referred to the area's fertility. Located in the peninsula's mountainous southwest, in what is now Yemen, it catches the warm, wet winds of the summer monsoon and receives an average of ten inches of rain annually. The southwestern port city of Aden derives its name from the Arabic word for Eden, which accurately describes this rare patch of moist climate. (The rest of the otherwise arid peninsula was known as Arabia Deserta.)

Incense is the general term for frankincense, myrrh, and rarer exotic aromatics that have grown for millennia in Arabia Felix. The earliest Sabaean and Minaean inhabitants, as well as peoples across Bab el Mandeb in Somalia, pioneered its cultivation and export.

Before the arrival of silk and pepper in the West, incense was the premier luxury product of antiquity. To anyone living in Arabia around 1500 BC, the most obvious use for the newly domesticated camel would have been the transport of incense to consumers in the Fertile Crescent and Mediterranean basin. As far back as 3500 BC, Egyptian and Babylonian aristocrats acquired a taste for these fragrant products. Stone monuments from around 2500 BC celebrate incense-trading voyages to the land of Punt: modern-day Yemen and Somalia. The traders might have sailed the Red Sea down its entire length, but, as we've already seen, shallow waters, pirates, and adverse winds cursed this route. It was safer and more reliable to use the overland path north along the Arabian coast of the Red Sea, then west through the Sinai.

The growing cycle also favored the camel route. Growers harvested the crops mainly in autumn and spring, out of sync with the winter monsoon for sailing to Egypt or the summer monsoon for sailing to India, whereas the camel trains could operate year-round.[10] The rigors of navigation in the Red Sea and the peculiarities of the harvests and monsoons drove the peoples of the peninsula to domesticate the camel specifically to carry incense.

The bulk of the trade consisted of two somewhat different products: frankincense, a gum resin produced from *Boswellia sacra;* and myrrh, a fragrant oil produced by *Commiphora myrrha.* Both plant species are scruffy trees several feet tall that grow mainly at high altitude in southern Arabia and neighboring northern Somalia.

Frankincense and myrrh acquired their status as premier luxury items for reasons both sacred and profane. Although our imagination allows us to conceive the sights and sounds of ancient civilizations, their smells are well beyond modern comprehension. In cramped cities lacking effective sanitation, the nose discerned location as well as any map: the odor of feces from main sewer lines and slaughterhouses; the scent of urine surrounding government buildings, temples, and theaters; or the particularly offensive olfactory assaults of the tannery, the fishmonger, and the cemetery.

Amid such stenches, and where regular bathing in clean water and regular changes of clothes were reserved for only the wealthiest citizens, few substances were as prized as myrrh oil, easily applied as a body lotion and capable of hiding the rank smells of everyday life. Physicians used myrrh liberally in medicinals, and it was also the ancient world's embalming fluid of choice. In addition, incense was the aroma of eros, as attested in this come-on from a well-known, wicked, and deadly biblical adulteress:

> *I have decked my bed with coverings of tapestry, with carved works,*
> *   with fine linen of Egypt.*
> *I have perfumed my bed with myrrh, aloes, and cinnamon.*
> *Come, let us take our fill of love until the morning: let us solace*
> *   ourselves with loves.*
> *For the goodman is not at home, he is gone a long journey:*
> *He hath taken a bag of money with him, and will come home at the day*
> *   appointed.*[11]

Frankincense, while also fragrant, possessed more mystic qualities. This even-burning gum produced delicate, wispy curling smoke that, as envisioned by the ancient world, slowly rose to the heavens, where its appearance and scent pleased the gods. In China and India, funerary rites required the burning of frankincense. In the tabernacles of the early Jews, its opaque tendrils were said to veil the Almighty's very presence.[12]

Pliny wrote that Alexander the Great was particularly fond of burning large amounts of incense on holy altars. Alexander's tutor Leonides admonished him that "he might worship the gods in that manner when he had conquered the frankincense producing races." According to Pliny, Alexander then subjugated Arabia, whereupon "he sent Leonides a ship with a cargo of frankincense, with a message charging him to worship the gods without any stint."[13]

Pliny also gives us a vivid description of the frankincense trade in Arabia Felix. The trees secrete a slick, foamy liquid which collects under the bark. Growers incised the tree, and the fluid spurted onto the ground or onto palm mats, where it dried and thickened. This was the purest, most desirable frankincense, whereas the residual product, stuck to the tree and contaminated with bark, was of second quality. The integrity of the growers amazed Pliny:

> The forest is divided up into definite portions, and owing to the mutual honesty of the owners is free from trespassing, and though nobody keeps guard over the trees after an incision has been made, nobody steals from his neighbor.[14]

Today, bedouin men and women still harvest trees marked to indicate ownership, in accordance with Pliny's observations. Before the Common Era, the growing of incense was confined to the trees' natural habitat in southwest Arabia, and local peoples tapped them only during the hottest part of the year, in May, before the arrival of the cooling, moist southwest monsoon. After drying for a few weeks, the final product either began its northward journey by camel to markets in the Fertile Crescent and Mediterranean, or else was stored for a few more months until the worst of the monsoon storms had cleared and was then sent by sail east to India. The Greek naturalist Theophrastus described the highly trusting "silent trade" transactions that characterized the initial purchases:

> And that when they have brought it, each man piles up his own contribution of frankincense and the myrrh in like manner, and leaves it on guard; and on the pile he puts a tablet on which is stated the number of measures which it contains, and the price for which each measure should be sold; and that, when the merchants come, they look at the tablets, and whichsoever pleases them, they measure and put down the price on the spot whence they have taken the wares, and then the priest comes and, having taken the third part of the price for the god, leaves the rest where it was, and this remains safe for the owners until they come to claim it.[15]

The freshly dried frankincense, a fragile, gummy substance, was packaged in protective wooden cages; myrrh oil, more prone to evaporation, was transported in animal hides. For thousands of years, these two precious substances, produced in remote and secretive kingdoms, traversed a complex route from the southwest corner of the Arabian peninsula to their ultimate destinations in Babylon, Athens, and the ancient Egyptian capital of Memphis. The historian Nigel Groom writes, "One can visualize the camels of the ancient caravans with frankincense baskets bulging on either side of their saddles or swinging to the weight of myrrh in more compact, tightly closed goatskins."[16]

The Pax Romana changed this pattern. A significant part of the Roman booty went toward the purchase of incense. The earliest Greeks and Romans had probably propitiated the gods with human sacrifice, but in classical Greece and the early Roman republic, this had been replaced with animal offerings. Alongside the sacrificial altar, standing on a tripod, was the *acera,* in which frankincense was placed.[17] So central was the burning of this aromatic to Roman ritual that it was admitted into the empire duty-free, in contrast to the 25 percent duty on most other imports. (The Arch of Titus in the Forum depicts the emperor carrying a balsam shrub in his triumphant march through the capital after the conquest of Jerusalem in AD 70. This plant yielded one of the most expensive aromatics.)[18] With the prosperity of the empire grew its demand for incense, and the gradual extension of Roman control south toward Arabia Felix during the first and second centuries AD made both the maritime and the camel routes safer and cheaper.

As demand rose, growers added a second and third annual crop, which yielded a lower-quality product than the traditional May harvest. Cultivation spread eastward to Zufar, in modern Oman.

This expansion shift added inhospitable distance to cargoes bound for Rome. Some of the frankincense and myrrh from these new growing areas was shipped directly from the eastern Arabian ports of Qana and Moscha to Berenice on the Red Sea and thence to Alexandria. But most of the incense trade was conducted by camel; the king of Arabia Felix, wishing to control the lucrative market, saw that the bulk of it passed overland through the city of Shabwah, in the east of Arabia Felix.

Pliny described how the incense, after being collected, was carried to Shabwah, where "a single gate is left open for its admission." Failure to use the assigned gate—a sure sign of smuggling—was punishable by death. The land route seems to have been the monopoly of a single tribe,

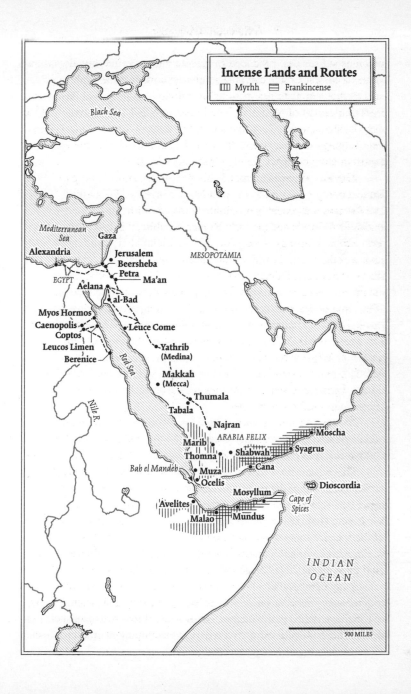

Incense Lands and Routes

IIII Myrrh ⊟ Frankincense

Black Sea

Mediterranean Sea

MESOPOTAMIA

Gaza
Alexandria
Jerusalem
Beersheba
Petra
EGYPT
Ma'an
Aelana
al-Bad

Myos Hormos
Caenopolis
Coptos
Leucos Limen
Berenice

Leuce Come

Yathrib (Medina)

Makkah (Mecca)

Red Sea

Thumala
Tabala

Nile R.

Najran

ARABIA FELIX

Moscha

Marib
Thomna
Shabwah
Syagrus

Bab el Mandeb
Muza
Cana
Ocelis

Dioscordia

Mosyllum
Cape of Spices

Avelites
Malao
Mundus

INDIAN OCEAN

500 MILES

whose priests oversaw the harvesting and transport of the crop. Pliny variously identifies the tribe as the Gebanitae or the Minaeans.

The priests at Shabwah took 10 percent of the cargo as an import tax. The incense then had to travel to Thomna, the capital of the country of the Gebanitae or Minaeans, who controlled the onward trade. Pliny records that the journey from Thomna to Gaza, about 1,500 miles, took sixty-five days, about twenty-three miles per day. Along the way, expenses were incurred. Among others:

> Fixed portions of the frankincense are also given to the priests and the king's secretaries, but beside these the guards and their attendants and the gate-keepers and servants also have their pickings: indeed, all along the route they keep on paying, at one place for water, at another for fodder, or the charges for lodging at the halts.[19]

Each camel's load to Rome incurred a total purchase and transport cost of approximately a thousand denarii, or about two denarii per pound. The highest-grade frankincense—so judged by its whiteness, brittleness, and ease of burning—sold in Rome for six denarii per pound. The lowest grade sold for three denarii per pound, about the same price as black pepper. (The denarius, a small silver coin weighing one-eighth of an ounce, roughly corresponded to a day's wage of a skilled laborer. Thus, a pound of frankincense represented roughly a week's worth of wages for a skilled laborer; a pound of myrrh, about two weeks' worth.) By comparison, the most precious aromatics, such as balsam from Palestine, sold for up to 1,000 denarii per pound.

What frankincense lacked in price, it more than made up for in quantity. Alone among the aromatics, frankincense was shipped in camel-load (about 500 pounds) quantities and was therefore by far the most important trade commodity of the era. If we take Pliny's accounting at face value and estimate the total cost of transporting a camel load of incense from Arabia Felix to Rome at approximately 1,000 denarii, then, at an average retail price of five denarii per pound, a total profit of 1,500 denarii per camel load was possible.

Incense generated prosperity all along its supply chain. This wealth was distributed among middlemen, those who serviced the caravans, and the camel drivers themselves, each capable of guiding up to six animals at a time. Snaking their way slowly along the western (Red Sea) coast of the peninsula, these caravans connected the incense sources of Arabia Felix with well-off consumers in the Fertile Crescent, and later, in Greece, Rome, and Byzantium. All along this route, great marketplaces prospered, particularly at the Sabaean-Gebanite cities of Shabwah, Thomna, and Marib. Another group, nomadic tribesmen, also prospered by plundering the rich incense supply chain. The product that arrived from eastern Arabia via Gaza and Alexandria on the wharves of Puteoli had traveled as much as four thousand miles.

The confusion over exactly who controlled the trade is in large part due to the difficulties of doing research in modern-day Yemen and Saudi Arabia. For most of the twentieth century, the key ancient Minaean-Gebanite town of Marib was off-limits to Westerners. When in 1951 the imam of Yemen finally granted permission to the renowned American archaeologist Frank Albright to visit Marib to help solve this mystery, his party was immediately driven off at gunpoint by unhappy locals. Archaeologists have found fragmentary but tantalizing Minaean inscriptions as far away as Memphis in Egypt and Delos in Greece, suggesting the presence of Arabian trade diasporas thousands of miles from their homeland.

As the domestication of camels for transport spread north and east, other legendary inland hubs, such as Palmyra, Samarkand, and Shiraz (in modern-day Syria, Uzbekistan, and Iran, respectively), swarmed with camel traders, caravan drivers, and the merchants of many nations. Each city became, in its turn, wealthy and powerful. Today, perhaps the most visible remnants of the incense trade are the magnificent stone temples and tombs at Petra, the capital of Nabataea, in what is now southern Jordan.

This mysterious kingdom of sun worshippers flourished between 300 BC and the fall of Rome, and their prosperity hinged on their control of the northern third of the Arabian incense track. Likewise, the Mediterranean terminus of the camel route at Gaza also thrived on the trade. The incense sent by Alexander to Leonides—fifteen tons of frankincense, three tons of myrrh—came from Gazan warehouses plundered by Alexander on his way from Tyre to Egypt in 332 BC. By that date, Gaza was already a very old and wealthy place, sitting on a large funeral mound and having been besieged several times in the preceding centuries by the Assyrians.

By the time the incense reached Egypt, the easygoing honesty of Arabia Felix had completely disappeared. Again, Pliny:

At Alexandria, on the other hand, where the frankincense is worked up for sale, by Hercules, no vigilance is sufficient to guard the factories! A seal is put upon the workmen's aprons, they have to wear a mask or a net with a close mesh on their heads, and before they are allowed to leave the premises they have to take off all their clothes.[20]

The ancient incense trade was thus no different from the modern cocaine and heroin trades: relatively safe around the raw agricultural source, but highly risky around the finished product and its ultimate consumers.

The effects of incense in its ultimate destination, Rome, were less salutary. Along with silk, aromatic imports drained the empire of silver; Nigel Groom estimates that about fifteen million denarii per year were spent on the ten thousand camel loads of incense bound for the capital. As long as plunder from abroad arrived on the wharves, there was no problem; Seneca's fortune alone was reputed to be almost one hundred million denarii. But in the second century, as the conquests ceased and Romans became ever more extravagant, those more poetically than economically inclined may be forgiven for concluding that the power of the empire evaporated in a haze of incense.[21]

Although frankincense and myrrh spread prosperity to cities and towns all along the caravan route, one place among them—a small western Arabian oasis situated about halfway between Yemen's producers of incense and its consumers in the faraway eastern Mediterranean and Fertile Crescent—would mesmerize the civilized world. There, the incense trade catalyzed the birth of Islam, whose military, spiritual, and commercial impacts transformed medieval Asia, Europe, and Africa. Riding on a rising tide of global trade along the land and sea routes of Asia, Islam came to dominate that continent's spiritual as well as its commercial life.

The saga of the new religion begins with the ancestors of the desert Arabs, who were sedentary farmers working marginal oasis plots. About 3,000 to 3,500 years ago, they first mastered camel domestication, which gave them the ability to challenge the stark, terrifying Arabian wilderness. Even with this newfound mobility, their situation was precarious, huddling in oases during the deadly, rainless summers and foraging the desert fringes with goats and camels the rest of the year.

This grim nomadic existence afforded them a precious geographic remoteness that spared them conquest. The two great western predator states of the post-Roman era, the Byzantine and the Persian Sassanid empires, both sought to regain the past glories of Trajan and Darius from each other: Byzantium endeavored to grab Mesopotamia from Persia, while Persia in turn hoped to regain Syria and Egypt from Byzantium. Locked in a continuous life-and-death struggle, these powers devoted no significant attention to the exotic, impoverished desert dwellers to the south. There was one exception to Arab remoteness and independence, and that was the monsoon-swept, fertile, incense-producing Arabia Felix, which became a luckless pawn in this ancient version of the Great Game.

The harsh and lawless environment of the desert shaped both economic and religious life on the Arabian Peninsula and has to this day left its mark on the culture of the Muslim world. Survival in Arabia, with its lack of a central authority, was, and remains, utterly dependent on the good efforts of the family and the tribe.

Western notions of individual autonomy and rule of law simply do not apply in the desert. An attack on one tribesman is an attack on all, and in a landscape where a murderer can quickly and quietly slip away, it matters little whether the accused is guilty or innocent. His entire clan is held accountable for *thar*—retribution. The resulting skein of honor and revenge, so familiar in the modern Middle East, is eternal, seemingly without beginning and without end. When the first recourse of victims is to their cousins, and not to the police or to an independent judicial system, poverty and political instability are the usual outcomes.

In such a barren and impoverished landscape, a major source of sustenance is often theft from the tents and caravans of neighboring tribes. The signal military operation of the desert is the *ghazu*—a raid mounted on horses (which are both faster and easier to control at a full gallop than the camel). The raiders swiftly and deftly execute these attacks so as to avoid causing casualties that would trigger *thar*.[22] Recall the trilemma of trade: whether to trade, protect, or raid. In the absence of any authority beyond the tribe, entrepreneurs will invariably choose to raid.

The pre-Islamic desert dwellers prayed to many gods, and Islam appropriated many early Arab religious beliefs and practices. The early Arabs erected shrines to numerous deities; the holiest was Kaaba at Mecca, a large granite block in one corner of which was embedded black stone, probably of meteoric origin. It is not certain if the Kaaba was dedicated to the main Arab deity, al-Llah, or to one of the lesser Arab deities, Hubal. The people of the ancient Middle East commonly worshipped meteoric fragments; the silk-loving Roman emperor Elagabalus, described in the Introduction, was a Syrian who began his career as the high priest of a temple housing such a celestial remnant in the town of Emesa (modern-day Homs in Syria). When he became emperor, he dismayed the Romans by bringing the rock along with him and building another temple for it in the capital.[23] (Twenty-two years after the death of Elagabalus, the leadership of that most ecumenical of empires would fall to Emperor Philip, an Arab.)

By AD 500, the desert Arabs had come into frequent contact with Christians and Jews. The Jews likely had migrated south after the conquest of Jerusalem by Nebuchadnezzar in 586 BC and established palm plantations in the Hejaz. Similarly, Christianity diffused into Arabia both from Byzantium in the north and from the south across Bab el Mandeb in Coptic Christian Abyssinia. Christians and Jews often taunted the Arabs about their polytheistic beliefs and their lack of an overarching creed and an afterlife. Consequently, a sense of religious inferiority arose among the desert dwellers, along with a pent-up desire for a comprehensive belief system of their own.

Exactly how Mecca became a bustling commercial center is something of a mystery; it produced nothing of value, was not a great center of consumption or of government, and had little strategic worth. Some historians have suggested that its main advantage was its position: Mecca lay approximately midway on the two-month journey up the Arabian Peninsula, so far from both Byzantium in the north and Abyssinian-run Yemen in the south that it was relatively safe from the depredations of both. This cannot be the major reason for its prominence, however. The role of the incense trade in the city's rise is also uncertain: there is controversy as to whether or not the main caravan route bypassed the town (in contrast to Medina, through which the incense highway almost certainly ran).[24] Mecca sits in a dry and barren valley, and during the pre-Islamic period was utterly dependent for its food on the gardens and farmlands of Taif, seventy-five miles away.[25] In a narrow sense, Mecca may be thought of as a miniature, parched, landlocked Arabian version of Venice, whose food supply and rhythms of daily life hummed to the tunes of trade, whether or not it actually sat on the main incense route.

The real reason for the early prominence of Mecca in pre-Islamic Arabia may lie in the Kaaba stone and the several nearby shrines to the other desert gods. Each year, the faithful made the pilgrimage, known as the hajj (which was only much later adopted by Islam), to venerate and circumambulate the Kaaba stone and black stone. The hajj in no small part contributed to Mecca's wealth and power.

By the late fifth century AD, the Quraish tribe, led by a sheikh named Qussay, moved in from the north, took over Mecca, and then fended off invasions by both the Byzantines and Abyssinnians. Qussay next convinced the Quraish and the surrounding tribes that it was more profitable to trade and to protect the caravans than to raid them. Taxing traders and selling them safe conduct, it turned out, paid better than plundering a shrunken, fearful traffic.[26] The Quraish continued to settle in Mecca in increasing numbers, grew wealthy, and gradually drifted away from their intensely communal, nomadic heritage. Their lives henceforth revolved around trade, not the precarious existence of oases and desert tents.

Beginning around AD 500, Abyssinia converted to Christianity and became a regional power closely associated with its co-religionists in Byzantium. The last ruler of an independent Arabia Felix, the handsome Yusuf Asai (also known as Dhu Nuwas and "the man with the hanging locks"), converted to Judaism in the early sixth century and proceeded to slaughter and enslave thousands of Christians in his kingdom. In AD 525, in response to the anti-Christian atrocities of Yusuf Asai, the Abyssinians attacked across Bab el Mandeb and overwhelmed his army. The despondent king was said to have ridden into the sea on horseback.[27]

The defeat of the Yemenite Jewish monarch and the resultant domination of Arabia Felix by Abyssinian Christians set in motion a chain of events whose effects reverberate to the present day. In AD 570, an Abyssinian proconsul in Arabia Felix named Abraha rebelled against his king and established a rival empire on the peninsula. A staunch Christian, with an army backed by African elephants transported from across Bab el Mandeb, Abraha was goaded by the Byzantine emperor Justinian into attacking Mecca, by that time the last pagan holdout in Arabia. The unfortunate elephants, however, although fearsome weapons on most of the ancient world's battlefields, were not well-suited to the searing sands of

Arabia and succumbed, either to disease or to the harsh climate, just outside the gates of the city. The Meccans had never seen such creatures and,
being unfamiliar with the basics of animal ecology and microbiology,
credited divine intervention. The year AD 571 became known in Arabia
as the "Year of the Elephant."[28] That same year saw the birth of the Prophet
Muhammad into a lesser branch of the Quraish, and his arrival was imbued forever after by Muslims with the mythic elephantine event. He
became, of course, a trader.

Had Abraha and his pachyderm allies succeeded at Mecca, Muhammad, had he been born at all, might have wound up a Christian monk.
The historical Muhammad is at best an indistinct figure; the first written accounts of his life did not appear for more than a century following his death, and even these were distorted by the ideological needs of
his early chroniclers. Certain basic facts, however, seem beyond dispute. Orphaned at an early age, he was raised by an uncle, Abu Talib, a
prosperous trader. Although Muhammad probably spent his formative
years observing and participating in his uncle's business, there is no
direct record of his early professional endeavors. What is more certain
is that at around age twenty-five, he found himself in the employ of
an older widow, Khadija, who also ran a prosperous trading enterprise.
We do not know precisely what goods her caravans carried, but dates,
raisins, and leather from nearby Taif; frankincense from Yemen; and
textiles from Egypt and beyond would certainly have been among
them.

As a woman, she did not travel with these cargoes, and so Muhammad
rapidly gained experience as her agent in Syria. Impressed with the young
man's competence and charmed by his personality, she proposed marriage,
and he accepted; Muhammad was now a man with standing and resources.

In his travels, Muhammad encountered Jews and Christians—the
"people of the Book"—and felt the power of their seductive belief systems. The fact that both Judaism and Christianity were associated with
hated foreign powers limited their appeal and drove Muhammad and his
Arab countrymen to seek their own path. The Arabs' sense of longing was
amplified by their revulsion at the materialistic ways of Mecca's newly
wealthy Quraish commercial aristocracy, perceived as having turned their
back on the ancient tribal codes of behavior.[29] In the words of Islam's great
Western historian, Maxime Rodinson:

The traditional virtues of the sons of the desert were no longer the sure road to success. Greed, and an eye to the main chance, were much more useful. The rich became proud and overbearing, glorying in their success as a personal thing—no longer a matter for the whole tribe. The ties of blood grew weaker.[30]

By the late sixth century, then, many Arabs were moved by twin needs: to create a single unifying identity in opposition to the two foreign-derived monotheistic religions, and to develop a political force to counter the wealth and corruption of the Quraish. In this turbulent socioeconomic atmosphere, al-Llah, who emerged alone from the gods of the desert, forcibly dictated through the angel Gabriel's voice the first verses of the Koran to an agonized Muhammad on Mount Hira, just outside Mecca, in 610. The dry tinder of religious fervor was now lit, and almost immediately flared up into the conflagration of conversion and conquest that would engulf much of Asia, Africa, and Europe.

Muslims have long recognized that Khadija's support was critical to the Prophet's ultimate mission: a common Arab saying has it that "Islam did not rise except through Ali's sword and Khadija's wealth." (Ali, Muhammad's cousin and son-in-law, eventually became the Prophet's fourth successor; his murder would split the Muslim world into a Shiite minority and a Sunni majority, who believe and disbelieve, respectively, that the leadership should pass directly through Muhammad's lineage by way of Ali.)

Alone among the world's religions, Islam was founded by a trader. (Muhammad's immediate successor, the cloth merchant Abu Bakr, was also a trader.) This extraordinary fact suffuses the soul of this faith and guides the historical events that ricocheted over the land routes of Asia and the sea-lanes of the Indian Ocean through the next nine centuries. Its traces are visible in today's world, from the modern colonies of Muslim Indians in East Africa to the Lebanese merchants still active in West Africa to the "Syrians" who populated the third-world outposts of Graham Greene's novels.

The most sacred texts of Islam resonate with the importance of commerce, as in this famous passage from the Koran: "O you who believe! Do not devour your property among yourselves falsely, except that it be trading by your mutual consent."[31] The most important passages on trade and commerce, however, are found in the hadith, the collected stories of

Muhammad's life, which offer advice on the conduct of trade from the general: "There is no harm for you [to trade] in the Hajj season," to the specific:

> The buyer and the seller have the option to cancel or to confirm the deal, as long as they have not parted or till they part, and if they spoke the truth and told each other the defects of the things, then blessings would be in their deal, and if they hid something and told lies, the blessing of the deal would be lost.[32]

One narrator, Jabir bin Abdullah, tells of a personal encounter with Muhammad, who offers to buy his troublesome camel, and for which one gold piece is paid. In a demonstration of charity, Muhammad later returns the camel and allows Jabir to keep the gold, informing posterity that at that point in his life, the Prophet might have been taken out of the trade, the trade had not yet been taken out of the Prophet.[33]

Within a very few decades, the new creed would sweep from Mecca to Medina and back, next across the Middle East, and then west to Spain and east to India. In a commercial sense, early Islam can be thought of as a rapidly inflating bubble of commerce; outside lay unbelievers, and inside lay a swiftly growing theological and institutional unity. A detailed recounting of Islam's astonishing initial spread is beyond the scope of this book, but it's worth noting that its lightning speed was due in no small part to the conflict between the new creed, which forbade stealing from fellow believers, but not from infidels, and the economic imperative of the *ghazu* (raid). The Prophet may have been born a trader, but he died a raider. Soon after he was expelled from Mecca in 622, he began attacking that city's infidel caravans. The new religion dictated that all the property of conquered nonbelievers was forfeit, with one-fifth earmarked for Allah and the *umma*—the people—and the rest divided between the victorious troops and their leaders.[34] If a people converted peacefully, their property was spared. Thus, as more distant tribes converted, it became necessary to raid ever farther afield to obtain sustenance from resistant nonbelieving tribes. After the Prophet's death in 632, this process accelerated as some peoples were conquered while others, driven both by the political, spiritual, and military power of the new creed and by a desire to retain their assets, saw the light and converted. Both mechanisms—conquest and peaceful conversion—rapidly drove the boundaries of Islam farther and farther from their starting point deep in the peninsula.

The Arab armies were stopped six years later at the gates of Constantinople by a string of unusual circumstances, that included the recent ascent of Emperor Leo the Isaurian, a master strategist, and unusually cold winter weather that proved deadly to troops bred in the Arabian climate and to an army supplied by camel. In the words of the Islamic scholar J. J. Saunders, "Had [Constantinople] fallen, the Balkan Peninsula would have been overrun, the Arabs would have sailed up the Danube into the heart of Europe, and Christianity might have lingered, an obscure cult, in the forests of Germany."[35]

The Arabs' first order of business was to feed the newly converted and hungry masses of the peninsula. Since time immemorial, Egypt had been the granary of the Mediterranean, and the Muslim conquest opened wide this supply to the demanding markets of Arabia. The caliph first sent grain by caravan down the incense route, but the new Islamic empire soon began clearing the old sea-level canal between the Nile and Red Sea to create a cheap maritime route between Arabia and its Egyptian food source. As in modern times, strategic considerations dictated the fate of this ancient version of the Suez Canal. Initially, the leaders considered extending it directly to the Mediterranean. This would have made its route nearly identical to that of the present-day canal, but Caliph Omar (the Prophet's second successor, after Abu Bakr) decided against the project, fearing that the Byzantines would use a connection between the Mediterranean Sea and the Red Sea to interfere with the hajj. What can feed can also starve: the grain now flowing down the Red Sea had previously sailed north to Constantinople. The loss of this vital food store in no small part contributed to the decline of Byzantium. A century later, Caliph Abu Jaffar shut down the canal for the last time in order to cut off provisions to Arabian rebels.

Next, Muslim forces wrested control of the eastern Mediterranean from the Byzantines at the battle of Dhat al-Sawari—the Battle of the Masts—in 655. At this early date, the Arabs had yet to assemble a working navy and so manned their vessels with experienced Christian Coptic seamen who, ironically, despising their Greek overlords, abetted one of Islam's greatest victories. At a stroke, the sea routes between the West and India, and China as well, were severed, and would remain so until

Vasco da Gama became the first European to break through into the Indian Ocean eight and a half centuries later.[36]

After their victory at the Battle of the Masts, Muslim navies gradually extended their control over the Mediterranean. In 711 a freed Berber slave, Tariq ibn Ziyad, successfully commanded a daring raid at a rocky promontory in southern Spain, then under the rule of the Goths. The Umayyad invaders celebrated this famous victory, which preceded the Muslim conquest of all Spain by just three years, by naming the rock Jabil Tariq: the mountain of Tariq, or, as it later became pronounced, Gibraltar.

Of the strategic islands in the Mediterranean Sea, Cyprus fell nearly in the first flush of Arab conquest in 649. Crete fell in 827, Malta in 870, and, after more than a century of conflict, the sea's greatest prize, Sicily, in 965. As the new millennium dawned, it must have seemed to the forces of Christendom that what the Romans once called *mare nostrum*—our sea—now swarmed with Muslim ships. So wide was the domain of Muslim conquest and trade in Europe that large numbers of Islamic coins dating to the ninth and tenth centuries have been found as far away as central Europe, Scandinavia (particularly on the island of Gotland, off eastern Sweden), England, and Iceland.[37]

The early Umayyad and Abbasid empires ruled, respectively, before and after 750. They controlled an area greater than that ruled by the Romans and as the sheer extent of their conquests dried up the supply of potential booty, commerce increasingly drove their military priorities. Poor and backward western Europe did not interest them as much as central Asia, with its rich silk route. The Umayyads did not return to Gaul after their defeat at the French city of Poitiers in 732, nor did they react vigorously to the *reconquista* of Spain and Portugal, which began in 718 and culminated in the expulsion of the last Moors (and of the Jews) in 1492.

Muslim armies, by contrast, attacked the far reaches of central Asia again and again, not succeeding until they defeated the Tang Chinese at Talas (in present day Kazakhstan) in 751 and delivered that part of the world, with its profitable caravan routes, into Muslim hands, where it remains to this day. Dramatic conquests often lead to startling serendipities: the most momentous Muslim acquisition at Talas was not territory or silk, but a commodity at once prosaic and precious. Among the

Chinese prisoners taken at Talas were papermakers, who soon spread their wondrous craft into the Islamic world, and then to Europe, changing forever human culture and the course of history.

The early Muslim conquests essentially recreated the Pax Romana, but on an even grander scale. The Umayyad and Abbasid empires were in effect large free-trade areas in which old borders and barriers had been swept away, especially along the Euphrates River, since remotest antiquity the traditional frontier between the East and West. No longer were the three great routes to Asia—the Red Sea, the Persian Gulf, and the Silk Road—competing alternatives; rather, they were an integrated global logistic system available to all parties who recognized the suzerainty of the caliphate.

For nearly the next millennium, Muslim seafaring ran well ahead of Muslim conquest and conversion. Astoundingly, by the mid-eighth century, barely a hundred years after the death of the Prophet, thousands of Muslim (likely Persian) traders had arrived not only in Chinese coastal ports, but in Chinese inland cities as well.[38] By contrast, the first large Chinese oceangoing junks did not venture into the Indian Ocean until about AD 1000, and the legendary eunuch admiral Zheng He would not sail his massive fleet to Sri Lanka and Zanzibar for another four hundred years after that.

Arabic was the lingua franca of the new empire, and Muslim navies patrolled ports and sea-lanes from Gibraltar to Sri Lanka. By the ninth century, Islamic rulers in central Asia had established contact with Volga Khazars, and through them, the Scandinavians; in the East, Muslim contact with China grew brisk via both the Silk Road and maritime routes, and North African traders sent caravans south across the Sahara. Within a few centuries of the Prophet's death, his followers had knitted almost the entirety of the known world into a vast emporium in which African gold, ivory, and ostrich feathers could be exchanged for Scandinavian furs, Baltic amber, Chinese silks, Indian pepper, and Persian metal crafts.[39] Further, the Arabs, invigorated by their conquests, experienced a cultural renaissance that extended to many fields; the era's greatest literature, art, mathematics, and astronomy was found not in Rome, Constantinople, or Paris, but rather in Damascus, Baghdad, and Cordova.

The Pax Islamica was not an unmixed blessing; the border between Occident and Orient shifted west into the Mediterranean, through which free passage was lost to Muslim and Christians alike. In the words of the historian George Hourani, "Instead of a highway, the Mediterranean became a frontier, a sea of war—a change which ruined Alexandria."[40] Although the Muslim commercial web possessed many advanced features, including bills of exchange, sophisticated lending institutions, and futures markets, no Islamic state ever established the bedrock financial institution of the modern world: a national or central bank.[41]

But this was beside the point. For several centuries after the fall of Rome, the fragments of the old empire suffered in obscurity as backwaters of world commerce, largely ignorant of the commercial and technological revolutions taking place in the Middle East, India, and especially China. Even so, Mediterranean shipping did benefit from the introduction of the Arab triangular lateen sail, which enabled vessels to tack into the wind, a feat not possible with the square rigging of Western antiquity.

This Pax Islamica went completely unchallenged until the eleventh century, when a resurgent Christendom recovered substantial territory in Spain, Sicily, and Malta. Emboldened by these gains, in 1095 Pope Urban II convened the Council of Clermont and called forth the First Crusade, which temporarily regained the Holy Land.

In the twelfth century Saladin followed his conquest of the Fatimids with the ejection of the crusaders from Jerusalem (although he was more than happy to trade with his Christian enemies) and consolidated Muslim power in the Middle East. With Saladin's victories came Islam's high point. Thereafter came a devastating series of misfortunes: the Mongol invasions in the thirteenth century, the plague in the fourteenth, and Vasco da Gama's penetrations of the Indian Ocean in the fifteenth and sixteenth.

In spite of Islam's long decline, Muslim traders dominated long-distance commerce until the sixteenth century, and in many areas, well into the early modern period.

4

THE BAGHDAD-CANTON
EXPRESS: ASIA ON FIVE
DIRHEM A DAY

As the thirteenth century drew to a close, Genoa and Venice, the two great maritime powers of the Mediterranean Sea, savaged each other in a life-and-death struggle over trade routes. In a dank Genoese prison sometime around 1292, a Venetian naval commander whiled away the days and weeks dictating his memoirs to a fellow captive, a Pisan writer of modest renown named Rustichello.

And what a tale this prisoner, captured off the Dalmatian island of Curzola, had to tell his new friend! For at least a century before he was captured, his family had grown rich in trade with the East and maintained a warehouse filled with spices and silks in the Venetian quarter of Constantinople, the great trade hub of that era. Venice earned its wealth not only from rare Oriental goods, but also from the pilgrim and crusader traffic to and from the Holy Land.

Although the Venetian prisoner knew the East well, he was no pioneer. For centuries, European merchants, emissaries, and missionaries had ventured along the Silk Road in search of wealth, power, and converts. Indeed, about forty years previously, just after his birth, his father and uncle had struck out from their base in Constantinople and ventured deep into Mongol-ruled central Asia, where they eventually found themselves trapped by warring tribes in the trading town of Bukhara (in modern-day Uzbekistan). There they met an ambassador of Hulagu, the great khan of central Asia; fascinated by the brothers' Italian tongue, the khan's envoy invited them east. The two astute merchants did not need to be asked twice on an excursion to the lands of silk and spices.

By 1265 or so the brothers had arrived in the court of Hulagu's brother Kublai Khan in China, where they spent the better part of a decade before returning to Venice with a letter from Kublai to Pope Clement IV. The curious and ecumenical Kublai, it seems, needed a hundred Christian missionaries to teach the Chinese about this powerful Western faith. By the time the Venetians arrived home in 1269, however, Clement had died, and the brothers, Maffeo and Niccolò Polo, had to bide their time until a new pontiff could supply them with the monks requested by Kublai. While they were away seeking their fortunes in China, Niccolò's wife had died, and he was left to care for his now fifteen-year-old son Marco, who had grown from a toddler to the brink of manhood.[1]

The original version of *The Travels of Marco Polo,* reconstructed by Rustichello from Marco Polo's recollections and notes requested from Venice, was probably first written down in French, then Europe's lingua franca, so to speak. The fantastical stories—of lands where cows were sacred, where widows threw themselves onto their husbands' funeral pyres, and where young men were abducted, drugged with hashish, plied with women and luxury, and trained as assassins (all of which occurred in India); of a place where the ground oozed with a gooey substance that burned (the oil fields of Mesopotamia); and of a place which was so far north that the sun never set in summer or rose in winter—struck Europeans as the product of a fevered imagination. The accuracy of *Travels* was, in fact, remarkable, including Polo's descriptions, passed to him at second and third hand, of places he did *not* visit, such as Burma, Siberia, Java, and the even more mysterious Spice Islands.

Although the family ran a well-known merchant house, and although *Travels* imparted a great deal about foreign mores, goods, dress, and customs, Marco Polo did not leave posterity many useful details about the texture of medieval long-distance trade. Perhaps the lack of quantitative data is the work of Rustichello, a seasoned writer who likely intuited that the medieval literary market responded better to self-immolating spouses and cities scores of miles in circumference than to pepper prices or to the precise patterns of monsoon sailing.[2]

Just as the stability afforded by the Pax Romana and the Han Empire encouraged the long-range and highly indirect commerce between Rome and China in the first and second centuries after Christ, the power of the early Islamic and Tang empires stimulated a far more direct intercourse between the lands of the caliphate and China during the seventh through ninth centuries. Chinese sources suggest that Islam arrived in Canton in about 620, a full dozen years *before* the death of the Prophet.[3]

Before the Chinese invented the magnetic compass, in around the twelfth century, mariners depended on celestial navigation; fog and overcast skies often proved as deadly as the fiercest storms. Although sailors since Greek times knew how to measure latitude, accurate determination of longitude did not become possible until the eighteenth century. The constant companion of the medieval traveler on the open seas was terror. As vividly recounted by a fifth century Chinese pilgrim who had voyaged to India and back:

> The Great Ocean spreads out over a boundless expanse. There is no knowing east from west; only by observing the sun, moon, and stars was it possible to go forward. If the weather was dark and rainy, the ship went forward as she was carried by the wind, without any definite course. In the darkness of the night, only the waves were to be seen, breaking on one another, emitting a brightness like that of fire. . . . The merchants were full of terror, not knowing where they were going. The sea was deep and bottomless, and there was no place where they could drop anchor.[4]

As early as the seventh century, the Chinese had seen enough Middle Eastern merchants to distinguish among the Muslims flooding into their ports: the "Po-ssi," or Persians, with their long Gulf-based tradition of seafaring, were far more numerous than the more landlocked "Ta-shih," or Arabs. The Chinese also clearly differentiated the world of Islam from a more mysterious land farther to the west called "Fu-lin"—the Byzantine Empire—known for its wondrous gemstones and glass.[5] By 758, there were enough Muslims in Canton that they were able to sack the city, burn it, and make off to sea with their booty.[6]

The Muslims, especially the Persians, knew China much better than the Chinese knew them. While the existence of pre-Islamic Persian trade with China is controversial, it is certain that not long after the Muslim armies defeated the Persian Sassanids at the battle of Ctesiphon (just south of modern Baghdad) in 636, Arab and Persian vessels voyaged directly

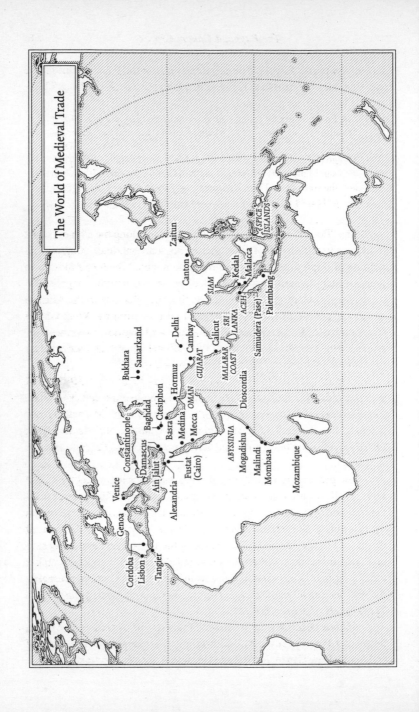

The World of Medieval Trade

to Chinese ports. As good a description as any of the Islamic world trade system under the caliphate is found in a Chinese document from 727:

> The Po-ssi being by nature bent on commerce, they are in the habit of sailing in big craft on the [Mediterranean] sea, and they enter the Indian Ocean to Ceylon, where they get precious stones. . . . They also go to the K'un-lun country [probably Africa] to fetch gold. They also sail in big craft to China straight to Canton for silk piece goods and the like ware. The inhabitants enjoy the killing of cattle; they serve Heaven [Allah] and do not know the law of Buddha.[7]

The "Po-ssi" established trade diasporas all along the Chinese coast —large populations of Muslim merchants who handled an increasing volume of imports and exports. Jews accompanied them or followed in their footsteps. Nearly simultaneously, Nestorian Christians, expelled for their heresies from the Byzantine Empire but tolerated in the Muslim world as "people of the book," began to arrive from the West via the overland route. It is easy to see how a splinter Christian movement, repelled by the savage intolerance of the Catholic Church and attracted by the relative tolerance of Islam, spread ever eastward.

Contact between the East and West intensified with the triumph of the Abbasids over the Umayyads in 750; this moved the center of Islam from the landlocked capital of Damascus to riverine Baghdad, with its easy connection to the Gulf. One Abbasid ruler exclaimed, "This is the Tigris; there is no obstacle between us and China; everything on the sea can come to us on it."[8]

The premodern record provides few statistics regarding trade, and history's flashlight illuminates the commerce between China and the Islamic world only with sporadic manuscript finds. One of the best-known manuscripts is the Arabic *Akhbar Al-Sin wa'l-Hind*—"An Account of China and India." Supposedly written in the mid-ninth century by several Arab merchants, particularly one Sulayman, this compilation takes the reader on a whirlwind journey from Baghdad to Canton, presaging the wonder and adventure evoked more than four hundred years later in *The Travels of Marco Polo*.

Akhbar describes the loading of the ships in Basra and at Siraf, a deepwater Persian Gulf port, followed by a monsoon-driven passage of one month from Oman, just outside Hormuz, to the Malabar coast of India, where the local ruler collected a tax of between ten and thirty dinars per vessel (approximately $800 to $2,400 in today's money). The Persian ships then set sail for another monthlong reach across the Bay of Bengal, provisioning midway in the Andaman Islands:

> The inhabitants are cannibals. They are black with curly hair, and have ugly faces and eyes and have long legs. Each one has a penis that is nearly a cubit [twenty inches] long; and they are naked. . . . Sometimes the cannibals catch some of the sailors, but they escape.[9]

The merchants made landfall in Southeast Asia on the coast of Kedah, just north of Penang in present-day Malaysia, where they could choose between proceeding south around the Strait of Malacca or portaging across the narrow waist of the Malay Peninsula. The journey from Kedah past Malacca to Indochina took about twenty days; from Indochina to Canton an additional month. Although *Akhbar* suggests that the entire voyage from Basra to Canton consumed only about four months' sailing time, the dance of the monsoons, as well as bureaucratic obstacles along the route, would have lengthened the transit time to well over a year.

Because merchants and captains preferred to ride the monsoons to and from their home port on an annual schedule, individual boats and crews tended to ply only one segment of the route year after year (if they were lucky enough to survive so many journeys). A Gujarati merchant, for example, would typically load his ship with the fine cotton cloths and indigo of his native land, sail the summer monsoon to Malacca, exchange there his goods for silk, spices, and porcelain, and return home on the winter monsoon. Or he might choose to sail west in the winter and return in the summer from Aden with horses and incense, or to Malindi on the East African coast and return with gold and slaves. Because of the pattern of the monsoons and the need to return home, goods traveling the entire length of the Baghdad-Canton route sailed in at least three different bottoms.

The Chinese sought from *Akhbar*'s Arab and Persian traders copper, ivory, incense, and turtle shells, while in Canton the Muslims loaded up on gold, pearls, and, naturally, silk and brocade. The exchange process was agonizing and appears to have been conducted through a government monopoly; the Chinese held the goods brought from Baghdad in Canton warehouses for six months until "the next batch of sailors come in." Thirty percent of the goods were taken as an import duty, and then, "Whatever the government wishes to take, [it] buys at the highest price and pays the amount immediately, and in the transaction do not act unjustly."[10]

Akhbar kicked off the venerable Western tradition of the China travelogue, later amplified by Marco Polo, Ibn Battuta, and numerous subsequent voyagers. The mostly anonymous authors of *Akhbar* wondered at the size and sophistication of the Celestial Empire, with its more than two hundred large cities, its exotic lifestyle, and its advanced institutions: "Everyone among the Chinese, whether he is poor or rich or young or old, learns calligraphy and the art of writing." Those concerned with the current debate over Social Security would do well to consider *Akhbar*'s description of the Chinese system of taxes and old-age pensions:

> [Tax] is collected per head on the basis of personal possession of wealth and land. If a son is born to anyone, his name is registered with the authority. When he reaches eighteen years of age, poll-tax is collected from him, and, when he reaches eighty years of age, no poll-tax is collected from him. He is then paid a [pension] from the treasury. They say, "We took from him when he was a youth, and we pay him a salary when he is old."[11]

Not all things Chinese pleased the sensibilities of pious Muslims. Particularly disagreeable were the diet high in pork and the use of toilet paper, both serious violations of Muslim sanitary rules. Finally, the Muslims made note of a most peculiar beverage:

> Among the important sources of revenue of the king is . . . an herb which they mix in hot water and then drink. It is sold in every town at a very high price. It is called *al-sakh*. It is more leafy than the green trefoil and slightly more perfumed, and has a soury taste. They boil water and then sprinkle the leaves over it. It is a cure for them for everything.[12]

The West had just encountered tea, a commodity that almost a thousand years later would spawn its own trading empire and multiply the world's demand for sugar, slaves, and porcelain.

About a century after *Akhbar* was written, a Persian sea captain, Burzug Ibn Shahriyar, recorded 123 brief stories, which came to him first- or secondhand from sailors and traders. It was entitled *The Book of the Marvels of India* and featured unreal, fearsome beasts and man-eating giants worthy of a South American novelist; there was even an island of women who fell upon shipwrecked men:

> a thousand women or more to every one man, and carried them away towards the mountains and forced them to become the instruments of their pleasure. . . . One after the other, the men dropped off and died of sheer exhaustion."[13]

Strewn, however, throughout the fantastic narratives are vignettes illuminating the nature of medieval trade on the Indian Ocean. The book makes clear that the fear of shipwreck looms over both trader and sailor; almost every story involves at least one broken boat. The voyage to China is so fraught with peril that the story of a captain who made seven journeys there astonishes the author:

> Before his time, no one had ever accomplished this journey without accident. To reach China and not perish on the way—that, in itself, was regarded as a considerable feat; but come back again, safe and sound, was a thing unheard of.[14]

Only the promise of fantastic wealth could drive men to risk such nearly certain disaster. *Marvels* tells of a Jewish merchant, Ishaq, the owner of a ship that was

> laden with a million dinars of musk, as well as silks and porcelain of equal value, and quite as much again in jewelry and stones, not counting a whole heap of marvelous objects of Chinese workmanship.[15]

Marvels goes on to describe a gift given by Ishaq to a Muslim friend, a vase of black porcelain with a gold lid. When his friend asked what was in it, Ishaq replied, "A dish of *sekbadj* [fish] I cooked you in China." His friend replied that the delicacy, now two years old, must be quite spoiled. When he opened the vase, he found inside "a golden fish, with ruby eyes, garnished with musk of the finest quality. The contents of the vase was worth fifty thousand dinars." In the end, Ishaq is cheated out of his fortune by mendacious Muslim neighbors and then murdered by a Sudanese governor after failing to produce an expected bribe.[16]

The longest story in *Marvels* poignantly describes two other features of the medieval Indian Ocean trade: the unself-conscious, unscrupulous, highly profitable slave trade; and the power of Islam to tie together Chinese, Arabs, Persians, and Indians into a commercial system whose customs and laws were well understood by all between Baghdad and Canton.

The tale begins, as usual, with a shipwreck, this time on the shores of East Africa. Fearful of cannibals, the marooned traders are pleasantly surprised to be taken in and treated well by the local king, who even allows them to conduct their business: "and excellent business for us it was, with no restriction and no duties to pay." After completing their trades, the ruler and his underlings accompany them onto their newly repaired vessels. As the merchants are about to depart, the narrator finds himself calculating his hosts' value in the slave markets:

> That young king would fetch at least thirty dinars in the marketplace in Oman, and his attendants one hundred and sixty dinars the lot. Their clothes are worth twenty dinars at the lowest. Altogether, we should make a profit of not less than three thousand dirhems, without stirring a finger.[17]

Away they sail with their captives. The king attempts to shame the merchants by reminding them of the kind treatment received under his care, but his pleas fall on deaf ears. Along the way, over two hundred other slaves are added to the cargo hold; all, including the king and his retinue, are duly sold into slavery in Oman.

Years pass, and as luck would have it, the narrator finds himself once again shipwrecked on the exact same East African shore. Worse, he finds himself greeted by the very same king he had long ago sold into slavery. Staring directly into the eyes of the fearsome justice that is his due, the narrator is amazed when the king calmly and politely describes how his buyer in Oman took him to Basra and Baghdad, where the king-slave converted to Islam. Soon after arriving in Baghdad, he escaped, and after a series of hair-raising adventures in Cairo, on the Nile, and in the African bush, found himself back in his old kingdom, which had also converted to Islam in his absence.

Observing the commercial customs and laws of Islam rewarded the trading nation; both now dictated that the king treat the treacherous merchant well. As put by the king, "Musulmans shall know that they may come to us like brothers, since we are Musulmans too." The king laments that his fondest desire is to reimburse his old master in Baghdad for his loss, "a sum ten times what he paid, as recompense for the delay." Unfortunately, this wish must remain unfulfilled, since this is a job for an honest man—something the narrator clearly is not.[18]

This first flush of direct trade centering on China, so well described in *Akhbar* and *Marvels,* came crashing down as the Tang dynasty spiraled into instability in the ninth century. In a scenario painfully familiar to modern Chinese in Indonesia, Indians in East Africa, and Jews nearly everywhere, the colonies of foreign traders on China's coast became convenient scapegoats during tough times.

As early as AD 840, the emperor Wuzong sought to blame foreign ideologies for China's plight. In 878, the rebel Huang Chao sacked Canton, slaughtering 120,000 Muslims (mainly Persians), Jews, and Christians living in that city's trade community.[19] Not content to massacre traders, Huang Chao also tried to kill China's main export industry by destroying the mulberry groves of south China.[20] After the calamitous events of 878 in Canton, China's foreign trade gradually migrated north to the port of Tsuan-chou on the Taiwan Strait—the legendary Zaitun of Marco Polo and Ibn Battuta. Canton, which had been China's main portal for foreign goods, would not regain its preeminence until the modern period.

This more northerly entrepôt had long-standing connections with Korea and Japan, whose wares attracted Arab and Persian traders. The size and cargoes of the Muslim ships, some of which required ladders dozens of feet tall for boarding, astounded the Chinese of the eighth and ninth centuries. The emperor soon appointed an inspector of maritime trade, whose job was to register these vessels, collect duties, and prevent the export of "rare and precious articles."[21] One such inspector was a nobleman, Chau Ju-Kua, who oversaw foreign trade at Zaitun in the early thirteenth century. A methodical compiler of knowledge, he cataloged the recollections of hundreds of homesick sailors and traders in *Chu-Fan-Chi:* "A Description of Barbarous Peoples." The book was a sort of reverse *Travels of Marco Polo;* although Chau never left China, the *Chu-Fan-Chi* describes in some detail places as remote as Asia Minor and Alexandria, including details (some accurate, some not) of that city's famous lighthouse.[22]

By the time the Mongols roared out of the northern steppes into China in the thirteenth century, Persian and Arab traders had more or less monopolized the long-distance trade in China, with two large and relatively self-governing Muslim communities at Canton and Zaitun. According to Chau:

> In its watchful kindness to the foreign Barbarians, our government has established at [Zaitun] and Canton Special Inspectorates of [maritime trade], and whenever any of the foreign traders have difficulties or wish to lay a complaint they must go to the Special Inspectorate. . . . Of all the wealthy foreign lands which have a great store of precious and varied goods, none surpasses the realm of the Arabs.[23]

Numerous other medieval travelers speak to us from differing perspectives. In the mid-twelfth century, a Spanish rabbi, Benjamin of Tudela, journeyed widely through Europe and the Middle East and reported on the bustle and splendors of Alexandria and Constantinople. He was particularly impressed by the intellectual life of Baghdad: "the place of meeting of philosophers, mathematicians, and all the other sciences." Almost at the same time, the Muslim merchant Shereef Idrisi, under the patronage of the Viking king of Sicily, Roger II, produced a geography, *Pleasure for the Man Who Wants to Know Thoroughly the Various Countries of the World,* which describes in great detail the Red Sea trade of the period. Idrisi was especially taken with the port of Aden, where he encountered Chinese junks laden with "pepper, some strong smelling, other odorless, wood of aloes, as well as bitter aloes, tortoise shell and ivory, ebony and rattan, porcelain, [and] leather saddles."[24]

The trading world of these accounts also found expression in a series of anonymous stories told by the fictional Scheherazade in her attempt to postpone her death at the hands of her husband: the famous *Book of the Thousand Nights and a Night.* Among its contents are the well-known tales of Ali Baba, Aladdin, and, of course, Sinbad the Sailor, which were probably recorded sometime in the fourteenth century.[25]

Sinbad's adventures were anything but children's stories. Many of them are remarkably similar to those told in *The Book of the Marvels of India;* the reader of both works will suspect that many of the Sinbad legends, if not lifted in whole cloth from the earlier book, at least share the same oral tradition.

In each of his seven trading voyages in search of spices and gems, our hero is shipwrecked or otherwise becomes separated from his ship. He then battles a series of deadly monsters or human villains. On his third trip, for example, he and his companions are captured by a grotesque giant who first examines potential victims "as a butcher feeleth a sheep he is about to slaughter." The gorgon finally settles on the ship's most plump and delectable morsel, its *rais* (master). The gorgon

> seized him, as a butcher seizeth a beast, and throwing him down, set his foot on his neck and brake it; after which he fetched a long spit and thrusting up his backside, brought forth of the crown of his head. Then, lighting a fierce fire, he set it over the spit with the Rais thereon, and turned it over the coals, till the flesh was roasted, when he took the spit off the fire and set it like a Kabab-stick before him. Then he tare off the body, limb from limb, as one jointeth a chicken and, rending the flesh with his nails, fell to eating of it and gnawing the bones, till there was nothing left but some of these, which he threw on one side of the wall.[26]

All of Sinbad's companions meet the same end except for our skinny hero, who is deemed an unworthy tidbit and released. In addition to his far-fetched escapades, the tales of Sinbad also provide a picture of the gritty day-to-day reality of long-distance commerce in the Abbasid and Fatimid periods. Even a cursory reading of *Nights* reveals that Sinbad was no sailor at all, but rather the scion of a wealthy Baghdad trading family that possessed many palaces and warehouses. Sinbad did not own, command, or, as far as we can tell, even crew on any of the vessels he sailed.

In fairness, a fine line separated the trader from the sailor on the Indian Ocean, as few crew members received a salary; rather, most of them made their living carrying trade goods on their own account.[27] Whatever Sinbad's precise job description, he recounts the modus operandi of traders familiar to the reader of the Geniza papers:

> I bought me goods, merchandise all needed for a voyage and, impatient to be at sea, I embarked, with a company of merchants, on board a ship for Bassorah [modern Basra, at the head of the Persian Gulf]. There we again embarked and sailed many days and nights, and we passed from isle to isle and sea to sea and shore to shore, buying and selling and bartering everywhere the ship touched.[28]

As already discussed, the Red Sea challenged the merchant with pirates, narrow channels, dangerous shoals, and adverse winds, and the Silk Road suffered from the inherent physical inefficiencies and even greater dangers and political problems of a land route. Of the three great conduits between Asia and Europe, the remaining path—"Sinbad's Way," via the Mediterranean, across the Syrian desert, down the Tigris or Euphrates, and out the Persian Gulf into the Indian Ocean—was clearly the preferred route.

Each of Sinbad's expeditions begins with the laying in of goods from his Abbasid homeland to be exchanged abroad, in particular the fine textiles of Baghdad. From that city, Sinbad proceeded by small river craft downstream to Basra, thence onto a larger oceangoing vessel for the journey through the Persian Gulf and Indian Ocean.

In the course of his travails, he usually managed to lose and later regain his Baghdadi trade goods, then proceed to make "a great profit on them, and bought me goods and gear of the growth and fashion" to fill his family's warehouses back home. Soon after he avoided being a dinner course for the gorgon, Sinbad recounts:

> We ceased not to buy and sell at the several islands till we came to the land of Hind [India], where we bought cloves and ginger and all manner of spices; and thence we fared on to the land of Sind [China], where we also bought and sold. . . . Then we set sail again with a fair wind and the blessing of Almighty Allah; and after a prosperous voyage, arrived safe and sound in Bassorah. Here I abode a few days and presently returned to Baghdad where I went at once to my quarter and my house and saluted my family and familiars and friends.[29]

What drives this mythical hero? Nothing more and nothing less than a faithful medieval Islamic rendition of Adam Smith's propensity to truck and barter: a desire for "the society of the various races of mankind and for traffic and profit," to which has been added more than a dab of romance and adventure along the sea-lanes between Baghdad and Canton.[30]

Sinbad's mythical creatures—gigantic, ferocious birds who fed on jewel-encrusted carrion (identical to the beasts in *Marvels*), fish so large that sailors mistook them for islands, and man-eating gorgons—merely reflected the limited geographical horizons of the premodern world. Europeans spun equally fabulous yarns about the East: the lands of Gog and Magog, of a breed of hairy kneeless humanoids whose blood yielded the precious red dye used in Chinese fabrics, and of a Far Eastern Christian empire ruled by Prester John. The Chinese spun equally wild tales of the West, such as water-dwelling sheep from which cotton was sheared.[31]

These fictional and nonfictional accounts from the era of the medieval Indian Ocean trade, scattered and incomplete as they are, make clear that the four main luxury products of China—silk, sandalwood, spices, and porcelain—were somehow exchanged for what the East desired from Arabia and Africa: thoroughbred horses, ivory, incense, cottons, gold, and copper. Grain, as always, was shipped, particularly as ballast: rice, which in some cases actually improves with age, was heavily favored over wheat, which is far more prone to spoilage.[32]

Since ancient times, the great civilizations of both East and West had been beset by bordering tribes of plundering herdsmen. Stretching in a broad band from northern Europe to Mongolia, and usually of Turkic origin in Asia or of Germano-Scandinavian origin in Europe, these nomadic raiders deployed skills honed over millennia of attacks on settled farmers. Periodically, they overwhelmed their more agriculturally proficient, institutionally advanced, and culturally accomplished sedentary neighbors, as occurred to Rome in the fifth century after Christ.

Their most spectacular success, however, occurred in the early thirteenth century, when Genghis Khan roared out of the steppes to conquer all of central Asia; within a few decades, the Great Khan's descendants ruled over a group of empires comprising more territory than any dynasty before or since.

In 1255, one of Genghis Khan's grandsons, Mongke, sent his brother Hulagu (whose ambassador had invited the Polo brothers east) to conquer the Muslim world. Hulagu destroyed Baghdad in 1258 and massacred hundreds of thousands in the process, a tragedy still mourned in the Muslim world today. The Mongols surely would have continued into the Mediterranean had not Mongke died at that moment, forcing Hulagu to return to Mongolia in an attempt to claim his dead brother's mantle. He left behind a rump force that fell prey to the Mamluk Egyptians in 1260 at Ain Jalut in Palestine. Adding insult to injury, Hulagu failed to grab

Mongke's crown, which instead fell to a third brother, Kublai, who would subsequently wrest China from the Song dynasty.

For over a century, from the mid-1200s to the mid-1300s, the overland route from China to the gates of Europe lay in the hands of a more or less stable chain of Mongol states, which enthusiastically embraced commerce as well as the religions and cultures of the peoples they conquered. Three of Asia's four great Mongol empires eventually converted to Islam; the only one that did not, the legendary Kublai's Chinese dynasty, rapidly assimilated China's ancient culture. The Mongols adopted Islamic and Christian influences as well. Kublai, distrusting the preexisting Mandarin bureaucracy, hired into his service many foreigners, whose numbers included all three Polos.

For about a century, beginning around 1260 after the conquests of Genghis's grandchildren and ending with the dissolution of Mongol dynasties from internal strife and the plague, the Silk Road lay unobstructed. Large numbers of Europeans and Muslims exploited this relatively brief opportunity and shuttled with ease between China and the West, but the names of two burn brightest in the light of history—Marco Polo and Ibn Battuta.

The Polos, a clan of consummate traders, exploited the window first, just as it was being opened up by Ghengis's grandchildren. Ibn Battuta, on the other hand, was not even a trader, but rather a *qadi*—a Muslim judge. Born into a scholarly family in Tangier, Morocco, in 1304, he studied Islamic law, as had generations of his male relatives. On completion of his studies he made the mandatory hajj to Mecca in 1325, one year after the death of Marco Polo.

The road must have appealed to him, for over the next three decades he journeyed approximately 74,000 miles throughout Asia, Africa, and Europe. A sort of medieval Islamic version of the modern Eurailpass-carrying flower child used to supplementing family money with guitar, harmonica, and donation box, he flogged his expertise in sharia (sacred law) for all it was worth and in the process acquired an ever-increasing amount of wealth, power, and female company. When boredom, adverse circumstances, or, on occasion, out-and-out self-preservation required him to, he moved on, not infrequently leaving behind a trail of discarded concubines and unhappy ex-wives, offspring, and in-laws.

Around 1300, a vigorous line of Turkic Muslims wrested northern and central India from its ancient Hindu dynasties and established their sultanate in Delhi. The most famous of these early Muslim masters of India was Sultan Muhammad Ibn Tughluq, who ruled from 1325 to 1351, a period roughly corresponding to the span of Battuta's epic journey. Tughluq became notorious for his hare-brained military, agricultural, and institutional schemes. These included an ill-fated attempt to move his capital four hundred miles south into the dusty, desolate Deccan plain of south India; a regimentation of Indian agriculture that ended in starvation and revolt; and the raising of a vast army to conquer the central Asian Mongols. (He largely abandoned the last plan, except for a force sent to Kashmir that was destroyed by mountain tribes.)

But Tughluq's real passion was Islamic law. Shortly after taking power, he began to import eminent scholars from the Islamic world. He spared no expense, offering fabulous sinecures, accommodations, and privileges to the most attractive recruits. By this time, Battuta was traversing the Hindu Kush mountains of northwest India. On the road for approximately eight years and accustomed to traveling in style (which in that era meant a train of pack mules, luxurious portable furniture and tents, and a small army of slaves and women), he was on the brink of exhausting his family funds. When word reached him of the opportunities at the Delhi court, he heeded the call.

Along the way, Battuta passed through the lower Indus Valley, revered by Muslims as the first part of the subcontinent to receive Islam in the eighth century. While he was en route, Hindu bandits attacked his party. He casually noted:

> The inhabitants of India are in general infidels [Hindus]; some of them live under the protection of the Mohammedans, and reside either in the villages or cities: others, however, infest the mountains and rob by highways. I happened to be of a party of two and twenty men, when a number of Hindus, consisting of two horsemen and eighty foot, made an attack upon us. We, however, engaged them, and by God's help put them to flight, having killed one horseman and twelve of the foot.[33]

Such was the day-to-day business of the medieval traveler; Battuta and his companions hung the heads of the thirteen unlucky bandits on the walls of the next government fort along their route.[34] He also encountered (as had the Polos) suttee:

> The woman adorns herself, and is accompanied by a cavalcade of the infidel Hindus and Brahmins, with drums, trumpets, and men following her, both Muslims and Infidels for mere pastime. The fire had already been kindled, and into it they threw the dead husband. The wife then threw herself upon him, and both were entirely burnt. A woman's burning herself, however, is not considered absolutely necessary among them. . . . But when she does not burn herself, she is ever after clothed coarsely, and remains in constraint among her relatives, on account of her want of fidelity to her husband.[35]

Battuta finally arrived in Delhi, where he encountered what was surely one of the most curious credit markets in the history of finance. The favor of Muhammad Tughluq, on which much enterprise (and certainly the fortunes of a foreign *qadi* such as Battuta) rested, had to be bought with lavish gifts. These gifts, in turn, were rewarded with favors from Tughluq of far greater value, creating a further sense of financial obligation to the court. Since such expensive presents went well beyond the means of the average person, enterprising supplicants almost always had to borrow:

> The merchants of China and India began to furnish each newcomer with thousands of dinars as a loan, and to supply him with whatever he might desire to offer as a gift. . . . They place both their money and their persons at his service, and stand before him like attendants. When he reaches the sultan, he receives a magnificent gift from him and pays off his debt to them. This trade of theirs is a flourishing one and brings in vast profits.[36]

Even if the supplicant was successful, the lavish lifestyle of the court usually swept him into a downward credit spiral. Although Battuta eventually found himself *qadi* of Delhi, in charge of a royal mausoleum, and the tax farmer of several villages, he still accumulated a debt of 55,000 silver dinars (roughly 4,000 gold dinars).

Battuta had mounted not only a financial tiger in Delhi, but a political one as well. Even for his time, Tughluq was a particularly bloodthirsty master. His interest in Islamic law imparted to him the menace of the ideologically pure, so familiar to the modern world. Disloyalty, real or imagined, hastened the end of many of his subjects, and a lack of doctrinal purity was also a reliable shortcut to the next world. As one modern scholar put it:

> It was one thing to chastise rebels by having them cut in half, skinned alive, or tossed about with elephants with swords attached to their tusks (the latter of which Battuta was to witness more than once). It was quite another thing to inflict such humiliations on distinguished scholars and holy men for merely questioning public policy.[37]

A brief association with a dissident Sufi cleric earned Battuta nine days under armed guard, during which he imagined one unpleasant end after another. Disillusioned with his terms of employment, he pleaded with the sultan to allow him to depart on the hajj; instead, he was made an offer he couldn't refuse: the ambassadorship to Kublai Khan's China. Preferring escape east with a retinue of ambassadorial slaves, concubines, and an escort of one thousand horsemen to escape west as a pilgrim, he left for China.

Even in the best of times, danger plagued the overland journey from Delhi to the Malabar Coast, from where his enormous party would embark for China. And with Tughluq's regime tottering, these were not the best of times. A few days out of New Delhi, a force of four thousand rebels attacked his entourage. Although they greatly outnumbered the ambassador's party, the attackers were slaughtered, apparently at little cost. Shortly thereafter, another rebel force captured Battuta, who escaped just before he was to be executed.

He rejoined his party and embarked from the northwestern Indian port of Cambay in four relatively small Indian craft for the southwestern port of Calicut. (Calicut is on the other side of the subcontinent from Calcutta, which would be settled two centuries later by the British.) This was pepper country, and the farther south he went, the richer the towns became. As the land grew more fertile and prosperous, the more frequent became his sightings of the huge Chinese junks sent to fetch the mountains of black spice used by Kublai's subjects to flavor their dishes. Fifty years before, Marco Polo had observed of Zaitun's spice markets, "The quantity of pepper imported there is so great that what is carried to Alexandria to supply the demand of the western parts of the world is trifling in comparison—perhaps not more than a hundredth part."[38]

Ibn Battuta cared little for such details of maritime technology or the volume of trade between India and China (or, for that matter, almost everything else besides Islamic law and the finer things in life). He was, however, smitten by the luxurious Chinese vessels, with their multiple decks, private enclosed toilets, steward service, lifeboats, and, of course, a cabin door "which can be bolted by the occupant, who may take with him his female slaves and women."[39]

To Battuta's annoyance, Chinese officials had already reserved the best rooms in the huge ships, leaving him with a smaller cabin, sans private bathroom. This simply would not do, so he took a larger room on a smaller Indian vessel. While he was at Friday prayers, the flotilla of large junks and smaller Indian ships put to sea to ride out a sudden storm; the junks went aground and sank, while the smaller vessel he was supposed to be on, carrying his servants, luggage, and concubines (one of whom was pregnant with his child), sailed south without him, and later was captured in Sumatra by "heathen" (i.e., Hindus).

Battuta eventually found passage to China on yet a smaller boat and in greatly reduced company. Along the way, on the western Malay Peninsula, he was the guest of a king and witnessed a strange spectacle. One of the ruler's subjects, wishing to demonstrate his loyalty, held a knife to his own neck:

> He then made a long speech, not a word of which I could understand; he then firmly grasped the knife, and its sharpness and the force with which he urged it were such that he severed his head from his body, and it fell to the ground. . . . The King said to me: Does any among you do such a thing? I answered, I never saw one do so. He smiled and said: "These our servants do so, out of their love to us."[40]

Shortly thereafter, Battuta spent several months in the northern Sumatran city of Samudera, awaiting the reversal of the monsoons that would blow him north to China. At the time of his visit there, it was the first place in Southeast Asia to come under Islamic rule, spread by Muslim traders from India. The year was 1345, and Battuta had no way of knowing that he was witnessing the vanguard of a religious conversion that would produce the modern world's most populous Muslim nation, Indonesia.

Battuta's travelogue grows increasingly sketchy as he arrives in China. He recounts extensive travel there, supposedly covering thousands of miles of roads and canals between Beijing and Canton in a few months, an impossibly short period of time. He was not pleased with what he saw. As he so often does in *Travels,* Battuta affects the mood of a surly Western package tourist who consorts only with his own countrymen and is fed strange food, housed in substandard hotels, and cheated at every turn by the locals:

> I was greatly troubled thinking about the way paganism dominated this country. Whenever I went out of my lodging, I saw many blameworthy things. That disturbed me so much that I stayed indoors most of the time and went out only when necessary.[41]

Neither was Battuta pleased with the remarkable Chinese innovation of paper currency. Like the archetypal American abroad exasperated with foreign "funny money," he complained: "When any one goes to the market with a dinar or a dirhem in his hand, no one will take it until it has been changed for these notes."[42] (Polo, by contrast, thrived on China's religious and cultural diversity: "The country is delightful. The people are idolators."[43])

Not everything Battuta saw in China displeased him. Like Marco Polo, he marveled at the size of Zaitun, which by then was a city with six separate boroughs: one for ordinary Chinese, one for the city's guards, one for the Jews and Christians, one for sailors and fishermen, one for the seat of government, and, of course, one for Muslims. This metropolis, probably the world's largest at the time, took three full days to circumnavigate. He also could not help commenting favorably on the safety of travel within China, an unimaginable luxury to someone inured to the perils of the road in Asia and the Middle East. His most enthusiastic entry, naturally enough, came when he encountered in the port city of Fuzhou a fellow Moroccan from near his home in Tangier, who gave Battuta many wonderful gifts, among which were two white male slaves, and in addition, two local females.[44]

In many regards, the Genoese Polo and the Moroccan Battuta provided mirror images of the epic medieval wanderer: Polo was Christian, intensely curious about the peoples, customs, and places he visited, and almost completely dependent on the goodwill of the Mongol khans of China and central Asia. By contrast, Battuta was Muslim, profoundly uncurious about the non-Islamic world, and achieved his greatest degree of wealth, fame, and influence in the Muslim court of Delhi.

The Polos eagerly sought contact with the non-Christians of Asia, if for no other reason than simply to survive and conduct business. Polo's fascination with and openness to outside influences shines through every page of his memoirs; the same cannot be said of Battuta, who exudes a remarkable lack of interest in non-Muslim peoples and affairs. About all that ties the two accounts together is that they concerned the East and were transcribed by a professional writer.

It is precisely Battuta's lack of interest in peoples outside *Dar-al-Islam*—the world of Islam—that testifies to Muslim dominance of medieval Asian trade. In the fourteenth century, Battuta could travel 74,000 miles through Morocco, East Africa, India, central Asia, Southeast Asia, and China and remain entirely within the Muslim cultural envelope, never having to interact in a meaningful manner with those outside it in order to survive, to travel, or even to make a living.

The Muslim spice importer in Cairo or Tangier obeyed the same religious, ethical, and—most important—commercial code (and was just as likely to need the services of a *qadi* like Battuta) as his Muslim supplier in Cambay or Malacca. The Muslim ruler, whether in Africa, Arabia, India, or Southeast Asia, observed the same basic rules regarding tax and customs rates. Typically, 2.5 percent was charged to believers, 5 percent to protected *dhimmi* (Christians and Jews), and 10 percent to nonprotected nonbelievers, such as Hindus and animist natives.[45]

The hajj, the Muslim obligation to visit Mecca and Medina, served to unite the world of Indian Ocean trade. Not all could afford the hajj, and many, if not most, who did undertake the expensive voyage paid for it with baggage of spices, silks, and cottons, in the process making the port city of Jeddah one of the era's great commercial centers.[46]

Certainly, the Indian Ocean, studded with more or less autonomous trading states, was no Muslim lake. The rulers of these states belonged to different nationalities and sects, and some were not even Muslim. Calicut, for instance, was ruled by the Hindu *zamorin*. Nonetheless, it is no exaggeration to state that the world of fourteenth-century medieval Indian Ocean trade was essentially one and the same with *Dar-al-Islam*.

In Battuta's obsession with *sharia* and the Muslim world and in his lack of interest in nearly everything outside it (besides the comforts of Chinese junks) we clearly see the double-edged sword of Islam so visible in today's world: an ecumenical but self-satisfied faith capable of uniting far-flung peoples under one system of belief and one regime of law, but also severely limited in its capacity to examine and borrow from others.

The Chinese leviathans of the Indian Ocean so admired by Battuta were the technological wonders of the medieval age. Beginning around the eleventh century, the Song Dynasty, forced to the south coast of China by steppe nomads, shifted their strategic focus toward the sea. In 1132, the emperor established a permanent navy, a nearly unheard-of innovation in the East. The Chinese military leadership made maritime engineering a high priority, and their boatyards began to turn out many types of huge military and maritime vessels with iron-nailed, multiple nested hulls; several decks; highly effective stern-mounted rudders; magnetic compass guidance (which allowed accurate navigation even in cloudy weather); and advanced fore-and-aft sails (which enabled ships to tack almost directly into the wind). The Chinese even briefly abandoned their famous cultural chauvinism and borrowed the sophisticated navigational techniques of the Persians and Indians.[47]

Compared with these advanced Chinese craft, the traditional Indian Ocean dhow, with its single hull stitched with coconut fiber, its clumsy lateen rigging (which had to be hauled up and down with each change of tack), and its lack of decks, was so flimsy that Marco Polo chose to endure the rigors, expense, and dangers of the Silk Road rather than embark on one at Hormuz.

One Westerner noted that the dhows were

> mighty frail and uncouth with no iron in them and no caulking. They are sewn like clothes with twine! And so if the twine breaks anywhere there is a breach indeed! Once every year, therefore, there is a mending of this, more or less, if they propose to go to sea. They have a flimsy rudder like the top of a table . . . and when they have to tack, it is done with a great deal of trouble; and if it is blowing in any hard way, they cannot tack at all.[48]

Another European observed that the Chinese junks tended to

> be very big, and have upon the ship's hull more than 100 cabins, and with a fair wind they carry ten sails, and they are very bulky,

being made of three thicknesses of plank, so that the first thickness is as great as in our ships, the second cross-wise, and the third again long-wise. In sooth 'tis a very strong affair.[49]

Nautical historians have in fact wondered why the Indians and Arabs stuck with the dhow so long, almost to the present day, and did not adopt the superior Chinese and European designs. The answer is at least three-fold. First, the weight of tradition among Indian shipbuilders overwhelmed the needs of sailors for secure oceangoing craft. Second, India's west coast did not produce enough iron for construction. Third, although the sewn craft may have been less seaworthy, they were more "beachworthy"— that is, more pliable, and thus better able to survive the frequent encounters with the reefs, rocks, and shallows of the coasting trade than were the more rigid planked and ribbed Chinese and European ships.[50]

Given China's advantage in maritime technology, the relatively low profile of its traders west of Malacca is remarkable. Only during the period between 1405 and 1433 did the Chinese intentionally flex their muscle in the Indian Ocean. Perhaps the inferior status accorded traders by Confucianism, which viewed merchants as parasites, steered the brightest and most ambitious away from trade and into the economically stifling Mandarin bureaucracy. Then too, China's (and later, Japan's) centralized political structure could quickly shut off contact with the outside world.

In contrast, the highly decentralized nature of the medieval world of Indian Ocean trade produced a bubbling stew of Darwinian economic competition, in which those states whose political "mutations" were best suited to trade and commerce thrived, and those whose institutions were not withered. In much the same way, the political environment of Europe, fractured by its mountainous and riverine geography into thousands of competing states, favored those nations with the most economically efficient institutions. One of them, England, would emerge as history's first truly global hegemon.[51]

In 1382, the army of the first Ming emperor, Zhu Yuanzhang, which had been pursuing the remnants of the Mongol army, captured a ten-year-old Muslim peasant boy named Ma. The commanding general asked the young captive the whereabouts of the Mongol pretender and received this impertinent answer: "He jumped into a pond." Ma's insouciance earned him captivity in the royal household, and three years later, as was the custom, he was castrated and added to the eunuch staff of the royal household, in this case of Zhu Di, the fourth of the emperor's twenty-six sons.

Unlike most eunuchs, he did not develop a shrill tongue or a feminine manner, but instead grew into a huge, fierce, intelligent warrior with a deep booming voice. When his master, Zhu Di, finally became emperor after a brutal civil war against his older brother, the young protégé was promoted to the powerful position of superintendent of the office of eunuchs.[52] His new name was Zheng He, or, as he was until recently called in the West, Cheng Ho, the commander of the treasure fleet and master of the Indian Ocean.

History associates the voyages of the great Chinese treasure fleets—seven in all between 1405 and 1433—with Zheng He, but these spectacular missions were for all intents and purposes just one cog in the grand design of the expansionist Emperor Zhu Di, and, in the end, a pawn in the age-old antagonism between the Confucian scholars and the eunuchs.

Zhu Di, unlike his isolationist peasant-warrior father, was a cultured ruler with an internationalist worldview who engaged China in dozens of costly foreign adventures. These efforts included diplomatic and military missions to the Mongol former enemy and, less successfully, an invasion of Vietnam that started a long and brutal guerrilla war (and from which modern France and America failed to learn the appropriate lessons).

None of Zhu Di's many spectacular projects left their mark on history as did the great treasure fleets, the gargantuan successors to the vessels so coveted by Ibn Battuta. These ships ranged in size from relatively small support boats "only" a hundred feet in length to the massive three-to four-hundred-foot-long "treasure ships," with their multiple nail-bound, watertight hull compartments; up to nine masts; dozens of spacious cabins; and sophisticated stern-post rudders of a type that would not be seen in Europe until the early modern period.[53]

Most voyages consisted of about three hundred vessels manned by approximately thirty thousand crew members, and sailed on two-year expeditions to Malacca, Sumatra, Java, and India, and on later journeys to Hormuz, the Red Sea, and much of the East African coast. The treasure fleets were hardly opening new markets for Chinese commerce; we know from Polo, Battuta, and Chinese and Muslim observers that they had been preceded into Asian ports by previous generations of Chinese diplomats and merchants. Rather, the primary purposes of the seven successive missions were diplomatic, military, and symbolic.

The monsoons drove the carefully choreographed arc of each voyage. Zheng He's fleets assembled in the fall at an anchorage at Taiping in southern China, where they waited for the winter northeast monsoon to carry them to Surabaya in Java. There they remained until July, when the southwest monsoon blew them past Sumatra and Malacca to Sri Lanka and the Malabar Coast of India. Smaller detachments then ranged as far as Hormuz and Africa. Over the next twelve months, the process was reversed: south to Java with the winter northeast monsoon, then homeward on the summer southwest monsoon.

First and foremost, the ventures stabilized the critical Strait of Malacca, ruled by a renegade Sumatran sultan but claimed by the Siamese, who controlled Chinese access to the Indian Ocean. Zheng He not only suppressed the piracy that was rampant in the strait, but also adroitly reconciled competing Siamese and Malaccan interests in the vital waterway, keeping it open to the commerce of all parties. An additional, unspoken charge of Zheng He may have been to search for Zhu Yunwen, the brother Zhu Di supplanted, who was reported to have fled overseas.[54]

Much of what is known about the treasure fleets comes from the memoirs of a Chinese Muslim translator, Ma Huan, who was fluent in Arabic. He accompanied Zheng He's later voyages, and his description of the visit to the sultan of Malacca speaks eloquently to the nature of "treasure fleet diplomacy":

> [The emperor bestowed upon the sultan] two silver seals, a hat, a girdle, and a robe. [Zheng He] set up a stone tablet and raised [Malacca] to a city, and it was subsequently called the country of Malacca. Thereafter [the king of Siam] did not dare to invade it. The sultan, having received the favor of having been made a king, conducted his wife and son and went to the court [in China] to return thanks and present tribute of local products. The court also granted him a sea-going ship, so that he might return to his country and protect his land.[55]

In India and Arabia, Ma Huan encountered the wellsprings of Western monotheism. In Calicut he recorded this wonderful whispering-down-the-lane story of Exodus, concerning one

> Mou-hsieh, who established a religious cult; the people knew that he
> was a true man of Heaven, and all men revered and followed him. Later
> the holy man went away to another with [others] to another place, and
> ordered his younger brother to govern and teach the people.

Unfortunately, this younger brother taught the people to worship a golden ox, saying, "It always excretes gold. The people got the gold, and their hearts rejoiced; and they forgot the way of Heaven; all took the ox to be the true lord." The prophet Mou-hsieh returns, destroys the ox, and banishes his brother, who "mounted a large elephant and vanished."[56]

Whatever his diplomatic and cross-cultural accomplishments, Zheng He earned little economic reward for an effort that consumed most of the nation's timber, shipbuilding capacity, and much of its military force. The most famous and prized of the fleets' cargoes produced only evanescent symbolic value: several African giraffes obtained from Arabian and Indian rulers as tribute. The beasts were valued not only because of their exotic and pleasing appearance, but also because they were thought by the Chinese to be an animal known as the *qilin*. This mythical beast had a unicorn's horn, horse's hooves, wolf's forehead, ox's tail, and musk deer's body, and was said to appear only at times of peace and prosperity. Another tribute gift from Malacca that captivated the Chinese were strange clear glass objects which magnified the size of tiny written characters —almost certainly the first eyeglasses, which had recently been invented in Venice.[57]

Worse, much of both the fleets' cargoes—outbound, porcelain and silk; and inbound, spices, precious stones, woolens, and carpets—passed through the warehouses of Zheng He's fellow eunuchs, who controlled most of the nation's overseas commerce. On the death of Zhu Di in 1424, the eunuchs and the xenophobic Confucian bureaucracy faced off in a power struggle. The Confucians' victory ended the great age of Chinese exploration. Zheng He died in command of the seventh voyage; after it returned up the Yangtze River in July 1433, none would follow.

Within a few generations, the Chinese allowed their naval and merchant fleets to wither; in 1500, an imperial edict made the construction of vessels with more than two masts a capital offense. In 1525, another decree forbade the building of *any* oceangoing vessel. Where navies are absent, pirates pillage. By the middle of the sixteenth century, Japanese *wako* marauders so terrorized China's coastline that to this day women in Fujian province hide their faces with blue scarves originally designed to shield the wearer from the lecherous gaze of foreign bandits.[58]

Recently, Zheng He's voyages have become a subject of revisionist history. In *1421: The Year China Discovered America,* the retired English submarine commander Gavin Menzies suggested that a detachment from Zheng He's sixth expedition visited America (as well as Australia, New Zealand, the Atlantic coast of Brazil, and the Cape Verde Islands); his claims, for the most part, are not taken seriously by maritime historians.[59]

Today, as China begins to flex its newfound military and economic power, it uses Zheng He's voyages to illustrate to the outside world the historically benign and nonaggressive nature of Chinese foreign policy. It would do better not to draw too much attention to the details of the missions, which on many occasions kidnapped and slaughtered those who did not pay proper homage to imperial authority. For example, on his first expedition, Zheng He killed over five thousand pirates in the Strait of Malacca; their leader was returned to China, presented to the emperor, and decapitated. On later voyages, Zheng He captured and carried back the rulers of Sri Lanka, Palembang in eastern Sumatra, and Semudera (near modern Banda Aceh), and on numerous occasions led his troops into battle.[60]

Da Gama and Zheng He missed each other by just sixty-five years; it can only be imagined what might have occurred had the first Europeans to visit the Indian Ocean encountered the treasure fleet, whose smallest support junks would have towered over the puny Portuguese caravels. Fortunately for the Portuguese, the fickle mistress of history spared them this humiliation. When Vasco da Gama breached the Indian Ocean, the playing field had just been vacated by the one force capable of repelling him.

On April 20, 1511, Tomé Pires, an apothecary (and thus knowledgeable about rare spices), shipped out from Lisbon to seek his fortune in India. He never returned to his mother country, for he was sent as the first official European ambassador to the Celestial Empire, where he died in captivity at age seventy. His story might have remained unknown had not a Portuguese researcher visiting the French National Library in the 1930s come across the "Paris Codex." This volume contained, among other documents, Pires's *Suma Oriental,* an account of his travels. He described the Indian Ocean emporium trade just before it disappeared under the boots of the Europeans, and he affords us a detailed and intimate last look at the indigenous world of Asian commerce.

At that time, the primary axis of Asian trade ran from the massive Gujarati port at Cambay (about sixty miles south of the modern western Indian metropolis of Ahmadabad), the marshalling point for Indian textiles and European goods moving east toward Malacca. There, they would be traded for rare spices and Chinese silks and porcelains.

Pires described the broad estuary of the Mahi River, on which Cambay sits, as stretching out "two arms; with her right arm she reaches out towards Aden, and with the other towards Malacca."[61] Although Cambay was ruled by Muslim Mughals, the city's long-distance commerce was dominated by its Hindu trading castes:

> There is no doubt that these people have the cream of the trade. They are men who understand merchandise; they are so properly steeped in the sound and harmony of it, that the Gujaratis say that any offense connected with merchandise is pardonable. There are Gujaratis settled everywhere. . . . They are diligent, quick men in trade. They do their accounts with figures like ours and with our very writing. . . . There are also Cairo merchants settled in Cambay, and many Khorasans and Guilans from Aden and Hormuz, all of whom do a great trade in the seaport towns of Cambay. . . . Those of our people who want to be clerks and factors ought to go there and learn, because the business of trade is a science in itself which does not hinder any other noble exercise, but helps a great deal.[62]

The Portuguese of the sixteenth century were perhaps the most outrageously chauvinistic of the Western intruders in Asia and the Americas. Pires's observation that his countrymen had much to learn from the heathen Gujaratis thus spoke volumes about the scope and sophistication of the indigenous Asian trade.

Pires worked no more than nine months in India before Portugal's master of the East, Afonso de Albuquerque, dispatched him to Malacca, which had just fallen to the Portuguese. At the time of his arrival there, Malacca was a relatively new city, whose indigenous origins predated by little more than a century its conquest by the Portuguese. Sometime around 1400, a Hindu sultan, Parameswara, the local ruler of the Sumatran city of Palembang (which lies about halfway between modern Singapore and Java) defied the Hindu Majapahit ruler of Java and was forced to flee north toward Singapore and the strait. After first conquering Singapore, Parameswara then settled in Malacca, which derives its name from an old Malay word, *malaqa*, meaning "hidden fugitive."[63]

The Hindu Majapahits, under attack from Muslim enclaves in Java and Sumatra and riven internally by strife and corruption, were on the way out. Parameswara proved the right man in the right place at the right time: canny, attuned to commerce, and possessed of innumerable contacts among both local and foreign traders in Palembang and beyond. Further, he was now in control of a fine natural port just out of range of the strife in Java and southern Sumatra, but still commanding the strait. That Parameswara concentrated his efforts on commerce through the strait was no accident—he was one of the last in a line of princes of the seafaring empire of Crivijaya. From its capital in Palembang, this empire had at one point ruled over large parts of Sumatra, Java, and the Malay Peninsula. Its wealth and power derived from its control of the local and long-distance trade through the strait.

Parameswara's heirs proved just as talented, and Malacca soon became one of the world's commercial fulcrums. What Singapore is to the modern world—a sprawling entrepôt commanding one of the world's key maritime choke points—Malacca, which lies 130 miles northwest of modern Singapore, was to the Middle Ages. Just as Singapore does today, medieval Malacca connected India, the Arab world, and Europe to its west with China and the legendary Spice Islands to its east.

Malacca dazzled Pires, and the city's sights, smells, and activity evoked in him a vision of the promised land. A meticulous observer, Pires possessed both a ready facility with numbers—rare among colonial officials of that era—and an eye for the fine points of government and trade. Although *Suma Oriental* is no one's idea of beach reading, the magic of Malacca at the very moment the Portuguese conquered it shines through. Pires counted eighty-four tongues being spoken, in a city as multicultural as London or New York, by the likes of:

> Moors from Cairo, Mecca, Aden, Abyssinians, men of Kilwa, Malindi, Hormuz, Parsees, Rumes, Turks, Turkomens, Christian Armenians, Gujaratis, men of Chaul, Dabhol, Goa, of the Kingdom of Deccan, Malabars and Klings, merchants from Orissa, Ceylon, Bengal,

Arakan, Pegu, Siamese, men of Kedah, Malays, men of Pahang, Patani, Cambodia, Champa, Cochin China, Chinese, Lequeos, men of Brunei, Luçoes, men of Tamjompura, Laue, Banka, Linga (they have a thousand other islands), Moluccas, Banda, Bima, Timor, Madura, Java, Sunda, Palembang, Jambi, Tongkal, Indragiri, Kappatta, Menangkabau, Siak, Arcat, Aru, Bata, country of the Tomjano, Pase, Pedir, Maldives.[64]

As pointed out by the historian and sociologist Janet Abu-Lughod, "No single other fact can quite capture the 'shape' of the world system by the fifteenth century as this cast of characters."[65] The presence of "Rumes" is especially intriguing, as this term was variously applied to southern Europeans, Turks, or Byzantine Greeks (Constantinople having been conquered sixty years previously by the Turks). Were there Italians already in Malacca before the Portuguese arrived? By 1326, following the enthusiastic reports of Marco Polo, Genoese merchants were a common sight in Zaitun, China's greatest port, so it would not have been surprising if Pires had found them in Malacca as well. The Genoese were at least as well traveled as the Venetians, but also famously close-mouthed about the particulars of their fabulously profitable trade routes. It is no accident that the first detailed reports of the Far East came from more voluble Venetians such as Marco Polo.[66] Even if there were no Italians in Malacca, their signature merchandise, transshipped from Alexandria and brought by Indian traders via the Red Sea and Cambay, abounded there: scarlet dye, colored woolens, beads, glass, and weapons of every type.

The massive flow of goods into the port was overseen by four harbormasters, one each for cargoes from the Arab Middle East and India, from Siam and China, from the local Sumatran ports, and from the rest of Indonesia. Pires observed that the main axis of trade was between Gujarat in western India, particularly its main port of Cambay, and Malacca. The most prized of Indian commodities was cloth, of which he documented thirty types, as well as opium and incense from farther west. More varied goods—mace, nutmeg, cloves, sandalwood, and tin, as well as Chinese silk and porcelain—flowed west, some bound for India, some for the Gulf, and some for Egypt and Europe. Pires mentions that four ships per year came from the smaller ports of Gujarat, each carrying a cargo worth up to thirty thousand cruzados (about $2.4 million in today's money), whereas just one giant annual shipment came from Cambay, valued at about "seventy or eighty thousand cruzados, without any doubt."[67] And all this from just the western coast of India; vessels to and from India's east coast likely carried a similar amount of goods as well.

What went right at Malacca? Its prosperity did not flow simply from its favorable location at one of the maritime world's critical choke points, "at the end of the monsoons."[68] After all, the strait stretches several hundred miles along the Malay and Sumatran coasts and is far easier to control at its narrower Singapore end. Further, both the Malay side and the Sumatran side were studded with trading cities for centuries before Parameswara founded Malacca in 1400.

Rather, the city's wealth and prominence can be credited to the institutional genius of Parameswara and his heirs. Alone among the many trading cities that lined the strait, Malacca had found the answer to the question of whether to trade, raid, or protect. The Malaccans levied import duties less onerous than those prescribed by traditional Islamic custom, the maximum being just 6 percent (instead of the usual 10 percent), payable on imports from "the West"—that is, those brought by Indians and Arabs. If a Westerner and his wife were both settled in the port, they paid only 3 percent. Easterners —local Malays, Indonesians (including the Moluccans with their precious spices), Siamese, and Chinese—paid no formal import duties at all. From all imports, even from "Easterners," were subtracted "presents" to the sultan and his lieutenants, estimated by Pires at a cost of 1 or 2 percent of cargo value. No trader, Eastern, Western, or local, paid an export duty.

A reasonably solid, if informal, legal structure seems to have been in place, rivaling even the advanced common law of medieval England. The sultan's chief civil officer, called the *bendara,* was a sort of mayor cum chief justice, who oversaw disputes and ensured that business ran smoothly. (He was also one of the recipients of the aforementioned "presents.") A brother of the *bendara* was usually appointed *tumungam,* or customs judge, who together with a panel of local and foreign traders valued the cargo; duties were then collected and the cargo was thrown open to bids from a yet larger group of merchants:

> And because time was short and the merchandise considerable, the merchants were cleared [i.e., the cargo fully sold], and then those of Malacca took the merchandise to their ships and sold them at their pleasure; from which the traders received their settlement and gains,

and the local merchants made their profits. . . . And that it was thus
done orderly, so that they did not favor the merchant from the ship,
nor did he go away displeased; *for the law and the prices of merchandise in Malacca are well known.* (italics added)[69]

Adam Smith would surely have approved, for here, in fewer than a
hundred short words, is the essential recipe for free-market success: an
auction process conducted with well-described and well-known rules at
a single point in time by a large number of well-informed participants,
backed by government institutions considered honest by the participants—
a sort of medieval eBay in the tropics, in which good rules attracted good
traders, who in turn insisted on even better rules.

Neither did it hurt that Parameswara, in order to fend off the Majapahits
of Java, converted to Islam so that he might marry the daughter of the
Muslim king of Pase (in northern Sumatra) and thus acquire the king's badly
needed protection against the Hindu enemy. By 1400, the majority of the
merchants in the strait were disciples of the Prophet, even if the local population was not. That Muslim commerce proceeded ahead of conversion in
Southeast Asia was no accident; whereas theology is the primary driving
force behind Christianity and the great Eastern religions, Islam's backbone
is a system of law covering all areas of conduct, including commerce. Thus,
the new monotheism from Arabia was especially attractive to those engaged
in any organized economic activity that flourished wherever rules were
plainly visible and vigorously enforced by disinterested parties—again, as
in the more secular English common law.

Even if one was not moved by religious fervor, embracing Islam at
least did wonders for one's credit rating. Only later would the general population, impressed with the wealth and piety of their Muslim merchant neighbors, follow their path.[70] The conversion of much of Southeast Asia was
accomplished not by conquerors roaring out of Arabia and Persia, but rather
by cloth and spice merchants from Cambay and Calicut, who often married native women. Their mixed-race offspring, regardless of their mother's
religion, were almost always raised as Muslims and served to spread the
word of the Prophet among their peers and their mothers' friends and families.[71] (When Pires arrived in Malacca, Muslim traders were still actively
spreading the word of Muhammad across the Hindu empires of Java,
Sumatra, and eastern Indonesia, even as the West was reclaiming Islam's
western domains in Spain and southeastern Europe.)

Like the previous Crivijaya, Parameswara kept open his lines of communication to China, which included Zheng He's fleets. The sultan and the Chinese cultivated each other, partly to keep the Siamese, who were rivals of both the Malaccans and the Chinese, at bay; between 1411 and 1419, Parameswara is thought to have visited China and paid tribute to Zhu Di on many occasions. By the time the Chinese left the Indian Ocean in 1433, the Malaccans were more than capable of filling the vacuum in the strait.

Malacca was certainly not the only Indian Ocean principality to hit on the essential formula for a prosperous coastal trading state—Pires's memoirs simply highlight the virtues of one of the most successful. The cities and ports between Venice and Canton that blossomed during the Middle Ages must have followed more or less the same precepts. In Calicut a series of hereditary Hindu rulers, the *zamorin,* maintained the legal, commercial, and maritime military institutions necessary for commercial success. Unfortunately for Calicut, it would be da Gama's first stop in India.

Alas, as Britons today will attest, even the most vigorous royal lines eventually peter out. Unluckily for Malacca, just as the Portuguese were appearing on the horizon, its leadership fell into the hands of a dissolute sultan, Mahmud Shah, from whom the Europeans plucked the city like a plump avocado. The rules of the game would soon change for the Muslims and other Asians engaged in the ancient trade of the Indian Ocean, and not for the better. In one of history's most bizarre chains of causation, the brutal, efficient newcomers were driven by a hunger for, of all things, culinary ingredients that today lie largely unused in most Western kitchens.

THE TASTE OF TRADE AND THE CAPTIVES OF TRADE

Few European institutions characterize everyday life on the Continent as do the weekly markets of the countryside. These gatherings, which delight both local resident and tourist alike, have their historical roots in the periodic gatherings of traveling merchants in towns too small to support their permanent presence.

During the medieval period, the layout of these markets was very different from today's rows of tidy stands. Back then, a more centrifugal pattern prevailed. The "dirtiest" operations—animal sales and butchering—occurred around the periphery of the market. Food stands, scribes, metalsmiths, barbers, dentists, rug weavers, and potters plied their wares and trades closer in. The focal point of the festivities was more often than not occupied by the aristocrats of the commercial hierarchy: the spice merchants. During the fourteenth to seventeenth centuries, cinnamon, nutmeg, mace, and cloves were not workaday flavorings, but rather the world's most sought-after commodities. Their sources and supply lines dealt wealth or poverty to nations; spices were as critical as oil and palladium are in the twenty-first century.

The most visible legacy of the wealth and splendor generated by the medieval spice trade still dazzles the eye today in Venice, whose grand palazzi and magnificent public architecture were built largely on profits from pepper, cinnamon, nutmeg, mace, and cloves. A hundred pounds of nutmeg, purchased in medieval Alexandria for ten ducats, might easily go for thirty or fifty ducats on the wharves of Venice. Even after payments for shipping, insurance, and customs duties at both ends, profits well in excess of 100 percent were routine; a typical Venetian galley carried one to three hundred tons between Egypt and Italy and earned vast fortunes for the imaginative and the lucky. During the medieval period, a corpulent Croesus was called a "pepper sack," not a thorough-going insult, since the price of a bag of pepper was usually higher than that of a human being.[1] The historian Frederic Lane estimates that on the eve of the Portuguese penetration of the Indian Ocean in the last years of the fifteenth century, swift Venetian galleys hauled 3,500,000 pounds of spices annually, most of it loaded in Alexandria, across the Mediterranean.[2]

The massive trade in spices raises an obvious question: just how did the West pay for this voracious appetite? Before silver from the mines of Peru and Mexico flooded across the Atlantic in the sixteenth century, Europe suffered from a severe shortage of coins with which to pay for imports. Further, the West fashioned few products that were desired in the Orient.

Before the modern era, the words "manufacturing" and "textiles" were virtually synonymous. Of Europe's two major cloth products, linen competed only poorly with Indian cotton, and wool did not appeal greatly to the inhabitants of hot climates. True, the Mediterranean yielded huge quantities of red coral, and the Italians were especially skilled at producing fine glass, but the Eastern markets for these luxury products filled only a tiny corner of the medieval Western trade deficit.

Did the Europeans produce any other commodity that could be traded at Alexandria and Cairo for the spices they so intensely desired? Indeed they did: slaves to fill the insatiable appetite of the Muslim armies for soldiers. Between roughly 1200 and 1500, Italian merchants became the world's most prosperous slave traders, buying humans on the eastern shores of the Black Sea and selling them in Egypt and the Levant. The cargo passed through the twin choke points at the Dardanelles (the ancient Hellespont) and the Bosphorus, guarded by the once mighty Byzantine Empire, which inevitably found itself in the gun sights of the two great Italian trading powers: Venice and Genoa.

Long-distance trade in the medieval period thus revolved around three stories: the spice trade, the slave trade, and the age-old struggle for mastery of the Bosphorus and Dardanelles.

Pepper and cinnamon came, respectively, from India and Sri Lanka, places that Europeans had at least heard of. Mace, nutmeg, and cloves came from the Spice Islands, which remained terra incognita until the fifteenth century.[3]

So remote were these fabled lands that even the Genoese and Venetian merchants who acquired the islands' precious products at ports in Egypt, the Levant, and the Black Sea were unaware of their precise location. The very name Spice Islands, like the Tin Islands of Herodotus, informs us that everything else about them—their peoples, geography, and language —was unknown or ignored in favor of the single purpose they served for the West.

If the importance of these spices in the medieval period is difficult to comprehend, think of the snob appeal of today's high-status items: the boxed Godiva chocolate, the BMW automobile, the Gucci shoe. Then surround the mystiques with a splash of uncertainty as to origin; all that we know about, say, the wonderful footwear is that it arrives on our wharves from somewhere in the East. In such an environment, a Gucci store is not simply a profitable business opportunity but a license to print money, and an established position anywhere along the shoe supply chain becomes a ticket to prestige and uncountable wealth. What would happen if these mythical consumers found out that the shoes came from an ordinary union-shop factory in Florence?

Such was the case with nutmeg, mace, and cloves during the medieval period. Certainly, Europeans had easy access to other appealing spices and herbs: saffron had been produced in Spain and England since it was first imported by Arab traders in the eighth century; pepper was easily available from India; coriander and cumin came from the Near East; and bay leaves, thyme, rosemary, marjoram, and oregano all originated in Europe. But nutmeg, mace, and cloves were far more desirable precisely because they were rare, expensive, and, above all, mysterious. Their gustatory appeal paled into insignificance compared with the message conveyed by their aroma and taste: here resides someone of wealth and status.

As had the Romans, Europeans became infatuated with spices. Physicians treated all manner of ailments with them, and Chaucer versified about fantasy forests filled with cloves to fumigate clothes chests and with nutmeg for flavoring ale. Spices and perfumes permeated gloves, hot beverages, liqueurs, and most of the recipes used in wealthy households. Historians have suggested that rare spices were originally valued because of their medicinal properties. For example, one authority points out that the contents of a medieval French spice store and a nineteenth-century American pharmacy would have been nearly identical.

But were these "drugs" effective? The placebo effect, one of the most powerful forces in the therapeutic armamentarium, derives in no small part from the exoticism of the ingredients or methods used. None of the spices mentioned in this chapter has any scientifically proven medicinal value, and those plant products that do are often quite common, such as the heart drug digitalis, from the lovely but lowly foxglove. Roman and Greek physicians prescribed the rare spice galangal "for the kidneys."[4] Precisely what medical conditions were meant by this? Whatever diseases these ancient medicos were treating probably had little to do with renal function.

It is more likely that rare spices found use as pharmaceuticals precisely *because* of their prestige. Superstitions die hard; even today, the rhinoceros has been hunted nearly to extinction because of the supposed aphrodisiac qualities of a powder made from its horn; such is the magic of rare animal and plant products that it is doubtful that the advent of Viagra will save the species.

Not all spices traveled eastward. Coriander, a modern favorite, is native to the eastern Mediterranean. It was well known to the Minoans and Egyptians by 1300 BC and reached China when the Han Empire opened the Silk Road a millennium later. Far more ominous was the eastward spread of another Mediterranean spice, the poppy seed, later to be cultivated in India under the watchful eyes of Europeans eager to improve their balance of trade by exporting the plant's highly addictive extract, opium.

Unlike the Tin Islands of Herodotus, there really were Spice Islands. Cloves, the unopened flower bud of *Syzygium aromaticum*, a tall fir, until recently grew only in the volcanic soil of five tiny islands—Ternate, Tidore, Moti, Makian, and Bacan—in the north Moluccas, an island group in eastern Indonesia. Nutmeg and mace come from different parts of the fruit of *Myristica fragrans*, a tree that grew only on nine flyspecks—the Bandas—in the southern part of the Moluccas.

The Moluccans had been selling spices long before the Europeans arrived. First occupied by aboriginal peoples tens of thousands of years ago, the archipelago was subsequently enveloped about 2000–1000 BC by the "Austronesian expansion," in which tribes from China and Taiwan, equipped with double outrigger-canoes, peopled the shores of the Indian and Pacific oceans from Madagascar to Easter Island. Empowered by the local spice trade, the aboriginal inhabitants of Ternate and Tidore

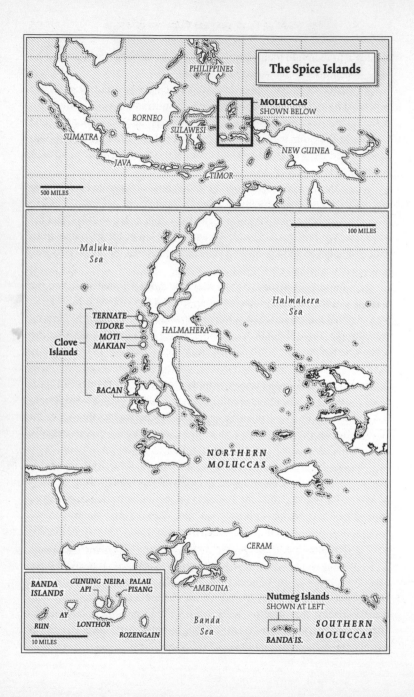

The Spice Islands

managed to maintain their identity and culture while the surrounding islands succumbed to the Austronesian tide.

These tiny volcanic "inner islands" grew only spices and coconuts and depended for their sustenance on the highly nutritious and productive sago palm produced on larger Moluccan "outer islands" such as Halmahera and Ceram. At first, this trade was purely an interisland affair, in which Bandanese plied the waters between the inner and outer islands in small craft and bartered sago for spices.

Like the Chinese silk imported into Rome, nutmeg and mace were probably known to the Romans—Pliny seems to have described them in *Historia Naturalis*. Similar also to silk, their source lay well beyond the horizon of Western knowledge, and the supply chain that first brought them to the Middle East and Europe was long, dangerous, indirect, and, of course, ridiculously expensive.[5]

As the export markets for nutmeg and mace expanded during the ancient and medieval periods, the spice-producing islands prospered to the point that they dominated most of the Moluccan archipelago. Ternate, for example, ruled the much larger island of Ceram until well after the arrival of the Dutch. The aboriginal Bandanese, though skilled at growing spices, did not trade them much beyond their home islands. It would be the descendants of the lighter-skinned, seafaring Austronesians, particularly the legendary Bugis from the large island of Sulawesi (about halfway between Java and the Spice Islands), who carried the spices far beyond the Moluccas to Java and Sumatra, from where they eventually arrived in China, India, and finally, Europe.[6]

Mace, the product of the thinner, outer layer of the fruit, was more precious than the more voluminous nutmeg-yielding core. During the early period of Portuguese rule, the Bandas yielded about a thousand tons of nutmeg per year, but only about a hundred of mace; consequently, mace was about seven to ten times as expensive as nutmeg. Occasionally, this price differential led to odd market behavior, some merely ironic, such as the burning of nutmeg by the Bandanese to increase its price, and some ridiculous, such as the famous (and probably apocryphal) order by the Dutch East India Company to its governor of the East Indies to grow only mace.[7] (Today, the situation is reversed, with nutmeg the more sought-after ingredient, and mace reserved for light-colored offerings in need of a fruity flavor, such as pound cake or cream soup.)

Occupying the middle ground between pepper and the Spice Islands flavorings was cinnamon, since its source in Sri Lanka hovered just at the eastern edge of the world known to the Romans. It first appeared in the capital at the height of the Empire and occupied the apex of culinary and aromatic luxury. Its flower juice sold for 1,500 denarii per pound—approximately its weight in gold. Those of more modest means settled for cinnamon oil, a relative bargain at only one-fourth of that price.[8] Still, Westerners would not be reliably informed about the cinnamon trees of Sri Lanka until Ibn Battuta described how Indian traders casually picked up their precious bark from beaches strewn with them.[9]

The same principle operated in reverse for China, which treasured items that were relatively common in Europe, such as ivory and incense, but whose provenance in Africa and Arabia was wrapped in the mystique of distance. By the same token, cloves from the relatively close Moluccas were considered less exotic by the Chinese, who used them as breath mints as early as the Han Dynasty: "They have the property of removing smells from the mouth, and high officials at Court put cloves into their mouths when they have to lay matters before the Emperor."[10]

The decay of the Roman Empire attenuated the supply of pepper and raised its prices. At the apex of the empire, a pound of gold bought almost three hundred of pepper, whereas by the beginning of the fourth century, it bought only ninety, and probably even less when Alaric ransomed Rome for a ton and a half of it. No matter how scarce and expensive pepper became, its flow to Europe was never to be interrupted, even during the depths of the Dark Ages.[11]

When the forces of Islam snapped shut Bab el Mandeb almost immediately after Muhammad's triumphant return to Mecca in the early seventh century, Greek ships could no longer sail east toward India's Western Ghats on the warm and turbulent southwest monsoon. While pepper still flowed easily westward through Muslim hands, knowledge of the East ceased. India, which had been well known to Greek and Roman geographers such as Strabo, Ptolemy, and Pomponius Mela, and whose ambassadors had fawned over Augustus, faded below the horizon of reality and into a sea of myth—a land of mountains of emeralds and gold guarded by fabulous dragons and flying monsters. During the nine centuries between the victory of the Prophet and the rounding of the Cape of

Good Hope by Bartholomew Diaz and Vasco da Gama, a European could not so much as dip an oar into the Indian Ocean.

For nearly a thousand years after nutmeg, mace, and cloves first appeared in the West, both Europeans and Muslims remained clueless as to their actual source. Writing in the tenth century, the Arab historian Ibn Khurdadhbih listed cloves and nutmeg among the produce of India, an error of only four thousand miles. Marco Polo, Ibn Battuta, and the Chinese (from whom the two travelers likely obtained much of their knowledge of the spice trade) all thought that the flavorings came from Java. Getting warmer: the Spice Islands were in fact about a thousand miles east-northeast of Java.[12]

The two major sea routes, via the Red Sea and the Persian Gulf, from India and the Moluccas to Baghdad and Alexandria, were under the control of the Umayyad and Abbasid caliphates. The Abbasids ruled the Middle East until about AD 910; before that date, the safer Gulf route, Sinbad's Way, was greatly favored, but afterward, the primacy of the Egyptian Fatimids and Mamluks made the Red Sea the main thoroughfare for spices arriving from India and the Moluccas.

A smaller portion of the spice traffic went overland, but the Silk Road, fractured among hundreds of warring tribes and principalities, required political stability over its entire length in order to compete with the Indian Ocean routes. This almost impossible trick was turned just once during the premodern period—by the Mongols during the thirteenth and fourteenth centuries. Even then, the khans, no strangers to maritime trade and power, directed a good deal of their long-distance traffic south through the Persian highlands to their Gulf port at Tabriz, from which China and the Spice Islands could be reached by ship with relative ease.

Needless to say, all three of these routes—via the Red Sea, Persian Gulf, and Silk Road—were well outside the control of the great Italian merchant states, Genoa and Venice. As the chauvinistic inhabitants of Christendom grew ever more fond of Oriental flavorings, they found themselves faced with the uncomfortable fact that wherever there were spices, there were infidels.

Nowhere was the Muslims' commercial advantage over Europe more glaring than in the China trade. Even during the period when they had free passage through the Indian Ocean, the Greeks and Romans never had direct knowledge of the nation that produced silk. Likewise, for the medieval European, China might just as well have been on another planet—this in a period when the Middle Kingdom hosted large Arab and Persian merchant colonies. Nor was the situation for the Europeans much better in the Mediterranean, which was battered by a rising tide of Muslim influence: at its eastern end, Arab armies conquered Jerusalem and the Levant coast within two years of Muhammad's death in 632, then vanquished the Byzantine navy at the Battle of the Masts shortly thereafter.

Notwithstanding the high-water mark of Muslim power in the Mediterranean in the ninth and tenth centuries, Italian ships from Salerno, Amalfi, and Venice were able to make the first substantial challenges to the Muslim dominance of world trade. As the first millennium ended, Europe grew slowly more prosperous and powerful. The Italians, now led by the Venetians and Genoese, exchanged Western goods for spices in Alexandria, Cairo, and Tyre, and supplied the thin edge of the wedge with which the West would prise long-distance commerce from the grip of Muslims in the Levant. Between 1072 and 1091, the Normans overran Palermo, Malta, and then the remainder of Sicily; meanwhile, the Spanish recaptured Toledo. These victories emboldened the Christians and set the stage for an event that reverberates to the present day; in 1095, Pope Urban II convened the Council of Clermont, at which the assembled temporal rulers of Christendom pledged to regain the Holy Land. By 1099, Jerusalem was in the hands of the First Crusade, which completed its sacred mission by slaughtering nearly every Muslim, Jewish, and Armenian man, woman, and child inside the city's gates.

Truth be told, the crusaders had gotten lucky—the Seljuk Turks and Fatimid Egyptians had been fighting over Jerusalem for decades before the arrival of the Christians, and at that moment, both Muslim nations were so weakened by the struggle and by internal dissension that neither could dislodge the infidels.

Much of the Holy Land remained under Christian rule until 1187—nearly a century after the crusaders' conquest of Jerusalem—when Saladin inflicted a disastrous defeat on the forces of Guy de Lusignan at the Battle of Hattin, then captured Jerusalem three months later. In contrast to the slaughter wrought by the crusaders of 1099, Saladin spared the civilian population of the city. Acre soon fell as well, leaving only a rump Christian force huddled in the fortress of Tyre, whose famous ramparts briefly protected the crusaders, just as its ancient walls had temporarily held off the forces of Alexander 1,500 years earlier.

On hearing the news of Jerusalem's fall, Pope Urban III was said to have died of shock. That his successor, Gregory VIII, would call for a Third Crusade was a foregone conclusion; it set sail two years later. The Venetians participated enthusiastically, particularly in the recapture of Acre (near modern Haifa), with its large Venetian quarter. However, despite (or perhaps because of) its most famous participant, Richard Coeur de Lion, the Third Crusade failed to retake the Holy City from Saladin.

The sorry history of the Fourth Crusade illuminated not only the extent to which the Western obsession with retaking the Holy Land benefited Genoa and Venice, but also the bilateral trade in the two key commodities of the era: spices and slaves. At this point, one of the most remarkable players in human history, Enrico Dandolo, took center stage. About eighty years of age and nearly blind when elected Doge of Venice in 1193, he agreed to convey to the Holy Land on the republic's galleys a Frankish force of 4,500 knights and their horses, 9,000 squires, and 20,000 foot soldiers—and all for a payment of just 84,000 silver marks (about $20 million in current value) plus half of the land and booty seized from Saladin.

The leader of the Frankish force, Geffroi de Villehardouin, had no intention of attacking the Holy Land, for he had been told years earlier by the English king, Richard, to concentrate his attack at the weak point of the Muslim Empire in Egypt. Moreover, Villehardouin's men were kept in the dark about their not actually being bound for the Holy Land. Dandolo not only was well aware of the Frankish leader's true intentions, but was at that very moment negotiating a profitable trade deal with the Egyptians, that involved a promise not to invade.

Dandolo had other plans, that included the capture of the Adriatic town of Zadar. The last thing he wanted was to invade Egypt, Venice's wealthiest trading partner. What to do? Simple: he leaked to the crusade's soldiers waiting on the city's wharves their true destination. On hearing that they were not going to the Holy Land, the largely Frankish troops deserted en masse, and on the appointed day, only one-third of the planned force formed up for boarding. Worse, the funding for the Frankish force had also decamped along with its deserting troops. The Venetians, naturally, were not willing to embark their precious galleys without sufficient up-front payment.

By the time the galleys finally cast off their anchors in November 1202, the crusaders had agreed to sack Zadar in lieu of further payment. As soon as this had been accomplished, Dandolo received an offer he could not refuse: in exchange for helping the deposed Byzantine emperor, Isaac Angelus, return to the throne in Constantinople, Isaac's son-in-law King Philip of Swabia would foot the bill for the rest of the expedition to Egypt.

Dandolo did not need to be told that this was his chance to sack the richest city in Christendom, and in the process frustrate the invasion of Egypt. The invasion forthwith sailed toward the Bosphorus. In the words of Villehardouin:

> The Doge of Venice, who was an old man and saw not, stood fully armed, on the prow of his galley and had the banner of Saint Mark before him; and he cried to his people to put him on land, or else that he would do justice upon their bodies with his hands.[13]

After a long and fearsome siege, Constantinople was taken and stripped of its riches. The four huge bronze horses from Constantine's hippodrome were taken to the Basilica of Saint Mark in Venice. (The animals looking out over the Piazza San Marco are copies; the originals are in the basilica's museum.) Beyond the baubles, the Venetians also became the "Masters of a Quarter and a Half-quarter of the Roman Empire," i.e., entitled to three-eighths of Constantinople proper plus a like amount of Byzantine territory. In addition, the peace terms included free passage throughout the empire's former territories, plus the exclusion of Venice's rivals, Genoa and Pisa, from trade with the empire. As Dandolo had hoped, the Fourth Crusade never made it to the Holy Land, thus preserving the Venetians' trade with Egypt. Not bad for a now ninety-year-old blind man.[14]

And what a trade Venice had with Egypt! Those crusaders lucky enough to return from the Holy Land greatly amplified the European demand for the exotic spices of the Orient to suffuse continental homes with the scents of status and wealth. German monks, for example, used to distribute a gingerbread known as *Lebkuchen;* after the crusades, they began to prepare it with pepper—the traditional *Pfefferkuchen*.[15]

The stage was now set for one of history's most momentous deals: the Europeans were mad for spices, the Muslims were desperate for conscripts to fight wars with the Mongols and crusaders, and the Italians now effectively controlled the straits through which the vital human cargo flowed.

The first Arab Empire, that of the Umayyads, had little trouble filling its armies with the original converts to Islam: the proud, fiercely independent, militarily skilled bedouin. As the Muslims' radius of conquest spread over the entire Middle East, Arabia's tiny population could not provide the requisite numbers of these formidable desert dwellers for Islam's ever-expanding armies.

The inhabitants of the more agricultural, and thus "civilized," newly Muslim lands bred farmers, not fighters. This was particularly true in Abbasid Mesopotamia and Fatimid Egypt. These settled subsistence farmers generally made poor soldiers, and it was equally difficult to turn a Cairo merchant or a Baghdad scribe, used to a relatively soft and prosperous existence, into a competent officer.[16]

Like any other scarce commodity, soldiers had to be imported from places where they were hungry, ferocious, and abundant. The historian Daniel Pipes notes that these fighters would of necessity hail from "marginal areas" with no strong tradition of central government. The inhabitants of such places were forced by dire conditions

> to protect themselves by grouping together and reinforcing the bonds of mutual trust. . . . Elaborate codes of honor and vigilant acts developed to ensure order. The total effect was to sharpen each person's wits and military capacity. Raiding for booty and feuding were endemic; for reasons of both defense and attack, every male practiced the martial arts from infancy, was trained as a soldier, and stayed in practice at all times.[17]

Where were Pipes's "marginal areas," from which the Muslim empires drew their soldiers? Primarily in Anatolia and the Caucasus, whose mounted fighters periodically swept south and west to raid and conquer the more "advanced" inhabitants of the Middle East and Europe. The most desirable source of captives was Circassia in the Caucasus, whose male and female slaves were highly prized for their beauty.

Prime among the "martial arts" practiced in Pipes's marginal areas was archery, and its mastery served as well on the battlefield as on the hunting field. Another skill mastered at an early age by the inhabitants of the medieval steppe was the devastating combination of horse and stirrup. Probably invented in China in the fifth century after Christ, the stirrup spread slowly throughout central Asia to the Islamic world. By uniting the horse and rider into a single, powerful mass and allowing the mounted combatant to multiply the force delivered by his lance, sword, or club, this seemingly ordinary device revolutionized warfare.[18]

As early as the mid-ninth century, the Abbasid army consisted primarily of slave soldiers from these areas. In Egypt, the Buyid Empire, which preceded the Fatimids, purchased large numbers of Turks; the Fatimids cast their net even wider, acquiring Turks, Slavs, and Berbers.

This peculiar Islamic institution, the mamluk slave system, flowed naturally from the military, demographic, and political imperatives of the medieval Muslim world and the laws of human nature. During the medieval and ancient periods, slavery was not a racial phenomenon; as a practical matter, the mamluk system was largely a brown-on-white affair. In the words of one historian, "African slave markets were disregarded as far as Mamluk cadres were concerned."[19]

The females went into households and harems; the males were sent off to training camps and into military units where "they were turned from infidels into Muslims, from boys into grown men, from raw recruits into full-fledged soldiers, and from slaves into free men." The age-old techniques of military bonding strengthened their *élan,* and the promise of freedom and riches from their trainers and commanders (themselves manumitted slaves) ensured their loyalty.[20] According to the foremost modern scholar of the system, David Ayalon:

> Those mamluks who were bought and set free by the ruling sultan constituted the chief support of his rule. The Mamluk system of servitude instilled in the mamluk a feeling of profound loyalty toward his master and liberator on the one hand, and for his fellows in servitude on the other. . . . The sultan and his mamluks formed a tightly-knit association, whose members were united by strong bonds of solidarity. There existed between the sultan and his mamluks a sort of double bond: they were in power only so long as he ruled, and he ruled only so long as his power was based on them.[21]

As soldiers, the freed slaves rose through the ranks to positions of high command; soon enough, they began deposing the native sultans. The perquisites and luxuries of power eroded the martial instincts and skills of the most successful mamluks within a generation or two, leaving the way open to a new crop of lean and hungry slave-soldiers, fresh from the hinterlands of Circassia and their Egyptian training camps, to seize power from their soft, indolent masters. The new Mamluk sultan would then purge the top rank of the old sultan's troops, the so-called "Royal Mamluks," and replace them with his own followers, and the cycle began anew. The replacement in power of one group with another could be rapid or gradual; it could be done with the sword or with a pension. At any one time, it was not unusual for several generations of cashiered mamluks to coexist both in civilian life and in the lower hierarchy of the army.[22]

The entire system was corrupted by a sense among the mamluks that the current sultan held power only through their grace. According to Pipes, "These soldiers considered the ruler in their debt and tolerated him only as an arbiter."[23] Before too long, the sultan, pressed by his "old friends," would feel the need for "new friends," unencumbered by the sense of entitlement felt by his current supporters. Where did these "new friends" come from? Naturally enough, from the training camps of the recently arrived slave-soldiers, who were offered freedom and power in return for their support.[24] Toward the end of the Kurdish-led Ayyubid dynasty, a member of the royal court was said to have inquired of a colleague about the peculiar uniforms of the sultan's mamluk guards. The answer, which would come true within less than a generation: "This is the dress of those who will conquer our country and will seize our property and treasures."[25]

The mamluk slave system, as already noted, began at most a century or two after the initial Arab conquests, then built slowly under the Abbasids, Buyids, and Fatimids, who thus had a constant and voracious appetite for fresh slaves. The Venetians, with their commercial instincts and newly won control over the Bosphorus, could supplement Egyptian needs during the first half of the thirteenth century.

Prior to his 1187 conquest of Jerusalem, the Kurd Saladin had already toppled the last Fatimid ruler of Egypt and would establish his own short-lived Ayyubid dynasty. Besides being skilled horsemen, Saladin's Turkish and Caucasian mamluks wielded the bow and arrow to devastating effect, especially during the crusades. At the Battle of Hattin, the predominantly mamluk archers were provided with four hundred loads of arrows, with reserves of additional missiles packed onto seventy camels and placed "in the thick of the fray." Without their mamluk core, Saladin's Kurds would surely not have dislodged the Franks from the Holy Land; even his legendary shock troops, the *Halqa,* consisted mainly of mamluk

Turks.[26] Further, without mamluk troops, Muslims would probably not have conquered the Byzantine Empire, India, or central Asia, and would likely be today a relatively small sect confined to tiny enclaves in the Middle East and northern Africa.[27]

As the thirteenth century dawned, the Ayyubid Egyptian state founded by Saladin was still highly dependent on slave troops, shipped by local merchants overland in caravans south through Anatolia (present-day Asian Turkey) and Mesopotamia. The Egyptians soon found themselves under siege from the Mongols, and around 1243, Anatolia and Mesopotamia, through which the land route from the Transcaucasus to Egypt ran, came under Mongol control, threatening to strangle the Ayyubids' supply of mamluk soldiers.[28]

The Venetians, who had grabbed power in the eastern Mediterranean, Bosphorus, and Black Sea in the wake of the Fourth Crusade, and who had a virtual trade monopoly in these seas and straits, were only too happy to help out. Dandolo's conquest of Constantinople in 1204 allowed Venice to supply slaves to the Ayyubids via the relatively Mongol-proof maritime route. The Venetians had long traded with Egypt, even during the height of crusades, all the while supplying ships, troops, and arms to the various Christian kingdoms of the Holy Land, particularly those, such as Acre, that held large Venetian merchant communities. Saladin famously boasted to his caliph that the Europeans were happily selling him arms to use against other Europeans; soon enough, they would be selling his descendants soldiers as well.[29]

At this critical juncture, in 1250, firmly entrenched Mamluk soldiers murdered the last Ayyubid sultan, Turan-Shah, and established an outright Mamluk dynasty, which was to last for more than 250 years, and whose soldiers would continue to be the mainstay of Egypt's military until the nineteenth century.[30]

The mid-thirteenth century was one of history's great cockpits, featuring not only the birth of the Mamluk dynasty in 1250, but also the disastrous invasion of Egypt by King Louis IX of France in the same year, the destruction of Baghdad by the Mongols in 1258, the defeat of Hulagu's Ilkhanid Mongols by the Mamluk Egyptians at Ain Jalut (probably located near modern Israel) in 1260, and the fall in 1261 of the Latin kingdom of Constantinople, the puppet state established by the Venetians and Franks after the Fourth Crusade. As David Ayalon put it, "In the battle of Ain Jalut, which had been fought out between the people of the same race, the infidels of yesterday had defeated the Muslims of tomorrow."[31] In other words, the Caucasian mamluks were closely related to the Mongols, the former having converted to Islam during their training whereas all the Mongol domains, save that of Kublai, would convert later. This series of events established the Mamluk Egyptians as the preeminent power in the eastern Mediterranean and put paid to Western ambitions in the Levant.

Of all the Italian powers, the Genoese, who had long played second fiddle to the Venetians, were most affected by the defeat of the Mongols and the fall of the Latin kingdom at Constantinople. Initially, the defeat of the Egyptian expedition of Louis IX, which the Genoese had vigorously supported, not only weakened them militarily, but devastated them commercially as well, since they had been Louis's shipbuilders. Then, just as abruptly, the tables turned in their favor; in 1261 their other major ally, the Byzantines, regained control of Constantinople from the Latin puppet state established by Dandolo and the Franks. The briefly resurgent Byzantines then tossed the hated Venetians out of the old imperial city and the vital straits through which they had previously held exclusive trading rights. Now, by virtue of prior treaties between the Genoese and the Byzantines, the monopoly of Black Sea trade passed to Genoa.

The Mamluk Egyptians, badly in need of military slaves via the only way open—the maritime route—pursued friendly relations with the Genoese and Byzantines, and even with the Golden Horde, the Ilkhan's northern Mongol neighbor, who actually controlled the slaves' homelands in the Caucasus and Crimea. A number of formal treaties between the Mamluks and Byzantines specifically granted the right of free passage through the Bosphorus for Egyptian slaving vessels; in addition, the Mamluk Egyptians allowed the Mongols to establish a slaving *funduq* (warehouse) in Alexandria.[32]

Despite the Mamluk Egyptian's open access to the Black Sea, their maritime capacity could not meet the demand for slaves; for that, they would need Genoese ports and bottoms. Genoese ships loaded their slave cargoes at their Crimean port of Kaffa, which had been built at the site of the ancient Pontic grain port of Theodosia, itself purchased from the Golden Horde in the mid-thirteenth century. (The city has since reverted back to the Slavic pronunciation of the original Greek name, Feodosiya, and is now in the Ukraine.) For their part, the Genoese turned a blind eye

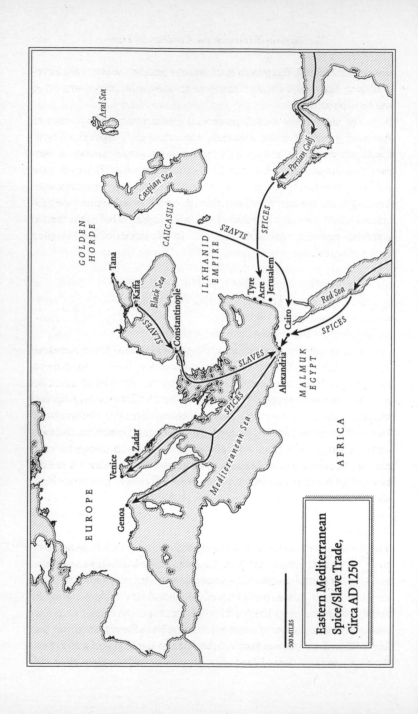

Eastern Mediterranean
Spice/Slave Trade,
Circa AD 1250

500 MILES

toward the Mamluk Egyptian's final assaults against the last crusader re-doubts at Acre and Tyre, and may even have promised naval support to the Muslim attackers.

The slave-laden vessels proceeded on the southbound journey to Alexandria (one of whose entrances was called the Pepper Gate) or to Cairo, where they filled their holds with pepper, ginger, cinnamon, nut-meg, and cloves brought by Arab traders from points east. This trade gave the Genoese a financial and strategic leg up against their Venetian rivals. The end of the crusader outposts in the Levant was clearly hastened by the slave-soldiers conveyed by the Genoese, who seemed to have little trouble choosing between God and Mammon. In the words of the historian Andrew Ehrenkreutz,

> When compared with all the materialistic benefits obtained from the businesslike relations with the Mamluks, the final humiliation of the Cross in the Levant was of small concern to the hard-headed Chris-tians of Genoa.[33]

Just as quickly as the demand for the Bosphorus–Black Sea slave route arose, it collapsed with the dissolution of the Ilkhan Mongol threat and the fall of Acre and Tyre in 1291. Not only was the need for mamluks greatly reduced by these events, but the retreat of the Ilkhans reopened the traditional slave caravan route through Anatolia and Mesopotamia. Despite Genoa's loss of its maritime slave routes, the expertise, commer-cial contacts, and shipbuilding capacity it had accrued during the brief period of conflict among Mamluks, Mongols, and crusaders during the last half of the thirteenth century long outlived the war-driven maritime slave trade.

The Italians were not the only ones to get fabulously rich from the spice trade. After the Genoese and Venetians had unloaded their slaves, glass, and textiles on the wharves of Alexandria and into the *funduq* of Cairo, they bought up all the spices they could find. At the eastern end of the supply chain, Indian and Malay Muslim traders purchased cloves, cinna-mon, nutmeg, and mace at straits entrepôts such as Pase, Palembang, and later Malacca, where these products had been brought by local traders from their sources in the Spice Islands. These precious cargoes then sailed with

Indian merchants across the Bay of Bengal to India on one winter north-east monsoon, then onward to Yemen on the next. There, the Indians were met by the Karimi, a guild of fabulously wealthy merchants who accompanied the ascension of the Mamluks; it would be the Karimi who wheeled and dealed with the Italians in the *funduqs* of Cairo and Alexandria.

Of the two, Cairo was described by European travelers as the more vibrant, with narrow, winding streets filled with traders from Turkey, Arabia, Yemen, Persia, Italy, France, and India and reeking of the aromatic treasures of the Orient. Then, as now, traders took time off from bazaars pulsating with the rhythms of commerce to ride out to gawk at the Pyramids: "All along the way from Cairo were gardens full of date palms, orange, lemon, and pomegranate trees—a delight to the eye."[34]

The origins of the Karimi are lost to history, and their commercial interactions are equally opaque, but they form the essential link in our understanding of the medieval world's greatest source of concentrated wealth. The historical record suggests that sometime around 1150, toward the end of the Fatimid Empire, this group reached a critical mass, possibly by virtue of its ability to purchase the protection of the Fatimid navy in the pirate-infested waters of the Red Sea and Bab el Mandeb. Smaller traders, such as the Jewish merchants of the Geniza papers, could not afford such expensive naval cover and were probably muscled aside by the Karimi. It is not known whether the Karimi were originally Hindu or Muslim, Indian or Egyptian, or even whether they were primarily merchants or shipowners, although according to the preponderance of the data they were the latter. The Indian and Hindu origins of the group are suggested by the fact that the term seems to derive from the Tamil word for business affairs, *karyam*.[35]

Somehow, by the Mamluk period the Karimi had evolved into a predominantly Arab Muslim, but by no means exclusively Egyptian, group known far and wide as "the merchants of pepper and spices," and had obtained command of the trade between Yemen and Egypt. A cooperative group of family enterprises handed from father to son and bound together by the commercial and social strictures of Islam and the special requirements of the spice trade, they established huge *funduqs* all along their long supply lines through the Red Sea. Based primarily at its ends in both Yemen and in Egypt, this chain snaked through many ports and way stations along the familiar ancient route that ran up the Red Sea to its Egyptian coast, across the desert by caravan, and then down the Nile. One thirteenth-century merchant, Muhammad bin Abd al-Rahman bin Ismail, spent his life shuttling among Syria, Mecca, Egypt, Iraq, and the Gulf states—nothing special for the time—but also made three separate journeys to China. He began his career worth five hundred dinars and ended it worth fifty thousand.[36]

Throughout the Muslim world, to "resemble the merchants of the Karimi" carried the same meaning as "rich as Rockefeller" in the early twentieth century. Many Karimi fortunes were estimated in excess of a million dinars, and one merchant—Yasir al-Balisi—was worth about ten million dinars, or nearly a half billion dollars in today's money, an almost unimaginable amount of wealth in the preindustrial world.[37] Karimi money built many a mosque, school, and hospital in Alexandria, Cairo, Mecca, and Jeddah. But by far the largest flows of Karimi money went to the state for military operations. When the Syrians rose against the Mamluks in 1352, and when the murderous Tamerlane threatened the Levant in 1394, three leading Karimi merchants financed Egyptian victories.[38]

Eventually, like all empires, the Mamluks grew greedy, corrupt, and unable to keep their hands out of the till; in 1428 Sultan Barsbay seized the spice monopoly from the Karimi and reduced them to the status of agents. In 1453, the Ottomans finally took Constantinople and shut off all trade with the Christians, but by then the jig was nearly up for the Muslim-Italian spice trade. The Portuguese were by then crawling down Africa's western coast; Bartholomew Diaz would double the southern cape in 1488, and a decade later da Gama would break into the Indian Ocean, ending forever the Muslim monopoly of Asian trade with the West.

The most momentous and lasting legacy of the spice-slave trade exploded out of a lethal gift bestowed by the Mongols on the Genoese at their newly established Black Sea port of Kaffa. Remember that name, for it would resonate with the deaths of millions of Europeans, the collapse of Mongol rule in Asia, the erosion of the Muslim trading empire, and ultimately, the phoenixlike rise of the West.

6

THE DISEASE OF TRADE

Kaffa resembled a medieval version of the American frontier railhead, the last European city before the border with the vast Mongol khanates that spread all the way east to China. Around 1266, the Horde—the Mongol empire of northwestern Asia and eastern Europe—sold the city's site to the Genoese, who valued its location on the Crimean Peninsula at the western terminus of the Silk Road. From Kaffa's wharves, merchants shipped slaves to Egypt and the luxuries of the Orient to Italy, France, and even the Atlantic ports of northern Europe.

The Mongols, observing Kaffa's prosperity under the Italians, suffered from seller's regret. They could not resist ravaging it, and an epic tug-of-war over this newly valuable piece of real estate ensued. The Horde's khan, Toqtai, found his pretext for plunder in the enslavement and exportation of his Turkic brothers and sisters. In 1307 he arrested the Italian residents in his capital at Sarai, some seven hundred miles east of Kaffa; later that same year, the Horde besieged Kaffa itself. The Italians resisted until 1308, when they burned and abandoned the city. After the Mongols had completed their pillage, the Genoese rebuilt it.

Just east of Kaffa, and thus more exposed to the Horde, was the Venetian slave-buying outpost of Tana. When it was bombarded in 1343, the Italians there fled west to Kaffa and presented Kipchak, the local Turkic ally of the Horde, with an even fatter opportunity. Over the next three years, Kipchak intermittently besieged Kaffa with his fearsome catapults. He failed. After the disaster of 1308, the Genoese had strengthened the city's maritime lifeline through the Bosphorus and had reinforced its ramparts with a set of two massive concentric walls.

Unbeknownst to either side, a doomsday weapon had just arrived from the East to inflict defeat on both sides. Initially, it devastated the attackers and provided blessed relief to the Italians huddled in Kaffa. But soon enough, it killed the defenders too, and then sailed silently south on

Genoese galleys to visit ashen ruin, first on Europe and next on the realm
of the Prophet.

The plague bacillus, *Yersinia pestis,* like many human pathogens, spends
most of its time in an "animal reservoir," a population of chronically infected rodents. During the medieval period, the ground squirrels and
marmots of the Himalayan foothills, the Asian steppes, and the Great
Lakes region of Africa served this function for the bacillus. Probably the
most important of these animals was the tarabagan, a burrowing animal
that most resembles an obese squirrel, grows to two feet in length, weighs
up to eighteen pounds, and hibernates in winter.

For millennia, the local inhabitants of the steppe kept their distance
from infected rodents, easily identified by their sluggish behavior. Occasionally, however, this cultural barrier to infection broke down, most often
when outsiders unfamiliar with local custom hunted the diseased animals.
When this occurred, the black death seared the land.[1]

We owe our modern appreciation of the origins and historical effects
of infectious disease to the great historian William H. McNeill of the
University of Chicago. Sometime around 1955, while reviewing the defeat
of the Aztecs by Hernán Cortés in 1521, he puzzled over how a population
of millions, many of them fierce and ruthless fighters, could have been
defeated by a force of only six hundred Spaniards. True, the horses, guns,
and steel swords of the Europeans conferred a great advantage, but McNeill
sensed that something else must have been going on.

In fact, the Aztecs had defeated Cortés the year before at the capital
city of Tenochtitlán and forced the Spanish to retreat—the infamous *noche
triste.* Four months later, a smallpox epidemic swept through the Aztec
nation. When McNeill came across mention of the death from smallpox of
the victorious Aztec commander, the steel trap of his mind snapped shut: in
an instant, he grasped the role of disease in the Spanish conquest of America
and opened up a new dimension in our understanding of world history.

McNeill realized that what had happened both in Tenochtitlán and
in Europe two centuries earlier were identical phenomena—the catastrophic introduction of a new disease into a population lacking immunity to it. He elucidated the mechanics of these collisions of civilizations,
in which trade often provided the primary motive force.

As is all too clear today, commerce and travel (as well as the increased population densities of the modern world) can spread pathogens, both novel and well-established, among continents with frightening speed. In many ways, the situation in the ancient and premodern world was even more dangerous. Back then, the world was an epidemiologic tinderbox consisting of several completely separate geographic "disease pools." The populations within each pool were reasonably resistant to its organisms, but not to those from other pools; an organism that had been benignly endemic in one nation for millennia could visit apocalypse several hundred miles away. As world commerce blossomed between the fourteenth and eighteenth centuries, the world's existing disease pools mixed together, with disastrous results. The good news is that today, relatively little further mixing of existing organisms can occur; pandemics result only when an organism from a nonhuman host, such as the HIV virus, mutates and acquires the ability to infect humans. This is a much higher bar than in the pre-Columbian era, when a merchant, sailor, or rodent from a neighboring disease pool could touch off a deadly epidemic.

McNeill seized on an episode, which began in 1859, when British settlers introduced rabbits into Australia, desiring to alleviate their homesickness for the English countryside and to have a familiar animal to hunt and eat. These adorable animals, unfortunately, found no predators in their new home. They multiplied, as rabbits are wont to do, stripped the continent of its scant and fragile pasturage, and threatened the nascent sheep industry. Fences, poisons, traps, and rifles proved of little use in keeping down the population of a creature that can reproduce just six months after it is born. The situation cried out for a more imaginative remedy.

In 1950, the Australians introduced the myxoma virus, uniquely lethal to rabbits, into their wild population, which had no prior exposure, and therefore limited resistance, to it. The situation was thus analogous to the Mexican and European experience with smallpox and plague. The ensuing years saw a rabbit holocaust which reduced their numbers by 80 percent; the death rate among infected rabbits was 99.8 percent.

Just at the point when the rabbit was about to disappear from Australia, natural selection kicked in, favoring those strains of rabbits most resistant to the disease. Further, this process worked equally well from the perspective of the virus. It did the myxoma organism no good to kill its host so rapidly; over time, it became less deadly, so that it lived longer and multiplied more effectively. By 1957, only one-fourth of infected rabbits succumbed. The one-sided relationship between a highly fatal disease and a completely defenseless host had changed into a standoff between a less virulent pathogen and a more resistant population.

The same process occurs when humans are exposed to new infections. At first, mortality is high, but natural selection results in both a more resistant population and a less lethal pathogen. This process of "disease equilibration," in which pathogen and host adapt to each other, seems to take about five or six generations—several years in the case of rabbits, and about 100 to 150 years in people. In the human population, such diseases as measles and chicken pox, which were once killers of adults, now affect mainly those who have not yet built up immunity to them, i.e., children. It is also no coincidence that these diseases arose originally from domesticated animals living in intimate proximity to humans: smallpox from cowpox, influenza from hogs, and measles from canine distemper or rinderpest.[2]

Plague presents a somewhat more complex case. While the disease has certainly not reached a similar equilibrium in humans—it is nearly as deadly now as it was when it tore through the Old World in the fourteenth century—this matters little to the organism, for whom human infection constitutes a mere sideshow. From the perspective of the plague bacillus, the only hosts that matter are ground rodents such as the tarabagan, millions of which are to this day infected all around the globe. The disease proves rapidly fatal to the creatures as well, but the degree of isolation among these burrowing animals is high enough to slow down colony-to-colony transmission. Only among gerbils in the southwest Asian deserts is plague infection believed to be indolent enough to allow chronic, low-grade infection of individual animals.[3] Scientists do not know for sure where the original reservoir population of infected underground rodents first arose; the best guess is somewhere in the Himalayan region of south China.

If humans, marmots, and ground squirrels were the only hosts of plague, then people would be protected from it by distance; however, two other animals are involved in this deadly disease chain. The first is the flea, whose bite transmits the bacillus from mammal to mammal. Fleas are unable to travel the miles between people and remote underground rodent populations; the second animal, the black rat, provides the essential "bridge" between ground rodent and civilization and allows the ground-animal reservoir to lap on human shores. The bacillus is just as lethal to the flea and the rat as it is to people. All that remains is for the rat to die; the infected fleas then abandon the dead rodent, and, just before they too succumb, span the final few feet to an unlucky human.

A particular species of flea, *Xenopsylla cheopsis,* became the crucial link in the chain of death. This unattractive insect has two characteristics that make it particularly well adapted to this role. First, the black rat is its host of choice. Whereas tarabagans seldom come into close contact with humans, the black rat is a so-called "commensal" animal. This term refers to the black rat's adaptation to close proximity to human habitation by feeding off garbage and discarded food scraps. The black rat also cohabits with tarabagans. This allows *Xenopsylla*, and the plague bacillus along with it, to hop from tarabagan to black rat. *Xenopsylla* leaves the rat only under duress, when the rat dies, freeing the flea to transmit the bacillus one final, spectacular step, to humans. *Xenopsylla*'s second deadly characteristic is that, uniquely among fleas, its digestive system is highly sensitive to the bacillus, which creates intestinal blockage and regurgitation of large amounts of infected material into the rodents and humans it bites.[4]

On the death of the rat, *Xenopsylla* can also find refuge in horses and camels, which become veritable flea hotels.[5] Both beasts of burden, as well as a large number of other mammal and bird species, are highly susceptible to the disease.

As far as the plague bacillus is concerned, *Xenopsylla,* the black rat, and man are two-bit players, unfortunate innocent bystanders. The organism's primary mission is to maintain itself in its reservoir population of ground rodents. Worse, successful settled agriculture results in dense, specialized cities, which in turn attract the commensal black rat, specifically adapted to the urban environment.

The black rat fills its deadly role brilliantly; it not only prefers close company to humans, but is also a world-class climber. Around the time when the Romans and the Han Chinese were in the ascendant, the species began to range far and wide along the Silk Road and the maritime monsoon routes. At some point early in the Common Era, the black rat gained passage to Europe via the mooring ropes of the dhows and Greek vessels plying the monsoon routes.

The term "plague" itself causes much confusion. Almost certainly, none of the outbreaks recorded in ancient sources were the work of *Yersinia pestis*. Sumerian sources mention epidemics as far back as 2000 BC, and the first books of the Old Testament, written between 1000 and 500 BC, described divine retribution in the form of outbreaks among the populations of the Fertile Crescent. Modern translators fell on the word "plague" to describe these episodes, but the Bible and other ancient sources rarely gave enough clinical detail to identify the responsible bacteria or viruses.

On only a few occasions did ancient observers provide enough such detail to identify the source of a specific outbreak. The very first passage in Hippocrates's *Of the Epidemics,* written around 400 BC, clearly details an outbreak of mumps (painless swelling about the ears, hoarseness, cough) on the island of Thasos. Nowhere in his works is found a description suggestive of *Yersinia pestis* infection.[6] The great historian of the Peloponnesian War, Thucydides, described perhaps the most famous epidemic of ancient history, the Athenian plague of 430 BC, which killed about one-fourth of the empire's army; its causative organism cannot be identified from the text with any accuracy.[7]

Outbreaks of infectious diseases regularly savaged Rome—both the republic and the empire, most famously in about AD 166, when Marcus Aurelius's legions brought back a pathogen from Mesopotamia. Contemporaneous accounts tell of the deaths of up to one-third of the inhabitants of the capital and the destruction of entire armies. Another outbreak struck Rome in the mid-third century and killed as many as five thousand people per day.[8] Once again, precise descriptions of these Roman pestilences are lacking; the best evidence suggests that these were the first European invasions of smallpox and measles from their origins in the stockyards and dwellings of the Fertile Crescent.

The clinical features of the plague caused by *Yersenia*—swelling in the groin and armpit, high fever, a black hemorrhagic rash, and rapid demise—are distinctive enough that had it occurred in the ancient world before AD 500, we should have record of it. This is even more true of the pneumonic form of the disease, in which airborne person-to-person transmission of the bacillus from coughing can by nightfall devastate entire urban quarters that at sunrise had appeared unaffected.[9]

* * *

Around the beginning of the Common Era, infected fleas or rodents somehow made the journey from the disease's probable ancient reservoir in the Himalayan foothills to India's Malabar Coast, where infected black rats scampered over mooring ropes onto westbound trading ships. The winter monsoon blew these vessels across the Indian Ocean to Alexandria (or alternatively, to intermediate ports such as the island of Socotra or Aden) quickly enough for the rats to survive and reestablish the disease on disembarkation. In AD 541, during the reign of the Byzantine emperor Justinian, the first convincing descriptions emerge of *Yersinia pestis* infection—the Black Death (so called because of the widespread hemorrhagic rash) emerged. The historian Procopius recorded that the "plague of Justinian" first appeared (at least to Western observers) in Egypt, just as would be expected from the maritime supply lines of the Eastern Empire, which ran through the ancient Red Sea route (the easier "Sinbad's Way" through the Gulf being blocked by Byzantium's archrival, the Persian Empire).[10]

Procopius observed the outbreak firsthand: "About the same time [the winter of 541–542] there was a Plague, which almost consumed mankind."[11] Procopius clearly described the buboes—painful, inflamed swellings of the lymph glands, "not only in the groin (called the Bubo), but in the armpits, under the ear, and in other parts," that are the disease's signature.[12] The lack of person-to-person transmission perplexed him:

> No physician, nor other, caught the disease by touching the sick or dead bodies, many strangely continuing free [of the disease] though they buried [the dead], and many catching it, they knew not how, and dying instantly.[13]

This first epidemic was transmitted from human to human by fleas, a path that proved less rapidly fatal than the person-to-person pneumonic route that affected Europe in the fourteenth century. Wave after wave of pestilence swept through the Eastern Empire at intervals of five to ten years following the initial outbreak and thus affected the young, who had not yet acquired immunity, disproportionately. About one-fourth of Constantinople's population died in AD 541–542—Procopius recorded peak death rates in the city of about ten thousand per day—and by the year 700 its population had fallen by half. Before the epidemic, Justinian seemed poised to reunify the empire; it is not too much of a stretch to conclude that *Yersinia*

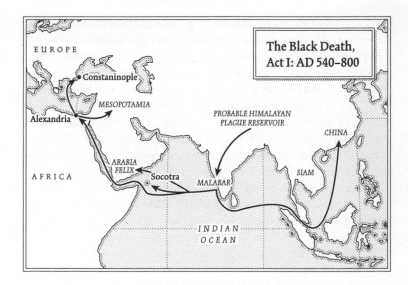

The Black Death, Act I: AD 540–800

EUROPE
Constaninople
MESOPOTAMIA
Alexandria
PROBABLE HIMALAYAN PLAGUE RESERVOIR
CHINA
ARABIA FELIX
Socotra
MALABAR
SIAM
AFRICA
INDIAN OCEAN

pestis was primarily responsible for dashing those hopes. The epidemic helped plunge Europe into the Dark Ages and provided a geopolitical vacuum into which the early adherents of Islam, protected from the disease by the desert climate (which is unfriendly to the black rat) and by a lack of large cities, could expand. The plague also aided the Muslims farther east; Procopius recorded its devastation in Persia, suggesting that succeeding waves of the pestilence may have abetted the historic Muslim triumph over that empire at Ctesiphon (in modern-day Iraq) in AD 636.[14]

By the time the plague finally burned itself out in the Eastern Empire, its trade with the Orient had reached low ebb. In AD 622, the same year as the last wave of plague at Constantinople, the Quraish expelled Muhammad and his followers from Mecca and precipitated their hegira to Medina. Within eight years, the Prophet's armies would control all of Arabia and close Bab el Mandeb to Western shipping for more than a millennium; over the next several generations, they would deny Westerners the Silk Road as well. The armies of Islam deprived Europe of the relatively open access to Asia it had enjoyed since nearly the beginning of the Common Era. The silver lining of this stinging defeat was that this isolation would protect Europeans from Asia's reservoirs of plague for the next seven centuries.

The hot, dry, and largely uninhabited Arabian Peninsula offered some protection against the disease, but the next venue of Muslim conquest, the densely populated Fertile Crescent, proved an ideal breeding ground for it. By AD 639, the plague raged through Syria, devastated the civilian population, and killed as many as twenty-five thousand Muslim soldiers. Caliph Omar, the Prophet's second successor, attempted to recall his great military commander Abu Ubaydah from Syria in an effort to save his life. Although the caliph concealed his purpose by telling his general that he was needed for urgent consultation, Abu Ubaydah saw through the ruse and, unwilling to thwart the will of Allah, remained in Syria. He soon succumbed to the disease, as did numerous succeeding Arab commanders.[15]

The plague may even be responsible for the schism in Islam. After Abu Ubaydah's death, another general, Muawiyah ibn Abi Sufyan, overthrew Caliph Ali (the fourth successor of the Prophet, and also his cousin and son-in-law), cleaving Muslims forever into Sunni and Shiite camps. Had Omar been successful in saving the capable Abu Ubaydah from the plague, it is possible that Islam would not have suffered this tragic split.

However much the "plague of Justinian" afflicted the newly triumphant warriors of Islam, it caused far greater damage to their Byzantine and Persian enemies. According to the historian Josiah Russell, "Neither Charlemagne, nor Harun, nor the great Isaurian and Macedonian dynasties could break the pattern set up by the flea, the rat, and the bacillus."[16] To the sword of Ali and the wealth of Khadijah must be added the Black Death, which killed the young religion's enemies—the Byzantines and Persians—with far greater regularity than it killed Arabs.

Within a few generations of the plague of Justinian, the bacillus had also spread eastward from India to China's seaports. Convincing Chinese descriptions of the disease appear by the early seventh century, and although confirmatory demographic data are few and far between, it seems likely that the plague devastated the Tang at least as much as it did Byzantium. One observer reported that in AD 762 half of the province of Shantung succumbed; between AD 2 and 742, the Chinese population appears to have decreased by about one-fourth.[17]

Then, nothing. The last wave of the plague engulfed Constantinople in AD 622 and the periphery of the empire in 767. After those dates, no further convincing descriptions of the Black Death in Christendom are found until the deadly invasion of the fourteenth century.

Why, then, did the plague not reach Europe until the middle of the first millennium, having been endemic among Asian ground rodents for thousands of years? Why did the next epidemic not occur for another eight hundred years? And why, finally, was the plague of Justinian confined largely to the Eastern Empire in Europe, whereas the later medieval epidemic engulfed all of the Continent?

First and foremost, plague is a disease of trade. Infected humans live no more than several days, infected rats no more than several weeks, and infected fleas no more than several months. In order to transport the bacillus to the next caravanserai or port, the human, rodent, and insect hosts must pass quickly across the seas and steppes.

While the plague of Justinian did strike scattered cities in northern Europe, it did not ravage the whole Continent for two reasons. First, in Europe the disease was conveyed primarily over Mediterranean routes, and the way west and north was blocked by the Goths, Vandals, and Huns. Second, by the sixth and seventh centuries, the essential intermediate host, the black rat, had not yet expanded much beyond the Mediterranean littoral, and certainly not yet to the continent's Atlantic ports.[18] The saving grace of the plague of Justinian was that the organism did not gain a foothold in Europe's population of ground rodents. In the fourteenth century, the Continent would not be so lucky. The centuries-long exclusion of European traders from Asia—the "Muslim quarantine"— ended with the Mongol conquests of the thirteenth century; the reopening of overland trade by the heirs of Genghis Kahn would in time loose the plague's fury on a Europe now much more vulnerable to the disease.

During the sixth century, the scourge emerged from the seas; in the fourteenth, it came overland. Political unification under the khans reopened the Silk Road, and along with the precious goods of China came the rats and fleas that infected the besiegers at Kaffa. Our understanding of exactly how the Mongols and their allies became infected is incomplete. McNeill believes that the steppe warriors acquired the disease in its ancient home among the ground rodents of the southern Chinese and Burmese Himalayan foothills when they invaded that region from the north in 1252.

In 1331, the first reports appeared of the plague's return to China. Almost immediately, the disease began barreling down the Silk Road, now running smoothly under Mongol rule. The infected fleas hitched rides westward, here in the manes of warhorses, there in the hair of camels, and elsewhere on black rats nestled in cargoes and in saddlebags. Just as the long-distance goods trade was indirect, with silks and spices changing hands along the way, so too did the bacillus pause many times before continuing the next leg of the journey.

McNeill believed that the caravanserais provided the essential link in the transmission of the disease and furnished sustenance not only to the camel and the trader, but also to the bacillus. At each caravanserai along the way, the plague devastated the workers, owners, and guests, and sped the progress of the outbreak by scattering the survivors in all directions and establishing the disease in the local ground rodent population. In 1338, seven years after the Chinese outbreak of 1331, an epidemic may have torn through a trading post near Lake Issyk-Kul (in what is today Kyrgyzstan), about halfway along the Silk Road. By 1345 the disease enveloped Astrakhan on the northern Caspian coast, and shortly thereafter, Kaffa.[19, 20]

In 1346, the bacillus reached Kipchak's troops at Kaffa, and they seemed to suffer a particularly malignant form of divine wrath. According to the chronicler of the plague Gabriele de' Mussi, "The Tartars died as soon as the signs of the disease appeared on their bodies: swellings in the armpit or groin caused by coagulating humors, followed by a putrid fever."[21]

The ferocity of the epidemic among Kaffa's attackers quickly forced them to abandon their siege, but before they did, they unleashed history's most devastating bioterrorism attack. Again, de' Mussi:

> The dying Tartars, stunned and stupefied by the immensity of the disaster brought about by the disease, and realizing that they had no hope of escape, lost interest in the siege. But they ordered corpses to be placed in catapults and lobbed into the city in the hope that the intolerable stench would kill everyone inside. What seemed like mountains of dead were thrown into the city. . . . the stench was so overwhelming that hardly one in several thousand was in a position to flee the remains of the Tartar army.[22]

The attack may have been an act of inspired desperation, or, as the world's most expert catapult engineers, the "Tartars" (Mongols and their allies) may simply have found their machines the most efficient mecha-

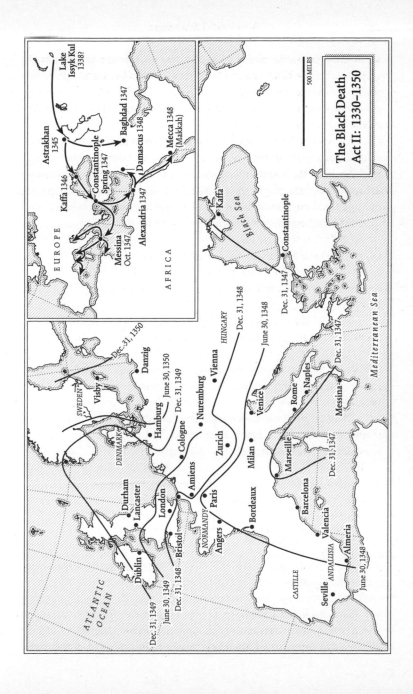

The Black Death, Act II: 1330–1350

500 MILES

Lake Issyk Kul 1338?
Astrakhan 1345
Baghdad 1347
Damascus 1348
Mecca 1348 (Makkah)
Kaffa 1346
Constantinople Spring 1347
Alexandria 1347
Messina Oct. 1347
EUROPE
AFRICA

Kaffa
Black Sea
Constantinople Dec. 31, 1347
Dec. 31, 1347
Mediterranean Sea

Dec. 31, 1350
Danzig
Visby
June 30, 1350
SWEDEN
Hamburg
Cologne Dec. 31, 1349
Nuremburg
Zurich
Vienna
HUNGARY
Dec. 31, 1348
June 30, 1348
Venice
Milan
Rome
Naples
Messina Dec. 31, 1347
Dec. 31, 1347
DENMARK
Durham
Lancaster
London
Bristol
Amiens
Paris
NORMANDY
Angers
Bordeaux
Marseille
Barcelona
Valencia
Almeria
June 30, 1348
Dublin
Dec. 31, 1349
June 30, 1349
Dec. 31, 1348
CASTILLE
ANDALUSIA
Seville
ATLANTIC OCEAN

nism available for removing corpses. By the thousands, Kaffa's defenders soon suffered the same fate, and within a few months, the Black Death tore through Europe and the Middle East.

After its arrival in Kaffa, there can be little doubt that its further spread was trade-borne. Among the few who survived the disaster at Kaffa were sailors who made their way back to their Italian home ports. Once again, it would be the much smaller stowaways on these vessels—black rats—that scampered down the ships' ropes and transported the plague bacillus to the wharves of Europe and touched off the medieval era's great apocalypse.[23] One Franciscan monk, Michele da Piazza, recorded the moment of the Black Death's arrival in Italy:

> In October 1347, about the beginning of the month, twelve Genoese galleys, fleeing from the divine vengeance which Our Lord sent upon them for their sins, put into the port of Messina. The Genoese carried such a disease in their bodies that if anyone so much as spoke with one of them, he was infected with the deadly illness and could not avoid death . . . and with them died . . . also anyone who had acquired or touched or laid hands on their belongings.[24]

The moment a plague ship docked, it was forced onward. As soon as a city became infected, the survivors fled, and the disease spread yet farther. Recorded da Piazza, "The Messinese were so loathed and feared that no man would speak with them, or be in their company, but hastily fled at the sight of them, holding his breath."[25]

Europe proved far more hospitable to the bacillus in 1347 than during the plague of Justinian. In the interim, the Mediterranean maritime trading network had grown swift, reliable, and voluminous; relays of infected rats could be shuttled from port to port more quickly, more regularly, and in far greater numbers than eight centuries earlier.

A half century before the outbreak, in 1291, a Spanish flotilla, led by the Genoese commander Benedetto Zaccaria, overcame a Moorish force near Gibraltar and opened the strait to western shipping for the first time since the Muslim conquest of Spain.[26] This allowed "plague ships" to sail directly out the newly opened passage into the Atlantic and deliver doom to northern Europe.

Whereas in the sixth and seventh centuries the black rat did not thrive much beyond the eastern Mediterranean, in 1346 it greeted its infected brethren wherever they disembarked and then transmitted the disease to the European ground rodent reservoir. This new ubiquity of the black rat set off a chain of recurrent outbreaks that was to last for centuries following the first onslaught. In addition, newly established pack animal routes served to spread the disease overland, probably via merchants in the early stages of pneumonic infection, at a rate of one to five miles per day across the continent.[27]

Between 1347 and 1350, the disease swept slowly and inexorably north from Italy; as can be seen on the map on page 141, its course followed both maritime and land routes, traveling, as did ordinary trade goods, more rapidly by sea than by land. Some small communities were entirely wiped out, while many larger cities escaped almost unscratched; according to the best estimates, approximately one of every three or four Europeans perished during those years. Although the initial onslaught burned itself out by 1350, repeated outbreaks occurred in the following decades, and then at more widely spaced intervals, as also happened after the plague of Justinian. Venice lost one-third of its inhabitants in the outbreak of 1575–1577, and again in 1630–1631.[28]

Nothing before or since terrorized Europe as did the first wave of the disease. That it was borne on ships was obvious; lord and commoner alike imagined the seas and ports teeming with merchant fleets bearing cargoes of death, and even in inland cities such as Avignon, newly arrived consignments of spices went untouched for fear that they harbored the disease. Just as the plague's flea-borne transmission (which would not be elucidated until modern times) perplexed Procopius, so would ignorance of this mechanism appall Europeans. De' Mussi recorded in amazement the story of four Genoese soldiers who temporarily left their unit in order to plunder. They then

> made their way to Rivarolo on the coast, where the disease had killed all the inhabitants. . . . They broke into one of the houses and stole a fleece which they found on the bed. They then rejoined the army and on the following night the four of them bedded down under the fleece. When morning comes it finds them dead. As a result, everyone panicked, and thereafter nobody would use the goods and clothes of the dead.[29]

Which was probably a good idea, since the purloined clothes were almost certainly crawling with infected fleas. After the initial landfall of the bacillus in Italy, messengers arrived in cities yet untouched and told petrified townspeople of a tide of death moving slowly their way. So high was the first wave's death rate that many thought it heralded the end of the world. The simple knowledge that some did survive the outbreak of 1346–1350 eventually lessened the terror of subsequent plagues, many of which were otherwise at least as awful as the first.[30]

During the medieval era, ignorance about the mechanism of the plague condemned tens of millions of Europeans, Africans, and Asians to death from a largely preventable infection. The lack of scientific knowledge also fanned the flames of anti-Semitism and consigned Jews to man-made fates arguably worse than the disease itself. Theories abounded as to the source of the pestilence. Punishment for corporeal or theological sins was a perennial explanation, as were the evil eye and the "miasma" (poisoned, if colorless, air). But by far the most pernicious theory held that Hebrews were poisoning wells. This delusion ignited panic among Christians. As a result, thousands of Jews falsely confessed to this imaginary crime under torture and then were burned at the stake or broken on the wheel. Typical of the deadly hysteria is the account left by a prominent German priest, Heinrich Truchess:

> On 4 January [1349] the citizens of Constance shut up the Jews in two of their own houses, and then burned 330 of them. . . . Some processed to the flames dancing, others singing, and the rest weeping. They were burnt shut up in a house which had been specially built for the purpose. On 12 January in Buchen and on 17 January in Basel they were all burnt apart from their babies, who were baptized.

Truchess goes on in the same vein for several paragraphs, recounting almost identical atrocities in cities great and small, finally concluding, "And thus, within one year . . . all the Jews between Cologne and Austria were burnt—and in Austria they await the same fate, for they are accursed of God."[31]

As with the Australian rabbit population in the years following the introduction of the myxoma virus in 1950, multiple rounds of the Black Death relentlessly drove down the populations of the nations of Europe to a nadir in the requisite five generations—about 125 to 150 years—

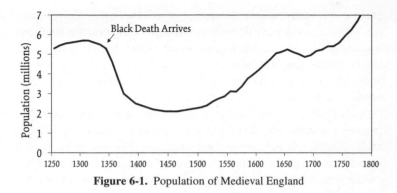

Figure 6-1. Population of Medieval England

before a modicum of immunity allowed the reproductive rate to gain the upper hand over this grimmest of reapers. In Britain, for which we have the most accurate demographic data of the period, the population decreased by well over half—from about 5.5 million on the eve of the plague in 1335 to 2.1 million in 1455. Figure 6-1 plots the fall and recovery of the English population; note that it did not return to its pre-plague level until four centuries after the initial outbreak.

The last outbreak in western Europe hit Marseilles in 1720, Russia and the Ottoman Empire were affected well into the nineteenth century, and early in the twentieth century a devastating outbreak killed thousands in China. Europe's population just before the outbreak of the Black Death was approximately fifty million. Thus, about twelve to fifteen million died in the initial onslaught, and probably far more over the next century, as wave after wave of pestilence overwhelmed the birthrate.

Even this greatest European apocalypse is only a small part of the story. If the cultural and demographic records of the Black Death are imperfect for Europe, those for the Middle East and Far East are essentially nonexistent; there is no Arab, Indian, or Chinese *Decameron*. However, medical practice in the medieval Muslim world far surpassed that in Europe, and the many precise clinical descriptions by Arab and Indian physicians leave little doubt that a massive outbreak of *Yersinia pestis* in the East

followed hard on the heels of the Black Death in Europe.[32] In the mid-
fourteenth century, perhaps five times as many people lived in the Orient
as in Europe, suggesting that the plague may have taken as many as one
hundred million souls in the East.

The disease spread most rapidly in the fur of horses and the holds
of ships, and it is reasonable to assume that the great overland and maritime hubs of the steppe and Indian Ocean would have been disproportionately affected, as occurred on the Continent. We know, for example,
that in Europe the plague particularly savaged port cities such as Bruges
and Genoa. Venice lost about 60 percent of its population after the first
wave of the plague washed over it in 1348. Major port improvements that
had been under way almost continuously before the plague came virtually to a halt for more than a century.[33]

Some idea of what must have happened in Oriental ports can be
surmised from the well-recorded events on Cyprus. This island, a
predominantly Christian focal point of Mediterranean trade, also had a
substantial Muslim minority. The disease struck there in 1348 and devastated the island's animal population before infecting humans. So many
Christians died or fled Cyprus that those left alive, fearing that Muslims would seize the opportunity to grab power, gathered up all Muslim prisoners and slaves and slaughtered them in the span of a few hours.
Within a week, three of four Cypriot princes died; the fourth fled, and
within a day of embarkation, he too perished, along with almost all his
shipmates.

Another merchant galley, that had probably started out with a comple-
ment of hundreds, arrived at Rhodes from parts unknown with just thirteen
merchants, then sailed on to Cyprus; when it arrived there, only four remained alive. Finding the island deserted, the four proceeded on to Tripoli (in modern Libya), where they related the fantastic narrative to their
amazed hosts.[34] European observers, overwhelmed as they were by the
catastrophe unfolding around them, did not realize that a simultaneous
tragedy was also devouring the East. One exception was Gabriele de'
Mussi:

> The scale of the mortality and the form which it took persuaded those
> who lived, weeping and lamenting, through the bitter events of 1346
> to 1348—the Chinese, Indians, Persians, Medes, Kurds, Armenians,
> Cilicians, Georgians, Mesopotamians, Nubians, Ethiopians, Turks,

Egyptians, Arabs, Saracens and Greeks (for almost all the East has been affected)—that the last judgment had come.[35]

De' Mussi estimated that during three months in 1348, over 480,000 inhabitants of Baghdad succumbed—this at a time when Europe's biggest city, Paris, had a population of just 185,000. In this case, he probably exaggerated. He also recorded that in China, "serpents and toads fell in a thick rain, entered dwellings and devoured numberless people."[36] Egypt too saw the wholesale destruction from plague of merchant galleys of the sort seen at Cyprus. One ship, presumably arriving from an affected Black Sea port with a cargo of hundreds of mamluks, docked in Alexandria with the following survivors: forty crew, four merchants, and exactly one slave-soldier. All died shortly after disembarkation.[37]

The disease sailed west into the Muslim ports of North Africa as well, reaching Morocco and Umayyad Spain. It killed, among many others, the mother of Ibn Battuta in 1349. Tunis was particularly hard hit. Muslim doctors were impressed that the tent-dwelling bedouin were rarely affected and, alone among the world's medical scholars, drew the appropriate conclusion: that the disease was due to some sort of contagion, not divine wrath, miasma, the evil eye, or poisoning by unbelievers.[38]

The medieval Arab civilizations had by then developed a strong historical (if nonquantitative) tradition, particularly in Mamluk Egypt. There, we find the richest sources of information about the effects of the pestilence in the nonwestern world. The plague arrived at Alexandria almost simultaneously with its first appearance on the Italian coast; Egypt seems to have suffered disproportionately from the virulent pneumonic form of the disease, which slowly churned south up the Nile Valley over the next eighteen months. At that time, wealthy Egyptians eagerly sought out Russian furs as fashion items. These proved to be not only frivolous luxuries in a hot climate, but also an ideal conveyance for fleas.[39]

The hajj traffic swept the pestilence south from Egypt to its next logical destination: Mecca's port city of Jeddah, and thence to Mecca itself. The carnage there threw Muslim theologians into turmoil, since the Prophet was believed to have promised the city protection from the plague; the fact that Medina was spared led many to believe that the outbreak was retribution by Allah for the presence of infidels in Mecca.

Although the initial death toll seems to have been about the same as that in Europe, the effects of the plague on the Mamluk Egyptian regime were even more severe and longer lasting than they were in the West. After the initial descent of the plague on Egypt in 1348, the native population eventually acquired a degree of immunity to it. Between 1441 and 1541, no fewer than fourteen epidemics occurred—approximately one every seven years. During this period, three groups would have lacked immunity: small children, adolescents, and newly purchased Caucasian slave soldiers—the latter being the most precious of the regime's resources. Packed together in Egyptian training facilities, the new mamluks suffered horrific mortality rates. Contemporary observers recorded that "the number of dead among the mamluks was too great to be counted" and that "the barracks in the citadel were emptied of the Royal Mamluks (those of the current sultan) because of their deaths."[40] Considering that these elite troops rarely numbered more than a few thousand, the losses must have been staggering:

> Death was terrible among the mamluks inhabiting the barracks; there
> died in this epidemic about 1,000. And there died of the castrated ser-
> vants 160 eunuchs; of the slave-girls of the sultan's household more
> than 160, besides 17 concubines and 17 male and female children.[41]

The plague thus hit hardest those just purchased by the current sultan and tended to spare the older, and therefore more likely immune, manumitted troops of the previous sultans—a surefire prescription for governmental instability.

Aside from the plague's destruction of its military power, Egypt lost much of its human and financial capital. The wealthy Karimi merchants, who spent their working lives in vast warehouses and bazaars teeming with rats and camels, were especially hard hit, becoming easy pickings for Sultan Barsbay in 1428.

The bacillus devastated not only fleas, rodents, and humans but other animals as well. In both Europe and the Middle East, the ground was strewn with the bodies of birds, farm animals, and even wild predators, many with the characteristic buboes at the base of their limbs. Cattle and camels died in large numbers, compounding the economic damage. At Bilbais, a major caravanserai between Cairo and Palestine, most of the sultan's dromedaries perished along with almost all the town's human inhabitants.

The European farmer lucky enough to survive the Black Death could at least escape to the forest and begin again. The same option was not open to his Egyptian counterpart, who was hemmed in by a fierce, endless desert that began only a few miles from the Nile's shores. Contemporary Egyptian accounts frequently mention completely depopulated towns. Egypt never recovered even a shadow of its former wealth, power, and influence. Its population, probably around eight million on the eve of the outbreak, was estimated by Napoleon's invading generals to be just three million in 1798. One recent authoritative account pegs Egypt's population in the early modern era at about the same level as at the birth of Christ.[42]

Economic statistics confirm the extent of the damage; before the Black Death, the government took in about 9.5 million dinars in taxes; by the time of the Ottoman conquest in 1517, revenues had fallen to 1.8 million dinars. In 1394, almost a half century after the first epidemic, about thirteen thousand weavers still worked in Alexandria. A half-century later, there were eight hundred.[43]

The primary human vectors of the disease, the Mongols, never recovered. In 1368, the Ming Chinese rebelled against their now plague-ridden overlords from the steppes and threw off their yoke. Mongol attacks grew less vigorous following the death of Tamerlane in 1405; after that date, the depredations of the fierce mounted warriors on their civilized agricultural neighbors to the south gradually tapered off. With the disappearance of the khanates, the steppe returned to its age-old Hobbesian state, and the access to China enjoyed by the Polos, Ibn Battuta, and generations of Genoese merchants disappeared. This drove spice-hungry Europeans to seek alternative routes to the East.

Mongol and Ming census data suggest that between 1330 and 1420, the population of China decreased from about 72 million to 51 million. Until the modern era, even in time of war, the microbe has usually proved a deadlier weapon than the sword against both soldier and civilian, and it seems most reasonable to blame the plague for the decline in population in China between these two dates. The decreased tax revenues from the shrunken Chinese population contributed in no small part to the withdrawal of the Middle Kingdom's navy from the Indian Ocean after the eunuch admiral Zheng He's last voyage in 1433.

The nearly total destruction of Egypt's trading and industrial structure, the disappearance of the Mongols from the world stage, and the withdrawal of China from the Indian Ocean created a vacuum that Europe—the last man standing, if just barely—filled only too happily. *Yersinia pestis*, which had helped smooth the way for the rise of Muslim power by attacking the Byzantine and Persian empires in the sixth and seventh centuries, greased the skids of Islamic decline in the fourteenth and fifteenth centuries.

Before the Common Era, trade was neither rapid enough nor direct enough to allow the widely separated "disease pools" of Asia, Europe, and Africa to interact; plague was isolated by time and distance to its probable birthplace in the Himalayan foothills, as were smallpox and measles to their origins in the Fertile Crescent. With the explosion of long-distance commerce during the Roman-Han era, and later under Islamic and Mongol influence, these diseases savaged distant, defenseless populations. Over the ensuing 1,500 years, the once-separated disease pools of the Old World collided and coalesced catastrophically, and in the end largely immunized Asians and Europeans. The first Western migrants to the New World could not even begin to comprehend the devastation they were about to visit on the native populations with their microscopic hitchhikers. In the words of William McNeill, by the dawn of the Age of Discovery, "Europe had much to give and little to receive in the way of new human infections."[44]

Even more amazingly, the reservoirs of the plague bacillus, once confined to only a few relatively small Asian locations, expanded to circle the globe. Why, then, does not the plague continue to vex the modern world? True, the bacillus has become less deadly to many species since 1346; dogs, cats, and birds, which died alongside humans in the fourteenth century, are no longer highly susceptible. Perhaps this has also occurred to a lesser degree in rats and humans.[45]

But this cannot be the whole story. The disappearance of the plague in England following the Great Fire of London in 1666 provides the essential clue. The brick houses that replaced the old wooden structures proved less hospitable to rats, and fleas found it far harder to drop onto occupants from the new tile roofs than from the old thatched ones. As wood became scarce in western Europe and brick came into increasing use, the distance between rat and human widened, interrupting disease transmission. By the twentieth century, modern sanitary precautions and antibiotics added yet another layer of insulation that protected human-kind from the large underground reservoirs of this deadly pathogen.

The interaction between trade and disease works both ways. Just as trade fanned the flames of pestilence, so too did epidemic outbreaks alter age-old trade patterns. Perhaps the most penetrating analysis of the ef-fect of the Black Death on the trajectory of world trade was offered by the great fourteenth-century Arab historian Ibn Khaldun:

> In the middle of the [fourteenth] century civilization in both the East and the West was visited by a destructive plague which devastated nations and caused populations to vanish. It swallowed up many of the good things of civilization and wiped them out. It overtook the Dynasties at the time of their senility. . . . Cities and buildings were laid waste, roads and way signs were obliterated, settlements and mansions became empty, dynasties and tribes grew weak. . . . The East, it seems, was similarly visited, though in accordance with and in proportion to its [wealthier] civilization. It was as if the voice of existence in the world had called out for oblivion and restriction, and the world responded to its call.[46]

In the fourteenth through the sixteenth centuries, the furies reached out and with a perverse will savaged the planet's long-distance trading apparatus, and along with it the most advanced commercial societies: the great Muslim civilizations of the Middle East and the entrepôts of India and China that so dazzled Marco Polo and Ibn Battuta. Europe too had been devastated, but within a few centuries its survivors, wielding a fear-some combination of religiously inspired brutality and quantitative ge-nius, would wade into the wreckage and establish the modern Western domination of trade.

7

DA GAMA'S URGE

Vasco da Gama, a gentleman of your household, came to my country, whereat I was pleased. My country is rich in cinnamon, cloves, ginger, pepper, and precious stones. That which I ask of you in exchange is gold, silver, corals, and scarlet cloth.—Letter from the *zamorin* of Calicut to the king of Portugal, 1498.[1]

In this year [1503] the vessels of the Frank appeared at sea en route for India, Hormuz, and those parts. They took about seven vessels, killing those on board and making some prisoner. This was their first action, and may God curse them.
—Umar al-Taiyib Ba Faquih, Yemenite historian[2]

Sometime around 1440, a Venetian merchant, Niccolò de' Conti, journeyed to Rome to request an interview with Pope Eugenius IV. While traveling in the Orient, he had committed a grievous sin: captured and threatened with the death of himself and his entire family, he converted to Islam. Soon after, his wife and two sons died of the plague, and the involuntary apostate hastened to the Vatican seeking absolution.

Happily for de' Conti, the Holy Father harbored a weakness for cinnamon-flavored beverages. Had the merchant encountered its source during his voyages? Indeed he had. Absolution granted! In return, de' Conti would dictate his observations in detail to the papal secretary, the brilliant and famous humanist Gian Francesco Poggio Bracciolini.

That de' Conti's narrative dovetailed nicely with Marco Polo's, and was in many regards superior to it, pleased the papal confidante, an astute and learned man. For example, de' Conti had made more careful notation of distances and travel times than his illustrious countryman had recorded more than a century before. Yes, he had seen the cinnamon trees of Sri Lanka, which he described to the rapt secretary. Moreover, he had encountered fields of pepper and camphor in Sumatra. He next sailed east for over a month until the winds blew no longer, to the island of "Sanday," where nutmeg and mace grew, and thence to the island of "Bandan," thick with clove trees. The secretary's amazed delight can only be imagined: the Venetian, it would seem, had found the legendary Spice Islands.[3]

Was de' Conti the first Westerner to lay foot on those fabled shores? Almost certainly not. Place yourself in the shoes of a medieval European merchant who has just discovered unlimited quantities of the world's most precious and sought-after commodity. Travelogue would not be among your first, or even last, concerns.

Although the primary objective of the crusades was not commercial (unless one was Venetian or Genoese), Christians clearly recognized the Muslim command of the spice trade for the money machine it was. During their campaigns in the Holy Land, the crusaders interrupted the caravan traffic between Egypt and Syria with a chain of fortresses that ran from the Mediterranean down to the Red Sea's northeastern extremity at the Gulf of Aqaba. In 1183 Reginald of Châtillon mounted a series of raids against Arab shipping in the Red Sea itself. The alarm of the Islamic world at the infidels' penetration of this critical maritime corridor, previously thought to have been a Muslim domain, must have been extreme. The Egyptians mounted a vigorous response and forced Reginald back north.

In 1249, events at Damietta, on the Nile delta, demonstrated the crucial importance of the spice trade in the Muslim world. In that year, Christian forces captured the town, and so anxious were the Ayyubid Egyptians to regain this strategic trade outpost that they offered to return Jerusalem to the Christians in exchange; the offer was refused.[4] When it came to the spice trade, Christian and Muslim alike usually favored Mammon over God.

During the fifteenth and sixteenth centuries, another quest drove Europeans toward the East: the search for an Asian Christian ally in the fight against the Saracen. These two goals—the search for spices and the search for Asia's warrior of the Cross—were inseparable in the minds of the first Iberian explorers, and it is impossible to understand their motivations without retelling the strange story of the mythical Prester John.

Although his name trembled on the lips of millions, little else was known about Prester John, especially his kingdom's location, save that it was in "the Indies." During the medieval period, this could mean Egypt, Japan, or anywhere in between. Exactly when, where, and how this shadowy figure first saw light of day is debated among medievalists. By the twelfth century, the crusaders held much of the Holy Land, but were increasingly under siege from Islam's angry armies and grasping at straws. In 1141, an itinerant early Mongol warlord of indeterminate religious affiliation, Yeh-lü Ta-Shih, defeated a Muslim army near Samarkand. Since this city lay far beyond the geographic horizon of twelfth-century Europeans, it was unsurprising that news of the Muslims' defeat became hopelessly garbled by the time it reached Western ears: a Christian king had arrived from the Indies and vanquished the infidels.[5] Soon, he would attack them from the east and deliver the outposts of Christendom in the Holy Land from danger.

Three years later, in 1144, for the first time since the crusades began, a substantial Christian state, Edessa (located in what is now the Syrian-Turkish frontier), fell to Muslim forces. The victorious Saracens slaughtered Edessa's Christians, sending shudders through the Western world. A French bishop by the name of Hugh, from the coastal city of Jabala, in present-day Lebanon, hurried back to Europe to plead for help. His message was simple. Yes, there is indeed a Prester John, and he has already attacked the Saracens. Unfortunately, he was unable to cross the Tigris River, as it had not frozen over as expected, and his boats were not up to the task. According to Bishop Hugh, "He is a direct descendant of the Magi. . . . He had planned to go to Jerusalem, but was prevented."[6] Hugh's message to his European brethren was clear—salvation by Prester John was *not* on the way. Send help, and send it fast.

Years after the loss of Edessa, a letter was delivered from parts unknown to the Byzantine emperor Manuel Comnenus, purporting to have been written by Prester John. It exulted in the wealth and size of his kingdom and the virtue of his peoples: "I, Prester John, who reign supreme, exceed in riches, virtue, and power all creatures who dwell under heaven. Seventy-two kings pay tribute to me."[7] The most outrageous boast concerned his waiters' pedigrees:

> During each month we are served at our table by seven kings, each in his turn, by sixty-two dukes, and by three hundred and sixty-five counts, aside from those who carry out various tasks on our account. In our hall there dine daily, on our right hand, twelve archbishops, on our left, twenty bishops. . . . If you can count the stars of the sky

and the sands of the sea, you will be able to judge thereby the vastness of our realm and of our power.[8]

Needless to say, the letter was a fraud, and, given the nature and style of
the fabrications, almost certainly composed by a European, whose identity and motives remain unknown. For the next four hundred years, Western sovereigns and explorers alike sought two holy grails: Prester John,
who would deliver them from the Saracens; and spices, which would deliver them riches beyond counting.

While Muslims plied the vital trade routes through the Indian Ocean,
Red Sea, and Persian Gulf, Europeans dreamed of breaking into these
markets. The most powerful Asian trading states from west to east were
Aden, Hormuz, Cambay, Calicut, Aceh, and Malacca (located, respectively, in present-day Yemen, Iran, India, India, and Sumatra). None of
these nations projected naval power over the high seas. They prospered
instead on the strength of their trading institutions. Were customs officials too corrupt? Was the ruler too demanding of gifts? Or, in contrast,
did he not levy enough duties to pay for anti-piracy measures? Did resident foreign traders have too little autonomy to govern their own affairs? The merchant could easily bypass such problems by calling at
friendlier ports. Corruption and cruelty were not absent; this was, after
all, medieval Asia. The malfeasance simply needed to be kept down to
a dull roar.

A millennium ago, pirates roamed all of the world's seas, but large,
powerful, and potentially hostile navies did not trouble merchant ships
in the Indian Ocean as they so often did in the Mediterranean. The absence of maritime threats from the great trading states allowed Asian
vessels to sail largely unarmed, which greatly reduced manpower requirements and increased cargo capacity. That was just as well, since firing a
cannon from the deck of a sewn Asian ship was more likely to obliterate
it than sink its target.

Before the Europeans' arrival, the world of Asian trade was no Oriental Valhalla. But as long as merchants paid customs, provided local sultans with gifts, and kept pirates at bay, the Indian Ocean was, more or
less, a *mare liberum*. The idea that any nation might seek to control all

maritime traffic would have struck merchants and rulers alike as ludicrous.[9] All this was to change on the black day in 1498 when Vasco da
Gama, armed to the teeth, entered Calicut harbor.

As the fifteenth century drew to a close, there were only three ways for
Europeans to gain access to the Indian Ocean: directly penetrate it through
the Suez or the Persian Gulf, outflank it around Africa's southern cape,
or venture west into the unknown. The first Europeans known to attempt
one of these routes were two Genoese brothers, Vadino and Ugolino
Vivaldi, who in 1291—just a few months after their countryman Zaccaria
had captured Gibraltar from the Muslims—sailed through the strait into
the open Atlantic bound for India. They were never heard from again. To
this day, historians do not know whether their objective was the Cape of
Good Hope or a circumnavigation of the globe. Whatever its goal, their
expedition riveted Italians, who for years waited in vain for their return.
The mystery of the Vivaldis was said to have been inspired the passages in
Dante's *Inferno* describing the fatal voyage of Ulysses out through the
Pillars of Hercules.[10]

     That the first Europeans to sail the open Atlantic in search of the Indies
were Genoese was no accident. Fighting a losing battle for the spice trade
with the Venetians, the Genoese turned their commercial energies to the
bulk cargoes of the Mediterranean Sea and the Black Sea: minerals such as
salt and alum, lumber, agricultural products, and, of course, slaves. The sail-
driven round ships proved better equipped to carry bulk cargoes; these were
precisely the sort of vessels necessary for long voyages of discovery.[11]

     Even casual visitors to Genoa appreciate that the city, set into nearly
impenetrable coastal mountains, turns its back on the European mainland.
In the era before the railroad and asphalt, nearly everything that went into
or out of that entrepôt did so by ship. In place of the mule and horse cart,
many local businesses and manufacturers kept a small lateen-rigged craft
for procuring supplies and delivering goods. In Genoa, the leap from land-
lubber to sailor was a short one.

     By the fifteenth century, the sun was setting on the trading empire
of Genoa and was rising on that of Portugal, the western sliver of Iberia
where, in the words of the historian John H. Plumb, "Life was desperately cheap, the afterlife desperately real, the poverty of the world so great

that luxury and riches inebriated the imagination and drove men mad with a lust to possess."[12] It would be the Portuguese who perfected the maritime technology that allowed Europeans entry into the Indian Ocean. Through this breach would rush the ravenous wolf pack of the West, and Lisbon would attract the hungry, talented, and brutal young men of all nations who manned the vanguard of this attack.

By the mid-thirteenth century, Portugal had expelled the Moors—over two hundred years before Spain did. After a vicious succession fight and a Spanish invasion in the late fourteenth century, the nation achieved unification and independence in 1385 with the accession to the throne of João of Aviz (King João I) and his English bride, Philippa. This felicitous union yielded two historic dividends: an alliance between England and Portugal, which was to endure as well as any in the history of nations, and five capable and valiant sons.

Portugal found itself in an unaccustomed and uncomfortable state of peace, and so in 1415 the royal couple sent three of their progeny to seize the Moorish port city of Ceuta, just across the Strait of Gibraltar. Philippa herself planned this assault as a preliminary to loosening the Muslims' hold on the Indian Ocean—a beachhead to anchor the western end of a Portuguese caravan route heading eastward across the Sahara to the Indies. That Ceuta was also at the receiving end of caravans bearing slaves and gold from the African hinterland was considered a bonus. Better yet, capturing it struck a blow against the hated Moor.

When her youngest son, Infante Dom Henrique, beheld the endless desert that lay beyond Ceuta, he understood at once that his mother's plan was foolhardy. Although Henrique participated in subsequent North African campaigns, he eventually returned to Portugal, settled down as governor of the southern province of Algarve, and devoted himself to finding a sea route around Africa.[13]

Almost two thousand years after the death of Ptolemy, his dictum that Africa extended all the way to the Antarctic and could not be rounded still held sway. Henrique thought differently. From his castle at windswept Cape Saint Vincent at Europe's southwest extreme, Henrique, later known in the West as Prince Henry the Navigator, became Europe's greatest patron of the maritime sciences. From his parapets he beheld the departure of the earliest Iberian explorers down Africa's western coast and of colonists to the Azores, the farthest west of which lay just twelve hundred miles from Newfoundland. He also provided welcome financial support to cartographers of all nationalities and amassed the largest collection of navigational maps in the known world.

At some point, the Portuguese mariners supported by Henrique developed a new type of round-hulled ship with lateen rigging, the caravel. These craft were capable of sailing generous cargoes closer to the wind than any other European vessel. Without them, the subsequent Portuguese crawl down the African coast, and the later voyages to the Indies, would not have been possible.

Besides advancing Portugal's quest for a route around Africa, the caravel yielded more immediate benefits. It improved the speed and cargo-carrying capacities of Portuguese merchants to the point where they were able to divert the trade in Africa's two most profitable exports, slaves and gold, to their North African ports and away from the Muslim-controlled trans-Saharan camel routes. Portuguese agents, while unaware of the ultimate source of African gold in present-day Mali and in the upper reaches of the Niger and Volta rivers, penetrated far inland to trading towns such as the fabled Timbuktu, where they purchased gold cheaply for transport downriver to waiting caravels.[14]

By the time of Henrique's death in 1460, Portuguese vessels under his patronage had reached the waters of equatorial Africa, but had still not gained the southern passage into the Indian Ocean. Many people began to question Henrique's dream of an ocean route to the Orient around Africa, and the crown revived the idea of reaching the Indies by venturing eastward across Africa. In 1486, Portuguese traders in what is now Nigeria heard a strange tale of a fabulously wealthy ruler known as Ogané who reigned over a kingdom "twenty moons" march (about a thousand miles) east from the coast. This king always remained hidden behind curtains of silk, save for one foot thrust under the fabric at the conclusion of an audience—just like Prester John, who was said to never show his face. More than three centuries had passed since the Byzantine emperor Manuel Comnenus had received the boastful, fraudulent missive signed by the mythical king. The Portuguese, demonstrating a remarkable willingness to suspend the laws of human biology, concluded that he had been found. They decided to once again pursue an overland route to the Indies across Africa.

King João II promptly dispatched two of his most talented aides,

Pero da Covilhã and Afonso de Paiva, to travel to Abyssinia, which the royal geographers had identified as the kingdom of Ogané/Prester John, in order to negotiate with him a monopoly of the spice trade. Disguised as merchants, the two sailed the Mediterranean to Egypt, where they split up, Paiva heading for Abyssinia and Covilhã for India. They were to rendezvous in Cairo three years later.

After a few years, Paiva returned to Cairo from parts unknown and soon succumbed to illness. In the interim, he had communicated with no one, and his itinerary and discoveries remain a mystery to this day. Covilhã, having traveled the length and breadth of the Malabar Coast, also returned to Cairo, and after learning of Paiva's death, laid plans for his own return to Portugal. He was surprised to be met by two Portuguese Jews, emissaries from João II, who informed Covilhã of the extreme importance of concluding a trade agreement with Prester John. Since Covilhã had no idea whether or not Paiva had succeeded in this task, Covilhã would have to go to Abyssinia himself.

He never made it home, either. Shaving his head and disguising himself as a Muslim, he became one of the few Europeans to visit Mecca; then in 1493 he proceeded to Abyssinia, where he negotiated trade relations with its ruler, King Eskender. The king died the next year, and his brother, who assumed the throne, became so fond of this exotic European emissary that he kept him as a prisoner of luxury. Covilhã quietly died decades later with a large estate and many wives, but not having found hide or hair of Prester John, whose memory still stirred the spirits of European monarchs and explorers.

Both before and after arriving in Abyssinia, Covilhã sent to the Portuguese crown a treasure trove of information about India, including the operations of the local Hindu and Muslim merchants, wind and sailing patterns, and the prices of goods. He also traveled far down the East African coast and learned from local sailors that Africa could indeed be rounded, sending this message back home to be relayed to Bartholomew Diaz, who had set out to attain the Indian Ocean in 1487:

> If you keep southward, the continent must come to an end. When your ships have reached the Indian Ocean, let your men inquire for Sofala and the Island of the Moon. There they will find pilots who will take them to India.[15]

Diaz had by that time already rounded the Cape, and Covilhã's priceless intelligence was probably not passed on to subsequent Portuguese explorers.

In 1451, about the same time the aging Henrique was sending his last expeditions south, the son of a wool weaver was born in Genoa, who later became known to history as Christopher Columbus. The nautical temptations that abounded in Genoa must have appealed to the young man. His first trading voyage likely sent him to the western Aegean island of Chios, where a Genoese cartel, the *moan Giustiniani,* controlled the local mastic industry. This chewy resin (whence derives the word "mastication") cannot be cultivated outside a dozen sites on the southern half of Chios. Its rarity imbued it with supposed medicinal qualities, and so its monopolized trade was especially profitable.

By the time of Columbus's first voyage to Chios in about 1474, both the Genoese and the Venetians were slowly being driven out of the Aegean by the Ottomans, who had conquered Constantinople two decades before. From that point forward, Genoese seeking their fortunes headed west, not east, and Columbus proved no exception. A year or two later, the young able-bodied seaman found himself a common sailor on a cog—a medium-size round freighter of the period—carrying a load of mastic in a convoy bound for Lisbon. Off Portugal's southern shore, a fleet of Burgundian privateers set upon the convoy. The attackers had miscalculated badly; after the Genoese vessels were grappled and boarded, a vicious, inconclusive battle ensued in which hundreds on both sides perished by the sword or were swallowed by the sea. One version of the story, perhaps an embellished bauble of the Columbus legend, has the swashbuckling young sailor, in true Indiana Jones style, fighting valiantly, leaping into the water off his sinking ship, then swimming several miles to shore, where he was nursed back to health in the local Genoese colony at Lagos in the Algarve.

Eventually, he made it north to Lisbon, home of the main Genoese trade diaspora in Portugal. Columbus could not have found a more stimulating maritime environment. In Lisbon's labyrinthine streets, the babble of tongues from Iceland to Guinea overwhelmed the ears, the smells of cloves, cinnamon, and myrrh informed the well-tutored nose just which wharf lay close by, and one might not be surprised to encounter a Danish sailor or a Senegalese prince.

Meanwhile, his younger brother Bartholomew had already established himself in Lisbon as a cartographer, and over the next decade, Columbus gathered mapmaking expertise from Bartholomew and broadened his maritime skills by shipping out on Portuguese vessels. During this period, he sailed as widely as any mariner of his era: as far south as the African Gold Coast (present-day Ghana), as far west as the Azores, and as far north as Ireland, and perhaps even Iceland.[16] During the medieval period, it was not uncommon for seamen, both Asian and European, to receive a freight allowance in lieu of a salary, so Columbus had almost certainly transported, bought, and sold goods on his own account.

Around 1480, a series of events transformed the young mariner, cartographer, and trader into the iconic figure he would become. As befitted any up-and-coming merchant, he married well. His wife, Felipa Perestrello e Moniz, came from a well-to-do Lisbon commercial family who owned a small island near Madeira, settled earlier under the direction of Prince Henry. At the same time, he learned Latin and Portuguese and acquired, among other skills, a smattering of Castilian, mathematics, shipbuilding, and astronomy. Before his arrival in Portugal, Columbus already boasted solid connections to Genoa's largest trading concerns, and his marriage to Felipa and wide-ranging commercial and maritime experience gave him easy access to the Lisbon court.

In 1481, Afonso V, who had been king for over half a century, died, and was succeeded by his son, Dom João II, great-grandson of João I and a protégé of his great-uncle Henrique, and thus an ardent proponent of Atlantic and African exploration. Sometime around 1484, Columbus returned from equatorial Africa with a daring proposal for the new king.

As with any gigantic historical figure of whom we have a less than complete documentary record, Columbus acquired more than his share of apocrypha and tall tales, particularly the famous stories of Queen Isabella pawning her jewels to finance his first voyage and of "Columbus and the egg."[17] But none of the Columbus tales was to prove more hardy, well-known, or iconic than his pioneering the idea that the earth was round. More importantly, this myth also cuts to the heart of why he had such a difficult time selling his scheme to Europe's rulers.

By the medieval era, no educated person thought the world flat. As early as 205 BC, Eratosthenes, a Greek living in Alexandria, deduced that the earth was a sphere, and even calculated its size with an accuracy that would not be surpassed for nearly another two thousand years. Nor was Columbus the first to propose reaching the Indies by sailing west. The transatlantic route to India had been suggested as far back as the first century after Christ by the Roman geographer Strabo, and perhaps even by Aristotle before him. Some historians, in fact, believe that the Vivaldi brothers were attempting to reach the Spice Islands by acting on Strabo's advice. By the late fifteenth century, it became apparent to even the hidebound Afonso V that his uncle Henrique's dream of navigating to India around Africa might not be the best way to accomplish the deed.

Afonso went so far as to consult the canon of the cathedral of Lisbon about the possibility of a westward route. In turn, the canon passed the inquiry on to the famous Florentine physician and mapmaker Paolo dal Pozzo Toscanelli, who wrote back from Florence that, yes, the sailing distance from Lisbon to China was only about five thousand miles—a gross underestimate.

From precisely which of the above legacies, if any, Columbus gathered the idea for the westward route may never be ascertained, but we do know that he corresponded with Toscanelli, who wrote back that he approved of his fellow Italian's desire to "pass over to where the spices grow." Columbus would later feature Toscanelli's written endorsement prominently in his efforts to obtain funding for his enterprise.[18]

Like many single-minded men, Columbus deluded himself at almost every turn. The feasibility of the westward route depended on its being short. Although the westward distance from Europe to Asia had of course never been directly measured, it could be estimated by subtracting the approximately known eastbound distance from the estimated circumference of the earth. For example, today we know that the eastbound distance from Lisbon to Malacca, as the crow flies, is approximately 7,000 miles. Since the earth's circumference is 25,000 miles, it follows that the westbound distance (at least along the equatorial route) must be approximately 18,000 miles.

Unfortunately for Columbus, geographers had already done such calculations, which invariably yielded a westbound distance so large as to be incompatible with survival at sea. For example, Ptolemy calculated that the Eurasian landmass stretched approximately halfway around the globe, in which case the westward route must stretch about the same distance as the eastward distance, about 12,500 miles. This proved an accurate estimate: if the Americas did not block the way, sailing the mid-latitudes from Lisbon to China would cover about 12,000 miles, with another 4,000 miles beyond that to India. Even at an optimistic four knots, the voyage to China would take about four months, but no vessel of the period could stock supplies adequate for so long a journey. Further, long before food and water would run out, most of the crew would have succumbed to scurvy. Had Columbus not collided with America in his quest for the Orient, he and his men would certainly have vanished like the Vivaldis.

Faced with inconvenient contrary data, Columbus behaved like all true believers from Saul of Tarsus to George Bush the Younger: he fudged.[19] He did so in a plausible and straightforward manner, by using the lowest possible estimate of the earth's circumference—about 17,000 miles—and the highest possible estimate of the east-west size of Eurasia. He was particularly drawn to Marco Polo's description of Cipangu—Japan—as lying another thousand miles east of Cathay. So great, Columbus rationalized, was the eastward distance from Portugal to Japan and so small was the globe that the golden roofs of Cipangu must be just over the western horizon from his proposed starting point, the Azores, located almost a thousand miles southeast of Lisbon.

What drove Columbus on his journey into the great unknown over the western horizon? Was he really looking for new worlds, or "merely" a faster way to China, India, and Japan? Was he propelled by a hunger for gold and spices? Was he motivated by the desire for respectability that suffuses the personalities of those of great ability and ambition but humble birth? Or was he looking for souls to save? For hundreds of years scholars have debated the provenance and meaning of the documents and marginalia he left behind, and the truth will probably never be known.[20] Perhaps projecting his own motives onto the settlers he carried on his subsequent journeys, he later complained that none of them

came save in the belief that the gold and spices could be gathered in by the shovelful, and they did not reflect that, though there was gold, it would be buried in mines, and the spices would be on the treetops and that the gold would have to be mined and the spices harvested and cured.[21]

Columbus, with his newly acquired connections at court, began to lobby João II. Initially, the monarch was friendly to the ambitious proposal of the young Genovese, and acted as any enlightened ruler would in such circumstances—he referred Columbus's idea to a committee of eminent astronomers, mathematicians, and geographers, the *Junta dos Mathemáticos*. Although we have no record of its deliberations, it must have found Columbus's estimate of the westward distance from Portugal to Japan ludicrous.

Worse, with his scheme came demands: generous underwriting of the voyage, including the use of a royal vessel, a hereditary title, and a huge cut of the profits from the Indies trade. These provisos did little to enhance Columbus's credibility. Despite the fact that Columbus was the son-in-law of one of the realm's most prosperous merchants, no backing was forthcoming from the Portuguese crown.

With no immediate prospect of funding from João II, Columbus decamped to Cordova in 1484. There, he pitched his scheme to Isabella and Ferdinand, who had united their respective kingdoms of Aragon and Castile into the modern nation of Spain just sixteen years previously. A nearly identical sequence of events played out at the Spanish court as had at Lisbon. Columbus, who came from the same ethnic stock as the Spanish queen, made a favorable initial impression, but once again he had to face a rather more hardheaded committee of experts, this time organized by the queen's confessor, Hernando de Talavera. Even before the committee reached a verdict, Ferdinand and Isabella cut off his modest stipend, and he returned to Portugal.

While Columbus licked his wounds in Lisbon, his luck turned from bad to worse. There, he personally witnessed the tiny vessels of Bartholomew Diaz, who had doubled the Cape of Good Hope in 1488, straggle up the Tagus River. As he did so, he must have realized that the rounding of southern Africa eliminated Portugal's need for a western route. He returned to Spain, where he glumly awaited the final verdict of Talavera's committee. In 1490, that ax fell too. The committee reported to the crown that it "judged his promises and offers were impossible and vain and worthy of rejection." Columbus tenaciously appealed to the queen, who granted an examination by a second committee. Again, his proposal was rejected.[22]

At the same time, Bartholomew Columbus probably traveled to England and presented his brother's proposal to the court of Henry VII. There is more solid documentation that Bartholomew arrived in France in 1490 and approached Charles VIII. Rejected in both courts, he remained in France until well after his brother returned from his first voyage.

In early 1492, the Spanish court informed Columbus that his mere presence in the kingdom was no longer welcome. Then, just before he disappeared over the horizon with his worldly belongings and donkey, a messenger commanded him to return. At the last minute, one of his staunchest supporters in Ferdinand's retinue, Luis de Santangel, convinced the queen that funding the voyage west was a low-cost proposition and that it carried the possibility of enormous gain. Further, Santangel offered to underwrite the voyage himself. It appears that Isabella did indeed proffer her jewels as collateral, but Santangel reassured her that this sacrifice would not be required.

As with any great enterprise, mere vision, courage, intelligence, attention to detail, and dogged hard work—Columbus was said to have inspected every timber on his three ships before embarking in 1492—do not suffice. Luck, too, is required: had João II accepted his proposal, then Columbus would have staged his expedition from the Portuguese Azores, which he knew well, and he probably would have foundered and perished in the unfavorable winds at that latitude. As fortune would have it, all four of his journeys were mounted from the more southerly Spanish Canaries, freshened with easterly trade winds blowing straight toward the Caribbean.

Columbus, Santangel, and Isabella had all been right, but for all the wrong reasons. Contrariwise, the scholarly advisers to the crowns of Portugal, England, France, and Spain were far better informed than Columbus about geography, and must have been astounded when Columbus returned after his momentous first voyage from "the Indies."[23] None could imagine that a vast new world, whose outlines had been dimly and fleetingly perceived by Norse explorers, and perhaps by others from Europe and Asia centuries before, now lay within their grasp.[24]

So single-mindedly did Columbus pursue the westerly route that he failed to take along on his journeys the specialists instinctively sought by later, and far more competent, conquistadors: Arabic translators to tell him that the primitive Carib "Indians" he encountered and brought back with him to Spain were certainly not residents of India; jewelers to ascertain that the massive quantity of yellow metal weighing down his holds was iron pyrite, fool's gold; or apothecaries like Tomé Pires to warn him that the "cinnamon" and "pepper" he presented to Ferdinand and Isabella on his return were, respectively, a nondescript bark and chilies of a sort never before seen in the Old World. Even had he brought such experts along, he would not have believed them. So thick-skulled was the discoverer of the New World that not until his third voyage would it slowly dawn on him that he had not reached Asia after all.

That the discovery of the New World would excite the avarice of little, greedy men should have come as no surprise to the ambitious son of a wool weaver. The path to "easy" riches he had supposedly found was no less admirable than the rent stream of the aristocrat, and the social upheaval caused by his return from the New World was considerable. As the poet, dramatist, and biographer Stefan Zweig put it:

> Everyone in Europe who was discontented with his means and his position, everyone who felt himself thrust into the background and was too impatient to wait; younger sons, unemployed officers, bastards of the nobles, fugitives from justice—one and all wanted to go to the New World.[25]

In the train of Columbus's voyages came ethnic cleansing and genocide, both deliberate and unintentional, and the extraction of every available ounce of silver and gold, first from the Amerindian ruling elite, and then from the ground. Modern economic historians have described a striking correlation between the economic development of the native peoples, their initial population densities, disease rates among white settlers, and subsequent economic development.[26] In those lands with relatively low initial native economic development and population densities, and a healthy climate for Europeans—the New World, Australia, and New Zealand—the white invaders were able to survive, settle, and subdue or kill off the indigenous peoples. The conquerors then went on to produce unimaginable wealth. Although much of the prosperity was due to trade, such as that from the sugar plantations of the Caribbean, the primary work of the settlers was mining, agriculture, and, later, manufacturing.

This sequence of events was impossible in those lands with high initial native populations, high disease rates among Europeans, and relatively prosperous native trading and manufacturing economies—that is, almost all the shores touched by the Indian Ocean. In such places, white men could not hope to survive and conquer vast numbers of advanced, relatively wealthy, and highly organized natives. Here, at least at first, trade would be the order of the day for Europeans.

Put more simply, the Portuguese and Dutch sent hundreds of thousands of Europeans to their deaths during and after the seven- or eight-month journey to the populous and disease-ridden lowlands of Africa, India, Sri Lanka, Malaya, and Indonesia. For example, during the seventeenth century alone, approximately 25,000 European soldiers died within the squalid confines of the Royal Hospital at Goa from malaria, dengue, typhoid, and cholera.[27] By contrast, European settlers sailed for only five or six weeks and then faced better odds in the less populated and far healthier highlands of Mexico and Peru, and later in North America.

Of more immediate import to the story at hand was the ongoing duel between the two great seafaring nations of the fifteenth and sixteenth centuries—Portugal and Spain. This competition was in full swing by the time Columbus's tiny fleet left the harbor at Palos de la Frontera in the wee hours of August 3, 1492.

We can better understand these two Iberian brethren as the favorite offspring of doting parents—in this case the mother church, which adored their Iberian extremist theological purity and fervor; and the Holy Father, for whom keeping peace between the two squabbling progeny amounted to a full-time job. Like children, they derived much of their legitimacy from parental authority, in this case the papal imprimatur, to which even the mightiest European monarchs were theoretically vassals, their crowns leased back to them in return for a not inconsiderable regular tribute to the Vatican.

The parent also played favorites. The pontiffs of the mid-fifteenth century were particularly fond of Dom Henrique's piety and crusading zeal against the Moors of North Africa. Pope Nicholas V, for example, issued a bull, *Romanus Pontifex,* just before his death in 1455. Called the "charter of Portuguese imperialism," it praised Henrique, authorized him to conquer and convert all the pagans between Morocco and the Indies, and, most importantly, awarded Portugal a trading monopoly in all territories between Africa and the Indies.[28]

Then, in August 1492, just eight days after Columbus slipped his moorage at Palos, a Spaniard ascended to the papacy as Alexander VI, owing his vestments to the financial backing and good efforts of Ferdinand and Isabella. In 1493, with Columbus's feet barely dry on his return from the first voyage, Alexander issued the first of several bulls awarding Spain possession of all territories newly discovered by its subjects. Later that same year, Alexander issued yet another bull drawing a demarcation line one hundred leagues (about 350 miles) west of the Cape Verde Islands, beyond which all terra firma, discovered or not, belonged to Ferdinand and Isabella. A final bull seemed to extend Spain's ambit south and east all the way to India. This infuriated the Portuguese, since it ignored three generations of their pioneering down the African coast, contradicted *Romanus Pontifex,* and made no mention of the doubling of the Cape by Diaz just five years earlier.

João II, disgusted with the corrupt Spanish pope, decided to deal directly with Ferdinand and Isabella. For their part, the Spanish monarchs, fearing the ruthless Portuguese and busy enough digesting the New World, were more than happy to seek a reasonable compromise. On June 7, 1494, a momentous treaty, known to history by the town in central Spain in which it was negotiated, was inked at Tordesillas.

The Treaty of Tordesillas divided the world into two hemispheres along a longitudinal (north-south) line placed 370 leagues, or about 1,270 miles, west of the Cape Verdes. This demarcation line was located at about forty-five degrees west of Greenwich, giving Asia to the Portuguese and the New World to the Spanish.[29]

In normal times, nations will expend blood and treasure over minuscule scraps of territory. These, however, were not normal times; Portugal had just achieved a goal sought by Westerners since the death of the Prophet—access to the Indian Ocean—and the Spanish had just discovered two new continents. Such was the excitement of this era that these bitter rivals could partition the entire planet between them as easily as two schoolchildren swapping marbles at recess.

What must have been going through the minds of João II's envoys that hot June day in the sleepy town of Tordesillas? All of Africa and all of

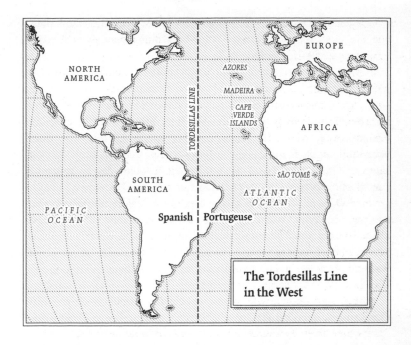

The Tordesillas Line in the West

Asia now supposedly belonged to Portugal, but at the time the treaty was signed, only the vessels of Bartholomew Diaz had, fleetingly, attained the extreme southwest corner of the Indian Ocean. Did the Portuguese have any inkling that they, just emerging from the Black Death with a population of barely more than one million, a few thousand able-bodied sailors, and a few hundred blue-water ships, were about to confront the world's largest and most sophisticated trading apparatus? So thinly stretched were the Portuguese that on their largest merchantmen, often only a few European officers and soldiers commanded crews consisting of hundreds of Asians or African slaves.[30] Portugal was truly the dog who had caught the car. This particular canine was fast and vicious and would leave many a fang mark, but was ultimately doomed to be left in the roadside dust.

João II could not have chosen a better man to make the first lunge at the two impossible quests: Asian spices and the still elusive Prester John. Vasco da Gama's voyage of 1497–1499 was simply the most remarkable maritime accomplishment of its time, a round trip across 28,000 miles of open ocean to attain its goal—India. Columbus, in spite of his blandishments, had done no such thing. Further, Columbus's definition of his target, the "Indies," left much to be desired in terms of geographical precision. Did he mean Japan, Cathay, India proper, or the realm of Prester John?

Unlike Columbus, da Gama gathered painstaking nautical intelligence before weighing anchor. He identified Calicut on India's southwestern Malabar Coast as the richest entrepôt on the subcontinent—almost precisely where the southwest monsoon deposited his ships after they departed the coast of East Africa. Da Gama accomplished his staggering nautical feat with the aid of two innovations.

Earlier, in 1488, on his way to the Cape, Diaz had followed the time-honored coastwise route pioneered by the first Portuguese expeditions sent by Henrique. South of the equator, as southerly trade winds increasingly blew against his ships, progress became ever more difficult. Sometime during the eight-year hiatus between his return in 1489 and da Gama's departure in 1497, a mariner unknown to history found the solution to this problem. As da Gama's ships passed the coast of what is now Sierra Leone, they turned right, departed the coast for the open Atlantic, and headed almost due west for several hundred miles. Then, the ships gradually executed a counterclockwise semicircle thousands of miles wide, enabling them to tack across the wind blowing directly on their port sides. This slowly brought them back to the Cape. So generous was the arc that da Gama's fleet came within several hundred miles of Brazil. Even so, he did not swing wide enough to achieve his objective of bypassing the treacherous Cape of Good Hope to the south, instead striking Africa's southwest coast at Saint Helena Bay.

Da Gama's small fleet had been out of sight of land an astounding ninety-five days; by contrast, Columbus's transit during his first voyage from the Canaries to the Bahamas took thirty-six. So great was da Gama's navigational skill that his measured latitudes were never off by more than two degrees. Columbus, by contrast, was notorious for his navigational inaccuracy, placing, for example, Cuba at forty-two degrees north latitude —that is, even with Boston.[31]

Not long after reaching the southern African coast, da Gama's crews suffered a strange illness, "their feet and hands swelling, and their gums growing over their teeth, so that they could not eat."[32] The caravel, by making

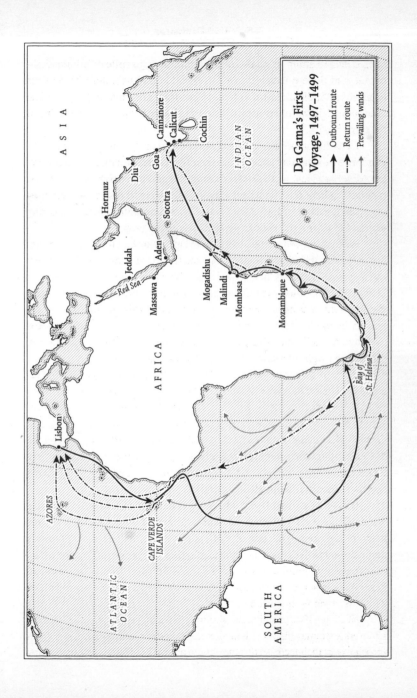

Da Gama's First
Voyage, 1497–1499

→ Outbound route
-·→ Return route
↑ Prevailing winds

possible journeys of up to several months out of sight of land, allowed sailors' bodies to deplete their stores of vitamin C, causing scurvy, the great killer of European mariners. On the outbound leg of the journey, the timely arrival of da Gama's crew in prosperous East African ports apparently spared them the brunt of the disease. They would not be so lucky on the way home.

Although da Gama's nautical preparation was excellent, the same cannot be said for his commercial planning. In order to apprise native traders of the goods they sought, the Portuguese did carry with them samples of gold, spices, and ivory, but they failed to also bring along adequate goods to barter for these desired items. Whether this was the result of ignorance, arrogance, or both, we shall never know.

At first, da Gama's trading operations in southern Africa went reasonably well; the natives seemed happy to exchange local goods for small quantities of European linen, which they prized greatly. However, as the Europeans proceeded north and began to encounter the Muslim-dominated Indian Ocean trade emporium, market conditions changed drastically. The traders became lighter-skinned, and they spoke Arabic. On the island of Mozambique, the Portuguese encountered a Muslim sheikh, to whom they offered

> hats, (silk garments), corals, and many other articles. He was, however, so proud that he treated all we gave him with contempt, and asked for scarlet cloth, of which we had none. We gave him, however, all of the things we had. One day the captain-major [da Gama] invited him to a repast, when there was an abundance of figs and confits, and begged him for two pilots to go with us.[33]

For the first time, and not the last, scraggly Europeans bearing inferior goods in puny ships with limited navigational expertise had failed to impress rulers grown rich and jaded on the well-oiled machinery of the Muslim Indian Ocean trade. Not only did Asian goods awe the European visitors; so did their maritime technology. As an anonymous crew member remarked:

> The vessels of this country are of good size and decked. There are no nails, and the planks are held together by cords. . . . The sails are made of palm matting. Their mariners have Genoese needles [magnetic compasses] by which they steer, quadrants, and navigating charts.[34]

The levers of this commercial machine were manipulated by the Muslim trade diaspora—merchants from Persia. For example, in Mombasa (in modern-day Kenya), the Portuguese observed: "There were colonies of both Moors and Christians in this city . . . these latter lived apart under their own lords."[35] At first, both the local sultans and the trade communities showed generous hospitality to the initially cautious and courteous Portuguese, from whom profitable commerce was expected. Native traders soon tumbled to the Portuguese obsession with Prester John and learned to indulge it—the great Christian ruler seemed always to be just over the horizon, beyond the next kingdom, or in the next port. Da Gama's men, for their part, assumed that anyone who was not visibly Muslim must be a Christian:

> These Indians are tawny men; they wear but little clothing and have long beards and long hair, which they braid. They told us that they ate no beef. . . . On the day on which the captain-major went up to the town in the boats, these Christian Indians fired off many bombards from their vessels, and when they saw [da Gama] pass they raised their hands and shouted lustily, *Christ! Christ!*[36]

Obviously, da Gama's men had mistaken as Christians Hindu Indian traders, who were more likely than not shouting the name "Krishna" than that of the Son of God. This dark religious comedy would continue in India, which the Portuguese at first assumed to be a largely Christian nation with exotic churches (Hindu temples) adorned with multiple-limbed and scantily clad versions of the Father, the Son, the Holy Spirit, the Virgin, and the saints.

Besides the wide south Atlantic arc, da Gama's other "innovation" was his reliance on Indian Ocean pilots. None other than Ibn Majid, the legendary Arab pilot and author of the most authoritative medieval text on Indian Ocean navigation, is said to have guided da Gama to India, and he is to this day cursed in the Islamic world for this act of unintended treachery. Although the story of how the generous and open Majid was ill-used by the perfidious Portuguese makes for a delicious morsel of anti-imperialist propaganda, Majid cannot possibly have been the guilty pilot. Da Gama's pilot, hired or abducted at Malindi (about sixty miles north of Mombasa), was a Gujarati who was taken back to Portugal; Majid, an Omani, made no mention of visiting Portugal in his extensive memoirs.[37]

Whatever da Gama's many virtues, he was not known for having a sweet or gentle nature; he ordered his crew to rob, kidnap, and murder at the slightest provocation. The two pilots taken on in Mozambique, who had been flogged for alleged disloyalty, escaped at the first opportunity in Mombasa. By the time the expedition reached its last port of call in Africa, Malindi, news of the Portuguese reputation for blood thirst preceded them, and no local vessels ventured out to do business. This posed a problem, since by that point they were short on supplies and in desperate need of a guide to India. At Malindi, necessity forced da Gama to behave tolerably well, going so far as releasing Muslim hostages taken in Mombasa and Mozambique as a sign of goodwill.

On April 24, 1498, resupplied and in the company of a Gujarati pilot provided by the sultan of Malindi, da Gama's three tiny ships left that port city and headed northeast into blue water on the first breaths of the summer monsoon. Five days later, they recrossed the equator and sighted the old friend of the European mariner, the north star, and on May 18, they beheld the mountains of the Malabar Coast. In only twenty-three days, they had flown across 2,800 miles of open ocean, missing their target, Calicut, by just seven miles. The world's most brutal trading nation had "discovered" the secrets of the monsoon; the wolf had entered the sheepfold, and world commerce would never be the same.

The Portuguese sought not a trading empire, but rather a protection racket that coerced local merchants into selling spices and other goods at below market rates and excluded others, particularly Muslims, from honest commerce. The dividing line between protection and piracy is a fine one indeed, and the Portuguese crossed it routinely. During this first voyage to India, da Gama developed a well-rehearsed routine. The flotilla waited until boats came to greet it; its crew then grabbed hostages. The captains of the three ships—da Gama, his brother Paulo, and Nicolau Coelho—remained on board whenever possible, and force was liberally used as part of subsequent "trade negotiations."[38]

Both in Africa and in India, da Gama employed condemned men called *degradados* from Portugal's jails, selected for their language abilities, to be the first ashore in strange lands. The *degradado* chosen for this honor at Calicut was João Nunez, a recently converted Jew who spoke some Arabic. He was met by Tunisians speaking both Spanish and Italian and was asked, "May the devil take thee! What brought you hither?" to which Nunez responded, "We come in search of Christians and of spices."[39]

As in East Africa, the Indians were less than awed by the quality of European trade goods. In preparation for a meeting with Calicut's Hindu ruler, the *zamorin,* da Gama sent to him "twelve pieces of [striped cloth], four scarlet hoods, six hats, four strings of coral, a case containing six hand-wash basins, a case of sugar, two casks of oil, and two of honey." Such gifts would likely not have impressed even the lowliest *geniza* merchant, let alone the ruler of the richest entrepôt in India. The *zamorin*'s retainers, on seeing these gifts, howled with derision and informed da Gama's messengers that, "It was not a thing to offer the king, that the poorest merchant from Mecca, or any other part of India, gave more, and that if he wanted to make a present, it should be in gold."[40]

The *zamorin* was not the only inhabitant of Calicut unhappy with da Gama. The city's powerful Muslim merchants worried, justifiably, that the appearance of European Christians did not bode well for their own future welfare, and they must certainly have advised the *zamorin* to be circumspect: he kept the captain-major waiting an entire day.

Things went from bad to worse. The captain-major, his offerings disparaged, brought nothing, and when the *zamorin* upbraided him for coming empty-handed, da Gama answered that his purpose was discovery, not trade. The *zamorin* then acidly asked "What it was he had come to discover: stones or men? If he had come to discover men, as he said, why had he brought nothing?"[41]

If da Gama's commercial preparation was inadequate, his understanding of Indian culture and customs was atrocious. The pitiful trade goods, the overweening arrogance, and the paranoia of the Portuguese combined to produce a downward spiral of hostage-taking and deteriorating relations with the Muslim merchants, who had probably already learned of the captain-major's demands for their expulsion from the city. The merchants spat on the ground exclaiming "Portugal! Portugal" each time one of da Gama's men passed by.

Remarkably, almost a decade before, Pero da Covilhã, in the course of his epic journey, had already gathered the commercial and diplomatic wisdom that da Gama so sadly lacked. Such, however, was the state of communication in the medieval era that da Gama, like Diaz, apparently never received Covilhã's priceless intelligence.

Despite these strained circumstances, commercial transactions between Indian merchants and da Gama's crews eventually took place. Even if the Muslim traders correctly perceived the religiously inspired hatred and mortal danger borne by the new arrivals, and even if the *zamorin* was unimpressed with the Westerners' gifts, his Hindu subjects were more than happy to exchange da Gama's European textiles for spices. Although the Portuguese were dismayed by the low prices fetched by their finest linen shirts—one-tenth, in terms of gold and silver, what they would command in Lisbon—they were delighted that they could purchase spices even more cheaply.

Although the Hindu *zamorin* was initially agreeable about trading with the Europeans, he rapidly tired of the captain-major's duplicity. He finally allowed the three ships, which had slowly loaded their holds with pepper and other treasures in the three months they had been in port (and had failed to pay the usual customs duties), to weigh anchor and depart Calicut on August 29, 1498.[42]

The rigors of da Gama's first voyage to the Indies were typical. Of the approximately 170 men who set out from Lisbon, less than half returned. The majority of the deaths were due to scurvy on the return leg across the Indian Ocean,[43] when the disease attacked with far greater fury than on the outbound journey, killing and sickening so many that one of the three ships had to be abandoned merely to muster enough able-bodied seamen to control the other two. Paulo da Gama succumbed to the disease the day after arriving in the Azores, the last stop before reaching Lisbon in September 1499. No matter. Da Gama's crews had loaded enough pepper, cinnamon, and cloves in Calicut to pay the expedition's cost sixty times over, and when the sorry remains of the expedition limped into Lisbon, no one questioned the awful human toll.[44]

The Portuguese crown quickly followed up on this momentous navigational and commercial accomplishment. Less than six months later, in March 1500, Pedro Alvares Cabral departed with thirteen ships and approximately 1,500 men. He made an even more effective "wide sweep" of the Atlantic, passing safely well to the south of the feared Cape and in the process becoming the first European to visit Brazil, which happily for Portugal lay on its side of the Tordesillas line.

This set the pattern for most subsequent European expeditions to the Indies. They left in late winter so as to take maximum advantage of the south Atlantic trade winds, then caught the summer monsoon across the Indian Ocean to arrive in India in September, just six months after departing Lisbon. (In the words of one captain, "The last day of February is time enough, but the first day of March is late."[45]) After spending the fall in India swapping cargoes and repairing sails and timbers, the Europeans could return on the winter monsoon. The late-winter departure from Europe proved not only more rapid but often more dangerous, as this schedule threw the expeditions into the teeth of southern hemisphere storms on the outbound leg. Four of Cabral's vessels were lost in a south Atlantic tempest, and of the nine that survived it, only six reached India. Again, no matter. Huge were profits and cheap were lives; hundreds of souls were a small price to pay for the pepper, cinnamon, and cloves demanded by a covetous Europe.

On arriving in India, Cabral stirred up the poisonous diplomatic brew concocted two years before by da Gama's paranoia and brutality. In the interim between the two voyages, the old and proud *zamorin,* who had had a tempestuous but ultimately satisfactory commercial relationship with da Gama, had died and been replaced by his son. Like da Gama, Cabral demanded that the Portuguese receive priority over Muslim merchants. Initially, things went well; the Europeans captured a ship from a neighboring Indian kingdom carrying an elephant, which was given to the flattered *zamorin,* and the largest vessels were loaded with pepper and fine spices. Hearing that a Muslim ship had just been loaded with spices and was bound for Jeddah, Mecca's port on the Red Sea, Cabral seized it, since in the eyes of the Portuguese, any commerce with the hated "Moors from Mecca" violated the "agreement" with the *zamorin.* This angered the city's Muslims, who attacked the Portuguese trading post and killed fifty-four men.

The Portuguese waited a day for word from the *zamorin.* When none came, they assumed the worst—that the *zamorin* was behind the massacre of the trading post—and captured about a dozen Indian ships, slaughtered their crews, and devastated the town with cannon fire for a full day. The Portuguese then decamped for Cochin, Calicut's rival to the south. In Cochin, and in Cannanore, about forty miles to the north of Calicut, they loaded their smaller ships with more spices. Fearing a counterattack

by the *zamorin* and betrayal by Cochin's ruler, they departed in such haste
that they abandoned their traders onshore, in spite of having significant
reserves of silver and cargo space. On the way back to Lisbon, Cabral
lost one more ship.[46]

The crown was less than pleased with the commander, who had lost
two-thirds of his vessels and blundered into a war with the new *zamorin*.
The king could pardon these sins. Far more serious was his purchase of a
large cargo of inferior-grade cinnamon. Better to give the next large India
fleet to da Gama, who departed in 1502 with twenty-five ships.

The three-year interlude between his first and second voyages had
not made da Gama a kinder, gentler captain-major. He had, it seemed, an
agenda that now ran far beyond mere commerce: in punishment for the
trading post massacre at Calicut of two years before, he planned to shut
off all Muslim traffic between the Malabar Coast and the Red Sea. In early
September 1502, seven months after departing Lisbon, his fleet took up
station off Cannanore and waited.

About three weeks later, on September 29, the fleet intercepted the
hajj vessel *Mîrî*, carrying several hundred men, women, and children returning from Mecca. Over the next five days, da Gama's crew slowly and
deliberately stripped the ship of its cargo and its passengers of their pos-
sessions and listened with deaf ears as the pilgrims bargained for their
lives with offers of far greater booty ashore.

A crew member and chronicler on that voyage, Tomé Lopes, wrote
that on October 3, 1502, after the looting had stopped, events occurred
which "I will remember all the days of my life."[47] Da Gama ordered the
ship set ablaze. The passengers, men and women alike, with little to lose,
responded by attacking da Gama's men with stones and their bare hands.
The doomed Muslims next rammed one of the Portuguese vessels, pre-
venting da Gama's men from bombarding the *Mîrî* lest they hit their own
ship, and a ferocious close-quarters combat ensued. All the while, Muslim women waved their jewelry and held their infants aloft in the hope
that da Gama, observing the action through a porthole, might take pity.
He did not. The only passengers spared were the children, who were removed and baptized, and, of course, the pilot.

The young *zamorin* sued for peace, diplomatically suggesting that
the carnage and plunder on the *Mîrî* more than made up for the attack on
the Portuguese trading post; let bygones be bygones. This only further

inflamed da Gama, who fulminated, "Since the beginning of the world, the Moors have been the enemies of the Christians, and the Christians the Moors, and they have always been at war with each other."[48]

Da Gama arrived in Calicut in the foulest of moods, and bombarded the port even more ferociously than had Cabral. On November 1, he hanged dozens of Muslim hostages from the masts, cut them down, and

> had the heads, hands, and feet of the hanged men cut off, and put on a boat with a letter, in which he said that if those men, though they were not the same as those responsible for the death of the Portuguese [at the trading post two years before] . . . had received that punishment . . . the authors of that treachery would await a manner of death that was even more cruel.[49]

This was no isolated incident. The Portuguese often boasted of hanging the bodies from pillaged dhows for target practice, then sending the bits to the local ruler, suggesting that he use them in a curry.[50] Their brutality was exceptional even for the times, intensified by fundamentalist Catholic temperament of the era. Medieval Christians embraced the damnation of nonbelievers as an axiom of faith; if Jews, Muslims, and Hindus were condemned to roast eternally in the afterlife, they could not expect much sympathy in the here and now.

As a result of these largely unprovoked Portuguese atrocities, da Gama and the *zamorin* were now engaged in all-out war. In January 1503, the Hindu ruler lured the captain-major from the safety of Cochin into an ambush in Calicut. This was followed by several direct attacks by swift Indian vessels; all were repulsed.

As winter wore on and the monsoonal clock ticked ever louder, the Portuguese finally departed. This time, they left behind permanent posts at Cannanore and Cochin along with several ships to serve as a sort of permanent Indian Ocean fleet. The departing vessels straggled home with an enormous quantity of spices—by one estimate, about seventeen hundred tons of pepper, and an additional four hundred tons of cinnamon, cloves, mace, and nutmeg loaded in Cochin following the *Mîrî* massacre. The captain-major himself was reputed to have carried about forty thousand ducats' worth of the fragrant cargo back up the Tagus.[51]

In the five years following da Gama's appearance in East Africa and India in 1498, the Portuguese not only had established a fabulously profitable trade but also had made enemies in virtually every port along the way. Even if they had exerted a lighter touch, they still would have earned the enmity of displaced Muslim merchants. The new spice route, so long, tenuous, and vulnerable, had to be protected and supported by a chain of fortified Portuguese outposts, whose cultural and architectural ghosts are still visible today, strung all the way from the Azores to Macao.

The building of this empire began quickly. In 1505, Francisco de Almeida assumed his duties as the first viceroy of India. His first stop was Kilwa (on what is now the coast of Tanzania), which he assaulted and subdued, leaving behind a puppet Arab sultan and a large garrison. Next, he sacked Mombasa, and while he sailed off to India, the garrison troops captured the island of Mozambique. Within a few months, Portugal was in command of East Africa's most important ports. These bases and trading posts also served as a source of African gold to trade for Indian spices. The gold, in turn, was bought with Gujarati textiles. There was nothing new about this triangular commerce in textiles, gold, and spices; Arab and Asian merchants had been plying the same trade for centuries. But for Europeans, it also held the advantage of adding a few profitable extra Indian Ocean legs to their missions and avoided the treacherous journey around the Cape.

Once in India, Almeida began to systematically subdue the Malabar ports. At first, the two great Muslim powers—the Mamluk Egyptians and the Muslim rulers of Gujarat—resisted. In 1508, they deployed a combined taskforce at the port of Chaul, south of modern day Bombay, where they unleashed a devastating ambush against Portuguese vessels in which Almeida's son was killed. The viceroy avenged his death a year later by destroying the combined Muslim fleet at Diu (just north of modern Bombay), thus eliminating the one threat to European naval supremacy in the Indian Ocean. Demonstrating once again that ducats trumped devotion, Venice backed the Muslim expedition against their brothers in Christ by providing the Gujarati-Mamluk navy with military advisers.

In addition to the East African and Indian campaigns, a third Portuguese offensive was commanded by a naval officer whose name, more than any other, symbolized European conquest in the Indian Ocean: Afonso de Albuquerque. In rapid succession, this legendary commander took control of several Somali ports and two islands pivotal to trade—

Socotra, the multicultural gateway to the Red Sea, and Hormuz, guard dog of the Persian Gulf. Not for the last time would the latter, a parched scrap best known for its sand, stone, salt, and sulfur, vex a Western power. When the capable Albuquerque was called away to India to become viceroy, the inhabitants of Hormuz threw the Portuguese out and forced him to recapture it several years later.

The Portuguese enterprise in the Indian Ocean did not run smoothly. When Albuquerque arrived in India in 1508, Almeida refused to recognize his commission and clapped him in irons for several months before another fleet arrived from Portugal with documents confirming his appointment. Wealthy, powerful, and hostile Calicut resisted conquest, and Cochin, already in Portuguese hands, proved inadequate as a harbor. Albuquerque's eye finally settled on the island of Goa, which he subdued in 1510; there, he established the headquarters of the *Estado da Índia,* the name given to the entirety of the Portuguese colonial empire in Asia and Africa.

Next, Aden had to be secured. It proved to be a thorn in Albuquerque's side, and ultimately, a stake through the *Estado*'s heart. Built on top of an extinct volcano in a coastal cordillera, the walled city commanded the "Gate of Sorrows," Bab el Mandeb, through which passed most of the Asian trade goods bound to Europe. From Abyssinia, across the strait, came slaves, ivory, coffee, and the city's food; through a gap in the mountains to the east came incense and the finest Arabian horses. Northbound cargoes sailed in large, deep draft vessels that called at Jeddah, halfway up the Red Sea. There, the huge cargoes of pepper, cloves, nutmeg, fine Gujarati cottons, Chinese silks and porcelains, and other exotic goods were transferred to smaller ships capable of negotiating the shallows and reefs of the sea's northern half and the Gulf of Suez.[52]

Even though the Portuguese controlled many of the Indian spice centers and Hormuz, they did not command Aden. Thus, supple Muslim and Hindu mariners could easily bypass the Iberian strongholds and sail up the unguarded Red Sea to Egypt: no Aden, no Portuguese spice monopoly.

Albuquerque never conquered it. Initially, he calculated that possession of the island of Socotra was adequate to blockade Bab el Mandeb, but it proved too distant from the strait for the purpose. He abandoned Socotra just a few years after its capture, and in 1513 finally mounted a direct assault on Aden itself. It failed miserably. He then sailed up the

Red Sea before being forced by adverse winds to return to his viceregal duties in India. This unsuccessful foray into the Red Sea had been the first significant Western military presence in that vital waterway since the crusaders' brief mission from the north three centuries before in 1183 by Reginald of Châtillon. It would also be the last for more than three centuries thereafter.

Still, the viceroy dreamed of commanding Bab el Mandeb, if not at Aden, then from the island of Massawa on the Abyssinian side of the strait. Like Aden, and like every other strategic port in this part of the world, Massawa had long been in Muslim hands; it was captured from the Christian Abyssinians in the eighth century. If only he could seize Massawa, Albuquerque wrote to the king of Portugal in 1515, the island could be kept supplied, armed, and out of Muslim hands with the help of Prester John, who reigned nearby:

> We have no unsettled question left in India now but that of Aden and the Red Sea. May it please Our Lord that we should fix ourselves at Massawa—the port of Prester John.[53]

Albuquerque died three months after he wrote this letter. Having failed to capture Aden, the Portuguese settled for second best. They deployed from India a naval blockade of Bab el Mandeb with each winter monsoon, timed to the commercial and hajj traffic. But because of the great distance, the limited number of warships at their disposal, and the enormous expense of sending them, this seaborne embargo never succeeded.

The window of opportunity for a Portuguese spice monopoly finally closed in 1538, when the Ottomans annexed Aden. Historians have suggested that it was more profitable for Portuguese captains and colonial officials to turn a blind eye to Asian traders transiting the strait than exert total control. Command of a Portuguese fort at Aden, in contrast, would have been a scorching, dangerous, and thankless billet.[54]

Piri Reis, the great Ottoman admiral, was Albuquerque's Muslim counterpart. Unfortunately for the Portuguese, his career lasted far longer; during the decades of his service to the sultan, he ranged over the Red Sea, Indian Ocean, and Persian Gulf, harassing, outwitting, and outflanking his European rivals. He was publicly beheaded at age ninety by the

Ottoman governor of Basra after refusing to support hostilities against the Portuguese in the northern Persian Gulf.

The Ottoman admirals who followed Reis continued his tradition, raiding and occasionally conquering Portuguese bases from East Africa through South Arabia and Oman, and even on the Malabar Coast. On one occasion, a lone Turkish warship virtually ejected the Portuguese upstarts from their fortresses and trading posts in the Swahili-speaking ports of East Africa.[55] Neither the Iberians nor even the far more powerful Ottomans could control the maritime traffic between Asia and Europe. Soon enough, the Portuguese would find themselves challenged by new competitors.

In 1505, two young Portuguese cousins and minor aristocrats, Fernão de Magalhães and Francisco Serrão, decided to seek their fortunes in India and shipped out among the thousands of troops and sailors in Almeida's fleet. Their subsequent adventures, while fantastic to the modern ear, were typical of the era. Throughout their lives, they drew on each other's ideas and experiences. Eventually, they would alter the course of history.

Over the next several years, Magalhães fought in countless battles and was wounded in several, including the naval Battle of Cannanore in 1506, where Almeida succeeded in repelling an offensive by a combined fleet of the *zamorin* and the Mamluk sultan. On that occasion, Magalhães was invalided back home, but having tasted adventure and opportunity in the Orient, he found Portugal's atmosphere impoverished and stifling. Both he and Serrão returned to sea with the next India fleet.

Their expedition this time was much smaller than the fleet of 1505. That, however, did not lessen its importance, for the Portuguese king had charged its leader, Lopez de Sequeria, with no less than the establishment of trade with Malacca. What Aden was to the western end of the Indian Ocean, controlling the stream of goods to Europe, Egypt, and Turkey, Malacca was to the ocean's eastern end—the narrow funnel through which the bounty of the Spice Islands and the luxury products of China and Japan flowed. In April 1509, the flotilla arrived in Cochin, resupplied and repaired its ships, and on August 19 ventured east on the summer monsoon into waters unknown to European mariners. It arrived in Malacca just twenty-three days later, on September 11.

On that day, Portuguese and Asians alike must have experienced an uneasy mixture of amazement, anticipation, curiosity, and dread. Even the wonders of India could not have prepared the Europeans for the sparkling tropical beauty, the wealth, the massive fleets of trading ships, the thousands of merchants and shops, and the cultural diversity expressed in dozens of tongues in one of the greatest entrepôts of the era. To say nothing of the knowledge that all of it might soon be theirs, and of the terrible cost that might be paid for it. Malacca's aristocracy and merchant community, by the same token, had so far seen only a few Europeans— enough, however, to have heard about Portuguese brutality.

On the surface, all was serene and cordial. The delight of the Portuguese sailors who, after months of grim existence aboard ship and in the repair yard, now reveled in the succulent food, sweet drink, and exotic women of the world's most exciting port city, can only be imagined. Yet Garcia de Sousa, the captain of one of the five Portuguese ships bobbing lazily in the harbor, worried about the hundreds of smiling Malaccans clambering aboard the vessels from their small catamarans and bearing local goods for sale. Smelling an ambush, he sent his most experienced and reliable sailor, Magalhães, to the command vessel to warn Sequeria. When he got to Sequeria's ship, he found the captain playing chess and observed that behind each of the players was a native with a curved Malay knife—the deadly kris. He whispered a quiet warning to Sequeria, who in turn sent an observer aloft.

At that very moment, the attack signal, a puff of smoke, wafted up from the royal palace. The fleet was saved, but just barely; Sequeria, Magalhães, and the other Portuguese dispatched the Malays in the stateroom before they could effectively deploy their krises, threw the natives on deck overboard, and gunned down the approaching catamarans.

The crewmen lured onshore by Malacca's tropical delights were not so fortunate. Many ran, but to no avail, since the Malays had already stolen their boats. Only one of the Portuguese ashore that day survived: Francisco Serrão. Surrounded by natives intent on his imminent demise, he was plucked off the beach by his cousin Magalhães, who had come to his rescue in a rowboat. Soon after, the expedition's survivors sailed off in haste.

Heretofore, Magalhães had seen plenty of action and acquitted himself well, but his exploits did not qualify as exceptional for a simple sol-

dier of the *Estado da Índia*. The events at Malacca brought him com-
mendation and promotion. In 1510, Albuquerque himself commissioned
Magalhães as an officer, and he accompanied the viceroy's fleet, which
took Malacca the next year and thus captured a prize as rich as Constantinople or Venice. With their Western obsession with maritime choke
points, the Portuguese had instinctively grasped by the throat the rich trade
of China, Japan, and, of course, the Spice Islands, spread throughout the
larger Moluccan chain, about 1,800 miles due east of Malacca.

At this moment of supreme triumph, the two cousins went their separate ways. Magalhães had had enough. Wealthy from his share of the
spices and other booty taken at Malacca; his reputation ensured, or so he
thought; and still alive, he cashed in his chips and returned home in the
company of a Malay slave purchased in Malacca, of whom we shall hear
more later. Serrão, on the other hand, decided to spin fortune's wheel one
more time and took command of a ship in a three-vessel detachment from
Albuquerque's fleet, led by António de Abreu and bound for the Spice
Islands.

Abreu, Serrão, and their crews could hardly believe their great good
luck. At Banda and Amboina they filled their holds to bursting with
cloves, mace, and nutmeg bought for bracelets, bells, and other trinkets,
and quickly set sail for the return journey. But Abreu had been greedy.
He so overloaded the ships that one of them, the vessel commanded by
Serrão, broke apart and was stranded on a reef.[56] Valiantly, Serrão led
the survivors off and made it back to Amboina. Military procedure dictated that he return to Malacca with all deliberate speed and place himself at the disposal of the crown. But by this point, he, like his cousin,
had reached his limit. He had risked his skin for the greater glory of the
king once too often; the contrast between the rigors of service to the
crown and Amboina's tropical landscape and friendly inhabitants was
just too much for his tired flesh to bear. Never again to see Portugal, he
went native, and found employment as military adviser to the king of
Ternate and happiness with a young wife and a household full of children and slaves.

Serrão did not entirely cut his ties with home. First and foremost,
he continued to write to his cousin, to whom he owed his life. Centuries
before the Treaty of Berne and the establishment of the Universal Postal
Union, Serrão's letters somehow found their way back to Europe from a

land below the wind and beyond Western consciousness. Besides entreat-
ing his beloved cousin to return east to join him in his earthly paradise,
he also supplied detailed, accurate navigational and commercial data.
Before long, Magalhães knew more about the Spice Islands than almost
any other European, and he formulated a plan to exploit his knowledge.
In his last letter to his cousin Serrão, he promised to rejoin him, "if not
by Portugal, by another way."[57]

When Magalhães returned to Lisbon in 1512, he found himself a
stranger in his own home, an anonymous, unsung veteran of the colonial
wars, in a city bursting at the seams with the trappings of the spice trade's
fabulous wealth. Bored and uneasy as a low-level hanger-on at court, he
shipped out with the army to Morocco, where he saw more action and
received one more serious wound, this time a knee laceration that dis-
abled him for combat and left him with a permanent limp. Accused of
theft as a quartermaster and facing a court-martial, he slipped away to
Lisbon to argue his case before the king, Dom Manuel, who refused him
an audience and ordered him to return to Morocco for trial. He complied,
stood trial, and was cleared.

Like any self-respecting conquistador of the age, he trembled before no man, not even his monarch. Rather than keep his mouth shut and
collect his pension, this loyal subject, who had repeatedly confronted the
cruel demons of the era for king and country, yet again demanded an
audience from Dom Manuel. This time, it was granted. The confrontation probably took place in the same chamber where Dom Manuel's
cousin, João II, turned down Christopher Columbus. It would have the
same costly outcome for Portugal.

Unlike Columbus, Magalhães had in mind no grand scheme of discovery or conquest. He merely wanted a bump in his pitiful pension and
an elevation in his standing at court above the callow youths who now
lorded it over him. Magalhães also asked for the only post commensu-
rate with his bravery, his dedication to the crown, his ability, and his long
experience: command of a vessel bound for India.

Coldly refused on all three accounts, a stunned Magalhães asked
Manuel: since Portugal no longer needed his services, was he free to find
employment elsewhere? Manuel, who wished only to be rid of this brash,
demanding upstart, informed him that where he wound up was of little
consequence to Portugal.

Magalhães coolly remained at court for more than a year, biding his time and diligently scouring the royal library for useful information from the charts and logs of Portugal's most recent expeditions to Asia and Brazil. He was particularly interested in the South American coast.

He also formed a partnership with a brilliant geographer and astronomer, Ruy Falerio, who instantly recognized Magalhães's extraordinary skill set and repaired the one gap in it—his lack of navigational expertise. Which of the two men concocted the plan for the first successful circumnavigation of the globe remains a mystery, but somehow they deduced the presence of a "southern strait" at the extreme end of South America, at about forty degrees south latitude, which like the Cape of Good Hope led to the Indies, but from the opposite direction.

Like Columbus's underestimation of the earth's circumference, Magalhães's placement of this passage was overly optimistic; the straits that would be named for him and the cape below them lay a brutal thousand miles beyond a relatively balmy, calm forty degrees. Similar to Columbus's miscalculation, this inaccuracy gave Magalhães the courage to proceed with his plan.[58] Finally, like Columbus, Fernão Magalhães found support and encouragement in the court of Spain, where he had changed his name to a Castilian spelling and pronunciation: Fernando de Magallanes, or, as he is known in the English-speaking world, Ferdinand Magellan.

This time around, the Spanish crown was easier to convince. Two decades before, the Treaty of Tordesillas had moved the demarcation line eight hundred miles to the west of the original papal line in order to protect Portuguese claims in Africa. Magellan told the Spanish that Portugal would now have to pay the piper; since the treaty bisected the globe, the dividing line in the eastern hemisphere had also moved eight hundred miles to the west, to what is now about 135 degrees east longitude. In Magellan's considered opinion, this shifted the Spice Islands into the Spanish zone. Within a few months of his arrival in Spain in the fall of 1517, he had secured backing for his plan, and two years later his multinational crew launched into the Atlantic on the most astonishing, and nearly the most deadly, of all the voyages of discovery.

Only thirty-one of the approximately 265 men—those who were not killed by the Filipinos, the Portuguese, or scurvy, or who did not desert—completed the circumnavigation. In one of history's saddest coincidences, the two cousins were killed within several weeks and several hundred miles of each other: Magellan by Filipino spears on the beach at Mactan, and Serrão by poison at the hands of a local sultan after becoming embroiled in an ancient rivalry between the two main clove islands, Ternate and Tidore.

The most remarkable tale of the circumnavigation concerns a slave, "Enrique of Malacca," brought back to Lisbon by Magellan in 1512. Having served his master in the Atlantic and Pacific during the circumnavigation, he had been promised freedom on his master's death. Angered when he was not manumitted after Magellan was killed, he escaped. Although his birthplace and subsequent history are unknown, he probably became the first man to circle the globe.

Of the five vessels that began the circumnavigation, only two, manned, almost literally, by skeleton crews and guided by captured local pilots, finally reached Tidore. Their crews loaded the holds so full of cloves that the sultan (the same one who had poisoned Serrão), observing how low to the water the vessels were set, recommended against firing farewell salutes for fear the shock would rupture their hulls.

Only one of these two vessels, the *Victoria,* completed the circumnavigation. Yet the twenty-six tons of cloves it had loaded in Tidore paid for the entire expedition.[59] The king of Spain awarded the commander who guided the crippled ship back to Spain, Juan Sebastián de Elcano, a pension and a coat of arms of two cinnamon sticks, three nutmegs, and a dozen cloves.

In the early sixteenth century, who controlled these tiny volcanic scraps was a matter of life and death to Spain and Portugal, and when the news reached Lisbon that Magellan had sailed on his mission, Dom Manuel feared that Portugal's fabulously profitable lock on the spice trade was at risk. He panicked. Since Magellan's route was a well-kept secret, and it was not even known whether the Spanish vessels were heading east or west, Manuel knew not where to send his ships. So he scattered them from Argentina to the Cape of Good Hope to Malacca in hopes of locating the Spanish fleet. The Portuguese eventually found just one of Magellan's ships, the *Trinidad,* which, in need of more extensive repairs at Tidore than the *Victoria,* had missed the winter monsoon and was then forced to attempt a suicidal easterly return across the Pacific. On reaching the latitude of northern Japan, its shattered crew gave up and returned to the Moluccas, where they were captured and imprisoned by the Portuguese, who had arrived too late to catch the *Victoria*. Only four of the *Trinidad*'s original sailors eventually made it back to Spain.

Manuel needn't have worried. Although the Spanish did leave a small trading post on Tidore, the pilots on the *Trinidad* and *Victoria* had by that point probably realized that Magellan and Falerio's original computation had been incorrect; the Spice Islands lay, regrettably, in the Portuguese zone. (So did the Philippines, an inconvenience that Philip II of Spain rectified in 1565 by invading the islands.) It would be another 250 years before longitude could be measured accurately enough to know for sure, and by that time, nutmeg, mace, and cloves had become so commonplace and cheap that it no longer mattered.

The Spanish crown, on learning of the harrowing journey, realized that even the long, deadly, and expensive Cape route was a cake walk compared to circumnavigation. The Portuguese, who controlled the Cape route, thus held an insuperable advantage over the Spanish. In the end, diplomatic requirements and the high cost of sending ships to the Spice Islands put paid to the Spanish attempt at the spice trade. Charles V of Spain had just married the sister of the new Portuguese king, João III, and so needed to maintain friendly relations with Portugal. In addition, Spain's military adventures kept it chronically in debt. Needing both cash and peace on its western border, in 1529 Spain sold its claims in the Spice Islands to Portugal for 350,000 ducats.[60]

The Portuguese, though freed from Spanish competition, still had to face the Asian trading powers. Portugal, with its tiny population and limited resources, could not cope with the enormous task of policing the entire Indian Ocean. Even within the relatively small confines of the Spice Islands, there were too many spice-bearing trees, too many beaches, too many native catamarans, and too many corrupt *Estado* officials willing to turn a blind eye for a few gold coins or a few sacks of nutmeg. As a result, Portugal, hopelessly strapped for manpower, could manage just one dilapidated trading post in the Moluccas. Consequently, only about one-eighth of the cloves unloaded in Europe traveled in Portuguese bottoms.[61] Cinnamon was even harder to monopolize, and pepper proved impossible, since the latter grew not only over the entire length of the Western Ghats, but in Sumatra as well.

Portugal's only realistic chance of stopping Muslim ships, their hulls packed tight with spices, from reaching Egypt, and ultimately Europe, was to blockade the Red Sea. This, as we've already seen, it could not do. During the first decades after Almeida and Albuquerque established their bases in the western Indian Ocean, the Portuguese did appear to impede traffic through Bab el Mandeb. Even so, *Estado* officials and naval officers were easily corrupted. As one Venetian diplomat observed, spices were

> allowed to pass by the Portuguese soldiers who govern . . . the Red Sea for their profit against the command of their King, for [the Portuguese soldiers] can make a living only in that region by selling cinnamon, cloves, nutmeg, mace, ginger, pepper, and other drugs.[62]

It was to be expected that Venice would charge its diplomats with keeping tabs on the Portuguese, who were, in the words of Tomé Pires, in the process of applying their cold and greedy hands to its long, slender throat, at Malacca and elsewhere. Venetian merchants had reacted with horror at the news of da Gama's return to Portugal, and at first saw their worst fears confirmed: Venice's spice trade did plummet, by perhaps as much as three-fourths, in the decades following 1498. The falloff was not, however, the result of a Portuguese blockade. Rather, large amounts of spices were now flowing around the Cape to Lisbon, then onward to Antwerp, the main Habsburg trading hub in an increasingly prosperous northern Europe. When da Gama left Lisbon on his first voyage in 1497, Europeans consumed less than two million pounds of pepper per year. By 1560, this amount had grown to between six and seven million pounds.[63]

Perhaps even more detrimental to the Venetian spice trade than competition from the Cape route was the deterioration in relations between Venice and the ever-expanding Ottomans. During the first few decades of the sixteenth century, the Turks drove the swift Venetian galleys, which carried luxury goods throughout the western Mediterranean, off the high seas.[64] Even so, only briefly during the first flush of Portuguese expansion immediately after 1500 did the flow of spices to Egypt completely dry up.[65] Otherwise, Venetian merchants found that they could always find spices piled high and offered at fair prices in Cairo and Alexandria— if they could but get there.

By the 1560s, Venice had reestablished trade with the Turks. With Bab el Mandeb, the Red Sea, and Egypt itself under the thumb of the Ottoman Empire, and with demand for luxury goods burgeoning in Europe, more pepper may have flowed through Venice than before da Gama opened the Cape route. Venice was not alone in mending fences in Constantinople; France and the German kingdoms were also on good terms with the Ottomans, and their ships soon began to muscle Venetian galleys aside.[66]

Just as the Venetians worried about the Portuguese, the Portuguese fretted about the power of the Islamic trading network. Today, it is difficult to imagine that in the sixteenth century, Portugal's greatest single rival in the Indian Ocean was the western Sumatran city-state of Aceh, now best known as the remote, underdeveloped victim of the tsunami of 2004. In the mid-1500s, however, it was a commercial powerhouse, the beneficiary of the seafaring tradition that had spread its Austronesian ancestors across most of the Indian and Pacific oceans. Aceh also had a head start from its thirteenth-century adoption of Islam, which appealed to Asian merchants eager to avoid dealing with the heathen Portuguese at Malacca. The rise of Aceh largely explains Portugal's difficulties in controlling the Indian Ocean. Asian vessels avoided Malacca and Goa, as they would avoid any port ruled by a corrupt, grasping sultanate, and instead favored entrepôts offering the merchant an honest deal. In the mid-sixteenth century, Aceh filled the bill perfectly.[67]

Aceh was influential throughout the Indian Ocean and beyond. At the eastern end of its trading range, it competed successfully with Portugal in the Spice Islands and terrorized Malacca with repeated deadly raids mounted from swift oared craft. At the western end, Aceh's close relations with the Ottoman Empire froze the Portuguese with fear.

During the medieval period, spies loitered around wharves and warehouses in the same way that agents cased missile and nuclear facilities during the Cold War. In 1546, two Portuguese agents stationed in Venice sent back word that 650,000 pounds of spices—enough to supply Europe for approximately a month and destined for Venice—had landed in Cairo. Much of this cargo came from Aceh, which each year exported west as much as seven million pounds of pepper—approximately equal to the entirety of European consumption. Even if some was bound for the Ottoman Empire, this suggests that Aceh, and thus Venice, may have controlled more of the Indian Ocean spice trade than Portugal.[68]

Portuguese agents reported that "These Acehnese are those who most frequent this commerce and navigation," and that because of them, spice markets everywhere were glutted and prices were falling. The Portuguese spies also noted that the Acehnese had sent ambassadors to the Ottoman sultan in Constantinople and requested expert gunsmiths in exchange for pearls, diamonds, and rubies. According to one Portuguese observer, the Acehnese sultan Ri'ayat Shah al-Kahhar "never turned over in his bed without thinking how he could encompass the destruction of Malacca."[69]

The Portuguese recognized that unless they disrupted the Aceh-Ottoman-Venice trading axis, their spice empire would wither. They laid grand plans to clear the Red Sea and to invade Aceh; for the latter task, they would need the cooperation of the Manila fleet of the hated Spaniards. All came to naught; the Portuguese simply did not have the manpower, the ships, or the money to retain control of the spice trade. One Portuguese observer noted that Javanese ships freely carried cloves, nutmeg, and mace through the Strait of Malacca to Aceh, where "we cannot stop them doing, as we have no fleet in those parts to prevent them."[70] Worse, an alternative route south of Sumatra, then north through the Sunda Strait (between Sumatra and Java) lay entirely beyond the reach of the Portuguese.

As Portugal's dominance of the spice trade gradually deteriorated during the sixteenth century, things were looking up for it, at least temporarily, farther east. Occasionally, the human urge to trade takes a backseat to war and racism. For centuries, trade between China and Japan had been stunted by the latter's piracy and coastal raiding. Ming emperors forbade any commercial relations with the "dwarf empire"—Japan—drying up the export market for the silver from Japanese mines. With the loss of their export markets, Japanese silver miners saw prices, and their incomes, fall. Further, although the Japanese produced silk, they greatly preferred the Chinese product, which, again, because of the embargo, commanded spectacularly high prices in Japan.[71] But if China and Japan could not do business with each other, each could at least do business with the Portuguese.

And what a business it was! Almost immediately after Albuquerque conquered Malacca in 1511, the Portuguese began trading actively with China. After just a decade, they attempted to conquer Canton, but were fended off by small Ming coastal vessels. In 1557, they gained a toehold at Macao, which they would rule for almost half a millennium.

Around the same time that the *Estado da Índia* established itself in Macao, Portuguese merchants also began trading in the southern Japanese island of Kyushu. The huge amount of silver carried from Japan into Macao harbor by one ship, captained by Vasco da Gama's son Duarte, electrified the Portuguese trading community in China. One member recounted:

> Ten or twelve days ago a Great Ship from Japan arrived here, and she came so richly laden that now all the other Portuguese and ships which are in China intend to go to Japan, and they wish to winter here on the China coast so that they may be able to leave for Japan next May, which is the season for the monsoon for voyaging thither.[72]

The Portuguese had hit a jackpot on a par with the spice trade, and in 1571 the *Estado* established permanent port facilities—run by Jesuits—at Nagasaki to exploit it. Initially, the crown awarded licenses to conduct voyages from India to both Japan and Macao as gifts to Portuguese officials or officers for meritorious service. Portugal quickly appreciated the potential of the Japan-China trade in silver and silk and strove to extract maximum advantage: it would license a limited number of ships (one per year at first, slowly increasing to several per year during the early seventeenth century) to ply this route. The licensee paid tens of thousands of cruzados (a cruzado being roughly the same as a ducat, or about $80 in modern value) for this privilege, and in return he would stuff his vessel to the gunwales with raw and finished silk in Macao and silver at Nagasaki. Local merchants at either end awaited this "great ship," and both ports became wealthy from the expeditions. Returns from a single round-trip were estimated at two hundred thousand ducats—more than half of what Portugal had paid Spain to permanently relinquish its claims to all of the Spice Islands.

Initially, the ships were about the same size as the typical merchantman of the period, usually a carrack of about five hundred tons. As the sixteenth century gave way to the seventeenth, they grew into behemoths of up to two thousand tons, the largest seagoing vessels of the era. Portuguese merchants, who accompanied the goods and actually accomplished the trade, presumably paid off the license-holding captain-major. An early Dutch visitor to Japan recorded this account of events following the arrival of a "great ship" at Nagasaki:

The ship coming from Macau usually has about 200 or more merchants on board who go ashore at once, each one of them taking a house wherein to lodge with his servants and slaves. They take no heed of what they spend and nothing is too costly for them, and sometimes they disburse in the seven or eight months that they stay in Nagasaki more than 250,000 or 300,000 [ounces of silver], through which the populace profit greatly. This is one of the reasons why they are still very friendly to them.[73]

As occurred elsewhere in Asia, the Portuguese were eventually undone by an excess of religious zeal. The early Tokugawa shoguns, having come to power just after the establishment of the "great ship" trade, were none too pleased with the increasing conversions by the Jesuits who infiltrated Kyushu from Nagasaki. After the Christian-led Shimabara rebellion of 1637–1638, the Tokugawa threw the missionaries out. When a Portuguese delegation arrived from Macao to appeal the decision, its members were beheaded.[74]

The "great ship" trade aside, the Portuguese could not effectively control the maritime commerce of the Indies. They were thus forced to protect, and at times even raid. Their protection racket was named after the *cartaz,* or pass, which Asian vessels were coerced into buying, and without which they were subject to seizure and worse.

The Portuguese did not have the muscle to enforce even the *cartaz* system. The pass, which itself sold for a nominal price, merely served as a device to force Asian ships to call at Portuguese-controlled ports where customs duties were collected. For example, in 1540 a Gujarati ship was seized because the final destination in the Persian Gulf, as specified in its *cartaz,* was inconsistent with its position far out in the Indian Ocean. That the customs duties were low—about 6 percent of cargo value—was itself evidence of Portugal's inability to control Indian Ocean shipping.[75] Although Asian merchants grudgingly purchased *cartazes* along the Hormuz-Gujarat-Malabar-Malacca route, they quickly learned that even this was not necessary when they sailed directly between Aden and Aceh. This route, which could be spanned in a single monsoon, was too far south to be reached by Portuguese patrols.[76]

Although the crown and its favored merchant elite made fabulous profits from the spice, silk, and silver trades, Portugal still went broke in the grand Iberian tradition: through court extravagance and the crushing expense of military adventurism. Even today, that one of Europe's tiniest kingdoms could deploy a blue-water navy all the way from Brazil east to Macao defies the imagination; Portugal's demand that Malabar commercial hubs such as Calicut, which was not under its control, expel all Muslim traders bordered on the surreal.

Perhaps had Portugal thrown its resources into trade, instead of an expensive protection racket of *cartazes,* war fleets, and fortified harbors, it could have sent enough spices, silk, fine cotton, porcelain, and pearls around the Cape to make it Europe's wealthiest nation. The royal family and its favored merchants and captains earned fabulous wealth from the spice trade, but the nation itself was bankrupted by the staggering military expenses of a global empire. Portugal became known as the "Indies of the Genoese," chronically in debt and beholden to Italian merchants and German banks run by the Fugger family, the kingdom's major creditors.[77]

Even during the sixteenth century, Portugal was an impoverished nation of subsistence farmers with little excess capital or functioning credit markets with which to provision the expeditions with ships, sailors, silver, and trade goods. The Portuguese were so short of cash that often, having paid the inevitable price in men and ships, they lacked the silver and trade goods with which to purchase spices when their fleets finally arrived in the Indies. For example, on one occasion in 1523, several decades before other Europeans were able to challenge the Portuguese in Asia, the royal trading post on Ternate simply did not have the wherewithal, even at the low prices prevailing in the Moluccas, to purchase a large shipment of cloves.[78] Instead, the cargo was bought by a private Portuguese merchant. When the Dutch appeared eighty years later with bales of fine Flemish fabric and chests of silver coins, local pepper and spice merchants flocked to them. It did not go unnoticed in Amsterdam, Madrid, and Lisbon that most of the silver coins carried by the Dutch had been minted in Mexico City and Lima by Spain.

To make matters worse, even though a soldier in the *Estado* could rise through the ranks to wealth and power, as did Francisco Serrão, the path was long and hard, and the outcome capricious. Not only did the *Estado* discourage capable men like his cousin Magellan, but appointments to high office lasted just three years. Those ambitious, brave, and lucky enough to earn such positions (or rich enough in the first place to buy them) were compelled to make the best of their limited tenure, squeezing local traders, their own troops, and the crown itself in a thirty-six month frenzy of self-dealing.

When Serrão came to Ternate in 1512 after his vessel sank, the sultan treated him almost as a deity, for the ruler had prophesized that "men of iron" would arrive from afar to aid Ternate in its struggle with other sultanates, particularly Tidore. A decade later, Tidore welcomed Magellan's men for exactly the same reason. When the Spanish left, the Portuguese burned down the Tidoran royal palace as a punishment for cooperating with their Iberian brethren.

Over the following decades, the Portuguese cursed the northern Moluccas with a series of increasingly brutal governors. One, Jorge de Menese, ordered his troops to pillage Ternate when a supply ship did not arrive. When the Ternatans, defending themselves, killed some of his men, he took a local official hostage, supposedly as security against further violence. Without provocation, Menese had the man's hands cut off, his arms tied behind his back, then set upon with dogs. The victim somehow managed to escape into the water, where he grasped the canines one by one with his teeth and drowned them before slipping below the waves himself.

Portuguese missionary zeal did not sit well with the Islamic sultans on the islands. They became increasingly alarmed at the Jesuits' success in converting commoners, who were reported to be highly susceptible to both church ritual and the church's protection from the rapacious Muslim Ternatan rulers.[79] By the mid-1530s, the Portuguese had managed the impossible: Ternate and Tidore were now allied, along with neighboring kingdoms, in revolt against the European presence. The central character in this drama was Sultan Hairun of Ternate. Placed on the throne as a puppet by the Portuguese in 1546, he found himself in and out of power over the next quarter century at their whim, even spending several years in Goa as an involuntary guest of the *Estado*.[80] Although Hairun had at first considered Christianity, he gradually turned against the cruelty of the Portuguese. This revulsion reinforced his Islamic identity, which in turn gained him the support of other Moluccan Muslims.

Events came to a head when the Portuguese assassinated Hairun in 1570. He was succeeded by his son Babullah, who swore to avenge his father's death. He soon became a rallying point for Muslim leaders throughout, and even beyond, the Moluccas. The insurrection acquired an increasingly Islamic flavor. Alarmed Jesuits reported that imams from as far away as Aceh and Turkey were exhorting the faithful to seek their heavenly reward through jihad in the archipelago. The Moluccans proved themselves every bit as vicious as the Europeans, ripping babies from the wombs of local Christian women, then chopping both mother and child to bits. The revolt swept the Portuguese from much of the area. Babullah's forces overran the *Estado*'s fort in 1575 and converted it into a royal palace. At the time of his death in 1583, Babullah ruled over much of the Spice Islands, becoming hugely wealthy in the process.

It is easy to draw the obvious modern connection—a jihadist uprising uniting traditional enemies against a distant Christian power attempting to control a strategic commodity—but the situation in the Moluccas during the late sixteenth century was more complex. Most strikingly, the Moluccas warmly greeted other Europeans as potential allies against the Portuguese. The first was Francis Drake, who in the course of his circumnavigation conferred extensively with Babullah in 1579. Drake gave a detailed description of his extensive kingdom, which leaves no doubt that the sultan, with a love of luxury and over a hundred wives and concubines, was not the most devout of Muslims. Twenty years later, the first expeditions from Holland arrived, and Babullah and his successors also courted these newcomers as a counterweight to the hated Portuguese.[81] Alas, the Dutch would soon prove even more brutal.

Portugal exploited not only Asians but also its own citizens. So miserable was the life of the common soldier that soon after arriving in India, thousands fled the ranks for monasteries. Portuguese recruits often went without shelter and during the monsoon season could be seen begging naked by the roadside.[82] The tens of thousands who died of tropical diseases and malnutrition in the Royal Hospital at Goa may well have been the lucky ones.

Ultimately, events in northern Europe sealed the fate of the Portuguese spice empire. The early seventeenth century would see a struggle for wealth and power among three nations—Portugal, Spain, and the Netherlands—whose newly acquired mastery of the earth's wind systems allowed them to compete both commercially and militarily over a planet completely encircled by trade routes.

8

A WORLD ENCOMPASSED

In June 1635, the Spanish barbers (that is, bloodletters) of Mexico City protested to the viceroy about the presence of Chinese barbers there. The viceroy referred the matter to the city council, which in its turn recommended to the viceroy that he limit the number of Asian barbershops to twelve, and that they be restricted to the suburbs, as was the practice with foreign merchants in Spain. Exactly what the viceroy eventually decided is not known.[1]

Less than a generation later, in 1654, twenty-three Portuguese-speaking Dutch Jews arrived in New Amsterdam—supposedly the first of their religion to come to North America. The Dutch governor of the city, Peter Stuyvesant, tried to deport them, but his bosses—in the West India Company, not in the Dutch government—allowed them to stay. The Company's decision carried restrictions: the Jews could not engage in business on their own, and "The poor among them should not become a burden to the Company or the community but be supported by their own nation."[2] That they arrived from Brazil on a French ship attracted no particular notice.

Nearly three centuries later, in 1931, an eleven-year-old Australian boy took an afternoon walk along sand dunes near the beach about sixty miles north of Perth. He came across forty silver Spanish coins dating to the same era as the Chinese barbers and Dutch-Portuguese Jewish immigrants. Not until 1963 would spearfishers several miles offshore come across the mother lode of this booty—the shipwreck of the *Vergulde Draek* ("Gilt Dragon"), a ship of the Dutch East India Company containing thousands of coins, which had sailed from Holland in 1655.

How, in the middle of the seventeenth century, had Chinese barbers gotten to Mexico City? What, less than two decades later, were a shipload of Jewish Portuguese-speakers from Holland doing in Brazil? Why was the West India Company, a privately held concern, making government policy decisions in New Amsterdam? And how, nearly a century before Australia was "discovered" by Captain James Cook, did a Dutch ship full of Spanish silver coins come to rest on the seabed off its far western edge?

Answering these four questions tells us a great deal about the remarkable worldwide expansion of the global economy that began in the wake of the voyages of discovery. In doing so, we shall expose the roots of today's globalization and its discontents. But first, we must understand five things.

First, within a few decades of Columbus's second voyage in 1493, the exchange of crop species such as corn, wheat, coffee, tea, and sugar between continents had revolutionized the world's agricultural and labor markets. The changes did not always improve the human condition.

Second, by the early seventeenth century, Spanish and Dutch mariners had decoded the last great secrets of the planetary wind machine, allowing them to cross the vast expanses of the world's oceans with relative ease. By 1650, goods of all kinds and people of all nations ranged over most of the globe.

Third, the discovery of huge silver deposits in Peru and Mexico produced a new global monetary system (along with a fearsome inflation caused by the coining of too much silver money). The most common piece of currency, the Spanish eight-real coin, was as ubiquitous as the American hundred-dollar bill and the Visa card are today.

Fourth, the seventeenth century saw the rise of a completely new trading order—the publicly held joint-stock corporation. These organizations had considerable advantages over what had preceded them: individual peddlers, their families, and royal monopolies. Large corporations soon came to dominate global commerce, a position they have not since relinquished.

Finally, change always makes some people unhappy. In the new global economy of the sixteenth and seventeenth centuries, textile manufacturers, farmers, and service workers were all hurt by cheaper and better products from abroad. They were just as vociferous then as French farmers and American autoworkers are today.

To untangle the mystery of the Chinese barbers in Mexico, we must delve a little more deeply into the history of silk. Sometime around 3000 BC, the first woven fragments, red-dyed ribbons and threads, appear in the

Chinese archaeological record. Chinese myth credits Lady His-Ling, who lived around 2650 BC and was the chief wife of the emperor, with discovering the fabric when she rescued a cocoon that had accidentally dropped from a mulberry tree into a cup of hot tea.

Unlike nutmeg and clove trees, which grow in only a few habitats and climates, the silkworm and the mulberry tree thrive in many locales. Sooner or later, the Chinese were bound to lose their monopoly on silk production. Amazingly, this did not happen until the Han-Roman trade explosion of 200 BC to AD 200, when the blind and almost immobile worms were transplanted to Korea and Japan. They then traveled west toward central Asia, the Middle East, and Europe along both the overland and the maritime routes.

In the sixth century after Christ, the Byzantine emperor Justinian gave two monks the task of procuring the treasured worms from China. (It was not necessary to purloin mulberry trees, since various species already grew throughout Eurasia.) At great peril, they eventually succeeded, and their feat gave rise to a vigorous silk industry in Spain and Italy.[3] Not all the European efforts at sericulture did as well; a nascent silk industry in England fizzled in its cold, wet climate. Nor did silkworms thrive in England's American colonies. The Spanish had only slightly better luck in Mexico, where almost from the time of Cortés, Eurasian silkworms produced a coarse, inferior fabric.

By the late sixteenth century, Spain had given up on its attempt to eject the Portuguese from the Spice Islands and retreated north to the Philippines. When the Spanish founded Manila in 1579, within relatively easy sailing range of south China, they eclipsed these meager European and American efforts at sericulture. Almost instantly, an immensely profitable trade in New World silver and oriental silk exploded over the unimaginable expanse of the Pacific Ocean. This semicircular route, shown in the map on page 201, pushed the limits of the era's maritime technology.

In order to understand how Spanish ships made this twenty thousand-mile round-trip, the earth's prevailing wind patterns must be understood. Mariners had for centuries harnessed the Indian Ocean monsoons, but away from Asia these seasonal phenomena play only bit roles, overshadowed by two main wind systems, both of which blow constantly through-

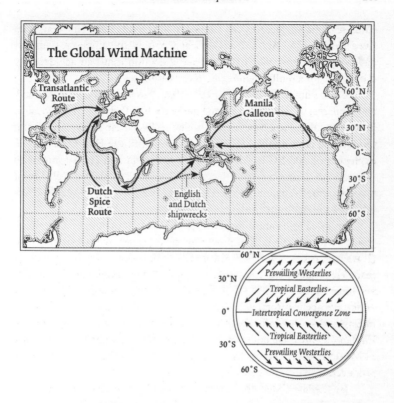

The Global Wind Machine

Transatlantic Route

Manila Galleon

Dutch Spice Route

English and Dutch shipwrecks

60°N
30°N
0°
30°S
60°S

60°N
30°N
0°
30°S
60°S

Prevailing Westerlies
Tropical Easterlies
Intertropical Convergence Zone
Tropical Easterlies
Prevailing Westerlies

out the year. The first system, taken advantage of by Columbus, and even more spectacularly by Magellan, blows from east to west in the tropical latitudes (or, more accurately, from the northeast above the equator, and from the southeast below it). The second system blows in the opposite direction—from west to east—in the temperate latitudes, most strongly between forty and fifty degrees latitude in both the northern and southern hemispheres (roughly even with Venice and the southern tip of New Zealand, respectively).[4]

The *Trinidad,* from Magellan's expedition, was the first to sail this high-latitude wind system across the Pacific during its ill-fated attempt to flee eastward in 1522. In 1565, two ships from another Spanish expedition—one under the command of Alonso de Arellano, and another,

two months later, under Friar Andrés de Urdaneta—became the first to
ride the west-to-east system completely across the northern Pacific in the
course of their twelve-thousand-mile journeys from Manila to Acapulco.
They covered the distance in just four months.[5]

These two ships were the forerunners of the annual "Manila galleons." Once a year, a treasure flotilla from Mexico, usually consisting of
two large merchantmen, weighed down with silver and guarded by a
heavily armed galleon, ventured westward along the equatorial route,
pioneered by Magellan, to Manila. The silver was exchanged for oriental
luxury goods, mainly high-quality Chinese silk, which had been brought
in junks from the southern coast of the Ming Empire to the Philippines,
and then shipped on the Manila galleon east to Acapulco.

In this manner, the Spanish wealth of Croesus was exchanged for
the sublime luxuries of the East. In 1677 an Irish friar, Thomas Gage, wrote
of Mexico City, "Both men and women are excessive in their apparel,
using more silks than stuffs and cloths." He was amazed at the thousands
of coaches cruising back and forth across the colonial city's fabled main
street, the Alameda, which were "full of gallants, ladies, and citizens, to
see and be seen, to court and to be courted." In the jewelry district, "A
man's eyes may behold in less than an hour many millions worth of gold,
silver, pearls, and jewels."[6]

The discovery of the "silver mountain" at Potosí in the colony of
Peru (now in modern-day Bolivia) occurred nearly simultaneously with
that of the ground-level Mexican silver veins at Guanajuato (in 1547 and
1548, respectively). The same excesses played out in Lima as in Mexico
City. In the Calle de Mercaderes ("Street of Merchants") in Lima, luxuries could be purchased in dozens of grand shops, some of which were
said to contain goods worth over one million silver pesos. In 1602, the
viceroy of Peru wrote to Philip III:

> All these people live most luxuriously. All wear silk, and of the most
> fine and costly quality. The gala dresses and clothes of the women
> are so many and so excessive that in no other kingdom of the world
> are found such.[7]

This vast redistribution of wealth jolted an already turbulent global
economy. As always, there were losers as well as winners. Who was

hurt? The Spanish barbers of Mexico City saw themselves as victims, exposed to a seventeenth-century version of unfair competition from cheap immigrant labor. They assured the viceroy that their desire to exclude the Chinese bloodletters was based only on the national interest. They sought merely to protect the public health from the inferior ethics and ability of their Chinese counterparts, noting that whereas the Europeans had "with so much diligence . . . cared for the prevalent sicknesses," many having died in the process, "the supposition is that these Chinese are of no benefit."[8]

Far larger interests were being hurt, of course, than a few Spanish barbers. Foremost among them were the Spanish and Mexican silk industries, which could not compete in either price or quality with the bales of Chinese fabric conveyed by the Manila galleon to Acapulco.

In 1581 direct voyages between Manila and Peru commenced; the very next year the Spanish crown, at the behest of Spain's silk growers, forbade such shipments. But merchants and bureaucrats alike in Lima and Mexico City routinely ignored crown edicts, and this one was no exception. In a futile effort to stop the trade between Manila and Peru, the edict was repeated in 1593, 1595, and 1604.

In 1611, the viceroy in Mexico City, under pressure from producers in and around Puebla, just southeast of the capital, argued unsuccessfully that the Manila galleon trade should be forbidden entirely. Spanish and Mexican silk producers even saw the coastal commerce between Peru and Mexico as a threat, fearing that Chinese silk, once unloaded in Mexico from the East, might be transshipped to Peru, or if smuggled into Peru from Manila, reshipped to Mexico. At their behest, the crown, amazingly, prohibited trade between its two biggest New World colonies: "Therefore, we order and command the viceroys of Peru and New Spain [Mexico] to prohibit and suppress, without fail, this commerce and trade between both kingdoms."[9] As with the ban on Manila-Peru traffic, this unenforceable edict was reissued, in this case no fewer than five times after its original proclamation in 1604.

Trade diasporas soon formed around the Filipino-Mexican trade in silk and silver. Silk merchants from both the Philippines and Mexico crossed the Pacific to establish trade colonies. Those who had settled in the Philippines, called Manileños, struck first, sailing east to Mexico and making vast middleman profits from their warehouse stores in Acapulco and the capital. The Mexican merchants then turned the tables by sending their own agents west to Manila.

Once again, established interests objected. The Manileños saw themselves as the founders and rightful beneficiaries of the silk trade. Unhappy at the loss of their monopoly with the arrival of the upstart Mexicans in Manila, they complained to the governor of the Philippines. As the Spanish barbers had done before them and generations of protectionists would do after them, the Manileños attempted to state their case in terms of the national interest: "One of the things which has ruined this land is the large consignments of money which rich persons in Mexico send here."[10] The crown responded with an easily evaded edict prohibiting the sending of money and agents from Mexico; its ineffectiveness was underscored by its repeated reissuance over subsequent decades.

The Spanish in the Philippines got not only their silk exports from China, but also their food staples and labor, both in short supply in the new Asian colony. Colonial authorities established Parián, just outside Manila, as a residence for Chinese immigrants, and within a few decades more than twenty thousand Chinese were living there. In 1628, the Spanish governor admitted of the Chinese, "There is no Spaniard, secular or religious, who obtains his food, clothing, or shoes, except through them."[11] Wealthy Manileño merchants, Mexican agents, and colonial officials all acquired Chinese servants, many of whom made their way from Parián to Acapulco on the Manila galleon. Hence the protectionist reaction to Mexico City's Chinese barbers, four centuries before cheap Asian electronics and riots at meetings of the World Trade Organization.

North America's first Jews came an even greater distance. Their story begins in 1496, when King Manuel I of Portugal issued an ultimatum to them—convert or leave. Many departed for Amsterdam. (The Jews who converted and stayed became known as *cristãos novos*—new Christians—and many of them served the *Estado* in the East. Manuel extended to the Jews the medieval version of "Don't ask, don't tell"; thus those who remained and did not convert should have been protected from inquiry until 1534. But Manuel's offer was a ruse; in 1504 and 1505 many were slaughtered.) When, a hundred years later, Portugal and Holland battled for control of long-distance trade, Portuguese Jews in Holland found themselves at the center of the conflict. In Asia, this struggle revolved around spices; in the New World, another cargo took center stage: sugar.

Today sugar, a bulk commodity, sells so cheaply that it is given scarcely a second thought: the average American today consumes sixty-six pounds per year; the average European consumes eighty-seven pounds. Yet during the medieval period, it was considered a "fine" spice, as rare and expensive as cloves, nutmeg, mace, and cinnamon. Economic historians estimate that during the fifteenth century, per capita consumption in Europe was just one teaspoon per year.[12]

It is not too much of an exaggeration to call sugar the heroin of foodstuffs. Babies will consume a solution of glucose in preference to water, and no human society or culture rejects the consumption of granulated sugar, even when a population is physically intolerant to it, as some Inuit tribes are.[13] Sucrose is the only chemical that humans will happily consume in pure form. In virtually every part of the world, its per capita consumption has increased steadily over the course of recorded history.[14]

The English, in particular, have a sweet tooth, and it dates back centuries. Consider the description of Queen Elizabeth by the German traveler Paul Hentzner, from around 1595:

> Her face oblong, fair but wrinkled, her eyes small, yet black and pleasant, her nose a little hooked, her lips narrow and her teeth black, a defect the English seem subject to, from their too great use of sugar.[15]

If sugar is so addictive and grows so easily, why didn't it spread more rapidly from its southeast Asian homeland? The cane plant, *Saccharum officinarum,* requires a frost-free growing season of about twelve to eighteen months, steady and copious rainfall or irrigation, and year-round temperatures averaging more than seventy degrees Fahrenheit. Cane harvesting and the subsequent extraction of pure, granulated sugar from the cut stalks are hot, backbreaking work that consumes vast amounts of both fuel and human effort.

The production of sugar is as much an industrial process as an agricultural one, and occurs in three stages. First, the cane is crushed to release the sweet cane juice. For millennia, this was accomplished with crude, inefficient mortar-and-pestle devices, and cane juice was therefore a luxury product, even where abundant slave labor was available. Next, the sweet juice has to be reduced by boiling it down to a concentrated sucrose solution, a process that requires a large amount of fuel. Finally, the solution is repeatedly heated and cooled in a refining process that separates out the sugar into granules of purity ranging from clear crystalline rocks to a brown residue—treacle or molasses—that cannot be further crystallized. This final process, sugar refining, not only consumes yet more fuel but also requires great skill, so much so that during the colonial age it was accomplished mainly in the advanced industrial centers of Europe.[16]

The natives of New Guinea were probably the first to domesticate sugarcane, sometime around 8000 BC. Its cultivation spread rapidly to southern China, Indochina, and India, where it flourished in their warm climates. Solid sugar does not appear in the historical record until its mention in Indian religious documents from AD 500.[17] Later, Muslim conquerors and traders exported both the cane plant and the techniques for refining it to the Middle East and Europe. Thus the old adage: "Sugar followed the Koran."[18]

But just barely. Muslims grew *Saccharum officinarum* in the few narrow strips of the Middle East and Mediterranean blessed with water from rainfall or irrigation: the Nile Valley, the coasts of Palestine, northern Sicily, Spain, Crete, and a few mountainous river valleys in Morocco. Farther north, the climate was too cold; farther south, there was not enough water.

When Europeans took over many of these areas after AD 1000, they inherited cane cultivation and the craving for sugar. The Portuguese transplanted production to their newly discovered tropical Atlantic colonies: first to the Atlantic island of Madeira, then to the Azores, and later to São Tomé, an island off the coast of equatorial Africa. These fertile islands had easy access to slave labor and provided plantation owners with far better conditions than those in the Middle East or the Mediterranean. Growers were particularly attracted to São Tomé, which was uninhabited when the Portuguese arrived in 1470, yet close to the heart of the central African slave trade.

Even with the cultivation of the Atlantic islands, sugar remained a luxury item, as production was still not widespread enough to make it a mass good. Two problems continued to hamper growers: a lack of efficient cane-crushing devices and a shortage of fuel. The first problem was remedied sometime around 1500 with the invention of the three-cylinder mill, which could be driven by water or animal power. This device consisted of three adjacent vertical rollers and could be run by only three men: one tended the waterwheel or draft animals that provided the power, and two continuously fed the cane through the rollers to each other. The second problem, lack of fuel, resulted from the deforestation of the Middle East, Europe, and soon enough, the Atlantic Islands. With the discovery of the endless forests of the New World, this last barrier disappeared.

By the time of Columbus's transatlantic voyages, cane had just been transplanted to the Spanish Canaries, from where his expeditions were staged. It quickly spread throughout the tropics of the New World and touched off an explosion of cane production that powered much of the world economy for the next three centuries. The "sugar belt" of the New World, which spread from northern Brazil to Surinam and up the Caribbean chain all the way to Cuba, attracted large numbers of European settlers lured by the relatively short transatlantic passage, the lack of organized native opposition, and agricultural profits unimaginable in their homelands.

The Spaniards soon lost their newcomer's advantage in the Caribbean to the more industrious Portuguese in Brazil. The first place to feel the shock of the New World's production was the Portuguese island of Madeira. Not only had it been the world's premier source of sugarcane before the discovery of the New World, but it was also the major staging point on the Brazil-Lisbon route. Local producers, hurt by the large amount of Brazilian sugar being dumped into the local markets, demanded, and got, protection. In 1591, authorities in Funchal, the island's capital, forbade the importation of New World sugar and imposed imprisonment or fines of up to a few years' wages on violators.

By 1591, protectionism was already an old story. One reason why the Spanish fell behind in the sugar race was the crippling of the industry in Cuba, Jamaica, and Puerto Rico by political pressure from the original growers in the New World, those on Hispañola.[19]

Over the course of the sixteenth century, Portugal became further disadvantaged by the growing economic strength of Holland and England. Both of these new powers in northern Europe licked their lips at the rich, far-flung, and poorly defended trading empire that Lisbon only loosely controlled, and its great prizes: Asian spices and Brazilian sugar.

The Dutch struck first at the Portuguese overseas empire. The results were mixed. One of their more notable failures to snatch trade and territory from Portugal occurred in South America. In 1630, the Dutch West India Company (WIC), which had been organized seven years before with the goal of cornering the sugar trade, chose as its main base in the New World some delta islands on the Brazilian coast, whose flat, maritime setting reminded its members of home. There they built the city of Mauristaad (modern Recife) at Brazil's easternmost extremity. Initially, things went well for them; over the subsequent decade, they conquered most of Brazil's northern coastline—from Mauristaad to the Amazon's mouth, a distance of about a thousand miles—and thus controlled the lion's share of the world sugar trade. In the seventeenth and eighteenth centuries, sugar and slaves were inextricably linked, so the WIC became a master of the slave trade as well; between 1636 and 1645, it sold at least 23,000 slaves in Brazil alone.

It was natural that the Brazilian expedition of the WIC would be spearheaded by Amsterdam's Portuguese-speaking Jews, who not only possessed the requisite language skills but also were deeply involved in the city's sugar trade, refining operations, and financial markets. The initial success of the WIC greatly improved the status of Dutch Jews. For example, the WIC, unlike the Dutch East India Company, had many Jewish shareholders. At the height of the WIC's operations in Brazil in the mid-1640s, over one-third of its four thousand settlers were Jewish.

At that point, history conspired against the WIC, and, along with it, the Jews of Brazil. Sixty years before, in 1580, Philip II of Spain inherited the crown of Portugal when its own royal line died out. (To Philip, this was only natural; he had Portuguese blood, had been raised by Portuguese courtesans, spoke Portuguese as his main language, and parodied Caesar by saying, "I inherited, I bought, I conquered.") The resultant loose union of Spain and Portugal, which left Brazil and the *Estado da Índia* independent of Spanish control, split apart following the Portuguese uprising of 1640.

Portugal's independence from Spain in 1640 produced two consequences that combined disastrously for the WIC. First, the new Portuguese king, João IV, negotiated a truce in 1641 with the Dutch government, as distinct from the WIC, forcing the company to halt its expansion and suspend its offensive operations against Portuguese ships. Second, the revolt against Spain galvanized Brazil's Catholic Portuguese settlers, who soon rose up against their Protestant and Jewish Dutch overlords. Passions ran high in the cities, particularly Mauristaad, where many Portuguese were deeply indebted to Jewish moneylenders.[20] By 1654, the Portuguese settlers had retaken Mauristaad, and Brazil's Dutch invaders scattered north to Surinam, the Caribbean, and back to Amsterdam.

During the seventeenth century, the Inquisition still raged in both Spain and Portugal. Fortunately for the Jews, the Portuguese commander who captured Mauristaad, Francisco Barřeto de Menezes, honored the letter of canon law, which stated that only Jews who had been converted from Christianity were subject to the Inquisition—a nicety not always observed in either Spain or Portugal, where unconverted Jews were regularly persecuted.

Twenty-three of the Jewish settlers boarded a Dutch vessel that was driven by adverse winds to Spanish Jamaica, and for a second time they wound up under the Inquisition's sword. Once again, fortune smiled: the Spanish governor, not wishing to anger the Portuguese or the Dutch, let them go. The refugees found passage on a French vessel, the *Sainte Catherine*, whose captain, after extorting from them what he could, deposited the Jews in Manhattan in 1654.[21]

Again, the modern reader may find the events leading up to the seventeenth-century arrival of the first Jews in New York disturbingly familiar: the sudden displacement of commodity production halfway around the planet, the inevitable calls for protection from the old centers of production, and the migration far from their native lands of those with specialized skills.

That the governor of New Amsterdam, Peter Stuyvesant, worked for a private concern, the WIC, seemed perfectly natural. After all, the Dutch outposts in Indonesia, southern Africa, and the New World (as well as the English bases in India) were almost exclusively trading enterprises; it was only logical that they be run by company men, not government officials.

* * *

By the early seventeenth century, mariners had mastered the world's winds so well that there was nothing unusual about a group of Jews from Amsterdam showing up in New York via Brazil, or about Chinese silk arriving in Mexico, or even Peru, by way of Manila. But one final wind system remained to be discovered.

How or when mariners encountered the southern version of the high-latitude westerlies that blew the Manila galleon from the Philippines to Mexico is unknown. But blow they did in the south Indian Ocean, more fiercely than in the North Pacific, because the Indian Ocean has fewer intervening landmasses—the "roaring forties" of the southern hemisphere. Da Gama and his Portuguese followers briefly took advantage of their weak northern edge on the last segment of the "wide swing" across the south Atlantic around the Cape of Good Hope. Had they but known, they could have ridden these winds almost all the way to the Spice Islands.

In 1611, Captain Henrik Brouwer of the Dutch East India Company passed the Cape, and instead of heading northeast toward India on the summer monsoon, boldly turned southeast into the void and became the first mariner to ride the roaring forties all the way to Java. He reached Batavia (modern Jakarta) just five months and twenty-four days after leaving Holland; by comparison, the usual monsoon route took over a year. Not only was the new route cheaper and quicker, but the crew remained healthier and the supplies fresher in the cooler mid-latitudes. As a bonus, Brouwer was able to avoid the Portuguese at Malacca.

Brouwer's method—round the Cape of Good Hope, head east for seven thousand miles, then turn left—became standard procedure for European mariners for the next three centuries.[22] The trick was knowing when to head north to thread the Sunda Strait between Java and Sumatra. John Harrison's marine chronometers, which could accurately measure longitude, would not come along for another 150 years, and many a Dutch and English ship failed to make the turn and got carried "beyond the bend" (as Coleridge's ancient mariner, cursed for shooting an albatross, had sailed south of Australia and shot straight into the Pacific). Only the lucky ones returned to tell of their accidental discoveries of Australia's northern and western coastlines.

More often than not, such missed turns proved disastrous, and Australia's coral-studded coastlines became a graveyard for dozens of European vessels. The most infamous of these wrecks was the *Batavia,* which foundered on a reef in Western Australia in 1629. About one-fourth of her three hundred passengers and crew drowned, but the rest made it onto a desolate strand of coral virtually devoid of fresh water. The ship's captain and its head merchant (the latter Brouwer's brother-in-law) reached Java in a small open boat. When rescue crews arrived three months later, they found a horror beyond description: a small group of mutineers had brutally and methodically murdered most of the remaining survivors. The Dutch East India Company attempted to censor the episode, and given the distances and lack of effective communication and transport, it nearly succeeded. The lurid events took decades to leak out and transfix the world with the story of how Europeans, in a wild place beyond the reach of law and civilization, slaughtered each other.[23] (Hereafter, the Dutch East India Company will be referred to by its Dutch initials—VOC—or, in the appropriate context, simply as "the Company.")

Mankind's hard-won command of the world's winds gave rise to a new monetary system, in many ways the forerunner of today's global credit and payment mechanisms, that bought the imported luxuries demanded by the covetous of both the Old and New worlds. Ships that traveled east on the roaring forties route carried the trade goods most in demand in Asia: fine European textiles and precious metals, most of which had been minted in Mexico and Peru into eight-real "Spanish dollars," or pieces of eight. This coin, which flooded the European currency markets in the sixteenth century, was approximately the same size and weight as the Bohemian thaler—from which the word "dollar" derives. (Since eight reales equaled one "dollar," and the coins were too unwieldy for everyday use, they were frequently broken up into eight one-real pieces, hence the term "piece of eight," and the nickname of the quarter-dollar, "two bits.")

The Spanish minted an enormous number of these coins. Their total production is unknown, but in the decade between 1766 and 1776, more than two hundred million coins, each weighing slightly less than an ounce, were produced in Mexico alone.[24] Between the sixteenth and nineteenth centuries, the piece of eight, particularly the trusted Mexican coin, was the de facto world currency. Whether in the hands of the mighty trading companies or a lowly local merchant, Spanish dollars paid for nutmeg in the Bandas, calicoes in Gujarat, silk in Manila and Mexico, coffee in Yemen, and cinnamon in Sri Lanka.

The coin tended to disappear and reappear according to monetary conditions. For example, in India in the late seventeenth century, when silver was highly sought-after, it rapidly found its way into crucibles where it was melted into rupees or jewelry.[25] By contrast, in the United States the Spanish dollar was considered legal tender until 1857.

From the perspective of the Dutch Company, the loss of treasure on Australia's reefs was at least as grievous as the loss of life. The rescue mission sent to the *Batavia* carried expert Dutch and Gujarati divers, who recovered ten of the ship's twelve chests of Spanish silver. When the *Vergulde Draek* failed to make the turn in 1656 and ran aground north of what is now Perth with its eight chests of silver, the crew, passengers, and Company fared even worse than those on the *Batavia*. Only seven of the *Vergulde Draek*'s survivors made it back to Java. The rest were never heard from again, and no trace of the ship's silver was found until three centuries later, when an Australian boy stumbled over some old coins on the beach.

In the 1960s, Australian archaeologists recovered approximately half of the estimated 46,000 coins loaded into the vessel's chests in Holland. The wreckage had been partially ravaged by looters, some of whom used explosives; this caused a public outrage that resulted in legislation protecting Australian archaeological sites.[26] Interestingly, almost all the coins carried the "M" stamp of the Mexico City mint, even though about 60 percent of New World silver came from Potosí in Peru and was minted in Lima. The reason for this was simple: the VOC avoided Peruvian coins, since the mint in Lima was notoriously corrupt, and its coins were often debased. In 1650 the officials responsible were punished—at least one was executed—and the VOC did not resume using the Peruvian coins until 1661, well after the shipwreck of the *Vergulde Draek*.[27]

That this huge treasure was the property of the VOC hints that by the mid-1600s, long-distance global commerce had become the domain of multinational corporate capitalism. Over the course of the seventeenth century, the Dutch company would methodically roll up the corrupt, ramshackle Portuguese trading empire, only to face a far more serious threat from another corporate challenger, the English East India Company. The advances in navigation outlined in this chapter would enable these battles to center on European trading posts and plantations around the world. For the most part, they would not be clashes of sovereign armies and navies, but of corporations.

THE COMING OF
THE CORPORATIONS

On December 13, 1577, a five-vessel flotilla under the command of Francis Drake left Plymouth, England. Drake's secret charge from Queen Elizabeth was threefold: to repeat Magellan's circumnavigation, to establish trade with the Spice Islands, and to plunder Iberian shipping.

Nothing could have suited Drake better. Just thirty-seven years old, he had already earned a reputation for navigational skill and bravery under fire. Nine years earlier, he had sailed the Caribbean to traffic in slaves with his cousin John Hawkins. While repairing their boats at the Mexican port of San Juan de Ulúa, they were double-crossed and nearly captured by the Spanish, an experience that left Drake with a lifelong hatred of Iberians. Five years later, he got even by robbing a Spanish silver train in Panama. He returned to England with a fabulous £20,000 booty for the queen.

Drake's circumnavigation succeeded beyond both his and Elizabeth's wildest expectations. On September 26, 1580, his remaining ships returned to Plymouth harbor, not only having reached the Moluccas but also having sailed the west coast of the New World from Cape Horn to Vancouver Island. During his epic voyage, Drake had explored, traded, and raided. Now his boats lay low in the water with Spanish treasure and Portuguese trade goods wrested from galleons and caravels between Africa and Peru, and with cloves and nutmeg obtained more honestly from Babullah, the rebellious sultan of Ternate in the Spice Islands.

In Europe, peaceful trade was the province of rich and powerful nations such as Spain and the Netherlands, who had a vested interest in keeping the seas free from piracy. Like many poor, weak, backward states, Britain in the late sixteenth century could not afford the luxury of permitting foreign merchantmen to sail undisturbed; there was simply too much profit in plunder. The majestic, liberal, and free-trading British Empire was more than two centuries in the future; Tudor England was a nation of bankrupt monarchs, crown monopolies distributed to court favorites, and royal letters of marque granting freebooters a piece of the action.

The most valuable cargo landed that day at Plymouth was neither spices nor silver, but rather intellectual capital. Early in Drake's odyssey, he had captured the Portuguese vessel *Santa Maria* near the Cape Verde Islands, off the west coast of Africa. His men were delighted to relieve the one hundred-ton caravel of its trade goods: woolens, linens, velvets, silks, and wine that had been bound for Brazil. It was also loaded down with canvas, nails, and tools—precisely the matériel needed on a long sea voyage.

However, Drake was far more interested in the pilot, Nuño da Silva, one of Europe's most experienced mariners. The Portuguese officer and the English pirate spent countless hours together examining and translating the *Santa Maria*'s charts; within a short time, Silva spoke English fluently. Over the ensuing months, the pilot dined at the captain's table and was accorded his every wish, except, of course, his immediate release. (Drake did let him go a year later.) Through Silva and his charts, Drake appropriated for England the most closely kept naval and trade secret of the era: celestial navigation in the strange skies "below the line" in the southern hemisphere.[1]

Nor was the transfer of this vital intelligence from southern to northern Europe the only historic symbolism to play out that day in Plymouth. When Drake arrived, crown authorities immediately spirited him away from public view. It would be five months before Elizabeth knighted him on the deck of the *Golden Hind*. State piracy was going out of fashion, and although in 1587 he would distinguish himself further with his daring raid on the war fleet of Philip II at Cádiz—the famous "singeing of the king of Spain's beard"—for the moment, he had become an embarrassment. England's future lay with trading, not raiding. The ledger book was soon to prove mightier than the sword, and the pirates, heroic lone traders, and swashbuckling naval commanders of the previous era were about to be replaced by the faceless managers of the two great multinational corporations of the premodern period.

The first of these was the VOC, which dominated long-distance commerce in the seventeenth century; the second was the English East India

Company (known hereafter as the EIC, or more simply, in the appropriate context, as "the Company"), which inherited its mantle in the eighteenth century. For two hundred years these two companies, with very different institutional origins and philosophies, battled each other for global trade supremacy, and their fortunes reflected the nations that gave them birth.

Before Drake's expedition, northern European ships had ventured east only as far as the Mediterranean via Gibraltar. If a Dutchman or an Englishman wanted to travel to the East, it would have to be on a Portuguese, Spanish, or Asian vessel, or by the overland route.

Early in the sixteenth century, the Tudors began granting monopolies to trading syndicates. Probably the first of these was a group known as the Merchant Adventurers, chartered in 1505 to send vessels laden with wool to Cypress, Tripoli, and Sicily. When successful, they returned to England with silks, spices, cottons, and carpets. Further charters followed, most notably to the Muscovy Company in 1555, to the Eastland Company's operations in Scandinavia and the Baltic in 1579, and to the Levant Company for trading with Turkey in 1581.

When the *Golden Hind* returned to Plymouth in 1580 laden with the riches of the East, its contents repaid Drake's backers fifty pounds for every one invested, not counting, of course, the £50,000 in Spanish pieces of eight and gold bars removed to the Tower's vault as crown property.

Inspired by Drake's success, a steady stream of adventurers headed to the Indies by various routes. In 1583 four traders from London—James Story, John Newberry, Ralph Fitch, and William Leeds—traveled overland to India and presented a letter of friendship from Elizabeth to the Mogul emperor Akbar. Fitch's written descriptions of the vast amounts of rubies, diamonds, silks, gold, and silver on display at the Mogul court galvanized London. In 1586, Thomas Cavendish conducted the third circumnavigation (after Magellan's and Drake's). He returned in 1588 laden with Spanish booty, his men clad in Chinese silk, his topsails trimmed with gold cloth, and his mainsail made entirely of damask. He departed on another circumnavigation in 1591 and was never seen again.

An expedition commanded by James Lancaster also departed in 1591 for India via the Cape. Lancaster's mission was plunder, not trade. During his three-year voyage, he roved between the Cape and the Moluccas, relieved several Portuguese Indiamen of their cargoes, and lost 90 percent of his crew to scurvy and storms. After unsuccessfully attempting to take the eastern coastal Brazilian province of Pernambuco from the Portuguese, he returned to London, where he would become a prime mover in a new venture, the EIC.[2]

The origins of the VOC were radically different, and in order to understand them, we must first describe its political and social roots. Before the mid-sixteenth century, what is today Holland and Belgium consisted of seventeen mainly lowland provinces that were part of Burgundy. They were inherited in 1506 by the Habsburg King Carlos I of Spain, who later became the Holy Roman emperor. When Carlos's son Philip II invaded this territory in 1568 to suppress the Protestant Reformation, the five northern provinces revolted. They formally declared their independence in 1579 with the Union of Utrecht, which banded them together into the United Provinces—what is now the Netherlands.

At that time, Antwerp (now in Belgium) was northern Europe's trading hub. This wealthy city attracted both Catholic and Protestant merchants from England, Germany, and the new United Provinces. All were more than happy to trade with Spain and Portugal, not just for spices but in other goods as well, most importantly the Iberian salt used to preserve Dutch herring. In exchange, the Dutch sent south their increasingly sophisticated textile products, as well as grain and timber from the Baltic.

In 1585, Philip's nephew the duke of Parma (in Italy) captured Antwerp, and with a decency uncharacteristic of the times allowed the city's Protestants to leave peaceably. Nearly simultaneously, his uncle embargoed the United Provinces and seized its vessels in Spanish and Portuguese ports. Each of these three actions was a colossal mistake. At a stroke Philip had created a network of the hardest-working, most commercially savvy traders in the world—Antwerp's now exiled Protestants, who were now dedicated to bypassing Iberian ports.[3]

The largest number of the refugees settled in Amsterdam, which was the capital of Holland but heretofore an unimportant port. ("Holland," strictly speaking, during that period referred to the largest of the United Provinces, not to the nation itself.) Between 1585 and 1622, Amsterdam's population swelled with Protestant refugees, increasing from 30,000 to 105,000 and becoming one of the largest European cities. The rebels blockaded Antwerp, which shrank to insignificance.[4]

In the late 1500s, a Dutchman, Jan Huyghen van Linschoten, would provide the final impetus for Holland's push into the Indian Ocean. For several years he served as a secretary to the Portuguese archbishop of the Indian city of Goa, and after the death of the prelate in 1588, he decided to seek his fortune and head even farther east. He dreamed not of great fortune, but only of a small-time peddling trade: "If I possessed only two or three hundred ducats, they could easily be converted into six or seven hundred."[5]

On his eventual return home to Holland in 1592, van Linschoten began work on a book, best known by its nickname, *Itinerario,* describing the botany and commercial geography of southeast Asia, as well as offering advice on navigation. The book's most useful recommendation concerned the East Indies trade:

> In this place of Sunda there is much pepper, and it is better than that of India or Malabar, whereof there is so great quantity that they could lade yearly from thence [500,000 pounds]. . . . It hath likewise much frankincense, camphor, and diamonds, to which men might very well traffic without much impeachment, for that the Portugals come not thither, because great numbers of Java come themselves unto Malacca to sell their wares.[6]

In other words, sail south of Sumatra, then pass north through the Sunda Strait (between Java and Sumatra) to avoid the Portuguese, who were happy to have Indonesian merchants come to them well to the west at Malacca. Even though the book was not printed until 1596, van Linschoten's observations and advice became common knowledge and were put to good use in Holland, soon after his return in 1592. Subsequently translated into several languages, *Itinerario* excited interest in France, England, and Germany.

In 1594, spurred by van Linschoten's observations and navigational charts (as yet unpublished), four Amsterdam merchants founded the "Company of Far Lands," and a year later this syndicate sent four ships and 249 sailors to India. As was typical of the era, just eighty-nine men arrived home in 1597. Worse, they landed only a small cargo of pepper, and no fine spices at all. In spite of their poor luck and planning, the merchants still made a handsome profit, and this did not go unnoticed. Within the next twelve months, Far Lands and five new competing companies sent no fewer than twenty-two ships to the East. Again, only fourteen of the vessels and less than half of the men made it home, but the ships of Far Lands returned fully laden with six hundred thousand pounds of pepper, earning the investors an enormous profit.[7]

When the first of these ships arrived back in Amsterdam in 1601, church bells rang with joy. According to one observer, "So long as Holland has been Holland, such richly laden ships have never been seen."[8] The Dutch were seized by a righteous commercial fervor that would do any modern free-trade enthusiast proud. Jacob van Neck, the commander of the successful expedition, noted that their modus operandi was "not to rob anyone of their property, but to trade uprightly with all foreign nations."[9] That would soon change.

At the same time, events were also moving rapidly in England, where, as in almost every other nation of the period, no one doubted the appropriate course of action: the crown would either arrogate monopoly rights to the trade for itself, or else award them to a court favorite in return for a piece of the action. Elizabeth was a past master at this sort of quid pro quo; in 1583, for example, she had granted Sir Walter Raleigh the monopoly on sweet wines throughout England.

The crown rushed to pursue the spice trade because of the success of the Dutch, whose merchants in 1599 cornered the pepper market and promptly tripled its price. English traders could not sit idly by.[10] A group of London merchants, many of whom were already principals in the Levant Company, petitioned the privy council with papers entitled "Certain Reasons Why English Merchants May Trade in the East Indies." The council indicated its approval, and over the next year and a half the organizers held meetings and solicited capital subscriptions totaling £68,000. Given the queen's history of awarding monopolies on a whim, the organizers took no chances: they presented her with a fait accompli. Even before they formally requested a charter, they had purchased, overhauled, and supplied five vessels, and then filled them with trade goods and gifts for local rulers.

By the time the petition reached Elizabeth, it bore more than two hundred signatures. On December 31, 1600, Elizabeth affixed her stamp and signature to the new company's charter, good for fifteen years; just six weeks later, the flotilla, under the command of James Lancaster, slid down the Thames.[11]

The year 1601 was eventful in Holland as well. In response to the success of the second Far Lands expedition, the six existing Dutch companies sent fourteen expeditions consisting of sixty-five ships around the Cape of Good Hope. By now, it was obvious that the rush for spices was getting out of hand, as the competing companies were crowding each other out at both ends of the supply chain, simultaneously bidding up prices in Indonesia and glutting the market in Amsterdam. If the profits were not to be entirely squeezed out of the trade, the Dutch government would have to regulate it.

In England, as we've already seen, the natural inclination of merchant venturers to the Indies was to seek a monopoly charter from the crown. But Holland was not a typical medieval absolutist European nation, and the Dutch government was far more inclined to act in the interest of the nation as a whole, particularly when this was politically expedient.

Just what was meant by the term "Dutch government"? For two centuries after 1579, when the Union of Utrecht established the northern provinces in revolt against Spain, the only national political institution was the States General. This representative body met in The Hague and decided military and diplomatic policy in conjunction with the stadholder, a hereditary prince of the House of Orange. Otherwise, each of the provinces governed itself, regulated its own merchants and businessmen, and championed its own companies in the States General, which was itself frequently at odds with the House of Orange. Creating a national trading company would not be easy.

Fortunately for the Dutch, in 1602 the gifted leader of the States General, Johan van Oldenbarnevelt, and the influential stadholder Prince Maurice were able to cajole the provinces into accepting a single combined monopoly organization to handle all commerce to the Indies.

The new organization, the VOC, strongly resembled the nation that gave it birth. Each of the original six companies was given its own regional head office, or chamber. A national board of seventeen over-seers, the Heeren XVII, oversaw these six offices. The Heeren were ap-portioned roughly in accordance with the national population: one each from the four smaller provinces; four from the second-largest province, Zeeland; and eight from Holland. So that the latter did not command an absolute majority, the seventeenth member alternated between Zeeland and one of the four remaining provinces.

The Company's charter granted it the ability to hire military person-nel, with the sole proviso that they swear fealty to the States General, and to wage war, so long as it was "defensive." (The EIC was also allowed to conduct military operations, and, as we'll soon see, the English and Dutch companies frequently exercised this privilege against each other.) Given that communication with the East Indies took a year in each direction, the VOC behaved as a sovereign nation wherever it went, with a free hand to physically destroy its Asian competitors whenever the Heeren XVII, or a particularly aggressive local governor or commander, felt like it.

The VOC, and along with it the West India Company (WIC), char-tered twenty years later with the same military potential, were not slow to use force of arms. Between 1602 and 1663, the two companies tried to pick off Portuguese and Spanish settlements in Chile, Brazil, East and West Africa, the Persian Gulf, India, Sri Lanka, Indonesia, China, and the Philippines. In reality, the WIC and VOC, two private companies, con-ducted the first world war, a grab for spices in Asia, sugar in Brazil, and slaves and gold in Africa.[12]

The results were mixed. The Dutch largely succeeded in India and Indonesia; by the late seventeenth century, the Portuguese were left with only tiny enclaves at Goa and Timor. The Dutch failed miserably at Ma-nila, Macao, and, most importantly, in Africa. Unable to seize the Portu-guese bases in Angola and Mozambique, the VOC was forced to establish a new outpost at Africa's remote southern tip, the Cape Colony, in order to protect its Indian Ocean routes.

Impressive as was the war-making machinery of the VOC and WIC, their most potent weapon was Dutch finance. In 1602, investors provided the VOC with 6.5 million guilders in initial funding—about $100 mil-lion in today's money—to hire men, purchase ships, and acquire silver and trade goods to exchange for spices. This capital was permanent, that is, if things went well, it would yield profits that would go mostly to pay for the expansion of business. Although the investors hoped for a modest annual dividend, they had no reason to expect to see their original 6.5 million guilders back anytime soon. This may not seem at all unusual to the modern investor, but at the beginning of the seventeenth century, the appearance of permanent capital in Holland demonstrated an extraordinary degree of confidence in Dutch financial institutions.[13]

By the early seventeenth century, all roads led to the Netherlands. This nation, physically smaller than Portugal and with only a slightly larger population (1.5 million in 1600), assembled the first truly global trading system. To this day, success or failure in the global marketplace depends not on size but on advanced political, legal, and financial institutions; by 1600, the Netherlands had far and away the world's finest, putting it in the best position to challenge the Portuguese trading empire. True, Holland was still in the midst of a fight for independence from Spain—the Eighty Years' War, which would not end until 1648, with the Treaty of Münster. In spite of that conflict, the Netherlands was still in far better shape than Spain, England, or any other European nation. Drake's exploits, the defeat of the Armada, and the EIC's slight head start aside, the realm of the Tudors and the Stuarts was roiled by religious strife, had only primitive and unstable financial markets, and was eventually to be plunged into a devastating civil war. France and Spain were even further behind, plagued with crown monopolies and chronic bankruptcy. By contrast, the Dutch confederation was one of the few European states free of the curse of absolute monarchy, possessed of vigorous legal and financial institutions, and relatively tolerant of the ambitious and able of all religions.

Two simple pairs of statistics tell the tale. Economic historians estimate that in 1600, per capita gross domestic product in England was around $1,440 in current dollars, versus $2,175 in Holland. (The comparable figures for Spain and Portugal were $1,370 and $1,175, respectively.)[14] These figures hint at the yawning technological and commercial gap separating Holland and England as the race for colonial supremacy began, but institutional and financial differences between the two nations proved even more important. In England, reputable borrowers (that most certainly did *not* include the crown), paid 10 percent on their loans, versus 4 percent in Holland, with the Dutch government getting its credit at the lowest rates of all. By contrast, in England, where the crown could, and often did, repudiate its loans, lenders charged it higher rates than those for good commercial borrowers.[15]

Why were Dutch interest rates so low? By the year 1600, because of its curious lowland geography and cultural capital, the Netherlands had become the most financially advanced nation in Europe. Much of its best farmland lay below sea level, laboriously reclaimed over the centuries with dikes and windmills (the latter used to power pumps). These projects were locally run and financed, and the rich new lands they exposed yielded not only an agricultural bounty, but also a population of empowered and prosperous peasants unbeholden to any crown or feudal overlord.

These reclamation projects stimulated the nation's credit markets. Dikes and windmills were expensive, and local church and municipal councils raised the required funds in the form of loans. This turned Holland into a nation of capitalists; merchants, aristocrats, and even rich peasants tended to invest their spare guilders in the bonds used to finance the reclamation projects. This tradition carried over into trade; after 1600, Dutch citizens would consider it just as natural to own a fractional share in a trading vessel to the Baltic or the Spice Islands.[16] Eventually, merchants and brokers sliced ownership into ever smaller pieces: not just half or quarter shares, but thirty-seconds and even sixty-fourths. To this day, the Dutch are among the world's most aggressive international investors.

Dividing ownership in this way was the essence of "Dutch finance," whose genius lay in allowing entrepreneurs and investors to spread risk. In 1610, court documents showed that the estate of one petit bourgeois merchant consisted of shares in twenty-two ships: thirteen 1/16 shares, seven 1/32 shares, one 1/17 share, and one 1/28 share.[17] Fractional shares not only made it easier for merchants to bear prudent risks, but also allowed investors to increase their margin of safety by blunting the damage done by the loss of an individual ship or an unsuccessful commercial outcome. This in turn increased the willingness of investors to provide capital, which further lowered interest rates.

Another Dutch financial innovation that served to decrease risk (at least when used properly) was the futures market—the "buying of herrings before they be catched."[18] Essentially, such markets assigned prices to given amounts of commodities at some point in the future—say for a thousand pounds of herring one year hence. These financial instruments could then be bought and sold just like the actual item. The Dutch did not invent this concept—it was well known in both southern Europe and the Muslim world—but they refined and institutionalized it to a degree never before seen. By selling futures, Dutch farmers and merchants could be assured of a given price for their products six or twelve months hence. By purchasing futures, buyers could avoid disastrous price rises in the interim. Shippers could also acquire maritime insurance as a hedge against loss of their cargoes at sea, yet another risk-sharing device. Fractional shares, futures contracts, and maritime insurance all served to stimulate commerce.

As Josiah Child, a seventeenth-century English merchant, economist, and governor of the English East India Company, explained, "All nations are at this day richer or poorer in exact proportion to what they pay, and have usually paid, for the Interest of Money."[19] For millennia merchants have had to borrow to finance their trading ventures, and governments have had to borrow to support their military ambitions. All other things being equal, a Dutch company could borrow at a 4 percent interest rate two and a half times more money than an English company could at a 10 percent rate.

The same was also true of a nation's ability to support its military. Four percent interest rates meant wealth and power; 10 percent, poverty and impotence. The ability of the Dutch to borrow, combined with the turbulence of English politics, gave Holland a head start that England would not overcome until its financial and political institutions were reformed generations later.

The sad state of England's financial markets manifested itself in the EIC's puny initial capitalization: £68,000, just one-tenth of that of the VOC.[20] Moreover, the English company's capital was *not* permanent; it had to be completely returned to investors as soon as the company's ships sailed back up the Thames and their merchandise was sold. On more than one occasion, investors were paid with spices instead of specie and took delivery of bags of pepper in place of pounds sterling.[21]

Imagine for a moment how hobbled Microsoft and Boeing might be in their competition with foreign companies if they had to return the entirety of their initial investment capital each time they completed development of a software product or an aircraft, then had to repeat the process with each new project. Imagine further that they occasionally sent their shareholders a stack of software disks or a wing spar in lieu of a dividend check. This describes, more or less, the handicap borne by Holland's competitors.

For almost a century, the EIC played the role of the obnoxious kid brother of the VOC. In 1622, for example, the Dutch company had eighty-three ships under its command in Asian waters, while the English had just twenty-eight, roughly the ratio of interest rates between the two nations. One Dutch observer noted:

> It is a great mistake on the part of Your Honors to suppose that the finest trading opportunities in all the world can be seized and held in the face of all the world by keeping 30, 40, or perhaps 50 ships and yachts in the fairway.[22]

Finance and ships were not the only edge the Dutch had on the English. Even though the VOC's structure reflected the divisions within the United Provinces, the EIC was even more decentralized. Less a trading company than a guild, the English company allowed each of its members to trade on his own account, owning only the ships in common with other members. Since both the voyages and the merchants were separately financed, there was almost no cooperation where it mattered: at the EIC's trading posts. When disputes broke out among English traders in Asia, they had to be sorted out in London, half a world and a two-year round-trip away. At Bantam in Java, near modern-day Jakarta, there were three different English trading offices. Not only did the merchants of EIC trade their own goods; they were free to compete directly with their own company.[23] The VOC, by contrast, sent to Indonesia a strong governor-general with full authority over all of the company's officers.

Since the States General had been its midwife, the VOC could count on government support, both military and political. But the EIC, a private company of loosely confederated merchants, could not expect shelter from attack by foreign trading powers abroad or from protectionism at home.

The decentralization of the EIC also made it more susceptible to corruption than the VOC. Although the behavior of Dutch traders and sailors was hardly upstanding in this regard, the employees of the EIC treated its ships as their own, transporting large amounts of trade goods for their accounts to and from Asia. As one EIC official wrote to his directors:

Concerning the private trade of the English . . . Your Honours must
believe that if the Company of England were served according to
the manner in which Your Honours are served it would long since
have surpassed the Dutch Company.[24]

Another great advantage that the Dutch had over England, and over
its other European rivals, was in maritime technology. The decrease in piracy in northern European waters after 1595 allowed the development of a
round, slow, but highly efficient vessel known as the *fluitschip,* or "flute
ship," which required less than half the crew of other vessels of similar
tonnage. Initially, the craft was victimized by its own success; its efficiency
threw so many sailors out of work that many turned back to piracy.[25]

By 1605, the VOC realized that if profits were to be maximized, it
needed a monopoly not just in Holland's spice markets but in those in the
rest of the world as well. In order to accomplish this, it would need permanent bases in Asia where it could store trade goods, repair and provision ships, and coordinate activities without interference from local rulers
or the Portuguese. The following year, the Company unsuccessfully attacked Portuguese Malacca, then turned its attention eastward to the Spice
Islands and Java.

Spanish forces from Manila had occupied the Moluccan island of
Ternate in 1606, and when the sultan appealed to the VOC for help against
them, the company sent troops. Over the next several decades the Dutch
slowly pushed the Spanish out of the Moluccas.[26] Because of the delay in
communication between the Indies and Europe, the last battle in the Dutch
war of independence from the Spaniards took place on Ternate in 1649,
fully one year after the signing of the Treaty of Münster in 1648.[27]

The subsequent course of the takeover of Asian trade by the VOC
pivoted on Holland's takeover of the Bandas, Moluccan flyspecks placed
in history's crosshairs by a unique soil that made them the world's only
source of nutmeg and mace.

During the sixteenth century, the Portuguese and the Spanish had reduced the clove-producing north Moluccans to vassalage by exploiting the
rivalry among their islands, particularly that between Ternate and Tidore.
At the same time, the south Moluccans, especially the Bandanese, prospered. Left relatively undisturbed by the Iberians, they collected nutmeg
and mace from the forests that covered their islands as they had done for
more than a thousand years. They grew wealthy by shipping to Malacca,

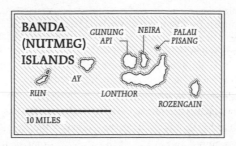

two thousand miles to the west, their own nutmeg and mace, as well as cloves from their northern neighbors.

The VOC quickly recognized that if it was to monopolize the spice trade, the Bandanese would have to go. And go they did, with a brutality and efficiency that would become the trademark of Dutch policy in Asia. The largest, and most important, part of the Bandas consists of three island remnants of a caldera—Lonthor, Neira, and Gunung Api. A few miles west lies tiny but fertile Ay; and a few miles farther west, the most isolated of the group, the even tinier Run.

Like the north Moluccans, the Bandanese welcomed the Dutch, when they first arrived in 1599, as a counterweight to the overbearing, proselytizing Portuguese. The VOC easily hoodwinked the islanders into yielding their nutmeg exclusively, at artificially low prices. It is not clear whether or not the Bandanese understood the documents they signed, but whatever the case, disputes soon arose. The islanders were totally dependent on barter with neighboring islands for their food supplies, a fact the Dutch seemed not to appreciate at first. Simply to avoid starvation the Bandanese almost immediately "violated" the "agreements" with the VOC. Worse, in 1609 the inhabitants of Neira granted Captain William Keeling of the EIC permission to build a trading post.

Both the disregard of the Bandanese for the niceties of European contractual propriety and the insouciance of the freeloading Britons, who had expended no military capital in the Moluccas, enraged the Dutch, in no small part because English competition had driven up purchase prices. That same year the VOC sent a delegation to Lonthor to "negotiate" a new agreement. The islanders fell on the Dutchmen as soon as they landed and cut to pieces forty-seven soldiers and officers. A Dutch rescue party arrived too late.

Among the members of that party was a young "junior merchant" whose name later became synonymous with Dutch efficiency and brutality: Jan Pieterszoon Coen. Before embarking for the Indies, he had spent his teenage years as an apprentice to a branch of a Dutch merchant company in Rome, where he learned the new science of double-entry bookkeeping, which was not yet in widespread use in Holland.

Coen shipped out in 1607 to the East Indies for three years (during which he served on the unsuccessful Lonthor rescue party). He then returned to Holland for two years. In 1612 he was sent out again as a "senior merchant." In this capacity Coen submitted a brilliant analysis, based on the new bookkeeping techniques, of the VOC's operations, *Discoers Touscherende den Nederlantsche Indischen Staet,* which soon caught the attention of the Heeren XVII. In his report, Coen, a true spiritual ancestor of the modern bean-counting MBA, wielded the cutting-edge management tools of the seventeenth century, and observed that the company was turning very little profit on its complex operations. He recommended two courses of action: first, that a monopoly be obtained on the three precious "fine spices"—nutmeg, cloves, and mace—and second, that this be done at any cost, including the ruthless exploitation of local workers and the importation of Dutch colonists and slave labor.

Whether or not Coen's involvement with the Lonthor massacre informed the recommendations of the *Discoers* and his later brutality is not known. One thing, however, was perfectly clear. The new trade was to be accomplished with force of arms:

> Your Honors should know by experience that trade in Asia must be driven and maintained under the protection and favor of Your Honors' own weapons, and that the weapons must be paid for by the profits from the trade, so that we cannot carry on trade without war, nor war without trade.[28]

The first to feel the force of those arms were the British. Even though the English captain Keeling had recently protected a VOC delegation at Ay from an attack by natives, the Dutch still suspected him, probably wrongly, of conspiring with the Bandanese. Outmanned and outgunned by the Dutch, Keeling filled his boat with spices and sailed away.

By this point, Neira was already under Dutch control. Lonthor, starving under a blockade, submitted next. In 1610, Captain David

Middleton of the EIC arrived at Neira. Stonewalled by the VOC, he did not load a single nutmeg. He then decamped a few miles west to Ay, where the locals happily loaded his holds with fine spices, a trick that was turned by subsequent EIC captains over the next few years.

By 1615, the VOC had lost patience with both the English and Ay's inhabitants. It invaded, only to be repulsed by the islanders. This time, its suspicions of British scheming were well-founded. English weapons were discovered on the island, and English boats had observed the action and perhaps even fired on VOC forces. The Dutch attacked the next year, with devastating results. They slaughtered hundreds, dispersed thousands, and enslaved the rest. On losing its trading post at Ay, the EIC simply moved its base of operations a few miles farther west to Run. At this point Coen, who had been appointed the local VOC commander in Bantam on Java a few years earlier, warned the English that he would consider any further support of the Bandanese an act of war.

The escalation of hostilities between the VOC and EIC aroused concern not only at the companies' headquarters in London and Amsterdam, but also at Windsor and in The Hague. Between 1613 and 1619, the two governments conducted trade negotiations as contentious as any WTO or GATT conference. It galled the English that the Dutch sent as their chief negotiator none other that Hugo Grotius, the era's towering legal scholar and author of the principle of *Mare Liberum*—the concept that God had given all nations the right to navigate the seas and to trade freely.

Although the English embarrassed him by quoting his own theories, Grotius was a brilliant rhetorician and had no difficulty arguing the opposite case—that the English, having contributed nothing to the establishment of trade with the Spice Islands, had no business there. Just as the fleets of the EIC and VOC were about to come to blows off Bantam in March 1620, the English vessel *Bull* arrived with a message for Coen from the Heeren XVII: nine months before, the companies had signed a treaty of cooperation.

The agreement infuriated Coen, who wanted to destroy every last English trading post and merchant ship in the East Indies. Its terms gave the EIC one-third of the profits from the Moluccas, but also made EIC liable for one-third of the costs.

The arrangement gave Coen the tools with which to eject the British, albeit more peacefully than he would have liked. Since the English could not compete financially with the Dutch, outsmarting them was child's play, especially for an operator like Coen, as skilled at double-entry bookkeeping as with a cannon. Repeatedly he presented the EIC with enormous bills for spice purchases, ships' provisions, and military expenses that the English could hardly hope to pay. When the English pleaded insufficient funds or declined to supply warships in support of Coen's attacks on the islands, the Dutch refused to let them load spices.

Later that year, the VOC, without English support, committed one of the bloodiest outrages of the colonial era when they assaulted the main island of Lonthor and slaughtered most of its approximately thirteen thousand inhabitants. The few survivors were sent off to forced labor in Java or enslaved to work the clove trees that had once been theirs. In the decades that followed, those who had been packed off to Java were sent back home when the Dutch found themselves in need of native expertise to salvage their mismanaged nutmeg groves.

A number of islanders escaped westward, particularly to the Buginese port of Makassar (situated along the sea-lanes running from the Spice Islands to Java and Malacca), where they became an important part of this key trading community.[29] Meanwhile, the English were left in nominal control of Run and a tiny neighboring island. Although the Dutch did not physically eject the British from Run, for fear of violating the 1619 treaty, they destroyed the island's nutmeg trees.[30]

While the VOC was consolidating its monopoly in the Spice Islands at the eastern end of the Indonesian archipelago, it also established a more important foothold at the western end in Java. In defiance of orders of the Heeren XVII, the brilliant and monomaniacal Coen, who had just been appointed governor-general, seized the small fishing village of Jakarta from the sultan of Bantam on May 30, 1619, and renamed it Batavia.

In two decades, the Dutch had accomplished what the Portuguese had not been able to do in the preceding century—acquire a nearly complete monopoly on cloves, nutmeg, and mace. But like the Portuguese, they could not control the pepper trade, which was spread too diffusely between India and Indonesia.

The conquest of the Spice Islands was part of a grander VOC strategy for seizing control of Asian trade from the Portuguese. In 1622, the Dutch got unwitting assistance from the Persians and English when their

This ancient rock carving from Bergbuten in Norway clearly shows a hunter in the bow of a sewn skin boat. The paddler stands in the rear. Source: *The Earliest Ships*, Conway Maritime Press.

The north Arabian saddle, which has been in continuous use for the past two thousand years, solved the difficult problem of mounting cargo over the soft, moveable hump of the dromedary camel. In one day, a single driver leading three to six animals could convey over two tons of goods thirty miles. Source: *The Pastoral Taureg*, Thames & Hudson.

A Bactrian camel struggles to rise under its load. This Tang Dynasty (ca. ninth century AD) ceramic was found in the tomb of a Chinese Silk Road merchant. *By courtesy of the Field Museum, Chicago.*

Marco Polo's fantastical but true tales of places where widows threw themselves on their husbands' funeral pyres, where hashish-addled assassins thought themselves in heaven, and where the sun never set in summer nor rose in winter evoked widespread ridicule in Europe.

The modern government of China has revived the story of eunuch admiral Zheng He's seven massive expeditions into the Indian Ocean in the fifteenth century in order to demonstrate its peaceful intentions in the twenty-first century. *By courtesy of David Kootnikoff.*

Doge Enrico Dandolo saw the Fourth Crusade as a threat to Venice's spice trade with Egypt. He sabotaged the expedition and at age ninety led its remaining forces in the sacking of Constantinople. *From the Granger Collection, New York.*

Infante Dom Henrique (later known as Prince Henry the Navigator), the youngest son of King João I and Queen Philippa of Portugal, participated in the kingdom's Moroccan campaigns. On beholding the edge of the vast North African desert, he realized the futility of his mother's dream of a trans-Saharan route to the Indies. After returning home, he sponsored the fifteenth-century Portuguese exploration of the African coast, which eventually lead to the rounding of the Cape of Good Hope by Diaz and da Gama.

Portugal's slow crawl down the African coast in the fifteenth century foundered on the adverse winds which grew stronger the farther the vessels proceeded south. Vasco da Gama solved the problem with a "wide swing" to the southwest before heading eastward to the Cape of Good Hope. His reputation for brutality preceded him in most of the African and Asian ports he subsequently visited and snarled trade and diplomatic relations. *By courtesy of National Maritime Museum, Greenwich, England.*

Afonso de Albuquerque built Portugal's empire in the Indian Ocean. He seized the critical chokepoints at Malacca and Hormuz, but could not stanch the flow of spices on Muslim ships through Bab el Mandeb. *From the Granger Collection, New York.*

In the sixteenth century, Ottoman Admiral Piri Reis harassed the thinly stretched Portuguese forces in the Indian Ocean, Red Sea, and Persian Gulf over a career that spanned several decades. *By courtesy of business-with-turkey.com.*

The Portuguese soldier of fortune Fernão de Magalhães, spurned by King Manuel, convinced the Spanish crown that the Spice Islands lay on its side of the Tordesillas Line in the East, and accomplished the first circumnavigation of the globe. He is today known in the English-speaking world as Ferdinand Magellan. *From the Granger Collection, New York.*

The three-cylinder mill, which could be operated by three or four slaves, revolutionized sugar production in the New World. Note the three counter-rotating vertical rollers at the center of the device, and the two slaves feeding cane stalks to each other from opposite directions. *By courtesy of the University of Virginia special collections.*

In 1611, Dutch East India Company captain Henrik Brouwer rounded the Cape of Good Hope, sailed southeast into the vastness of the Indian Ocean, and became the first commander to exploit the speed and temperate weather of the roaring forties route to the Spice Islands.

After serving as the secretary to the Portuguese archbishop of Goa, Jan Huyghen van Linschoten returned to his native Holland and acquainted his countrymen with the secrets of the Spice Islands. The navigational and trade data contained in his *Itinerario*, published in 1596, paved the way for the success of the Dutch East India Company.

Dutch East India Company merchant Jan Pieterszoon Coen wielded the ledger book and the sword with equal efficiency and brutality in his monomaniacal pursuit of a spice trade monopoly.

The great Dutch legal scholar Hugo Grotius preached the principle of *Mare Liberum*: the right of every nation to freely navigate the open ocean. But he would not extend this privilege to the English when they challenged the Dutch East India Company's monopoly in the Spice Islands.

Sir Josiah Child, governor of the English East India Company, spoke forcefully against protectionism in public and liberally greased palms in private. In 1697, anti-globalization mobs attacked his home, along with Parliament and the East India House. *By courtesy of the National Portrait Gallery, London.*

Josiah Wedgwood's technical skill and marketing savvy made his cups and pots, filled with tea and sugar from opposite sides of the globe, the essential totem of England's upwardly mobile masses. *From the Granger Collection, New York.*

Before 1757, the English East India Company's territorial presence in India was limited to small trading colonies needed to support the cotton trade. In that year, a young colonel, Robert Clive, defeated a French-supported native force at Plassey and gained for the Company its first substantial conquest in India, a huge swath of territory in the Bengal. *By courtesy of the National Maritime Museum, Greenwich, England.*

This schematic drawing demonstrates the conditions of extreme crowding on a slave ship. *From an abstract of Evidence delivered before a select committee of the House of Commons in 1790 and 1791.*

William Jardine began his career with the English East India Company as a surgeon's mate, earned vast profits in the China opium trade, and founded a trading venture with James Matheson that still bears their names.

Jamsetjee Jeejeebhoy, a Bombay Parsi unhappy with his inherited profession of bottle merchant, set out for China on the ill-fated East Indiaman *Brunswick*, where he formed a life-long association with William Jardine. Both would earn fortunes and knighthoods.

James Matheson, the scion of a wealthy Scottish family, was able to buy his way directly into the "country trade" between China and India, thus avoiding the long apprenticeship with the East India Company endured by William Jardine. The two would eventually join forces to dominate the opium trade.

David Sassoon, a Jewish merchant from Bombay whose ancestors hailed from Baghdad, seized the China opium trade from his larger English rivals in the wake of the legalization forced by the Second Opium War. His descendants would achieve distinction in the arts and business in England. *From the Jewish Encyclopedia.*

The issue of a wealthy Portuguese Jewish merchant family, David Ricardo formulated the law of comparative advantage, which demonstrated how all nations could benefit from trade.

Richard Cobden, a textile printer by trade, became the foremost opponent of the corn laws. His exploitation of the transport and communication advances of the day—the railroad, telegraph, and penny post—finally led to repeal in 1846.

Tory prime minister Sir Robert Peel eventually saw the wisdom of corn law repeal, famously commenting to his deputy, Sidney Herbert, in response to a speech by Richard Cobden, "You must answer this, for I cannot." This heroic decision, which saved the ruling class of aristocratic landowners from itself, cost him his political career. *From the Granger Collection, New York.*

PAPA COBDEN TAKING MASTER ROBERT A FREE TRADE WALK.

This *Punch* cartoon satirizes the persuasive Richard Cobden's conversion of prime minister Sir Robert Peel toward support of corn law repeal. *By courtesy of Punch Limited, London.*

DAME COBDEN'S NEW PUPIL.

After his triumphant 1846 parliamentary victory in the fight over corn law repeal, Richard Cobden turned his attention to the Continent, where he influenced Napoleon III and eventually pushed through the Cobden-Chevalier Treaty, which lowered tariffs between France and England and brought both nations back from the brink of war. *By courtesy of Punch Limited, London.*

Vice president under both John Quincy Adams and Andrew Jackson, John C. Calhoun shared the anger of his fellow South Carolinians against northern protectionism and was the architect of the nullification crisis of 1833, which nearly triggered the Civil War a generation early.

English scientist Henry Bessemer's blast technique for the manufacture of inexpensive high-quality steel led, in turn, to steel tracks and high-pressure steam engines, the flooding of Europe with cheap New World grain, and a wave of worldwide protectionism. *From the Granger Collection, New York.*

French farmers, devastated by the avalanche of New World grain, found their voice in Félix Jules Méline, who engineered the passage of a drastic tariff law in 1892. *Photograph by Harlingue-H. Roger-Viollet.*

Economists Eli Heckscher (left) and Bertil Ohlin (right) described how the prices of land, labor, and capital converged in an increasingly globalized economy. *Heckscher photo by courtesy of the Stockholm School of Economics.*

Representative Willis Hawley and Senator Reed Smoot congratulate each other on the signing of their 1930 tariff bill. This disastrous legislation gave rise to virulent anti-Americanism, devastated international commerce, and contributed in no small part to the outbreak of the Second World War.

Cordell Hull, the longest-serving American secretary of state, clearly discerned the damage to world security done by the tariff wars of the early twentieth century and laid the groundwork for the GATT and WTO. *By courtesy of the United States House of Representatives.*

This photograph of economists Wolfgang Stolper (left) and Paul Samuelson (right) was taken fifty years after they developed a theorem that explained who wins, and who loses, with free trade. *By courtesy of the University of Michigan Press.*

combined forces captured the island of Hormuz, the guardian of the narrow Persian Gulf entrance, from the Portuguese. The Persian emperor, Abbas I, had long wanted to regain the port's commanding position over the gulf in order to open it up to silk exports, a royal monopoly. Previously, silk had to travel by caravan through the territory of the Persians' archenemies, the Ottomans.

Hormuz, once one of the world's busiest and most cosmopolitan trading posts, became deserted, never to rise again, and its fall changed the face of Asian trade. First, the British received a base at Gombroon on the Persian mainland, later renamed Bandar Abbas ("Port of Abbas") which has dominated the strait down to the present day. Second, the Gulf was now closed to the Portuguese, as well as to the Gujaratis and the Acehnese of western Sumatra. This in turn shut down the ancient caravan trade across the Syrian desert, which had for a thousand years brought spices from the Indian Ocean to the Levant and Venice.

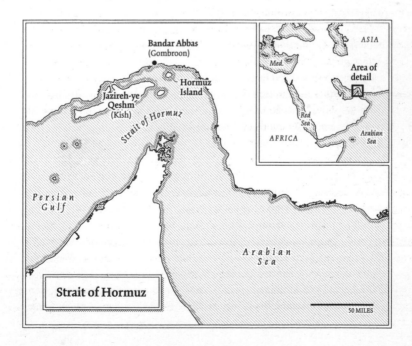

Paradoxically, the real beneficiary of the Anglo-Persian seizure of Hormuz was the VOC.[31] The nominal victors at Hormuz, the Persians and the English, derived little benefit from their newly won command of the Gulf, the former because they had no merchant fleet, and the latter because they no longer had Moluccan spices to ship to the caravans at Persian Gulf ports. The Dutch had almost totally frozen the English out of the spice trade, and not until the end of the seventeenth century would the EIC be able to exploit other commodities and once again challenge the VOC.

The Dutch followed this stroke of good luck by taking Sri Lanka from the Portuguese in a long and bloody campaign lasting from 1638 until 1658 and added the hugely profitable cinnamon monopoly to their portfolio. Finally, they completely sealed off the last leakages from the Spice Islands by bringing the Buginese port of Makassar, an important spice market for Asian traders, under VOC domination in 1669 and by taking Bantam, the main English base in Indonesia, in 1682.

With the fall of Hormuz and the virtual elimination of Portuguese power from the Indian Ocean, the only route open to Asian competitors was through the Red Sea. After 1630, the Turks lost control of its entrance at Bab el Mandeb to a local Yemenite imam, who reopened trade to all comers, including the Europeans, through the port of Mocha, near Aden. Although the Red Sea was theoretically open, Holland's competitors had no spices to ship through it. The Acehnese, who had so successfully defied the Portuguese *cartaz* system in the sixteenth century, had disappeared from the western Indian Ocean. The exact reasons for their decline are not clear, but it seems likely that merchants from Aceh could not buy spices because of the increasing VOC presence on Sumatra.

Dutch maritime technology had improved to the point where the route around the Cape of Good Hope at last became decisively cheaper and faster than "Sinbad's Way" and the Red Sea route. So complete was the VOC's control of the Spice Islands, so efficient was Dutch shipping, and so well financed and well managed were Company accounts, that by the early seventeenth century it was intentionally glutting the Mediterranean with pepper and fine spices from the *west* via Gibraltar. While this decreased profits, the low prices rendered the overland spice routes uneconomical and thus doomed the age-old Venetian trade via the eastern shore of the Mediterranean.[32] A century and a half later, Venice, its major source of revenue gone, would be easy pickings for Napoleon's army.

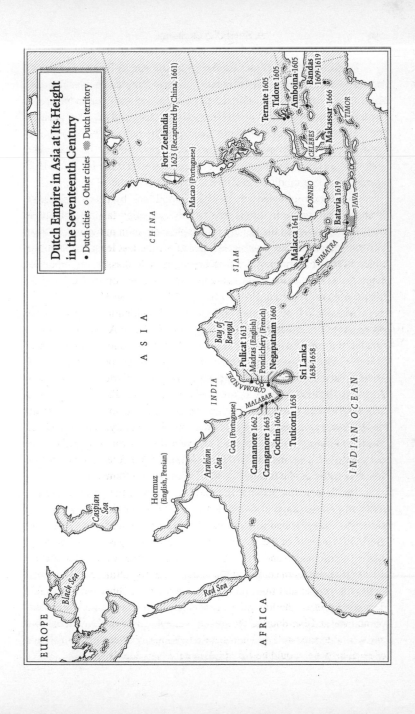

Dutch Empire in Asia at Its Height in the Seventeenth Century

● Dutch cities ○ Other cities ▨ Dutch territory

EUROPE

Black Sea

Caspian Sea

A S I A

CHINA

Fort Zeelandia
1623 (Recaptured by China, 1661)

Macao (Portuguese)

Ternate 1605
Tidore 1605
Bandas
Amboina 1605
1609-1619
CELEBES
Makassar 1666
TIMOR

SIAM

BORNEO

Malacca 1641

Batavia 1619
JAVA

SUMATRA

Bay of Bengal

Pulicat 1613
Madras (English)
Pondichéry (French)
Negapatnam 1660

Sri Lanka
1638-1658

INDIA

COROMANDEL

Arabian Sea

MALABAR

Goa (Portuguese)

Cannanore 1662
Cranganore 1663
Cochin 1662

Tuticorin 1658

Hormuz
(English, Persian)

INDIAN OCEAN

Red Sea

AFRICA

In the end, Tomé Pires, the Portuguese apothecary, adventurer, and author we met in Chapter 4, had not quite gotten it right when he famously said, "Whoever is lord of Malacca has his hand on the throat of Venice." In order to strangle it, one needed to be lord not only of Malacca, but also of Sunda, the Cape of Good Hope, and the Spice Islands. The Portuguese had not quite been up to it, but by the mid-seventeenth century, the Dutch had finally cornered the spice market and throttled Venice.

The most profitable part of the VOC's business took place entirely within Asia and thus avoided the long and treacherous Cape route altogether. When the Tokugawa shogunate threw out the Portuguese in 1638, the VOC acquired a Japanese trading post on the small island of Deshima in Nagasaki harbor. The Japanese created this artificial island from landfill for the express purpose of enforcing isolation from what the Tokugawas saw as the two most dangerous Western influences: Christianity and firearms. At Deshima, silver was loaded onto Dutch boats until the Tokugawas forbade its export in 1668, and the Dutch replaced it with gold and copper.

The Dutch were a good fit with their isolationist hosts. Both enjoyed strong drink and carousing (which were eschewed by the abstemious Portuguese), and the Calvinists were far less obsessed with saving heathen souls than with making profits. (Charles X of Sweden, in reply to a diplomat from Holland who lectured him about freedom of religion, famously pulled a Dutch coin from his pocket with a sly, "*Voilà votre religion.*"[33])

During the more than two centuries that the Tokugawas locked Japan away from the outside world, Deshima served as its sole window to the West. Initially, the Dutch at Deshima received only the basics, "provisions and prostitutes," but before long, curiosity got the better of the Japanese. The lure of Western culture and technological knowledge, or "Dutch learning," would help open Japan long before the appearance of Perry's black ships in 1854.[34]

Whereas the Dutch got along tolerably well with the Japanese, they offended the Chinese by refusing to sell spices to China's merchants in Sumatra and Java. Recall that the Chinese consumed spices, particularly pepper, on a larger scale than Europeans, and that the VOC now controlled the lion's share of the trade. The Chinese responded by sending their silk directly to Japan and Spanish Manila (whence it sailed on Manila galleons to Mexico). Coen retaliated by seizing junks on the Canton-Manila route, further alienating the Chinese, and in 1622, he tried to take Macao. When this attempt failed, Coen forced the Chinese to knuckle under by sinking eighty junks along the south China coast. Their foreign trade at a standstill, the Chinese granted the VOC a permanent trading post on Taiwan—Fort Zeelandia—whose warehouses soon bulged with spices, silks, porcelain, and drugs.[35]

The hub of Asian commerce remained western Java, easily reachable via the roaring forties route discovered by Brouwer. Had the Messiah returned to earth in 1650, he would almost certainly have changed ships in Batavia. Nearly all shipping to and from Holland went through that great port, and it also served as the nerve center of a complex intra-Asian trade network. Fine spices from Indonesia; gold, copper, and silver from Japan; and tea, porcelain, and silk from China transited its warehouses to the east and west coasts of India, where they were traded for cotton. The Indian fabric was in turn sent back to Batavia to pay for more spices, silks, and other goods. This internal Asian trade was as close to a perpetual-motion money machine as the world has ever seen.[36] Only the most exquisite goods—the finest silks, the best-quality spices, gold, porcelain, and precious jewels—went back around the Cape to Amsterdam.

A seventeenth-century English prisoner in Batavia estimated that at any one time, the VOC had up to two hundred ships and thirty thousand men throughout the Indies. Given the high mortality rate among employees —about one-fourth of the men were lost on the outbound journey alone— the VOC required a constant stream of enlistees, and not only from the streets of the United Provinces. So great were its manpower requirements that from the mid-seventeenth century on, most of its soldiers and sailors came from abroad, particularly Germany.

This grisly recruitment effort was run by a specialized corps, com-posed mostly of women, the *zielverkoopers* (literally, "soul sellers"). Their marks were the young foreign men, mainly from Germany, who swarmed into Dutch cities seeking their fortune. In return for a cut of their signing advance and future pay from the Company, the women advertised room, board, and the sort of entertainments usually sought by unattached young men, during the weeks and months until they sailed for Asia.

The reality fell far short of the promise. One contemporary report described three hundred men in a single attic,

> where they must stay day and night, where they perform their natural functions, and where they have no proper place to sleep, but must lie higgledy-piggledy on top of each other. . . . the death rate is so alarming that the owners, not daring to report the correct number of deaths, sometimes bury two bodies in one coffin.[37]

Holland being Holland, this Faustian transaction yielded a financial instrument, in this case the *transportbrief*—a marketable security entitling the *zielverkooper* to a cut of the recruit's wages, paid by the Company as they were earned. Other investors then bought these securities at a discount that reflected the high death rate of VOC personnel and assembled them into profitable, diversified pools of human capital. These magnates were called, naturally enough, *zielkoopers*—*buyers* of souls. When, in the eighteenth century, the mortality among the VOC's soldiers and sailors soared because of lax Company procedures, many *zielkoopers* went bankrupt.

Over half of the million or so men who embarked from Holland's wharves for the East never returned. In the words of the economic historian Jan de Vries, "It is hardly an exaggeration to say that the Company swept the city streets of beggars and the unemployed."[38] The low quality of these recruits would eventually be the Achilles' heel of the VOC. By contrast, the EIC realized that it needed men who could sail, handle cargo, and fight to serve on its relatively small and undermanned Indiamen. The English Company selected only the most qualified applicants and granted them exemption from the Royal Navy's press gangs.[39]

If hundreds of thousands left Holland's wharves to meet a miserable and terrifying end at sea or in pestilential Asian ports, the return of cargoes from the East was something else again. The VOC posted lookout ships on constant patrol in home waters, and prize money went to the captain whose crew first espied the homebound East Indiamen.

High-ranking Company representatives sailed out to the returning vessels on sloops. Their first destination was the flagship, where the expedition's commander gave them a brief report. What goods were on board? How many men and vessels had been lost? Had any strange vessels come near the fleet on their approach to the harbor? The greeting party then split up among the returning vessels. Each ship's master gave up the leather bag containing diamonds and jewels as well as the ship's log, which was carried back on the delegates' sloop. The delegates then inspected the crew's personal trading accounts and bags. They questioned the officers and crew about the voyage. Did the officers and mates have anything to say about the crew? Did the crew have any complaints about the ship's command? The delegates used specialized shallow-draft boats called lighters to collect cargoes and prisoners, as well as the crew's equipment, clothes, and personal trade goods, and inspected the ships' guns and ammunition.

Specially bonded lightermen came to break down the bulkheads and chute the spice bales down to the waiting boats. This hot dusty work burned the throat; the lightermen relieved their discomfort with gin and sugared pretzels. Finally, the delegates descended to the ship's bottoms, where they supervised the unloading of the heavy ballast goods: Javanese rice, Japanese copper, and lesser-grade Chinese porcelain. (Higher-grade porcelain traveled on the upper decks.) The filled lighters now sailed into the inner harbor, where they dispersed among Holland's complex network of inland canals to the warehouses of the *kamers* (the Company's regional branches). Their shipboard duties done, the delegates departed in their sloops and reassembled at the company's headquarters, where they presented the leather bags of gems to the Heeren XVII to be opened.

Now came the hard part: distributing the vast amount of goods without depressing prices. The VOC used many different arrangements, but the most common involved selling the entire stock of a given commodity at a fixed price, with the promise that the Company would refrain from releasing any future stocks for a predetermined period—in Dutch, the *stilstand*—so as to protect the buyer. For example, in 1624 a syndicate of three spice merchants contracted to buy over two million pounds of pepper at a wholesale cost of four million guilders with a *stilstand* of twenty-four months. It would be more than a century before the trading companies and merchants of any other nation were able to regulate commerce on so grand a scale.[40]

So complete was the VOC's control of the spice markets that for more than five decades after 1690, it could fix nutmeg and clove prices at a nearly constant level. This ability did not come without effort, especially considering the wild fluctuation in crop yields. In 1714, 1.5 million pounds of cloves were harvested in the north Moluccas; in 1715, two hundred thousand pounds. In 1719, the harvests were so large, and European demand was so small that 4.5 million pounds of cloves and 1.5 million pounds of nutmeg had to be destroyed. One year, the Dutch would plant aggressively; the next, they would exterminate tens of thousands of trees.[41]

Just as the arriving fleets, lighters, and warehouses groaned with the opulence of Asia, the bounty of Europe could be seen on its way out: German rope, Russian canvas, Norwegian lumber, Iberian salt, French soap, English leather, cheese from Edam, coal from Newcastle, herring from Holland, and coins minted from New World silver.

Few things excite the envy and belligerence of other nations as much as wealth derived from commerce. This emotional undercurrent permeated Anglo-Dutch relations during the seventeenth and eighteenth centuries, when England and Holland would engage in four full-scale armed conflicts. These were literal trade wars, not the sterile commercial and diplomatic pantomime of our era.

The signing of the Treaty of Münster in 1648, which ended the Eighty Years' War between the Dutch and the Spanish and granted the Netherlands its independence, unleashed the full potential of Dutch trading capacity, which before then had been restrained by the threat of Spanish seizure and blockade.

Holland's new commercial power came as a rude shock to England. With the Spanish threat gone, the English were even less of a match for Holland's merchants. Suddenly, the Dutch were everywhere in the Baltic, in Spain, and on the Mediterranean, loading onto their flute ships timber, salt, wines, and olive oil that had previously sailed under the flag of Britain.[42]

The resultant slump in the English economy, as well as the highhandedness of the Dutch in the Indian Ocean and their rejection of Oliver Cromwell's overtures at forming an anti-Catholic union after the beheading of Charles I in 1649, led to the passage of the Navigation Act in 1651. This legislation prohibited third-party trade into England—that is, although it was perfectly legal for a foreign ship to land its own nation's goods on the wharves of London, landing the goods of another nation was outlawed. Since this law applied to most cargo on Dutch vessels, the act amounted to a declaration of war against Holland.

Cromwell's navy and privateers began seizing hundreds of Dutch flutes, and within seven months of the act's passage, the first of the Anglo-Dutch wars began. All together, three such conflicts broke out between 1652 and 1672. Each was closely fought, and the Dutch generally came out on top.

In the first war, which lasted until 1654, Holland's shipping in northern Europe was devastated by the capture or sinking of more than 1,200 of its ships. Yet in the end, the Dutch carried the day through their ability to control the choke points at Gibraltar and at the strait between Sweden and Denmark. English merchants, trapped in Swedish, Italian, and German ports, and the Royal Navy, with its supplies of Scandinavian timbers threatened, pressured Parliament to sue for peace.

But only for the time being. Holland was most vulnerable at the Oresund, a strait 2.4 miles wide between what is now the Danish city of Helsingør (Hamlet's Elsinore) and the Swedish city of Helingsborg. Vital Scandinavian and German grain, timber, and metals, which fed and supplied Holland, and the herring and manufactured products that paid for them, all flowed through this vital passage. In the sixteenth and seventeenth centuries, the Danes, who could fire on any ship in the strait from forts on either side, collected tariffs—so-called "sound dues"—on all merchant traffic through it. As Dutch naval and merchant power grew, so grew the importance of stability and a reasonable tariff structure at the strait, and the weaker Denmark found itself Holland's client state.

In 1658 Charles X of Sweden attacked Copenhagen and the strait. Since Sweden and Denmark were allied with England and Holland, respectively, this became an Anglo-Dutch proxy war. The Dutch, although bloodied and exhausted from the conflict of 1652–1654, mustered their last naval and land reserves to force the Swedes and the English, whose navy had begun patrolling Danish waters, to back down. In a dramatic series of engagements, the Dutch admirals Obdam and de Ruyter broke the Swedish siege of Copenhagen, flushed the English out of the Danish archipelago, and opened the Oresund by escorting a large merchant convoy through a withering Swedish crossfire and under the astonished eyes of Charles X, watching from Helsingør castle.

Resentment of the commercial hegemony of the Dutch was not limited to England. In 1667, France challenged Holland's Baltic trade when Colbert, the finance minister of Louis XIV, set up the Compagnie du Nord to ship French salt and wine to Sweden and Germany, a trade dominated by the Netherlands. At the same time, Colbert imposed draconian tariffs on Dutch fabric, tobacco, and whale oil.

Holland's formidable financial firepower won the day; the Compagnie could not equal the ability of the Dutch to pay French merchants in advance for their wine and salt. Colbert should have known better than to match fiscal wits with the Dutch, who, adding insult to injury, targeted the Compagnie by dumping Scandinavian wood on French markets at reduced prices, greatly lowering the value of the timber imported by the Compagnie du Nord.

The French responded with trade competition by other means and invaded Holland in 1672. Stadholder Willem III defeated the French by opening up the dikes and flooding the approaches to Amsterdam. Frustrated both in the rough-and-tumble of commerce and on the field of battle, Louis XIV and Colbert folded the Compagnie in 1675. Adding insult to injury, in 1688 Willem essentially invaded England and ascended the British throne as King William with the express purpose of establishing an anti-French alliance.

The period after 1648 marked the golden age of Holland, captured so well by Rembrandt and Vermeer. Not only did it sit astride the world's trade routes, but its manufactures had few peers. By the late seventeenth century the Turks had grown so fond of the almost silken Leiden wool that Venetian craftsmen were unable to compete; in 1670, Venice's senate concluded that the only way to revive its textile industry would be to import Dutch equipment. English importers sent Holland their raw sugar for refining, their raw tobacco for processing, and their raw diamonds for cutting. Continental housewives demanded Delftware, an inexpensive imitation of Chinese blue porcelain, and the soap and lamp oil obtained from Dutch whaling advanced European standards of hygiene and made the nighttime streets safe. Even paper, the traditional preserve of Italian and French manufacturers, fell to the smooth, white reams of the northern city of Zaan.[43]

The decisions of merchants and politicians in London, as well as the shifting tastes of Western consumers, would soon end the Dutch golden age. Ironically, Willem III's capture of the English crown set in train events that cleared the way for England to replace Holland as the world's economic and military superpower. The era of spices was coming to an end, and Britons, frozen out of the East Indies, turned their attention north to India and China, and west to the Caribbean and Africa, where they would prosper from the commodities of the future: cotton, tea, sugar, opium, and slaves.

10

TRANSPLANTS

Few images in American history are as familiar as that of the nation's earliest patriots, costumed as Indians with blankets and blackened faces, dumping tea into Boston harbor on December 16, 1773, ostensibly demanding "No taxation without representation." This stirring slogan better reflected the revolutionaries' propaganda needs than the facts.

When Arthur M. Schlesinger Sr.—the father of the distinguished Harvard historian and aide to John F. Kennedy—addressed this topic in a 1917 essay, he entitled it "The Uprising Against the East India Company."[1] A historian writing today about the event might easily label it "the first American antiglobalization rally."

By the late eighteenth century, Britons everywhere were addicted to tea, and the colonists in the New World were no exception. Just before the American Revolution, Governor Thomas Hutchinson of Massachusetts, who was also a merchant, estimated that Americans consumed about 6.5 million pounds of tea each year: 2.5 pounds per capita. In actuality, the only levy on tea was an import duty of about 10 percent imposed by the Townshend Act a full six years before the Boston Tea Party. Colonists easily circumvented this modest tax by smuggling the dried leaves via Holland and France. Only about 5 percent of consumption was actually declared to the crown. Why, then, were Bostonians so riled up in 1773, six years after the fact? Simple: they dumped the tea into the harbor because they feared that the East India Company (EIC) was dumping it on them.

In the global downturn following the Seven Years' War—a devastating worldwide conflict between France and England lasting from 1756 to 1763—Britain found itself in fiscal difficulties and decided to repair its finances with funds from the colonies. The Stamp Act of 1765, which taxed legal documents, newspapers, pamphlets, and even playing cards in British North America, provoked widespread protest; it was repealed the next year. It was followed the year after by the more moderate Townshend Act, which also sparked cries of taxation without representation.

The war had also hit the EIC hard, and by the early 1770s it was in dire need of assistance from the government. The Townshend Act forbade the Company from selling its goods directly to the colonists. Instead, the EIC had to auction merchandise to middlemen, who then shipped the cargoes to American wholesalers, who finally sold to local shop owners. In May 1773, Parliament, at the request of the EIC, passed the Tea Act. It imposed no new taxes, but rather allowed the Company, for the first time, to import tea directly from Asia into America. The act cut the price of tea in half and was therefore a boon to colonial consumers.[2]

The middlemen cut out by the act, local smugglers and tea merchants, were not as happy with the new legislation. When news of its passage arrived in Boston in September 1773, these two groups took action against the "unfair foreign competition" from the EIC. Ignoring the inconvenient fact that the act would save their countrymen a substantial amount of money, merchants and smugglers couched their arguments in the familiar protectionist language of national interest. An editorialist writing under the pen name "A Consistent Patriot" pointed out that the new legislation would cost honest, hardworking American merchants their livelihood "in order to make room for an East India factor, probably from North-Britain, to thrive upon what are now the honest gains of *our own* merchants."[3] Others, relying on the ignorance and partisanship of their audience, raised the shibboleths of taxation without representation and the far-fetched threat of a British takeover of all American commerce. At least one town council, however, saw things more clearly and resolved that those objecting to the act did so "because the intended Method of Sale in this Country by the East India Company probably would hurt the private Interest of many Persons who deal largely in Tea."[4]

In November 1773, the East Indiamen *Dartmouth, Beaver,* and *Eleanor* entered Boston Harbor with the first loads of the EIC's tea. The conspirators, probably led by Samuel Adams, were well prepared and highly disciplined; they cleaned the decks when they were finished and took no tea for personal use or later sale.

By the time of the American Revolution, the familiar elements of globalization were in place. International corporations shipped their products across the face of the planet and molded consumer preferences to the point that a hot drink brewed from dry leaves was considered a "necessary and common article of subsistence." Colonial special-interest groups deployed protectionist cant against the welfare of the many and against the big companies, improbably tarred as the agents of a foreign culture.

Before 1700, global commerce revolved around armed trading that sought to preserve monopolies in fabled commodities from exotic locations. Only once, in the seventeenth century, did the Dutch actually attain this ideal when they cornered the market in fine spices from the Moluccas and Sri Lanka.

After 1700, the pattern changed completely. New commodities—coffee, sugar, tea, and cotton—which were previously little known in the West and whose production could be easily transplanted across continents, came to dominate global commerce. No longer could huge profits be earned by offloading a few tons of spices, silk, or incense onto the wharves of Antwerp, London, Lisbon, Amsterdam, or Venice. Further, the companies would have to stimulate demand for the new mass-market goods.

Figure 10-1, which plots the percentage of imports into Amsterdam by the Dutch East India Company (VOC), clearly shows the primacy of these new products. (This plot actually understates their importance in Europe, since the EIC came to control the lion's share of textile and beverage imports, but carried very little of the spice commerce.) No one could hope to maintain a monopoly in items that were so easily grown and produced, and the nation most proficient at the new high-volume commerce, England, slowly realized that peaceful free trade served its interests best.

The story of the rise of the multinationals and mass-market commodities began with another beverage, coffee, which for more than half a millennium has been far more than just a drink. Nutmeg, cloves, cinnamon, and pepper once hypnotized the high and mighty, but eventually, they fell out of fashion. By contrast, the dark liquid concocted from the roasted beans of the *Coffea arabica* bush still commands the attention of corporate chairmen, prime ministers, and an ever-increasing number of the world's population. For the five centuries following its introduction into the Islamic

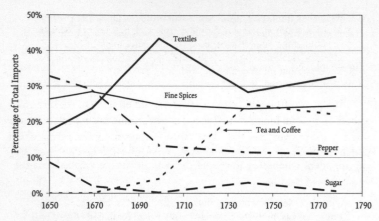

Figure 10-1. Imports to the Dutch East India Company at Amsterdam

world, this hot, flavorful beverage has stimulated social intercourse, financial transactions, and at times, revolution.

Legend has it that around AD 700 an Ethiopian herder noticed that on reaching a certain upland pasture, his camels and goats never rested, but pranced about all night. He investigated and found his animals feeding on the red berries of a small shrub. When the herder chewed some of these berries, he too found himself invigorated.[5] Although this story is almost certainly apocryphal, most authorities agree that coffee was first cultivated in Ethiopia sometime shortly after AD 1000 and then made its way across the Red Sea to Arabia Felix (modern Yemen), where members of the Sufi sect—a mystic offshoot of Islam—began consuming it regularly.

Sufis were seldom full-time priests; like most believers, they held day jobs. Almost uniquely among the world's faithful, they solved this problem by performing their rituals, in which they strove for a state of detached, trancelike otherworldliness, late at night. Around the midfifteenth century, Sufis began drinking coffee to keep them awake, instead of the traditional Yemeni stimulant, the leaves of the *qat* shrub.

The fact that Sufis were not monastic hermits, but rather men of ordinary affairs, quickened coffee's spread from the religious to the secular sphere. One of the first non-Sufis to notice its healing effects was the mufti of Aden, who, on falling ill, took some [coffee] in the Hopes it might do him good. Not only the Mufti's health was restor'd by the Use of it, but he soon became sensible of the other Properties of Coffee; particularly, that it dissipates the Heaviness of the Head, exhilarates the Spirits, and hinders Sleep without indisposing one.[6]

In the late fifteenth century, coffee assumed its dual modern roles as both as a social lubricant and an aid in performing the monotonous and tiring work of everyday life.[7] One early European observer, impressed with its promotion of honest human interaction and business relationships, noted that it

qualifies Men for entering onto the Bonds of Society, and strict Engagements, more than anything else . . . and for making their Protestations so much the more sincere, as they proceed from a Mind not overcast with Fumes, and are not easily forgot, which too often happens, when they are made by Men in their Wine.[8]

With increased demand, organized cultivation soon sprang up in the hills north of the Yemeni port of Mocha, just inside Bab el Mandeb. Its coffee groves fed a habit that spread rapidly north via the Red Sea trade routes. Around 1500, coffee arrived in Jeddah, the transfer point between large Indian Ocean trading vessels and the shallow draft ships that plied the northern Red Sea. There, it became an instant hit and assumed a Seattle-like importance. One European observer in Jeddah noted:

They made its Use so common, that it was sold publicly in Coffee-Houses, where they flock'd together, under that Pretence to pass away the Time more agreeably; there they play at Chess, and at Mancalah, even for money. There they fling, play on Instruments and dance; Things which the more rigid Mahometans cannot endure; which did not fail to bring Trouble in the End.[9]

Wherever the coffeehouses were full and the mosques empty, trouble indeed came. In Mecca, its messenger was the Mamluk governor, Khair Beg al-Mimar, a typical killjoy bureaucrat obsessed with a fear that somewhere, somehow, people were having fun. In 1511, with the collaboration of two Persian physicians, he forbade the beverage, for both medical and moral reasons. Meccans thumbed their noses at the decision, and a formal ruling from Cairo wisely allowed home consumption. Within a few years, Khair Beg and the two physicians met terrible deaths, although this probably had more to do with the Ottoman conquest than espressos.[10]

The same morality play ensued as the drink spread north and east throughout the Muslim world. Small dishes of the strong, unsweetened liquid, occasionally flavored with cloves, anise, or cardamom, found their way into the harem; women considered a steady supply of the roasted beans an essential spousal obligation, and failure to provide it constituted grounds for divorce.[11]

In 1555, a Syrian businessman named Shams carried the beans, and the sensation, to Constantinople, where within a few decades several hundred cafés sprang up. These were "thronged night and day, the poorer classes actually begging money in the streets for the sole object of purchasing coffee."[12] Not long after, the familiar drama unfolded on the Bosphorus when the wicked and uneducated vizier Mahomet Kolpili, the power behind Sultan Murat IV, closed the coffeehouses, fearful that they might foment revolution. At nearly the same time in Persia, the wife of Emperor Abbas I proved more politically adept; she did not shutter these establishments but rather infiltrated them with agents who diverted conversation from politics to more acceptable subjects.[13]

By the early seventeenth century, Western visitors could not help noticing the phenomenon. One European estimated that between two thousand and three thousand coffeehouses flourished in Cairo. In Constantinople, the traveler Pietro della Valle observed that in the houses of the wealthy,

> a large fire is kept going [to keep the coffee hot] and little porcelain bowls are kept by it ready-filled with the mixture; when it is hot enough there are men entrusted with the office who do nothing else but carry these little bowls to all the company . . . also giving each person a few melon seeds to chew to pass the time. And with the seeds and this beverage, which they call *kafoue,* they amuse themselves . . . for a period of seven or eight hours.[14]

Any commodity popular in Constantinople soon found its way to the rest of Europe via Venice, which had by then repaired its relations with the Ottomans.[15] Italy's Catholic theologians, like their Muslim counterparts, harbored suspicions about the brew's moral properties, but Pope

Clement VIII spared Europe the caffeine controversy when, around 1600, he sampled a cup and blessed coffee as a Christian beverage. The French physician Pierre de La Roque brought coffee to Marseille in 1644, and his son Jean would later write *A Voyage to Arabia Felix,* a popular book describing his journeys as a merchant and the early history of coffee.

In 1669, the Turks sent an ambassador, Suleiman Aga, to Versailles. Insolently wearing a simple wool coat and refusing to bow before the bejeweled Louis XIV, he addressed the Sun King as an equal and was instantly banished to Paris. His embassy may have failed, but his coffee succeeded. In Paris, he rented a large house in a fashionable neighborhood. Aristocratic women, drawn by rumors of the residence's exotic, perfumed atmosphere, eagerly sought audiences inside, where Nubian slaves served them coffee in exquisitely gilded eggshell porcelain. Their tongues loosened by caffeine, they revealed to Suleiman that Louis had invited the Turks to Paris for the sole purpose of making the Austrians anxious that he might not support them during the expected Ottoman siege of Vienna. This further soured relations between Versailles and the Turks.

The fashion soon spread throughout Paris as Armenians, costumed as Turks in turbans and caftans and carrying trays of pots and cups, sold the beverage from street to street. These roving peddlers gave way to stalls at fairs, and these ultimately evolved into cafés. One of the best known was the Procope, established in 1686 and named after the Italian waiter of one of the first Armenian stall owners. A century later, Robespierre and Marat would conspire at the Procope, and it still serves customers today, as does Venice's even more famous and overpriced Café Florian, founded around the same time.

Brought not by merchants but by soldiers, coffee also came to Vienna from Constantinople. In 1683, the Ottomans surrounded and besieged Vienna for two months before being driven back by an Austrian army largely made up of Poles, among whom was Franz George Kolschitzky. Having previously served as an interpreter with the Turks, he was ideally suited for the dangerous courier duty between the defenders within the city and their Polish allies waiting outside. He cheated death several times by bluffing his way through enemy lines with his Turkish uniform and linguistic ability.

When the Poles finally relieved the city, the Turks left behind not only their hope of conquering Europe, but also large stocks of oxen, camels, tents, and gold that were distributed among the victorious troops. Vienna's defenders also inherited bales of coffee, but they found no takers. Hearing of this, Kolschitzky said, "If nobody wants those sacks, I will take them."[16] Having lived among the Turks, he knew just what to do with the beans. Retracing the beverage's Parisian history, Kolschitzky first began selling the drink on the street and door to door. Later, he rented a small house, which became the first Viennese café.

By 1700 most coffee served in Europe came not to Venice, Paris, or Vienna, but to the banks of the Thames. That the British were now consuming the lion's share of one of the era's great luxury commodities hints that European commercial supremacy had shifted to London, and no group welcomed coffee's pharmacological boost to stamina and mental sharpness more than England's new merchant class. Wherever it spread, the beverage became the "drink of commerce."[17]

England's rapid commercial ascent followed the Glorious Revolution of 1688, in which the Dutch Protestant stadholder Willem III, along with his royal English wife, Mary, overthrew the last Catholic monarch, James II. Willem, now King William, had sought the English crown to unite Britain and Holland in a Protestant alliance against Louis XIV. In order to accomplish this, he willingly dealt away the ancient divine right of kings and elevated Parliament to governmental supremacy. In exchange, Parliament gave William a robust tax base of excise levies (especially on luxury commodities such as coffee) to pay for his war against France.

This grand bargain—the Revolutionary Settlement of 1689—had far-reaching effects. First, the transfer of power from an absolute monarch to a representative legislative body invigorated the rule of law, the essential soil in which nations thrive economically.[18] Second, the establishment of a crown excise tax made it easier for the government to pay off debts, thus making it a better credit risk and dramatically lowering interest rates. As a bonus, lenders perceived that a dominant legislature made up of wealthy bondholders and businessmen was less likely to default on its loans. Between 1690 and 1727, prime interest rates in England plummeted from over 10 percent to 4 percent.[19] Third, after the events of 1688–1689, the Dutch financiers deduced that the commercial wind had shifted and decamped en masse for London. One of the émigrés was Abraham Ricardo, father of the economist David Ricardo, about whom we shall hear more later.

The Revolutionary Settlement turbocharged England's economy. It also made the British the most avid coffee drinkers in Europe, as the nation's merchants, financiers, and stockbrokers congregated in London's coffeehouses. In these establishments, situated by the city's wharves, where news from foreign markets first arrived, the movers and shakers of England's new trading economy met to do business, their wits not dulled by wine and beer as in days of old, but rather sharpened by the elixir of enterprise.

As long as only Yemenis grew the berries, coffee remained scarce and expensive. In the first decades of the eighteenth century, an increasing number of European traders converged on Yemen, first at Mocha, then at the dusty highland town of Beit-el-Fakih in the growing district north of the port. Agents of the VOC and EIC were joined by representatives of French, Flemish, and German trading companies, and an even larger number of Muslim merchants.

The Europeans were Johnny-come-latelies to the trade. In the mid-eighteenth century, most coffee was still going north to its traditional markets in Egypt, Turkey, and Mesopotamia, or east to Persia and India. During the 1720s, for example, Yemen exported about sixteen million pounds (forty thousand *bahars,* or camel loads) annually to the Muslim world, as compared with only about six million to Europe, most of which went to England.

The EIC agents usually ran rings around their VOC counterparts, often leaving the Dutch to purchase overpriced, mildewed beans. The VOC's lack of success resulted from both corruption and laziness. In particular, the Dutch traders were unwilling to leave the relative comforts of Mocha and venture to Beit-el-Fakih, as their competitors were increasingly doing.[20]

As the coffee craze spread in Europe after 1700, more ships appeared in Mocha, as well as in Hodeida and Lohaya, two smaller ports closer to Beit-el-Fakih. The European agents dreaded the entrance of any trading vessel into these harbors, even from their own company, as this invariably raised prices. At one point, beans at their Yemeni source sold for as much as 0.8 guilder per pound, or about $12 in modern value; at such a cost, only the wealthiest could frequent Europe's coffeehouses.[21]

By about 1725, cutthroat competition among the European companies at both ends of the supply chain had squeezed the profit out of the business. The most noteworthy aspect of the Yemeni coffee trade was an event that *didn't* occur. While the British, Dutch, French, Flemish, and

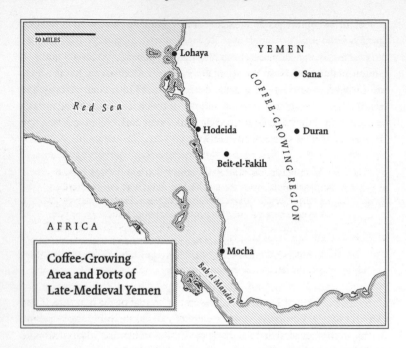

Coffee-Growing Area and Ports of Late-Medieval Yemen

German companies competed viciously, this time they avoided outright war. For their part, the Yemenis greedily savored the frantic bidding among the Europeans. When Parliament rashly directed the EIC to arrest all British subjects in Mocha outside its employ, the local factor recommended against it, as this would anger the sultan, "who we believe would interfere to protect the people of any ship that came to the port as they show an equal respect without distinction to Europeans."[22]

If the Dutch could not outtrade their British and French rivals, they could at least out-cultivate them by transplanting coffee bushes to Surinam, Sri Lanka, and the Malabar Coast. After some initial setbacks, bushes originally transplanted from Yemen to the Malabar Coast were successfully cultivated in the Javanese highlands near Batavia. By 1732, Indonesia grew about 1.2 million pounds of coffee annually, and bales of beans from Surinam and Brazil joined those from the Indies on Amsterdam's wharves. The increase in supply broke the Yemeni monopoly and finally lowered prices. Growers in the new areas could produce coffee more cheaply than in Yemen, assuring the Dutch of healthy profits.[23]

The plunge in prices brought about by the new growing areas in Indonesia and the New World changed European drinking habits. Suddenly, everyone could afford the odd cup. In 1726 a Dutch clergyman complained that seamstresses would not so much as pass a thread though a needle until they had consumed their morning coffee, and in 1782, one French aristocrat sarcastically sniffed:

> There is no bourgeois household where you are not offered coffee, no shopkeeper, no cook, no chambermaid who does not breakfast on coffee with milk in the morning. . . . There is usually a wooden bench near the merchant's stall or shop. Suddenly, to your surprise, you see a woman from Les Halles or a porter arrive and ask for coffee. . . . These elegant people take it standing up, basket on back, unless as a sensuous refinement they want to place their burden on the bench and sit down.[24]

The quality of Javan beans was not up to that of the real thing from Mocha. While Europeans could generally not tell the difference (except, perhaps, for the fact that the transplanted coffee contained 50 percent more caffeine than coffee from Yemen), more discerning Muslim consumers could, and they would not touch the cheaper Indonesian brew. Nothing better demonstrated the complacent obstinacy of the eighteenth-century VOC than the response of its directors—the Heeren XVII—to reports of the Muslim's disdain for the cup of Java. This august group solemnly reported that they had sampled coffee from both Javan and Mochan beans and could not distinguish between them. They could not believe that "a bunch of boorish Turks and Persians should have so much tastier tongues than we and others like us."[25]

That England was able to achieve primacy in the coffee trade (and later, in tea) did not augur well for its European competitors. These products, after all, originated in places—Yemen and China—where the Dutch and French had a long head start on the British. The worst-case scenario for England's rivals, then, would be a new commodity that grew in many locations and for which there was widespread demand.

Cotton filled the bill precisely. This fabric so pervades modern life that it is easy to lose sight of its unique biological and geographic properties. First and foremost, *Gossypium hirsutum*—the plant species responsible for more than 90 percent of global production today—contains four complete sets of chromosomes, instead of the two sets in most plants and animals. (In scientific terms, it is a tetraploid organism, as opposed to the usual diploid configuration.) Many varieties, including *G. hirsutum,* contain one pair of chromosomes of Asian origin and another of American origin.

Amazingly, recent scientific studies using DNA "molecular clocks" suggest that this hybridization between Old and New World strains occurred about ten million years ago, long before human beings evolved. For the past several million years, various species have grown in places as diverse as Peru, India, eastern and southern Africa, Egypt, New Guinea, Arabia, the Cape Verdes, Australia, the Galápagos, and Hawaii.

How did cotton develop this unique ability to spread, and even crossbreed, across the face of the earth without human help? The answer seems to lie in two unusual properties of its seeds: first, their ability to survive immersion in salt water for up to several years; and second, their natural buoyancy and their propensity to attach themselves to flotsam.

Ancient cotton plants produced fibers only a fraction of an inch long, in contrast to the modern domesticated agricultural product, which yields fibers up to several inches long. Most commercially important plants and animals were domesticated just once, but ancient farmers in both the Old World and the New World independently turned this trick on at least four separate occasions—twice in the Americas (*G. hirsutum* and *G. barbadense*), once in Asia (*G. arboreum*), and once in Africa (*G. herbaceum*).[26]

India's highly varying soils yielded different varieties of cotton, which in turn produced the rich diversity of Indian manufactured cloths, such as fine muslin from Dacca in east Bengal and sateens and printed chintz from the Gujarat. Just as today's automobile, movie, and software industries crystallized around the technical expertise that accumulated in Detroit, Hollywood, and Silicon Valley, respectively, in the sixteenth century Indian cities such as Kasimbazar and Ahmadabad attracted spinners, weavers, and finishers, and their products became world famous. Of

India's four major textile centers—the Bengal, the Punjab, the Coromandel (southeast) Coast, and Gujarat—the last was by far the most important and supplied the Muslim empires of the Middle East with both common cloth and the finest luxury fabrics, via the Red Sea and Persian Gulf routes.

Until well into the modern era, textiles were the world's primary manufactured product. Often woven with silver, gold, and silk, they were also the chief form of stored wealth for both rich and poor; most families wore their estate on their backs and hung it on their walls and windows. More to the point, people inherited these textile treasures from their parents; fashions would remain relatively unchanged for centuries, and all but the wealthiest possessed only a few items.[27] Styles not only were static over time but were also rigidly segregated by class. An inflexible social structure, reinforced by sumptuary laws, determined just who could wear what. In the mid-seventeenth century, the EIC disrupted this age-old state of affairs, turning the worlds of English industry, trade, fashion, and social rank upside down in just a few decades. The Company's instrument in this commercial revolution was cotton.

The fabric's evolution into a major trade commodity bears a striking resemblance to that of sugar. At the EIC's birth in 1600, cotton was a high-end product on a par with silk; that it was affordable at all, even as a luxury item, depended on the cheapness of Indian labor. Like sugar, cotton is easy to grow but requires an enormous amount of labor to process. At the dawn of the industrial age, growing a hundred pounds of the crude mixture of fibers and seeds—the bolls—consumed only about two person-days of work. Removing the seeds from the bolls (ginning), arranging the fibers in parallel order (carding), and packing (bailing) took another seventy person-days and yielded just eight pounds of raw cotton ("cotton wool").[28] Female spinners (whence "spinster") required another thirty-five person-days to transform this amount of cotton wool into thread. Thus, about thirteen days labor were needed to produce each pound of cotton thread, compared with one or two per pound of wool, two to five for linen, and six for silk.[29]

India had not only a large and inexpensive workforce, but also centuries of expertise with cotton textiles. The assembly of millions of short, fragile cotton fibers into a durable thread is no mean task. Before 1750, English spinners could not produce cotton thread strong enough to use in the lengthwise fabric warp, so domestically made cloth was usually a mix of linen or wool warp and cotton weft; only the more highly skilled Indian spinners manufactured thread adequate for bolts of pure cotton fabric. Thus, before the invention of practical spinning machines in the eighteenth century, almost all of the West's cotton cloth came from thread spun in India.

In the early 1600s, the EIC commanded only a small portion of the all-important spice trade; its major business was in Persian silks, shipped by camel over the Syrian desert to Turkish ports. Before long, the EIC began tapping the Indian fabric markets as well. At that early stage, no one could imagine that the trade in these textiles would eventually ignite the Industrial Revolution, destroy Indian textile manufacturing, spark a controversy over free trade in Britain as contentious as any seen in today's globalized economy, and, last but not least, give birth to the British Empire.

Within several decades of the Company's chartering by Elizabeth I on the last day of the sixteenth century, England was gazing at a kaleidoscope of fabrics, colors, and patterns the like of which had never been seen before in Europe. England's traditional heavy, monochrome woolens could not compete with clothes, drapery, and upholstery made of the light, gaily colored printed Indian fabric. Nor did it hurt that one of the world's most efficient commercial organizations now ran the cotton trade.

The EIC was not content to let mere market demand drive its sales and imports. In the mid-seventeenth century, the Company began to actively manipulate consumer tastes, and in the process invented both the fashion industry and consumer society as we know them today.

The EIC realized that if "fashion leaders" wore Indian chintz and hung calico drapery, others would quickly follow. In a corrupt and class-obsessed monarchical society, it was relatively easy to identify and seduce these fountainheads—the royal family. If they adopted a given style, the aristocracy would follow, and the aristocrats would in turn be aped by the minor nobility, who would in turn be slavishly copied by the commercial elites, and so on down the line to the humblest peasant with a few shillings to spare.

By the late seventeenth century, Indian chintzes had already found limited favor among small numbers of the English middle class because they mimicked the more expensive silks, satins, and taffetas worn by the aristocracy. The royals themselves, however, shunned the new imitators from the subcontinent, preferring the "real thing." Sir Josiah Child, governor of the EIC, set out to change things. The Company had previously made a "gift" of silver tableware worth £3,000 to Charles II in 1660, but the directors decided that it was useless to dole out such small change. In 1684 they extended to the monarch "voluntary contributions" of £324,250, and in addition both the king and the Duke of York were granted company shares. The birth of constitutional monarchy in 1689 did not stop such favors. In 1698 one courtier observed that in the queen's chamber "all [the] Indian Embroidery on white satin [was] presented to her by the Company."[30] Other members of the nobility were not forgotten; to them went not only calicoes and shares, but also committee memberships and free freightage on EIC ships.[31]

By the early eighteenth century, cotton fabrics had deposed silks and woolens at the apex of the fashion world. Daniel Defoe observed:

> Our wrought silks and our fine stuffs submit to that noble usurpation of printed calico; striped muslins have most gallantly deposed your manufacture of bordelace, and are sometimes sold for as great a price.[32]

The EIC had also discovered the salutary effects of annual changes in style. Defoe sniffed, "[That] the clothes [are] thrown by in *England,* not for their being worn out, *but merely for their being out of Fashion* is incredible, and perhaps are equivalent to the Clothing Expense of some Nations."[33] The Company also encouraged the concept of "undress," or what we today call leisure wear—lightweight gowns and shifts worn in the privacy of the home.[34]

While enlisting high and low fashion in the service of the EIC, Josiah Child did not neglect the status of its Indian outposts. Less than a decade after its founding in 1600, the Company established its first base of operations at Surat (north of Bombay), the chief Mughal port, which had succeeded Cambay after the latter silted up. By the time Child became a director in 1677, the EIC had already established "presidencies," or trading posts, in Madras (on India's southeast coast) and Bombay. (Bombay derives its name from *Bom Baia,* or "good bay," the name given to it by the Portuguese. In 1661, England's Charles II had acquired it as a dowry from his

Portuguese bride, Catherine of Braganza, and the port soon overshadowed nearby Surat.[35]) In 1690, under Child's leadership, a third presidency was established in Calcutta. Eventually, these trading posts, whose main purpose was the purchase of textiles, would become the cornerstone of the British Empire.

An unabashed admirer of the Dutch system of fortified trading posts, Child rapidly built up the EIC's military presence at the three presidencies. This policy paid off during the conflict between the Mughals and Hindu Marathas that raged between 1681 and 1707. He also solidified the complex "trading rules" required by the two-year "feedback loop" between the initial departure of cargoes of silver and trade goods from England and the arrival back home of calicoes.

By the end of the seventeenth century, the Company was shipping home more than 1.5 million cotton bolts and clothing items per year, which represented 83 percent of the total value of its imports.[36] Spices were dead; cotton was now truly king.

Needless to say, the EIC's competitors howled in protest. For example, the Levant Company sought in 1681 to prohibit importation of India's superior cotton fabrics.[37] Its arguments had the familiar ring of protectionist sanctimony, charging that purchases by the EIC had drained Britain of gold bullion in order to acquire

> calicoes, pepper, wrought silks, and a deceitful sort of raw silk— calicoes and wrought silks manufactured in India being an evident damage to the poor of this nation and the latter of raw silks an infallible destruction of the Turkey trade.[38]

This was not all. The EIC also stood accused of exporting advanced English technology to India, having sent

> into India throwsters, weavers, and dyers, and actually set up there a manufacture of silk . . . importing them ready made and dyed into England is an unspeakable impoverishment of the working people of this kingdom who would otherwise be employed therein and to the ruin of many thousands of families here.[39]

Josiah Child, recently elevated to the governorship of the EIC, carried the day, as he so often did:

> The truth of the case at bottom is this: the importation of better and cheaper raw silk from India may probably throw some Turkey merchants' profit at present though it doth benefit the kingdom. . . . What then? Must one trade be interrupted because it works upon another? At that rate there would be nothing but confusion in a nation ad infinitum.[40]

Modernize the grammar and change a few nouns, and the above exchange could easily pass for television talk show repartee between opponents and supporters of the latest international trade agreement.

In the closing years of the seventeenth century, three groups in England coalesced into a strange protectionist alliance dedicated to shutting down cotton imports from Asia: the moralists, angered by the social disruption caused by the new finery; the silk and wool weavers, made redundant by a cheaper and better foreign product; and the mercantilists, angered by the outflow of silver to pay for mere fashion. These forces rose against the EIC and caused dire consequences for the Company and also revolutions in England's economy, social structure, and empire. In addition, as we shall see in chapter 11, they also destroyed the bedrock of India's economy, its textile industry.

Of the three groups opposed to the India trade, the mercantilists were the most influential. The debate between them and the free-traders supporting the EIC engaged the nation's most talented economic minds and found expression in that era's equivalent of the political blog, the pamphlet, which generally sold for a few pence per piece. Mercantilist theory was simplicity itself: a nation's wealth was measured by the amount of gold and silver it possessed.

In other words, international commerce constituted a zero-sum game in which one nation's gain came only at the expense of another, and the only way for a country to grow rich was to garner gold and silver from abroad by exporting more than it imported. In modern parlance, the route to wealth lay in a positive trade balance. This, too, was a grim tug-of-war, since every gold sovereign or piece of eight accrued by one nation had to come from a competitor. In the words of an early EIC merchant, Thomas Mun, "We must ever observe this rule: to sell more to strangers yearly than we consume of theirs in value."[41]

Not all imports and exports were equal in the mercantilist scheme of things. Ideally, a nation should import only raw materials and export only finished manufactured products, as this practice would maximize employment. Likewise, a prudent people eschewed the consumption of foreign luxury products, since these vaporized large amounts of gold and silver and weakened domestic employment, a tenet aimed squarely at the EIC. The mercantilist sought to minimize imports with high tariffs or, occasionally, outright prohibition, and to encourage exports by eliminating embarkation duties, and even by subsidizing exports.

Today, the fallacy of these arguments is obvious: nations grow wealthy mainly by improving their industrial and agricultural productivity. The consumption of foreign luxuries causes little concern, and few Americans care how many bars of gold sit in vaults in Fort Knox or in the New York Federal Reserve Bank. (The ghost of mercantilism still haunts the modern world in the form of import duties and restrictions, and, most perniciously, agricultural subsidies.)

Three hundred years ago, as England debated the India trade, few detected the flaws in mercantilism.[42] One observer, Roger Coke, noted that Holland, the world's wealthiest nation on a per capita basis, "imported everything," whereas impoverished Ireland exported far more than it imported.[43] Another, Charles Davenant, cogently explained that the benefits of keeping a nation "more Cheaply supply'd" with foreign imports far outweighed the damage done to domestic employment. He perceptively argued that trade was not in fact a zero-sum game, "For all Trades have a Mutual Dependance upon one another, and one begets another, and the loss of one frequently loses half the rest." In his view, protectionist measures were "needless, unnatural, and can have no Effect conducive to the Publick Good"; further, they encouraged inefficient domestic industries with artificially high prices and threw good money after bad.[44]

By far the most remarkable early free-trader was Henry Martyn, whose *Considerations upon the East India Trade* preceded by seventy-five years Adam Smith's *Wealth of Nations*. Martyn saw clearly that mercantilists, by equating gold with wealth, repeated the mistake of King Midas. Precious metals are useful only because they can be exchanged for things we want or need. A nation's true wealth, Martyn realized, was defined by how much it *consumed:*

> Bullion is only secondary and dependant, Cloaths and Manufactures are real and principal riches. Are not these things esteem'd Riches

over the World? And that Country thought richest which most abounds in them? *Holland* is the Magazin of every Country's Manufactures; *English* Cloth, *French* Wines, *Italian* Silks, are treasur'd up there. If these things were not riches, they wou'd not give their Bullion for 'em.[45]

Martyn gloried in the cornucopia of trade:

Why are we surrounded by the Sea? Surely that our Wants at home might be supply'd by our navigation into other Countries, the least and easiest Labour. By this we taste the spices of *Arabia,* yet we never feel the scorching Sun which brings them forth; we shine in silks which our Hands have never wrought; we drink of Vinyards which we never planted; the Treasures of those Mines are ours, in which we have never digg'd; we only plough the Deep and reap the Harvest of every Country in the World.[46]

Martyn freely admitted that allowing in cheap Indian goods cost English weavers their jobs, but he saw their labor as wasted "make work" that could be more profitably employed elsewhere:

If the Providence of God wou'd provide Corn for *England* as *Manna* heretofore for *Israel,* the People wou'd not be well imploy'd to Plough, and Sow, and Reap. . . . In like manner, if the *East-Indies* wou'd send us Cloaths for nothing, as good or equivalent of those made in *England* by prodigious labour of the People, we shou'd be very ill imploy'd to refuse the Gift.[47]

Martyn's brilliant economic insights strayed too far ahead of their time, and unlike Adam Smith he did not become a household name. In the case of the EIC's Indian imports, the legislative records barely mention him or Coke and Davenant; only the mercantilist John Pollexfen, a member of the Board of Trade, influenced parliamentary debate in the way that Smith would do in the nineteenth century.[48]

The real battle—the political one—began in 1678. In that year, Parliament, mindful of the difficulty of mandating fashion for the living, required that the dead, at least, be buried in wool. Over the next decade, the EIC and its allies narrowly defeated a series of bills aimed at their imports. One would have required the wearing of wool by all students, faculty members, judges, and lawyers; another, the wearing of wool by all citizens six months of the year; yet another, the wearing of felt hats by all female servants earning less than £5 per year.

By the time of the Glorious Revolution of 1688, the calico contro-versy had grown more contentious. With the ascension of the Dutch King William, the Company lost much of its previous influence over the mon-archy. A newly adjusted Land Tax paid for King William's conflict with France and burdened English landowners. In turn, the landowners saw the merchant class as villains perpetrating the cardinal sin of mercantilist dogma: draining the kingdom of gold and silver to pay for Asian frivoli-ties. The new merchant class, represented by the EIC, found itself gener-ally outgunned by the moralists, weavers, and mercantilists and fighting a rearguard action against the forces of protectionism.

In 1696, weavers and spinners from Canterbury, Norwich, Norfolk, and Cambridge, impoverished by competition from calicoes, petitioned Parliament for relief. The House of Commons responded with a draco-nian bill which would have outlawed the importation of any cotton fabric into the kingdom and penalized violators with a £100 fine—five to ten years of wages for the average worker. Proponents of the bill mustered a steady stream of witnesses who had been damaged by the India trade—not just wool and silk makers, but also domestic lacquer workers and makers of furniture and fans put out of work by less expensive Indian products. Opposition came from the EIC and its supporters—upholsterers, linen drapers, dyers, and calico printers.

The bill sailed through the House of Commons, but it was killed be-hind closed doors in the House of Lords, probably in a hail of bribes from Child. The weavers, stung by this treachery, marched on Parliament, which took the bill up again later in 1696. In January 1697, five thousand weav-ers, agitated by the false rumor that the bill had yet again been thrown out, surrounded Parliament and managed to break into the Commons lobby. The members locked the door to the main chamber, whereupon the weavers pro-ceeded to the EIC headquarters, where they also failed to break in. Secu-rity was tightened at both Parliament and the EIC, and a cowed House of Commons placated the weavers by once again passing the bill. Once more, Child greased the skids in the House of Lords by "pouring gold in plente-ous showers in ladyes' laps who bore great powers."[49] Yet again, thousands of weavers marched in anger, this time on Child's house, where soldiers fired on the mob, killing one and injuring several others.

Wealthier sponsors now acted against the EIC. For many years, small private merchants had traded in Asian ports in violation of the Company's monopoly. In 1698, Parliament gave official status to these "interlopers," as they were called, and granted them a charter for the New East India Company. To reestablish its monopoly, the original EIC was forced to buy a majority of shares in the new company and then merge its operations into the old one.

At this critical juncture, in 1699, Child died. Absent his intellectual presence and deep pockets, the forces of protection finally triumphed. In April 1700, the party of the landed interests, the Tories, succeeded in passing the Prohibition Act, which forbade the importation of painted or dyed calicoes and silks; unpainted fabrics were still permitted, though they became subject to a 15 percent import duty.[50]

The 1701 Act (named for the year it actually became effective) backfired, for three reasons. First, calicoes became forbidden fruit, and thus even more desirable. Second, smuggling, the inevitable accompaniment of prohibition, flared up in the years following the act's passage. In the words of one pamphleteer, "England being an Island, there are a thousand places for putting goods on shore."[51] Though most of the smuggled calicoes were brought in by French and Dutch merchants, no small amount entered England in the private baggage of the EIC's employees. Third, and worst of all for the weavers, the act aided domestic cotton manufacturers by providing them with large amounts of plain Indian cloth to feed their advanced printing machinery. The wool manufacturers soon realized that the act had worsened their situation. Before its passage:

> Calicoes printed in India were most used by the richer sort of people whilst the poor continued to wear and use our woolen goods. The calicoes now printed in England are so very cheap and so much the fashion that persons of all qualities and degrees clothe themselves and furnish their houses in great measure with them.[52]

This overstated the case. Because of the enormous amount of labor required to turn raw cotton into fine cloth, finished calicoes were still more expensive than wool or silk garments. The economic downturn of 1719, caused by war with Spain, pushed silk weavers and wool weavers to desperation. On June 10 of that year, several hundred workers from Spitalfields, the silk-weaving district of London, attacked stores that sold calicoes, cotton printing shops, and even people unfortunate to be caught wearing the fabric. In some instances the "calico chasers" ripped the hated fabric off wearers' backs, soaked the garments in corrosive nitric acid, mounted them on sticks, then paraded these motley trophies through the streets. For months, weavers terrorized London. The disturbance ended only with the onset of winter, when even the most fashionable ladies clad themselves in warmer wool.[53]

The specter of insurrection frightened Parliament and the new Hanoverian monarchy. They debated how to mollify mobs of weavers, who on at least one other occasion again angrily surrounded Parliament, chanted, and demanded action. The legislative battle raged for two years. Finally, in 1721, following the economic chaos caused by the collapse of the South Sea Bubble, Parliament banned even the importation of plain Indian cloth. Wearing it also became a crime; violators were fined £5, which could be claimed by the informer. Thenceforth, only thread or raw cotton could be imported. Curiously, Parliament allowed one exception to the ban on whole cloth: women were allowed to wear imported cottons if dyed an unfashionable plain blue.[54]

Inevitably, these protectionist measures backfired against the woolen industry and the silk weavers. At the beginning of the eighteenth century, calico was the classic "high value-added commodity." The wealth of Croesus awaited those who could bridge the gap between cheap raw cotton and the expensive, smooth, light cloth desired by consumers. High demand and high prices for calicoes, combined with the unavailability of Indian cloth, drove innovators to improve the spinning and weaving processes.

Improve they did. Just a dozen years after the passage of the act of 1721, John Kay perfected the flying shuttle, which doubled weavers' productivity. This served to increase the demand for thread, whose spinning was more difficult to mechanize. In 1738, Lewis Paul and John Wyatt patented the first mechanical spinning machine, but no commercially feasible device became available until the mid-1760s, when such machines were invented by James Hargreaves, Richard Arkwright, and Samuel Crompton. (These were, respectively, the spinning jenny, the water frame, and the mule, the latter so-called because it was a hybrid of the first two.)[55]

As the economic historian Eric Hobsbawm famously said, "Whoever says Industrial Revolution says cotton." The new machines that were the heart of the great transformation made redundant untold thousands of spinners and weavers, who engaged in spasms of "machine breaking" in the eighteenth and nineteenth centuries before finally disappearing into the new mills.[56] (The term "Luddite" derives from the probably fictional leader of the machine-breaking riots in the 1810s, Ned Ludd.)

Immediately after the act of 1721, the EIC's favored import had been Indian thread, but with the advent of these ingenious new machines raw cotton became the fodder of the Industrial Revolution and the trade commodity of choice. In the early 1720s, the EIC imported about 1.5 million pounds of cotton wool per year from India; this figure rose to about thirty million pounds by the late 1790s.[57]

Over the next seventy-five years, the English cotton industry increased demand for its inexpensive new products by inventing the multipronged consumer marketing machine so familiar today: fashion magazines, an ever-shorter style cycle, retail showrooms, and regional warehouses fed by the country's newly privatized roads and turnpikes.[58]

Asia's cotton crops were no longer sufficient to satisfy the hungry maw of the dark, satanic mills. England's factories turned out half a million pounds of finished cloth in 1765, two million in 1775, and sixteen million in 1784. English settlers began to plant cotton in tropical South America and the West Indies, which were already well supplied with slave labor, but even these could not satisfy Lancashire's demand for raw cotton. The supply would come not from the empire, but rather from the newly independent United States.

At the time of the first census in 1790, the young republic contained roughly seven hundred thousand slaves (about one-sixth of the total population), most of whom lived in the South. But owing to an agricultural depression, the South at that time actually exported more slaves than it imported. In 1794, this situation changed when Eli Whitney invented the cotton gin—a crude nail-and-cylinder device that efficiently separated fiber from seed. This machine converted the South's huge arable basin into England's cotton farm, just a few weeks' sailing time away from Bristol and Liverpool (versus six months around the African cape from India).

By 1820, American cotton exports, primarily to England, would grow to two hundred million pounds annually, and by the eve of the Civil War that number would swell to two billion pounds.[59] England, indignant over the Confederacy's aggressive defense of slavery and disdainful of the

Scotch-Irish rabble who settled the South, should by rights have sided with
the Union. Such, however, was the dark influence of King Cotton that Britain
remained neutral throughout the conflict.

Just as the loss of the Spice Islands to the Dutch in the seventeenth century had forced the EIC to shift its focus to Indian textiles, the loss of the
highly profitable trade in finished cottons and silks in the eighteenth century once again shifted its center of gravity. This time, it would turn to
China and the tea trade.

Whereas India was a fractious land divided along ethnic, religious,
and political lines, and thus highly susceptible to manipulation by Europeans, China was an ethnically coherent, centralized country. It easily kept
Western merchants at arm's length and permitted them entrance only into
Canton. Worse, the Chinese had little appetite for Western goods besides
mechanical novelties, such as watches, clocks, and "singsongs" (the in-
tricate European music boxes favored by the imperial household), or the
exceptional strategic commodities they lacked, such as copper. This trade
imbalance would explode into open warfare in the mid-nineteenth century, and that conflict yet poisons present day Sino-Western trade and
politics.

The EIC's China ships were dedicated to tea transport, crafted for
speed and crammed with specially designed sealed chests to protect their
precious but perishable cargo. As the Dutch had avoided the Portuguese
by bypassing Malacca, so too did the English steer clear of the strait to
avoid the Dutch. Outbound, the sleek China boats followed the route of
the Ancient Mariner on the frigid roaring forties south of Australia before turning north. Homebound, they avoided Dutch patrols by steering
southeast into the open Pacific before threading past the eastern tip of New
Guinea and the shallow Torres Strait north of Australia.

Since China largely excluded Westerners, Europeans knew little more
about growing tea than they did in the time of Marco Polo. The production
process was far more complex than merely growing and drying the leaves.
By the time tea appeared on Canton's wharves, it had been processed, transported, and stored numerous times. At each stage it was tasted and blended
with leaves from other towns and provinces, and adulterated with ingredients as exotic as scented bergamot or as dishonest as sawdust.

Coffee had a century's head start on tea; the VOC brought the first cargoes of the dried tea leaves to Amsterdam around 1610; the first shipments reached England around 1645; and in 1657 Garroway's Coffee House in London's financial district began selling the beverage.[60] When Portugal's Catherine of Braganza married Charles II, she brought to the English court not only the dowry of Bombay, but also tea brewing, which had by then become well established in Lisbon. As with cotton, the road to commercial success in England ran directly through the royal chambers; it was not long before the nobility, the lesser aristocracy, and aspiring commoners soon followed. In 1685 the EIC informed its buyers in Canton:

> Thea is grown to be a commodity here and we have occasion to make presents therein to our great friends at Court; we would have you send us yearly five or six canisters of the very best and freshest Thea.[61]

In 1700, a pound of leaves for which a Chinese peasant was paid one penny sold in European shops for about £3. By 1800, that price had plummeted 95 percent to about three shillings, making tea affordable for most citizens. In 1700, only the wealthiest drank tea; at midcentury, most members of the bourgeoisie (including, famously, Dr. Johnson) consumed it regularly; by 1800 it was swilled even in the workhouses.

The Company more than made up for the drop in price with the rise in volume, which over the eighteenth century rose from fifty tons per year to fifteen thousand. Even if most tea was reexported to places such as Paris and Boston, that still left one or two pounds per year for every Englishman. The EIC made perhaps a shilling per pound—not an enormous profit margin, but multiplied over thousands of tons per year, enough to inspire hatred and envy at all levels of British society. Even more venom was reserved for the crown, which levied taxes totaling as much as 100 percent of the landing price in England. As Englishmen grew addicted to tea, the crown grew addicted to duties on its import.

Smuggling inevitably followed high tariffs. England's south coast and West Country became a paradise for landing contraband tea, while French traders favored the Channel Islands. Typically, local entrepreneurs rowed out to waiting foreign vessels to purchase the illicit cargo that eventually found its way into caves, castles, private homes, and even church crypts. Women traveling abroad equipped their petticoats with hidden pockets. As much as three-quarters of the brew consumed in England was contraband, a proportion surpassed only in the American colonies. By the middle of the eighteenth century, the conflict between tea runners and customs agents verged on open warfare. The tombstone of one smuggler reads:

> A little tea, one leaf I did not steal
> For guiltless bloodshed I to God appeal
> Put tea on one scale, human blood in t'other
> And think what 'tis to slay a harmless brother.[62]

Ironically, the smugglers, by dramatically bringing down the cost of tea, increased its consumption. In 1784, the government finally came to its senses and reduced the tariff from 120 percent to 12.5 percent.

The explosion in tea imports during the eighteenth century cannot, however, be credited entirely to the smugglers, let alone to the marketing genius of the EIC. Because tea was relatively cheap at its source in China, it was served there lukewarm with little aplomb in a handle-less cup. The Japanese, because of its expense, poured it with far greater ceremony, and Europeans served it hot so as to quickly dissolve the sugar used to make it palatable to the Western tongue. This custom required a new invention: the cup handle.

The handle-less Chinese cups stacked easily and could be shipped as ballast and sold for a few pence. The handles were added later, and by the mid-eighteenth century, handle makers had become a fixture in most large European cities. Gradually, the secrets of making fine porcelain were solved by European craftsmen such as Josiah Wedgwood, whose technical skill was exceeded only by his marketing genius.

Tea consumption burgeoned as beverage and cup combined to change the very rhythm of daily life in England, punctuating the day with ceremonial occasions around which social activity and organized conversation flowed, from the most stylish households to the humblest of workplaces. It amazed and annoyed the aristocratic fountainheads of fashion that the great unwashed had adopted their once exclusive preserve.[63] As early as 1757, one observer scoffed:

The laborer and the mechanic will ape the lord. . . . Your servants' servants, down to the very beggars, will not be satisfied unless they consume the produce of the remote country of China.[64]

The histories of tea and sugar are also intertwined and their consumptions rose nearly in tandem. The sugar planters encouraged the consumption of tea, realizing that it was in their interest, and the EIC did the same for sugar, in which it otherwise had little direct trade. By the eighteenth century, it amazed few observers that these two items, considered necessities from the high to the humble, grew thousands of miles from England and on opposite sides of the world from each other.

The story of sugar cannot be grasped without an understanding of Caribbean history. Since 1492, Spain had claimed the Caribbean as its exclusive preserve, while the Dutch, English, and French sought for centuries to prise it from Spanish hands. In 1559, the French and Spanish agreed that the region was "beyond the line"—that is, exempt from whatever treaties and agreements bound them in the rest of the world. The region was up for grabs—the Wild West of the 1600s and 1700s—and exerted an irresistible pull on adventurers all over Europe.

The Caribbean was no late-medieval tropical paradise, but rather a Hobbesian maelstrom of avarice and barbarity. Europeans who sailed west flouted not only the treaty obligations of their home countries, but also the mores and boundaries of normal behavior. These deviations manifested themselves in all manner of excess: drinking, overspending, and violence toward natives, slaves, and each other. When a Frenchman could find no Dutchman, Spaniard, or Briton to kill, his own countrymen sufficed quite nicely. In the spirit of the times, the first English efforts in the region were led by pirates such as Drake and his cousin Hawkins, who traded slaves to European planters when they were not plundering the shipping of Portugal and Spain.

Traditionally, geographers have divided the Caribbean islands into the Greater Antilles—Cuba, Hispañola, Puerto Rico, and Jamaica—and the Lesser Antilles: the numerous smaller islands curving south toward Venezuela. The Spanish quickly settled the Greater Antilles, which then became a backwater, second fiddle to the far greater riches of Mexico and

South America. This left only the scraps, the Lesser Antilles, to the French, Dutch, and English. Although the Spanish had little direct territorial interest in these flyspecks, they could not be ignored, since the treasure ships bearing silver from Mexico and South America had to thread the strategic, narrow passages through them on the way home.

The British began modestly in the Caribbean by acquiring the tiny island of Saint Christopher (modern-day Saint Kitts), in 1623. It would soon be lost to France, then regained by diplomatic means. (More than a century later, Alexander Hamilton was born on neighboring Nevis.) In 1627, England began planting subsistence crops on Barbados, a larger (166 square miles), uninhabited, isolated island well to the east of the main chain.

In 1625 the crown awarded Barbados to two competing royal "patent holders," William Courteen and the Earl of Carlisle. When the latter won out around 1630, he distributed the land among 764 settlers, with grants ranging from about thirty acres up to a thousand. These first immigrant farmers produced food for themselves and also planted cash crops, the most important of which were tobacco and cotton.

Each of the new landholders in turn typically attracted paid laborers and indentured servants from England with promises of small plots, generally ten acres, at the completion of their service. Early on, most of these promises were kept, but when the land ran out in the 1630s, new immigrants were faced with the unpleasant choice of leaving for other islands in search of land, remaining on Barbados, or returning empty-handed to England.

Initially, then, Barbadian society was not radically different from English society, with few, if any, slaves. Around 1640, the inhabitants noted the rapid increase in European demand for sugar and decided to band together to plant cane, which had arrived from Surinam shortly after Barbados was first settled.

Fate smiled on the island, for just at that moment small-time Dutch interlopers, seeking to carve out a sugar-carrying trade independent of the monopoly held by the Dutch West India Company (WIC), appeared in the Caribbean offering French and English settlers expertise in sugar growing and slaves. Further assistance became available between 1645 and 1654, when the Portuguese settlers drove the WIC out of Brazil, and Dutch-Portuguese Jewish growers, not eager to stay in a colony

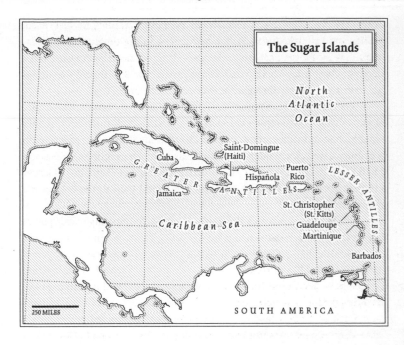

The Sugar Islands

North Atlantic Ocean

Cuba

Saint-Domingue (Haiti)

Puerto Rico

Hispañola

Jamaica

GREATER ANTILLES

LESSER ANTILLES

St. Christopher (St. Kitts)

Caribbean Sea

Guadeloupe

Martinique

Barbados

250 MILES

SOUTH AMERICA

newly reconquered by Portuguese Catholics, made their services available in the Caribbean.

Within a few decades, the first British farmers and their servants had almost completely cleared Barbados and planted it with cane. By 1660, it had more settlers than Virginia or Massachusetts, four hundred inhabitants per square mile, or four times the population density of England. It had become the world's largest sugar producer, supplying almost two-thirds of England's consumption.[65] Just how was this tiny island able to rival its much larger competitors in Brazil and the Greater Antilles? Some of the answer can be found in the agreeable soil and availability of wind power on its leeward side, which was relatively protected from hurricanes. Credit also belongs to the capitalist mind-set of the English farmer, who owned his own land (or at least paid his own rent to the landowner), hired his own labor, and reaped his own profits. The Brazilians, by contrast, used a paternalistic sharecropping model in which small farmers sent their cane to the landowner's mill and received in return only a fraction of the refined sugar it yielded.[66] With sugar prices so high and land at such a premium in Barbados, farmers planted little acreage with subsistence crops, and the island had to import much of its food, a pattern that would be repeated later on the larger Caribbean sugar islands.

Of all the islands, Barbados held the firmest grip on the British imagination. Its fertile soil yielded cane in abundance, and its cool, rolling uplands reminded homesick settlers of England. One early settler, Richard Ligon, rapturously described his first visit:

> The nearer we came, the more beautiful it appeared to our eyes. . . . There we saw the high, large, and lofty Trees, with their spreading Branches and flourishing tops . . . as to grow to that perfection of beauty and largeness. Whilst they in gratitude return their cool shade . . . The plantations appear'd to us one above the other, like several stories in stately buildings, which afforded us a large proportion of delight.[67]

The easterly trades provided the cane crushers with reliable power, and by 1660 the island was dotted with hundreds of picturesque windmills. But the settlement's true appeal was a rather less aesthetic quality: it had become one of the world's wealthiest places, and its planter aristocracy the stuff of gaudy legend.

Before the rise of the New World sugar plantations, the far-flung plantations of the Mediterranean and eastern Atlantic islands usually shipped hogsheads of raw brown "muscovado" to industrial refineries in the home country for final processing into the fine white sugar craved by consumers. As Barbadian production rose, the planters acquired the sophisticated crystallization technology and bypassed the European refineries. English refiners reacted in the predictable protectionist language of national interest:

> One ship of white brings the lading of three of brown. . . . Is this the way to maintain Nurseries for our Seamen? Since refining in England hath been a trade before ever we had plantations [it was absurd that] it should be lost by having them.[68]

They needn't have worried, for the sugar industrialists of Barbados soon turned their efforts away from the white gold to a cane product whose very name became synonymous with the island: rum. The sweet alcoholic beverage, first fermented by Barbadian slaves from molasses, the waste product of the refining process, soon found itself in demand in Africa, where it was greatly preferred to English brandy. Before long Caribbean traders dispatched ships loaded with rum to the Gulf of Guinea to exchange for slaves. Barbadian planters directed their factories toward rum production and kept the island the richest place in the Caribbean well into the eighteenth century, even as its sugar output fell well behind that of Jamaica, Saint-Domingue (modern Haiti), and the Leewards.[69]

While some of the original settlers stayed on to join the new planter elite, many sold their property, which had appreciated tenfold in the 1640s alone, and retired to England. Those who took their place were nothing like the doughty yeomen who hacked farms out of the tropical forest in the 1620s and 1630s. The optimal size for a Barbadian sugar plantation seemed to be about two hundred acres, large enough to make its mill economical. After 1650, buying one of the increasingly pricey plantations required a healthy line of credit; many of the new arrivals were the poor but creditworthy younger sons of the landed aristocracy, usually fresh from the battles of the English civil war. Typical of the new breed was Thomas Modyford, who

> had taken a Resolution to himself not to set his face towards England,
> till he had made his voyage, and imployment there, worth him a
> hundred thousand pounds sterling; and all by this sugar plant.[70]

England, its appetite whetted by the wealth of Barbadian sugar, cast its eyes on other Caribbean islands. There was now no avoiding conflict with Spain, which had long occupied the choicest Caribbean real estate. The English finally settled on Jamaica, twenty-six times the size of Barbados. By 1655, the larger island had been raided and its cities burned by both pirates and English regulars on several occasions. In that year, British soldiers invaded it (under the direction of Admiral William Penn, father of Pennsylvania's founder), and by 1658 they had driven out the last Spaniards. From that moment, the British strove to make Jamaica their sugar pantry, at one point drawing one third of the African slave traffic.[71]

Barbados's heyday was relatively short-lived. After 1680, falling sugar prices, English tariffs, and depleted soil and forests ruined its plantations, and many planters fled to greener pastures in the New World. Modyford, for example, already one of the world's wealthiest men, went to Jamaica, where he became governor. Others returned as estate holders to England, where they became the prototypical nouveau riche of the eighteenth century, portrayed endlessly in the literature of the period. Yet another group went to an even larger and more promising venue: what is now South Carolina, where they re-created the plantation society they had left behind on the island. This Barbadian heritage manifested itself in the most slave-intensive society on the North American continent, and in a political style that centuries later yielded Fort Sumter and Strom Thurmond.[72]

The Portuguese, English, and Dutch operating "beyond the line" in the New World were to become three of the largest consumers of slave labor in the history of mankind. This was an unplanned and unforeseen fallout of the logistics of the plantation economy.

Growing cane requires vast amounts of manpower, which the European homelands could not supply. As the historian Richard S. Dunn described events in the British Caribbean: "The rape's progress was fatally easy: from exploiting the English laboring poor to abusing colonial bondservants to ensnaring kidnaps and convicts to enslaving black Africans."[73]

The first workers in the cane fields of the English Caribbean were white freemen, but by the late seventeenth century almost one-third of the field hands were prisoners.[74] It was not unheard of for youths to be kidnapped (or "barbadosed," a term analogous to the more modern "shanghaied") off the streets of Bristol or Liverpool to work in the cane fields. Even when available, English laborers were often surly and uncooperative; in the best of circumstances they remained on the plantation for only a few years before their indenture, their contracts, their prison terms, their patience, or their lives expired. A more permanent solution was needed.

Sometime around 1640, a group of Barbadian planters visited Dutch plantations in Brazil and were mightily impressed with the advantages of black slave labor. Africans had for millennia been accomplished farmers; not only were they skilled with plow and hoe, but they were also, unlike the English, well used to the heat and resistant to the great killers of the sugar islands—yellow fever and malaria. Best of all, they were cheap in comparison with free English labor, in terms of both initial price and upkeep. After 1660, plantation crews consisting of scores, and then hundreds, of Africans became the norm.[75]

Initially, the Portuguese, who were familiar with the West African coastline, supplied British needs in the Caribbean, but soon Englishmen entered the trade. Just four months after the restoration of the monarchy in 1660, and in the tradition of the time, Charles II established a monopoly company, jauntily named the "Royal Adventurers into Africa," to deal in African trade. Its shareholders included most of the royal family, Lord Sandwich, and Lord Ashley, who, in one of history's more delicious ideological ironies, was the philosopher John Locke's principal patron and protector. The Company concerned itself mainly with Africa's major export, gold, but also delivered several thousand slaves to Barbados.

The chronically mismanaged Adventurers were disbanded in 1672 and replaced with a far more formidable monopoly organization—the Royal African Company (RAC). This time, perhaps tipped off by Ashley about the profitability of traffic in slaves, Locke himself became a minor shareholder. A creature of the monarchy, the RAC did not fare well after the Glorious Revolution of 1688 and lost its monopoly a decade later. (With monopolies, timing is everything, and the RAC's was not good; Charles II had granted it the exclusive right to trade with Africa for a thousand years.) After it lost its slaving monopoly, the RAC did collect a one-tenth royalty on sales by independent slavers—"ten percenters," as they were known. Before the RAC faded into obscurity in the seventeenth century, it had shipped 75,000 slaves across the Atlantic. Of this number, about one in six did not survive the journey. (The death rate was almost certainly higher among the white crew members, who were not only more susceptible to tropical disease than the slaves but also less expensive to replace).[76]

Millions more would follow. Even in the absence of religious and cultural strictures against slavery, it is difficult and expensive to hunt, capture, and transport human beings; the majority of black slaves initially fell into the hands of opposing tribal armies, not slave traders. The Europeans' susceptibility to infectious diseases dictated a minimal white presence on the African slave coasts, limited to visiting crews and a few permanent agents, whose primary expertise lay in plying local rulers with gifts and bribes of all descriptions.

Since the local inhabitants of the slaving ports would not countenance such inhuman treatment of their ethnic brethren, the captives themselves had usually passed through several hands before reaching the coast in order to ensure that they were of different tribal origin from their final African jailers. Until well into the nineteenth century, the Portuguese, English, Dutch, and French remained largely unaware of just how their human cargoes had been acquired, and often of their precise geographic origin. Even had they wanted to capture the slaves themselves, Europeans could not have survived long enough to do so. The RAC's records show that 60 percent of its personnel in Africa died in the first year and 80 percent by the seventh year, and that only one in ten was discharged alive from company service.[77] One of the most prominent historians of slavery, David Brion Davis, points out:

> There has long been a widespread mythology claiming that Europeans were the ones who physically enslaved Africans—as if small groups of sailors, who were highly vulnerable to tropical diseases and who had no supply lines to their homelands, could kidnap some eleven to twelve million Africans.[78]

Just how did Europeans pay for their slaves? Largely in cloth. The RAC's records show that in the late 1600s, nearly three-quarters of the value of trade goods bound for Africa were in textiles, mostly of English manufacture, but with a considerable fraction of Indian calicoes as well. The non-textile items consisted mainly of raw iron, firearms, and cowrie shells.[79]

After exchanging trade goods for captives, the Europeans continued the barbarity. Each captive was allotted approximately four square feet of shipboard space—about the same as the space per passenger on a packed subway car or commercial airliner, but minus elemental sanitation, ventilation, or relief from a sweltering environment, and not for minutes or hours, but for weeks. Even in the best of circumstances—that is, in the absence of the epidemic diseases that almost always swept the slave holds—the captives were packed together spoon-style in pools of their own waste. Add to this miasma gastrointestinal illnesses and festering open sores from chains and immobility, and the circumstances on transatlantic slavers soon exceeded the bounds of human imagination. Testimony to Parliament from an officer on one ship, the *Alexander,* revealed that:

> When employed in stowing the slaves, he made the most of the room and wedged them in. They had not so much room as a man in his coffin, either in length or in breadth. It was impossible for them to turn or shift. . . . He says he cannot conceive of any situation so dreadful and disgusting as that of the slaves when ill of the flux: in the *Alexander,* the deck was covered with blood and mucus, and resembled a slaughterhouse. The stench and foul air were intolerable.[80]

Few subjects carry the emotional freight of the slave trade, and until very recently most of the approximations of its volume, nationality, and mortality reflected the ideological needs of the estimators more than objective reality. Only after 1950 did the subject become an object of serious historical inquiry, as scholars such as Philip Curtin and David Eltis strove to obtain a meaningful and accurate census of the trade.

The picture their data draw is stunning.[81] Between 1519 and the end of the slave trade in the late 1860s, 9.5 million African slaves arrived in the New World; Figure 10-2 plots the annual transatlantic traffic. Since the best estimates of mortality on the middle passage are around 15 percent, this means that eleven million captives began the journey in Africa.

The majority of the 9.5 million who survived the middle passage cut, crushed, and boiled cane.[82] Fully 80 percent of slaves came to Brazil and the Caribbean, while most of the rest went to Spanish North America and South America. So massive was this involuntary migration that as early as 1580, slaves constituted well over half of voyagers to the New World; by 1700, three-quarters; and by 1820, 90 percent. Truly, the settlement of the Americas would not have been possible without black slaves, who constituted fully 77 percent of those who crossed the Atlantic before 1820.[83] Only after the mid-nineteenth century, when the institution was finally outlawed, did the majority of immigrants have white skin.

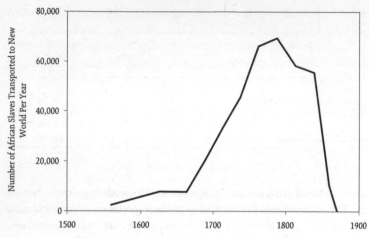

Figure 10-2. Annual Transatlantic Slave Trade

Surprisingly, only about four hundred thousand—about 4.5 percent—came to the British North American colonies. Table 10-1, which summarizes the proportions of slaves arriving in the New World according to destination and the proportions of their descendants living there in 1950, lays.out the puzzle. First, note that in spite of the fact that the United States and Canada received fewer than one slave in twenty, these two nations now contain nearly one in three of their descendants. The opposite pattern holds for the Caribbean, which received over two-fifths of the slaves, but now contains just one-fifth of their descendants, suggesting that it was difficult to maintain the slave population in the islands.

How did the slaves manage to increase their numbers in Canada and the United States? The answer is that sugar is the deadliest of crops, and for the most part British North America did not grow it. The cutting, grinding, and boiling meant overwork and an early death for millions of Africans—most of them men, since vigorous males were the import of choice on the plantations. Nothing like the sugar islands, as exemplified by Barbados, Jamaica, the Windwards and Leewards, and Saint-Domingue, had ever been seen before, and hopefully nothing like them will ever be seen again. These societies were peopled almost en-

Table 10-1. Proportions of New-World Slave Imports between 1500 and 1880, and Their Descendant Populations in 1950.

	Proportion of Slaves Imported into New World between 1500 and 1880	Proportion of New-World African Descendants in 1950
U.S. and Canada	4.5%	31.1%
Mexico and Central America	2.4%	0.7%
Caribbean Islands	43.0%	20.0%
Brazil	38.2%	36.6%
Other South America	11.8%	11.6%

tirely by black Africans and largely devoted to producing one commodity. The sugar islands thus depended on the importation of food and most other essential items. So ravaged by overwork, malnutrition, and disease were their slave workforces that a constant stream of fresh humanity was required merely to keep their numbers level.

This was not the bondage of the household or harem slave of the Middle East, who was often treated as a member of the family and allowed to conduct business; nor of the mamluk, who could gain manumission, and even rise to power, through conversion and service. Rather, it was an unrelenting hell of hot, killing work in fields and factories under the hour-by-hour and minute-by-minute supervision of gang bosses.[84]

The "grinding season" proved especially deadly. Since cane juice goes sour unless crushed and boiled within twenty-four hours of cutting, the production sequence had to be condensed into round-the-clock shifts of backbreaking work in the fields, at the three-cylinder mills, and in the inferno-like boiler rooms. This put robust male slaves at a premium, and that in turn meant a relative deficiency of women in the islands. A reduced birthrate naturally followed, not merely because there were fewer females, but also because of the social instability resulting from this imbalance. Further, plantation owners had no use for slave children, since they would have to be fed for more than a decade before they yielded economic benefit; it was better to import healthy young males, who could be bought for three or four years' upkeep. Slave children were so undesirable that an infant sold for one-twentieth to one-tenth the price of an adult.[85]

Death on the plantation was sugar's constant companion, and those colonies that relied most heavily on cane had the most trouble maintaining their slave populations. The black population of British North America, which grew little cane, increased nearly as fast as the white population. The one exception to the pattern of lower mortality among slaves in North America was found in the southernmost parishes of Louisiana, one of the few places on the continent that grew cane. Conversely, one exception to the high mortality among slaves in Brazil was found in the province of Minas Gerais, which was more dependent on "easier" labor: coffee and dairy production.[86]

The deadly face of "sugar demographics" is easily seen today in the cultural differences between the black population in the United States and Canada and that in the rest of the hemisphere. British North America, because of its vigorous population growth, required ever-smaller infusions of African slaves. After 1800, the relatively high fertility and low death rates among slaves in the United States meant that southern plantation owners simply did not need to import more Africans. The American prohibition of the slave trade in 1808 easily passed through the southern-dominated Congress for just this reason: the Americans' abolition of the slave trade crippled their Caribbean and Brazilian competitors. By 1808, almost all North American slaves were native-born, and by the Civil War, relatively little cultural memory of Africa remained.[87] The Caribbean islands and Brazil, on the other hand, required a constant flow of Africans; well into the twentieth century, the Yoruba language flourished in Cuba, the last bastion of the New World plantation society, and African influences still pervade Caribbean culture.

The transatlantic commerce of the seventeenth through nineteenth centuries—coffee, cotton, sugar, rum, and tobacco from the New World to Europe; manufactured goods, particularly textiles, from Europe to Africa; and slaves from Africa to the New World—has been described as the "triangular trade pattern" and taught to most schoolchildren. This oversimplified picture neglects the real-world reality of shorter hauls. An English ship might carry indigo from Jamaica to Philadelphia, then corn from there to London, then wool cloth from there to Le Havre, then French silks to Africa's slave coast, and so on.

In the East, things did not run as smoothly. Even though Britons might have been crazy for calicoes and besotted by tea, it was more difficult to find trade goods to exchange for them, particularly with the self-sufficient and self-satisfied Chinese. A more even-flowing system, similar to that achieved in the Atlantic, was needed. Just as the slave-trade arm of the Atlantic triangle poisoned race relations for centuries thereafter, so would the inequities of the nineteenth-century India and China trades profoundly affect East-West relations to the present day.

11

THE TRIUMPH AND TRAGEDY OF FREE TRADE

There is cause for apprehension lest in centuries or millennia to come China may be endangered by collision with the nations of the West.—Kang Hsi, emperor of China, warning of the British presence at Canton in 1717[1]

On March 30, 1802, William Jardine, an eighteen-year-old Scot, shipped out as a surgeon's mate on the *Brunswick,* bound for China. He was typical of up-and-comers in the East India Company (EIC). After the death of his father, a humble Highlands farmer, William managed to make it through medical school at Edinburgh with the help of an older brother.

In those days, a berth on an Indiaman was a rare plum. Its advantage derived not from the Company's salary—a miserly two-month £5 signing advance in Jardine's case, or about $800 in today's currency—but because of the "privileged tonnage" allotted to crewmen. The EIC granted a surgeon's mate two tons; a surgeon, three; and a captain, fifty-six outbound and thirty-eight homebound. An Indiaman's crew members could rent out their personal allowances to private merchants at £20 to £40 per ton, but an enterprising man like Jardine could do far better on his own account. The career of this young medical officer, who later founded one of the modern world's great trading empires, eloquently portrays the changes that swept through world commerce in the early nineteenth century.

Though no record of Jardine's medical ability exists, there is little doubt that he discharged his duties competently and conscientiously, since on the very next passage he was promoted to ship's surgeon. But his real talent lay elsewhere. On his six voyages to the East with the EIC, he amassed a considerable personal fortune by exchanging silver and merchandise from England and India for Chinese goods, mainly tea and silk.

By nineteenth-century standards, his fifteen-year tenure in the EIC was fairly routine, despite the fact that four of his six voyages took place in wartime. On his second voyage in 1805, his ship, the ill-fated *Brunswick,* was captured off Sri Lanka by the French, who transferred him to a prison on the Cape of Good Hope, then controlled by Napoleon's newly conquered Dutch Republic, and allowed him to return home on an American vessel. Since it was Company policy to pay only those who served on successful missions, his salary for the journey was forfeit.

The most fateful event on this voyage, however, was Jardine's introduction to a flamboyant and ambitious Parsi merchant, Jamsetjee Jeejeebhoy, who even by the standards of the time exuded an extraordinary exoticism. Although the Parsis were an ethnically Indian sect and lived in the Bombay area, they practiced an offshoot of Persian Zoroastrianism. Given their Persian-Indian roots, it is not surprising that they were deeply involved in the ancient Indian Ocean emporium trade. They were familiar with China, to which they had for centuries shipped both raw and finished cotton, myrrh, ivory, shark's fins, and a myriad of other goods, earning a reputation as the "Jews of India."[2] (This term overlooked the fact that real Jews had lived on the subcontinent for millennia, perhaps as early as Solomon's reign.)

Born to a poor but priestly family in 1783, Jeejeebhoy was apprenticed to his uncle, a bottle wallah (that is, a bottle seller). The young man soon became bored with the profession his family had chosen for him and within a year shipped out to China, the first of several sojourns there in the subsequent decade. Like Jardine, he lost his cargo and purse to the *Brunswick*'s captors, but over the next four decades these two brothers in commerce would amass fortunes and knighthoods—Jeejeebhoy's being the first ever awarded an Indian—in the morally ambiguous world of maritime commerce between India and China, the so-called "country trade."[3]

If Jardine epitomized the new breed of English merchant in Canton, then Commissioner Lin Tse-hsü personified the Chinese society and culture that greeted the ambitious Scot in Canton. Hailing from a long line of scholars and statesmen, Lin followed the traditional Mandarin meritocratic pathway of academic immersion—success in rigorous qualifying examinations followed by advancement through the government bureaucracy. He served successively as secretary to the governor of coastal

Fukien province, compiler at the provincial academy, chief provincial examiner, circuit judge, salt controller, judicial commissioner, financial commissioner, director of river conservation, provincial governor, and provincial governor-general, before finally being appointed to the coveted position of imperial commissioner in 1838. Along the way, he advised the emperor on opium policy, and as imperial commissioner he would face off against the English in a momentous struggle that sours East-West relations to this day.[4]

The trading world in which Jardine, Jeejeebhoy, and Lin operated ran according to long-established rules and customs. In 1650, the Manchu Ching, the last Chinese dynasty, conquered Beijing and dethroned the Mings. A dozen years later began the sixty-year reign—from 1662 to 1722—of Emperor K'ang-hsi, the Asian counterpart of Louis XIV. Initially, K'ang-hsi reversed Ming isolationism and opened the country to foreign merchants, but he soon pulled back and established a restrictive set of diplomatic and trading rules that became known as the "Canton System," named after the southern city to which Western merchants were confined.[5] That Canton was nearly as far from the center of power in Beijing as it could be and still have a deepwater port was no accident.

The main European player in this time-honored system that greeted young Jardine on his first visit to Canton was, of course, his employer, the EIC (or, as it had become known by that time, the "Honourable Company"). For more than a century, its monopoly on traffic with the Orient had been threatened by "interlopers," who were increasingly its former employees.

As the eighteenth century drew to a close, a new and more potent domestic enemy appeared to bedevil the Honourable Company—Adam Smith and his disciples, who practiced the new science of "political economy." Their credibility derived from their *not* having a dog in the age-old fight between monopolists and free-traders. However persuasive were Thomas Mun and Josiah Child, they had been, after all, Company directors who benefited from its monopoly on Eastern trade, and, at the same time, were hurt by the protectionism of the domestic textile manufacturers.[6] Now, respected scholars with no financial interest in the outcome of the debate were making powerful arguments in favor of free trade.

Smith's compelling analysis of the EIC would ultimately deal the death blow to its Eastern monopoly. The Company was not only the world's largest commercial enterprise but also a crown monopoly, and it is not surprising that Smith had a great deal to say about its operations.

Smith's analysis of Company policy in India, as well as its China trade, cannot be understood without some knowledge of Indian history. In 1757, a brash young colonel of the EIC, Robert Clive, defeated the Mogul Nawab of Bengal and his French allies at the battle of Plassey (about a hundred miles north of present-day Calcutta). He thus acquired for the EIC its first significant territorial holdings on the subcontinent —roughly, present-day Bangladesh and adjoining eastern India, about the size of New Mexico. More important, Clive also inherited the old Mogul *diwani*—the ruler's right to tax—which in that day meant receiving, in lieu of money, a portion of the land's produce, particularly cotton.[7] The undermanned Company now directly ruled a small portion of the Indian landmass, and it wisely left the Mogul institutional structure intact. One of the EIC's edicts reflected the looseness of its control at the local level: "There should be no restriction whatever upon the Princes taking as many women, either wives or concubines, as they may think proper. They cannot employ their money in a more harmless way."[8]

Smith, writing less than two decades after the battle of Plassey, described the Bengal as a declining society whose benighted citizens were doomed to "starve, or be driven to seek a subsistence either by begging, or by the perpetration of the greatest enormities."[9] He laid the blame for this sad state of affairs squarely in the lap of the Honourable Company. The job of government, Smith asserted, was to look after its people and to ensure that a multitude of enterprises would compete with each other for business and investment capital, precisely what a monopoly wishes to avoid. To let a monopoly run a government was thus a prescription for disaster, as occurred when the Company restricted the rice trade in the Bengal and precipitated a famine that killed one-sixth of the population.[10]

As revered as Smith is today, in his own time he was just one man of ideas among many, with little direct influence over policy. The victory of free trade in England during the nineteenth century would be won not by economists but by their disciples, the hard-nosed captains of the

Industrial Revolution, Manchester's factory owners, who had a vested interest in open international markets for their inexpensive wares.

The first skirmish came with the Charter Act of 1793, in which Parliament grudgingly allowed private traders a piddling annual allowance of three thousand tons (about fifteen shiploads) to be divided among them. Napoleon's "Continental System," which forbade his allies to trade with England, was met with the equally infamous British "orders in council" of 1807 and 1809, which forced all traffic heading to Europe to call first in Britain. This set off the War of 1812, which disrupted the flow of American cotton to England. Now suddenly dependent on higher-priced cotton from the EIC's Indian monopoly, the Lancashire mill owners were infuriated. Parliament repealed the orders in June 1812, too late to stop the war with the Americans, and in July 1813 voted to end the EIC's monopoly in India. Since the Canton trade was at that time important to neither the private traders nor the Lancashiremen, the Company retained its China monopoly, and the Canton System remained viable for another twenty years.[11]

The Canton System limited European merchants to dealing only with a few officially sanctioned Chinese trading companies, or hongs, and allowed a tiny colony for foreigners, just a few hundred yards square. Further, the merchants could not reside there permanently, but only during the several months between the summer monsoon, which blew them in, and the winter monsoon, which blew them out.

The Pearl River estuary provided the geographic stage for the great drama that would blight East-West relations. A sailor approaching Canton first saw a group of islands guarding a bay approximately twenty miles wide at its entrance. At its western end lay the small peninsula of Macao, the Portuguese trading post, and at its eastern end, the islands of Lantau and Hong Kong, with its magnificent harbor. The bay stretches north for forty miles, and roughly in its middle lies mountainous Lintin Island, an ideal locale for smuggling.

At the north end of the bay is the entrance to the Pearl River, called the Bogue, where the emperor had positioned an impressive array of artillery, designed to prevent enemy ships and pirates from proceeding upriver to Canton. There was just one problem with the configuration of these guns—they were permanently attached to the ground on fixed mounts. In other words, they could not actually be *aimed*. As one historian put it, "They

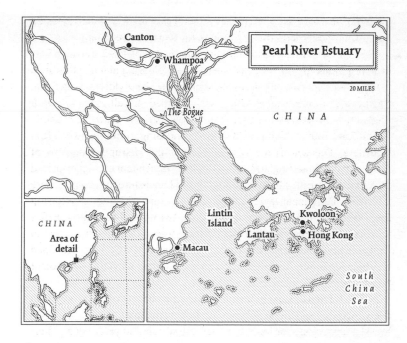

were more like fireworks than pieces of ordnance," a deficiency that would become painfully obvious during the coming Opium Wars.[12] The river then curves another forty miles to the north, then west, toward Canton. Along its course lay numerous low islands, the most important of which was Whampoa, just east of Canton, where the Canton System required foreign ships to anchor and transfer their cargoes to small junks.

The barriers between East and West in China were not merely geographic. Technically, China did not engage in trade at all; rather, it accepted tribute to the emperor, who then reciprocated with gifts to the foreign supplicants. In practice, however, the tribute-for-gift exchange looked remarkably like the normal trade in the other Asian emporia. China spectacularly mistook England for an ordinary vassal state like Siam, an error that was to cost it dearly.

The trading and diplomatic misunderstandings could be simultaneously tragic and comic. In 1793, when George III sent Lord George Macartney to Beijing as ambassador, the Chinese affixed to his riverboat a sign that proclaimed, "Tribute from the Red Barbarians." Contrary to popular legend, Macartney did agree to kowtow (a complex maneuver consisting of bowing once, kneeling once, and touching the forehead to the floor nine times), but only on the condition that the emperor's courtiers do the same before a portrait of the British monarch, which Macartney had thoughtfully provided for the occasion. The horrified Chinese politely refused, so no kowtows took place that day on either side.[13]

Although some Europeans became fluent in the Chinese dialects, the Chinese almost never became fluent in any European language. For example, Commissioner Lin hired the best translators he could find; later examination of their work showed it to be at the level of pidgin. More fundamentally, a chasm of culture and class separated China and Britain; by the eighteenth century, English traders occupied the higher rungs of British society, whereas in China, merchants had been despised as scum for millennia.[14]

At first, the Canton System suited the EIC well. The hongs had a monopoly on the trade from the Chinese side, and the Company, having effectively frozen both the Portuguese and the Dutch out of China during the preceding century, controlled all trade from the European side. Consequently, the hongs and the EIC monopoly fit together like a jigsaw puzzle.

Under the surface, all was not well. First, the EIC could finance its operations with the abundance of capital available in London, whereas China was a subsistence-level society with only the most rudimentary financial markets, scant capital, and sky-high interest rates. This greatly weakened the EIC's hong partners.

The high interest rates were a two-edged sword. On the one hand, they afforded the Company, and subsequent private English traders, enormous profits through borrowing at low rates in England and lending at astronomical rates in China. But it did the EIC no good to have chronically insolvent trading partners who were in constant need of rescue. Even today, international commerce is a highly uncertain enterprise, and merchants frequently have to bear losses. Adequate credit is to trade what altitude is to aircraft; without it, the odds of coming to grief over perilous commercial terrain are great. All merchant enterprises sooner or later lose cargoes or encounter soft markets. Without ample capital reserves and the ability to borrow at low rates of interest, bankruptcy is inevitable. Stretching the analogy a bit, if the hong system was an aircraft unable to attain a safe altitude, it also operated on only one engine. The Chinese had no functioning insurance markets; when fire swept Canton in 1822, most of the local traders were wiped out.[15]

By the mid-eighteenth century, an even more serious problem arose: the English had developed an increasing thirst for tea, but the Chinese desired relatively little from England. In the words of the nineteenth-century British trade commissioner for China, Robert Hart:

> [The] Chinese have the best food in the world, rice; the best drink, tea; and the best clothing, cotton, silk, fur. Possessing these staples and their innumerable native adjuncts, they do not need to buy a penny's worth elsewhere.[16]

The revenues from copper and mechanical novelties—the only things China wanted from the West—did not pay for even a small fraction of tea purchases. If the English wanted tea, they would have to pay in silver. Eighteenth-century records of the EIC show that about 90 percent of the value of England's exports to China was in the form of bullion.[17] In 1751, for example, four British vessels arrived in China bearing £10,842 in trade goods and £119,000 in silver.[18]

Although the Chinese did not value English merchandise, they did crave Indian cotton, a commodity the EIC now possessed in abundance from the old Mughal *diwani* won at Plassey. Though China had grown cotton for millennia, before 1800 domestic production had been inadequate, and the Chinese had to import both raw bales and calicoes from India. A triangular system, similar to that in the Atlantic, began to flourish: British manufactured goods to India, Indian cotton to China, and Chinese tea back to England. Increasingly, England also began to export cotton from the new Lancashire factories to China and India.

By the 1820s China's demand for Indian cotton slacked off, because of hard economic times and increased domestic planting. The English, once again reduced to exchanging their precious silver for tea, turned their eyes to another *diwani* crop, opium, whose prime Indian fields lay in the territories surrounding Patna and Varanasi won by Clive in 1757.

For several thousand years, humans have dried the juice of the common poppy, *Papaver somniferum,* into opium. As with many modern crops, the poppy is a cultivar, that is, a cultivated variety that does not grow easily in the wild, which suggests that agricultural societies take their drugs as seriously as their food.

Humans probably first extracted opium for consumption in southern Europe, and the Greeks and Romans used it extensively. Arab traders transplanted the poppy to the more hospitable soils and climates of Persia and India, and then to China, where its use is recorded as early as the eighth century after Christ.[19]

For almost all of recorded history, no particular opprobrium was attached to consuming opium as a painkiller, relaxant, work aid, and social lubricant. The Dutch in Indonesia were the first to smoke opium, in the early 1600s, when they began adding a few grains to a recent New World import, tobacco. The Chinese probably acquired the practice from the Dutch base in Formosa, whence the opium pipe rapidly spread to the mainland.[20] As early as 1512, Pires observed opium commerce in Malacca, centuries before the British and Dutch became involved in the trade. This indicates that the drug was a high-volume item in Indian Ocean emporium commerce well before the English came to dominate it.[21]

Nineteenth-century Europeans swallowed enormous amounts of opium, whereas the Chinese smoked theirs. Since inhaled opium is more addictive than opium taken orally, it was considered much more dangerous in China than in the nations of the West. In England, horticultural organizations awarded prizes for particularly potent domestically grown poppies (although most opium used in Britain came from Turkey), and opium was consumed guiltlessly by both high and low, most famously by Samuel Taylor Coleridge ("Kubla Khan"), Thomas de Quincey (*Confessions of an Opium Eater*), and Arthur Conan Doyle's Sherlock Holmes. The drug could be purchased freely in England until the Pharmacy Act of 1868; other Western nations did not restrict its use until around 1900.

At the time the EIC acquired the Bengal, the Portuguese had been shipping opium from Goa to Canton for some time. Chinese authorities first outlawed its use in 1729, and their reasons for doing so were far from clear.[22] By the end of the eighteenth century, the EIC could not be seen as directly involved in bringing opium into China, which would incur the wrath of the emperor. In response, the Honourable Company, in the words of the historian Michael Greenberg, "perfected the technique for growing opium in India and disowning it in China."[23]

It did so by establishing strict oversight of production and maintaining both monopoly pricing and quality control at the Indian end of the supply chain. The Company's Patna and Varanasi trademarks (named after the northern Indian cities housing its main opium agencies) came to signify excellence to Chinese users, and opium boxes bearing them commanded a premium.

The EIC sold its high-end branded product to private traders such as Jardine, who shipped it to the mountainous Pearl River estuary island of Lintin, where they based themselves on easily defended floating hulks just off its shore (as opposed to Canton's downriver wharf at Whampoa, where legitimate cargo was unloaded). Local smugglers brought the contraband upriver and slipped it past Canton's customs inspectors. The smugglers paid Chinese silver to the English private traders, who then exchanged it at Company offices for silver bills drawable by them on Company accounts in Calcutta and London. The EIC, in turn, used the silver obtained from the private traders to pay for tea.[24]

The popular image of an entire Chinese population and its economy ravaged by opium is a misconception. In the first place, the drug was quite expensive and largely the province of the mandarin and merchant elite classes. Second, like alcohol, it was catastrophically addictive in only a small proportion of its users. Even the infamous opium dens did not live up to their seedy reputation, as a disappointed Somerset Maugham discovered:

> And when I was taken to an opium den by a smooth-talking Eurasian, the narrow, winding stairway up which he led me prepared me sufficiently to receive the thrill I expected. I was introduced into a neat enough room, brightly lit, divided into cubicles the raised floor of which, covered with clean matting, formed a convenient couch. In one an elderly gentleman, with a grey head and very beautiful hands, was quietly reading a newspaper, with his long pipe by his side. . . . [In another room] four men squatted over a chess-board, and a little further on a man was dandling a baby. . . . It was a cheerful spot, comfortable, home-like, and cozy. It reminded me somewhat of the little intimate beer-houses of Berlin where the tired working man could go in the evening and spend a peaceful hour.[25]

Academic research on opium consumption in China bears out Maugham's observation: it was largely a social drug that harmed only a tiny percentage of users. One modern scholar estimates that although as many as half of men and one-fourth of women were occasional users, in 1879 only about one Chinese person in a hundred inhaled enough opium to even be at risk of addiction.[26]

The emperor and the mandarins did express some moral outrage over the debilitation caused by opium, but they were far more concerned about the drug's damage to their balance of trade. China subscribed to European-style mercantilism as faithfully as any seventeenth-century Western monarchy. Before 1800, the tea trade was, at least in the terms of the mercantilist ideology of the day, grossly favorable to the Chinese. The EIC's records pinpoint 1806 as the year when the silver flow reversed. After that date, the value of opium imports exceeded that of tea exports, and Chinese silver began flowing *out* of the Celestial Kingdom for the first time. After 1818, silver constituted fully one-fifth of the value of Chinese export goods.

In the 1820s, a powerful group of mandarins began to support legalizing opium as a way to reduce its price and staunch the outflow of silver. One of them, Hsü Nai-chi, wrote a memo to the emperor noting that some users were indeed enfeebled, but the fiscal damage to the nation was far worse. He recommended legalization, with the stipulation that opium should be purchased only by barter (presumably for tea), not with silver. The wide circulation of this memo among Canton's foreign traders gave them hope that legalization was imminent. Hsü's proposal was defeated, however, in a bitter battle at the imperial court.[27]

In the early nineteenth century, the British controlled only a small part of the Indian subcontinent, and it was not long before Parsi merchants, particularly Jamsetjee Jeejeebhoy, got around the EIC's opium monopoly in Bengal by shipping their local product, called *malwa,* out of Malabar and Gujarati ports. (*Malwa* was the generic term for non-EIC opium shipped out of the western ports, as opposed to the EIC-branded Patna and Varanasi blocks exported from the eastern port of Calcutta.) Eventually, the Company realized the advantage in centralizing *malwa* shipments from its convenient Bombay wharves, and after 1832 it began collecting a modest transit duty from local merchants.

By the early nineteenth century, cracks had begun to appear in the Honourable Company's monopoly. In addition to using private traders to ship opium to China, the EIC began to license a few private "country traders" to conduct legitimate trade to Whampoa as well, using what was left of its monopoly power to keep these entrepreneurs under its thumb. American fur merchants, led by John Jacob Astor, forced some of the first openings in the monopoly system with seal and sea otter skins from the Pacific

Northwest, items highly prized in China.[28] The EIC, afraid to offend the fierce, unpredictable independent nation which had handed the mother country a stinging defeat in the Revolutionary War, left the Americans alone.

Even before the appearance of the former colonials, other English private merchants had hit on a ruse for getting around the EIC's monopoly: foreign diplomatic cover. In 1780, an Englishman, Daniel Beale, sailed to China under Austrian colors bearing an appointment as Prussia's consul. He would use his appointment to engage in the profitable country trade between India and China, free of EIC control. Another Englishman, John Henry Cox, the preeminent importer of singsongs to China, attempted to avoid interference from the EIC with a Swedish naval commission; when the Company still refused to let his vessel enter, he replaced the Swedish flag with a Prussian one. Poland, Genoa, Sicily, and Denmark would graciously and, presumably for a price, extend diplomatic privileges to British traders.[29]

When Jardine returned to London in 1817 and left the service of the Company a wealthy man, he formed a partnership with another former EIC ship's surgeon, Thomas Weeding, who had obtained a prized license from the Company to engage privately in the country trade. The two joined forces with a Bombay Parsi, Framjee Cowasjee, and in 1819 Jardine left for Bombay, where he assembled 649 chests of *malwa* that the partnership then sold for $813,000 in Canton.[30] (Henceforth, in this chapter, the dollar-sign signifies eight-real pieces, or Spanish dollars. This familiar sign probably has its origins in the coat of arms inscribed on these coins). It would be the first of many profitable smuggling ventures for Jardine. In Bombay, he reconnected with Jeejeebhoy, with whom he would also have a long and lucrative commercial relationship. There, he also met James Matheson; the two would later found the great firm that still bears their names—Jardine Matheson and Company.

Matheson came from a Scottish family wealthy enough to afford the necessary EIC license to privately ply the country trade. This allowed him to avoid the long apprenticeship with the Company endured by Jardine. Eventually, Matheson became the "Danish consul" in Canton, a position that enabled him to escape altogether the strictures imposed by his EIC license.

Matheson also invented another ruse, which would later assume global importance. Whereas the transport of goods directly from India to China by private traders violated the EIC's China monopoly, it was perfectly legal to ship merchandise sent from, say, Calcutta to the Strait of Malacca or from the strait to Canton. In 1822, the wily Scot first took advantage of this legal nicety by transferring his cargoes from ship to ship at the newly settled port of Singapore, just three years after Stamford Raffles had founded it on a marshy, malarial island.[31]

Matheson's wealth gave him the freedom to pursue both scholarship and journalism. Like many bright young merchants of his day, he adopted the free-trade ideology espoused by Adam Smith in *Wealth of Nations.* In 1827 Matheson founded the first English-language newspaper in China, the *Canton Register,* a broadsheet that printed local shipping news, tabulated opium prices, and editorialized against the tyranny of the EIC. That same year, after the death of his original partner, a Spaniard, Xavier Yrissari, he informed his Chinese customers that henceforth the overall management of the business would be undertaken by William Jardine. By 1830, the new firm, Jardine Matheson and Company, was smuggling about five thousand chests of opium per year into China, and like any young, vigorous organization, it sought efficiency in every direction.

It fell to a remarkable member of Jardine Matheson, the linguist and medical missionary Karl Friedrich August Gutzlaff, to blow apart the Canton System. He did so by operating from small smuggling craft that ranged as far up the coast as Manchuria, selling *malwa* to local merchants, in direct defiance of the Chinese authorities.[32] Gutzlaff, an intensely anglophilic Pomeranian Lutheran who spoke most of the major Chinese dialects, successively married three Englishwomen and believed strongly in the ability of commerce to bring salvation to the pagan Chinese.[33] Unfortunately for his historical reputation, he chose opium as his preferred vehicle of Christian redemption.

The historian Carl Trocki provides this vivid glimpse into everyday life on one of the coastal opium clippers. After anchoring in a secure bay, the crew of one ship found it

> overrun with Chinese, while [the captain], the shroff [a tester and changer of coins], and another European sat up far into the night selling opium to "all comers, high and low." While waiting, some smoked opium and fell asleep on the couch in his cabin and others occasionally napped on the floor while the abacus rattled, and Chi-

nese and Europeans communicated by sign language. In four days,
[the crew] sold opium worth . . . about \$200,000.[34]

Although the EIC was steadily losing market share to private traders,
it pioneered a sailing advance that would have momentous economic and
historical impact. For nearly two thousand years, the monsoon allowed
mariners only one annual round-trip between India and China. This limita-
tion would be conquered not by the new steam technology, but rather by
improved hull and sail design. During the War of 1812, the Americans came
up with a revolutionary vessel whose speed enabled their privateers to ravage English shipping and outrun blockades—the Baltimore clipper. The
most famous, the *Prince de Neufchatel,* seized numerous British merchantmen before being cornered by three Royal Navy frigates just prior to the
war's end. The British towed the clipper to drydock and plumbed the secrets of its speed: a clean, narrow hull that kept the ship upright sailing
into the strongest winds; and massive, tightly hung sails, characteristics easily visible in racing yachts even today. The fatal mistake of the
Prince de Neufchatel's captain, in fact, had been to overload the boat with
too much weight in canvas sail, which had to be hauled down during the
blustery conditions that prevailed during its final engagement.[35]

A Royal Navy skipper, William Clifton, eventually came into possession of the clipper's specifications. After leaving the navy, he commanded EIC vessels and realized that the Baltimore clipper's sleek hull and
tight sails were just the ticket for conquering the monsoons. In 1829 the
EIC, with the backing of its governor-general, Lord William Bentinck,
commissioned production of the *Red Rover,* a 255-ton craft that combined
a Baltimore clipper–type hull with the bark (or barque) sail configuration
favored by the navy.[36] On January 4, 1830, the sleek new vessel slipped its
moorings on the Hooghly River and headed downwind to Singapore, arriving just sixteen days later. Less than a week after that, it sailed north into
the teeth of the monsoon and arrived in Macao in only twenty-two days.
Clifton went on to complete three round-trips between India and China that
year, a performance that earned him acclaim and a £10,000 prize from the
EIC.[37] The *Red Rover* finally met its end, along with all hands, in a stormy
Bay of Bengal in 1853, an unusually long career among China clippers that
spent much of their careers beating into the rough monsoons.[38]

Clipper ships, to be sure, did not come cheap. One vessel, the *Lanrick,* cost the firm $65,000. But it carried 1,250 chests of opium, which would have earned $25,000 per voyage, thus paying off the entire purchase price of the ship by its third round-trip: that is, within one year.

Although the EIC introduced clipper ships into the China trade, in the end the private companies most successfully exploited the new vessel's potential. Jardine Matheson and others in the country trade had learned that it was more profitable to act as go-between and connect the sellers of *malwa* in Bombay to the buyers on Lintin Island. The commission, $20 per chest, was more reliably profitable than directly buying and selling opium themselves.[39]

In 1830, a coalition of country traders and Manchester factory interests, led by an eager Jardine, eyed the coming expiration of the EIC charter and petitioned Parliament in favor of a "new commercial code." In the spirit of the times, Parliament complied. The EIC's monopoly on Eastern trade finally lapsed permanently in April 1834. Almost immediately, the private merchants, already in control of opium, captured the venerable and profitable trade in tea, the Company's last major protected product.

What a difference 150 years had made. In 1700, the Honourable Company was in the vanguard of free trade, while England's protectionist textile industry sought to maintain its eroding monopoly. By the early nineteenth century, these positions had been reversed: the sclerotic EIC desperately sought to maintain its privileged position, while the cotton producers pushed for unrestricted commerce, envisioning that "if we could only persuade every person in China to lengthen his shirt tail by a foot, we could keep the mills of Lancashire running around the clock."[40] Before 1700, the globalist creed of Child and Martyn gained remarkably little public traction, but by 1830, Adam Smith's free-market principles, as personified by Willam Jardine and James Matheson, carried the day. For centuries before the arrival of the Europeans, the emporia of the Indian Ocean had known reasonably open markets. Now the West, wielding superior new military and maritime technologies, would forsake its armed monopolist ways and embrace free trade, whether or not the Chinese and Indians wanted it to.

The year 1828, for which we have particularly good records, provides us with a snapshot of the China trade just before the abolition of the Company monopoly. Of roughly $20,000,000 worth of imports into Canton, over three-quarters was carried by the private country traders, and three-quarters of that was opium. In other words, opium made up over half of the British trade, the lion's share of which was in private hands. Over 99 percent of the EIC's exports from China consisted of tea, which before 1834 the private merchants, who were paid mainly in silver, were not allowed to carry.[41]

After 1834, with the Company monopoly gone, private traders expanded the scope of their operations; they were now free to ignore the Canton System, which had been enforced almost as vigorously by the EIC as by the emperor. The sleek, fast clippers proved ideal for high-value cargoes such as opium and tea. By the late 1830s, these ships allowed companies such as Jardine Matheson to control both the older country trade and the newer coastal trade pioneered by Gutzlaff. Opium imports had grown relatively slowly from about four thousand chests per year in 1800 to about ten thousand in 1825. After the private companies took over the China trade from the EIC, volume mushroomed to forty thousand chests in the late 1830s.[42]

When the EIC relinquished its monopoly in 1834, its select committee, which regulated English trade, gave way to a superintendent of British trade in China, who was appointed by the crown and was greatly influenced by the powerful private traders and their hatred of the Chinese government. The misadventures of the first superintendent, the inept Lord William John Napier, symbolized the cultural gulf between China and the West. Napier arrived unannounced at the EIC's factory in Canton at 2 AM on July 25, 1834; by daybreak, he had already hoisted the Union Jack, a gross affront to the Chinese. This faux pas was only the beginning. Napier next had an introductory letter translated into Chinese and delivered to the local Chinese governor-general. Within forty-eight hours of his arrival in Canton, the superintendent had thus violated several imperial edicts relating to barbarians: he had traveled upriver to Canton without approval, taken up residence there, delivered a letter to the governor-general directly (not through the hong merchants), and written in Chinese (instead of in English). The Chinese rebuffed Napier, shut down all commerce with the English, and fired on English vessels. Jardine and the other private traders, who had egged Napier on, realized that they had overplayed their hand and mollified the Chinese by negotiating the hapless envoy's hasty exit.[43]

Four years later, it was the emperor's turn to overreach, when he appointed the brilliant but equally maladroit Lin as commissioner and set the stage for a far more disastrous confrontation between the two governments. Even before Lin's appointment, the Chinese authorities had begun to jail large numbers of local opium smugglers, and brought trade to a standstill. In March 1839, Lin increased the pressure by making foreign merchants criminally liable for any illicit shipments. Shortly thereafter, Lin ordered the public beheading of Chinese opium dealers under the eyes of horrified Europeans and then held all the resident foreigners—English, American, Parsi, and French—hostage in their factories for several weeks until they agreed to turn over more than twenty thousand chests of opium. Only after Lin's forces had destroyed the huge haul were the foreigners released.

The new superintendent of trade, Charles Elliot, was a retired Royal Navy captain and a veteran of the West African anti-slave patrols. (At one point he held the office of "protector of slaves.") A strict Calvinist who deplored opium, he compartmentalized his religious beliefs and official duties well enough to mollify the increasingly desperate private traders by compensating them for their confiscated opium. This action drew the English government directly into the fray.

Just a spark sufficed. Several months later, in August 1839, following the murder of a local villager by a drunk English seamen, Lin cut off food and water to the British naval forces and demanded that the sailor be handed over for trial. Elliot refused and instead submitted the defendant to a British jury of merchants, who meted out a fine and a six-month sentence, to be served in England. (When the sailor arrived in England, he was set free on the grounds that the jury, which included James Matheson, had been improperly constituted.[44]) At about noon on September 4, Gutzlaff, under orders from Elliot, presented letters to the commanders of two Chinese junks off Kowloon and informed them that if supplies were not forthcoming within thirty minutes, their ships would be sunk. No food or water arrived, and HMS *Volage* fired on the vessels.

In retaliation, Lin ordered that all trade with Britain be forever banned and that English ships would be fired on.

Meanwhile, Jardine and other veterans of Lin's blockade of the Canton factories made their way back to England. On arrival, they asked the cabinet of the Whig prime minister, Lord Melbourne, to demand an apology from the Chinese and negotiate a more "equitable" treaty that would open several other ports to the West. Dispatches from Elliot, whose pride and reputation were stung by Lin's ham-handedness, also favored taking a firm hand with the Chinese.

Jardine and his allies further recommended that their demands be backed up with naval force. All that remained was a means to finance the war. Thomas Babington Macaulay, the war minister, supplied it: have the Chinese pay reparations. Melbourne dispatched a force consisting of a dozen men-of-war and several thousand marines that arrived in China in June 1840.

The first Opium War had started. It would not end until 1842 and the infamous Treaty of Nanking, which awarded Britain monetary recompense, eliminated the hong monopoly, set Chinese export and import tariffs at a low rate, and opened Canton and four other treaty ports (Shanghai, Amoy, Foochow, and the island of Ningbo). In these ports, Britons had the privilege of extraterritoriality (immunity from Chinese law) and were governed by British consuls. No mention was made of opium, whose continued importation was tacitly understood by both sides. To this day, the humiliation of the Treaty of Nanking burns in China's national consciousness. That not one American in a hundred has heard of it does not augur well for Sino-American relations in the twenty-first century.

The English sought, in addition, a permanent colony. Matheson had long desired Formosa, but from London Jardine argued that this island was too large to pacify and pushed for the port of Ningbo. Neither had his way; Elliot, a former naval officer, coveted Hong Kong's superb harbor, and on his own initiative had its transfer written into the treaty. Even before the treaty was signed, Matheson moved the partnership's headquarters to Hong Kong, beginning the island's and the firm's dual ascent to prosperity.

To be sure, Elliot was not the only Englishman who entertained doubts about the morality of the opium trade. The Anglican clergy and the Tory opposition leader Robert Peel spearheaded a movement against it. The most eloquent advocate of prohibition was a thirty year-old back-bencher, William Gladstone, whose sister had been ravaged by opium addiction. When Peel moved in Parliament in 1840 to condemn the attack on China, young Gladstone gave an impassioned speech in the Commons that launched him into public prominence. Decades later he would serve four terms as prime minister.

For the most part, in mid-eighteenth-century England opium was still a benign nostrum dispensed to colicky babies and swallowed by little old ladies to ease the infirmities of age. The nascent prohibition movement was no match for what the historian W. Travis Hanes called "big opium"—the consortium of Chinese merchants and their allies in London led by William Jardine.[45]

Opium traffic grew even more rapidly after the First Opium War. In 1845, for example, the auditor-general of the new colony of Hong Kong estimated that at any one time, there were eighty clippers carrying opium to China or tea from it, one-fourth of them Jardine Matheson's. Gradually, Jardine Matheson became the focus of the increasing anti-opium sentiment in England.

In private, Jardine Matheson was happy with the illicit trade and greatly feared the possibility of legalization, which the Chinese entertained from time to time, as this would open the traffic up to competition from "men of small capital."[46] Its fears were well founded. In 1858, the Treaty of Tianjin, which concluded the Second Opium War, forced the Chinese to legalize opium (in addition to granting ten more treaty ports, paying further reparations, and handing over Kowloon). The legalization of the trade meant that anyone could purchase *malwa* in Bombay, ship it on one of the new vessels of the Peninsular and Oriental Steamship Company, and sell it in Hong Kong. Within a few years, Jardine Matheson found itself forced out of the opium trade by men like David Sassoon, a Bombay merchant of Baghdadi Jewish origin. Sassoon's knowledge of local Indian producers, his family's extensive business connections, and legalization enabled him to wrest control of the trade from the "old" English country traders. Sassoon would be joined in the opium trade by many Indian traders, especially Jeejeebhoy's Parsi heirs.

The displacement of Jardine Matheson from the opium trade proved a blessing in disguise, as it was forced to diversify. Imports of opium peaked at approximately a hundred thousand chests per year by 1880.[47]

Societal norms can change with great rapidity. For example, in 1600, even the most enlightened Europeans saw nothing wrong with black slavery; in 1800, few Europeans, and not very many Chinese, faulted Britain for exporting opium to China. It should not go unnoticed that tobacco, which is at least as addictive as opium and has killed far more people, is today aggressively marketed around the globe by the corporate heirs of William Jardine and James Matheson.

If the importation of a harmful product, opium, did China no good, the importation of a harmless good, machine-manufactured cotton cloth, is today blamed for plunging India into poverty. Certainly, that was how Karl Marx saw it when he quoted the EIC's governor-general, William Bentinck: "The misery hardly finds a parallel in the history of commerce. The bones of the cotton weavers are bleaching the plains of India."[48] India's founders saw it the same way, as do many Indians today.

The standard narrative goes something like this. The English forbade the export of Indian manufactured goods, while allowing British goods "free entry." The result was the destruction of India's vaunted textile industry. In the words of Jawaharlal Nehru, modern India's founding father and first prime minister:

> The liquidation of the artisan class led to unemployment on a prodigious scale. What were all these scores of millions, who had so far engaged in industry and manufacture, to do? Where were they to go? Their old profession was no longer open to them, the way to a new one was barred. They could die, of course; that way of escape from an intolerable situation is always open. They did die in the tens of millions.[49]

Marx and Nehru did capture an essential truth: in 1750, India provided nearly one-fourth of the world's textile output; by 1900, its output had shrunk to less than 2 percent.[50]

The overall loss to the Indian economy was relatively modest, since most of the nation's output was agricultural: somewhere in the range of two million to six million jobs—at most, 3 percent of the labor force— not the scores of millions in Marx's and Nehru's apocalyptic prose.[51] (By comparison, unemployment in the United States during the Great

Depression exceeded 30 percent.) Some economic historians argue that because of imports of superior and cheaper English thread, the domestic weaving industry actually expanded. Curiously absent from most discussions is the indisputable fact that hundreds of millions of Indians, poor and wealthy alike, were able to clothe themselves in English cloth that was both less expensive and better made.[52]

India had not gotten poorer; rather, the rapidly industrializing West had gotten vastly richer. Modern economic historians, in both Europe and India, now ascribe India's troubles in the eighteenth and nineteenth centuries to a number of factors unrelated to British trade policy: poor soils, the frequent failure of the monsoon rains, inadequate inland transportation systems, a lack of functioning capital markets, and the death, in 1707, of the last great Mughal emperor, Aurangzeb.[53]

Can we blame the British, as Nehru did, for letting British goods into India scot-free while barring the flow of Indian goods in the opposite direction? Only to a relatively small degree: by the mid-nineteenth century, most English imports into India were subject to a duty of either 3.5 percent and 7 percent (depending on whether they arrived on British or non-British vessels). The comparable duty paid on foreign (including Indian) goods landing in England was between 15 and 20 percent; agricultural goods, such as Indian sugar and raw cotton, incurred a much lower rate.[54] This was discriminatory, to be sure, but not prohibitive. Nor can it be plausibly argued that abuse of the *diwani* by the English drained India of its wealth. The British spent a much greater proportion of the *diwani* on public works, such as the subcontinent's massive rail system, than was ever spent under the luxury-loving Mughals, and in any case the revenues did not amount to much more than 1 percent of national income.[55, 56]

Having surveyed Britain's checkered dealings in Chinese opium and Indian cotton, we now turn to the final, and most historically significant, episode in the nineteenth-century history of free trade: its commerce with the Continent in grain.

Since at least the fifteenth century, the crown saw fit to micromanage its vital grain trade with a series of "corn laws." In common English usage, "corn" meant all grain—barley, rye, and particularly wheat. (Maize was unknown in Europe before Columbus.) Between 1660, when detailed statutory records begin, and the final repeal in 1846, no fewer than 127 corn laws were enacted to govern every imaginable facet of commerce in grain and other foodstuffs: retail and wholesale transactions, storage, import, export, and most critically of all, government tariffs. The great nineteenth-century battle over free trade was in many ways a debate over the wisdom of such intrusive involvement by government in what was increasingly an international trade.[57]

Until the mid-eighteenth century, England's wealth and power derived not from trade or manufacturing, but from the strength of its agriculture, which had become so efficient that by 1800 just two-fifths of the country's workforce was needed to feed it.[58] During the turbulent seventeenth century, English farmers exported little grain. When peace and institutional stability finally came in the wake of the Revolutionary Settlement of 1689, England became the granary of northern Europe.

Then, just as quickly as the surplus had appeared, it vanished. Four events consumed the bounty. First, a series of massive conflicts gripped Europe and crippled the regional grain trade. Between the Seven Years' War in 1756 and the end of the French-Napoleonic wars in 1815, England was either engaged in global conflict or preparing strenuously for it. Second, during the eighteenth century, England's population nearly doubled, to nine million. Third, rapid industrialization after 1760 shifted workers and financial capital from farms to factories. Finally, a series of crop failures began in 1756 and continued, on and off, for nearly two decades. In most years after 1780, Britain was a net importer of grain, mostly from Denmark, Poland, and coastal Germany. The year 1808 was the last time that England sent abroad more grain than it purchased.[59]

During the years of self-sufficiency and bounty, not many people, even farmers, had given the corn laws much notice. Sometimes these statutes favored the landed aristocracy by imposing high taxes and thus discouraging imports, or even by paying traders a bounty on exports, and sometimes they favored urban dwellers by doing the opposite. But for the most part, the laws were irrelevant: the medieval economy was largely self-sufficient, and in any case, law-enforcement manpower was spread so thin in medieval societies that it rarely got around to enforcing these obscure statutes.

The importance of the corn laws increased with the outbreak of the Seven Years' War in 1756; food shortages swept the industrial centers in the north, and rioters sacked granaries and even bakeries. Grain merchants, who for centuries had ignored or been blithely unaware of the sales strictures of the corn laws, suddenly found themselves condemned to hang by hastily assembled tribunals. (In the end, most were pardoned or "transported" to Australia.)

Suddenly, agricultural trade policy moved to the forefront of public debate. Over the next several decades, Parliament passed a series of corn laws designed to increase supplies to consumers and maintain the interests of the landed aristocracy. They usually did neither. After 1793, war with revolutionary France and a series of disastrous crop failures again caused scarcity. Wheat prices, which had averaged forty shillings per quarter (five hundred pounds, or a quarter ton) during the century before 1790, spiked to well above a hundred shillings, as shown in Figure 11-1. On October 29, 1795, when the king was on his way to deliver the opening speech to Parliament, a mob surrounded his entourage. Shots were fired into his carriage while the mob shouted "Peace! Peace!"

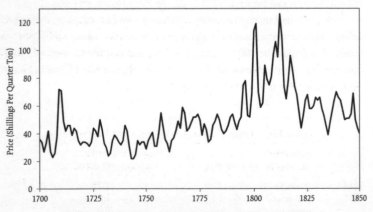

Figure 11-1. Price of Wheat in England 1700–1850

The government pulled out all the stops. It forbade the export of grain and its use in distilleries, eliminated all import duties, and purchased Baltic wheat through official channels. The navy seized grain from neutral ships bound for France. These actions not only fell short of stopping widespread starvation, but also enraged wealthy landowners no longer able to gouge an impoverished and hungry populace.

The government then offered bounties for *imports* and encouraged consumers to eat bread made from wheat flour mixed with barley or rye. But by the late eighteenth century, even the poor had long been accustomed to white wheaten loaves, and bakers refused to make mixed breads that were doomed to go stale and unsold.[60]

After 1800, favorable harvests temporarily reduced prices, and in November 1804 landowners took advantage of the overall wartime scarcity and forced through Parliament a corn law using a traditional "sliding scale" of duties on foreign wheat.

Placing such an onerous import duty on foreign wheat, for which transport costs were already higher than for domestic wheat, assured English farmers of a minimum price of sixty-three shillings per quarter, more than 50 percent higher than its historical level. The Corn Law of 1804 served to reveal the mind-set and political power of England's growers, and also clearly illustrated the double-edged sword of protectionism, which seeks to shelter domestic producers (in this case, Britain's landed aristocracy) at the expense of consumers. Essentially, England's landowners sought to make permanent the high wartime grain prices.

The law had nearly no effect, because poor harvests and the intensifying French wars soon drove market prices once again well above a hundred shillings. In 1809, scarcity in England combined with a French bumper crop to give Napoleon the irresistible opportunity of reaping huge profits by selling grain to the enemy.[61]

Table 11-1. Import Levies on Wheat: Corn Law of 1804

Grain Price (shillings per quarter ton)	Import Tax (shillings per quarter ton)
Below 63	24.25
Between 63 and 66	2.5
Above 66	0.5

In October 1813, Britain and its allies invaded France, and by April 1814 Napoleon had been sent to Elba. Between those two dates the price of wheat fell from approximately 120 shillings to seventy shillings, and English landholders, now accustomed to triple-digit market prices, again pleaded for legislation to extend their windfall profits into peacetime. Once again, the poor marched in the streets and besieged Parliament.

At this point, the centuries-old history of the corn laws converged with a family saga of similar vintage—that of the Ricardos. Not long after the expulsion and slaughter of Portugal's Jews in the early sixteenth century, many members of this remarkable clan found refuge in the free port of Livorno, or Leghorn, north of Rome. Uniquely among the Italian city-states, Livorno did not force Jews to wear badges, live in ghettos, or tolerate harangues from priests.

The chief business of Livorno's Jews was the ancient Mediterranean red coral trade, but as supplies dried up, tolerant and up-and-coming Amsterdam beckoned to one clan member, Samuel Israel, who moved to the Dutch republic sometime around 1680. There, the family prospered; Samuel's grandson, Joseph Israel Ricardo, became a successful stockbroker, helped set up the Amsterdam stock exchange, and was intimately involved in financing Holland's military effort during the Seven Years' War.

Joseph Ricardo's missions to fund Holland's armed forces often took him to London. His son, Abraham Israel Ricardo, could not help noticing that the English capital had replaced Amsterdam as the world's financial center. Sometime around 1760, Abraham Israel Ricardo established the family in the city on the Thames. His son David would become the great advocate and theoretician of free trade, and also the most influential and vocal early opponent of the corn laws.[62]

David had been born in 1772, four years before the publication of Adam Smith's *Wealth of Nations,* which vigorously espoused free trade. He apparently came across the book for the first time at age twenty-seven in a library in Bath, where his wife had been taking the cure. In subsequent years, he surpassed his father's success in the London stock exchange, and in 1815 the young broker profited hugely by his ownership in government bonds that increased in value after the victory at Waterloo (along with Nathan Mayer Rothschild, who had gotten early word of the victory). David used his newfound wealth to obtain a seat in the House of Commons and to pursue intellectual interests. At some point he acquired his own copy of Smith's book, in which 150 notations were later found. These scribbles formed the basis of his famous *Principles of Political Economy and Taxation,* published in 1817.

Principles proved a worthy successor to *Wealth of Nations;* in the words of the historian David Weatherall, "Adam Smith explained what the capitalist system was. David Ricardo explained how the capitalist system works."[63] Ricardo's famous chapter on foreign trade begins with this forthright statement, which turns mercantilism on its head: "We should have no greater value if, by the discovery of new markets, we obtained double the quantity of foreign goods in exchange for a given quantity of ours." Ricardo proceeded to describe the law of comparative advantage, in which he poses the following hypothetical situation. Imagine that it takes 120 Englishmen to produce a given quantity of wine and 100 to produce a given quantity of cloth, whereas it takes only eighty and ninety Portuguese, respectively, to produce the same quantities of wine and cloth. Even though Portugal was more efficient than England in producing both wine and wool, Ricardo argued that it was better for Portugal to concentrate on what it did best—wine, which it needed only eighty workers to produce—and exchange the wine it did not consume for cloth made in England, rather than make its own cloth.[64] But Ricardo's conclusions proved too opaque for his contemporary audience, and even today, the law of comparative advantage is often misunderstood.[65]

A more cogent example will suffice. Imagine for a moment a famous attorney whose services are so highly desired that his hourly fee is $1,000. Further imagine that he is also very skilled at woodworking—so proficient that he is twice as productive as the average carpenter. Remodeling a kitchen, for example, which might take a carpenter two hundred hours, would take our talented attorney only one hundred. Since the average carpenter earns $25 per hour, our attorney's woodworking skills are worth $50 per hour in the marketplace.

If the attorney's family needs a new kitchen, shouldn't he do the job himself, since he is twice as productive as the average carpenter? Not when his legal skills are worth $1,000 per hour. In the hundred hours he spent on the kitchen, he could have earned $100,000 in his office. He is far better off hiring the less efficient carpenter for two hundred hours, which would cost him only $5,000. Put a different way, the attorney is better off working five hours in his own profession to pay for the carpenter to do the kitchen job than working one hundred doing it himself. In economic terms, the attorney has a *comparative advantage* in legal work and a *comparative disadvantage* in woodworking. (Note that pleasure and preference do not enter into Ricardo's analysis. Our attorney may *enjoy* carpentry and decide to do the job himself—a valid emotional choice, but not an economically rational one.)

Alas, *Principles,* and Ricardo himself, arrived too late to save England from the draconian Corn Law of 1815. In response to a pro-Corn Law tract by Thomas Malthus, Ricardo wrote an anti-Corn Law pamphlet, "An Essay on the Influence of a low Price of Corn on the Profits of Stock." In it, he pointed out that the major advantage of the "real" England (as opposed to the hypothetical England of *Principles*) lay in its factory machinery. The corn laws, he wrote, impeded the purchase of foreign grain and forced England to waste its precious labor in less productive farmwork. This benefited no one except the landowning aristocracy. Ricardo's pamphlet convinced few. His more influential *Principles* did not appear in print until 1817, and he himself did not enter Parliament until 1819.

The thought of German, Polish, and Danish warehouses bulging with cheap grain incited England's working poor. In the end the mob proved more influential than the forces of rational discourse, but not in the direction intended. In March 1815, anti–Corn Law rioters raged through London's streets and broke into the houses of the bill's supporters, including those of Lord Castlereagh, the notoriously repressive foreign minister, and Frederick Robinson, who had introduced the bill. In the aftermath of the French wars, starving workers rioted *for* free trade, just as today more comfortable workers riot against it. Their lawlessness proved similarly counterproductive, forcing pro-repeal politicians and newspapers to disown their raucous allies.

In 1815 the landed interests ruled the day. That year's infamous legislation, whose passage required not only majority votes in both houses but also fixed bayonets outside them, absolutely forbade grain imports when wheat fell below eighty shillings per quarter.[66] Not long after, grain prices briefly fell well below eighty shillings, and Ricardo participated in a successful rearguard action through further pamphleteering and speeches in the Commons against the demands of landowners for even more protection.[67] He died in 1823 at age fifty-one, his dream of global free trade unfulfilled.

Protectionist legislation usually strikes hardest at the weak and powerless, and the Corn Law of 1815 was no exception. Since the price of wheat rarely rose above eighty shillings in peacetime, and since England's agricultural self-sufficiency was rapidly disappearing, the act effectively kept foreign grain out and forced England's poor to pay an artificially inflated price for their daily bread. The subsequent enforcement of the act did not cause the kind of violence attending its passage, but expensive grain was still high on the list of grievances behind the political reform efforts in postwar England. These efforts often turned nasty, as in the "Peterloo Massacre" of 1819, a senseless attack by panicked constables at a peaceful demonstration in Manchester. [68, 69]

Later in the nineteenth century, the increasingly prosperous manufacturers, who would benefit from cheap grain with which to feed their hungry labor force, began to challenge the landed aristocracy. In 1828, the Lancashiremen rammed through a bill that replaced the rigid eighty-shilling barrier with a more gradual sliding scale, similar to that of 1804.[70] By 1840, the intellectual tide had clearly turned in favor of free trade, yet the new act, albeit somewhat less brutal than that of 1815, still plagued England's hungry poor. An unlikely visionary, Richard Cobden, administered the coup de grâce to the statutes, and his ultimate success still speaks volumes about today's controversy over globalization, as well as the democratic process in general.

Cobden was born to a poor family of yeoman farmers in 1804, and would enter public life at the right time—in the wake of the Reform Act of 1832. At age ten, Richard experienced his father's loss of the family farm. His uncle, a cloth merchant, packed him off to the sort of boy's institution made notorious by Charles Dickens. (On later reading *Nicholas Nickelby,* Cobden felt a shock of recognition at the novel's boarding school, Dotheboys Hall.[71]) At fifteen, he was apprenticed as a clerk to his uncle, a calico merchant, and by age twenty he was traveling the countryside selling printed cottons. By age thirty he and his older brother Frederick had established their own printing factory in Manchester and became men of independent means.

Although he undoubtedly had the talent to do so, Cobden never acquired great wealth, enjoying intellectual pursuits, travel, and politics far more than the cotton trade. By thirty-three he had been to the Continent, the Middle East, and the United States, recording of the last, "If knowledge be power, and if education give knowledge, then must the Americans inevitably become the most powerful people in the world."[72] His travels taught him that England could prosper if only it was able to sell its manufactures cheaper than other nations. Military intervention consumed taxes, which drove up the price of England's exports, and spending too much for expensive protected domestic grain to feed English workers did the same. Both damaged the nation.[73] From this reasoning naturally flowed his belief in pacifism, international cooperation, and, most importantly, free trade. By 1840, Britain sent one-third of its exports —mainly cotton fabric and clothing—to the United States, in return for the South's raw cotton. It did not escape the young factory owner that this trade demanded no expensive naval protection.

Cobden was hardly alone in these sentiments. By the 1830s, two very strange bedfellows had also arrived at the conclusion that the Corn Law had to go: the Manchester cotton interests and the Chartists, a group of often lawless radicals dedicated to broadening the voting franchise beyond the landholding aristocracy. In September 1838, representatives of these two groups met in Manchester and founded the Anti-Corn Law League. The best-known free-trader in England, Cobden, assumed its leadership later that year.[74]

In 1838 the League found itself in the right place at the right time. Before the 1830s, communication and transportation were prohibitively expensive. A world in which only the wealthy can write letters or travel long distances utterly disenfranchises those unable to do so. In England, this meant that the entrenched, established landholders easily held the upper hand in their struggle with poor consumers for protection of grain.

The era's rapidly evolving technologies, particularly steam power, greatly reduced this imbalance. The Anti-Corn Law League was now able to send its charismatic speakers—the charming, persuasive Cobden and the fiery, emotional John Bright—speeding around the country to organize and marshal support.

The League developed many of the sophisticated tools used by today's major political parties and special-interest groups: mass mailings, carefully choreographed traveling campaigns, exploitation of religious subtexts, meticulous polling, and targeted legal challenges.

Soon after assuming the League's leadership, Cobden found himself in the company of another visionary of humble background, Rowland Hill, a passionate advocate of the "penny post." By 1838 England was well on its way to being served with high-speed rail transport, which radically reduced carrying costs. The government, however, did not pass the savings along to letter writers. In those days, postage was paid by the *recipient* and came dear: a letter sent from Edinburgh to London, for instance, cost a shilling—almost a day's wages for a farmer or factory worker.

Payment by the recipient and high costs led to all sorts of expediencies and abuses. Travelers routinely carried letters for friends, relatives, and strangers, and several letters would be written on a single sheet that was sent to a distant city, where it was then cut up and sent onward to different recipients there. Books sent from printer to shop carried much of the mail, sandwiched among their pages. Employees had their mail addressed to their workplace, and legislative franking—the privilege of sending letters free of postage—was one of the important perks of public office.[75]

Hill reckoned that it cost the Post Office only one thirty-sixth of a penny to carry a letter from London to Edinburgh, and Cobden soon found himself persuaded by Hill to apply his legendary charm and persuasive skill for the benefit of a select committee of the Commons. Cheaper postage, Cobden told the committee, would allow the fifty thousand Irish working in Manchester to regularly write to their loved ones back home; when members questioned whether the Post Office could manage such a volume of letters, he coolly informed them that an elephant had recently been sent by rail from London to Manchester at twenty miles per hour.

Parliament passed the penny post measure, and it was put into operation on January 10, 1840. At first, confusion reigned over exactly how to implement the scheme; Cobden suggested "something similar to the stamp on patent medicines, something to be affixed by the party with gum on the envelope, then stamped at the post office," the result being modern adhesive postage.[76]

Cobden knew exactly what he was doing; when the penny post finally cleared the House of Lords, he is said to have shouted for joy, "There go the Corn Laws!"[77] Inexpensive mail became the most powerful weapon in the arsenal of the repeal forces, a veritable propaganda howitzer. Further, the Anti-Corn Law League could tap into the wealth of the mill owners, the very wellspring of the Industrial Revolution's riches.

The combination of generous funding and cheap postage enabled the League to blanket England's pitifully small number of voters—just 7 percent of adult males after the Reform Act of 1832.[78] The barrage was systematic and monotonously regular. It featured a daily newspaper, *The Anti-Corn Law Circular;* a well-written weekly, *The League;* and an incessant flow of pamphlets. At the height of the effort in the early 1840s, Cobden estimated that more than one-third of the nation's eight hundred thousand voters regularly received *The League.*[79]

The forces of repeal enlisted not only the new power of the rails and the penny post, but also a very old one: God's messengers on earth. The free-traders drew on the religious fervor of their Chartist and abolitionist allies. At one League meeting, seven hundred ministers in Manchester declared the corn laws "opposed to the law of God," perhaps the first and last time that the Almighty was so dramatically invoked on the side of tariff reduction.[80]

The League also deployed platoons of lawyers into the counties and boroughs to poll voters and ascertain their political leanings. Any landowner whose registration or qualification was questionable saw his franchise challenged, and in order to prevent the opposition from doing the same, the papers of likely free-traders were set right. This strategy quite often resulted in the disqualification of up to one in six Tory electors in a given district. Finally, the League was able to harness its mighty financial resources to purchase property blocks in the names of poor tenants so that each received forty shillings a year in rent—just enough to qualify for the franchise.[81]

When they were not busy in Westminster, Cobden and his colleague John Bright canvassed the country, the former leading off with his charm and quiet mastery of the facts, the latter sweeping away the audience with roaring moral indignation at the perfidy of the landowners. The new railroads whisked them from city to city on an almost hourly basis, and they arrived at each new venue fresh and rested, a feat unimaginable in the days of horse and coach.

In 1841 the Whig government of Lord Melbourne fell and precipitated a general election. Cobden had been narrowly defeated in a run for the Commons four years previously, but he was now such a well-known personality that he easily won election, along with a number of other League candidates, including John Bright.

The election also saw the Tories regain power and returned Robert Peel to 10 Downing Street, the residence he had lost in 1835. Peel's political vision and dogged empiricism put him far out in front of, and out of touch with, the reactionary and aristocratic landowning Tory rank and file. Over the next several years, Cobden sparred with him over the Corn Law, and while their exchanges occasionally became acrimonious, Cobden's command of the facts and his pleasing and logical demeanor slowly wore down the prime minister's opposition to repeal.

The essence of Cobden's argument was as follows. Allowing in cheap foreign corn helped the workingman in two ways: first, it provided him with easy bread; and second, this bread would be paid for by English manufactures, whose production gave the laborer work. In short, trade inward of necessity produced trade outward.[82] During one of Cobden's speeches in the Commons, Peel turned to his deputy Sidney Herbert and said, "You must answer this, for I cannot."[83]

Both sides sought to exploit the dismal labor conditions of the time. In particular, the Tories could thunder with righteous indignation (and not a little hypocrisy) at the dark satanic mills, owned, more often than not, by League members. No sooner had Cobden taken his seat in 1841 than he was attacked as a heartless mill owner and investigated for bookkeeping irregularities. Cobden's factories were, for the era, generally well run and humane, and he easily avoided indictment. In 1844, Lord Ashley Cooper, a Tory MP whose family owned huge agricultural estates, introduced a measure that would have radically restricted factory working hours and child labor. The bill was subsequently watered down and passed with Peel's intervention, and in 1845 Cooper took off after calico printers, a move obviously aimed squarely at Cobden. When Cooper pointed out that child factory workers labored long hours for a pittance of three shillings per week, Cobden retorted that at least they were working indoors, and that child farm laborers put in longer hours in all weather for half the salary.[84]

Victory in the battle for repeal came in fits and starts. In 1842, poor harvests drove Peel to persuade his cabinet to halve the 1828 sliding scale of import duties on grain, and in 1843 Parliament reduced the tariff on Canadian wheat to just one shilling per quarter.[85] In doing so, the prime minister pleased no one—certainly not Cobden, Bright, and their colleagues in the League, who scorned the halfhearted measure, and certainly not many of his fellow Tories, disgusted with Peel's perceived betrayal of his class. Two years later, however, bountiful harvests took the pressure off the landowners, and the League made little progress in Parliament.

Then, in 1845, the gods of agriculture let loose their fury on the British Isles, and precipitated one of the most dramatic episodes in English political history. July and August of that year saw a wet, cold "green winter" that savaged the wheat harvest. Almost simultaneously, a potato blight appeared in southern England and spread like wildfire to Ireland, throwing the populace well beyond the brink of starvation. As the nightmarish year wore on, Peel's government watched in horror. A relief commission was empowered to purchase American corn (maize), and a special scientific commission reported that the blight was even more disastrous than had been feared. On November 22, the other shoe dropped when the leader of the Whig opposition, Lord John Russell, declared for repeal.

By that point, even the staunchest Tories understood that in order to avoid mass starvation, English and Irish ports would have to be opened to foreign grain. Peel further realized that once open, they could not be shut without risking revolution; two weeks later, he assembled his cabinet and informed them that he intended to move for repeal.[86] When two of his ministers refused their support, he tendered his resignation to the queen. Russell proved unable to put together a Whig government, because the party had only a minority in the Commons, and Peel resumed office on December 20.

By January 1846 Peel had no choice but to admit publicly that Cobden and the League had long since proved their case, and that he himself had changed his mind about the Corn Law. Those of his fellow Tories who remained unconverted would have to be outmaneuvered.[87] This remarkable act of self-sacrifice sealed both his political fate as well as his reputation as arguably Britain's ablest nineteenth-century leader. On June 25, repeal passed the House of Lords, and within days the Tory party's landowning elite, spearheaded by Benjamin Disraeli, forced Peel's final resignation.[88, 89] Peel had saved his own class, the landowning aristocracy, from itself, and in the process became anathema to it.

Although the repeal in 1846 marks a historical watershed in world trade policy, by that date most of the heavy lifting had already been done. The act of 1842 had lowered tariffs even more than the final repeal, and modern scholarship suggests that by 1846 effective grain duties had been falling for decades; by the time of their final repeal, they had long since become economically unimportant.[90]

Cobden continued on in Parliament. In order to spread the free-trade gospel, he increasingly lived abroad. Late in life, he found a willing student in Emperor Napoleon III of France, the first Napoleon's nephew.

By 1859, Anglo-French relations had deteriorated nearly to the point of war, mainly because of hysteria stemming from Britain's distrust of its historic enemy, and Cobden found himself on an unofficial mission to Paris advocating for an English-French tariff-reduction treaty. He met with Napoleon III and the emperor's ministers on several occasions. The emperor remarked that while he would very much like to repeal his nation's import tariffs, "The difficulties are very great. We do not make reforms in France; we only make revolutions."[91] Napoleon III was more than receptive to Cobden's idealistic advice, but the captains of French industry and their allies in the government wanted no part of free trade. By now Cobden was a maestro in the art of dispatching protectionist assertions. A passage in his diary speaks as well to the modern world as it did to Napoleon III:

> [The Emperor] repeated to me the arguments which had been used by some of his ministers to dissuade him from a free-trade policy, particularly M. Mange, his Finance Minister, who had urged that if he merely changed his system from prohibition to . . . moderate duties which admitted a large importation of foreign merchandise, then, for every piece of manufactured goods so admitted to consumption in France, a piece of domestic manufacture must be displaced. I pointed out the fallacy of M. Mange's argument in the assumption that everybody in France was sufficiently clothed, and that no increased consumption could take place. I observed that many millions in France never wore stockings, and yet stockings were prohibited. He remarked that he was sorry to say that tens of millions of the population hardly ever tasted bread, but subsisted on potatoes, chestnuts, etc.[92]

That Napoleon III was so receptive to free trade is no surprise; he had been exiled to England in 1846, just as repeal was enacted, and remained there for two years, a time when the nation was under the intellectual sway of Smith, Ricardo, and Cobden himself. French cotton manufacturers, devastated by cheaper and better English cloth, bombarded the emperor with protectionist special pleading, but he also heard from those who supported free trade: producers of wine, silk, and fine furniture, all eager to export their wares. Many French manufacturers who depended on foreign materials, such as machinery makers who consumed large amounts of imported iron, also pushed for lower tariffs.[93]

By the 1850s, the catechism of free trade had spread across the Channel; anti-tariff organizations sprang up in Belgium and France and inspired a generation of liberal economists. The most prominent of these was a professor of political economy who was also a deputy in the National Assembly, Michel Chevalier. He wrote:

> Britain's adoption of the freedom of trade is one of the greatest events of the century. When such a powerful and enlightened nation not only puts such a great principle into practice but is also well known to have profited by it, how can its emulators fail to follow the same way?"[94]

In 1860 Cobden and Chevalier guided the Anglo-French treaty through a hailstorm of opposition on both sides of the Channel, evoking this tribute to Cobden from the Liberal Party MP William Gladstone:

> Rare is the privilege of any man who, having fourteen years ago rendered to his country one signal service, now again, within the same brief span of life, decorated neither by land nor title, bearing no mark to distinguish him from the people he loves, has been permitted to perform another great and memorable service to his sovereign and his country.[95]

The Cobden-Chevalier Treaty slashed import tariffs on both sides. Over the next several years, Italy, Switzerland, Norway, Spain, Austria, and the Hanseatic cities also entered into the spirit of the times. This period saw, for the first time, the widespread use of the most-favored-nation (MFN) clause. MFN status, which goes back to twelfth-century treaties, is similar to the "I will beat any price" offer from your local car dealership. The nation granting it promises tariff rates as low as that offered to any other country, and if, in the future, it further lowers tariffs for goods from another country, it must then do the same for all of its MFN partners. Once the MFN ball began to roll in the 1860s, tariff "disarmament" spread throughout the Continent. Duties that had been as high as 50 percent disappeared entirely on some manufactured goods.[96]

Between the publication of *Wealth of Nations* in 1776 and the repeal of the Corn Laws in 1846, Smith, Ricardo, and Cobden had laid the theoretical and political foundations of the new global economy, which had its heyday in the decades after the signing of the Cobden-Chevalier accord. Protectionists predicted a catastrophe for farmers because of cheap grain imported from abroad. At first, this did not happen, as Europe's increasing population ensured high food prices. But a generation after repeal, an avalanche of inexpensive grain from the Americas, Australia, New Zealand, and Russia buried English and continental farmers. By 1913, England imported 80 percent of its wheat from abroad, but as the twentieth century dawned, no sane Englishman would have traded his nation's industrial present for its agricultural past.[97]

The invasion of New World grain played out differently on the Continent, where the 1880s saw the beginnings of a devastating backlash against free trade that would last until the middle of the twentieth century. This nineteenth-century reaction against the new global economy speaks forcefully to the twenty-first: although free trade benefits mankind in the aggregate, it also produces losers who cannot be expected to passively accept the new order.

WHAT HENRY BESSEMER WROUGHT

If people would transport their manufactories to America or China whenever they could save a small percentage of their expenses by it, profits would be alike . . . all over the world, and all things would be produced in the places where the same labor and capital would produce them in the greatest quantity and quality. A tendency may, even now, be observed toward such a state of things.—John Stuart Mill, 1848.[1]

The dance of modern international manufacturing dazzles the imagination. The myriad of components in your laptop computer, digital music player, and automobile were designed, produced, and assembled on different continents, some making two or more transoceanic journeys before you purchased the final product.

Those who think that this is something new should visit the former copper mining town of Jerome in northern Arizona. Today, an old smelter sits in the middle of this tiny, picturesque tourist site, mute witness to a storied past. With a little coaxing, this squat, ugly machine yields up a remarkable narrative of global trade in the late nineteenth century.

Its tale begins during the late medieval period in the extreme west of Britain, where the Cornish and Welsh became leaders in mining and metallurgy. They had long provided the lion's share of Europe's copper, tin, and iron ores. Almost as important, their mines produced some of the world's best sulfur-free coal, critical for the smelting process. By 1820, the efficient new reverberatory smelters (in which the flame and the mix of ore and coal or charcoal were separated) had begun to exceed the outputs of English and Irish mines. The smelting factories imported ore from wherever they could find it: first from Spain, Cuba, and Australia, and then around the Horn from Chile and Arizona. In return, the coal of western England filled the outgoing vessels.

The sleepy Welsh port of Swansea, with a shallow moorage guarded by a dangerous sandbar, was the center of this long-distance bulk trade. The peculiarities of its cargoes—coal and ore—and the primitive port facilities at both ends of the routes dictated vessels of shallow draft built for capacity, not speed. Ironically, though Wales produced and exported much of the world's coal, the craft that carried it—the ore barques—were powered by sail until the dawn of the twentieth century.

The novelist and seaman Joseph Conrad captured the spirit of the trade after a visit to a dying former captain:

> He had "served his time" in the . . . famous copper-ore trade of the old days between Swansea and the Chilean coast, coal out and copper in, deep-loaded both ways, as if in wanton defiance of the great Cape Horn seas—a work, this, for staunch ships, and a great school of staunchness of West-Country seamen. A whole fleet of copper-bottom barques, as strong in rib and planking, as well-found and great as ever was sent upon the seas, manned by hardy crews and commanded by young masters, was engaged in that now long-defunct trade.[2]

Both inbound and outbound cargoes could kill in unique ways. The rich copper ores of the New World were extraordinarily dense, sometimes containing more than 50 percent of the metal.[3] If not tightly packed into special chests, the ore could shift and lethally unbalance a vessel. Further, iron and copper do not get along well, and ore that found its way to the hull's bottom could sink a ship by corroding its nails.

Outbound from Swansea, coal brought its own peril—fire. The propensity of coal dust to spontaneously combust ensured that during an average year in the late nineteenth century, about six of the roughly 150 barques plying the trade burned at sea. A coal fire that smoldered deep in a hold, undetected for days, was nearly impossible to put out, its one saving grace being that it often burned slowly enough to be jettisoned, or at least to allow the crew to abandon ship in orderly fashion.

At first, foreign ore, profitable because of its high purity, seemed to answer the prayers of the Welsh smelting industry. If factory owners were particularly lucky, the ore also contained a large amount of recoverable silver. As late as 1850, most of the world's copper ore was still being smelted in south Wales.

In the long run, Cornwall and Wales could hardly expect to keep the profitable copper smelting industry to themselves. Their miners, made redundant by the closure of played-out pits, had long carried their skills with them across the ocean; few mining camps in the New World lacked a contingent of "Cousin Jacks" (as the Cornish men were known). In the late nineteenth century, Welsh smelting workers also began to migrate abroad. With their help, American refining technology soon surpassed that of the Old World factories.

With the arrival of the railroad in the copper regions of Montana, Utah, and Arizona, a new trading pattern arose. Jerome's experience was typical. By 1882, smelting operations were under way there, and it became a major center of both mining and smelting operations.[4] Fine Welsh coke (charred coal) went around the Horn to San Francisco; thence by rail to Ashfork, Arizona, where the tracks ended; and then by mule-drawn wagon the final sixty miles over the mountains to Jerome. There, the coke smelted the local ore into pure copper, which was shipped back to Europe via the reverse route—in all, a round-trip of over thirty-two thousand miles, a manufacturing cycle that would impress even a modern computer maker.[5]

The nineteenth century brought changes in world trade that would not be matched by even those of the twentieth. By 1900, transcontinental trade in both luxury and bulk commodities had become part of everyday life. Imagine for a moment two time travelers: the first sent from the year 1800 to the year 1900, and the second from 1900 to 2000. Our twentieth-century time traveler, starting out in 1900, would already be familiar with instantaneous global communication, passenger trains speeding at more than sixty miles per hour, and perishable foods sent from the antipodes in refrigerated railcars and ships. By contrast, our nineteenth-century time traveler, starting out in 1800, would never have seen information, people, or goods travel faster than the speed of a horse. For this traveler, the very idea of buying tulips grown across the continent, eating out-of-season strawberries from across the ocean, or reading the news the day it happened anywhere on the planet—all things that were everyday occurrences in 1900—would have seemed fantastic.

The story of the nineteenth-century trade revolution cannot be told in linear fashion, for it involves several interwoven, nearly simultaneous strands. The 1800s saw the advent of the steamship, the railroad, the telegraph, and novel systems of both natural and artificial refrigeration, all augmented by a new process for the production of cheap, high-quality steel. These combined to open up the New World, Australia, and the Ukraine to agricultural exploitation, which in turn aroused a violent protectionist reaction in continental Europe that lingers today.

At its birth in 1776, the United States was a small agrarian confederation strung along the eastern seaboard of North America, huddled hard by the Appalachian range. The northern and southern states were divided not only by the peculiar institution of slavery, but also by deep and abiding differences in trade policy. It is not much of an exaggeration to consider the fight over tariffs equal to that over abolition as a cause of the Civil War. Only a minority of southerners owned slaves, and an even smaller minority of northerners were abolitionists, but nearly all Americans either consumed or produced trade items. In the early 1830s, the dispute over tariffs nearly triggered that Armageddon prematurely, an eventuality prevented only by the political skill of Andrew Jackson, Henry Clay, and the elderly James Madison.

The British industrial juggernaut frightened the small but growing manufacturing concerns clustered in New England and the Mid-Atlantic states. Alexander Hamilton felt strongly that America's infant industries needed protection from foreign behemoths, albeit in the form of subsidies, not tariffs. Almost as influential was a brilliant German-born economist, Georg Friedrich List, who had spent several years in America making his fortune in the railroad business. On his return to Germany in 1832 as an American consul, he applied himself to trade economics. Adam Smith and David Ricardo had erred, he thought; they had both written that nations benefited from a free-trade policy even in the face of protectionism from their neighbors, but List reckoned that retaliation served better. In the United States, he became enamoured of Hamilton's American System—a plan for a national infrastructure, largely paid for with import duties. List also agreed with Hamilton about infant industries; nations should protect their young enterprises from stronger and more established competitors, such as England.[6] List's leading American disciple was the influential Henry Carey, a Philadelphian insurance tycoon and economist who felt even more strongly that the road to national prosperity was paved with high tariffs.

When times are hard, both farmers and workers demand protection. This was most definitely the case when grain prices fell in the aftermath of the Napoleonic wars. American farmers sought to keep the domestic grain market to themselves, and factory owners in New England demanded shelter from murderous competition from the Lancashire mills.

Before the adoption of the income tax during the twentieth century, import duties financed 90 percent of American government.[7] This meant that tariffs had to be raised during economic depressions, precisely the wrong thing to do during a downturn. These three elements—the fear of British manufacturing, frequent economic downturns, and the need to raise revenue—drove the protectionism of the North, which would last well into the twentieth century.

The South, by contrast, favored free trade. The casual visitor to the ports of the antebellum South would have understood why this was so. On a single day in 1798, one observer counted no fewer than 117 vessels in Charleston harbor, either bearing goods from places like Liverpool, Glasgow, London, Bordeaux, Cádiz, Bremen, and Madeira, or outbound with cotton, tobacco, rice, and indigo, none of which needed even a whiff of tariff protection.[8]

Before 1820, the South had relatively little quarrel with the North; Dixie largely supported the American System. But that year the Missouri Compromise made the South aware of the ability of the growing Northern majority to restrict slavery. This in turn focused southerners' attention on other disagreements with the North, prime among which was the tariff issue. Both issues ended the "Era of Good Feelings."

Southern exports of cotton, indigo, and rice continued to flourish, but as the new nation's North and West grew, European goods increasingly came to New York City. This growing metropolis was fast becoming the nation's financial capital and, after 1825, the distribution point for the westward flow of export goods through the Erie Canal. Southerners smelled conspiracy in New York City's ascendancy, and Congress added insult to injury when it passed a series of dramatic tariff increases in the 1820s. In the eyes of southerners, the most egregious of these were those on low-quality British wool, or "negro cloths," worn by slaves. Members of the House of Representatives from the Mid-Atlantic states voted sixty to fifteen in favor of the act of 1824, whereas southerners voted sixty-four to three against it.[9] Had a direct vote on abolition been placed before Congress that year, the outcome could hardly have been more polarized.

The two protagonists of the tariff controversy of the 1820s and 1830s were Andrew Jackson and South Carolina's John Calhoun, the latter vice president under both Jackson and his predecessor, John Quincy Adams. Jackson's coalition assured Calhoun that it would not pass the even more restrictive tariff act threatened by the Adams men. The promise was not kept. The Jackson coalition voted with the Adams men to pass the draconian 1828 Act, better known as the "Tariff of Abominations." This legislation inflamed the growing estrangement between North and South.[10]

Nowhere was the anger greater than in South Carolina, which had been settled almost two centuries before by expatriate sugar planters from Barbados. Between the censuses of 1790 and 1830, the proportion of slaves had grown from 42 percent to 54 percent of the population. This made the state the American Sparta, with a tiny white elite sitting atop a massive population of black helots. South Carolina, anxious about both restive blacks at home and abolitionists in the North, led the opposition to the new tariffs and asserted the right of states to nullify those federal statutes it found unconstitutional. One South Carolinian congressman, the brooding George McDuffie, railed against the acts of 1824 and 1828 and propounded the "forty bale theory," which fallaciously equated the 40 percent tariff on imported textiles with a 40 percent reduction in the living standard. "The manufacturer actually invades your barns and plunders you forty out of every hundred bales that you produce."[11]

After the passage of the Tariff of Abominations in 1828, the South Carolina legislature asked Vice President Calhoun, the South's finest constitutionalist, for advice on how the state could nullify the act. He did so, but in secret. For four years the South pushed hard for the easing of duties.

Andrew Jackson, who had been born in South Carolina and raised in Tennessee, assumed the presidency in 1829 determined to assuage the ill feelings of Southern slaveholders and free-traders. But he also wanted to retire the national debt, and that required maintaining tariff revenue. Balancing these two conflicting goals, he kept the nation together by maintaining a "middle and just course": the moderate Tariff

Act of 1832.[12] Jackson was helped by the octogenarian James Madison, who warned his fellow southerners against pushing the North too hard. Madison focused his powers of persuasion on Henry Clay, leader of the newborn protectionist Whig Party and a staunch supporter of Hamilton's American System.

The act of 1832 lowered duties only slightly on some manufactured goods. Jackson had thought that these concessions would mollify the South, but they did not, since the act kept tariffs on imported textiles, particularly on negro cloths, at about 50 percent.[13] On November 24, 1832, a state convention in South Carolina applied Calhoun's secret legal strategy to pass the Ordinance of Nullification, which declared both the 1828 and 1832 tariffs illegal within its borders. By year's end, Calhoun had resigned the vice presidency, returned home, and been elected senator. Jackson replied swiftly, first with words (declaring that the South Carolinians were "in a state of insanity"), then by sending a naval squadron to Charleston, and even by threatening to arrest the governor of Virginia should he be so foolish as to impede federal troops sent through his state to pacify South Carolina.[14]

By this point, Jackson was brimming over with righteous anger against the South and seemed hell-bent on a violent confrontation. But the protectionist Henry Clay, "the Great Compromiser," saved the president from himself. Clay realized two things: first, that only a further reduction in import duties would prevent South Carolina from nullifying the previous tariff acts and precipitating a showdown; and second, that Jackson desired the authority to bring an increasingly radicalized South Carolina to heel.[15]

Clay accomplished both aims, and thereby postponed the Civil War for a generation. On March 1, 1833, the "Compromise Tariff," under which rates fell slowly over the next several years, passed Congress. This cleaved rabid South Carolina, petrified of her growing slave majority and committed to nullification, away from the rest of the South. On the same day, the "Force Bill," which authorized the president to take whatever action he saw fit to collect tariffs and maintain the Union, passed as well. Outmaneuvered, Calhoun had no choice but to go along, and on March 3 he raced in an open mail cart through freezing rain to Columbia, South Carolina, to prevent the state convention from passing the nullification decree.

Eight days later, having been convinced by Calhoun that the Compromise Tariff had stripped away the support of the other southern states, the convention backed down. It did nullify the Force Bill, but this was an empty gesture: its acceptance of the Compromise Tariff meant that there was now no need to invoke the Force Bill.

Thanks to the adroit political maneuvering of Jackson and Clay, South Carolina found itself alone in its power struggle with the federal government over the nullification of the tariff acts. In all fairness, Calhoun still believed strongly in the Union, even if many of his fellow South Carolinians did not. He saw nullification as a way to defuse secession and keep his native state within the national system, where it indeed remained for another generation.[16]

Two decades later, in 1856, the poor showing by the abolitionist John C. Frémont, the first Republican presidential candidate, against James Buchanan convinced the new party that its antislavery platform alone was inadequate. Pennsylvania, the most protectionist state in the Union, had been a pivotal one in the election, and it would remain pivotal in the election of 1860. Already under the spell of the arch-protectionist Henry Carey, Abraham Lincoln took up the cry for higher tariffs and won the Keystone State and the White House. Carey would become his chief economic advisor.[17]

When South Carolina again incited conflict in 1861, the secessionists had gained the upper hand in the entire South, and the North would not be as understanding as it had been a generation earlier. According to Confederate mythology, a Virginia Unionist, Colonel John Baldwin, offered Lincoln the adjournment of his state's secession convention in return for the evacuation of Fort Sumter. Lincoln is supposed to have replied, "What will become of my tariff?"[18]

By 1861, the balance of economic power and military potential had shifted in favor of the North. Had Jackson, Clay, and Madison acted less wisely, the tariff controversy of the 1830s and the subsequent nullification crisis could quite possibly have ended in the defeat of the Union.

The roots of southerners' discontent spread far beyond trade policy, of course; in 1833, moderates in Congress had accused the nullification forces, bent on states' rights and the survival of slavery, of using the tariff laws as a convenient excuse for tearing the Union apart.[19] Calhoun admitted as much. Speaking to a northerner friend, he explained, "The tariff is the occasion, rather than the real cause of the unhappy state of things."[20]

Nonetheless, there can be no doubting the importance of the split between free-traders and protectionists as a cause of the Civil War. After Lincoln's election, an editorial in the appropriately named *Natchez* (Mississippi) *Free Trader* stated:

> Ere the 4th of March next [Inauguration Day] the signs of the times are that a Southern Confederacy will be formed and the principle of free trade will be established. Then will the North, prostrate in the dust, too keenly feel what a precious jewel they have parted with, never to be regained. The South needs no Custom House and will thrive on free trade as she never can without it.[21]

In 1861, secession and war left the North with the need to fund its army, and later, pensions and Reconstruction; paying for all this would require billions in import duties. The Union, now shorn of Southern opposition, was free to erect one of the world's highest tariff walls. For more than a half century after the Civil War, this formidable barrier shielded American industries from British competition.

As much as the debate over protection roiled the United States and Europe at the beginning of the nineteenth century, this issue would be trumped by the dramatic fall in shipping costs. After 1830, cheap freight would create a revolutionary new global market for the world's most important bulk product, grain.

The economic historian Paul Bairoch calculates that in 1830, wheat sold for approximately $95 per ton in Europe, and the cost of transport per ton per thousand miles was $4.62 by ocean, $28 by canal or river, and $174 by road. (Prices have been converted into 2007 dollars.) America's fertile new lands could produce grain at roughly half the cost of that in Europe—$47.50 per ton, giving a price advantage of $47.50 over European-grown grain. It cost $17 to transport a ton of New World wheat 3,600 miles across the ocean; this left a $30 advantage over wheat grown in Europe. However, once the costs of transshipment, spoilage, and insurance were taken into account, the breakeven point was probably no more than a few dozen miles inland from American ports.[22]

These numbers demonstrate that in the mid-nineteenth century, transport costs were so high that grain and other bulk products from

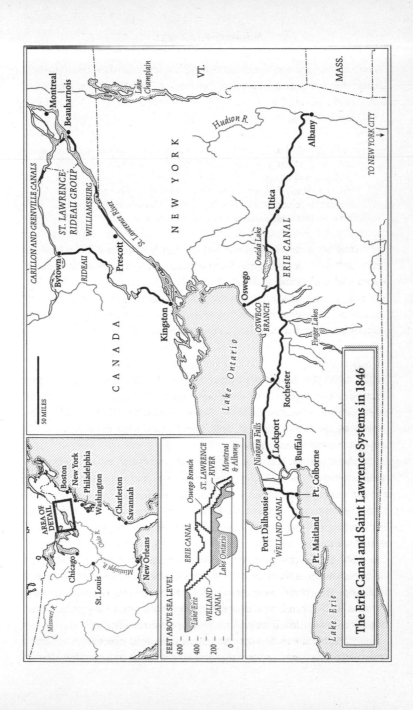

The Erie Canal and Saint Lawrence Systems in 1846

America could not compete in Europe. In other words, land transport costs for bulk goods were so high that the tariff rates levied on them were irrelevant.

Neither the Mississippi nor the Great Lakes system provided transportation that was cheap or efficient enough to fill the bill. The solution would be the Erie Canal, a 364-mile channel that cut through unsettled wilderness from just south of Niagara Falls to the Hudson River at Albany, traversing several hundred feet of elevation along the way.

At its opening in 1825, the canal carried 185,000 tons per year of eastbound cargo. Traffic on the new waterway grew so rapidly that it was soon widened and double-locked; in 1845, it carried one million tons; in 1852, two million; and in 1880, its peak year, 4.6 million. The success of the Erie set off a canal boom that provided America with 3,326 miles of artificial waterways by 1840.

Historians have long wondered how traffic on the Erie Canal continued to increase for fifty-five years in the face of competition from the railroads.[23] The canal's tonnage grew so prodigiously for more than half a century precisely *because* of the iron horse. Before the railroad, canal transport suffered from the same shortcoming as maritime shipping: because of the astronomic expense of road carriage, a load of grain grown more than twenty or thirty miles from a port might just as well have been sitting on the far side of the moon. The primitive steam and iron rail technology of the mid-nineteenth century was not capable of getting crops to the ports and efficiently powering them across the ocean. More advanced metallurgical technology was needed to make the new inland supply chain practicable.

The major stumbling block was the mechanical properties of iron. Wrought iron rails were too soft to bear the weight of heavy railcars, and wore out quickly; steam boilers made of iron were not strong enough to bear high pressures.

Strong, flexible steel was needed for both rails and boilers, but before Henry Bessemer invented his blast process in the mid-1850s, it was far too expensive for either application. After his technique was perfected by Charles William Siemens and Pierre Martin, the price of steel fell to just a few pounds sterling per ton, about one-tenth of what it had been.[24]

The switch from iron to stronger and more flexible steel for boilers and pistons allowed finer engine machining and, most importantly, higher

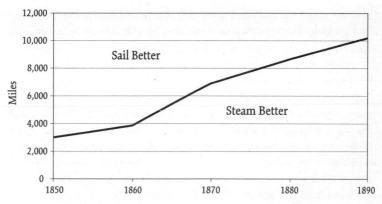

Figure 12-1. Break-Even Point between Sail and Steam

pressures and greater fuel efficiency. However, new improvements usually create new problems: wooden hulls could not tolerate the stress of the new propulsion system. Steel plates allowed for stronger and lighter hulls, and steel propellers and shafts bore high rotation speeds better than those of iron. The stage was now set for the triumph of steam on the oceans.

The victory of steam would not come easily on the deep seas. At the same time that the new steel engine and hull designs made ocean-going steamships possible, radical improvements were also being made in the designs of sails and of wooden hulls, particularly for the clipper ships described in Chapter 11. The steamship's need for refueling meant that the longer the route, the less price-competitive steam became. By the late nineteenth century "extreme clipper" designs, epitomized by the *Cutty Sark,* sustained speeds in excess of fifteen knots and dominated the long-haul routes.[25] In the roaring forties, a well-trimmed clipper could sustain runs of up to twenty knots, a speed no steamship of the era could match.[26]

Economic historians have calculated how the carrying capacity of steamships (the tonnage not used for coal, and thus available for cargo) fell off with distance, as shown in Figure 12-1. Below a carrying capacity of approximately 75 percent (that is, using more than one-fourth of displacement for coal), steam could not compete with sail. Over the course of the nineteenth century, this "steam-sail boundary" gradually lengthened as more efficient engines consumed less fuel. In 1850, steam lost out to sail beyond three thousand miles, but by 1890 the boundary had lengthened to ten thousand miles. The epic competition between steam and sail that raged throughout the nineteenth century had nearly ended. By the beginning of the twentieth century, steam propulsion was economical on all but the very longest ocean routes.[27]

Steam-driven metal ships suffered from other disadvantages. A steamship cost about 50 percent more than a wooden vessel of the same size and required 50 percent more crew. The steamship companies spent enormous sums cleaning iron bottoms, since metal hulls fouled easily with barnacles and seaweed. (Copper resists these pests much more effectively. A thin sheet of it could easily be nailed over a wooden hull but would rapidly corrode an iron or steel hull.) If a dockworker or shipping clerk did not know whether a scheduled arrival was sail- or steam-powered, all doubt was removed when the vessel became overdue. Joseph Conrad, again:

> The sailing ship, when I knew her in her days of perfection, was a sensible creature. . . . No iron ship of yesterday ever attained the marvels of speed which the seamanship of men famous in their time had obtained from their wooden, copper-sheeted predecessors. Everything had been done to make the iron ship perfect, but no wit of man had managed to devise an efficient coating composition to keep her bottom clean with the smooth cleanliness of yellow metal sheeting. After a spell of a few weeks at sea, an iron ship begins to lag as if she had grown tired too soon.[28]

Two other factors helped keep sail alive. The first was cheap American timber; in the mid-nineteenth century, the United States briefly surpassed England as the world's leading shipbuilder (although most of the American-built clipper ships sailed under the Union Jack). The second factor was improvements in meteorological observation. Beginning with the eighteenth-century voyages of Captain James Cook, both British and American mariners and geographers systematically mapped the world's winds and ocean currents. Sailing ships no longer groped their way through the seas using vague seasonal rules of thumb, but rather could maintain the most advantageous routing for the precise time of year. During the nineteenth century, these advances shortened the 11,000-mile voyage from England around the Cape to Australia from 125 days to 92 days.

Gradually, the improved efficiency of steam engines overwhelmed the valiant rearguard action of sail. By 1855, steamships carried one-third of England's trade with the western Mediterranean and almost all of its trade with northern Europe, and by 1865, steam powered cargoes to and from Alexandria as well. In 1865, the steamship *Halley* carried a load of coffee from Rio de Janeiro to New York, demolishing the myth that only wooden ships preserved the beans' flavor, and iron ships came to dominate the North and South American East Coast trade.[29]

The opening of the Suez Canal on November 17, 1869 shortened the distance between London and Bombay from 11,500 to 6,200 miles. This cut the heart out of the long-range advantage of sail. Since the steam-sail boundary (shown in Figure 12-1) for 1870 was about seven thousand miles, this meant that the canal's opening abruptly rendered sail uneconomical between Europe and Asia. Worse, sailing ships could not travel north up the Red Sea against its prevailing headwinds, and they had to be towed in both directions through the canal. During the first five years of the canal's operation, not even one in twenty craft transiting it was a sailing vessel.

Figure 12-2 plots the dramatic falloff in the construction of wooden ships caused by the Suez Canal. Over the next twenty years, the remaining old wooden sailing vessels wore out and were replaced with iron

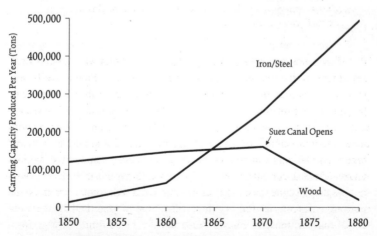

Figure 12-2. Annual World Ship Construction

ships; in 1890, total global steam tonnage permanently surpassed that of sail.[30]

Theoretically, sail should have competed well with steam over the very long distances of the China trade. But since China's exports consisted mainly of high-value tea, shippers happily paid the higher steam freight after the Suez Canal opened. The last of the fabled clippers departed Canton in the late 1870s.

Since the canal cut only one hundred miles off the Cape route between Sydney and London, most Australian traffic remained open to sail. Even so, high-value carriage—passengers and luxury goods—went by steam, leaving only low-value ores and nitrates to go by sail.[31] In 1914, the opening of the Panama Canal, which eliminated the long leg around the Horn, rang down the final curtain on the age of sail.

Steam and steel wrought a trade revolution not only on the world's oceans, but also on its rivers, canals, and land. These changes were particularly important in the vast open spaces of the New World unreachable by boat, and they return our narrative to the Erie Canal.

When it opened in 1825, the Canal dramatically decreased the price of inland waterborne transport, but the land barrier remained. Without efficient rail transport, the Great Lakes system gave access to only a thin crescent of territory within a few dozen miles of the shores of lakes Erie, Huron, and Michigan.

Strong, cheap steel rails and high-pressure steel boilers brought the American cornucopia to the rest of the world. In 1830, it cost $173.82 (in today's dollars) to move a ton of goods a thousand miles by wagon; in 1910, the price of the same haulage by rail was only $22.43, one-eighth as expensive as, and several times faster than it had been in 1830.[32]

No point in England lies more than seventy miles over relatively tame countryside from the sea. For centuries, this geographical fact combined with the prohibitive expense of overland carriage to give England an incalculable advantage over its continental neighbors. With the advent of cheap canal and rail transport, that edge vanished; for the world's farmers, the world became flat in a hurry after Bessemer poured the first steel out of his crucibles.

When the Mary's Fall Canal locks connected Lake Superior to the

Great Lakes system and the Erie Canal in 1855, they gave access not only to the agricultural produce of the Great Plains, but also to Minnesota's huge iron ore deposits, from which yet more steel rails, boilers, and ship's plates could be made.

Because the laws of physics dictate that water transport is inherently more efficient than land transport, canal shipment remained cheaper than rail shipment. With time, however, shippers increasingly valued the speed and reliability of rail. Grain sent direct by freight car to the East Coast arrived more quickly, was less likely to spoil in summer, and did not require the two expensive and risky transshipments of the lake system: from rail to lake steamer and from lake steamer to canal barge. Shippers paid high insurance premiums for cargoes in the lake system, whereas the railroads wisely assumed direct responsibility for the contents of freight cars. In addition, the railroads could be kept running in all but the worst weather in winter, when the lakes froze over.

During the nineteenth century, the advantages of rail grew. Before about 1873, wheat sent east through Chicago went by train only if the lakes were frozen; after that date, almost all wheat traveled directly by rail; the changeover for less valuable corn came in 1884. Chicago's rise to prominence as a rail hub was not accidental. From the southern shores of Lake Michigan, rail held a decided advantage over the lake route east, since a train journey from Chicago to the East Coast was much more direct than steaming the semicircular route around lakes Michigan and Huron. Although tonnage on the Erie Canal grew for over half a century after its opening in 1825, not peaking until 1885, the *value* of cargo carried began falling long before that, in 1853, because the railroads siphoned off high-cost goods and left the lakes and canals with cheap, bulky commodities such as iron ore.[33]

Before the opening of the Erie Canal, New York and Pennsylvania ranked first and second in American wheat production. After about 1870, Illinois and Iowa took over that honor. The opening of Lake Superior by the Mary's Fall Canal gave easy access to the northern Great Plains and dramatically altered the nation's agricultural landscape; by 1895, the Dakotas and Minnesota ruled the breadbasket.[34]

North American wheat and corn growers benefited mightily from being able to pour grain directly onto railcars that fed steamships bound for Europe, but they were not alone. Farmers from Argentina, Australia,

New Zealand, and deep in the Ukraine also benefited from the dawning age of cheap transport.

On September 5, 1833, the American clipper *Tuscany* appeared at the mouth of India's Hooghly River, took on a river pilot, and headed upstream to Calcutta. The news of its arrival was swiftly relayed upriver, throwing that city, whose name is synonymous with sweltering heat, into a state of excitement. The *Tuscany* carried a new and priceless cargo: more than a hundred tons of crystal-clear New England ice.

By that year, ice had been shipped over great distances for nearly three decades. This trade was the brainchild of an eccentric Bostonian, Frederic Tudor. On a visit to the Hades of Havana one summer in his youth, he imagined that he might make his fortune acquainting the city with cold drinks. He was right. Beginning in the Caribbean, he expanded his operations throughout Europe and the United States, particularly in New Orleans, where Tudor ice made the mint julep famous.

Getting a frozen cargo from Massachusetts to India on a sailing ship is not as difficult as it sounds—the larger the mass of ice, the more slowly it melts. A layer of sawdust insulation and a bit of ventilation were enough to keep two-thirds of 150 tons of ice frozen for the four-month journey.

The hard part of shipping ice to the tropics was harvesting the clear, cold cargo in sufficient quantity, quality, and shape. This problem was solved by Nathaniel Wyeth, a hotel keeper who sold ice to Tudor as a sideline. Wyeth's invention, patented in 1829, gave birth to one of New England's largest nineteenth-century industries. His horse-drawn contraption, which mounted cutting teeth on a rectangular frame, yielded twenty-inch blocks that loaded easily and stacked tightly.

Beginning with his first Caribbean shipments, Tudor began packing seasonal fruit into his refrigerated holds—typically, Baldwin apples southbound to Havana, and oranges northbound. Farther north, the very first barges on the Erie Canal carried ice-chilled Great Lakes fish to New York. Strangely, Tudor did little to exploit this advance. Until the day he died in 1864, he dealt almost exclusively in ice, and it fell to others to develop what would become a much larger business, the shipment of perishables.[35]

Well into the twentieth century, most of America's refrigeration was harvested from the ponds and rivers of New England and the Upper Midwest and packed into ships, barges, and specially designed railroad cars that chilled an increasing amount of produce bound for the East Coast, the Caribbean, and Europe.

One of Tudor's minor sources was Walden Pond. Henry David Thoreau, demonstrating an imperfect grasp of Indian Ocean trade routes, sea temperature, and the physics of heat transfer, mused about a wayward block of Tudor ice tumbling into the harbor at Calcutta:

> The pure Walden water is mingled with the sacred water of the Ganges. With favoring winds it is wafted past the site of the fabulous islands of Atlantis and the Hesperides, makes the periplus of Hanno, and, floating by Ternate and Tidore and the mouth of the Persian Gulf, melts in the tropic gales of the Indian Seas, and is landed in ports of which Alexander only heard the names.[36]

Refrigerated vehicles began to appear in the 1830s. Photographs taken at Promontory, Utah in 1869, just after the opening of the transcontinental railroad, reveal a long string of the distinctive Union Pacific fruit cars used to carry out-of-season grapes, pears, and peaches to astonished easterners. Other chilled cargoes ranged from cut flowers to sides of beef, and these bounteous luxuries fed consumers' demand for more. By the mid-nineteenth century, a higher tonnage of ice, bound for India, Europe, and around the Horn to the West Coast, was shipped out of Boston harbor than any other product. Occasionally, shipments traveled as far as China and Australia.[37]

Around the same time, a meat packer in New England, Gustavus Swift, decided to move his business to Chicago's rail hub. Finding the railroad companies both unwilling and unable to provide ice-chilled cars, he began to experiment with various railcar designs. He settled on one invented by Andrew Chase that featured easily loaded twin overhead ice tanks at either end, a configuration later improved on by another meat packer, Philip Armour, who added an effective cooling mixture of crushed ice and salt.[38] By 1880, the railroads and private shippers owned more than 1,300 ice-cooled refrigerated cars; by 1900, that number swelled to 87,000. The number finally peaked in 1930 at 181,000 cars.[39]

In 1875, the American beef distributor Timothy Eastman shipped the first chilled meat from New York to England. He packed about one-fourth of the volume of the hold with ice and cooled the adjacent cargo with ventilation fans. Queen Victoria deemed the beef "very good," continuing the centuries-old tradition of royal endorsement of novel consumer goods and bringing chilled American meat to English tables.

Not many populated areas of the world are blessed with a reliable ice-harvesting season. Even in the Boston area where Tudor operated, a mild winter often resulted in a "crop failure," inducing panic in the more refined parts of the South and moving the cutting crews to Maine. In the nineteenth century, the public also became concerned about the purity of ice harvested by horse-drawn Wyeth cutters from increasingly polluted ponds and rivers. Both Americans and Europeans began to investigate artificial chilling.

Before the mid-twentieth century, home refrigeration meant iceboxes. By the early twentieth century, most American families owned such "refrigerators"—insulated cedar or oak boxes designed to keep a small amount of meat or a dairy product cold with ice replenished every several days.

Mechanical refrigeration had no Alexander Graham Bell or Thomas Edison. The basic principles of artificial cooling had been known since prehistoric times by the chill of wind on wet skin. (In terms of modern physics, evaporation consumes heat, and thus produces cooling.) In ancient Egypt, wealthy people had their slaves moisten the outside of earthen jars, which chilled on exposure to night breezes; the Indians recorded the first production of artificial ice by a similar treatment of covered water-filled pits.

In 1755, William Cullen, a Scottish physician, made a simple but far-reaching breakthrough when he generated a vacuum in a water-filled vessel. This made the water boil at room temperature (or at least what passes for it in Scotland). Since boiling is essentially very rapid evaporation, it produces dramatic cooling—the same phenomenon that occurs when you emerge from a swim into a stiff breeze. Soon enough, Cullen was able to make ice at room temperature. Variations on Cullen's basic technique multiplied; the most alarming of them involved using concentrated sulfuric acid, which aggressively absorbs water, to hasten its evaporation.

Physicists improved Cullen's method with the use of ether, which boils at a much lower temperature than water and is thus a more effective cooling agent. Finally, the discovery of thermodynamics brought the realization that certain gases, particularly ammonia and carbon dioxide, could also exist as solids or liquids at a low enough temperature or high enough pressure, and thus provide yet more efficient cooling.

Figure 12-3 illustrates the operation of a simple, early mechanical refrigeration device. The compressor sucks ammonia from the system on the left of the diagram, producing low pressure there, and compresses it into the right half. As the ammonia boils off on the low-pressure side, it cools a jacket of brine (which has a low freezing temperature) that is circulated out to the task at hand—ice-making machinery in the case of an ice plant, or the refrigerated compartment of a ship. On the high-pressure side, the ammonia condenses, producing "waste" heat that is vented off.

These first heavy, inefficient steam-driven mechanical refrigerators, produced by dozens of inventors under numerous patents, were used in fixed ice-making plants far from natural ice sources—in the Caribbean, south of the Mason-Dixon Line, in West Coast cities, and particularly in Argentinean and Australian meatpacking plants. Tudor's Calcutta trade, which grew steadily more profitable for nearly half a century following his initial delivery in 1833, came to an abrupt end a few years after the opening of the city's first artificial ice plant in 1878.[40]

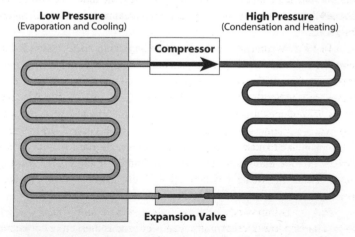

Figure 12-3. Schematic of Early Mechanical Refrigeration Unit

Artificial and natural production complemented each other nicely; ice made in plants in New Orleans or California filled the cooling tanks of northbound and eastbound refrigerator cars; blocks harvested from midwestern rivers and New England ponds cooled south- and westbound freights.

Timothy Eastman's partner, Henry Bell, suspected that the new artificial refrigeration machines might prove more economical than ice for marine shipping. In 1877 he approached the famous physicist Sir William Thompson (later Lord Kelvin) about the feasibility of transporting artificially chilled and frozen beef. (The American firm Kelvinator would subsequently appropriate his name.) Not having the time or inclination for commercial schemes, Thompson introduced Bell to his associate J. J. Coleman, and the two founded the Bell-Coleman Mechanical Refrigeration Company.[41] Together, they built a fleet of mechanically refrigerated ships, one of which, the *Circassia,* carried the first American beef kept chilled by the new machines.[42]

In 1881, Australia was home to sixty-five million sheep, eight million cattle, and just over two million people; artificial refrigeration allowed much of the mutton to find its way into English butcher shops. By 1910, the United States was sending about four hundred thousand tons of beef to Britain each year, and Argentina was shipping an even larger amount of both beef and mutton. (American beef was chilled, whereas Argentinian and Australian meat was deep-frozen to about sixteen degrees Fahrenheit because of the greater distance it had to travel.) On the eve of World War I, nearly 40 percent of meat consumed by Britons came from abroad.[43] The London correspondent of *Scientific American* observed:

> I frequently stood at the great warehouse on the Thames and have seen the barges that have taken out the carcasses of mutton . . . which are stacked up just like cord wood, handled like cord wood, and put under the great arches of the Cannon Street Bridge, in rooms holding 80,000. There you find mutton from New Zealand and South America, artificially frozen at the start, kept frozen on the voyage, stored in the storehouses under the great arches of the bridge, and delivered frozen to the retailers. All the meat is being sent by Armour, Hammond, Eastman, and other shippers.[44]

The refrigerated meat industry got yet another marketing boost from Edward L. Bernays, public relations pioneer and nephew of Sigmund

Freud. By the 1920s, busy Americans and Britons had cut their break-fasts down to rapidly prepared juice, toast, and coffee or tea. Bernays conducted the first "three out of four doctors recommend" campaign for New York's Beechnut Packing Company. It plugged a hearty breakfast (and plugged arteries), and established bacon and eggs as the traditional morning meal of English-speakers on both sides of the Atlantic.[45]

Throughout history, increases in trade volume have always benefited some and harmed others. Falling transport costs allowed farmers and ranchers in the United States, Canada, Argentina, New Zealand, Australia, and the Ukraine to bury Europe under mountains of grain and meat. On the other hand, American shipbuilders, who had relied on cheap domestic timber and their expertise with sailing vessels, lost out to British steam and steel tech-nology. Between 1850 and 1910, two-fifths of Atlantic tonnage sailed under the Union Jack, compared with only one-tenth under the Stars and Stripes.[46]

India also lost. Its cotton and jute growers prospered, but its sail-based maritime sector was devastated by the combination of steam and the Suez Canal. By the beginning of World War I, India's vessels could not even service its own coastal trade, and its shipbuilding industry dis-appeared almost entirely.[47]

While optimistic observers, like the correspondent for *Scientific American,* marveled at the miracles of global commerce, a backlash was building. The European reaction to the avalanche of agricultural prod-ucts from the New World would set back the free-trade movement for over half a century, contribute in no small part to two devastating world conflicts, and supply the backdrop for today's battles over globalization.

13

COLLAPSE

We learned that a prohibitive protective tariff is a gun that recoils upon ourselves.—Cordell Hull[1]

It was the worst of times to be an American. Around the world, political leaders and editorialists condemned our foreign policy, which was seen, correctly, as unilateralist, arrogant, and dangerous. Outraged Europeans organized boycotts of our products. Wrote one Italian businessman to another, "The driver of an American car, in our province, particularly in the environment of the city, is continually made the butt of obscene gestures and epithets unworthy of a civilized people."[2] The French, as always, fretted about the growing power of the United States. One Parisian editorialist viewed opposition to the monster across the Atlantic as the duty of all Europeans—"the only means of struggling against American hegemony."[3]

What had incited such vigorous anti-Americanism? The invasion of Iraq? The conflict in Vietnam? The global ubiquity of McDonald's, Microsoft, and Disney? The period in question was 1930–1933, and the issue was the Smoot-Hawley Tariff.

One of the most notorious pieces of legislation ever passed by Congress, it is also one of the most poorly understood. Smoot-Hawley did dramatically raise U.S. tariffs, but they were already quite high. More important, and contrary to popular perception, it did not cause, or even greatly deepen, the Great Depression, nor was it a significant departure from previous American trade policy. Rather, Smoot-Hawley represented the high tide of worldwide protectionism that flowed on the new global agricultural trade.

The story begins with a brief tour of twentieth-century trade theory. The great premodern thinkers in the field—Henry Martyn, Adam Smith, and David Ricardo—described the *overall* benefits of free trade. They understood but largely ignored the fact that a significant minority of inno-

cent people were usually harmed. Their twentieth-century descendants—
Bertil Ohlin, Eli Heckscher, Paul Samuelson, and Wolfgang Stolper—
provided a framework that identifies who wins, who loses, and how they
react.

By 1860, northern Europe, basking in the warm glow of the repeal of the
Corn Law, the signing of the Cobden-Chevalier Treaty, and the "tariff
disarmament" that followed, seemed firmly on the road to free trade. This
pleasant and profitable voyage would not last long.

Cheaper transport means price convergence. Between the late 1850s
and 1912, the cost of sending a bushel of grain from Chicago to Liverpool
fell from thirty-five cents to around ten cents. Since faster and more reliable shipping also meant lower handling and insurance costs, the actual
savings to consumers were even greater.

Predictably, during the six decades preceding World War I, wheat
prices in the Old World and New World moved closer together, as shown
in Figure 13-1.[4] A similar plot of price convergence in the late nineteenth
century could be drawn for raw and manufactured commodities alike: beef,
copper, iron, machinery, and textiles. In 1870, meat sold for 93 percent
more in Liverpool than in Chicago; by 1913 this gap had narrowed to just
16 percent.

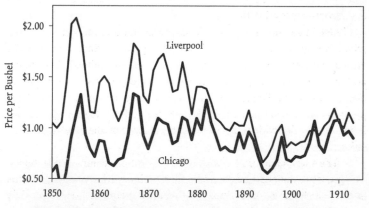

Figure 13-1. Wheat Prices in Liverpool vs. Chicago, 1850–1913

The dramatic increase in shipping efficiency not only produced convergence in agricultural prices but also eliminated the farmer's friend in hard times: high prices. In a world where it cost too much to import grain from the neighboring valley, let alone from across the ocean, a short crop was partially compensated for by a rise in price. In a global agricultural market with cheap shipping, even that comfort disappeared.[5] The loss of this familiar cushion provides as poignant an example as any of the risks of a globalizing economy.

The situation was reversed with manufactured products, which were initially cheaper in the labor- and capital-rich Old World. In 1870, pig iron was 85 percent more expensive in the United States than in England; by 1913, this gap had narrowed to 19 percent. Between these two dates the differential for smelted copper fell from 32 percent to zero, and the price structure for textiles actually reversed: textiles were 13.7 percent more expensive in Boston than in Manchester in 1870, and 2.6 percent more expensive in Manchester in 1913.[6]

Not only did the prices of the traditional grains begin to move together around the planet, they also danced in sync with the great staple of the East, rice. The nexus of the integrated rice-wheat market was India; a rise in the price of wheat in Bombay also increased that of rice, since Indians ate both. Further, the spread of long-distance submarine and land telegraph lines in the 1860s and 1870s meant that a movement in grain in Calcutta was instantly mirrored in the markets of London, Sydney, and Hong Kong.[7]

In the early twentieth century, two Swedish economists, Eli Heckscher and Bertil Ohlin, puzzled over these data and came to the conclusion that something even more profound was happening. The "classical economics" of Adam Smith, David Ricardo, and John Stuart Mill stipulated three inputs for all products: labor, land, and capital—paid for, respectively, with wages, rents, and interest.[8] Heckscher and Ohlin's essential insight was that decreased shipping costs created not only the global convergence of commodity prices, but also convergence of the prices of the three basic input factors: wages, rents, and interest rates.[9]

Recent research has confirmed their hypothesis. In the early nineteenth century, labor and capital were more abundant in the Old World than in the New World; therefore, wages and interest rates were low in the former and high in the latter. By contrast, land was far more abundant in the New World, so rents were lower there. The economic historians Kevin O'Rourke and Jeffrey Williamson note that in 1870 in the New World, average real wages (defined as actual purchasing power) were 136 percent higher than those in the Old World; by 1913 this gap had decreased to 87 percent. Even more amazingly, between those two dates real American rents rose by 248.9 percent, while British rents *fell* 43.3 percent.[10]

The reasons for the convergence of rents were clear enough. Cheap transport flooded Europe with grain and meat, driving down their prices in the Old World and raising them in the New World, where they previously would have gone to waste. This in turn lowered the value of farmland in the Old World while raising it in the New World.

The convergence in the capital markets is even easier to understand. The telegraph removed uncertainty about distant interest rates and even allowed the instantaneous "wiring" of capital and credit.

The reasons for wage convergence are more controversial. The most obvious, and likely, explanation is migration driven by higher wages in the New World. Europeans did not emigrate to the New World yearning for freedom or streets paved with gold; they simply wanted higher hourly rates. During the late nineteenth century, an Irish carpenter could earn a far better living in New York, and an Italian peasant could prosper on the endless Argentine pampas in a way he never could in the poor soil of his native land. But as large numbers of Europeans migrated across the Atlantic Ocean, these earning differentials gradually disappeared, reducing immigration even before legal restrictions were instituted. In 1900, real wages were almost three times higher in Argentina than in Italy. By 1950 they were equal, and by 1985, the average Italian earned four times as much as his emigrant Argentine relatives.[11]

Were we to score the nineteenth-century transport revolution on points, Old World laborers and New World landowners (mainly farmers) won, and Old World landowners and New World workers lost. Admittedly, the lot of American workers did improve between 1870 and 1913, but their enormous advantage over their British counterparts eroded considerably. The same cannot be said for English landowners, who saw their rents fall disastrously.

In 1941, in the aftermath of the Smoot-Hawley debacle and in the midst of the world war to which it had contributed, an Austrian-born instructor at Harvard University, Wolfgang Stolper, approached a young colleague, Paul Samuelson, with a question about trade theory. He wondered why classical economics taught that all nations benefited from trade when Heckscher and Ohlin's work implied that with increased trade, wages in some nations must fall, hurting workers. Samuelson realized that Stolper was on to something, and the two collaborated on what came to be known as the Stolper-Samuelson theorem, a framework that provides insight into the politics of global trade: who draws the long straw, who gets the short one, and, most important, how the political fallout affects the fate of nations.

Mathematics is the language of the economist, and in order to make their model work, Stolper and Samuelson could allow for only two products and two input factors—one that was scarce relative to that in other nations, and a second that was abundant relative to other nations. Their model predicted that protection benefited those who predominantly owned a relatively scarce factor and harmed those who owned a relatively abundant one.[12] With free trade, the opposite occurred. (The factors considered were typically the inputs of classical economics: land, labor, and capital.)

Let's see how this works. If labor is scarce in nation A and abundant in nation B, then wages will be lower in B, and labor-intensive products made in B will consequently be cheaper there as well. With free trade, merchants and consumers will prefer the less expensive goods made in B to those made in A. Workers in B will benefit, and workers in A will lose. This is true of the other two factors as well; free trade helps farmers in countries with abundant land and hurts those in countries with scarce land, and it helps capitalists in rich nations with abundant capital and hurts capitalists in poor nations.[13]

In Stolper and Samuelson's terms, "free trade" and "protection" refer not just to tariff levels and prohibitions, but also to the costs of transport. Reducing the price of shipping has the same effect as lowering tariffs: in other words, a reduction of fifty cents per bushel in transport costs and a reduction of fifty cents per bushel in tariffs should both increase grain commerce by roughly the same amount.

What does this mean in practice? Before 1870, England had, relative to other nations, abundant capital and labor, and scarce land. By contrast, the United States had relatively scarce capital and labor, but abundant land. Tariffs rose dramatically during that period around the world, especially in the United States after the Civil War, but trade grew more free as rapidly decreasing shipping costs more than compensated for the higher tariffs. Table 13-1 shows the "Stolper-Samuelson grid" for some representative nations and time periods.

The Stolper-Samuelson theorem predicts that the main beneficiaries of increased trade would be the owners of abundant factors in each nation: capitalists and laborers in England, and landowners (that is, farmers) in the United States. This is precisely what happened, and thus it was no coincidence that all these groups favored free trade. Likewise it is no surprise that the owners of scarce factors in each nation—English landowners and American laborers and capitalists—sought protection.

What about continental Europe? In general, these nations had scarce capital and land but abundant labor. Stolper-Samuelson predicts that falling transport costs after 1870 would have generated a wave of protectionism by continental capitalists and farmers. Again, the theory is dead-on: European farmers reacted vehemently and brought to an end the free-trade era that began with Corn Law repeal and the Cobden-Chevalier Treaty.

In truth, the French had never been happy with the treaty, which was seen by their democratic forces and farmers as a "royal coup d'état" by a despotic Napoleon III. When the humiliating Franco-Prussian War of 1870–1871 brought Napoleon III's Second Empire to an end, French support of free trade faded with it.

The birth of the new French state, the Third Republic, occurred almost simultaneously with the flood of New World wheat. From time immemorial, the walls of terrain and distance had protected France's farmers, particularly those in the hinterland. The railroad and steamship destroyed these comforting barriers, and by 1881, net French wheat imports

Table 13-1. Stolper-Samuelson Categories

	Abundant Factor(s) (Favor Free Trade)	Scarce Factor(s) (Favor Protectionism)
United States before 1900	Land	Labor, Capital
United States after 1900	Land, Capital	Labor
England, 1750–present	Labor, Capital	Land
Germany before 1870	Labor, Land	Capital
Germany 1870–1960	Labor	Capital, Land
Germany after 1960	Labor, Capital	Land

passed the million-ton mark. Cheaper imported grain forced an increasing number of French farmers out of business, and they clamored for a new insulation to replace the one formerly provided by the wagon and the rutted road. There were simply too many farmers in France for an elected government to ignore; even as late as the end of the nineteenth century, about half of the nation's labor force still worked the land. Their protectionism was supported by strapped French financiers, the owners of the other scarce factor, capital. The nation's financiers, saddled with debt from the disastrous Franco-Prussian War, also saw salvation in higher tariff income. This combination of French capitalists and farmers proved decisive. By contrast, in England, only one-sixth of the labor force worked the land. And English financiers, flush with capital from industry and trade, opposed protection.[14]

Once again, the different outcomes in England and France matched the predictions of Stolper-Samuelson: in Britain, the abundant factors of labor and capital that favored free trade teamed up to defeat the scarce factor favoring protectionism, the landowners. In France, the scarce factors favoring protectionism, capital and landowners, combined to defeat the abundant factor favoring free trade, labor.

By the mid- to late-nineteenth century, every major nation had its disciple of Friedrich List and his "nationalist economics," as this brand of protectionism became known: Henry Carey in the United States; Joseph Chamberlain in England; and in France, Paul-Louis Cauwès, dean of the Sorbonne's law school. In 1884, France repealed a law, passed nearly a century before by the revolutionary government, that prevented farmers and other workers from banding together in associations based on economic interest. Almost immediately after the repeal, agricultural *syndicats* sprouted and demanded a tariff wall. A resultant flurry of legislation slowly raised duties on imported grain, farm animals, and meat. The general election of 1889 sent to the Assembly a large number of protectionist deputies, especially from the agrarian strongholds of Normandy and Brittany.

A dramatic series of parliamentary maneuvers and debates followed, the high point of which was a verbal duel between Léon Say, liberal economist and finance minister, and the protectionist Félix Jules Méline, a disciple of Cauwès and a future premier of France. Inveighing against any further tariff increases, Say argued that the struggle was not just between protection and free trade, but rather a mere facet of "that great combat of the individual against the state."[15] Say's eloquence failed to move the Assembly, which in early 1892 passed the "Méline Tariff." It nearly doubled existing rates and was followed by even further increases that would continue until World War II.

The tariffs failed to stop the decline of agriculture in France and served only to burden its citizens with high food costs. Although many French observers decried their countrymen's fear of the new global economy, others were more fatalistic. In a commentary as descriptive of French national character today as it was when it was penned in 1904, the economist Henri Truchy noted:

> We judged it better to content ourselves with the untroubled posses-sion of the domestic market than to risk the hazards of the world mar-ket, and we built a solid fortress of tariffs. Within the boundaries of this limited, but assured market, the French live calmly, comfortably enough, and leaving to others the torment of great ambition, are no more than spectators in the struggles for economic supremacy.[16]

Few Englishmen, however, shed tears over the harm done to the landed aristocracy by grain and meat from the New World. In the words of the economic historian Charles Kindleberger:

> No action was taken to halt the decline in farm prices or to assist the farming community. . . . Rents fell, young men left the farm for the town, land planted to crops shrank rapidly. The response to the de-cline in the world price of wheat was to complete the liquidation of agriculture as the most powerful economic group in Britain.[17]

After 1890 some British industries, notably steel, sugar refining, and jewelry, began to feel the landowners' pain, and they met increased American competition with cries for "fair trade." England was beginning to catch the protectionist influenza, spread by Joseph Chamberlain, a prominent politician (first in the Liberal Party, and then the Liberal Union-ist Party), president of the Board of Trade, and father of the future prime minister Neville Chamberlain. His protectionism was of a different strain from the ordinary continental variety; it would have erected a high tariff wall around the entire empire and the commonwealths, within whose ambit there would be free trade—so-called "imperial preference." But England was not ready to abandon free trade. Chamberlain's proposals became the major issue in the general election of 1906, in which he and his supporters were roundly defeated.[18]

While most of continental Europe walled itself off from foreign imports, and even the English fretted over their free-trade policy, one nation took a different path, based on, of all things, pigs and cows. The best meat comes from the youngest animals, and earlier slaughter means more intense feeding to bring them up to weight. After 1870, the combination of high demand, inexpensive refrigerated shipping, and cheap feed corn brought the stars into nearly perfect alignment for the world's producers of beef, pork, cheese, milk, and butter. For centuries, northern European nations held the lead in high-end animal husbandry, but curiously, only Denmark opened its markets and took advantage of the situation.

Great industries are usually born of banal concerns in humble circumstances. In 1882 a group of dairy farmers in the village of Hjedding in western Jutland (Denmark's large, mainland peninsula) organized a cooperative in order to purchase one of the expensive new milk-separating machines and jointly sell their cream and butter. They elected three directors who, after a long night of negotiation, came up with a members' agreement that would become the cornerstone of Denmark's rise to prosperity in the early twentieth century.

The contract was a model of simplicity: each morning, milk was collected by the cooperative's truck, taken to the factory, and processed by skilled technicians. The skimmed milk was returned to the farmer, the butter was sold on the open market, and the co-op's profits were divided among the participants according to the quality and quantity of whole milk they contributed. The members agreed to deliver to the co-op every last drop that was not immediately consumed in the farmhouse, and to collect it according to rigorous hygienic standards. The arrangement proved wildly successful, and within less than a decade, Danish farmers had organized over five hundred co-ops.

But this was only a prelude to the main event: bacon. In 1887 a group of hog farmers in eastern Jutland, unhappy with their rail service, banded together under the Hjedding model and built a state-of-the-art meat-packing plant. This time, the government took a hand: hog quality varies more than milk quality, and the Danish Agriculture Department set up experimental stations in order to supply farmers with the best breeding stock. In 1871, Denmark had 442,000 pigs; by 1914, it had 2.5 million. Between those two dates, pork exports rose from roughly eleven million pounds to three hundred million. By the early 1930s, with over half of all Danish adults members of co-ops, this small nation exported 731 million pounds of pork—nearly half of the world's trade in it.

The government also gave farmers moral encouragement and suggested to national dairy and hog-farming organizations that they trademark the quality of their products abroad. The Lur brand, which evolved into the modern Lurpak label, is today featured in supermarket cases around the world.[19]

Both the creamery and the pork co-ops required relatively large amounts of borrowed capital to acquire factories, equipment, vehicles, and workers. The Danish experience remains to this day a powerful, though nearly forgotten, lesson on the appropriate government reaction to the challenge of global competition: support and fund, but do not protect.

In Germany, the specter of inexpensive agricultural products from the New World and manufactured goods from Britain had a far less positive result. For centuries, German economic and political life had been dominated by the Junkers, the Prussian counterpart of England's landed aristocracy.[20] These freewheeling farmers dominated Germany's "wild East" frontier with Poland and Russia, and over the centuries they accumulated an ever-increasing percentage of the nation's arable land. Nothing could stop them; even the abolition of serfdom in Prussia in 1807 allowed the Junkers to exploit their connections and appropriate more of the peasant's land. (And nothing did stop them until the Soviets confiscated their estates in 1945.)

Before 1880, the factor used most intensively by the Junkers, land, had been abundant, compared with land in Germany's neighbors at the time. Germany had been an exporter of wheat and rye and had been one of England's major sources of these two vital grains. Naturally, in those days the Junkers were free-traders. According to the economic historian Alexander Gerschenkron, they

> not very consistently, but very conveniently, had contrived to find a
> place for Adam Smith in the system of their general philosophy and
> had nothing but scorn and hatred for the protectionist doctrines of
> [their countryman] Friedrich List.[21]

After 1880, German landholdings looked puny relative to those in the new agricultural behemoths: the United States, Canada, Argentina, Australia, New Zealand, and Russia. Suddenly, the Junkers switched from being free-trading abundant-factor owners to being protectionist scarce-factor owners. As in France, a series of protectionist acts, most notably the "Bülow tariff" of 1902, dramatically raised import duties, particularly on grain.

This protectionist response benefited only the grain-growing aristocracy and was otherwise an unmitigated disaster. Along the way, the Junkers duped northern German peasants into supporting the tariffs by shielding their cows and pigs with high protective duties on imported animals and meat. As skilled at animal husbandry as their Danish neighbors, these poor farmers found themselves deprived of the cheap feed grain that would have made them prosperous. Protectionism's "silent killer"— the increased cost of raw materials to domestic industries—had struck again.

Worse was to come. Take another look at Table 13-1. Note that in every nation and time period, the factor owners square off against each other in a two-against-one configuration.[22] In both England and pre-1900 America, labor and capital found themselves on the same side—for free trade in the former, and for protection in the latter. In Germany, capital and land (the coalition of "iron and rye," so-called because the iron industry was an intensive consumer of the scarce capital factor) found itself opposed to urban laborers, who tended toward Marxism.

German urban workers favored free trade, not only because they represented the abundant factor, but also because of the perversities of the Marxist worldview. Free trade was an essential ingredient in the revolutionary recipe, since it supported industrial development and full-fledged capitalism, which then would inevitably crumble and clear the way for communism.[23] Marx, logical to a fault, thus opposed tariffs:

> The protective system of our day is conservative, while the free trade system is destructive. It breaks up old nationalities and pushes the antagonism of the proletariat and bourgeoisie to the extreme point. In a word, the free trade system hastens the social revolution. In this revolutionary sense alone, gentlemen, I vote in favor of free trade.[24]

By identifying who favors and who opposes open markets, Stolper-Samuelson helps to explain political alliances. In the twentieth century, the world would find out that the German coalition of xenophobic, protectionist landowners and capitalists arrayed against socialist, free-trading workers was a prescription for fascism. In nineteenth-century England, on the other hand, capitalists and workers united in favor of free trade against the old landowning oligarchy, a profoundly democratic development. (American capitalists and workers did the same, but with a different objective—protectionism.) Obviously, this interpretation of Stolper-Samuelson, developed by UCLA political scientist Ronald Rogowski, is a simple model that takes no account of race, culture, or history, and Rogowski himself repeatedly cautions that his model is only part of the story. That said, the insights it affords into political processes around the world are remarkable.[25]

The rapid erection of tariff barriers between 1880 and 1914 should have choked off global commerce. In fact, no such thing occurred; between those two dates, the volume of world trade approximately tripled, driven by two forces. First, the steam engine continued to prove mightier than the customhouse, as savings on shipping costs more than made up for increased import duties. Second, the planet had grown much richer, with total world real GDP nearly quadrupling during that thirty-four-year period. All other things being equal, wealthier societies trade more, since they have more excess goods to exchange. This means that, in general, the volume of trade grows faster than wealth; between 1720 and 1998, world real GDP grew by an average of 1.5 percent per year, while the real value of trade grew by 2.7 percent per year.[26]

Ever since the Civil War, American tariff policy had followed a monotonous cycle of protectionism under Republicans and moderation under Democrats. In the election of 1888, the Republican Benjamin Harrison narrowly defeated the Democrat Grover Cleveland (who actually won the popular vote). The Republican congressional delegation, led by Senator William McKinley, took this as a "mandate" to pass the notorious tariff named after him, which he rode to the presidency eight years later. After the election of the Democrat Woodrow Wilson in 1912, the McKinley Tariff was replaced by the Underwood Tariff, which gradually drove import duties to a historic low of 16 percent in 1920.

The Underwood Tariff was to be a short-lived victory for American free-traders. Not long after it was passed, the Republicans recaptured the presidency and Congress. Two years later, in 1922, the protectionist Fordney-McCumber Tariff was signed into law by President Harding. Soon enough, import duties stood at over 40 percent.

Besides being ludicrously high, Republican tariffs tended also to be "autonomous." That is, they were set by Congress, and while they gave the president power to punish trading partners with higher rates, they did not allow him to decrease levels. Democratic tariffs, such as the Underwood Act, generally left open the possibility of reductions and talks with trading partners, although these options were rarely exploited, for fear of arousing Republican legislators.[27]

Between 1830 and 1910, the costs of shipping by sea, canal or river, and land had fallen by 65, 80, and 87 percent, respectively. By World War I, most of the juice had been squeezed out of the transport efficiency orange. Certainly, great advances in transportation—the internal combustion engine, the airplane, and the shipping container—were made in the twentieth century. But by the outbreak of the Great War, even bulk cargoes such as ore, guano, and timber routinely rounded the Horn—and under sail at that. The slowing rate of improvement in transport efficiency no longer offset large tariff increases or a severe downturn in the world economy. Unfortunately, both a worldwide depression and a rapidly escalating tariff wall combined in the fiasco wrought by Herbert Hoover.

A successful mining engineer who had turned to public service, Hoover rose to prominence directing relief efforts in war-torn Europe. When questioned about the wisdom of feeding Russians, some of who were Bolsheviks, in the aftermath of the revolution, he is said to have replied, "Twenty million people are starving. Whatever their politics, they shall be fed!"[28]

Hoover had always been a protectionist, and he remained one during his tenure as secretary of commerce under Harding and Coolidge. Although conversant with mining textbooks, he had either not read or not understood Ricardo and believed that nations should import only those products that could not be produced domestically. In 1928 he overtly appealed to farmers, a traditional Democratic constituency, who had been hurt by falling crop prices:

> [We] realize that there are certain industries which cannot now suc-
> cessfully compete with foreign producers because of lower foreign
> wages and a lower cost of living abroad, and we pledge the next
> Republican Congress to an examination and where necessary a re-
> vision of these schedules to the end that American labor in these
> industries can again command the home market, may maintain its
> standard of living, and may count upon steady employment in its
> accustomed field.[29]

It would have been more accurate to call the bill he eventually signed the "Hoover Tariff," but that infamy fell instead to its two sponsoring Republicans, Senator Reed Smoot of Utah and Representative Willis Hawley of Oregon. Raising the average tariff on dutiable goods to nearly 60 percent, Smoot-Hawley was no bolt from the blue; it merely propelled the already high rates of the Fordney-McCumber Act into the stratosphere.

Even before Smoot-Hawley's passage, two groups reacted with horror: Europeans and economists. By the time the legislation reached the Senate, foreign ministries the world over sent protests to the State Department and boycotts were already under way; virtually all American economists of any stature—1,028 in all—signed a petition to Hoover pleading for a veto.[30]

To no avail. On June 17, 1930, he signed Smoot-Hawley into law and so set off retaliation and trade war. Covering tens of thousands of items, the bill seemed designed to offend every last trading partner. It deployed many "non-tariff barriers" as well. For example, bottle corks constituted about half of Spanish exports to the United States; not only did the new law increase the tariffs on corks to prohibitive levels, it also required that they be stamped with their country of origin, a process that actually cost more than the cork itself.

The act slapped high tariffs on foreign watches, particularly inexpensive ones that competed with American "dollar watches." One Swiss worker in ten either labored in, or was closely connected to, the watch industry, and the issue galvanized the normally agreeable and peaceable nation into righteous anger. The watches and corks nicely illustrate the impotence of small nations; whereas shipments to the United States accounted for 10 percent of Swiss exports, trade in the reverse direction accounted for only one tenth of 1 percent of American exports. The feeling of helplessness among the Swiss and Spaniards magnified their anger.

The Continent's large nations, Italy, France, and Germany, were in a better position to land punches, and they did so against the pride of American industry: its automobiles and radios, raising average import duties on these items well above 50 percent. It took no small provocation to goad Benito Mussolini into action on this issue; an auto aficionado who loathed the indifferent quality of Italy's largest manufacturer, Fiat, Il Duce had for years resisted the protectionist demands of its president, Giovanni Agnelli. Smoot-Hawley finally exhausted his patience, and he responded with tariffs approaching 100 percent that almost completely shut off imports of American vehicles.[31] (Some things really never do change: the Agnellis continued to control Fiat, produce lousy cars, and demand protection almost into the twenty-first century.) By 1932, even free-trading England piled on, passing a 10 percent tariff on most imported goods and convening a Commonwealth Conference in Ottawa that erected a protectionist wall around the empire.

So it went, all over the world, for three years after the passage of Smoot-Hawley in 1930, as French lace, Spanish fruit, Canadian timber, Argentine beef, Swiss watches, and American cars slowly disappeared from the world's wharves. By 1933 the entire globe seemed headed for what economists call autarky—a condition in which nations achieve self-sufficiency in all products, no matter how inept they are at producing them.

America had brought the world to the brink of international commercial collapse, and it would take an American to reverse the process. Born in a log cabin in tobacco-growing eastern Tennessee, Cordell Hull had acquired a homespun understanding of Ricardian economics and, more important, of the moral value of trade. His grasp of the subject is best revealed by this passage from his memoirs:

> When I was a boy on the farm in Tennessee, we had two neighbors— I'll call them Jenkins and Jones—who were enemies of each other. For many years there had been bad feeling between them—I don't know why—and when they met on the road or in town or at church, they stared at each other coldly and didn't speak.
> Then one of Jenkins' mules went lame in the spring just when Jenkins needed him the most for plowing. At the same time Jones ran short of corn for hogs. Now it happened that Jones was through

with his own plowing and had a mule to spare, and Jenkins had a bin filled with corn. A friendly third party brought the two men together, and Jones let Jenkins use his mule in exchange for corn for the hogs.

As a result, it wasn't long before the two old enemies were the best of friends. A common-sense trade and ordinary neighborliness had made them aware of their economic need of each other and brought them peace.[32]

As a Democratic congressman for nearly a quarter century, Hull fought a valiant rearguard action against both Fordney-McCumber and Smoot-Hawley, and in 1930 he won a Senate seat, only to resign it two years later when Roosevelt chose him as secretary of state. On his arrival at Foggy Bottom, he was confronted by no fewer than thirty-four formal protests against American tariffs from foreign governments.

Like Cobden a century before, he took his message to the country, and then he took it abroad. With trade approaching a standstill and the world in the throes of depression, he reasoned to anyone who would listen that in the present sorry circumstances: "It should be obvious [that] high tariffs could not be the infallible and inevitable producers of prosperity they had been represented to be."[33] Foreign nations, he continued, could not be expected to purchase our products if they could not earn cash by selling to us.

His toughest audience was the new president, whose fear of the Republicans drove him to almost immediately backtrack from his campaign promises of free trade. Hull gradually won him over by pointing out that the Fordney-McCumber and Smoot-Hawley tariffs emasculated the president's ability to conduct international commercial relations. The wily Hull proposed to Roosevelt that Smoot-Hawley be merely "amended" to allow the president to increase or decrease its rates by half and to unilaterally offer foreign nations other limited concessions, such as a guarantee that an item on the duty-free list would remain there. The resultant legislation, the Reciprocal Trade Agreements Act of 1934, checked the world's nearly half-century march toward protection and autarky. It ran for three years, and was then repeatedly renewed by Congress.

Hull began modestly and first negotiated an agreement with Cuba, then peeled Canada away from the Ottawa Accords. Next, he negotiated agreements with most of the rest of the hemisphere, followed by treaties

with the major European nations, Australia, and New Zealand before finally negotiating a largely symbolic agreement with England just as the
lights were going out in Europe for the second time in a generation. Hull
served the longest term as secretary of state in American history—just under
twelve years—before finally resigning in 1944 because of poor health.

There had, of course, been winners during the trade debacle of 1930–
1933: Fiat, wine growers in California, watchmakers in Waltham, Massachusetts, and radio manufacturers in Germany. But overall, damage had
been done. How much? From an economic perspective, surprisingly little.
In the first place, since economic growth is such a powerful driver of trade,
proving an effect in the opposite direction—that protectionism makes the
world poor (or that free trade makes it rich)—is problematic. Between
1929 and 1932, real GDP fell by 17 percent worldwide, and by 26 percent in the United States, but most economic historians now believe that
only a minuscule part of that huge loss of both world GDP and the United
States' GDP can be ascribed to the tariff wars.

A back-of-the-envelope calculation shows that this must have been
true. At the time of Smoot-Hawley's passage, trade volume accounted
for only about 9 percent of world economic output. Had all international
trade been eliminated, and had no domestic use for the previously exported
goods been found, world GDP would have fallen by the same amount—
9 percent. Between 1930 and 1933, worldwide trade volume fell off by
one-third to one-half. Depending on how the falloff is measured, this
computes to 3 to 5 percent of world GDP, and these losses were partially
made up by more expensive domestic goods.[34] Thus, the damage done
could not possibly have exceeded 1 or 2 percent of world GDP—nowhere
near the 17 percent falloff seen during the Great Depression.

Even more impressively, the nations most dependent on trade did
not suffer the most damage. For example, in Holland, trade accounted for
17 percent of GDP, and yet its economy contracted by only 8 percent in
those years. By contrast, trade constituted less than 4 percent of the United
States' GDP, yet its economy contracted by 26 percent during the
Depression.[35] The inescapable conclusion: contrary to public perception,
Smoot-Hawley did not cause, or even significantly deepen, the Great
Depression.[36]

If the 1930s trade war did not greatly harm the world economy, it
certainly choked off international commerce. As just mentioned, world

trade fell dramatically during the Smoot-Hawley years. Between 1914 and 1944, world trade volume remained stagnant, an unprecedented event in three decades of modern history, during which world GDP had approximately doubled in spite of two devastating global conflicts.

Recently, economic historians have calculated that the tariff wars of the 1930s caused less than half of this falloff in trade, the rest being due to the Great Depression itself, which decreased demand for trade products. Interestingly, the combination of "specific tariffs" and deflation caused at least as much unintentional damage as the intentional increases in tariff rates. Specific tariffs are those calculated on a per pound or per unit basis; if the price per pound falls and the amount of tariff per pound does not, this unintentionally increases the effective ad valorem rates. That is, a specific tariff of twenty cents per pound on meat worth forty cents amounts to a 50 percent tariff; if the price of the meat falls to twenty cents, the effective ad valorem rate is now 100 percent.[37]

The real long-term damage done by the tariff war was not to the world economy, which was minimal, or even to world commerce, which recovered relatively rapidly. Rather, it was the damage to the intangibles of trade: the expansion of consumption beyond domestic goods, commerce with and living among foreigners, and understanding their motives and concerns. Farmers Jones and Jenkins of Hull's parable were finally made to understand that they were worth more to each other alive than dead, but in the run-up to World War II, the nations of the world did not realize this until it was too late. The political and moral benefits of trade had in fact been eloquently described by John Stuart Mill nearly a century before:

> The economical advantages of commerce are surpassed in importance by those of its effects which are intellectual and moral. It is hardly possible to overrate the value, in the present low state of human improvement, of placing human beings in contact with persons dissimilar to themselves, and with modes of thought and action unlike those with which they are familiar. . . . Commerce first taught nations to see with goodwill the wealth and prosperity of one another. Before, the patriot, unless sufficiently advanced to feel the world his country, wished all countries weak, poor, and ill-governed but his own: he now sees in their wealth and progress a direct source of wealth and progress to his own country.[38]

During the first half of the twentieth century, patriots around the world less and less felt the world their country, and this would cause no little grief. America learned the hard way that protection invites retaliation; a nation cannot trade out without trading in.

America also learned that a trade war could start a real war, and even before the United States entered World War II, historians and statesmen sensed that its isolationism and protectionism had contributed to the cataclysm. The historian John Bell Condliffe, writing in 1940, presciently observed, "If an international system is to be restored, it must be an American-dominated system, based on *Pax America*."[39] Albert Hirschman, a participant in the events of the period, noted in 1945:

> [Trade wars] undoubtedly sharpen national antagonisms. They also provide excellent opportunities for nationalist leaders to arouse popular resentment . . . international economic relations provide them with an excellent instrument to achieve their ends, just as a promise of a quick and crushing victory by means of aerial superiority undoubtedly contributed in a most important way to the present war.[40]

As the United States emerged from the horrors of World War II, it began the long, difficult job of dismantling the tariff walls erected over most of the preceding century. Those seeking the origins of today's globalized, multinational-dominated economy will find it in a long-forgotten State Department report published in 1945, *Proposals for the Expansion of Trade and Employment.* Although this remarkable document originated within the American wartime bureaucracy, it was infused with the spirits of Smith, Ricardo, Cobden, and Hull.[41]

Its drafters sensed that they were actors on a unique historical stage— one on which everything around them was a shambles, and in which the fate of the entire world depended on just how they reassembled the pieces. As expressed in the opening sentence of *Proposals,* "The main prize of the victory of the United Nations is a limited and temporary power to establish the world we want to live in."[42]

Proposals went on to catalog the mistakes that had been made and to suggest how, in general, to avoid repeating them, and then, more specifically, how to negotiate the unraveling of the protectionism that had crippled international commerce since 1880. It was nothing more and nothing less than a road map for the new commercial *Pax Americana*. The economic historian Clair Wilcox, writing in 1948, neatly summarized America's transformation from autarky to leader of the new international commercial order:

> [After the First World War] we made new loans to the rest of the world; now, again, we are making such loans. But then, we sought to recover, with interest, sums that we had advanced to our allies to finance the prosecution of the war. And, at the same time, we raised our tariff so fast and so far as to make it difficult, if not impossible, for any of these debts to be paid. Now, however, we have written off the wartime balance of the lend-lease account and we have taken the lead in reducing barriers to trade. We have come, at last, to recognize the requirements of our position as the world's greatest creditor. We have demonstrated that we can learn from history.[43]

The first order of business was to get the British on board. By 1945, the positions of England and the United States had completely reversed; heavily indebted Britain sought to choke off imports so as not to erode its scarce currency reserves, whereas the U.S. State Department wanted to open up world commerce as rapidly as possible. After tough negotiations, the victors reached a compromise: multilateral trade talks would proceed, but with all participants allowed an "escape clause" if they determined that lower tariffs might produce "sudden and widespread injury to the producers concerned."

The newly opened world trade was, at least initially, an American creature, an accident of the singular international economic conditions at the end of the war. With the United States the last man standing, American farmers, workers, and capitalists had relatively little to fear from foreign competition in any sphere. In the immediate postwar years, Americans of all stripes offered little resistance to lower tariffs.[44]

In early 1947, trade officials from twenty-two major nations, using *Proposals* as their blueprint, paired off in Geneva in a dizzying round of more than a thousand bilateral conferences covering more than fifty thousand products. The negotiations yielded a document that became known as the General Agreement on Tariffs and Trade (GATT), signed by twenty-three nations (Pakistan having been born during the process) on November 18, 1947.

Table 13-2. GATT Rounds

Year	Round/Event	Action
1947	Geneva	45,000 reductions in bilateral tariffs covering one-fifth of world trade
1949	Annency, France	5,000 reductions in bilateral tariffs
1951	Torquay, England	8,700 reductions in bilateral tariffs, covering most of items not previously affected
1955–1956	Geneva	$2.5 billion reduction in bilateral tariffs
1960–1962	Dillon Round	$5 billion in bilateral tariff reductions; EEC talks begin
1964–1967	Kennedy Round	$40 billion reduction in bilateral tariffs, negotiation rules established
1973–1979	Tokyo Round	$300 billion reduction in bilateral tariffs, procedures on dispute resolution, dumping, licensing established
1986–1993	Uruguay Round	Further tariff reductions, difficulties in rationalizing agricultural tariffs
1995	WTO Established	WTO takes over GATT process
2001–present	Doha Round	Talks stalled on North/South issues and agricultural subsidies

Just three days later, fifty-six nations entered into negotiations in Havana for the formation of the International Trade Organization (ITO), which was to oversee succeeding GATT rounds. Curiously, the ITO died, a victim of indifference in the U.S. Congress and of the Republican victory in the congressional election of 1946, whereas GATT flourished.[45] By the end of its third round in Torquay, England, in 1951, the prewar barriers to industrial products had been largely demolished. This fall is reflected in the levels of the United States' import tariffs, plotted in Figure 13-2.

Proposals' anonymous authors had, perhaps unwittingly, cracked one of the central problems of free trade, which modern economists and sociologists refer to as the "logic of collective action."[46] Free trade provides modest benefits for most of the population while greatly harming small groups in specific industries and occupations. Imagine, for example, that the United States forbade the importation of foreign-grown rice. This would greatly enrich a few thousand domestic growers, as they would make millions, and most Americans would not notice the few extra dollars per year hidden in their grocery bills. Domestic growers, each of whom

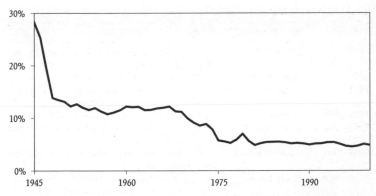

Figure 13-2. U.S. Import Tariffs on Dutiable Goods Under GATT

has a large stake in the issue, would resist any attempt to open the market up to foreign rice much more actively than the hundreds of millions of consumers who would each benefit a tiny amount each year from less expensive imported rice. The GATT, in essence, created a global "consumers' union" representing the world's billions of disenfranchised buyers, each nicked a few pennies, francs, or yen every time the cash register rang.

As a rough approximation, then, we can divide the history of modern globalization into four periods. The first period spans the years between 1830 and 1885, when rapidly falling transport and communication costs combined with relatively low tariffs (except in the United States) to dramatically increase the volume of trade and to produce global convergence of wages, land prices and rents, and interest rates. During the second period, roughly between 1885 and 1930, intense agricultural competition from the Americas, Australia, New Zealand, and the Ukraine caused a European protectionist backlash; this was easily overwhelmed by the continuing fall in transport prices.[47] The third period, which began with the passage of Smoot-Hawley in 1930, saw slowing improvements in transport technology swamped by large tariff hikes. These events resulted in a devastating fall in world trade.[48] During the fourth period, which began

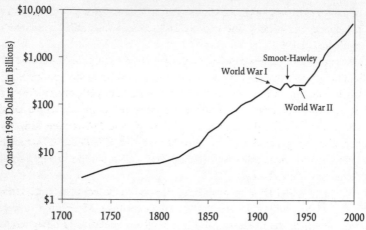

Figure 13-3. Real Value of World Trade: 1720–2000
(Constant 1998 Dollars)

in 1945, the free-trade initiative led by the United States, as outlined in *Proposals,* opened the floodgates of world trade. The real value of world commerce exploded and grew at the astonishing rate of 6.4 percent per year over the next half century. Between 1945 and 1998, the volume of world trade increased from 5.5 percent of world GDP to 17.2 percent.

The postwar increase in trade volume and the nearly simultaneous rise of longshoremen's unions combined to make the journey from cargo hold to freight car (or, increasingly, diesel truck) nearly as expensive as the journey across the ocean. An exhaustive government study of the freight carried on one transatlantic voyage by one vessel, the SS *Warrior* found that more than one-third of the cost of getting its cargo to its final destination was incurred on the pier. For cargoes to and from Hawaii, the cost was closer to 50 percent.

America's founding fathers made few missteps in crafting the Constitution, but surely none did more harm than the five "extra" words in the famous Commerce Clause of Article I, which gave the federal government the power "to regulate commerce with foreign nations, *and among the several states,* and with the Indian tribes." The power to regulate commerce among the states eventually gave rise in 1887 to the Interstate Commerce Commission (ICC), which regulated nearly every aspect of long-range transport in the United States, corroded nearly every industry it touched, and stifled American transport innovation until it was finally abolished in 1995.

For more than a century, merchants had sought an "intermodal" shipping device that could be seamlessly loaded and unloaded among train, truck, and ship. In 1837 a shipper in Pittsburgh, James O'Connor, devised a boxcar that could be either fitted with train wheels or mounted on a canal barge, and in 1926 the Chicago North Shore and Milwaukee Railway began to "piggyback" trailers onto flatcars. The ICC decided that such intermodal devices fell under its authority and promptly brought their development to a halt.

In the mid-1950s, two events revolutionized the technology. The first was the brainchild of a visionary trucking executive, Malcolm McLean: a prototype of the modern shipping container, specifically designed to stack inside a surplus military tanker, chosen because of its relatively rectangular hull. The second was a federal court ruling in 1956 that removed intermodal containers from the ICC's purview.

The widespread adoption of McLean's new system saw port costs plummet over the next few decades. If international freight had been cheap before 1960, afterward it became practically free—in the unlovely jargon of economics, "frictionless."[49] Freed of burdensome tariffs and shipping costs, goods began circulating more freely around the globe. If shirts or cars could be produced ever so slightly cheaper in a given country, then their production would shift there.

At the same time that shipping costs were shrinking almost to nothing, Europe was becoming rich. The Continent's new wealth aligned European capitalists, now the owners of an abundant factor, with labor in favor of lower tariffs. As predicted by Stolper-Samuelson, Europeans embraced both free trade and democracy. Although the European Community supported its farmers with subsidies under the so-called Common Agricultural Policy, this did not prevent the decline of agriculture: in 1950, farmers made up 35 percent of the Continent's workforce; in 1980, just 15 percent.

The post-World War II period would see an even greater flip-flop in the trade policies of America's major political parties. As the nation became increasingly prosperous and its capital became ever more abundant, the Republicans, the traditional party of capital, changed their allegiance from protectionism to free trade. (This switch occurred during the Eisenhower administration.) The Democrats, on the other hand, have traditionally represented the interests of laborers, the owners of a scarce factor, and farmers, the owners of an abundant factor. Over the course of the twentieth century, the relative size of the labor force grew while that of the farming population shrank; today, farmers constitute just 1 percent of the work force. As a result of this shift in their constituency, the Democrats swung toward protectionism, and in response, farmers defected en masse to the Republican Party.

Ronald Rogowski provides a final, intriguing twist to Stolper-Samuelson; just as his paradigm suggests who favors or opposes free trade, it also suggests which groups see their power enhanced or diminished by their nation's trade policy. The rise of protectionism in the 1930s empowered the owners of scarce factors both in the United States (labor, represented by the Democratic Party) and in Germany (land and capital, represented most ferociously by the Nazis). So too does the rise of free trade today empower those who favor it, most spectacularly the owners of America's abundant factors—land and capital—represented by the Republican Party. Rogowski observed in 1987:

> As far as one can now foresee, the Democrats . . . will increasingly embrace protectionism and, much as Labor in Britain, will be reduced to a regional party of industrial decay. In the burgeoning and export-oriented West and South the Republicans will achieve something close to one-party domination.[50]

Over the next twenty years, Rogowski's prediction came increasingly true. Only very recently has protectionism again begun to gain traction in the heretofore solidly Republican West and South. How well the Republicans will maintain their dominance of these regions in the face of the Bush administration's colossal mistakes in foreign policy remains to be seen.

Although GATT dramatically altered the balance of power in the battle between protectionism and free trade, it did not succeed with all cargoes. Agriculture and textiles represent two of the world's oldest and largest economic sectors. Over the centuries both sectors have acquired great expertise in politics and propaganda and have thereby managed to escape, at great cost to consumers, the rigors of the new global marketplace. In most countries, farmers have succeeded in portraying themselves as the "soul of the nation," in spite of the fact that they constitute no more than a small percentage of the workforce in most developed countries.

From the outset, the world's farmers and textile manufacturers were able to exclude themselves from the GATT framework and maintain high tariffs and, even more importantly, non-tariff barriers such as quotas, restrictions, and subsidies on both domestic production and exports.

The survival of protection for textiles and agricultural products has clearly cost the world's developing nations dearly, as these are the two areas in which they have the greatest comparative advantages. Exactly how and why this occurred is a matter of some controversy. One interpretation is that GATT is yet one more mechanism of rationing crumbs from the white man's table to the world's poorest nations, crippling them in precisely those areas in which they are best able to compete. According to an alternative explanation, the world's developing nations are hellbent on autarky and essentially indifferent to the GATT process, unwilling or unable to meet the developed nations halfway.

The evidence favors the latter explanation. Developing nations typically levy agricultural import tariffs in excess of 50 percent (over 100 percent in India), as compared with 30 percent in Europe and 15 percent in the United States. Second, until very recently, many developing nations, led by India, openly espoused a policy of "import substitution"—the encouragement of a broad range of domestic industries with high tariffs. (Indian autarky is symbolized in its original national flag by Gandhi's *chakra,* or spinning wheel. Just before independence, this was replaced, to Gandhi's dismay, with the *ashoka chakra,* the wheel of law.) Finally, as will be seen in Chapter 14, the developing nations that opened themselves to international commerce have prospered mightily.[51]

To see protectionism's modern face, meet the Fanjuls. The heirs of wealthy Cuban sugar growers who fled the island after Fidel Castro's victory in 1958, and one of Florida's wealthiest families, these three brothers today own 160,000 acres of prime Florida cane fields, in addition to 240,000 acres in the Dominican Republic. The Labor Department has repeatedly singled out their holding company, Flo-Sun, for abuse and underpayment of workers, and the Department of the Interior extracted from them a huge settlement for toxic runoff from their fields into the Everglades.[52]

One federal agency, however, takes a sunnier view of the Fanjuls: the Agriculture Department, which in recent years has paid them an average of $65 million annually for their sugar—more than twice the world price—as part of a broad system of agricultural supports costing taxpayers $8 billion per year.[53] To the Fanjuls, this $65 million subsidy is just so much change left under the plate; the main event is quotas, which jack up grocery prices by keeping foreign crops out of the United States and in 1998 robbed American consumers of an estimated $2 billion for sugar alone.[54] Not coincidentally, the Dominican Republic, home to huge Fanjul plantations, has the highest import quota among the world's sugar-producing nations. Nor is this all: the Army Corps of Engineers spends an estimated $52 million per year keeping these sugar fields dry, damaging the environment yet more.[55]

How did the Fanjuls and their peers manage to secure such government largess over the decades? By giving generously to various political campaigns in the form of both direct and "soft" money. One of the most fascinating passages in the independent counsel's referral to the House's impeachment proceedings against William Clinton related to his dalliance with Monica Lewinsky. The president demonstrated his famous talent for multitasking by combining these sessions with telephone conversations. On only one occasion did he ask his dedicated young aide to leave the room so that he could answer a call in private. The caller was neither the British prime minister nor the pope, but Alfonso ("Alfie") Fanjul.[56]

Since the inception of GATT, virtually all nations have sidestepped its best efforts to lower barriers to agricultural trade—the rich nations with non-tariff barriers (mainly subsidies) and the poor ones with direct tariffs.[57] After the September 11 attacks, the United States and Europe convened the Doha Round of GATT talks under the auspices of the newly formed World Trade Organization (WTO)—the successor to the ITO. The Doha Round explicitly sought to end all subsidies by 2013 in order to alleviate poverty in the developing world, the breeding ground for international terrorism.

Negotiations collapsed ignominiously in July 2006 in a hail of mutual recrimination. None of the three major parties to the talks—Americans, Europeans, and developing nations—could bring itself to offend its sacrosanct farmers. One observer noted that the failure of the Doha Round was a "big victory for the farm lobby groups," and the Indian representative declared, "We can't negotiate subsistence and livelihood . . . we should not even be asked to do that." The European negotiator, Peter Mandelson, noted even more candidly before the talks that the Continent would lose "next to nothing" if the negotiations failed.[58] There is one consolation: as the world has become a wealthier place, protected food and clothing constitute an ever smaller proportion of the global economy. (In 2006, for example, Americans spent less than 10 percent of their income on food, down from 24 percent in 1929.[59])

World trade has not quite evolved to the point described by John Stuart Mill in the epigraph of chapter 12, where "all things would be produced in the places where the same labor and capital would produce them in the greatest quantity and quality," but it is getting there rapidly. In the process, the frictions and crises described in the previous chapters will multiply and accelerate.

14

THE BATTLE OF SEATTLE

Our argument provides no political ammunition for the protectionist. . . . It has been shown that the harm which free trade inflicts upon one factor of production is necessarily less than the gain to the other. Hence, it is always possible to bribe the suffering factor by subsidy or other redistributive devices so as to leave all factors better off as a result of trade.—Wolfgang Stolper and Paul Samuelson[1]

In January 1999, Seattle's political leaders had every right to be proud when their bid to host the Third Ministerial Conference of the WTO later that year beat out San Diego's. Not only would thousands of visitors flood hotels and restaurants, but the meeting would showcase the city to world leaders, including the U.S. president and secretary of state.

Norm Stamper, Seattle's well-regarded police chief, also knew that the conference would draw tens of thousands of antiglobalization protesters, and that the last Ministerial Conference, held eighteen months before in Geneva, had turned ugly. But this was the United States, not Europe; the country had not seen significant violent political protest for a generation, and certainly the 1,200 well-trained officers under his command were up to any challenge. In addition, the AFL-CIO, the protest's largest contingent, had promised to keep the lid on.

Stamper and the AFL-CIO miscalculated. A large minority of protesters, well-stocked with bottles, gas masks, crowbars, masonry hammers, and tripods from which to suspend observers above the throng, wreaked mayhem. By the third day of the conference, Seattle's finest had lost control. Mobs slashed tires, broke windows, and looted shops, and more than a thousand attackers laid siege to a precinct house for hours before its astonished defenders dispersed the assault with tear gas and rubber bullets.[2]

The protesters forced the conference to adjourn early and focused the world's attention on the process of global free trade. Did the Battle of Seattle represent something new in the history of world trade?

Hardly. Almost no economic, ideological, or even tactical daylight separated the rioters in Seattle from the antiglobalists of preceding centuries: Madeiran growers incensed by sugar imports from the New World; Mexico City's Spanish barbers and silk growers anxious about cheap Asian labor and textiles; English refiners of muscovado angry at competition from Barbadian factories; the wool weavers who attacked Josiah Child's House, the EIC's headquarters, and Parliament; or the revelers at the Boston Tea Party. Were archaeologists to discover that four thousand years ago, Dilmun's farmers, unhappy with the dumping of Sumerian grain, had sacked the customhouse, we would scarcely be surprised.

This final chapter asks two simple questions: What has the history of world trade taught us? How can we apply those lessons to today's debates about globalization?

The instinct to truck and barter is part of human nature; any effort to stifle it is doomed to fail in the long run. Ever since men first challenged the world's seas and deserts with ships and camels, they have carried with them tradable commodities. At the dawn of the Common Era, the extremities of civilized Europe and Asia knew and coveted each other's luxury goods. By the end of the nineteenth century, most of the features we consider peculiar to modern global commerce—instantaneous communication, long-distance trade in bulk commodities and perishables, and an intercontinental manufacturing cycle—were well established. Today's debates over globalization repeat, nearly word for word in some cases, those of earlier eras. Wherever trade arrives, resentment, protectionism, and their constant companions—smuggling, disrespect for authority, and occasionally war—will follow.

Ships have always been, and for the foreseeable future will be, the most efficient method of long-distance transport. Seaborne commerce in turn requires political stability at critical maritime choke points. From ancient times, Europe's convoluted coastal geography taught its merchants and navies the value of strategic straits and passages, the capture of which could bring starvation to a nation or to its enemies. For at least 2,500 years, the Hellespont and the Bosphorus have been the quintessential maritime choke points; they remain so to this day. When Europeans ventured into the Indian Ocean in Vasco da Gama's trail, their first targets, not always attained, were the straits at Malacca, Hormuz, and Bab el Mandeb.

Little has changed, save for the addition of two more man-made choke points at Suez and Panama. Today, about 80 percent of world commerce travels by ship, most going through one, and sometimes two or three, of these seven critical passages.

By any measure—physical volume, monetary value, or strategic importance—petroleum is the most critical product carried, occupying at any given moment almost half of the planet's commercial tonnage. The world currently pumps and ships about eighty million barrels per day, of which the United States uses one-fourth: twenty million barrels. About three-fifths of this, or twelve million barrels per day, must be imported. Petroleum not only powers the world but also lubricates it, fertilizes it, and supplies the major ingredient of the modern world's most ubiquitous manufacturing material, plastic. Were oil supply lines seriously interrupted, much of the planet's activity would quite literally grind to a halt, and hundreds of millions of people would starve.

The volume of American oil imports roughly corresponds to the amount of crude passing daily through the Persian Gulf entrance at the Strait of Hormuz. A smaller, but still strategically important, amount also passes through the Dardanelles and Bosphorus (these two passages together hereafter are referred to as the Turkish Straits), Bab el Mandeb,

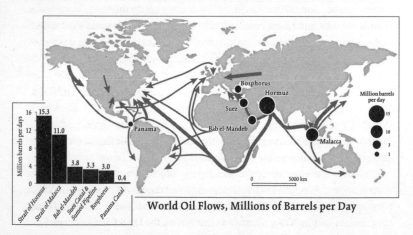

World Oil Flows, Millions of Barrels per Day

the Suez Canal, the Sumed pipeline (which parallels the Suez Canal), and the Panama Canal. Finally, most petroleum that exits through these Middle Eastern straits bound for East Asia must also pass by Malacca. The sudden closure of any of these passages would throw the world economy into turmoil.

Within the next few decades, such an event is not merely possible or probable, but nearly certain. Those who doubt this should consider some recent history. The Suez area has sparked two conflicts in the twentieth century alone: one in 1956 involving Egypt, Israel, Britain, and France; and another in 1967, the Six-Day War, after which it was closed for fifteen years.

Hormuz is even more problematic. In his 1980 State of the Union Address, President Carter enunciated what came to be known as the Carter Doctrine:

> An attempt by an outside force to gain control of the Persian Gulf region will be regarded as an assault on the vital interests of the United States of America, and such an assault will be repelled by any means necessary, including military force.[3]

During the war between Iran and Iraq in 1981–1988, these two nations engaged in a "tanker war": both combatant and neutral shipping (particularly Kuwaiti shipping) was attacked. Most ominously, the Iraqis repeatedly attempted to put Iran's main export facility at Kharg Island out of commission. When Lloyd's of London sharply increased insurance premiums on Gulf-bound vessels, both the Soviet Union and the United States chartered tankers and "reflagged" them under their own colors to force the combatants to think twice about continued assaults.

It didn't work, in spite of the fact that by the end of the 1980s, at least ten Western navies and eight regional ones patrolled the Gulf. On May 17, 1987, an Iraqi missile "mistakenly" struck the USS *Stark* and killed thirty-seven sailors. Since the United States had sided with Iraq, President Reagan blamed the incident on Iran for initiating the conflict, an accusation as untrue as it was bizarre.

When Iranians hit one of the reflagged tankers, the *Sea Isle City*, American forces retaliated by destroying two Iranian oil platforms.[4] After a truce in August 1988, the situation quieted down, only to be replaced by a new danger in 2000, when Al Qaeda struck the USS *Cole* in the harbor of Aden at Bab el Mandeb, killing seventeen. The world trade system is most vulnerable at these three choke points—the Suez Canal, the Strait of Hormuz, and Bab el Mandeb—for all lie in a highly unstable region, within easy striking range of both state and nonstate actors hostile to the West.

Even the "safe" passages have their problems. Although the Turkish straits have been placid for the past several decades, they saw fierce fighting in the Crimean War and World War I. In 1936, the Montreux Convention, while giving nominal control of the Straits to Turkey, granted all nations free right of passage through them. In practice, this convention allows Turkey to "meter" traffic through the straits, but not to board or inspect transiting vessels.

This is no small distinction, and to anyone who has seen the dramatic and beautiful Bosphorus, the meaning is obvious. Spanning little more than a thousand yards across at its narrowest point and fronted for twenty miles on both sides with expensive homes, it is packed around the clock with an unbroken line of tankers, freighters, long-distance ferries, and luxury liners choreographed into northbound and southbound lanes, along with thousands of smaller craft. The straits long ago reached their maximum carrying capacity, and deadly collisions and spills have become routine. Worse, when vessels more than five hundred feet long enter the Bosphorus, an almost constant occurrence, the opposite lane must be closed down because of the wide turning radius of these behemoths, causing horrendous delays.

The newly discovered oil reserves of the Caspian area flow through the straits, and the possibility of an accidental spill has caused the Turks to push the limits of the powers granted to them by the Montreux Convention, forbidding, for example, night transits by large tankers. In 2001, Turkey announced plans to impose significant fees on tankers, although such levies are at least technically a violation of both the Montreux Convention and international law.

With luck, these issues will be resolved diplomatically. More serious is the possibility of terrorism, from either Al Qaeda or Kurdish insurgents. Scientists have estimated that the detonation of a large liquid natural gas tanker in the Bosphorus would wreak havoc far exceeding that of a Richter 8.0 earthquake.[5]

Farther east, oil bound for Japan, Korea, and China passes through the Strait of Malacca, which is plagued by pirates, the terrorist group Jamal Islamiya, and disputes over high dredging costs among the three nations bordering its shores: Malaysia, Indonesia, and Singapore. The United States Seventh Fleet currently patrols this strait, and it is not difficult to imagine a future Sino-American conflict arising from China's concern over foreign control of its increasingly important oil and merchandise lifelines to the Middle East and Europe.

Insecurity haunts even the Western Hemisphere choke points. In 1989, when the strongman Manuel Noriega annulled the election of Guillermo Endara as Panama's president, the United States invaded, ostensibly to restore Endara to power. Had the same events taken place in Honduras or Paraguay, it seems unlikely that American troops would have become directly involved or that their leaders would have wound up in a Miami jail.

Choke points can estrange even the best of neighbors. The once obscure Northwest Passage, which had long frustrated European explorers until being conquered by Roald Amundsen in 1906, has recently provoked confrontation between the United States, which considers the passage an international waterway, and Canada, which claims sovereignty over its eastern entrance at the Davis Strait (between Baffin Island and Greenland). In 1969, the first commercial transit of the passage by the Humble Oil tanker *Manhattan* drew the notice of Canada, and when an American Coast Guard cutter made the transit in 1985, the Canadians lodged a formal protest.[6]

Because of global warming, the Northwest Passage is likely to become navigable year-round within a decade or two, and its emergence as a commercial sea-lane will produce lively discussion between Ottawa and Washington for years to come. Not long after the Northwest Passage opens, further increases in world temperatures will probably make practicable routes over the North Polar region via the Bering Strait from East Asia to Europe and the North American East coast, paring more than one-third of the distance off the current route via Suez. New routes from Europe to the North American West Coast would also become possible; these transpolar routes will almost certainly cause tension between the United States and Russia over control of the Bering Strait.[7]

* * *

Enthusiasts of free trade have overestimated its economic benefits. The history of the nineteenth century casts doubt on the notion that trade is an engine of growth. Were free trade the path to national wealth, then the United States, which for most of its history had sky-high tariffs, would never have prospered. The "golden era" of tariff reduction in Europe, from 1860–1880, should have been a time of much higher growth than between 1880 and 1900, a period of protectionism; in fact, growth was higher during the later period. Also, after 1880, the economy of protectionist northern Europe grew faster than that of free-trading England.

This point is not lost on the better-read American protectionists, such as 1996 presidential candidate Patrick Buchanan, who wrote

> Behind a tariff wall built by Washington, Hamilton, Clay, Lincoln, and the Republican presidents who followed, the United States had gone from an agricultural coastal republic to become the greatest industrial power the world had ever seen—in a single century. Such was the success of the policy called protectionism that is so disparaged today.[8]

Buchanan is not alone in this assertion; he is joined by a phalanx of economic historians, including the highly respected late Paul Bairoch.[9] Modern quantitative techniques confirm that the evidence for free trade as an engine of growth in the nineteenth century is weak at best. In fact, a number of rigorous quantitative studies have suggested that during the 1800s, protectionism actually may have fostered economic development. A detailed "what if" analysis of American protectionism during the early nineteenth century by the economic historian Mark Bils shows that Hamilton, the Adams men, and Carey may have been right all along: without high tariffs, "about half of the industrial sector of New England would have been bankrupted."[10] Another distinguished economic historian, Kevin O'Rourke, studied eight wealthy European nations, the United States, and Canada during the late nineteenth century and was startled to find a *positive* correlation between tariff levels and economic growth—the higher the tariff, the better a nation did. In the understated language of academic economics, he concluded:

It appears that the Bairoch hypothesis [that tariffs were positively associated with growth in the late nineteenth century] holds up remarkably well, when tested with recently available data, and when controlling for other factors influencing growth.[11]

A rigorously conducted study of England's break from free trade in 1932 also concluded that the tariffs of that year boosted its economy.[12]

Not all trade historians agree that America's high nineteenth-century tariffs were beneficial. Bradford DeLong of Berkeley notes that protectionism delayed the acquisition by New England entrepreneurs of leading-edge English steam and industrial technologies, stunting industries that might have benefited from them. Although Bils may be correct in saying that a lower tariff would have devastated existing New England factories, DeLong argues that the nation would have wound up with a different, and much more prosperous, capital-intensive "high-tech" industrial sector in its place.[13]

After 1945, however, the picture changes. A detailed analysis by the economic historian Edward Denison showed that the GATT tariff reductions between 1950 and 1960 did produce a small amount of excess growth, only 1 percent extra, overall, during that decade in northern Europe; there was no effect in the United States.[14]

After 1960, stronger evidence emerges in favor of the benefit of free trade, particularly in the developing world. In 1995, economists Jeffrey Sachs and Andrew Warner examined the experience with open international markets in the late twentieth century. They began by dividing the developing world into three groups: nations that have always had reasonably open trade policies, those that converted from protectionism at some point, and those that have always been highly protectionist. Table 14-1 lists the nations in the first and last groups.[15]

The two lists speak for themselves; in 2006 the average GDP for the "always open" group was $17,521, as opposed to $2,362 for the "always closed" group. Sachs and his colleagues next looked at the effect of trade policy on the ability of a nation to join the "convergence club" of the world's prosperous economies.[16] This time, they examined the relationship in both developed and developing nations between per capita GDP in 1970 and growth rates over the next twenty years. They found that free-trading nations had very high growth rates. This was especially true of

Table 14-1. Per Capita GDP in Nations Open and Closed to World Trade.

Always Open Nation	2006 Per Capita GDP	Always Closed Nation	2006 Per Capita GDP
Barbados	$17,610	Algeria	$7,189
Cyprus	$21,177	Angola	$2,813
Hong Kong	$33,479	Bangladesh	$2,011
Mauritius	$12,895	Burkina Faso	$1,285
Singapore	$28,368	Burundi	$700
Thailand	$8,368	Cent. Af. Rep.	$1,128
Yemen	$751	Chad	$1,519
		China	$2,001
		Congo	$1,369
		Cote d'Ivoire	$1,600
		Dom. Rep.	$7,627
		Egypt	$4,317
		Ethiopia	$823
		Gabon	$7,055
		Haiti	$1,791
		Iran	$7,980
		Iraq	$2,900
		Madagascar	$900
		Malawi	$596
		Mauritania	$2,535
		Mozambique	$1,379
		Myanmar	$1,693
		Niger	$872
		Nigeria	$1,188
		Pakistan	$2,653
		Papua NG	$2,418
		Rwanda	$1,380
		Senegal	$1,759
		Sierra L.	$903
		Somalia	$600
		Syria	$3,847
		Tanzania	$723
		Togo	$1,675
		Zaire	$774
		Zimbabwe	$2,607

those that began in 1970 with relatively low per capita GDPs; these nations grew at rates that often exceeded 5 percent per year. The initially wealthy nations tended to grow less rapidly, at 2 to 3 percent per year. In other words, poor nations that adopt free trade tend to catch up with rich nations.

Sachs and Warner next performed the same exercise for nations with generally protectionist policies over the same period. Their real per capita GDPs barely grew, clocking an average rate of just 0.5 percent per year.

When the poor protect, they stagnate and fall ever further behind the developed nations. (Of late, Professor Sachs has become famous for his controversial views about the need to redistribute wealth from developed nations to developing nations. His earlier research on the connection between growth and trade commands more respect among economists than his more recent pronouncements.)

How to reconcile the difference between the nineteenth- and twentieth-century data? Sachs and Warner begin by noting research by others which shows that in Japan and the United States, incomes in the prefectures and individual states, respectively, converged during the nineteenth and twentieth centuries, just as the developing nations' economies had converged through trade in the late twentieth century.

And therein lies the solution to the riddle: during the nineteenth century, trade within a nation was much more important than trade with other countries. As long as a country's internal markets were open, a tariff wall against foreign goods did relatively little damage. Before the twentieth century, external trade constituted only a tiny part of the economy of most nations. For example, in 1870 exports constituted just 2.5 percent of GDP in the United States; in France, 4.9 percent; and even in free-trading England, only 12.2 percent. As trade has grown, the world economy has become more dependent on it, with exports rising from 4.6 percent of world GDP in 1870 to 17.2 percent in 1998.

Geography contributes as well: the larger and more economically diverse a nation, the more self-sufficient it is, and the less important trade becomes. Since its independence, the United States has been the most self-sufficient of all major nations; today imports constitute only about 14 percent of its GDP. Holland lies at the other extreme, with imports making up 61 percent of its economy.[17] This is consistent with Edward Denison's data for the period 1950–1962, which showed the largest benefits of the worldwide fall in tariffs in the Netherlands, Belgium, and Norway; less benefit for the larger and more diverse economies of Germany and France; and none at all for the United States.[18]

In the nineteenth century, nations, particularly large, self-reliant nations such as the United States, could get away with protectionist trade policies. In the globally integrated economy of the twenty-first century, autarky becomes a much dicier proposition. Further, most of the damage done to the economies of the developing world has been self-inflicted; to paraphrase Cordell Hull, protectionism is a gun that recoils most forcefully upon the least fortunate.

The intangible rewards of free trade are underestimated. A century and a half ago, the French economist Frédéric Bastiat reportedly said, "When goods are not allowed to cross borders, soldiers will."[19] The Nobel Committee certainly agreed when it awarded the 1945 Peace Prize to Cordell Hull for his role in reopening world trade in the 1930s and 1940s.

Life on earth is slowly becoming less violent, mainly owing to the increasing realization that neighbors are more useful alive than dead. Those who doubt this rosy assessment should consider some data from the World Health Organization. Their statistics show that in 2004, violence accounted for just 1.3 percent of the world's deaths, an all-time low, and that at the beginning of the twenty-first century the number of battle deaths per year has decreased to one-thirtieth of what it was in the 1950s. This seems to be part of a longer-term historical trend; archaeological data suggest that upward of 20 percent of Stone-Age populations met violent deaths, a finding that is supported by research on modern hunter-gatherer societies.[20] Perhaps the strongest evidence supporting the connection between trade and peace is the European Union, which has rendered military conflict among its powers highly unlikely—this on a continent that saw more or less continuous warfare before 1945. In microeconomic terms, it makes little sense to bomb those who purchase and produce our shirts, laptops, and automobiles.

Today's greatest threats to world security come not from conventional armies, but rather from terrorism based in the world's failed states—precisely those parts of the globe that would benefit most from freer trade and a decrease in agricultural subsidies. To paraphrase Bastiat, if cotton, sugar, and rice can cross borders, then perhaps terrorists will not be able to.

* * *

Although free trade has benefited mankind in the aggregate, it has also produced many losers. The future expansion of world trade, resulting from increasing prosperity, falling tariffs, and vanishing transport costs, will create yet more winners, as well as a growing minority of losers. Not treating these losers fairly and compassionately is a prescription for failure. Again, Stolper-Samuelson provides the proper framework. Instead of two or three factors, consider only labor. Now divide it into two categories: high-skilled and low-skilled. Compared with the rest of the world, the developed nations are relatively well endowed with abundant high-skilled labor and have relatively little unskilled labor.

Whom does free trade hurt in the developed world? The relatively scarce factor: low-skilled labor. Who benefits? Highly skilled workers. Further, globalization increases income inequalities in the rich nations, as the inflation-adjusted incomes of the highly skilled rise rapidly and those of the low-skilled rise more slowly or even fall.

Once again, Stolper-Samuelson comes alive in the real world. For the past generation, income inequalities have grown dramatically in the United States. Figure 14-1 plots Census Bureau data with American families sorted into two groups—the top quintile, or 20 percent, and bottom 80 percent—and then computes their shares of total national income over the past thirty-five years.

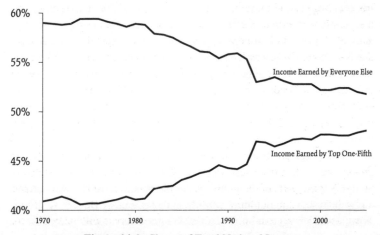

Figure 14-1. Shares of Total National Income

This graph clearly shows that in America, the top quintile, or 20 percent, of the population has become relatively richer, increasing its share of the income pie by one-sixth (from 41 percent to 48 percent) between 1970 and 2005, while everyone else has gotten relatively poorer.

Most people would describe those at the lower border of the top quintile, who earned $103,100 in 2005, as only modestly wealthy. To see how the rich are really doing, the population's top end needs to be sliced more thinly. Those in the top 5 percent, who earned more than $184,500 in 2005, saw their slice of the pie increase by more than one-third during the preceding thirty-five years; the top 1 percent, who earned more than $340,000 in 2005, saw their piece double in size.

Whereas the incomes of highly skilled professionals and managers have soared in recent decades, the inflation-adjusted salary of the median male worker (at the fiftieth percentile of income) has not risen for more than a generation.[21] There is more than a little truth in the popular American perception of globalization: highly paid factory jobs are disappearing overseas and being replaced with burger-flipping slots.

Worse, even though the unemployment rate has fallen during the past two decades, job insecurity has grown dramatically during the same period. Average workers are about one-third more likely to lose their job than they were two decades ago, and to be paid almost 14 percent less when they eventually do find work again, if they are lucky enough to do so. (One-third of workers are not so lucky.) A 1998 *Wall Street Journal* survey asked Americans if they agreed with the statement, "Foreign trade has been bad for the U.S. economy because cheap imports have cost wages and jobs here." As predicted by Stolper-Samuelson, this issue cleaves the nation along the abundant-scarce factor fault line: among those earning more than $100,000 per year, only one-third agreed, whereas among blue-collar workers and union members, two-thirds agreed.[22]

Stolper-Samuelson does fail in at least one area by predicting that freer trade should decrease inequalities in developing nations by helping low-skilled workers. In fact, the opposite occurs: the most highly skilled industrial workers earn better pay in call centers and multinational-owned plants, increasing the gap between those who are fortunate enough to find such work and those who are not.[23] Although working conditions in an Asian Nike factory may appall people in the developed world, positions in American-associated factories are the most sought-after jobs in Vietnam's "development zones." Far less desirable are jobs in the Spartan and more strictly run Chinese-owned factories. Worst of all are the alternatives to factory work: subsistence-level farming and prostitution.[24]

The developing world exports to the United States not only shirts, sneakers, and electronics but also its abundant human capital: low-skilled workers who compete with Americans depress domestic wages, increase the income gap, and fan anti-immigration sentiment. It is no accident that union members are among the most vocal proponents of stricter immigration policy.

Yet again, this is nothing new. In the nineteenth century, as inequality rose, so did fear of immigration. A century ago, the United States, Canada, Australia, Brazil, and Argentina all began to restrict immigration. This tightening did not correlate at all with the factors that traditionally have received blame for it: economic hard times and racism. Rather it took place precisely when income competition from recent European immigrants at the low end of the wage scale started to squeeze low-paid voters.[25]

Why all the fuss about income inequality? Isn't it simply a sign of a healthy economy that generously rewards the successful and ambitious? Well, no. Economists and demographers use a number of measures of inequality, the most popular being the Gini coefficient. This number varies between zero and one; a population in which everyone has exactly the same income has a coefficient of 0.0, and a population in which only one individual earns all the income has a coefficient of 1.0.

The Ginis of the world's twenty wealthiest nations range from 0.25 (Sweden) to 0.41 (United States). The list of the highest-Gini nations fails to impress: Namibia, 0.74; Botswana, 0.63; Bolivia, 0.60; and Paraguay, 0.58.[26] More systematic research strongly suggests that increasing inequality produces social and political instability, which in turn leads to decreased investment and decreased economic development.[27]

Modern developed nations have gotten into the habit of intentionally lowering their Ginis with redistributive tax policies and social welfare programs. These expensive schemes can harm economic development, but by reducing inequality, they can also buy social peace, which can offset the inefficiencies of social spending. One of the leading authorities in this area, Geoffrey Garrett, notes that:

> Since the welfare state mitigates conflict by reducing market-generated inequalities of risk and wealth, it may have a beneficial rather than deleterious consequence for business. Government spending may thus stimulate investment via two channels—increasing productivity through improvements in human and physical capital and increasing stability through maintaining support for market openness.[28]

In other words, it is important to find a happy medium between the Scylla of expensive and economically damaging social welfare systems and the Charybdis of too thin a safety net, which worsens inequality. The United States and northern Europe are nearly equally wealthy, yet the United States cycles about 30 percent of GDP through federal, state, and local governments, whereas the governments of northern Europe consume nearly half of GDP, most of which goes to pay for their social welfare schemes. This suggests that the "sweet spot" lies somewhere between these two points.

The problem is that not all, or perhaps even most, of this growing inequality and insecurity can be blamed on freer trade. Economists hotly debate exactly how much damage is caused by outsourcing and the loss of jobs to foreign factories, and how much is due to an increase in the wages paid to highly-trained and educated workers.

Consider two different farm hands, one who is able to harvest wheat with 99.5 percent efficiency, and another who is able to harvest it with 95 percent efficiency. Certainly, the first laborer might command a larger salary than the second, but not by very much. Now consider a factory making a complex microchip that requires a hundred manufacturing steps, an error in any one of which will ruin the end product. Here, a labor force that completes each step with 99.5 percent accuracy will result in a 39 percent defect rate, versus a 99.4 percent reject rate for a labor force with 95 percent accuracy. Thus, in advanced manufacturing and service economies, highly skilled workers will command a larger wage premium than in less advanced ones. (This paradigm has been called the "O–Ring Theory," after the minor design flaw which destroyed the Challenger space shuttle.)[29]

Paul Krugman believes that almost all of the growing inequality in wages in the United States is due to this increased skill premium (and more recently, changes in tax policy), whereas data from economist Adrian Wood suggest that much, if not most, is due to increased international trade. The consensus seems to be somewhere in the middle: perhaps one-fifth to one-quarter of the widening inequality in U.S. wages is due to trade, the rest to tax cuts aimed at the wealthy and the increasing rewards of domestic education and training.[30]

The Free Trade Act of 1989 between the United States and Canada gave researchers a nearly ideal lens through which to observe the globalization trade-off. The act slashed tariffs from about 8 percent to 1 percent on goods moving north, and from 4 percent to 1 percent on goods moving south. Both nations have stable legal, banking, and political institutions, and since the United States dominates the Canadian economy, the most dramatic effects of the act occurred north of the border.

The economist Daniel Trefler calculated that although the act produced a significant net benefit to Canada as a whole, with long-term productivity in some industries increasing by up to 15 percent, it also vaporized about 5 percent of Canadian jobs, up to 12 percent of existing positions in some industries. These job losses, however, lasted less than a decade; overall, unemployment in Canada has fallen since the passage of the act. Commenting on this trade-off, Trefler wrote that the critical question in trade policy is to understand "how freer trade can be implemented in an industrialized economy in a way that recognizes both the long-run gains and the short-term adjustment costs borne by workers and others."[31]

For almost two decades, economists and politicians have grappled with the problem of how, or even whether, those left behind by free trade should be compensated. In 1825, John Stuart Mill calculated that although the Corn Laws put a certain amount of extra money in the pockets of the landlords, these laws cost the nation as a whole several times more. He theorized that it would be far cheaper to buy the landlords off:

> The landlords should make an estimate of their probable losses from the repeal of the Corn Laws, and found upon it a claim to compensation. Some, indeed, may question how far they who, for their own emolument, imposed one of the worst of taxes upon their countrymen [i.e., the Corn Laws], are entitled to compensation for renouncing advantages which they never ought to have enjoyed. It would

> be better, however, to have a repeal of the Corn Laws, even clogged
> by a compensation, than to not have it at all; and if this were our
> only alternative, no one could complain of a change, but which,
> though an enormous amount of evil would be prevented, no one
> would lose.[32]

In other words, it is far cheaper and better for all to directly compensate the losers. Almost two centuries after those words were written, and half a century after Cordell Hull and *Proposals* started the world down the road to free trade, the resultant inequalities and dislocations are again beginning to derail the process. Can free trade, with all its benefits, indeed be saved by compensating the losers?

Many American advocates of free trade realize that in order for the current system of relatively free trade to survive, the nation's social safety net needs to be expanded, but lip service, at best, is all that is usually offered. Consider Jagdish Bhagwati, perhaps today's best-known proponent of trade liberalization and a formidable academician who has trained many of today's foremost economists. His book *In Defense of Globalization* spends three hundred pages living up to its title; it gives the issue of "adjustment assistance" less than two pages. The following passage from this book captures the tone used by many free traders in discussing displaced workers:

> If a steel mill closes down in Pennsylvania because steel in Califor
> nia has become cheaper, workers tend to accept that as something
> that happens, and the general unemployment insurance seems to be
> an adequate way to deal with the bad hand that an unpredictable fate
> has dealt one. But the same workers get indignant when the loss is
> to a steel producer in Korea or Brazil, and they go off agitating for
> anti-dumping action. . . . Or they ask for special relief in the form of
> additional unemployment compensation, with or without retraining
> benefits and requirements.[33]

Professor Bhagwati only grudgingly accepts the need for compensation. Referring to a safety net specifically intended for those put out of work by foreign products, he continues: "This quasi-xenophobia is just a fact of life. If trade liberalization is to occur and be sustained, one or more of these special programs and policies have to be considered."[34]

Such sentiments not only unnecessarily antagonize workers but also are unfair; American industry has in fact been much more adept than labor at getting protection, particularly in the form of non-tariff barriers: quotas, subsidies, antidumping legislation, and the like.[35] Trade economists are slowly beginning to realize that they must stop being their own worst enemies. Dani Rodrik of the Kennedy School of Government at Harvard has, with great sensitivity, extensively surveyed the social havoc caused by the increased mobility of goods and services, explored the necessity of compensation, and considered how it might work. He believes it is no accident that those developed nations with the highest ratio of trade to GDP also have the richest social welfare schemes.[36] Free trade and a generous safety net reinforce each other; stable, wealthy trading nations, if they want to remain that way, cannot afford to throw to the wolves those whose jobs can be so easily "exchanged" in an increasingly frictionless global economy. According to Rodrik:

> Social spending has the important function of buying social peace. Without disagreeing about the need to eliminate waste and reform in the welfare state more broadly, I would argue that the need for social insurance does not decline but rather increases as global integration increases.[37]

More than five decades after Stolper and Samuelson penned their treatise explaining who won and who lost, Paul Samuelson, considered by many the world's greatest living economist, again stunned his colleagues by suggesting that entire nations could lose from free trade. He explained, in dense quantitative language decipherable only by other economists, how such competition from foreign labor causes job displacement but not job loss. (Indeed, unemployment in the United States is currently just under 5 percent.) Yes, Americans are still working, but they are doing so in jobs that pay less and are shorn of benefits. Samuelson reckons that these losses in compensation and benefits are permanent, and that as a whole, the United States is relatively worse off as a nation because of free trade:

> High I.Q. secondary school graduates in South Dakota, who had been receiving . . . wages one-and-a-half times the U.S. minimum wage for handling phone calls about my credit card, have been laid off since 1990; a Bombay outsourcing unit has come to handle my inquiries. Their Bombay wage rate falls short of South Dakota's, but in India their wage far exceeds what their uncles and aunts used to earn.[38]

The historical irony here is almost too delicious: perhaps no place was hurt as badly by free trade during the eighteenth and nineteenth centuries as India. Revenge is sweet.

At the end of World War II, the United States accounted for almost half of world GDP; its share has since fallen to less than one-fourth. Had America in 1945 slammed shut the door first opened by Cordell Hull a decade earlier, it would have almost certainly retained a larger slice of the world's wealth, the only problem being that the pie itself would have been much smaller, and rancid to boot. In 1900, Britannia ruled the waves; today, it plays a weak second fiddle to the American hegemon. Yet who in his right mind would rather live in the England of 1900 than in the England of today?

Samuelson continues:

> It does not follow . . . that nations should or should not introduce selective protectionisms. Even where a genuine harm is dealt out by the roulette wheel of evolving comparative advantage in a world of free trade, what a democracy tries to do in self defense may often amount to gratuitously shooting itself in the foot.[39]

When governments erect tariff barriers, Samuelson asserts, the result is industrial stagnation; it is far better to protect workers than to protect industries. Even so, Samuelson is not overly optimistic about the ability to "bribe the suffering factor" in a nation where a majority of people are worse off. (Neither is Rodrik, who notes the difficulties of paying for such social welfare schemes with taxes in a world in which corporations can easily move their capital and factories across national borders.)[40]

World trade has yielded not only a bounty of material goods, but also of intellectual and cultural capital, an understanding of our neighbors, and a desire to sell things to others rather than annihilate them. A significant minority of citizens are unavoidably harmed in the process. As people, goods, and financial assets whiz around the world ever more easily, the inevitable dislocations caused by free trade will increase along with these blessings.

The dilemmas of free trade are reminiscent of Churchill's famous assessment of democracy: "the worst form of Government except all those other forms that have been tried from time to time."[41] From time to time, the forces of protectionism will indeed suggest reversing the movement toward free trade, but as the twentieth-century history of both the developed and the developing nations has shown, there really is no alternative.

Few would argue that mankind is not the better for having made the trading expedition from Sumer to Seattle. To turn back would risk revisiting the darkest episodes of the twentieth century. By remembering the straits navigated along the way, we might just avoid the shoals that lie ahead.

ACKNOWLEDGMENTS

No author writes a nonfiction work of any length and scope without shamelessly relying upon family, friends, colleagues, publishing staff, and total strangers for advice and direction. I could not have written this book without the help of numerous individuals.

Leonard Andaya, Liam Brockey, Peter Downey, Lee Drago, Christopher Ehret, David Eltis, Mark Garrison, Dermot Gately, Katheryn Gigler, Peter Gottschalk, Michael Guasco, Jonathan Israel, Glenn May, Joel Mokyr, J. P. McNeill, the late Clark Reynolds, Giorgio Riello, Patricia Risso, Dani Rodrik, Ron Roope, Bradley Rogers, Sanjay Subrahmanyam, Steve Vinson, David Warsh, Roger Weller, Jonathan Wendel, and Willem Wolters provided much needed referencing information.

In particular, I would like to thank the following for help in these specific areas: Walter Bloom and Jeremy Green, Australian silver coin finds; Roger Burt, British and American mining history; Fred Drogula and Jean Paul Rodrigue, maritime chokepoints; Michael Laffan, the Ternatan Rebellion; Jonathan Rees, the mysteries of early refrigerated shipping; Ronald Rogowski, the politics of the Stolper-Samuelson theorem; Richard Sylla, the early planning stages of the book; Daniel Trefler, recent Canadian trade history; Carl Trocki, opium addiction in nineteenth-century China; Shelly Wachsmann, early maritime history; and Jeffrey Williamson, the quantitative aspects of recent economic history.

I pestered several people unmercifully; they are owed not only thanks but apologies: Donald Kagan for helping me disguise, if only thinly, my deficiencies in Greek history; Mark Wheelis for reminding me of the things I should have learned in microbiology about the plague bacillus; Sidney Mintz for providing valued guidance on the history of the Caribbean sugar trade; and last, and most certainly not least, Doug Irwin for assistance in picking my way through the intellectual history of the never-ending battle between protection and free trade.

Two giants of economic and financial journalism—Peter Bernstein and Jason Zweig—offered priceless advice, as did other friends: Barney

Sherman, Bob Uphaus, and Ed Tower, as well as Ed's students in his Neat New Books in International Trade and Economic Development course at Duke University, particularly Eric Schwartz and Mark Marvelli.

Wesley Neff generously lent his long years of literary experience to the project from start to finish; Toby Mundy, Morgan Entrekin, Luba Ostashevsky, and Michael Hornburg at Grove/Atlantic Press provided expert editorial guidance; Matthew Ericson created the book's maps; Lewis O'Brien provided permission and imaging assistance; and Molly Blalock-Koral helped secure obscure reference materials.

Two editors at Grove/Atlantic, Brando Skyhorse and Jofie Ferrari-Adler, deserve special mention. Brando taught me a multitude of narrative skills that I sorely lacked and supplied the fortitude to attack what seemed an insurmountably broad topic, while Jofie polished it to a smoothness that I could not have achieved on my own and adroitly shepherded the book through the production process.

Finally, my wife Jane Gigler supplied, in addition to superhuman quantities of patience and large blocks of her precious free time, what can only be described as literary alchemy. Over the past several years, she showed me how to transform an amorphous mass of jumbled, disorganized prose into pages I could send to my editors with a clear conscience. I do not deserve her.

NOTES

Introduction

1. T. E. Page et al., eds., *The Scriptores Historiae Augustae* (Cambridge, MA: Harvard University Press, 1940), II: 115, 157.

2. G. G. Ramsay, trans., *Juvenal and Perseus* (Cambridge, MA: Harvard University Press, 1945), 105.

3. William Adlington, trans., *The Golden Ass of Apuleius* (New York: AMS, 1967), 233.

4. E. H. Warmington, *The Commerce between the Roman Empire and India* (New Delhi: Munshiram Manoharlal, 1995): 147–165, 174–175, 180–183. For cotton in the Roman Empire, see 210–212. For the extreme difficulty of cotton production in the preindustrial world, see this book, 253–254.

5. Modern comparisons are difficult, but in the ancient world the average daily wage of a skilled worker was about one Greek drachma, a small silver coin weighing about one-eighth of an ounce. At a ratio of twelve to one for gold to silver, then, one ounce of gold or silk represented ninety-six days' wages.

6. S. D. Goitein, *A Mediterranean Society* (Berkeley: University of California Press, 1967), I: 347–348.

7. Ibid., 298.

8. Ibid., 299–300.

9. Ibid., 340–342.

10. Ibid., 219. Only in the twentieth century did economists begin to fully appreciate the unpredictability of market prices. By a strange coincidence, the founder of chaos theory, Benoit Mandelbrot, drew his original inspiration by connecting the pattern of cotton prices with that of the flooding pattern of the Nile.

11. The dinar, like most of the standard gold coins of the premodern period, weighed about one-eighth of an ounce, worth about eighty dollars at current value. Thus, an annual income of one hundred dinars corresponds to about $8,000 per year in today's currency.

12. Adam Smith, *An Inquiry into the Nature and Causes of the Wealth of Nations* (Chicago: University of Chicago Press, 1976), I: 17.

13. Paul Mellars, "The Impossible Coincidence. A Single-Species Model for the Origins of Modern Human Behavior in Europe," *Evolutionary Anthropology,* 14:1 (February, 2005): 12–27.

14. Thomas L. Friedman, *The World Is Flat* (New York: Farrar, Straus and Giroux, 2005).

15. Warmington, 35–39; see also William H. McNeill, *Plagues and Peoples* (New York: Anchor, 1998), 128.

16. Warmington, 279–284. See also Ian Carapace, review of *Roman Coins from India* (Paula J. Turner) in *The Classical Review,* 41 (January 1991): 264–265.

17. Alfred W. Crosby, *The Columbian Exchange* (Westport, CT: Greenwood, 1973), 75–81.

18. Quoted ibid., 88.

19. Quoted ibid., 21.

20. Patricia Risso, personal communication.

21. John Maynard Keynes, *The General Theory of Employment Interest and Money* (New York: Harcourt, 1936), 383.

Chapter 1

1. Daniel Boorstin, *Hidden History* (New York: Harper and Row, 1987), 14.

2. Robert L. O'Connell, *Soul of the Sword* (New York: Free Press, 2002), 9–23.

3. Ibid.

4. Mellars, 12–27.

5. Herodotus, *The Histories* (Baltimore: Penguin, 1968), 307.

6. P. F. de Moraes Fairas, "Silent Trade: Myth and Historical Evidence," *History in Africa,* 1 (1974): 9–24.

7. Colin Renfrew, "Trade and Culture Process in European History," *Current Anthropology* 10 (April–June 1969): 151–169. A more readable and available version of this work may be found in J. E. Dixon, J. R. Cann, and Colin Renfrew, "Obsidian and the Origins of Trade," *Scientific American,* 218 (March 1968): 38–46.

8. Detlev Elmers, "The Beginnings of Boatbuilding in Central Europe," in *The Earliest Ships* (Annapolis, MD: Naval Institute Press, 1996), 10, 11, 20.

9. Phyllis Deane, *The First Industrial Revolution* (Cambridge: Cambridge University Press, 1981), 82.

10. Herodotus, 92–93.

11. Gil J. Stein, *Rethinking World Systems* (Tuscon: University of Arizona Press, 1999), 83–84.

12. Christopher Edens, "Dynamics of Trade in the Ancient Mesopotamian 'World System,'" *American Anthropologist,* 94 (March 1992): 118–127.

13. Jacquetta Hawkes, *The First Great Civilizations: Life in Mesopotamia, the Indus Valley, and Egypt* (New York: Knopf, 1973), 110–111, 138–139.

14. Ibid.; see also A. L. Oppenheim, "The Seafaring Merchants of Ur," *Journal of the American Oriental Society,* 74:1 (January–March 1954): 10–11.

15. Robert Raymond, *Out of the Fiery Furnace* (University Park: Pennsylvania State University Press, 1968), 1–18; and R. F. Tylcote, *A History of Metallurgy* (London: Metals Society, 1976), 9, 11.

16. Donald Harden, *The Phoenicians* (New York: Praeger, 1962), 171.

17. Christoph Bachhuber, "Aspects of Late Helladic Sea Trade," master's thesis, Texas A&M University, December 2003, 100.

18. James D. Muhly, "Sources of Tin and the Beginnings of Bronze Metallurgy," *American Journal of Archaeology,* 89 (April 1985): 276. See also Peter Throckmorton, "Sailors in the Time of Troy," in *The Sea Remembers* (New York: Weidenfeld and Nicholson, 1987), 32.

19. Oppenheim, 8.

20. H. E. W. Crawford, "Mesopotamia's Invisible Exports in the Third Millennium BC," *World Archaeology,* 5 (October 1973): 232–241.

21. Edens, 130.

22. Ibid., 118–119.

23. Albano Beja-Pereira et al., "African Origins of the Domestic Donkey," *Science,* 304 (June 18, 2004): 1781–1782.

24. Stein, 88.

25. Ibid., 117–169.

26. George F. Hourani and John Carswell, *Arab Seafaring* (Princeton, NJ: Princeton University Press, 1995), 7.

27. Shelley Wachsmann, "Paddled and Oared Boats before the Iron Age," in Robert Gardiner, ed., *The Age of the Galley* (Edison, NJ: Chartwell, 2000), 21–22.

28. 1 Kings 9:26–28, King James Version.

29. The identification of "Ophir" as India is a matter of some dispute; historians have also suggested Yemen, Sudan, and Ethiopia as possibilities. See Maria Eugenia Aubert, *The Phoenicians and the West,* 2nd ed. (Cambridge: Cambridge University Press, 2001), 44–45.

30. Harden, 157–179.

31. Herodotus, 255.

32. Not until 205 BC—well over two centuries after *Histories* was written— would Eratosthenes correctly calculate the circumference of the earth from the difference between the angles of the sun at Alexandria and Syene, putting the equator well south of even Alexandria.

33. Hourani and Carswell, 8–19.

34. Ibid., 19.

35. Carol A. Redmount, "The Wadi Tumilat and the 'Canal of the Pharaohs,'" *Journal of Near Eastern Studies,* 54:2 (April 1995): 127–135; and Joseph Rabino, "The Statistical Story of the Suez Canal," *Journal of the Royal Statistical Society,* 50:3 (September 1887): 496–498.

36. Jack Turner, *Spice* (New York: Vintage, 2004), 69–70.

37. Warmington, 183, 303–304.

38. Quoted in Sonia E. Howe, *In Quest of Spices* (London: Herbert Jenkins, 1946), 26.

39. Pliny, *Natural History* (Bury St. Edmunds: St. Edmundsbury, 1968), v 4, 21.

40. Ibid., 61 (12: 83).

41. Warmington, 261–318.

42. Ibid., 273.

43. Dennis Flynn and Arturo Giráldez, "Path dependence, time lags, and the birth of globalization: A critique of O'Rourke and Williamson," *European Review of Economic History,* 8 (April 2004): 81–86.

44. Rustichello, as told to Marco Polo, *The Travels of Marco Polo* (New York: Signet Classics, 2004), xxiv.

45. Flynn and Giráldez, 85. Italics added.

Chapter 2

1. Thucydides, *History of the Peloponnesian War,* VII: 68.

2. Tomé Pires, *The Suma Oriental of Tomé Pires and The Book of Francisco Rodrigues,* Armando Cortesão, ed., (Glasgow, Robert Maclehose, 1944), II: 87.

3. Thucydides, VII: 87.

4. The concept that an obsession with control of sea lanes and maritime choke points has its origins in Europe's uniquely convoluted and mountainous geography is best expressed by Chaudhuri: "The phenomenon that is in need of explanation is not the system of peaceful (Asian) but that of armed (European) trading. A comprehensive and convincing explanation has not been attempted as yet by historians. In the Mediterranean, however, from Graeco-Roman times, and perhaps even earlier periods of history, it was essential to exercise control over the vital sea-routes in order to control both economic resources and political settlements. Except in the Persian Gulf and the inland sea of the Indonesian islands, no such combination of geography, politics, economic factors, and historical experience was to be found in the Indian Ocean." See K. N. Chaudhuri, *Trade and Civilization in the Indian Ocean* (New Delhi: Munshiram Manoharlal, 1985), 14.

5. William H. McNeill, *Plagues and Peoples,* 112.

6. Thucydides, I: 2.

7. Ellen Churchill Semple, "Geographic Factors in the Ancient Mediterranean Grain Trade," *Annals of the Association of American Geographers,* 11 (1921): 47–48, 54.

8. Amasis was the pharaoh's Greek name. He was known in Egypt as Khnemibre Ahmose-si-Neit.

9. Herodotus, 172.

10. Ibid., 49.

11. Donald Kagan, *The Peloponnesian War* (New York: Viking, 2003), 8–9, 65, 85–86.

12. Thucydides, VI: 20.

13. Quoted in Semple, 64, from Xenophon, *Hellenes,* II: 2:3.

Chapter 3

1. Leila Hadley, *A Journey with Elsa Cloud* (New York: Penguin, 1998), 468.

2. Bertram Thomas, *Arabia Felix* (New York: Scribner, 1932), 172–174.

3. Richard W. Bulliet, *The Camel and the Wheel* (New York: Columbia University Press, 1990), 28–35.

4. Jared Diamond, *Guns, Germs, and Steel* (New York: Norton, 1999), 168–175.

5. Only the camel's sensitivity to moist climates and the tsetse fly, the vector for camel trypanosomiasis, prevents it from replacing the donkey over a much wider territory.

6. Bulliet, 37–78, 87–89, 281.

7. Ibid., 141–171.

8. Food and Agriculture Organization of the United Nations, accessed at http://www.fao.org/AG/AGAInfo/commissions/docs/greece04/App40.pdf; Australian camel population from Simon Worrall, "Full Speed Ahead," *Smithsonian,* 36:10 (January 2006): 93.

9. Janet Abu-Lughod, *Before European Hegemony* (Oxford: Oxford University Press, 1989), 176.

10. Nigel Groom, *Frankincense and Myrrh* (Beirut: Librairie du Liban, 1981), 5, 148–154, 177–213.

11. Proverbs 7:16–20, King James Version.

12. Numbers 16:18, King James Version: "And they took every man his censer, and put fire in them, and laid incense thereon, and stood in the door of the tabernacle of the congregation with Moses and Aaron."

13. Pliny, 45 (12:64).

14. Ibid., 43 (12:58).

15. T. E. Page et al., eds., *Theophrastus, Enquiry into Plants* (Cambridge, MA: Harvard University Press, 1949), 237–239.

16. Groom, 136.

17. Ibid., 6–7.

18. Pliny, 12:111–113.

19. Ibid., (12:65).

20. Ibid., 43 (12:59).

21. Groom, 149–162.

22. Maxime Rodinson, *Mohammed* (New York: Pantheon, 1971), 11–14.

23. Ibid., 39–40.

24. Groom states that the route ran about 100 miles east of Mecca, whereas Hodgson puts Mecca squarely on the main north-south caravan trail. See Groom, 192; and Marshall G. S. Hodgson, *The Venture of Islam* (Chicago: University of Chicago Press, 1974), I:152.

25. J. J. Saunders, *The History of Medieval Islam* (New York: Barnes and Noble, 1965), 22.

26. Bulliett, 105–106.

27. Rodinson, 32.

28. Saunders, 13–14.

29. Karen Armstrong, *Muhammad* (New York: Harper San Francisco, 1993), 65–86.

30. Rodinson, 36. This author's insights on Islam suffer neither from his Marxism nor from his atheism.

31. Sura 4:29.

32. Narrated by Ibn Abbas, 3:34:311, and by Hakim bin Hizam, 3:34:296, from http://www.usc.edu/dept/MSA/fundamentals/hadithsunnah/bukhari/034.sbt .html #003.034.264.

33. Ibid., narrated by Jabir bin Abdullah, 3:34:310.

34. Saunders, 47.

35. Ibid., 91.

36. Hourani, 57–61.

37. Bengt E. Hovén, "Ninth-century dirham hoards from Sweden," *Journal of Baltic Studies,* 13:3 (Autumn 1982): 202–219.

38. Edwin O. Reischauer, "Notes on T'ang Dynasty Sea Routes," *Harvard Journal of Asiatic Studies,* 5 (June 1940): 142–144.

39. Saunders, 115–122.

40. Hourani, 52.

41. Subhi Y. Labib, "Capitalism in Medieval Islam," *The Journal of Economic History,* 29:1 (March 1969): 93–94.

Chapter 4

1. Rustichello, *The Travels of Marco Polo* (New York: Signet Classics, 2004), vii–xxiv.

2. The numbers came much later as modern historians such as S. D. Goitein and Frederic Lane sifted through the account books and letters of Cairene and Venetian merchants with forensic exactitude.

3. Chau Ju-Kua, *Chu-Fan-Chi,* ed. and trans. Friedrich Hirth and W. W. Rockhill (New York: Paragon, 1966), 14.

4. Quoted ibid., 27.

5. Friedrich Hirth, "The Mystery of Fu-lin," *Journal of the American Oriental Society,* 33 (1913): 193–208.

6. Chau Ju-Kua, 15.

7. Ibid., 205.

8. Quoted in Hourani, 64.

9. S. Maqbul Ahmad, ed., *Arabic Classical Accounts of India and China* (Shimla: Indian Institute of Advanced Study, 1989), 36.

10. Ibid., 46.

11. Ibid., 51–52.

12. *Arabic Classical Accounts of India and China,* 38–40, 46–47, 52–52, 56.

13. Burzug Ibn Shahriyar, trans. L. Marcel Devic, *The Book of the Marvels of India* (New York: Dial, 1929). 23.

14. Ibid., 74.

15. Ibid., 93.

16. Ibid., 92–95.

17. Ibid., 45.

18. Ibid., 44–52.

19. Hourani, 77.

20. Edward H. Schafer, *The Golden Peaches of Samarkand* (Los Angeles: University of California Press, 1963), 16.

21. Chau Ju-Kua, 7.

22. Ibid., 146–147.

23. Ibid., 22–23.

24. Quoted in Howe, 37–39.

25. Ibid., 39.

26. Richard F. Burton, trans., *The Book of the Thousand Nights and a Night* (London: Burton Club, 1900), 6:25.

27. M. N. Pearson, "Introduction I: The Subject," in Ashin Das Gupta, ed., *India and the Indian Ocean 1500–1800* (Calcutta: Oxford University Press, 1987), 15.

28. *The Book of the Thousand Nights and a Night,* 5.

29. Ibid., 32–33.

30. Ibid., 34

31. Igor de Rachewiltz, *Papal Envoys to the Great Khans* (London: Faber and Faber, 1971), 202.

32. Chaudhuri, *Trade and Civilization in the Indian Ocean,* 29.

33. Samuel Lee, trans., *The Travels of Ibn Battuta* (Mineola, NY: Dover, 2004), 108.

34. Ross E. Dunn, *The Adventures of Ibn Battuta* (Berkeley: University of California Press, 1989), 196.

35. Lee, 108–109.

36. Labib, 90.

37. Dunn, 191.

38. Rustichello, 204.

39. Dunn, 223.

40. Lee, 204–205.

41. C. Defremery and B. R. Sanguinetti, *Voyages d'Ibn Battuta* (Paris: 1979), 4:282–283, quoted in Dunn, 258.

42. Lee, 209.

43. Rustichello, 204.

44. Lee, 216; and Dunn, 260.

45. Patricia Risso, *Merchants of Faith* (Boulder, CO: Westview, 1995) 19–20.

46. Pearson, 18.

47. Louise Levathes, *When China Ruled the Seas* (Oxford: Oxford University Press, 1994), 42–43.

48. M. H. Moreland, "The Ships of the Arabian Sea around AD 1500," *The Journal of the Royal Asiatic Society of Great Britain and Ireland* (January 1939): 67.

49. Ibid., 68.

50. Ibid., 182–192.

51. William J. Bernstein, *The Birth of Plenty* (New York: McGraw-Hill, 2004).

52. Ma Huan, *Ying-Yai Sheng-Lan* (Cambridge: Cambridge University Press for the Hakluyt Society, 1970), 6.

53. Joseph Needham, *Science and Civilization in China* (Cambridge: Cambridge University Press, 1971), IV:3:480–482. There is some controversy surrounding the precise size of the fleets' largest ships, with some scholars placing their maximum possible size at only three hundred feet. See Ma Huan, 31.

54. Levathes, 73–74.

55. Ma Huan, 108–109.

56. Ibid., 139.

57. Levathes, 119, 140–141.

58. Ibid., 186.

59. Gavin Menzies, *1421: The Year China Discovered America* (New York: Morrow, 2003). For a penetrating critique of Menzies's thesis, see Robert Finlay, "How Not to (Re)Write World History: Gavin Menzies and the Chinese Discovery of America," *Journal of World History,* 15:2 (June 2004): 229–242. From the abstract: ". . . based on a hodgepodge of circular reasoning, bizarre speculation, distorted sources, and slapdash research. In reality, the voyages described did not take place."

60. Ma Huan, 6–7, 10–11.

61. *The Suma Oriental of Tomé Pires and The Book of Francisco Rodrigues,* I:42.

62. Ibid., I:41–42.

63. Ibid., II:234.

64. Ibid., II:268.

65. Abu-Lughod, 309.

66. Robert Sabatino Lopez, "European Merchants in the Medieval Indes: The Evidence of Commercial Documents," *Journal of Economic History,* 3 (November 1943): 165.

67. *The Suma Oriental of Tomé Pires and The Book of Francisco Rodriguez,* II:270.

68. Ibid., II:253.

69. Ibid., II:273–274.

70. Risso, 54.

71. C. R. Boxer, *The Portuguese Seaborne Empire* (New York: Knopf, 1969), 45.

Chapter 5

1. E. Ashtor, "Profits from Trade with the Levant in the Fifteenth Century," *Bulletin of the School of Oriental and African Studies,* 38 (1975): 250–275. For quote, see Stefan Zweig, *Conqueror of the Sea* (New York: Literary Guild of America, 1938), 5.

2. Frederic C. Lane, "Venetian Shipping during the Commercial Revolution," *The American Historical Review,* 38:2 (January 1933): 228.

3. Abu-Lughod, 52–68.

4. Andrew Dalby, *Dangerous Tastes* (Berkeley: University of California Press, 2000), 16, 78.

5. Pliny, 12:30.

6. Joanna Hall Brierly, *Spices* (Kuala Lumpur: Oxford University Press, 1994), 4–8.

7. John Villiers, "Trade and Society in the Banda Islands in the Sixteenth Century," *Modern Asian Studies,* 15, no. 4 (1981): 738.

8. Warmington, 227–228.

9. Quoted in Dalby, 40.

10. Chau Ju-Kua, 209. See also Geoffrey Hudson, "The Medieval Trade of China," in D. S. Richards, ed., *Islam and the Trade of Asia* (Philadelphia: University of Pennsylvania Press, 1970), 163.

11. Turner, 85, 92.

12. Ibn Khurdadhbih, *Al-Masalik Wa'l-Mamalik* ("Roads and Kingdoms") in *Arabic Classical Accounts of India and China* (Shimla: Indian Institute of Advanced Study, 1989), 7. Henry Yule, ed., *The Book of Marco Polo* (London: John Murray, 1921), ii:272.

13. Geffroi de Villehardouin and Jean, Sire de Joinville, trans. Frank T. Marzials, *Memoirs of the Crusades* (New York: Dutton, 1958), 42.

14. Ibid., 122–143.

15. Howe, 33.

16. David Ayalon, *The Mamluk Military Society* (London: Variorum Reprints, 1979), IX:46.

17. Daniel Pipes, *Slave Soldiers and Islam* (New Haven: Yale University Press, 1981), 78.

18. Lynn White, Jr., *Medieval Technology and Social Change* (Oxford: Clarendon, 1962), 10–25. For criticism of this thesis, see P. H. Sawyer and R. H. Hilton, "Technical Determinism: The Stirrup and the Plough," *Past and Present,* 24 (April 1963): 90–100.

19. Andrew Ehrenkreutz, "Strategic Implications of the Slave Trade between Genoa and Mamluk Egypt in the Second Half of the Thirteenth Century," in A. L. Udovitch, ed., *The Islamic Middle East, 700–1900* (Princeton, NJ: Darwin, 1981), 337.

20. David Ayalon, "The Circassians in the Mamluk Kingdom," *Journal of the American Oriental Society,* 69 (July–September 1949): 146.

21. David Ayalon, "Studies on the Structure of the Mamluk Army—I," *Bulletin of the School of Oriental and African Studies, University of London,* 15 (1953): 206–207.

22. Ayalon, "The Circassians in the Mamluk Kingdom," 146.

23. Pipes, 83.

24. Ibid., 83–84.

25. Ayalon, *The Mamluk Military Society,* Xb:6.

26. Ibid., Xb:15.

27. Ibid., Xa:197, 221.

28. Ehrenkreutz, 336.

29. Saunders, 165.

30. Ibid., 47, 49.

31. Ayalon, *The Mamluk Military Society,* VIII:49.

32. Michael W. Dols, *The Black Death in the Middle East* (Princeton: Princeton University Press, 1977), 21, 56–57.

33. Ehrenkreutz, 343.

34. Howe, 98–99.

35. S. D. Goitein, "New Light on the Beginnings of the Karim Merchants," *Journal of Economic and Social History of the Orient* 1 (August 1957): 182–183.

36. Labib, 84.

37. Ibid., 83.

38. Walter J. Fischel, "The Spice Trade in Mamluk Egypt," *Journal of Economic and Social History of the Orient* 1 (August 1957): 161–173.

Chapter 6

1. This occurred as late as in the early twentieth century, when Han Chinese migrants flooded into Manchuria to hunt the creatures for their increasingly valuable skins. The migrants contracted the disease, touching off an epidemic that killed about 60,000. See Wu Lien-Teh et al., *Plague* (Shanghai Station: National Quarantine Service, 1936), 31–35.

2. Ibid., 74–75.

3. Mark Wheelis, personal communication.

4. Wu, 289–291. See also Rosemary Horrox, *The Black Death* (Manchester, England: Manchester University Press, 1994), 5.

5. A. B. Christie et al., "Plague in camels and goats: their role in human epidemics," *Journal of Infectious Disease,* 141:6 (June 1980): 724–726.

6. Hippocrates, *Of the Epidemics,* I:1, http://classics.mit.edu/Hippocrates/epidemics.1.i.html, accessed December 23, 2005.

7. Thucydides, 2:47–54. Recent isolates from the dental pulp of presumed victims demonstrated the presence of *Salmonella enterica,* suggesting typhoid fever as the causative organism. See M. J. Papagrigorakis et al., "DNA examination of ancient dental pulp incriminates typhoid fever as a probable cause of the Plague of Athens," *International Journal of Infectious Diseases* 10, no. 3 (May 2006): 206–214.

8. J. F. Gilliam, "The Plague under Marcus Aurelius," *The American Journal of Philology* 82, no. 3 (July 1961): 225–251. Also see McNeill, 131.

9. There is an even more rapidly fatal third form of the disease, "septicemic plague," which primarily involves the bloodstream. Although rare in the modern world, it was probably common during the Black Death. Wheelis, unpublished material. Also see Wu, 3, 317, 325.

10. Ibid., 178–179.

11. Procopius, *The History of the Persian Wars,* II:16, from *The History of the Warres of the Emperour Justinian* (London: printed for Humphrey Moseley, 1653).

12. Ibid.

13. Ibid.

14. Ibid., 23:31.

15. Dols, 21–27.

16. Josiah C. Russell, "That Earlier Plague," *Demography* 5, no. 1 (1968): 174–184.

17. McNeill, 147–148.

18. Ibid., 138–139, 142.

19. Ibid., 173–176.

20. Mark Wheelis, unpublished material, personal communication. This sequence of events is speculative. Medical historians have pointed out that the Chinese outbreak of 1331 was not well described, and that the evidence for the outbreak of 1338 at Issyk-Kul is largely anthropological. Other possible mechanisms for the spread of plague to Kaffa eight years later include a long-standing reservoir in the ground rodents of the Caspian area, spread northward from Persia, or slow migration westward from China of the infection via rats and tarabagans without any intervention whatsoever from man.

21. Horrox, 17.

22. Ibid.

23. Mark Wheelis, "Biological warfare at the 1346 Siege of Kaffa." Emerg. Infect. Dis. [serial online] September 2002 [accessed December 15, 2005]: 8. Available from URL: http://www.cdc.gov/ncidod/EID/vol8no9/01-0536.htm

24. Horrox, 36.

25. Ibid., 39. Gabriele de' Mussi, it seems, was a highly skilled collator of primary and secondary observations, since he never left his Italian hometown of Piacenza. Some have questioned the importance of Kaffa in the transmission of the plague to Europe. For at least a decade, the organism had been bouncing between flea, rat, ground rodent, horse, camel, and human, westward across central Asia. The Mongols controlled many other Black Sea ports, and it is possible that the disease was transported through these as well.

26. Allan Evans, review of *Genova marinara nel duecento: Benedetto Zaccaria, ammiraglio e mercante. Speculum* 11, no. 3 (July 1936): 417.

27. Mark Wheelis, unpublished material.

28. McNeill, 179, 182.

29. Horrox, 20.

30. Ibid., 9–13.

31. Ibid., 209–210.

32. Ibid., 13–18.

33. Frederic C. Lane, *Venice: A Maritime Republic* (Baltimore: Johns Hopkins University Press, 1973), 19. B. Z. Kedar, *Merchants in Crisis* (New Haven: Yale University Press, 1976), 5.

34. Dols, 58–59.

35. Horrox, 18.

36. Ibid., 25. For municipal population figures see Daron Acemoglu et al., "Reversal of Fortune: Geography and Institutions and the Making of the Modern World Income Distribution," *Quarterly Journal of Economics,* 117 (November 2002): 1231–1294.

37. Dols, 60.

38. Ibid., 65.

39. Ibid., 57.

40. David Neustadt (Ayalon), "The Plague and its Effects upon the Mamluk Army," *Journal of the Royal Asiatic Society* (1946): 67–73, quotes from 72.

41. Quoted in Dols, 188.

42. The most easily accessible and authoritative source of historical and world economic and population statistics is available at economic historian Angus Maddison's website in Excel format at http://www.ggdc.net/Maddison/Historical_Statistics/horizontal-file.xls.

43. Abu-Lughod, 236–239; Dols 197, 265.

44. McNeill, 130.

45. Ibid., 7–8.

46. Ibn Khaldun, trans. Franz Rosenthal, *The Muqaddimah: An Introduction to History* (New York: Pantheon, 1958), 64.

Chapter 7

1. Anon., *"Roteiro,"*: ed. E. G. Ravenstein, *A Journal of the First Voyage of Vasco da Gama* (London: Hakluyt Society, 1898), 75. This diary, which will be referenced hereafter as the *Roteiro,* or "journal," kept by an unknown member of da Gama's crew (quite possibly João de Sá, the scrivener on the *São Rafael,* commanded by da Gama's brother Paulo, or Álvaro Velho, who also served on the same vessel) is the most important primary record of da Gama's first voyage.

2. Robert B. Serjeant, *The Portuguese off the South Arabian Coast: Hadrami Chronicles* (Oxford: Clarendon, 1963), 43.

3. There can be little question that he had indeed done so, as the papal secretary's notes record Niccolò de' Conti's precise descriptions of Moluccan parrots and the particularly dark-skinned aboriginal inhabitants of the islands. See N. M. Penzer, ed., and John Frampton, trans., *The Most Noble and Famous Travels of Marco Polo*

Together with the Travels of Niccolò de' Conti (London: Adam and Charles Black, 1937), 133. See also Howe, 70–74.

4. Ehrenkreutz, 338–339.

5. Charles E. Nowell, "The Historical Prester John," *Speculum,* 28:3 (July 1953): 434–445.

6. Robert Silverberg, *In the Realm of Prester John* (Garden City, NY: Doubleday, 1972), 3–7, quote, 45.

7. Ibid., 43.

8. Ibid., 2.

9. Pearson, 83.

10. Dana B. Durand, review of *Precursori di Colombo? Il tentativo di viaggio transoceanio dei genovesi fratelli Vivaldi nel 1291* by Alberto Magnaghi, *Geographical Review,* 26:3 (July 1936): 525–526.

11. Felipe Fernández-Armesto, *Columbus* (Oxford: Oxford University Press, 1991), 9.

12. J. H. Plumb, Introduction, in C. R. Boxer, *The Portuguese Seaborne Empire,* xxvi.

13. Silverberg, 194–195.

14. Boxer, *The Portuguese Seaborne Empire,* 28–29.

15. Howe, 105.

16. Samuel Eliot Morison, *Admiral of the Ocean Sea* (Boston: Little, Brown, 1970), 24–26, 41.

17. This fictional story has Columbus sitting at dinner following his return from his first transatlantic voyage with a group of jealous noblemen, who proceed to denigrate his accomplishment—after all, anyone can sail west on the trade winds to the New World. Columbus asks them, "Who among you, gentlemen, can make this egg stand on end?" After each of the noblemen, in his turn, tries and fails, they declare the task impossible. Columbus then gently crushes the egg tip on the table and accomplishes the deed, adding, "Gentlemen, what is easier than to do this which you said was impossible? It is the simplest thing in the world. Anybody can do it—*after he has been shown how!*" http://www.mainlesson.com/display.php?author=olcott&book=holidays&story=egg.

18. Ibid., 33–34, 64.

19. Unlike most true believers, however, Columbus rarely alienated anyone. Even after João II rejected his initial proposal, he was repeatedly invited back for further discussions. Another of Columbus's old employers from his Mediterranean sailing days, the powerful Genoese Centurione trading family, underwrote his third voyage to the New World. (See Fernández-Armesto, 9.)

20. For a comprehensive discussion of the historiography of Columbus's motivations, see Cecil Jane, *Select Documents Illustrating the Four Voyages of Christopher Columbus* (London: Hakluyt Society, 1930), xiii–cl.

21. C. Varela, ed., *Cristóbal Colón: Textos y documentos completos* (Madrid: 1984), 256, quoted in Fernández-Armesto, 134.

22. Quoted in Fernández-Armesto, 97.

23. Ibid., 54–108.

24. Tantalizing hints of pre-Norse voyages to the New World abound, including Roman coins found in Venezuela and textile patterns characteristic of Asia found in pre-Columbian Latin American artifacts. See Stephen Jett, *Crossing Ancient Oceans* (New York: Springer, 2006).

25. Zweig, 26.

26. Acemoglu et al., 1231–1294.

27. A. R. Disney, *Twilight of the Pepper Empire* (Cambridge, MA: Harvard University Press, 1978), 21.

28. Boxer, *The Portuguese Seaborne Empire,* 20–22.

29. Morison, 368–374.

30. M. N. Pearson, "India and the Indian Ocean in the Sixteenth Century," in *India and the Indian Ocean,* 78.

31. *Roteiro,* xix.

32. Ibid., 20–21.

33. Ibid., 25.

34. Ibid., 26.

35. Ibid., 35.

36. Ibid., 45.

37. Sanjay Subrahmanyam, *The Career and Legend of Vasco da Gama* (Cambridge: Cambridge University Press, 1997), 121–128.

38. Ibid., 121.

39. *Roteiro,* 48.

40. Ibid., 60.

41. Ibid., 62.

42. Ibid., 68.

43. Ibid., 173.

44. Earl J. Hamilton, "American Treasure and the Rise of Capitalism," *Economica* 27 (November 1929): 348.

45. Boxer, *The Portuguese Seaborne Empire,* 206.

46. William Brooks Greenlee, trans., *The Voyage of Pedro Álvares Cabral to Brazil and India* (London: Hakluyt Society, 1938), xxiii–xxviii , 83–85.

47. Quoted in Subrahmanyam, 205.

48. Ibid., 214.

49. Ibid., 215.

50. Boxer, *The Portuguese Seaborne Empire,* xxiii.

51. Ibid., 227.

52. Genevieve Bouchon and Denys Lombard, "The Indian Ocean in the Fifteenth Century," in *India and the Indian Ocean,* ed. A. D. Gupta and M. N. Pearson (Calcutta: Oxford University Press, 1987), 55–56.

53. Quoted in Silverberg, 216.

54. Pearson, "India and the Indian Ocean in the Sixteenth Century," 67–68.

55. Ibid., 87.

56. Serrão's original vessel had become too decrepit to proceed. The ship that came to grief under his command was a local junk purchased en route. See Leonard Y. Andaya, *The World of Maluku* (Honolulu: University of Hawaii Press, 1993), 115.

57. Quoted in Zweig, 52.

58. Zweig, 33–69.

59. One of the vessels returned home after a mutiny; one was lost in rough seas; one (as with da Gama's voyage) was abandoned to combine crews; and one, the *Trinidad*, was captured by the Portuguese. Of the thirty-one men on the *Victoria* who completed the circumnavigation, thirteen were captured by the Portuguese in the Cape Verde Islands but were eventually returned to Spain. See Tim Joyner, *Magellan* (Camden, ME: International Marine, 1992), especially the crew roster and accounting, 252–265.

60. Ibid., 192–240.

61. Pearson, "India and the Indian Ocean in the Sixteenth Century," 90.

62. Quoted in Frederic C. Lane, "The Mediterranean Spice Trade: Further Evidence of Its Revival in the Sixteenth Century," *American Historical Review,* 45:3 (April 1940): 589.

63. Ibid., 587.

64. Frederic C. Lane, "Venetian Shipping during the Commercial Revolution," 228–234.

65. Om Prakash, "European Commercial Enterprise in Precolonial Europe," in *The New Cambridge History of India* (Cambridge: Cambridge University Press, 1998), II:5, 45.

66. Ibid., 581, 587–588. For a contrary view, see C. H. H. Wake, "The Changing Pattern of Europe's Pepper and Spice Imports, ca. 1400–1700," *Journal of European Economic History* 8 (Fall 1979): 361–403. Even Wake, however, admits that there was a significant flow of spices via the Red Sea and Venice in the sixteenth century.

67. M. N. Pearson, *The New Cambridge History of India* (Cambridge: Cambridge University Press, 1987), I:1, 44.

68. Boxer, *The Portuguese Seaborne Empire,* 59.

69. Charles R. Boxer, "A Note on Portuguese Reactions to the Revival of the Red Sea Spice Trade and the Rise of Atjeh, 1540–1600," *Journal of Southeast Asian History* 10 (1969): 420.

70. Ibid., 425.

71. Charles R. Boxer, *The Great Ship from Amacon* (Lisbon: Centro de Estudios Históricos Ultramarinos, 1959), 1–2.

72. Ibid., 22.

73. Ibid., 15–16.

74. Ibid., 16–18.

75. M. N. Pearson, *The New Cambridge History of India,* I:1, 37–39.

76. M. A. P. Meilink-Roelofsz, *Asian Trade and European Influence in the*

Indonesian Archipelago Between 1500 and About 1630 (The Hague: Martinus Nijhoff, 1962), 144.

77. Ibid., 43.

78. Prakash, 54.

79. John Villiers, "Las Yslas de Esperar en Dios: The Jesuit Mission in Moro 1546–1571," *Modern Asian Studies* 22, no. 3 (1988, special issue): 597.

80. Paramita R. Abdurachman, "'Niachile Pokaraga': A Sad Story of a Moluccan Queen," *Modern Asian Studies* 22, no. 3 (1988, special issue): 589.

81. Andaya, 116–141.

82. Disney, 20–21.

Chapter 8

1. Homer H. Dubs and Robert S. Smith, "Chinese in Mexico City in 1635," *Far Eastern Quarterly* 1, no. 4 (August 1942): 387.

2. Horace Stern, "The First Jewish Settlers in America: Their Struggle for Religious Freedom," *Jewish Quarterly Review* 45, no. 4 (April 1955): 289, 292–293, quote, 293. The assertion that the twenty-three were in fact the first Jews in North America is a matter of some dispute. See, for example, Jonathan D. Sarna, "American Jewish History," *Modern Judaism* 10, no. 3 (October 1990): 244–245.

3. Philippa Scott, *The Book of Silk* (London: Thames and Hudson, 1993), 22, 24, 33.

4. In tropical regions, the flow of surface air is toward the equator. As this air mass moves in that direction, it finds itself rotating toward the east more slowly than the earth below it, because of the increase in the diameter of the earth toward the equator (resulting in a higher velocity of rotation); thus, it moves relatively toward the west—the Coriolis effect. At higher latitudes in both hemispheres, the opposite occurs. The air masses move toward the poles, and as they do so, they find themselves moving eastward more rapidly than the earth below, since the decrease in the earth's diameter at higher latitudes means a smaller velocity of rotation; at the poles, the velocity of rotation is zero. This is also the reason why storm systems rotate clockwise in the northern hemisphere and counterclockwise in the southern hemisphere. (It has nothing to do, however, with the rotation of drain whirlpools, which is random—the Coriolis effect is not strong enough over small distances to affect the water in your sink or bathtub.)

5. J. H. Parry, review of "Friar Andrés de Uraneta, O.S.A.," *Hispanic American Historical Review* 47, no. 2 (May 1967): 262. Although Arellano, who had abandoned the main force of Urdaneta's expedition just after it left Manila, arrived in Mexico first, he kept poor logs and was later reprimanded; it is Urdaneta who is remembered as the route's pioneer. For the conventional view crediting Urdaneta, see Thor Heyerdahl, "Feasible Ocean Routes to and from the Americas in Pre-Columbian Times," *American Antiquity* 28, no. 4 (April 1963): 486.

6. William Lytle Schurz, "Mexico, Peru, and the Manila Galleon," *American Historical Review* 1, no. 4 (November 1918): 390.

7. Ibid., 394–395.

8. Dubs and Smith, 387.

9. Ibid., 398.

10. Ibid., 391.

11. Ibid., 387.

12. Sugar consumption from http://www.fao.org/documents/show_cdr.asp? url_file=/docrep/009/J7927e/j7927e07.htm. EU population of 457 million from http://www.cia.gov/cia/publications/factbook/rankorder/2119rank.html; U.S. population of 299 million from http://www.census.gov/population/www/popclockus.html. Medieval European consumption from Henry Hobhouse, *Seeds of Change* (New York: Harper and Row, 1986), 44.

13. Norge W. Jerome, in James M. Weiffenbach, ed., *Taste and Development: The Genesis of Sweet Preference* (Washington D.C.: National Institutes of Health, 1974), 243.

14. Sidney W. Mintz, *Sweetness and Power* (New York: Penguin, 1986), xxi, 6.

15. Paul Hentzner, from http://www.britannia.com/history/docs/hentzner.html.

16. J. H. Galloway, "The Mediterranean Sugar Industry," *Geographical Review* 67, no. 2 (April, 1977): 182–188.

17. Mintz, 23.

18. Galloway, 180.

19. Alberto Vieria, "Sugar Islands" and "Introduction," in Stuart B. Schwartz, ed. *Tropical Babylons* (Chapel Hill: University of North Carolina Press, 2004), 10, 62–73.

20. Jonathan I. Israel, *Dutch Primacy in World Trade, 1585–1740* (Oxford: Clarendon, 1989), 161–168.

21. Stern, 289. For a detailed historical analysis, see Arnold Wiznitzer, "The Exodus from Brazil and Arrival in New Amsterdam of the Jewish Pilgrim Fathers, 1654," *Publication of the American Jewish Historical Society* 44, no. 1 (September 1954): 80–95. By the latter account, the twenty-three Sephardic Jews from Brazil were not the first in New Amsterdam, since they were met and assisted by two Ashkenazic Jews.

22. J. E. Heeres, *Het Aandeel der Nederlanders in de Ontdekking van Australië 1606–1765* (Leiden: Boekhandel en Drukkerij Voorheen E. J. Brill, 1899), xii–xiv. Also see Estensen, 126–127.

23. Ibid., 156–164. For a more detailed description of the *Batavia* disaster, see Mike Dash, *Batavia's Graveyard* (New York: Crown Publishers, 2002).

24. John J. McCusker, *Money and Exchange in Europe and America, 1600–1775* (Chapel Hill: University of North Carolina Press, 1978), 7–8.

25. Kristof Glamann, *Dutch-Asiatic Trade 1620–1740* ('s-Gravenhage, Netherlands: Martinus Nijhoff, 1981), 64–65.

26. Jeremy N. Green, "The Wreck of the Dutch East Indiaman the *Vergulde Draek,* 1656," *International Journal of Nautical Archaeology and Underwater Exploration* 2, no. 2 (1973): 272–274, 278–279. For a more accessible discussion, see

Miriam Estensen, *Discovery, the Quest of the Great South Land* (New York: St. Martin's, 1998), 193–194.

27. Donald Simpson, "The Treasure in the *Vergulde Draek:* A Sample of V. O. C. Bullion Exports in the 17th Century," *Great Circle* 2, no. 1 (April 1980): 13.

Chapter 9

1. Derek Wilson, *The World Encompassed: Francis Drake and His Great Voyage* (New York: Harper and Row, 1977), 60–63.

2. Marguerite Eyer Wilbur, *The East India Company* (Stanford, CA: Stanford University Press, 1945), 5–9.

3. The most immediate effect of the closure of the Iberian ports on long-distance trade was that it cut off Holland, and other European nations, from supplies of Spanish salt, vital for the preservation of fish. As early as 1599, about 120 Dutch ships, along with dozens of others from England, France, and Italy, were calling annually at the salt flats at Punta de Araya in what is now Venezuela. See Philip Curtin, *The Rise and Fall of the Plantation Complex,* 2nd ed. (Cambridge: Cambridge University Press, 1998), 90.

4. Charles Boxer, *The Dutch Seaborne Empire* (New York: Penguin, 1988), 21.

5. Arthur Coke Burnell, ed., *The Voyage of John Huyghen van Linschoten to the East Indies* (New York: Burt Franklin, 1885), I:xxvi.

6. Ibid., 112.

7. John Bastin, "The Changing Balance of the Southeast Asian Pepper Trade," in M. N. Pearson, *Spices in the Indian Ocean World* (Aldershot: Variorum, 1996), 285.

8. Ibid., 25.

9. Ibid.

10. Michael Greenberg, *British Trade and the Opening of China* (Cambridge: Cambridge University Press, 1969), 2.

11. Wilbur, 18–24.

12. Charles R. Boxer, *The Portuguese Seaborne Empire,* 110.

13. Three centuries later, the American economist Irving Fisher would observe that where the houses were made of mud and straw, interest rates were high; where they were made of bricks, interest rates were low. See Irving Fisher, *The Theory of Interest* (Philadelphia: Porcupine, 1977), 375–382.

14. Data adjusted to year 2006 dollars from the year 1990 data from Angus Maddison, *The World Economy: A Millennial Perspective* (Paris: OECD, 2001), 264. Data recomputed for the U.S. CPI as of 2006.

15. Sidney Homer and Richard Sylla, *A History of Interest Rates* (New Brunswick, NJ: Rutgers University Press, 1996), 137–138.

16. Jan De Vries and Ad Van Der Woude, *The First Modern Economy* (Cambridge: Cambridge University Press, 1997), 26–28.

17. Israel, 21–22.

18. Ibid., 75.

19. Quoted in T. S. Ashton, *The Industrial Revolution, 1760–1830* (Oxford: Oxford University Press, 1967), 9.

20. At the exchange rate in 1600 of approximately ten guilders per English pound sterling.

21. Wilbur, 21. See also Jonathan B. Baskin and Paul J. Miranti, *A History of Corporate Finance* (Cambridge: Cambridge University Press, 1997), 75.

22. Meilink-Roelofsz, 195–196.

23. Vincent C. Loth, "Armed Incidents and Unpaid Bills: Anglo-Dutch Rivalry in the Banda Islands in the Seventeenth Century," *Modern Asian Studies* 29, no. 4 (October 1995): 707.

24. Meilink-Roelofsz, 193.

25. Boxer, *The Dutch Seaborne Empire,* 75.

26. Andaya, 152–155.

27. Israel, 185.

28. Boxer, *The Dutch Seaborne Empire,* 107.

29. Ibid., 164.

30. Loth, 705–740. The Dutch eventually took Run in 1666, during the Second Anglo-Dutch War, and they formally acquired it in the next year in the Treaty of Breda. Just as the Dutch had gained actual control of Run at the time of the treaty, so too were English troops in possession of Manhattan, for which it was famously "exchanged."

31. Niels Steensgaard, *The Asian Trade Revolution of the Seventeenth Century* (Chicago, University of Chicago Press, 1974), 345–397.

32. Meilink- Roelofsz, 222–225.

33. Boxer, *The Dutch Seaborne Empire,* 128.

34. Ibid., 265–267. Quote in C. R. Boxer, *Jan Compagnie in Japan, 1600–1850* (The Hague: Nijhoff, 1950), 90.

35. Israel, 172–175.

36. Ibid., 177.

37. Ibid., 91–92.

38. De Vries and Van Der Woude, 642–646; quote, 643.

39. Hobhouse, 105.

40. Glamann, 27–34.

41. Ibid., 108–111.

42. Israel, 199–202.

43. Ibid., 208–224, 262–269, 287.

Chapter 10

1. Arthur Meier Schlesinger, "The Uprising Against the East India Company," *Political Science Quarterly* 32, no. 1 (March 1917): 60–79.

2. Ibid., 67–68.

3. Quoted ibid., 69.

4. Quoted ibid., 70.

5. Jean de La Roque, *A voyage to Arabia fœlix through the Eastern Ocean and the Streights of the Red-Sea, being the first made by the French in the years 1708, 1709, and 1710* (London: Printed for James Hodges, 1742), 296–297.

6. Ibid., 309.

7. Ralph S. Hattox, *Coffee and Coffeehouses* (Seattle: University of Washington Press, 1988): 22–26.

8. La Roque, 335.

9. Ibid., 313.

10. Ibid., 321; Hattox, 36–37.

11. La Roque, 336; also Bennett Alan Weinberg and Bonnie K. Bealer, *The World of Caffeine* (New York: Routledge, 2001), 14.

12. Quoted in Weinberg and Bealer, 13.

13. Ibid., 15.

14. Quoted in Fernand Braudel, *Capitalism and Material Life 1400–1800* (New York: Harper and Row, 1967), 184.

15. The first known mention of coffee by a European was probably by the famous German physician Leonhard Rauwolf, who encountered it in the course of a journey to the Levant in the 1570s, searching for medicinals to trade. See William H. Ukers, *All About Coffee* (New York: Tea and Coffee Trade Journal Company, 1935), 21.

16. Ibid., 46.

17. David Liss, *The Coffee Trader* (New York: Random House, 2003), 15.

18. Douglass C. North and Barry R. Weingast, "Constitutions and Commitment: The Evolution of Institutional Governing Public Choice in Seventeenth-Century England," *Journal of Economic History* 49 (December 1989): 803–32.

19. Homer and Sylla, 124, 155. These figures are for loans to the crown, secured by taxes. In 1726, when attached to a lottery ticket—a common "kicker" to medieval government borrowing—rates fell as low as 3 percent.

20. Glamann, 204–206, calculated at four hundred pounds per *bahar*.

21. For coffee prices at Mocha, see Glamann, 205. The price of 0.8 guilder per pound is calculated from a lading price of 245 Spanish reales per local *bahar*, 735 pounds at Mocha, with a conversion rate of 2.4 guilders per real. For more on weights and currencies in the coffee markets, see Glamann, 304.

22. Ibid., 200–201.

23. Ibid., 207–211.

24. Re. Dutch Clergyman, Boxer, *Jan Compagnie*, 61, and quote, Braudel, 186.

25. Boxer, *Jan Compagnie*, 61–62.

26. Jonathan F. Wendel and Richard C. Cronin, "Polyploidity and the Evolutionary History of Cotton," *Advances in Agronomy* 78 (2003): 139–186.

27. Neil McKendrick, John Brewer, and J. H. Plumb, *The Birth of a Consumer Society* (London: Europa, 1982), 36–37.

28. A person-day is a measure of work, defined as that done by one person in one day.

29. Hobhouse, 144. The figure of thirteen person-days is arrived at from the sum of the total person-days divided by eight pounds.

30. Audrey W. Douglas, "Cotton Textiles in England: The East India Company's Attempt to Exploit Developments in Fashion 1660–1721," *Journal of British Studies* 8, no. 2 (May 1969): 29.

31. Ibid., 30.

32. *Defoe's Review* (New York: Columbia University Press, 1938); see no. 43 (January 6, 1712), 8.

33. Ibid., no. 11 (January 26, 1706), 3.

34. Douglas, 33.

35. Ramkrishna Mukherjee, *The Rise and Fall of the East India Company* (Berlin: VEB Deutsher Verlag der Wissenschaften, 1958), 226.

36. Ibid., 282.

37. Alfred C. Wood, *A History of the Levant Company* (London: Frank Cass, 1964), 1–11, 102–105.

38. Ibid., 103–104.

39. Ibid., 104.

40. Ibid., 104–105.

41. Thomas Mun, *England's Treasure by Foreign Trade,* in Lenoard D. Abbot, ed., *Masterworks of Economics* (New York: McGraw-Hill, 1973), 6. Mun occupied the curious position of being both a mercantilist and a supporter of the EIC; he argued that the EIC could acquire more specie from the reexport of the calicoes it sent to Europe than it spent in India for them. See William J. Barber, *British Economic Thought and India 1600–1858* (Oxford: Clarendon, 1975), 10–27.

42. The underlying theoretical flaw in the mercantilist argument is simple: if a country has a strongly positive balance of trade, its stock of specie will swell, causing an overall rise in prices (as indeed was the case in seventeenth-century Holland), thus making its exports more expensive. This would then reduce or eliminate the favorable trade balance. The opposite effect would occur in nations with a negative trade balance: specie would dry up, lowering prices, thus making their exports more attractive.

43. Quoted in Douglas Irwin, *Against the Tide* (Princeton: Princeton University Press, 1996), 48.

44. Charles Davenant, *Essay on the East-India-Trade* (London: Printed for author, 1696), 22, 26, 32.

45. Henry Martyn, *Considerations on the East India Trade* (London: Printed for J. Roberts, 1701), 10, photographic reproduction in J. R. McCullouch, *Early English Tracts on Commerce* (Cambridge: Cambridge University Press, 1970). There is some doubt as to the authorship of this tract. The frontispiece lists no author, but most scholars consider Martyn the author—see P. J. Thomas, *Mercantilism and the East India Trade* (London: Frank Cass, 1963), 171–173.

46. Ibid., 37.

47. Ibid., 32–33. Even more remarkably, Martyn clearly described the magic of the division of labor seventy-five years before Adam Smith. He noted that while

a cloth- or watchmaker might be able to perform every step in the manufacturing process, it was better for each to specialize in the task he performs best: "The Spinner, the Fuller, the Dyer or Clothworker, must needs be more skilful and expeditious at his proper business, which shall be his whole and constant imployment, than any Man can be at the same work, whose skill shall be pulsed and confounded with variety of other businesses," 43.

48. George L. Cherry, "The Development of the English Free-Trade Movement in Parliament, 1689–1702," *Journal of Modern History* 25, no. 2 (June 1953): 103–119.

49. Ibid., 110.

50. K. N. Chaudhuri, *The Trading World of Asia and the English East India Company* (Cambridge: Cambridge University Press, 1978), 294–295.

51. Quoted in Thomas, 136.

52. Beverly Lemire, *Fashion's Favourite* (Oxford: Oxford University Press, 1991), 32.

53. Ibid., 145–146.

54. Ibid., 34–42, 160.

55. T. K. Derry and Trevor I. Williams, *A Short History of Technology* (New York: Dover, 1993) 105–107, 558–561.

56. E. J. Hobsbawm, "The Machine Breakers," *Past and Present* 1 (February 1952): 57–70.

57. Lemire, 54.

58. McKendrick et al., 34–99.

59. Hobhouse, 148–154.

60. C. R. Harler, *The Culture and Marketing of Tea,* 2nd ed. (London: Oxford University Press, 1958), 109, 225.

61. Chaudhuri, *The Trading World of Asia and the East India Company,* 386.

62. James Walvin, *Fruits of Empire* (New York: New York University Press, 1997), 16–19.

63. N. McKendrick, "Josiah Wedgwood: An Eighteenth-Century Entrepreneur in Salesmanship and Marketing Techniques," *Economic History Review* 12, no. 3 (1960): 412–426.

64. Jonas Hanway, quoted in Walvin, 22.

65. Philip Curtin, *The Rise and Fall of the Plantation Complex,* 83.

66. Richard S. Dunn, *Sugar and Slaves* (Chapel Hill: University of North Carolina Press, 1972), 7–21, 61, 64–65.

67. Richard Ligon, *A True & Exact History of the Island of Barbadoes* (London: Peter Parker, 1673), 20–21.

68. Quoted in David Eltis, *The Rise of African Slavery in the Americas* (Cambridge: Cambridge University Press, 2000), 201.

69. Ibid., 127, 201–202.

70. Ligon, 96.

71. Hugh Thomas, *The Slave Trade* (New York: Simon and Schuster, 1999), 201–207.

72. Dunn, 112–116.

73. Ibid., 73.

74. Calculated from Eltis, 50, table 2-2.

75. Philip Curtin, *The Atlantic Slave Trade* (Madison: University of Wisconsin Press, 1969), 69, 81.

76. Paul Bairoch, *Economics and World History* (Chicago: University of Chicago Press, 1993), 146.

77. Curtin, *The Rise and Fall of the Plantation Complex,* 39–40.

78. David Brion Davis, *Inhuman Bondage* (Oxford: Oxford University Press, 2006), 90–91.

79. Eltis, *The Rise of African Slavery in the Americas,* from 176, table 7-3.

80. Quoted in Davis, *Inhuman Bondage,* 92.

81. Professor Curtin produced the first scientific census with the publication of his landmark *The Atlantic Slave Trade* in 1967. His basic conclusions were largely confirmed and refined by Professor Eltis; see *The Rise of African Slavery in the Americas;* "The Volume and Structure of the Transatlantic Slave Trade: A Reassessment," *William And Mary Quarterly,* 58, no. 1 (January 2001): 17–46, and David Eltis and David Richardson, "Prices of African Slaves Newly Arrived in the Americas, 1673–1865: New Evidence on Long-Run Trends and Regional Differentials," in David Eltis, ed., *Slavery in the Development of the Americas* (Cambridge: Cambridge University Press, 2004), 181–211.

82. Curtin, *The Atlantic Slave Trade,* from 268, table 77. For a more recent, and perhaps more accurate, quantitative assessment of the transatlantic slave flow, see Eltis, "The Volume and Structure of the Transatlantic Slave Trade: A Reassessment," 17–46.

83. Davis, *Inhuman Bondage,* 80.

84. Ibid., 11–12, 40–41.

85. Michael Tadman, "The Demographic Cost of Sugar: Debates on Slave Societies and Natural Increase in the Americas," *American Historical Review,* 105, no. 5 (December 2000): 1556.

86. Ibid., 1554–1555, 1561.

87. Ibid., 1536.

Chapter 11

1. Quoted in Greenberg, 45.

2. Ibid., 78–79.

3. Jehangir R. P. Mody, *Jamsetjee Jeejeebhoy* (Bombay: R.M.D.C. Press, 1959), 2–14, 21–28.

4. Hsin-pao Chan, *Commissioner Lin and the Opium War* (New York, Norton, 1964), 121–122.

5. Briefly summarized, the Canton System revolved around nine rules: (1) No foreign war vessels in the Pearl River. (2) No weapons in the factories. (3) Foreign merchants allowed at Canton only during the trading season (September–March). (4) All Chinese boat crews in employ of foreigners to be licensed. (5) Number of

servants of foreigners subject to strict limits. (6) Only very limited visits by foreigners to Canton city proper allowed. (7) No smuggling by or credit to foreigners permitted. (8) Foreign ships allowed no farther upriver than Whampoa; all goods to be carried the final thirteen miles to Canton in small local boats. (9) All transactions to be conducted through the government-sanctioned hong monopoly. See Maurice Collis, *Foreign Mud* (New York: New Directions, 2002), 15.

6. In 1772, four years before the publication of *Wealth of Nations,* Smith had been considered for membership in a commission of the EIC to travel to the Bengal to investigate malfeasance there, but because of parliamentary opposition, it was never sent. See William J. Barber, *British Economic Thought and India 1600–1858* (Oxford: Clarendon, 1975), 88–89.

7. Plassey was just one facet of the Seven Years' War, which yielded a particularly rich bounty for England: not only the Bengal, but also Canada and much of the Lesser Antilles.

8. Quoted in J. R. Ward, "The Industrial Revolution and British Imperialism, 1750–1850," *Economic History Review* 47, no. 1 (February 1994): 47.

9. Adam Smith, *An Inquiry into the Nature and Causes of the Wealth of Nations* (Chicago: University of Chicago Press, 1976), I: 82.

10. Ibid., II:33; Barber, 97.

11. Anthony Webster, "The Political Economy of Trade Liberalization: The East India Company Charter Act of 1813," *The Economic History Review* 43, no. 3 (August 1990): 404–419.

12. Jack Beeching, *The Chinese Opium Wars* (New York: Harcourt Brace Jovanovich, 1975), 51.

13. W. Travis Hanes III, *The Opium Wars* (Naperville IL: Sourcebooks, 2002), 13–19.

14. Hsin-pao, 9–10.

15. Greenberg, 86.

16. Ibid., 5.

17. Hsin-pao, 4.

18. Greenberg, 6, 8.

19. Carl Trocki, *Opium, Empire, and the Global Political Economy* (London: Routledge, 1999), 6, 14–21.

20. Hsin-pao, 16–17.

21. Trocki, 34.

22. Paul Johnson, *The Birth of the Modern* (New York: HarperCollins, 1991), 761–774; Hsin-pao, 95–96.

23. Greenberg, 110.

24. Robert Blake, *Jardine Matheson* (London: Weidenfeld & Nicholson, 1999), 44–45. The one exception to the EIC's abstention from direct opium sales occurred in 1782, when because of the Spanish War, no trade goods or silver had arrived to pay for tea exports, and the governor-general of Bengal, Warren Hastings, authorized the shipment of two opium vessels. See Greenberg, 108.

25. W. Somerset Maugham, *On a Chinese Screen* (New York: George H. Doran, 1922), 60–61.

26. R. K. Newman, "Opium Smoking in Late Imperial China: A Reconsideration," *Modern Asian Studies* 24, no. 4 (October 1995): 784.

27. Hsin-pao, 85–91.

28. Astor's wealth derived not just from the fur trade, but also from tea and sandalwood. In the early nineteenth century one of his trans-Pacific ships loaded some firewood in the Sandwich Islands. On arrival at Canton, the captain was astonished to be offered $500 per ton for it. Astor managed to keep this profitable secret over the two decades it took to denude the islands of sandalwood trees before moving on to Manhattan real estate. See Anonymous, "China and the Foreign Devils," *Bulletin of the Business Historical Society*" 3, no. 6 (November 1929): 15.

29. Greenberg., 22–28.

30. Chinese trade figures are quoted in the main medium of exchange, Spanish dollars. A Spanish dollar (an eight-real piece) was equivalent to one U.S. silver dollar, at an exchange rate of approximately five dollars to one pound sterling.

31. Ibid., 96–97.

32. Greenberg, 36–41, 136–139.

33. Blake, 46.

34. Trocki, 103.

35. Basil Lubbock, *The Opium Clippers* (Glasgow: Brown, Son, and Ferguson, 1933), 72–77.

36. A bark has three masts: a stern fore-and-aft rigging, with one square-rigged mast amidships and another in the bow. The original *Prince de Neufchatel* had been a brigantine, which has only two masts, the fore-and aft in the stern and square-rigged in the bow. There are other permutations of square- and fore-and-aft-rigged masts, among which are the barkentine, brig, and schooner, to name but a few. All these configurations could be tightened and mounted on a sleek, narrow hull to produce a "clipper."

37. The *Red Rover*'s triumphant first voyage followed many years of trial and error. In 1826 Clifton had married the daughter of François Vrignon, a successful Calcuttan shipwright; the result was a disastrous attempt to use a combination of a steam tug and clipper to reach China. At about the same time, a small private yacht designed along clipper lines, the *Falcon,* made an unsuccessful winter run from Singapore to China. The first vessel to successfully complete a full leg against the monsoons was probably the Baltimore-style schooner *Dhaulle* in 1827. However, it was much smaller and slower than the *Red Rover,* and only made one journey. See Lubbock, 62–78; Blake, 54.

38. Because of their short life span, there exists today only one example of an "extreme clipper," the renowned *Cutty Sark,* which was on display at Greenwich until it was damaged by fire in 2007.

39. Trocki, 106.

40. Anonymous eighteenth-century journalist, quoted in "Behind the Mask," *Economist,* March 18, 2004.

41. Greenberg, 13.

42. Ibid., 112–113, 142.

43. Hsin-pao, 51–61.

44. Ibid., 62.

45. Ibid., 189–203; see also Hanes, 66–83. Even within the firm, there were doubts; in 1849, Donald Matheson resigned his position in the firm cofounded by his uncle in protest against the trade. See Trocki, 163; and Peter Ward Fay, "The Opening of China," in Maggie Keswick, ed., *The Thistle and the Jade* (London: Octopus, 1982), 66–67.

46. Edward Le Fevour, *Western Enterprise in Late Ching China* (Cambridge, MA: Harvard University Press, 1968), 13.

47. Trocki, 110–115.

48. Quoted in Karl Marx, *Capital* (New York: International, 1967), 1:432. This passage is supposedly from a letter written by the governor-general in 1834, but Marx probably manufactured it. An examination of Bentinck's letters for 1834 and the years surrounding it does not yield a primary quotation. These two dramatic and eloquent sentences, while consistent with Marx's occasionally emotive prose, are quite inconsistent with Bentinck's uniformly dry and undistinguished output. See C. H. Philips, ed., *The Correspondence of Lord William Cavendish Bentinck, Governor-General of India, 1828–1835,* 2 (Oxford: Oxford University Press, 1977); and Morris D. Morris, "Trends and Tendencies in Indian Economic History," in *Indian Economy in the Nineteenth Century: A Symposium* (Delhi: Hindustan, 1969): 165.

49. Jawaharlal Nehru, *The Discovery of India* (Calcutta: Signet, 1956): 316.

50. Colin Simmons, "'De-industrialization,' Industrialization, and the Indian Economy, c. 1850–1947," *Modern Asian Studies* 19, no. 3 (April 1985): 600.

51. B. R. Tomlinson, "The Economy of Modern India," *The New Cambridge History of India,* vol. 3, 3. (Cambridge: Cambridge University Press, 1993): 102.

52. Morris D. Morris, "Towards a Reinterpretation of Nineteenth-Century Indian Economic History," *Journal of Economic History* 23, no. 4 (December 1963): 613.

53. See, for example, Morris; Tomlinson; and Tirthankar Roy, "Economic History and Modern India: Redefining the Link," *Journal of Economic Perspectives* 16, no. 3 (Summer 2002): 109–130.

54. Paul Bairoch, "European Trade Policy, 1815–1914," in Peter Mathias and Sidney Pollard, eds., *The Cambridge Economic History of Europe* (Cambridge: Cambridge University Press, 1989), VIII:109.

55. Jeffrey Williamson, working paper, "De-Industrialization and Underdevelopment: A Comparative Assessment around the Periphery 1750–1939" (December 2004): 15, accessed at http://www.economics.harvard.edu/faculty/jwilliam/papers/DeIndEHW1204.pdf, December 22, 2006.

56. Recent economic research shows a fairly strong relationship between length of European rule and subsequent economic progress; the longer the period of colonial governance, the higher a nation's modern GDP. See, for example, James Freyer and Bruce Sacerdote, "Colonialism and Modern Income—Islands as Natural Experi-

ments," Working Paper (October 2006), accessed at http://www.dartmouth.edu/~jfeyrer/islands.pdf, December 22, 2006.

57. Computed from Donald Grove Barnes, *A History of the English Corn Laws* (New York: Augustus M. Kelley, 1961): 295–296.

58. Interpolated from Maddison, *The World Economy,* 95.

59. Ibid., 299–300; and S. Fairlie, "The Corn Laws Reconsidered," *Economic History Review* 18, no. 3 (1965): 563.

60. Barnes, 72–73. This is not very different from the refusal of twenty-first-century Americans to drive fuel-efficient vehicles.

61. Ibid., 5–89.

62. David Weatherall, *David Ricardo, A Biography* (The Hague: Martinus Nijhoff, 1976), 1–3.

63. Ibid., 38–39; see also 69–71 for Waterloo loan.

64. David Ricardo, *Principles of Political Economy and Taxation* (London: Dutton, 1911), 77–93; quotation, 77.

65. In fact, John Stuart Mill described the principle much more clearly in his similarly titled *Principles of Political Economy,* published a generation later; and earlier writers of the seventeenth and eighteenth centuries, including Smith, Robert Torrens, and Henry Martyn, had described the concept in general terms. Nonetheless, economic historians generally award Ricardo pride of place for his groundbreaking mathematical description of free trade's win-win nature. See Irwin, 89–93.

66. Barnes 133–135, 177–179. The foreign minister's antipathy to the working class would later be immortalized by Shelley after the Peterloo massacre of 1819: "I met murder upon the way; He had a mask like Castlereagh." ("The Masque of Anarchy." Note to American readers: this rhymes.)

67. Weatherall, 101–106, 135–137.

68. For more than a century, there has been a lively debate among economic historians as to whether the corn laws did indeed serve to keep grain prices high, and if their repeal caused prices to fall. The consensus seems to be "yes" to both questions. For a comprehensive treatment of the subject, see Fairlie, 562–575.

69. Joyce Marlow, *The Peterloo Massacre* (London: Panther, 1969), 53–54.

70. The bill of 1828 imposed a $34^2/_3$-shilling duty when the price was below fifty-two shillings, which decreased gradually to just one shilling when the price reached seventy-two shillings. See Barnes, 200–201.

71. Wendy Hinde, *Richard Cobden* (New Haven, CT: Yale University Press, 1987), 1–2.

72. Richard Cobden, *England, Ireland, and America* (Philadelphia: Institute for the Study of Human Issues, 1980), 94.

73. Ibid., 29. This is a point that is almost always overlooked by proponents of protection: imposing high import tariffs and erecting trade barriers raises the prices of imported production materials, making domestically produced manufactures more expensive, and thus less competitive abroad.

74. Norman McCord, *The Anti-Corn Law League* (London: George Allen and Unwin, 1958), 34–36.

75. Johnson, 167.

76. Hinde, 50–52; quote, 51.

77. Ibid., 52.

78. Barnes, 254.

79. Henry Donaldson Jordan, "The Political Methods of the Anti-Corn Law League," *Political Science Quarterly* 42, no. 1 (March 1927): 66.

80. G. Kitson Clark, "The Repeal of the Corn Laws and the Politics of the Forties," *The Economic History Review* 4, no. 1 (1951): 5.

81. Jordan, 69–73. If one estimates the return on property at 6 percent per year, then this computes to a cost per vote of approximately £33 (the £2 per year freehold divided by 0.06), well within the league's budget in a tightly contested "pocket borough," where a dozen votes could easily decide a seat in the Commons.

82. Fay, 105.

83. Quoted in Hinde, 147.

84. The modern reader will find an obvious similarity between the pious concern of the English landowning aristocracy for working conditions in England's mills and that of the modern American labor movement for the treatment of workers in the developing world. Many on both sides of the Corn Law controversy thought, incorrectly as it turned out, that the League's factory owners would benefit from cheaper bread, which would enable them to pay workers less and thus exact greater profits. (Cobden, right as usual, realized that cheaper bread meant a higher standard of living for workers, not higher profits for mill owners.) A popular ditty went:

Who are that blustering, canting crew,
Who keep the cheap loaf in our view,
And would from us more profit screw?
                    The League.

Who cry "Repeal the curs'd Corn Law,"
And would their workmen feed with straw,
That they may filthy lucre paw?
                    The League.

Who wish to gull the working man,
And burk the Charter, if they can,
With their self-aggrandizing plan,
                    The League.

Quoted in Hinde, 70.

85. Lord Ernle, *English Farming* (Chicago: Quadrangle, 1961), 274.

86. Fay, 98; see also Fairlie, 571.

87. Barnes, 274–276. See also Michael Lusztig, "Solving Peel's Puzzle: Repeal of the Corn Laws and Institutional Preservation," *Comparative Politics* 27, no. 4 (July 1995): 400–401.

88. Hinde, 103–104, 135–168. Disraeli attacked Peel with the vituperation of a skilled novelist: "[Peel] has traded on the ideas and intelligence of others. His life

has been one grand appropriation clause. He is a burglar of other's intellect." Quoted in Barnes, 278.

89. In practice, "repeal" meant that duties were drastically lowered until February 1, 1849, at which point they were to be lowered yet further to one shilling per quarter. After 1869, they were abolished altogether. See Ernle, 274.

90. Jeffrey G. Williamson, "The Impact of the Corn Laws Just Prior to Repeal," *Explorations in Economic History* 27 (1990): 127–129.

91. J. A. Hobson, *Richard Cobden, the International Man* (London: Ernest Benn, 1968), 248.

92. John Morley, *The Life of Richard Cobden* (London: T. Fisher Unwin, 1903), 721.

93. Charles Kindleberger, "The Rise of Free Trade in Western Europe, 1820–1875," *Journal of Economic History* 31, no. 1 (March 1975): 37–38.

94. Quoted in Bairoch, 29–30.

95. Morley, 751. Gladstone was by this time the Liberal (the successor party to the Whigs) chancellor of the exchequer.

96. Bairoch, "European trade policy, 1815–1914," 39–45.

97. Fay, 106; Barnes 291. Britain's main grain suppliers before 1846, Poland and Germany, also became unable to feed themselves. See Fairlie, 568.

Chapter 12

1. John Stuart Mill, *Principles of Political Economy* (New York: Appleton, 1888), 378,

2. Joseph Conrad, *The Mirror of the Sea* (New York: Doubleday, Page, 1924), 11–12.

3. Copper has a very high specific gravity, weighing nine times its volume of water. Copper ore is a mix of copper-containing compounds and mineral contaminants, almost all of which are lighter than copper. Thus, the higher the copper content of the ore, the heavier it is.

4. Herbert V. Young, *They Came to Jerome* (Jerome, AZ: Jerome Historical Society, 1972), 17.

5. Ronald Roope, personal communication; Ronald Prain, *Copper* (London: Mining Journal Books, 1975), 17–18, 21–22.

6. W. O. Henderson, *Friedrich List* (London: Frank Cass, 1983), 68–75, 143–182.

7. The one exception on import duties was a brief period of high proceeds from public land sales during the 1830s. See Mark Thornton and Robert B. Ekelund Jr., *Tariffs, Blockades, and Inflation* (Wilmington, DE: Scholarly Resources, 2004), 13.

8. John G. Van Deusen, "Economic Bases of Disunion in South Carolina" (Ph.D. thesis, Columbia University, 1928), 182–183.

9. The representatives from New England also favored the tariff, albeit by a less impressive margin, enabling the bill to pass. See Thornton and Ekelund, 19–20.

10. F. W. Taussig, *The Tariff History of the United States* (New York: Capricorn, 1964), 68–110. See also Donald J. Ratcliffe, "The Nullification Crisis, Southern Discontent, and the American Political Process," *American Nineteenth Century History* 1, no. 2 (Summer 2000): 3–5.

11. William W. Freehling, *The Road to Disunion* (Oxford: Oxford University Press), I:256. The fallacy in McDuffie's argument is that South Carolinians spent only a small portion of their income on imported goods. Still, the fact remains that the South paid for the shielding of northern industry, while its own exports needed none.

12. Richard B. Latner, "The Nullification Crisis and Republican Subversion," *Journal of Southern History* 43, no. 1 (February 1977): 21.

13. Richard E. Ellis, *The Union at Risk* (Oxford: Oxford University Press, 1987), 46.

14. Ibid., 23, 33. This was not the first time South Carolina had nullified a federal law. In 1822, the state passed legislation requiring the jailing of foreign black seamen who arrived in its ports, in direct contradiction of federal law and of treaty obligations to England. The federal government, not wanting a confrontation, quietly let the state law stand, and thus granted South Carolina the de facto right of nullification. See Freehling, 254.

15. Ellis, 158–177.

16. Ratcliffe, 8, 22–23.

17. Reinhard H. Luthin, "Abraham Lincoln and the Tariff," *The American Historical Review* 49, no. 4 (July 1944): 612, 622.

18. Lyon G. Tyler, "The South and Self-Determination," *William and Mary College Quarterly Historical Magazine* 27, no. 4 (April 1919): 224.

19. John. L. Conger, "South Carolina and the Early Tariffs," *The Mississippi Valley Historical Review* 5, no. 4 (March 1919): 431–433.

20. Freehling, 272.

21. *Natchez Free Trader,* November 27, 1860, quoted in P. L. Rainwater, "Economic Benefits of Secession: Opinions in Mississippi in the 1850s," *The Journal of Southern History* 1, no. 4 (November 1935): 470–471.

22. Recomputed from Paul Bairoch, "European Trade Policy, 1815–1914," 56, at a 2007/1988 inflation conversion factor of 1.75.

23. F. Daniel Larkin, "Erie Canal Freight," *New York State Archives Time Machine,* http://www.archives.nysed.gov/projects/eriecanal/ErieEssay/ecf.html, accessed February 12, 2007.

24. See David Landes, *The Unbound Prometheus* (Cambridge: Cambridge University Press, 1969), 251–259; and W. T. Jeans, *The Creators of the Age of Steel* (New York: Scribner, 1884), 29.

25. Charles K. Harley, "The Shift from Sailing Ships to Steamships, 1850–1890: A Study in Technological Change and Its Diffusion," in Donald N. McCloskey, ed., *Essays on a Mature Economy* (Princeton: Princeton University Press, 1971), 215–225.

26. Gerald S. Graham, "The Ascendancy of the Sailing Ship 1850–1885," *Economic History Review* 9, no. 1 (1956): 79.

27. In a later paper, Harley estimated that in the late 1860s, the steam-sail boundary lay between 3,000 and 3,500 miles, considerably shorter than the approximately 7,000 miles predicted by this model. Still, the basic premise holds: evolutionary improvements in engine and hull design brought a gradual lengthening of the steam-sail boundary over the course of the nineteenth century. See C. Knick Harley, "Ocean Freight Rates and Productivity, 1740–1913: The Primacy of Mechanical Invention Reaffirmed," *Journal of Economic History* 48, no. 4 (December 1988): 863–864.

28. Conrad, 47–48. He may not have been an entirely disinterested observer. Trained on wooden ships and briefly a ship's master, Conrad found himself out of work with the ascendancy of the steamship and turned to writing. The steam age thus resulted not only in more efficient trade but also a better understanding of "the horror, the horror," of colonialism.

29. Juan E. Oribe Stemmer, "Freight Rates in the Trade between Europe and South America, 1840–1914," *Journal of Latin American Studies* 21, no. 1 (February 1989): 44.

30. Extrapolated from table IV, Lewis R. Fischer and Helge W. Nordvik, "Maritime Transport and the Integration of the North Atlantic Economy, 1850–1914," in Wolfram Fischer et al., eds., *The Emergence of a World Economy 1500–1914* (Wiesbaden, Commissioned by Franz Steiner Verlag, 1986), II:531.

31. Harley, 221–225.

32. Computed from Bairoch, 56.

33. Ronald W. Filante, "A Note on the Economic Viability of the Erie Canal, 1825–1860, *Business History Review* 48, no. 1 (Spring 1974): 100.

34. George G. Tunell, "The Diversion of the Flour and Grain Traffic from the Great Lakes to the Railroads," *Journal of Political Economy* 5, no. 3 (June 1897): 340–361.

35. Gavin Weightman, *The Frozen Water Trade* (New York: Hyperion, 2003), 7, 71, 105–109, 127–143. For a detailed description of Wyeth's invention and ancillary ice-harvesting tools, see Oscar Edward Anderson Jr., *Refrigeration in America* (Princeton: Princeton University Press for the University of Cincinnati, 1953), 13–35.

36. Henry D. Thoreau, *Walden* (Boston: Houghton Mifflin, 1938), 329.

37. Weightman, 163, 207.

38. Anderson, 21–22, 50–52.

39. John H. White, *The Great Yellow Fleet* (San Marino, CA: Golden West, 1986), 11–13.

40. Weightman, 223–224.

41. James Troubridge Critchell and Joseph Raymond, *A History of the Frozen Meat Trade,* 2nd ed. (London: Constable, 1912), 25.

42. Pride of place in artificially refrigerated shipping probably belongs to the Frenchman Charles Tellier, who in 1876–1877 shipped chilled beef in the *Frigorifique,* a steamer fitted with an ammonia compression device, from Buenos Aires to Rouen. See E. G. Jones, "The Argentine Refrigerated Meat Industry," *Economica* 26 (June 1929): 160.

43. Critchell and Raymond, 3, 9, 26–29. For a detailed discussion of the relative advantages of chilled and frozen beef, see Richard Perren, "The North American Beef and Cattle Trade with Great Britain, 1870–1914," *Economic History Review* 24, no. 3 (August 1971): 430–434.

44. "Coal Ammonia for Refrigeration," *Scientific American* LXIV (1891): 241.

45. Larry Tye, *The Father of Spin* (New York: Crown, 1998), 51–52.

46. Fischer and Nordvik, II:526.

47. Max Fletcher, "The Suez Canal and World Shipping, 1869–1914," *Journal of Economic History* 18, no. 4 (December 1958): 556–573.

Chapter 13

1. Cordell Hull, *International Trade and Domestic Prosperity* (Washington, DC: United States Government Printing Office, 1934), 5.

2. Joseph M. Jones Jr., *Tariff Retaliation* (Philadelphia: University of Pennsylvania Press, 1934), 74.

3. Ibid., 1931.

4. C. Knick Harley, "Transportation, the World Wheat Trade, and the Kuznets Cycle, 1850–1913," *Explorations in Economic History* 17, no. 3 (July 1980): 223, 246–247.

5. C. P. Kindleberger, "Group Behavior and International Trade," *Journal of Political Economy* 59, no. 1 (February 1951): 31.

6. Kevin O'Rourke and Jeffrey G. Williamson, "Late Nineteenth Century Anglo-American Price Convergence: Were Heckscher and Ohlin Right?" *Journal of Economic History* 54, no. 4 (December 1994): 900.

7. A. J. H. Latham and Larry Neal, "The International Market in Rice and Wheat, 1868–1914," *Economic History Review* 36, no. 2 (May 1983): 260–280.

8. Here, the term "rents" is used loosely to mean the price of land, as paid for with a mortgage, outright payment, or rental money.

9. Bertil Ohlin, *Interregional and International Trade* (Cambridge: Harvard University Press, 1957), 35–50; Eli Heckscher, "The Effect of Foreign Trade on the Distribution of Income," in *Readings in the Theory of International Trade* (Homewood IL: Irwin, 1950), 272–300. For the most succinct statements of their theorem, see Ohlin, 35; and Heckscher, 287.

10. O'Rourke and Williamson, "Late Nineteenth Century Anglo-American Price Convergence: Were Nechscher and Ohlin Right?", 894–895, 908.

11. Jeffrey G. Williamson, "The Evolution of Global Labor Markets since 1830: Background Evidence and Hypotheses," *Explorations in Economic History* 32 (1995), 141–196; Kevin H. O'Rourke and Jeffrey G. Williamson, *Globalization and History* (Cambridge: MIT Press, 1999), 286.

12. Wolfgang F. Stolper and Paul Samuelson, "Protection and Real Wages," *Review of Economic Studies* 9, no. 1 (November 1941): 58–73. The narrowest description of the Stolper-Samuelson theorem is as follows: when the relative price of

a good increases, so too will the return to the factor which is used most intensively in the production of it, and the return to the less intensively used factor will fall.

13. This is true in "segmented markets," that is, where capital does not flow easily across borders. It is certainly not true today.

14. Eugene Owen Golob, *The Méline Tariff* (New York: AMS, 1968), 22–23, 78–79; Angus Maddison, *The World Economy,* 95.

15. Golob, 83–85, 189–190.

16. Ibid., 245.

17. Kindleberger, "Group Behavior and International Trade," 32–33.

18. Douglas A. Irwin, "The Political Economy of Free Trade: Voting in the British General Election of 1906," *Journal of Law and Economics* 37, no. 1 (April 1994): 75–108.

19. Einar Jensen, *Danish Agriculture* (Copenhagen: J. H. Schultz Forlag, 1937), 251, 315–334, Harald Faber, *Co-operation in Danish Agriculture* (New York: Longmans, Green, 1937), 31–70, 105–106; Henry C. Taylor and Anne Dewees Taylor, *World Trade in Agricultural Products* (New York: Macmillan, 1943), 179; Alexander Gerschenkron, *Bread and Democracy in Germany* (Ithaca NY: Cornell University Press, 1989), 39.

20. The term itself likely derives from *junk Herr,* "young lord."

21. Gerschenkron, 42.

22. It is theoretically possible for a nation to have a relative abundance or scarcity of all three factors, but whether this actually occurs in practice is debatable.

23. Gerschenkron, 3–80.

24. Karl Marx, *The Poverty of Philosophy* (New York: International Publishers, 1963), 224. Marx had it wrong: later twentieth-century history would prove the Hungarian maxim that communism is "the longest road from capitalism to capitalism." William D. Nordhaus, "Soviet Economic Reform: The Longest Road," *Brookings Papers on Economic Activity* 1990, no. 1 (1990): 287.

25. In the preceding pages, I have adopted the controversial "broad" interpretation of Stolper-Samuelson offered by Rogowski in *Commerce and Coalitions* (Princeton: Princeton University Press, 1989), 1–60. On the one hand, Rogowski's interpretation of Stolper-Samuelson overextends their original two-commodity, two-factor model: see Douglas A. Irwin, Review: [Untitled], *Journal of Economic History* 50, no. 2 (June 1990): 509–510. Stolper and Samuelson themselves recognized this problem in their original paper, observing that while there may have been extreme cases where most laborers were made worse off by free trade, as in Australia or the colonial United States, this occurs only rarely in the modern world: "It does not follow that the American working man today would be better off if trade with, say, the tropics were cut off, because suitable land for growing coffee, rubber, and bananas is ever scarcer than is labor." (Stolper and Samuelson, 73). On the other hand, Rogowski's liberal interpretation of Stolper-Samuelson fits the historical record remarkably well despite its theoretical flaws. See O'Rourke and Williamson, *Globalization and History,* 109–110. For a further refinement of Rogowski's thesis, see Paul Midford, "International Trade and Domestic Politics: Improving on

Rogowski's Model of Political Alignments," *International Organization* 47, no. 4 (Autumn 1993): 535–564. Further, even when workers are, on average, not harmed by free trade, small groups of them certainly are. More important, the majority of workers or farmers may behave *as if* trade harms them, even if in fact it does not, as happened to the northern German peasants duped by the Junkers into supporting protectionism.

26. Real values, computed from W. W. Rostow, *The World Economy* (Austin: University of Texas, 1978), 669; and Maddison, 361, 362.

27. Carolyn Rhodes, *Reciprocity, U.S. Trade Policy, and the GATT Regime* (Ithaca, NY: Cornell University Press, 1993), 23–45.

28. http://www.whitehouse.gov/history/presidents/hh31.html accessed March 7, 2007.

29. Colleen M. Callahan et al., "Who Voted for Smoot-Hawley?" *Journal of Economic History* 54, no. 3 (September 1994): 683–684.

30. Charles P. Kindleberger, "Commercial Policy between the Wars," in Peter Mathias and Sidney Pollard, eds., *The Cambridge Economic History of Europe* (Cambridge: Cambridge University Press, 1989), VIII:170–171.

31. Jones, *Tariff Retaliation,* 40, 76–82, 105–109.

32. Cordell Hull, *The Memoirs of Cordell Hull* (New York: Macmillan, 1948), I:364–365.

33. Hull, *International Trade and Domestic Prosperity,* 2.

34. The precise amount of the falloff in world trade is difficult to quantify. Paul Bairoch estimates it at 60 percent in value and 35 percent in volume. Since this was a period of significant deflation, the true value is probably between these two figures. See Bairoch, *Economics and World History,* 9.

35. Maddison, *The World Economy,* 363; and *Monitoring the World Economy* (Paris: OECD, 1995), 182–183, 196.

36. See, for example, Giorgio Basevi, "The Restrictive Effect of the U.S. Tariff and its Welfare Value," *American Economic Review* 58, no. 4 (September 1968): 851. Some observers believe that protectionism actually *raised* national income in the larger nations, particularly in the United States and England. See John Conybeare, "Trade Wars: A Comparative Study of Anglo-Hanse, Franco-Italian, and Hawley-Smoot Conflicts," *World Politics,*" 38, no. 1 (October 1985): 169–170; and Michael Kitson and Solomos Solomu, *Protectionism and Economic Revival: The British Interwar Economy* (Cambridge: Cambridge University Press, 1990), 100–102.

37. Douglas A. Irwin, "The Smoot-Hawley Tariff: A Quantitative Assessment," *Review of Economics and Statistics* 80, no. 2 (May 1998): 326–334; Jakob B. Madsen, "Trade Barriers and the Collapse of World Trade during the Great Depression," *Southern Economic Journal* 64, no. 4 (April 2001): 848–868.

38. John Stuart Mill, *Principles of Political Economy,* 389–390.

39. J. B. Condliffe, *The Reconstruction of World Trade* (New York: Norton, 1940), 394.

40. Albert O. Hirschman, *National Power and the Structure of Foreign Trade* (Berkeley: University of California Press, 1980), 72–73.

41. *Proposals for the Expansion of World Trade and Employment,* United States Department of State Publication 2411, November 1945. The document was written by interested parties from various government departments under the direction of Assistant Secretary of State William Clayton. It is only a slight exaggeration to consider *Proposals* the blueprint of modern globalization. It is remarkable that it is so little known and difficult to access. It can be found at http://www. efficientfrontier .com/files/proposals.pdf.

42. Ibid., 1.

43. Clair Wilcox, *A Charter for World Trade* (New York: Macmillan, 1949), 24. For the history of *Proposals'* origins, see Wilcox, 21–24 and 38–40. It should be noted that during the past half-century the United States has gone from being the world's greatest creditor nation to being its greatest debtor nation.

44. Rhodes, 46–77.

45. T. N. Srinivasan, *Developing Countries and the Multilateral Trading System* (Boulder, CO: Westview, 1998), 9–11; John H. Jackson, *The World Trading System,* 2nd ed. (Cambridge, MA: MIT Press, 1997), 36–38. Jackson's book is considered by most scholars to be the "standard" English-language text on the legal and institutional foundation of the modern trade system.

46. Mancur Olson, *The Logic of Collective Action* (Cambridge, MA: Harvard University Press, 1965).

47. Bairoch, *Economics and World History,* 26.

48. Harley, "Ocean Freight Rates and Productivity, 1740–1913: The Primacy of Mechanical Invention Reaffirmed," 861.

49. Marc Levinson, *The Box* (Princeton: Princeton University Press, 2006), 7–53; Mark Rosenstein, "The Rise of Containerization in the Port of Oakland," New York Univerity master's thesis, 2000, 23–31, http://www.apparent-wind.com/mbr/maritime-writings/thesis.pdf, accessed on March 13, 2007. Both sources are entertaining and well written; Rosenstein's thesis is the more balanced, readable, and inexpensive of the two.

50. Rogowski, 100–101; quote, 121. The protectionist Patrick Buchanan and William Clinton, a supporter of NAFTA, are exceptions.

51. T. N. Srinivasan, "Developing Countries in the World Trading System: From GATT, 1947, to the Third Ministerial Meeting of WTO, 1999," *World Economy* 22, no. 8 (1999): 1052.

52. Jane Mayer and Jose de Cordoba, "Sweet Life: First Family of Sugar is Tough on Workers, Generous to Politicians," *The Wall Street Journal* (July 29, 1991), A1.

53. Technically, these payments are "loans" from the Agriculture Department collateralized by the producers' crops. The "borrowers" can choose at any time to repay the "loan" with sugar, wheat, cotton, corn, or rice valued at two to three times the market price. Which, of course, they always elect to do.

54. "Sugar Program: Supporting Sugar Prices Has Increased Users' Costs While Benefiting Producers," General Accounting Office GAO/RCED-00-126 (June 2000).

55. Timothy P. Carney, *The Big Ripoff* (New York: Wiley, 2006), 56–61.

56. Mary Anastasia O'Grady, "Americas: Clinton's Sugar Daddy Games Now Threaten NAFTA's Future," *The Wall Street Journal* (December 20, 2002), A15.

57. A discussion of the history of the relevant GATT "agreements" in agriculture and textiles—the Short-Term Agreement on Cotton Textiles, the Long-Term Arrangement Regarding International Trade in Cotton Textiles, the Multi-Fiber Arrangement, and the Uruguay Round Agreement on Agriculture—is well beyond this book's scope. For an excellent survey of this subject, see John H. Barton et al., *The Evolution of the Trade Regime* (Princeton: Princeton University Press, 2006), 92–108.

58. Scott Miller and Marc Champion, "At WTO Talks, Stances Are Hardening," *The Wall Street Journal* (January 27, 2006), A7; Scott Kilman and Roger Thurow, "Politics and Economics, U.S. Farm-Subsidy Cuts a Long Shot as Doha Falters," *The Wall Street Journal* (July 26, 2006), A10; Bernard K. Gordon, "Doha Aground," *The Wall Street Journal* (July 26, 2006), A14.

59. United States Department of Agriculture, "Food Spending in Relation to Income," *Food Cost Review, 1950–97,* http://www.ers.usda.gov/Publications/ AER780/, accessed March 23, 2007; Food Remains a Bargain for Oregon and U.S. Consumers," Oregon Department of Agriculture, http://www.oregon.gov/ODA/news/ 060719spending.shtml, accessed March 23, 2007.

Chapter 14

1. Stolper and Samuelson, 73.

2. Norm Stamper, "A Good Cop Wasted," excerpted in *Seattle Weekly* (June 1, 2005).

3. Quoted in Jean-Paul Rodrigue, "Straits, Passages, and Chokepoints: A Maritime Geostrategy of Petroleum Distribution," *Les Cahiers de Géographie du Québec* 48, no. 135 (December 2004): 357.

4. "The Tanker War, 1984–1987," from *Iraq,* Library of Congress Studies, accessed at http://lcweb2.loc.gov/cgi-bin/query/r?frd/cstdy:@field(DOCID+iq0105), March 26, 2007.

5. Yüksel İnan, "The Current Regime of the Turkish Straits," *Perceptions: Journal of International Affairs* 6, no. 1 (March–May 2001), accessed at http:// www.sam.gov.tr/perceptions/Volume6/March-May2001/inan06.PDF.

6. See Rodrigue; see also Donna J. Nincic, "Sea Lane Security and U.S. Maritime Trade: Chokepoints as Scarce Resources," in Sam J. Tangredi, ed., *Globalization and Maritime Power* (Washington, DC: National Defense University Press, 2002), 143–169.

7. Jessie C. Carman, "Economic and Strategic Implications of Ice-Free Arctic Seas," in *Globalization and Maritime Power* 171–188.

8. Patrick J. Buchanan, *The Great Betrayal* (Boston: Little, Brown, 1998), 224.

9. Bairoch, *Economics and World History,* 47–55, 135–138.

10. Mark Bils, "Tariff Protection and Production in the Early U.S. Cotton Textile Industry," *The Journal of Economic History,* 44, no. 4 (December 1984): 1041, 1045.

11. Kevin O' Rourke, "Tariffs and Growth in the Late 19th Century," *The Economic Journal* 110 (April 2000): 456–683; quote, 473. The papers by O'Rourke and Bils are representative of a much larger literature.

12. Kitson and Solomu, 102.

13. J. Bradford DeLong, "Trade Policy and America's Standard of Living: An Historical Perspective," working paper, 1995.

14. Edward F. Denison, *Why Growth Rates Differ* (Washington DC: Brookings Institution, 1967), 260–263.

15. Jeffrey D. Sachs and Andrew Warner, "Economic Reform and the Process of Global Integration," *Brookings Papers on Economic Activity* 1995, no. 1 (1995): 41. The central difficulty in attempting to assess the impact of free trade on the economy is called the "endogeneity" problem. That is, since economic growth is itself such a powerful driver of trade, proving an effect in the opposite direction becomes highly problematic. As put by Douglas Irwin, the simplistic analyses of Bairoch and Buchanan "rest on the dubious assumption that one can judge a trade regime simply by examining the economic growth that occurs on its clock. A major problem with this approach is that the effects of trade policy on growth are probably swamped by other factors." Douglas A. Irwin, "Tariffs and Growth in Late Nineteenth Century America," working paper, June 2000. Economists have recently brought to bear cutting-edge statistical tools in this quest, most importantly "instrumental variables" such as geographic location to disentangle these effects. Such techniques have confirmed and extended the work of Sachs and Warner. For a sampling of this literature, see O'Rourke, 456; Alan M. Taylor, "On the Costs of Inward-Looking Development: Price Distortions, Growth, and Divergence in Latin America," *The Journal of Economic History* 58, no. 1 (March 1998): 1–28; Nicholas Crafts, "Globalization and Growth in the Twentieth Century," IMF Working Paper WP/00/44; Douglas A. Irwin and Marko Terviö, "Does Trade Raise Income? Evidence from the Twentieth Century," *Journal of International Economics* 58 (2002): 1–18; Jeffrey A. Frankel and David Romer, "Does Trade Cause Growth?" *The American Economic Review* 89, no. 3 (June 1999): 379–399; Sebastian Edwards, "Openness, Productivity, and Growth: What Do We Really Know?" *The Economic Journal* 108, no. 447 (March 1998): 383–398.

16. The term "convergence club" was originally coined by the economist William Baumol. See William J. Baumol, "Productivity Growth, Convergence, and Welfare: What the Long-Run Data Show," *The American Economic Review* 76, no. 5 (December 1986): 1079.

17. Maddison, *The World Economy,* 363.

18. Denison, 262.

19. Those seeking a precise citation for this famous quotation will have difficulty. The sentiment permeates Bastiat's writings about trade but is never so succinctly stated. This phrasing may be the work of Cordell Hull, who was fond of quoting Bastiat. See Hull, *The Memoirs of Cordell Hull,* I:363–365.

20. Steven Pinker, "A History of Violence," *New Republic* (March 19, 2007); World Health Organization, http://www.who.int/whr/2004/annex/topic/en/annex_2_en.pdf, accessed March 28, 2007.

21. United States Census Bureau, "Historical Income Tables—People," http://www.census.gov/hhes/www/income/histinc/p05ar.html, accessed April 3, 2007.

22. Henry S. Farber, "What do we know about job loss in the United States? Evidence from the Displaced Workers Survey, 1984–2004," working paper, 2006. See also Peter Gottschalk et al., "The Growth of Earnings Instability in the U.S. Labor Market," *Brookings Papers on Economic Activity* 1994, no. 2 (1994): 217–272. For a general exposition of increasing inequality and job instability in the United States, see Jacob Hacker, *The Great Risk Shift* (New York: Oxford University Press, 2006). See also Jackie Calmes, "Despite Buoyant Economic Times, Americans Don't Buy Free Trade," *The Wall Street Journal* (December 10, 1998), A10. The key word here is "relatively"; the United States has *relatively* more skilled workers than the rest of the world, and has *relatively* fewer unskilled ones.

23. Susan Chun Zhu and Daniel Trefler, "Trade and inequality in developing countries: a general equilibrium analysis," *Journal of International Economics* 65 (2005): 21–48.

24. Katheryn Gigler, personal communication. See also "Secrets, Lies, and Sweatshops," *Business Week* (November 27, 2006).

25. Ashley S. Timmer and Jeffrey G. Williamson, "Immigration Policy Prior to the 1930s: Labor Markets, Policy Interactions, and Globalization Backlash," *Population and Development Review* 21, no. 4 (December 1998): 739–771.

26. *Human Development Report, 2006* (New York: United Nations, 2006), 335–338.

27. Alberto Alesina and Roberto Perotti, "Income Distribution, Political Instability, and Investment," *European Economic Review* 40 (1996): 1203–1228.

28. Geoffrey Garrett, "Global Markets and National Politics: Collision Course or Virtuous Cycle?" *International Organization* 52, no. 4 (Autumn, 1998): 798.

29. See Michael Kremer, "The O-Ring Theory of Economic Development," *The Quarterly Journal of Economics* 108, no. 3 (August 1993): 551–575.

30. See Adrian Wood and Cristóbal Ridao-Cano, "Skill, Trade, and International Inequality," working paper; and Paul Krugman, "Growing World Trade: Causes and Consequences," *Brookings Papers on Economic Activity* 1995, no. 1 (1995): 327–377. For a superb summary of this controversial area, see Ethan B. Kapstein, "Review: Winners and Losers in the Global Economy," *International Organization* 54, no. 2 (Spring 2000): 359–384. For a 100-step process with a 99 percent success rate at each step, the probability of overall success is 0.995^{100}, or 61 percent. At a 95 percent success rate for each step, the overall success probability is 0.95^{100}, or 0.6 percent.

31. Daniel Trefler, personal communication. See also Daniel Trefler, "The Long and Short of the Canada-U.S. Free Trade Agreement," *American Economic Review* 94, no. 4 (September 2004): 888.

32. *Westminster Review* (April 1825), 400–401. The article is anonymous; Mill's authorship is identified in Frank W. Fetter, "Economic Articles in the West-

minster Review and Their Authors, 1824–1851, *The Journal of Political Economy* 70, no. 6 (December 1962): 584.

33. Jagdish Bhagwati, *In Defense of Globalization* (Oxford: Oxford University Press, 2004), 234.

34. Ibid.

35. Daniel Trefler, "Trade Liberalization and the Theory of Endogenous Protection: An Econometric Study of U.S. Import Policy," *Journal of Political Economy* 101, no. 1 (February 1993): 157.

36. Dani Rodrik, *Has Globalization Gone Too Far?* (Washington, DC: Institute for International Economics, 1997), 5–7.

37. Ibid., 79.

38. Paul A. Samuelson, "Where Ricardo and Mill Rebut and Confirm Arguments of Mainstream Economists Supporting Globalization," *The Journal of Economic Perspectives,* 18, no. 3 (Summer 2004): 137. For a delightful radio interview with Professor Samuelson on the topic, see http://www.onpointradio.org/shows/2004/09/20040927_b_main.asp. As might be expected, Samuelson's article caused significant controversy among economists, not all of whom agree with the relevance and accuracy of his model. For the most cogent criticism, see Jagdish Bhagwati et al., "The Muddle over Outsourcing," *Economic Perspectives* 18, no. 4 (Fall 2004): 93–114.

39. Samuelson, 142.

40. Rodrik, 54.

41. *The Oxford Dictionary of Quotes,* 3rd ed. (Oxford: Oxford University Press, 1979), 150.

BIBLIOGRAPHY

Abdurachman, Paramita R., " 'Niachile Pokaraga': A Sad Story of a Moluccan Queen," *Modern Asian Studies* 22, no. 3 (1988, special issue): 571–592.

Abu-Lughod, Janet, *Before European Hegemony* (Oxford: Oxford University Press, 1989).

Acemoglu, Daron, et al., "Reversal of Fortune: Geography and Institutions and the Making of the Modern World Income Distribution," *Quarterly Journal of Economics* 117 (November 2002): 1231–1294.

Adlington, William, trans., *The Golden Ass of Apuleius* (New York: AMS, 1967).

Ahmad, S. Maqbul, ed., *Arabic Classical Accounts of India and China* (Shimla: Indian Institute of Advanced Study, 1989).

Alesina, Alberto, and Roberto Perotti, "Income Distribution, Political Instability, and Investment," *European Economic Review* 40 (1996): 1203–1228.

Andaya, Leonard Y., *The World of Maluku* (Honolulu: University of Hawaii Press, 1993).

Anderson, Oscar Edward Jr., *Refrigeration in America* (Princeton: Princeton University Press for University of Cincinnati, 1953).

Anonymous, "Behind the Mask," *Economist* (March 18, 2004).

Anonymous, "China and the Foreign Devils," *Bulletin of the Business Historical Society* 3, no. 6 (November 1929): 15.

Anonymous, "Coal Ammonia for Refrigeration," *Scientific American* 64 (1891): 241.

Armstrong, Karen, *Muhammad* (New York: Harper San Francisco, 1993).

Ashton, T. W., *The Industrial Revolution, 1760–1830* (Oxford: Oxford University Press, 1967).

Ashtor, E., "Profits from Trade with the Levant in the Fifteenth Century," *Bulletin of the School of Oriental and African Studies* 38 (1975): 250–275.

Aubert, Maria Eugenia, *The Phoenicians and the West*, 2nd ed. (Cambridge: Cambridge University Press, 2001).

Ayalon, David, "The Circassians in the Mamluk Kingdom," *Journal of the American Oriental Society* 69 (July–September 1949): 135–147.

Ayalon, David, *The Mamluk Military Society* (London: Variorum Reprints, 1979).

Ayalon, David, "Studies on the Structure of the Mamluk Army—I," *Bulletin of the School of Oriental and African Studies, University of London* 15 (1953): 203–228.

Bachhuber, Christoph, "Aspects of Late Helladic Sea Trade," master's thesis, Texas A&M University (December 2003).

Bairoch, Paul, *Economics and World History* (Chicago: University of Chicago Press, 1993).

Bairoch, Paul. "European Trade Policy, 1815–1914," in Peter Mathias and Sidney Pollard, eds., *The Cambridge Economic History of Europe*, vol. 8 (Cambridge: Cambridge University Press, 1989).

Barber, William J., *British Economic Thought and India, 1600–1858* (Oxford: Clarendon, 1975).

Barnes, Donald Grove, *A History of the English Corn Laws* (New York: Augustus M. Kelley, 1961).

Barton, John H., et al., *The Evolution of the Trade Regime* (Princeton: Princeton University Press, 2006).

Basevi, Giorgio, "The Restrictive Effect of the U.S. Tariff and Its Welfare Value," *The American Economic Review* 58, no. 4 (September 1968): 840–852.

Bastin, John, "The Changing Balance of the Southeast Asian Pepper Trade," in M. N. Pearson, ed., *Spices in the Indian Ocean World* (Aldershot: Variorum, 1996).

Baumol, William J., "Productivity Growth, Convergence, and Welfare: What the Long-Run Data Show," *American Economic Review* 76, no. 5 (December 1986): 1072–1085.

Beeching, Jack, *The Chinese Opium Wars* (New York: Harcourt Brace Jovanovich, 1975).

Beja-Pereira, Albano, et al., "African Origins of the Domestic Donkey," *Science* 304 (June 18, 2004): 1781–1782.

Bernstein, Peter L., *The Wedding of the Waters* (New York: Norton, 2005).

Bernstein, William J., *The Birth of Plenty* (New York: McGraw-Hill, 2004).

Bhagwati, Jagdish, *In Defense of Globalization* (Oxford: Oxford University Press, 2004).

Bhagwati, Jagdish, et al., "The Muddle over Outsourcing," *Economic Perspectives* 18, no. 4 (Fall 2004): 93–114.

Bils, Mark, "Tariff Protection and Production in the Early U.S. Cotton Textile Industry," *Journal of Economic History* 44, no. 4 (December 1984): 1033–1045.

Blake, Robert, *Jardine Matheson* (London: Weidenfeld and Nicholson, 1999).

Boorstin, Daniel, *Hidden History* (New York: Harper and Row, 1987).

Bouchon, Genevieve, and Denys Lombard, "The Indian Ocean in the Fifteenth Century," in Ashin Das Gupta and M. N. Pearson, eds., *India and the Indian Ocean 1500–1800* (Calcutta: Oxford University Press, 1987).

Boxer, Charles R., *The Dutch Seaborne Empire* (New York: Penguin, 1988).

Boxer, Charles R., *The Great Ship from Amacon* (Lisbon: Centro de Estudios Históricos Ultramarinos, 1959).

Boxer, Charles R., *Jan Compagnie in Japan, 1600–1850* (The Hague: Nijhoff, 1950).

Boxer, Charles R., "A Note on Portuguese Reactions to the Revival of the Red Sea Spice Trade and the Rise of Atjeh, 1540–1600," *Journal of Southeast Asian History* 10 (1969): 415–428.

Boxer, Charles R., *The Portuguese Seaborne Empire* (New York: Knopf, 1969).

Braudel, Fernand, *Capitalism and Material Life 1400–1800* (New York: Harper and Row, 1967).

Brierly, Joanna Hall, *Spices* (Kuala Lumpur: Oxford University Press, 1994).

Buchanan, Patrick J., *The Great Betrayal* (Boston: Little, Brown, 1998).

Bulliet, Richard W., *The Camel and the Wheel* (New York: Columbia University Press, 1990).

Burnell, Arthur Coke, ed., *The Voyage of John Huyghen van Linschoten to the East Indies* (New York: Burt Franklin, 1885).

Burton, Richard F., trans., *The Book of the Thousand Nights and a Night,* vol. 6 (London: Burton Club, 1900).

Butel, Paul, *The Atlantic* (London: Routledge, 1999).

Callahan, Colleen M., et al., "Who Voted for Smoot-Hawley?" *Journal of Economic History* 54, no. 3 (September 1994): 683–690.

Calmes, Jackie, "Despite Buoyant Economic Times, Americans Don't Buy Free Trade," *The Wall Street Journal* (December 10, 1998).

Carapace, Ian, Review of *Roman Coins from India* (Paula J. Turner), *Classical Review* 41 (January 1991): 264–265.

Carman, Jessie C., "Economic and Strategic Implications of Ice-Free Arctic Seas," in *Globalization and Maritime Power* (Washington, DC: National Defense University Press, 2002).

Carney, Timothy P., *The Big Ripoff* (New York: Wiley, 2006).

Chau Ju-Kua, *Chu-Fan-Chi,* Friedrich Hirth and W. W. Rockhill, ed. and trans. (New York: Paragon, 1966).

Chaudhuri, K. N., *Trade and Civilization in the Indian Ocean* (New Delhi: Munshiram Manoharlal, 1985).

Chaudhuri, K. N., *The Trading World of Asia and the English East India Company* (Cambridge: Cambridge University Press, 1978).

Cherry, George L., "The Development of the English Free-Trade Movement in Parliament, 1689–1702," *The Journal of Modern History* 25, no. 2 (June 1953): 103–119.

Christie, A. B., et al., "Plague in Camels and Goats: Their Role in Human Epidemics," *Journal of Infectious Disease* 141, no. 6 (June 1980): 724–726.

Churchill, Ellen Semple, "Geographic Factors in the Ancient Mediterranean Grain Trade," *Annals of the Association of American Geographers* 11 (1921): 47–74.

Clark, G. Kitson, "The Repeal of the Corn Laws and the Politics of the Forties," *The Economic History Review* 4, no. 1 (1951): 1–13.

Clayton, William, *Proposals for the Expansion of World Trade and Employment*, United States Department of State Publication 2411 (November 1945).

Cochran, Gregory, Jason Hardy, and Henry Harpending, "Natural History of Ashkenazi Intelligence," *Journal of Biosocial Science* 36, no. 5 (September 2006): 659–693.

Coleman, William, *Yellow Fever in the North* (Madison: University of Wisconsin Press, 1987).

Collis, Maurice, *Foreign Mud* (New York: New Directions, 2002).

Condliffe, J. B., *The Reconstruction of World Trade* (New York: Norton, 1940).

Conger, John L., "South Carolina and the Early Tariffs," *The Mississippi Valley Historical Review* 5, no. 4 (March 1919): 415–433.

Conrad, Joseph, *The Mirror of the Sea* (New York: Doubleday, Page, 1924).

Conybeare, John, "Trade Wars: A Comparative Study of Anglo-Hanse, Franco-Italian, and Hawley-Smoot Conflicts," *World Politics* 38, no. 1 (October 1985): 147–172.

Crafts, Nicholas, "Globalization and Growth in the Twentieth Century," IMF working paper WP/00/44.

Crawford, H. E. W., "Mesopotamia's Invisible Exports in the Third Millennium BC," *World Archaeology* 5 (October 1973): 232–241.

Critchell, James Troubridge, and Joseph Raymond, *A History of the Frozen Meat Trade,* 2nd ed. (London: Constable, 1912).

Crosby, Alfred W., *The Columbian Exchange* (Westport, CT: Greenwood, 1973).

Curtin, Philip D., "Africa and the Wider Monetary World, 1250–1850," in J. F. Richards, ed., *Precious Metals in the Later and Early Modern Worlds* (Durham, NC: Carolina Academic Press, 1983).

Curtin, Philip D., *The Atlantic Slave Trade* (Madison: University of Wisconsin Press, 1969).

Curtin, Philip D., *The Rise and Fall of the Plantation Complex*, 2nd ed. (Cambridge: Cambridge University Press, 1998).

Dalby, Andrew, *Dangerous Tastes* (Berkeley: University of California Press, 2000).

Dash, Mike, *Batavia's Graveyard* (New York: Crown, 2002).

Davenant, Charles, *Essay on the East-India Trade* (London: Printed for Author, 1696).

Davis, David Brion, "Impact of the French and Haitian Revolutions," in David P. Geggus, ed., *The Impact of the Haitian Revolution in the Atlantic World* (Columbia: University of South Carolina Press, 2001).

Davis, David Brion, *Inhuman Bondage* (Oxford: Oxford University Press, 2006).

Davis, David Brion, *Slavery and Human Progress* (Oxford: Oxford University Press, 1984).

de La Roque, Jean, *A voyage to Arabia fœlix through the Eastern Ocean and the Streights of the Red-Sea, being the first made by the French in the years 1708, 1709, and 1710* (London: Printed for James Hodges, 1742).

DeLong, J. Bradford, "Trade Policy and America's Standard of Living: An Historical Perspective," working paper, 1995.

de Moraes Fairas, P. F., "Silent Trade: Myth and Historical Evidence," *History in Africa* 1 (1974): 9–24.

de Rachewiltz, Igor, *Papal Envoys to the Great Khans* (London: Faber and Faber, 1971).

de Villehardouin, Geffroi, and Jean, Sire de Joinville, *Memoirs of the Crusades,* Frank T. Marzials, trans. (New York: Dutton, 1958).

De Vries, Jan, and Ad Van Der Woude, *The First Modern Economy* (Cambridge: Cambridge University Press, 1997).

Deane, Phyllis, *The First Industrial Revolution* (Cambridge: Cambridge University Press, 1981).

Defoe's Review (New York: Columbia University Press, 1938).

Defremery, C., and B. R. Sanguinetti, *Voyages d'Ibn Battuta* (Paris: 1979).

Denison, Edward F., *Why Growth Rates Differ* (Washington DC: Brookings Institution, 1967).

Derry, T. K., and Trevor I. Williams, *A Short History of Technology* (New York: Dover, 1993).

Diamond, Jared, *Guns, Germs, and Steel* (New York: Norton, 1999).

Disney, A. R., *Twilight of the Pepper Empire* (Cambridge, MA: Harvard University Press, 1978).

Dixon, J. E., et al., "Obsidian and the Origins of Trade," *Scientific American* 218 (March 1968): 38–46.

Dols, Michael W., *The Black Death in the Middle East* (Princeton: Princeton University Press, 1977).

Douglas, Audrey W., "Cotton Textiles in England: The East India Company's Attempt to Exploit Developments in Fashion 1660–1721," *Journal of British Studies* 8, no. 2 (May 1969): 28–43.

Dubois, Laurent, *Avengers of the New World* (Cambridge, MA: Harvard University Press, 2004).

Dubs, Homer H., and Robert H. Smith, "Chinese in Mexico City in 1635," *The Far Eastern Quarterly* 1, no. 4 (August 1942): 387–389.

Dunn, Richard S., *Sugar and Slaves* (Chapel Hill: University of North Carolina Press, 1972).

Dunn, Ross E., *The Adventures of Ibn Battuta* (Berkeley: University of California Press, 1989).

Durand, Dana B., Review of *Precursori di Colombo? Il tentativo di viaggio transoceanio dei genovesi fratelli Vivaldi nel 1291* by Alberto Magnaghi, *Geographical Review* 26, no. 3 (July 1936): 525–526.

Eccles, W. J., *France in America* (East Lansing: Michigan State University Press, 1990).

Edens, Christopher, "Dynamics of Trade in the Ancient Mesopotamian 'World System,'" *American Anthropologist* 94 (March 1992): 118–139.

Edwards, Sebastian, "Openness, Productivity, and Growth: What Do We Really Know?" *Economic Journal* 108, no. 447 (March 1998): 383–398.

Ehrenkreutz, Andrew, "Strategic Implications of the Slave Trade between Genoa and Mamluk Egypt in the Second Half of the Thirteenth Century," in A. L. Udovitch, ed., *The Islamic Middle East, 700–1900* (Princeton: Darwin, 1981).

Ellis, Richard E., *The Union at Risk* (Oxford: Oxford University Press, 1987).

Elmers, Detlev, "The Beginnings of Boatbuilding in Central Europe," in *The Earliest Ships* (Annapolis, MD: Naval Institute Press, 1996).

Eltis, David, *The Rise of African Slavery in the Americas* (Cambridge: Cambridge University Press, 2000).

Eltis, David, "The Volume and Structure of the Transatlantic Slave Trade: A Reassessment," *The William And Mary Quarterly* 58, no. 1 (January 2001): 17–46.

Eltis, David, and David Richardson, "Prices of African Slaves Newly Arrived in the Americas, 1673–1865: New Evidence on Long-Run Trends and Regional

Differentials," in David Eltis, ed., *Slavery in the Development of the Americas* (Cambridge: Cambridge University Press, 2004).

Ernle, Lord, *English Farming* (Chicago: Quadrangle, 1961).

Estensen, Miriam, *Discovery, the Quest of the Great South Land* (New York: St. Martin's, 1998).

Evans, Allan, Review of *Genova marinara nel duecento: Benedetto Zaccaria, ammiraglio e mercante, Speculum* 11, no. 3 (July 1936): 417.

Faber, Harald, *Co-Operation in Danish Agriculture* (New York: Longmans, Green, 1937).

Fairbank, John K., "The Creation of the Treaty System," in John K. Fairbank, ed., *The Cambridge History of China* (Cambridge: Cambridge University Press, 1978).

Fairlie, S., "The Corn Laws Reconsidered," *Economic History Review* 18, no. 3 (1965): 562–575.

Farber, Henry S., "What do we know about job loss in the United States? Evidence from the Displaced Workers Survey, 1984–2004," working paper, 2006.

Fay, Peter Ward, "The Opening of China," in Maggie Keswick, ed., *The Thistle and the Jade* (London: Octopus, 1982).

Fernández-Armesto, Felipe, *Columbus* (Oxford: Oxford University Press, 1991).

Fetter, Frank W., "Economic Articles in the Westminister Review and Their Authors, 1824–1851," *The Journal of Political Economy* 70, no. 6 (December 1962): 570–596.

Filante, Ronald W., "A Note on the Economic Viability of the Erie Canal, 1825–1860," *The Business History Review* 48, no. 1 (Spring 1974): 95–102.

Finlay, Robert, "How Not to (Re)Write World History: Gavin Menzies and the Chinese Discovery of America," *Journal of World History* 15, no. 2 (June 2004): 229–242.

Fischel, Walter J., "The Spice Trade in Mamluk Egypt," *Journal of Economic and Social History of the Orient* 1 (August 1957): 161–173.

Fischer, Lewis R., and Helge W. Nordvik, "Maritime Transport and the Integration of the North Atlantic Economy, 1850–1914," in Wolfram Fischer et al., eds., *The Emergence of a World Economy 1500–1914*, vol. 2, (Wiesbaden: Commissioned by Franz Steiner Verlag, 1986).

Fisher, Irving, *The Theory of Interest* (Philadelphia: Porcupine, 1977).

Fletcher, Max, "The Suez Canal and World Shipping, 1869–1914," *The Journal of Economic History* 18, no. 4 (December 1958): 556–573.

Flynn, Dennis, and Arturo Giráldez, "Path Dependence, Time Lags, and the Birth of Globalization: A Critique of O'Rourke and Williamson," *European Review of Economic History* 8 (April 2004): 81–108.

Food and Agriculture Organization of the United Nations, accessed at http://www.fao.org/AG/AGAInfo/commissions/docs/greece04/App40.pdf.

Frankel, Jeffrey A., and David Romer, "Does Trade Cause Growth?" *American Economic Review* 89, no. 3 (June 1999): 379–399.

Freehling, William W., *The Road to Disunion* vol. 1. (Oxford: Oxford University Press).

Freyer, James, and Bruce Sacerdote, "Colonialism and Modern Income—Islands as Natural Experiments," working paper (October 2006), http://www.dartmouth.edu/~jfeyrer/islands.pdf accessed December 22, 2006.

Friedman, Thomas L., *The World Is Flat* (New York: Farrar, Straus and Giroux, 2005).

Galloway, J. H., "The Mediterranean Sugar Industry," *Geographical Review* 67, no. 2 (April 1977): 177–194.

Garrett, Geoffrey, "Global Markets and National Politics: Collision Course or Virtuous Cycle?" *International Organization* 52, no. 4 (Autumn 1998): 787–824.

General Accounting Office, "Sugar Program: Supporting Sugar Prices Has Increased Users' Costs While Benefiting Producers," General Accounting Office GAO/RCED-00-126 (June 2000).

Gerschenkron, Alexander, *Bread and Democracy in Germany* (Ithaca, NY: Cornell University Press, 1989).

Gilliam, J. F., "The Plague under Marcus Aurelius," *American Journal of Philology* 82, no. 3 (July 1961): 225–251.

Glamann, Kristof, *Dutch-Asiatic Trade 1620–1740* ('s-Gravenhage, Netherlands: Martinus Nijhoff, 1981).

Goitein, S. D., *A Mediterranean Society* (Berkeley: University of California Press, 1967).

Goitein, S. D., "New Light on the Beginnings of the Karim Merchants," *Journal of Economic and Social History of the Orient* 1 (August 1957): 175–184.

Golob, Eugene Owen, *The Méline Tariff* (New York: AMS, 1968).

Gordon, Bernard K., "Doha Aground," *The Wall Street Journal* (July 26, 2006).

Gottschalk, Peter, et al., "The Growth of Earnings Instability in the U.S. Labor Market," *Brookings Papers on Economic Activity* 1994, no. 2 (1994): 217–272.

Graham, Gerald S., "The Ascendancy of the Sailing Ship 1850–1885," *The Economic History Review* 9, no. 1 (1956): 74–88.

Grant, William L., "Canada versus Guadeloupe, an Episode in the Seven Years' War," *American Historical Review* 17, no. 4 (July 1912): 735–743.

Green, Jeremy N., "The wreck of the Dutch East Indiaman the *Vergulde Draek*, 1656," *International Journal of Nautical Archaeology and Underwater Exploration* 2, no. 2 (1973): 267–289.

Greenberg, Michael, *British Trade and the Opening of China* (Cambridge: Cambridge University Press, 1969).

Greenlee, William Brooks, trans., *The Voyage of Pedro Álvares Cabral to Brazil and India* (London: Hakluyt Society, 1938).

Groom, Nigel, *Frankincense and Myrrh* (Beirut: Librairie du Liban, 1981).

Hacker, Jacob, *The Great Risk Shift* (New York: Oxford University Press, 2006).

Hadley, Leila, *A Journey with Elsa Cloud* (New York: Penguin, 1998).

Hamilton, Earl J., "American Treasure and the Rise of Capitalism," *Economica* 27 (November 1929): 338–357.

Hanes, W. Travis, III, *The Opium Wars* (Naperville, IL: Sourcebooks, 2002).

Hanson, Victor Davis, *The Other Greeks* (Berkeley: University of California Press, 1999).

Harden, Donald, *The Phoenicians* (New York: Praeger, 1962).

Harding, C. H., *The Buccaneers in the West Indies in the XVII Century* (Hamden, CT: Archon, 1966).

Harler, C. R., *The Culture and Marketing of Tea*, 2nd ed. (London: Oxford University Press, 1958).

Harley, C. Knick, "Ocean Freight Rates and Productivity, 1740–1913: The Primacy of Mechanical Invention Reaffirmed," *The Journal of Economic History* 48, no. 4 (December 1988): 851–876.

Harley, C. Knick, "The Shift from sailing ships to steamships, 1850–1890: a study in technological change and its diffusion," in Donald N. McCloskey, ed., *Essays on a Mature Economy* (Princeton: Princeton University Press, 1971).

Harley, C. Knick, "Transportation, the World Wheat Trade, and the Kuznets Cycle, 1850–1913," *Explorations in Economic History* 17, no. 3 (July 1980): 218–250.

Hartwell, Robert, "Markets, Technology, and the Structure of Enterprise in the Development of the Eleventh-Century Chinese Iron and Steel Industry," *The Journal of Economic History* 26, no. 1 (March 1966): 29–58.

Hattox, Ralph S., *Coffee and Coffeehouses* (Seattle: University of Washington Press, 1988).

Hawkes, Jacquetta, *The First Great Civilizations: Life in Mesopotamia, the Indus Valley, and Egypt* (New York: Knopf, 1973).

Heckscher, Eli, "The Effect of Foreign Trade on the Distribution of Income," in *Readings in the Theory of International Trade* (Homewood, IL: Irwin, 1950).

Heeres, J. E., *Het Aandeel der Nederlanders in de Ontdekking van Australië 1606–1765* (Leiden: Boekhandel en Drukkerij Voorheen E. J. Brill, 1899).

Henderson, W. O., *Friedrich List* (London: Frank Cass, 1983).

Herodotus, *The Histories* (Baltimore: Penguin, 1968).

Heyerdahl, Thor, "Feasible Ocean Routes to and from the Americas in Pre-Columbian Times," *American Antiquity* 28, no. 4 (April 1963): 482–488.

Hinde, Wendy, *Richard Cobden* (New Haven, CT: Yale University Press, 1987).

Hippocrates, *Of the Epidemics*, I:1, http://classics.mit.edu/Hippocrates/epidemics.1.i.html, accessed December 23, 2005.

Hirschman, Albert O., *National Power and the Structure of Foreign Trade* (Berkeley: University of California Press, 1980).

Hirth, Friedrich, "The Mystery of Fu-lin," *Journal of the American Oriental Society* 33 (1913): 193–208.

Hobhouse, Henry, *Seeds of Change* (New York: Harper and Row, 1986).

Hobsbawm, E. J., *Industry and Empire,* rev. ed. (London: Penguin, 1990).

Hobsbawm, E. J., "The Machine Breakers," *Past and Present* 1 (February 1952): 57–70.

Hobson, J. A., *Richard Cobden, the International Man* (London: Ernest Benn, 1968).

Homer, Sidney, and Richard Sylla, *A History of Interest Rates* (New Brunswick, NJ: Rutgers University Press, 1996).

Horrox, Rosemary, *The Black Death* (Manchester: Manchester University Press, 1994).

Hourani, George F., and John Carswell, *Arab Seafaring* (Princeton: Princeton University Press, 1995).

Hovén, Bengt E., "Ninth-Century Dirham Hoards from Sweden," *Journal of Baltic Studies* 13, no. 3 (Autumn 1982): 202–219.

Howe, Sonia E., *In Quest of Spices* (London: Herbert Jenkins, 1946).

Hsin-pao Chan, *Commissioner Lin and the Opium War* (New York: Norton, 1964).

Hudson, Geoffrey, "The Medieval Trade of China," in D. S. Richards, ed., *Islam and the Trade of Asia* (Philadelphia: University of Pennsylvania Press, 1970).

Hull, Cordell, *International Trade and Domestic Prosperity* (Washington DC: U.S. Government Printing Office, 1934).

Hull, Cordell, *The Memoirs of Cordell Hull* (New York: Macmillan, 1948).

Ibn Battuta, *The Travels of Ibn Battuta* (Mineola, NY: Dover, 2004).

Ibn Khaldun, *The Muqaddimah (An Introduction to History)*, trans. Franz Rosenthal (New York: Pantheon, 1958).

Ibn Khurdadhbih, "Al-Masalik Wa'l-Mamalik" ("Roads and Kingdoms") in *Arabic Classical Accounts of India and China* (Shimla: Indian Institute of Advanced Study, 1989).

Ibn Shahriyar, Burzug, *The Book of the Marvels of India,* trans. Marcel Devic (New York: Dial, 1929).

Irwin, Douglas A., *Against the Tide* (Princeton: Princeton University Press, 1996).

Irwin, Douglas A., "The Political Economy of Free Trade: Voting in the British General Election of 1906," *The Journal of Law and Economics* 37, no. 1 (April 1994): 75–108.

Irwin, Douglas A., Review [Untitled], *Journal of Economic History* 50, no. 2 (June 1990): 509–510.

Irwin, Douglas A., "The Smoot-Hawley Tariff: A Quantitative Assessment," *The Review of Economics and Statistics* 8, no. 2 (May 1998): 326–334.

Irwin, Douglas A., and Marko Terviö, "Does Trade Raise Income? Evidence from the Twentieth Century," *Journal of International Economics* 58 (2002): 1–18.

Israel, Jonathan I., *Dutch Primacy in World Trade, 1585–1740* (Oxford: Clarendon, 1989).

İnan, Yüksel, "The Current Regime of the Turkish Straits," *Perceptions: Journal of International Affairs* 6, no. 1 (March–May 2001), http://www.sam .gov.tr/perceptions/Volume6/March-May2001/inan06.PDF.

Jane, Cecil, *Select Documents Illustrating the Four Voyages of Christopher Columbus* (London: Hakluyt Society, 1930).

Jeans, W. T., *The Creators of the Age of Steel* (New York: Scribner, 1884).

Jensen, Einar, *Danish Agriculture* (Copenhagen: J. H. Schultz Forlag, 1937).

Jerome, Norge W., and James M. Weiffenbach, eds., *Taste and Development: the genesis of sweet preference* (Washington DC: National Institutes of Health, 1974).

Jett, Stephen, *Crossing Ancient Oceans* (New York: Springer, 2006).

Johnson, Paul, *The Birth of the Modern* (New York: HarperCollins, 1991).

Jones, E. G., "The Argentine Refrigerated Meat Industry," *Economica* 26 (June 1929): 157–172.

Jones, Joseph M., Jr., *Tariff Retaliation* (Philadelphia: University of Pennsylvania Press, 1934).

Jordan, Henry Donaldson, "The Political Methods of the Anti-Corn Law League," *Political Science Quarterly* 42, no. 1 (March 1927): 58–76.

Joyner, Tim, *Magellan* (Camden, ME: International Marine, 1992).

Kagan, Donald, *The Peloponnesian War* (New York: Viking, 2003).

Kapstein, Ethan B., "Review: Winners and Losers in the Global Economy," *International Organization* 54, no. 2 (Spring 2000): 359–384.

Kedar, B. Z., *Merchants in Crisis* (New Haven, CT: Yale University Press, 1976).

Keynes, John Maynard, *The General Theory of Employment Interest and Money* (New York: Harcourt, 1936).

Kilman, Scott, and Roger Thurow, "Politics & Economics, U.S. Farm-Subsidy Cuts a Long Shot as Doha Falters," *The Wall Street Journal* (July 26, 2006).

Kindleberger, Charles P., "Commercial Policy between the Wars," in Peter Mathias and Sidney Pollard, eds., *The Cambridge Economic History of Europe* vol. 8 (Cambridge: Cambridge University Press, 1989).

Kindleberger, Charles P., "Group Behavior and International Trade," *The Journal of Political Economy* 59, no. 1 (February 1951): 30–46.

Kindleberger, Charles P., "The Rise of Free Trade in Western Europe, 1820–1875," *The Journal of Economic History* 31, no. 1 (March 1975): 20–55.

Kitson, Michael, and Solomos Solomu, *Protectionism and economic revival: the British interwar economy* (Cambridge: Cambridge University Press, 1990).

Krugman, Paul, "Growing World Trade: Causes and Consequences," *Brookings Papers on Economic Activity,* 1995:1 (1995): 327–377.

Labib, Subhi Y., "Capitalism in Medieval Islam," *Journal of Economic History* 29, no. 1 (March 1969): 79–96.

Landes, David, *The Unbound Prometheus* (Cambridge: Cambridge University Press, 1969).

Lane, Frederic C., "The Mediterranean Spice Trade: Further Evidence of Its Revival in the Sixteenth Century," *American Historical Review* 45, no. 3 (April 1940): 581–590.

Lane, Frederic C., "Venetian Shipping during the Commercial Revolution," *American Historical Review* 38, no. 2 (January 1933): 219–239.

Lane, Frederic C., *Venice: A Maritime Republic* (Baltimore: Johns Hopkins University Press, 1973).

Larkin, F. Daniel, "Erie Canal Freight," *The New York State Archives Time Machine,* http://www.archives.nysed.gov/projects/eriecanal/ErieEssay/ecf.html, accessed February 12, 2007.

Latham, A. J. H., and Larry Neal, "The International Market in Rice and Wheat, 1868–1914," *The Economic History Review* 36, no. 2 (May 1983): 260–280.

Latner, Richard B., "The Nullification Crisis and Republican Subversion," *The Journal of Southern History* 43, no. 1 (February 1977): 19–38.

Le Fevour, Edward, *Western Enterprise in Late Ching China* (Cambridge, MA: Harvard University Press, 1968).

Lee, Samuel, trans., *The Travels of Ibn Battuta* (Mineola, NY: Dover, 2004).

Lemire, Beverly, *Fashion's Favourite* (Oxford: Oxford University Press, 1991).

Levathes, Louise, *When China Ruled the Seas* (Oxford: Oxford University Press, 1994).

Levinson, Marc, *The Box* (Princeton: Princeton University Press, 2006).

Leyburn, James G., *The Haitian People* (New Haven, CT: Yale University Press, 1966).

Library of Congress Studies, "The Tanker War, 1984–1987," from *Iraq,* http://lcweb2.loc.gov/cgi-bin/query/r?frd/cstdy:@field(DOCID+iq0105) accessed March 26, 2007.

Ligon, Richard, *A True & Exact History of the Island of Barbadoes* (London: Peter Parker, 1673).

Liss, David, *The Coffee Trader* (New York: Random House, 2003).

Lopez, Robert Sabatino, "European Merchants in the Medieval Indies: The Evidence of Commercial Documents," *Journal of Economic History* 3 (November 1943): 164–184.

Loth, Vincent C., "Armed Incidents and Unpaid Bills: Anglo-Dutch Rivalry in the Banda Islands in the Seventeenth Century," *Modern Asian Studies* 29, no. 4 (October 1995): 705–740.

Lubbock, Basil, *The Opium Clippers* (Glasgow: Brown, Son, and Ferguson, 1933).

Lusztig, Michael, "Solving Peel's Puzzle: Repeal of the Corn Laws and Institutional Preservation," *Comparative Politics* 27, no. 4 (July 1995): 393–408.

Luthin, Reinhard H., "Abraham Lincoln and the Tariff," *The American Historical Review* 49, no. 4 (July 1944): 609–621.

Ma Huan, *Ying-Yai Sheng-Lan* (Cambridge: Cambridge University Press for Hakluyt Society, 1970).

Maddison, Angus, *Monitoring the World Economy* (Paris: OECD, 1995).

Maddison, Angus, *The World Economy: A Millennial Perspective* (Paris: OECD, 2001).

Madsen, Jakob B., "Trade Barriers and the Collapse of World Trade during the Great Depression," *Southern Economic Journal* 67, no. 4 (April 2001): 848–868.

Marlow, Joyce, *The Peterloo Massacre* (London: Panther, 1969).

Martyn, Henry, *Considerations on the East India Trade* (London: Printed for J. Roberts, 1701). Photographic reproduction in J. R. McCullouch, *Early English Tracts on Commerce* (Cambridge: Cambridge University Press, 1970).

Marx, Karl, *Capital,* vol 1. (New York: International, 1967).

Marx, Karl, *The Poverty of Philosophy* (New York: International, 1963).

Maugham, W. Somerset, *On a Chinese Screen* (New York: George H. Doran, 1922).

Mayer, Jane, and Jose de Cordoba, "Sweet Life: First Family of Sugar Is Tough on Workers, Generous to Politicians," *Wall Street Journal* (July 29, 1991).

McCord, Norman, *The Anti-Corn Law League* (London: George Allen and Unwin, 1958).

McCusker, John. J., *Money and Exchange in Europe and America, 1600–1775* (Chapel Hill: University of North Carolina Press, 1978).

McKendrick, N., "Josiah Wedgwood: An Eighteenth-Century Entrepreneur in Salesmanship and Marketing Techniques," *Economic History Review* 12, no. 3 (1960): 408–433.

McKendrick, Neil, John Brewer, and J. H. Plumb, *The Birth of a Consumer Society* (London: Europa, 1982).

McNeill, William H., *Plagues and Peoples* (New York: Anchor, 1998).

Meilink-Roelofsz, M. A. P., *Asian Trade and European Influence in the Indonesian Archipelago Between 1500 and About 1630* (The Hague: Martinus Nijhoff, 1962).

Mellars, Paul, "The Impossible Coincidence: A Single-Species Model for the Origins of Modern Human Behavior in Europe," *Evolutionary Anthropology* 14, no. 1 (February 2005): 12–27.

Menzies, Gavin, *1421: The Year China Discovered America* (New York: Morrow, 2003).

Midford, Paul, "International Trade and Domestic Politics: Improving on Rogowski's Model of Political Alignments," *International Organization* 47, no. 4 (Autumn 1993): 535–564.

Mill, John Stuart, "The Corn Laws," *Westminster Review* (April 1825).

Mill, John Stuart, *Principles of Political Economy* (New York: Appleton, 1888).

Miller, Scott, and Marc Champion, "At WTO Talks, Stances are Hardening," *The Wall Street Journal* (January 27, 2006).

Mintz, Sidney W., *Sweetness and Power* (New York: Penguin, 1986).

Mody, Jehangir R. P., *Jamsetjee Jeejeebhoy* (Bombay: R.M.D.C. Press, 1959).

Moreland, M. H., "The Ships of the Arabian Sea around AD 1500," *Journal of the Royal Asiatic Society of Great Britain and Ireland* (January 1939): 63–74.

Morison, Samuel Eliot, *Admiral of the Ocean Sea* (Boston: Little, Brown, 1970).

Morley, John, *The Life of Richard Cobden* (London: T. Fisher Unwin, 1903).

Morris, Morris D., "Towards a Reinterpretation of Nineteenth-Century Indian Economic History," *Journal of Economic History* 23, no. 4 (December 1963): 606–618.

Muhly, James D., "Sources of Tin and the Beginnings of Bronze Metallurgy," *American Journal of Archaeology* 89 (April 1985): 275–291.

Mukherjee, Ramkrishna, *The Rise and Fall of the East India Company* (Berlin: VEB Deutscher Verlag der Wissenshaften, 1958).

Mun, Thomas, *England's Treasure by Foreign Trade*, in Leonard D. Abbot, ed., *Masterworks of Economics* (New York: McGraw-Hill, 1973).

Needham, Joseph, *Science and Civilization in China,* vol. 4 (Cambridge: Cambridge University Press, 1971).

Nehru, Jawaharlal, *The Discovery of India* (Calcutta: Signet, 1956).

Neustadt (Ayalon), David, "The Plague and Its Effects upon the Mamluk Army," *Journal of the Royal Asiatic Society* (1946): 67–73.

Newman, R. K., "Opium Smoking in Late Imperial China: A Reconsideration," *Modern Asian Studies* 29, no. 4 (October 1995): 765–794.

Nincic, Donna J., "Sea Lane Security and U.S. Maritime Trade: Chokepoints as Scarce Resources," in Sam J. Tangredi, ed., *Globalization and Maritime Power* (Washington, DC: National Defense University Press, 2002).

Nordhaus, William D., "Soviet Economic Reform: The Longest Road," *Brookings Papers on Economic Activity* 1990, no. 1 (1990).

North, Douglass C., and Barry R. Weingast, "Constitutions and Commitment: The Evolution of Institutional Governing Public Choice in Seventeenth-Century England," *The Journal of Economic History* 49 (December 1989): 808–832.

Nowell, Charles E., "The Historical Prester John," *Speculum* 28, no. 3 (July 1953): 434–445.

O'Connell, Robert L., *Soul of the Sword* (New York: Free Press, 2002).

O'Grady, Mary Anastasia, "Americas: Clinton's Sugar Daddy Games Now Threaten NAFTA's Future," *The Wall Street Journal* (December 20, 2002).

Ohlin, Bertil, *Interregional and International Trade* (Cambridge: Harvard University Press, 1957).

Olson, Mancur, *The Logic of Collective Action* (Cambridge: Harvard University Press, 1965).

Oppenheim, A. L., "The Seafaring Merchants of Ur," *Journal of the American Oriental Society* 74, no. 1 (January–March 1954): 6–17.

Oregon Department of Agriculture, "Food remains a bargain for Oregon and U.S. consumers," http://www.oregon.gov/ODA/news/060719spending.shtml, accessed March 23, 2007.

O'Rourke, Kevin, "Tariffs and Growth in the Late 19th Century," *The Economic Journal* 110, no. 463 (April 2000): 456–483.

O'Rourke, Kevin, and Jeffrey G. Williamson, *Globalization and History* (Cambridge, MA: MIT Press, 1999).

O'Rourke, Kevin, and Jeffrey G. Williamson, "Late Nineteenth Century Anglo-American Price Convergence: Were Heckscher and Ohlin Right?" *The Journal of Economic History* 54, no. 4 (December 1994): 892–916.

The Oxford Dictionary of Quotes, 3rd ed., (Oxford: Oxford University Press, 1979).

Page, T. E., et al., eds., *The Scriptores Historiae Augustae* (Cambridge, MA: Harvard University Press, 1940).

Paquette, Robert L., "Revolutionary Saint Domingue in the Making of Territorial Louisiana," in David Gaspar and David Geggus, eds., *A Turbulent Time* (Indianapolis: Indiana University Press).

Parry, J. H., Review of "Friar Andrés de Uraneta, O.S.A.," *Hispanic American Historical Review* 47, no. 2 (May 1967): 262.

Patterson, Orlando, *Freedom* (New York: Basic Books, 1991).

Pearson, M. N., "India and the Indian Ocean in the Sixteenth Century," in Ashin Das Gupta and M. N. Pearson, eds., *India and the Indian Ocean 1500–1800* (Calcutta: Oxford University Press, 1987).

Pearson, M. N., "Introduction I: The Subject," in Ashin Das Gupta and M. N. Pearson, eds., *India and the Indian Ocean 1500–1800* (Calcutta: Oxford University Press, 1987).

Pearson, M. N., *The New Cambridge History of India* (Cambridge: Cambridge University Press, 1987).

Penzer, N. M., ed., and John Frampton, trans., *The Most Noble and Famous Travels of Marco Polo Together with the Travels of Nicolo de' Conti* (London: Adam and Charles Black, 1937).

Perren, Richard, "The North American Beef and Cattle Trade with Great Britain, 1870–1914," *The Economic History Review* 24, no. 3 (August 1971): 430–444.

Pinker, Steven, "We're Getting Nicer Every Day," *The New Republic* (March 20, 2007).

Pipes, Daniel, *Slave Soldiers and Islam* (New Haven, CT: Yale University Press, 1981).

Pires, Tomé, *The Suma Oriental of Tomé Pires and The Book of Francisco Rodrigues,* ed. Armando Cortesão (Glasgow: Robert Maclohose, 1944), 1.

Pliny, *Natural History* vol. 4 (Bury St. Edmunds: St. Edmundsbury, 1968).

Prain, Ronald, *Copper* (London: Mining Journal Books, 1975).

Prakash, Om, "European Commercial Enterprise in Precolonial Europe," in *The New Cambridge History of India,* vol. 2, no. 5 (Cambridge: Cambridge University Press, 1998).

Procopius, *The History of the Persian Wars*, II:16, from *The History of the Warres of the Emperour Justinian* (London: Printed for Humphrey Moseley, 1653).

Rabino, Joseph, "The Statistical Story of the Suez Canal," *Journal of the Royal Statistical Society* 50, no. 3 (September 1887): 495–546.

Rainwater, P. L., "Economic Benefits of Secession: Opinions in Mississippi in the 1850s," *The Journal of Southern History* 1, no. 4 (November 1935): 459–474.

Ramsay, G. G., trans., *Juvenal and Perseus* (Cambridge, MA: Harvard University Press, 1945).

Ratcliffe, Donald J., "The Nullification Crisis, Southern Discontent, and the American Political Process," *American Nineteenth Century History* 1, no. 2 (Summer 2000): 1–30.

Ravenstein, E. G., ed., *A Journal of the First Voyage of Vasco da Gama* (London: Hakluyt Society, 1898).

Raymond, Robert, *Out of the Fiery Furnace* (University Park: The Pennsylvania State University Press, 1968).

Redmount, Carol A., "The Wadi Tumilat and the 'Canal of the Pharaohs,'" *Journal of Near Eastern Studies* 54, no. 2 (April 1995): 127–135.

Rees, Ronald, *King Copper* (Cardiff: University of Wales Press, 2000).

Reischauer, Edwin O., "Notes on T'ang Dynasty Sea Routes," *Harvard Journal of Asiatic Studies* 5 (June 1940): 142–164.

Renfrew, Colin, "Trade and Culture Process in European History," *Current Anthropology* 10 (April–June 1969): 151–169.

Rhodes, Carolyn, *Reciprocity, U.S. Trade Policy, and the GATT Regime* (Ithaca, NY: Cornell University Press, 1993).

Ricardo, David, *The Principles of Political Economy & Taxation* (London: Dutton, 1911).

Risso, Patricia, *Merchants of Faith* (Boulder, CO: Westview, 1995).

Rodinson, Maxime, *Mohammed* (New York: Pantheon, 1971).

Rodrigue, Jean-Paul, "Straits, Passages, and Chokepoints: A Maritime Geostrategy of Petroleum Distribution," *Les Cahiers de Géographie du Québec* 48, no. 135 (December 2004): 357–374.

Rodrik, Dani, *Has Globalization Gone Too Far?* (Washington DC: Institute for International Economics, 1997).

Rogowski, Ronald, *Commerce and Coalitions* (Princeton: Princeton University Press, 1989).

Rosenstein, Mark, "The Rise of Containerization in the Port of Oakland," New York University master's thesis (2000), 23–31, http://www.apparent-wind.com/mbr/maritime-writings/thesis.pdf, accessed March 13, 2007.

Rostow, W.W., *The World Economy* (Austin: University of Texas, 1978).

Roy, Tirthankar, "Economic History and Modern India: Redefining the Link," *The Journal of Economic Perspectives* 16, no. 3 (Summer 2002): 109–130.

Josiah C. Russell, "That Earlier Plague," *Demography* 5, no. 1 (1968): 174–184.

Rustichello, *The Travels of Marco Polo* (New York: Signet, 2004).

Sachs, Jeffrey D., and Andrew Warner, "Economic Reform and the Process of Global Integration," *Brookings Papers on Economic Activity* 1995, no. 1 (1995): 1–118.

Samuelson, Paul A., "Where Ricardo and Mill Rebut and Confirm Arguments of Mainstream Economists Supporting Globalization," *The Journal of Economic Perspectives* 18, no. 3 (Summer 2004): 135–146.

Sarna, Jonathan D., "American Jewish History," *Modern Judaism* 10, no. 3 (October 1990): 343–365.

Saunders, J. J., *The History of Medieval Islam* (New York: Barnes & Noble, Inc., 1965).

Sawyer, P. H., and R. H. Hilton, "Technical Determinism: The Stirrup and the Plough," *Past and Present* 24 (April 1963): 90–100.

Schafer, Edward H., *The Golden Peaches of Samarkand* (Los Angeles: University of California Press, 1963).

Schlesinger, Arthur Meier, "The Uprising against the East India Company," *Political Science Quarterly* 32, no. 1 (March 1917): 60–79.

Schurz, William Lytle, "Mexico, Peru, and the Manila Galleon," *The American Historical Review* 1, no. 4 (November 1918): 389–402.

Schwartz, Stuart B., *Tropical Babylons* (Chapel Hill: University of North Carolina Press, 2004).

Scott, Philippa, *The Book of Silk* (London: Thames and Hudson, 1993).

Serjeant, Robert B., *The Portuguese off the South Arabian Coast: Hadrami Chronicles* (Oxford: Clarendon, 1963).

Silverberg, Robert, *In the Realm of Prester John* (Garden City, NY: Doubleday, 1972).

Simmons, Colin, "'De-Industrialization,' Industrialization, and the Indian Economy, c. 1850–1947," *Modern Asian Studies* 19, no. 3 (April 1985): 593–622

Simpson, Donald, "The Treasure in the Vergulde Draek: A Sample of V. O. C. Bullion Exports in the 17th Century," *The Great Circle* 2, no. 1 (April 1980): 13–17.

Smith, Adam, *An Inquiry into the Nature and Causes of the Wealth of Nations* (Chicago: University of Chicago Press, 1976).

Srinivasan, T. N., "Developing Countries in the World Trading System: From GATT, 1947, to the Third Ministerial Meeting of WTO, 1999," *World Economy* 22, no. 8 (1999): 1047–1064.

Stamper, Norm, "A Good Cop Wasted," excerpted in *Seattle Weekly* (June 1, 2005).

Steensgaard, Niels, *The Asian Trade Revolution of the Seventeenth Century* (Chicago: University of Chicago Press, 1974).

Stein, Gil J., *Rethinking World Systems* (Tucson: University of Arizona Press, 1999).

Stemmer, Juan E. Oribe, "Freight Rates in the Trade between Europe and South America, 1840–1914," *Journal of Latin American Studies* 21, no. 1 (February 1989): 23–59.

Stern, Horace, "The First Jewish Settlers in America: Their Struggle for Religious Freedom," *The Jewish Quarterly Review* 45, no. 4 (April 1955): 289–296.

Stolper, Wolfgang F., and Paul Samuelson, "Protection and Real Wages," *The Review of Economic Studies* 9, no. 1 (November 1941): 58–73.

Subrahmanyam, Sanjay, *The Career and Legend of Vasco da Gama* (Cambridge: Cambridge University Press, 1997).

Tadman, Michael, "The Demographic Cost of Sugar: Debates on Slave Societies and Natural Increase in the Americas," *The American Historical Review* 105, no. 5 (December 2000): 1534–1575.

Taussig, F. W., *The Tariff History of the United States* (New York: Capricorn, 1964).

Taylor, Alan M., "On the Costs of Inward-Looking Development: Price Distortions, Growth, and Divergence in Latin America," *The Journal of Economic History* 58, no. 1 (March 1998): 1–28.

Taylor, George Rogers, *The Transportation Revolution* (New York: Harper and Row, 1951).

Taylor, Henry C., and Anne Dewees Taylor, *World Trade in Agricultural Products* (New York: Macmillan, 1943).

Theophrastus, T. E. Page, et al., eds., *Enquiry into Plants* (Cambridge, MA: Harvard University Press, 1949).

Thomas, Bertram, *Arabia Felix* (New York: Scribner, 1932).

Thomas, Hugh, *The Slave Trade* (New York: Simon and Schuster, 1999).

Thomas, P. J., *Mercantilism and the East India Trade* (London: Frank Cass, 1963).

Thoreau, Henry D., *Walden* (Boston: Houghton Mifflin, 1938).

Thornton, Mark, and Robert B. Ekelund, Jr., *Tariffs, Blockades, and Inflation* (Wilmington, DE: Scholarly Resources, 2004).

Throckmorton, Peter, "Sailors in the Time of Troy," in *The Sea Remembers* (New York: Weidenfeld and Nicholson, 1987).

Thucydides, *History of the Peloponnesian War* (New York: Penguin, 1972).

Timmer, Ashley, and Jeffrey G. Williamson, "Immigration Policy Prior to the 1930s:

Labor Markets, Policy Interactions, and Globalization Backlash," *Population and Development Review* 21, no. 4 (December 1998): 739–771.

Tomlinson, B. R., "The Economy of Modern India," *The New Cambridge History of India*, vol. 3, no. 3 (Cambridge: Cambridge University Press, 1993).

Trefler, Daniel, "The Long and Short of the Canada-U.S. Free Trade Agreement," *The American Economic Review* 94, no. 4 (September 2004): 870–895.

Trefler, Daniel, "Trade Liberalization and the Theory of Endogenous Protection: An Econometric Study of U.S. Import Policy," *The Journal of Political Economy* 101, no. 1 (February 1993): 138–160.

Trevelyan, George Macaulay, *The Life of John Bright* (Boston: Houghton Mifflin, 1913).

Trocki, Carl, *Opium, Empire, and the Global Political Economy* (London: Routledge, 1999).

Tunell, George G., "The Diversion of the Flour and Grain Traffic from the Great Lakes to the Railroads," *The Journal of Political Economy* 5, no. 3 (June 1897): 340–361.

Turner, Jack, *Spice* (New York: Vintage, 2004).

Tye, Larry, *The Father of Spin* (New York: Crown, 1998).

Tylcote, R. F., *A History of Metallurgy* (London: Metals Society, 1976).

Tyler, Lyon G., "The South and Self-Determination," *William and Mary College Quarterly Historical Magazine* 27, no. 4 (April 1919): 217–225.

Varela, C., ed., *Cristóbal Colón: Textos y documentos completos* (Madrid: Alianza, 1984).

Ukers, William H., *All About Coffee* (New York: Tea and Coffee Trade Journal, 1935).

United Nations, *Human Development Report, 2006* (New York: United Nations, 2006).

United States Census Bureau, "Historical Income Tables—People," http://www.census.gov/hhes/www/income/histinc/p05ar.html, accessed April 3, 2007.

United States Department of Agriculture "Food Spending in Relation to Income," *Food Cost Review, 1950–97,* http://www.ers.usda.gov/Publications/AER780/, accessed March 23, 2007.

Van Deusen, John G., "Economic Bases of Disunion in South Carolina," Ph.D. thesis, Columbia University (1928).

Villiers, John, "Trade and Society in the Banda Islands in the Sixteenth Century," *Modern Asian Studies* 15, no. 4 (1981): 723–750.

Villiers, John, "Las Yslas de Esperar en Dios: The Jesuit Mission in Moro 1546–1571," *Modern Asian Studies* 22, no. 3 (1988, special issue): 593–606.

Wachsmann, Shelly, "Paddled and Oared Boats Before the Iron Age," in Robert Gardiner, ed., *The Age of the Galley* (Edison, NJ: Chartwell, 2000).

Wachsmann, Shelly, *Seagoing Ships and Seamanship in the Bronze Age Levant* (College Station: Texas A&M University Press, 1998).

Wake, C. H. H., "The Changing Pattern of Europe's Pepper and Spice Imports, ca. 1400–1700," *The Journal of European Economic History* 8 (Fall 1979): 361–403.

Walvin, James, *Fruits of Empire* (New York: New York University Press, 1997).

Ward, J. R., "The Industrial Revolution and British Imperialism, 1750–1850," *The Economic History Review* 47, no. 1 (February 1994): 44–65.

Warmington, E. H., *The Commerce between the Roman Empire and India* (New Delhi: Munshiram Manoharlal, 1995).

Weatherall, David, *David Ricardo: A Biography* (The Hague: Martinus Nijhoff, 1976).

Webster, Anthony, "The Political Economy of Trade Liberalization: The East India Company Charter Act of 1813," *The Economic History Review* 43, no. 3 (August 1990): 404–419.

Weightman, Gavin, *The Frozen Water Trade* (New York: Hyperion, 2003).

Weinberg, Bennett Alan, and Bonnie K. Bealer, *The World of Caffeine* (New York: Routledge, 2001).

Wendel, Jonathan F., and Richard C. Cronin, "Polyploidity and the Evolutionary History of Cotton," *Advances in Agronomy* 78 (2003): 139–186.

Wheelis, Mark, "Biological Warfare at the 1346 Siege of Caffa." Emerging Infectious Diseases (September 2002), accessed 12/15/05 (Serial online).

White, John H., *The Great Yellow Fleet* (San Marino, CA: Golden West, 1986).

White, Lynn, Jr., *Medieval Technology and Social Change* (Oxford: Clarendon, 1962).

Wilbur, Marguerite Eyer, *The East India Company* (Stanford, CA: Stanford University Press, 1945).

Wilcox, Clair, *A Charter for World Trade* (New York: Macmillan, 1949).

Williamson, Jeffrey, G., "De-Industrialization and Underdevelopment: A Comparative Assessment around the Periphery 1750–1939," working paper (December 2004), http://www.economics.harvard.edu/faculty/jwilliam/papers/DeInd EHW1204.pdf, accessed December 22, 2006.

Williamson, Jeffrey G., "The Impact of the Corn Laws Just Prior to Repeal," *Explorations in Economic History* 27 (1990): 123–156.

Wilson, Derek, *The World Encompassed: Francis Drake and His Great Voyage* (New York: Harper and Row, 1977).

Wiznitzer, Arnold, "The Exodus from Brazil and Arrival in New Amsterdam of the Jewish Pilgrim Fathers, 1654," *Publication of the American Jewish Historical Society* 44, no. 1 (September 1954): 80–95.

Wood, Adrian, and Cristóbal Ridao-Cano, "Skill, Trade, and International Inequality," working paper.

Wood, Alfred C., *A History of the Levant Company* (London: Frank Cass, 1964).

Woodward, C. Vann, *American Counterpoint: Slavery and Racism in the North/South Dialogue* (Boston: Little, Brown, 1964).

Worrall, Simon, "Full Speed Ahead," *Smithsonian* 36, no. 10 (January 2006): 93.

Wu Lien-Teh et al., *Plague* (Shanghai Station, China: National Quarantine Service, 1936).

Young, Herbert V., *They Came to Jerome* (Jerome, AZ: Jerome Historical Society, 1972).

Yule, Henry, ed., *The Book of Marco Polo* (London: John Murray, 1921).

Zhu, Susan Chun, and Daniel Trefler, "Trade and Inequality in Developing Countries: A General Equilibrium Analysis," *Journal of International Economics* 65 (2005): 21–48.

Zweig, Stefan, *Conqueror of the Sea* (New York: Literary Guild of America, 1938).

ILLUSTRATION CREDITS

Figure 1-1, page 33, Expedition of Queen Hatshepsut, reproduced with permission from Torgny Säve-Söderbergh, *The Navy of the Eighteenth Egyptian Dynasty* (Uppsala: Uppsala Universitets Arsskrift, 1946), 14.

Figure 6-1, page 145, Population of Medieval England. Source Data: *British Population History from the Black Death to the Present Day* Michael Anderson ed., (New York: Cambridge University Press, 1996), 77.

Figure 10-1, page 244, Imports to Dutch East India Company at Amsterdam. Source Data: Kristoff Glamann, *Dutch-Asiatic Trade, 1620–1740* ('s-Gravenhage, Holland: Martinus-Nijhoff, 1981), 14.

Figure 10-2, page 276, Annual Transatlantic Slave Trade. Source Data: David Eltis and David Richardson, "Prices of African Slaves Newly Arrived in the Americas, 1673–1865: New Evidence on Long-Run Trends and Regional Differentials," in David Eltis, ed., *Slavery in the Development of the Americas* (Cambridge University Press, 2004), 188–189.

Figure 11-1, page 302, Price of Wheat in England 1700–1850. Source Data: Donald Grove Barnes, *A History of the English Corn Laws* (New York: Augustus M. Kelley, 1961), 297–8.

Figure 12-1, page 327, Break-Even Point between Sail and Steam. Computed from Charles K. Harley, "British Shipbuilding and Merchant Shipping: 1850–1890," *The Journal of Economic History* 30, no. 1 (March 1970), 264.

Figure 12-2, page 329, Annual World Ship Construction. Source Data: Gerald S. Graham, "The Ascendancy of the Sailing Ship 1850–1885," *The Economic History Review,* 9, no. 1 (1956), 77.

Figure 12-3, page 335, Schematic of Early Mechanical Refrigeration Unit. Courtesy of Lewis O'Brien.

Figure 13-1, page 339, Wheat Prices in Liverpool vs. Chicago, 1850–1913. Source Data: C. Knick Harley, "Transportation, the World Wheat Trade, and the Kuznets Cycle, 1850–1913," *Exploration in Economic History* 17, no. 3 (July 1980), 246–247.

Figure 13-2, page 359, U.S. Import Tariffs on Dutiable Goods Under GATT. Source Data: *Historical Statistics of the United States, Millennial Online Edition* (Cambridge University Press, 2006) Table Ee424–430.

Figure 13-3, page 360, Real Value of World Trade: 1720–2000. Source Data: W. W. Rostow, *The World Economy* (Austin: University of Texas, 1978), 669, and Angus Maddison, *The World Economy* (Paris: OECD, 2001), 362.

Figure 14-1, page 377, *Shares of Total National Income*. Source Data: United States Census Bureau.

Tables

Table 10-1, page 277, Proportions of New World Slave Imports between 1500 and 1880, and Their Descendant Populations in 1950. Source Data: Philip D. Curtin, *The Atlantic Slave Trade* (Madison, WI: University of Wisconsin Press, 1969), 91.

Table 13-1, page 343, Stolper-Samuelson Categories. Adapted from Ronald Rogowski, *Commerce and Coalitions* (Princeton: Princeton University Press, 1989), 1–60.

Table 13-2, page 358, GATT Rounds. Source Data: T. N. Srinivasan, *Developing Countries and the Multilateral Trading System* (Boulder, CO: Westview Press, 1998), 9–11, and John H. Jackson, *The World Trading System,* 2nd ed. (Cambridge MA: The MIT Press, 1997), 36–38.

Table 14-1, page 374, Per Capita GDP in Nations Open and Closed to World Trade. Source Data: Jeffrey D. Sachs et al., "Economic Reform and the Process of Global Integration," *Brookings Papers on Economic Activity,* 1995, no. 1 (1995): 22–38 and Angus Maddison dataset, http://www.ggdc.net/maddison/Historical_Statistics/horizontal-file_03-2007.xls.

Maps

Ancient Canals at Suez, page 37, based on Joseph Rabino, "The Statistical Story of the Suez Canal," *Journal of the Royal Statistical Society*, 50, no. 3 (September 1887): 496–497.

Incense Lands and Routes, page 63, based on Nigel Groom, *Frankincense and Myrrh* (Beirut: Librairie du Liban, 1981), 99, 192.

The Black Death, Act II: A.D. 1330–1350, page 141, based on Elizabeth Carpentier, "Autour de la Peste Noir: Famines et Epidémies dans l'Histoire du XIVᵉ Siècle," *Annales: Economies, Sociétés, Civilizations* (1962), 1062–1092.

Da Gama's First Voyage, 1497–1499, page 171, based on Sanjay Subrahmanyam, *The Career and Legend of Vasco da Gama* (Cambridge: Cambridge University Press, 1997), 90–91.

Dutch Empire in Asia at Its Height in the Seventeenth Century, page 233, based on Jonathan I. Israel, *Dutch Primacy in World Trade, 1585–1740* (Oxford: Clarendon Press, 1989), 182–183.

The Erie Canal and Saint Lawrence Systems in 1846, page 325, reproduced with kind permission from Cambridge University Press, Thomas F. McIlwraith, "Freight Capacity and Utilization of the Erie and Great Lakes Canals before 1850," *The Journal of Economic History* 36, no. 4 (December 1976), 854.

World Oil Flows, Millions of Barrels per Day, page 368, reproduced with kind permission from Jean-Paul Rodrigue, "Straits, Passages and Chokepoints: A Maritime Geostrategy of Petroleum Distribution," *Les Cahiers de Geographie du Quebec* 48, no. 135 (December 2004): 364.

INDEX